MANAGEMENT

MANAGEMENT

Third Edition

Michael A. Hitt
Texas A&M University

J. Stewart Black
INSEAD

Lyman W. Porter
University of California, Irvine

Prentice Hall

Boston   Columbus   Indianapolis   New York   San Francisco   Upper Saddle River
Amsterdam   Cape Town   Dubai   London   Madrid   Milan   Munich   Paris   Montréal
Toronto   Delhi   Mexico City   São Paulo   Sydney   Hong Kong   Seoul   Singapore   Taipei   Tokyo

Editorial Director: Sally Yagan
Editor in Chief: Eric Svendsen
Acquisitions Editor: Kim Norbuta
Director of Editorial Services: Ashley Santora
Editorial Project Manager: Claudia Fernandes
Editorial Assistant: Carter Anderson
Director of Marketing: Patrice Lumumba Jones
Marketing Manager: Nikki Ayana Jones
Marketing Assistant: Ian Gold
Senior Managing Editor: Judy Leale
Production Project Manager: Ilene Kahn
Senior Operations Supervisor: Arnold Vila
Operations Specialist: Cathleen Petersen
Creative Director: Christy Mahon

Senior Art Director: Janet Slowik
Interior Designer: Bobby Starnes/ElectraGraphics, Inc.
Cover Designer: Wanda España
Cover Photo: Paul Chauncey/Alamy
Manager, Rights and Permissions: Hessa Albader
Editorial Media Project Manager: Denise Vaughn
MyLab Product Manager: Joan Waxman
Media Project Manager: Lisa Rinaldi
Full-Service Project Management and Composition: Integra Software Services, Inc.
Printer/Binder: RR Donnelley
Cover Printer: RR Donnelley
Text Font: 10/12, Times Roman

Credits and acknowledgments borrowed from other sources and reproduced, with permission, in this textbook appear on appropriate page in the text. The credit for the part opener is Calvio/istockphoto.

Library of Congress Cataloging-in-Publication Data

Hitt, Michael A.
    Management/Michael A. Hitt, J. Stewart Black, Lyman W. Porter. — 3rd ed.
        p. cm.
    Includes bibliographical references and index.
    ISBN 978-0-13-255328-5
    1. Management.   I. Black, Stewart.   II. Porter, Lyman W.   III. Title.
    HD31.H5327 2012
    658—dc22

                                                    2010045859

10 9 8 7 6

Prentice Hall
is an imprint of

www.pearsonhighered.com

ISBN 10:   0-13-255328-7
ISBN 13: 978-0-13-255328-5

Brief Contents

Contents

Preface

What Makes This Book Unique?

One of our fundamental objectives as an author team was to create a textbook for students and instructors that was both relevant and rigorous. Despite the number of good textbooks on the market, many of them tend to lean in one of two directions: Some textbooks do a good job of presenting material and integrating research, but students struggle to make the connection between theory and practice. Other textbooks do a good job of relating the material to the real world, but they are not always based on the most current research. Our experience in teaching students, talking with other instructors, and working with practicing managers has led us to develop a textbook that is both relevant and strongly based on current research literature. This combination meets the needs of students for developing skills and having a good working knowledge of management.

As an author team we are fortunate to have, collectively, more than 100 years of in-depth experience directly conducting research, reviewing articles, and studying management literature—particularly in the international sphere—and working with colleagues from a variety of different countries and cultures. The breadth and depth of our experience has helped us identify the key theories, concepts, and empirical findings that inform the practice of management in both domestic and global contexts.

We have also had a great number of opportunities over the years to teach many students, work with a large number of managers, and consult with various companies, all focused on the practice of management. Like our research, these experiences have taken place in a variety of locations around the world. We have worked with managers from every part of the globe. We believe this experience has helped us understand the challenges that students of management face in tying theory to practice. As a consequence, we have worked hard to relate the findings from current research to the implications they hold for practicing managers.

Why a New Edition?

The dual objectives of relevance and rigor were the basis of the first two editions of *Management,* and they continue to be the basis for this third edition. However, as a team, we are great admirers and try to be good examples of the principle of continuous improvement. Toward this end, in this new edition we have made several changes that we believe enhance the book. Additionally, the recent changes in the economic environment and enhanced global interdependencies necessitated changes in many of the cases and examples that are used liberally throughout the book. Following is a summary of the major revisions made in this edition:

- We have updated the information on management concepts based on the most current research. In doing so, a number of new references were inserted into each chapter. In several chapters, 20 to more than 30 new references were used (many published in 2009 and 2010).
- Each chapter contains several "Managerial Challenge" segments (mini-cases showing application of the managerial concepts explained in the chapter). Approximately 50 percent of these are new. The others were reviewed and revised where appropriate to ensure currency and continued accuracy.
- All "Managerial Challenges from the Front Line" (chapter-opening managerial profiles with the "Rest of the Story" at the end of the chapter) were updated, and three new managerial profiles were inserted (Chapters 3, 4, and 15).
- All in-text examples were checked for currency and accuracy, and many examples are new or updated.

- All end-of-chapter cases were updated except for two new ones that replaced existing cases (Chapters 11 and 14).
- All in-chapter exhibits were checked for continued relevance and currency. Several were updated and a few new ones were inserted (for example, in Chapters 9, 10, and 11).
- There were a number of small, but nontrivial, changes to the content designed to ensure that the content is "cutting-edge" in the literature and both rigorous and relevant.

We continue to emphasize the connection between relevance and rigor for students and instructors. For example, we again use the feature that appeared first in the second edition, titled Managerial Challenges from the Front Line. It includes a focused example of a managerial challenge faced by a real person. Several of these people are recent college graduates, and others are more experienced managers. The feature helps students understand and relate the chapter content to managerial practice. We also provide a "Rest of the Story" feature at the end of the chapter that briefly describes how the manager resolved the challenge. A few of the people profiled in them and their stories are new; all others have been updated.

Because many undergraduates have not yet had extensive practical experience working in organizations, they are not always able to benefit from the personal insight and awareness that experience can provide. Yet, as we also know, much of a manager's approach to various managerial activities, such as decision making or communicating, are influenced by his or her own tendencies, orientations, and the like. As a consequence, we continue to have a "Self-Assessment" feature at the end of each chapter to help students evaluate and understand their capabilities (especially related to the material covered in the chapter).

This third edition retains our intent to be comprehensive but concise, with 15 chapters. We also continue to include an appendix titled "The History of Managerial Thought and Practice" for students who desire to learn more about the historical development of the management field. Overall, we believe this third edition provides students with a solid and stimulating understanding of the scope and challenges of the function of management in organizations.

Supplements to This Book

This third edition of *Management* has been designed specifically to support the instructor teaching the course and to be user friendly for students. The following support materials have been developed to accompany the third edition:

Instructor Supplements

At the Instructor Resource Center, www.pearsonhighered.com/irc, instructors can access a variety of print, digital, and presentation resources available with this text in downloadable format. Registration is simple and gives you immediate access to new titles and new editions. As a registered faculty member, you can download resource files and receive immediate access to and instructions for installing course management content on your campus server. In case you ever need assistance, our dedicated technical support team is ready to help with the media supplements that accompany this text. Visit http://247.pearsoned.com for toll-free user support phone numbers and answers to frequently asked questions.

The following supplements are available for download to adopting instructors:

- Instructor's Manual
- Test Item File
- TestGen (test-generating program)
- PowerPoint Slides

VIDEOS ON DVD   Video segments that illustrate the most pertinent topics in management today and highlight relevant issues that demonstrate how people lead, manage, and work effectively. Contact your Pearson representative for the DVD.

Student Supplements

COURSESMART eTEXTBOOK   CourseSmart is an exciting new choice for students looking to save money. As an alternative to purchasing the print textbook, students can purchase an electronic version of the same content. With a CourseSmart etextbook, students can search the text, make notes online, print out reading assignments that incorporate lecture notes, and bookmark important passages for later review. For more information or to purchase access to the CourseSmart eTextbook, visit www.coursesmart.com.

PEARSON mymanagementlab

(www.mymanagementlab.com) is an easy-to-use online tool that personalizes course content and provides robust assessment and reporting to measure individual and class performance. All of the resources that students need for course success are in one place—flexible and easily adapted for your students' course experience. Some of the resources include an eText version of all chapters, quizzes, video clips, simulations, assessments, and PowerPoint presentations that engage your students while helping them study independently.

Acknowledgments

We owe a debt of gratitude to Kim Norbuta, our editor, and the rest of the Prentice Hall team, including Claudia Fernandes, Ilene Kahn, and Lynn Savino Wendel, for their efforts to support and help us develop this edition. Grace McLaughlin also again did an excellent job in the development of the accompanying Instructor's Manual.

We extend special thanks for the excellent feedback from reviewers, users, and focus group participants (designated as "FG") for the third and previous editions of this textbook. These include:

David Albritton, Northern Arizona University

Forrest Aven, University of Houston-Downtown

Richard Babcock, University of San Francisco

Stacy Ball-Elias, Southwest Minnesota State University

Stephanie Bibb, Chicago State University

Gene Blackmun III, Rio Hondo College (FG)

Rochelle Brunson, Alvin Community College

Gary Bumgarner, Mountain Empire Community College

John Bums, North Harris Montgomery CC District-Tomball College (FG)

Barbara Carlin, University of Houston

Macgorine Cassell, Fairmount State University

Bruce Chamov, Hofstra University

Michael Drafke, College of DuPage

N. Mai Lai Eng, San Antonio College

Mary Fanning, College of Notre Dame of Maryland

Maruffi Fordham, Fordham University

Pat Hafford, Wentworth Institute

Gary Hensel, McHenry County College

Tammy Hunt, University of North Carolina-Wilmington

Karen Jacobs, LeTourneau University

Connie James, Pepperdine University (FG)

James H. Kennedy, Angelina College (FG)

Jerry Kinard, Western Carolina University

Frank Krafka, St. Edward's University

Sal Kukalis, California State University, Long Beach

Leslie Ledger, Central Texas College (FG)

Lianlian Lin, California State Polytechnic University-Pomona (FG)

Tom Mahafey, Siena College

Mark Nagel, Normandale Community College

Abdul Qastin, Lakeland College

R. Nicholas Panepinto, Flagler College

Mark Poulos, St. Edward's University

Lois Shelton, Chapman University (FG)

Randi Sims, Nova Southeastern University

Tom Sy, California State University-Long Beach (FG)

Pat Tadlock, Horry-Georgetown Technical College

Spence Tower, Central Michigan University

Julia Underwood, Azusa Pacific University (FG)

David G. Vequist, University of the Incarnate Word

Bruce Walker, University of Louisiana-Monroe

Randy Westgren, University of Illinois, Urbana/Champaign

Johnnie Williams, Texas Southern University

Nancy Zimmerman, Community College Baltimore/Catonsville

Part One
Managing Ethically and Globally

1

The Nature of Management

LEARNING OBJECTIVES

After studying this chapter, you should be able to:

Define the term *management*.

Explain the major challenges that managers must address.

Describe how historical research on management has contributed to the current practice of management.

Identify and discuss the primary managerial functions.

Explain the three general roles involved in managerial work and the specific roles within each.

Explore and describe the three dimensions of managerial jobs.

Discuss the primary skills required to be an effective manager.

Photo Courtesy of Blaine Halvorson, Junk Food Clothing

Name: Blaine Halvorson

Position: Chief Creative Officer (CCO), Junk Food

Alma mater: Montana State University (BA in Fine Arts/Graphic Design)

Outside work activities: Leisure time, travel, and painting (mainly pop art)

First job out of school: Designed clothes for rock bands and MTV while in college; post-college, worked for a short time at a Los Angeles apparel company followed by Planet Golf, where he oversaw the Japanese distribution of the company's products.

Hero: Jean-Michel Basquiat—I think that he is an amazing artist.

Motto to live by: Everyone should take a leap of faith once in their lives and see if they can do something great.

What drives me: The desire for accomplishment and to take something to the next level.

Management style: Not following a straight line—thinking outside of the box and having tremendous drive.

Graphic designer Blaine Halvorson, along with his business partner Natalie Grof, are the founders of the multimillion-dollar clothing-design business Junk Food, Inc. They worked together at Planet Golf prior to starting their own company. They built the company from a two-person business operating out of an apartment into the world's largest licensing T-shirt manufacturer.

Halvorson experienced early success designing clothes, showing that he had talent and that there was a market for his ideas. He attended trade shows and received a lot of positive press. Then, he started receiving large orders for his designs, but did not have the capacity to mass-produce his products. He realized that he had to learn more about managing a business. His subsequent learnings helped him make Junk Food a success a few years later.

While working at Planet Golf, Halvorson developed a business on the side that was the forerunner of Junk Food. After an investor bought Planet Golf, Halvorson sent him a new design and his idea for a different T-shirt line .

The owner of Planet Golf became an angel investor in Junk Food (a silent partner who provided money while Halvorson and Grof managed the company). The basic idea for the company was to provide a different product that customers valued. Halvorson and Grof built the brand name by using popular icons. Until then, licensing was used only for mass market merchandise, not "designer clothes," especially T-shirts. Starting with names like Twister, Candy Land, and My Little Pony, Halvorson and Grof moved to other licensees, such as Sesame Street, Rolling Stones, DC Comics, and Looney Tunes. They developed a strong following for the Junk Food brand, with even the products becoming collectibles because of the Junk Food brand label. Most recently, the Junk Food brand has moved into sports and entertainment, with licenses with the NFL, the NBA, and Disney. Junk Food's products are now sold globally, in Australia, Japan, Mexico, and many European countries, with a strong focus on Germany and Asian countries.

To do what Halvorson did—that is, build a successful company—requires the willingness to take risks and a desire to create something on your own. It also requires sacrifice, investing substantial amounts of time and effort to make the business work. What's more, it takes significant management skills. For example, Halvorson had to attract, hire, and manage a high-quality team to make Junk Food a success. It also requires perseverance and knowing the market. He learned how to mass-produce products and manage the business's cash flow, among other challenges. Halvorson describes the process as "moving in 50 different directions simultaneously and trying to solve 10 problems at the same time."

Even in the recent economic recession, Junk Food sales increased and the company grew. Because of severe price competition, however, the company moved more of its production overseas (products made in the United States have decreased from 80 percent to 10 percent). Still, as a known and respected brand, Junk Food has increased market share. For example, Gap now co-brands products with the company. Halvorson obviously learned well and has become not only a successful entrepreneur but also a highly effective manager.

As described in the opening profile, Blaine Halvorson has built a highly successful company. He did so by developing an idea for a different type of clothing design that customers valued. While Halvorson is a creative and excellent designer, his success was due to much more. For example, early in his career, he showed his talent for developing creative clothing designs that the market desired. However, he also learned how to build and manage a business. Halvorson had to learn how to organize the company to design, manufacture, and distribute Junk Food's products. He had to hire and manage people to complete these tasks. And finally, he had to ensure that the company used resources efficiently to make a profit and ensure that the business was successful.

The profile on Halvorson shows that management is a challenging and necessary part of a successful business. It also depicts management as exciting and yet requiring a lot of hard work and dedication. In this chapter, we introduce the concept of management and show how it is done. We explore the challenges that managers face on a regular basis and the skills they must have to successfully handle them.

Now, we turn to a set of basic questions that are the focus for the remainder of Chapter 1: (1) What is management? (2) What are the primary challenges that managers face? (3) What do managers do? (4) What skills do managers need?

What Is Management?

To begin, we examine the concepts that form the base of this book.

Management is an activity or process. More specifically, **management** is the process of assembling and using sets of resources in a goal-directed manner to accomplish tasks in an organization. This definition can be subdivided into its key parts:

1. Management is a process: It involves a series of activities and operations, such as planning, deciding, and evaluating.
2. Management involves assembling and using sets of resources: It is a process that brings together, and puts into use, a variety of resources: human, financial, material, and informational.
3. Management involves acting in a goal-directed manner to accomplish tasks: It is an activity with a purpose and direction. The purpose or direction may be that of the individual, the organization or, usually, a combination of the two. It includes one's efforts to complete activities successfully and to achieve particular levels of desired results.
4. Management involves activities carried out in an **organization:** It is a process undertaken in an organization by people with different functions intentionally structured and coordinated to achieve common purposes.

In addition to being "a process" or set of activities, management can also have several other meanings. The term sometimes designates a particular part of the organization: the set of individuals who carry out management activities. Thus, some may use the phrase "the *management* of IBM decided…." or "the *management* of University Hospital developed a new personnel policy…." Often, when the term is used this way, it does not necessarily refer to all members of management but rather to those who occupy the highest-level positions within the organization (top management).

Another similar use of the term is to distinguish a category of people (that is, "management") from those who are members of collective bargaining units ("union" members or, more informally, "labor") or those who are not involved in specific managerial activities, whether or not they are union members ("nonmanagement employees" or "rank-and-file employees"). The term *member* refers to any person (any employee) in an organization without regard to that individual's role in the organization. In this book, we use the term *manager* to refer to anyone who has designated responsibilities for carrying out managerial activities, and *managing* to refer to the process of completing those activities.

However, *management* is too complex a concept for one definition to capture accurately. Next, we explain several of the challenges that managers must address.

management
the process of assembling and using sets of resources in a goal-directed manner to accomplish tasks in an organizational setting

organization
an interconnected set of individuals and groups who attempt to accomplish common goals through differentiated functions and their coordination

Managerial Challenges

Managers face a number of challenges on a regular basis. The nature of the environment in which managers operate requires that they manage change effectively. Managers are responsible for managing resources—financial, human, and otherwise. To ensure that their organization is competitive and survives in a rapidly changing environment, they must manage strategically. Because of the major changes occurring rapidly in the business world today, managers must be entrepreneurial and innovative. Essentially, they must continuously find ways to create more value for customers than do competitors. Managers' activities take place within organizations. Although managers are the primary "drivers" of their organizations, organizations place boundaries on what managers can and cannot do. We examine each of these challenges next.

Managing Change

Managing change is the most persistent, pervasive, and powerful challenge with which all managers have to deal, regardless of the nature of their organization or its location. No matter how new or experienced managers are, they will be confronted with both the need for change and the opportunity to create change.[1] Not making any changes is unlikely to be an option. As a Greek philosopher once wrote many centuries ago, "Change alone is unchanging," and that statement remains appropriate today.[2]

Managing change is no simple task, especially because most people naturally resist change. Thus, managers must find ways to gain employees' acceptance of change in order to implement it effectively. To gain acceptance, it is useful for managers to create "small wins." For example, the manager might implement the change in one smaller area and make it successful. This success then makes the change legitimate in the eyes of the employees.[3] Two major causes of change that managers must address are new technology and globalization.

TECHNOLOGY No managers in today's world can ignore the impact of technology and the way it affects their jobs and firms. Technology developments often force managers to make changes—whether they want to or not. The Internet is a case in point. The Internet has had far-reaching effects on how managers do their jobs.

The introduction of a new technology often leads to the development of new products and new processes for accomplishing tasks. The Internet has created many opportunities to market products differently, to reach distant markets, and to communicate internally and externally in more effective ways. And, some of the technologies developed to use the Internet in more and effective ways have led to the development of complementary technologies and products, such as Apple's iPod and iPad. Therefore, the Internet has provided many opportunities for managers. Yet, managers must identify these opportunities and find ways to exploit them. If they do not, their competitors are likely to do so and take market share from them. Essentially, the development of new technologies has increased the speed of change, the flow of information, the competitive reach into international markets, and the amount of competition in all markets.

The continued development of new technologies and information about them has emphasized the importance of knowledge and increased the importance of human capital (the holder of the knowledge).[4] It has helped many small- and medium-sized firms enter and compete in international markets, thereby enhancing globalization.[5]

GLOBALIZATION Globalization is the development and observation of the increasing international and cross-national nature of everything from politics to business. Managers must maintain an awareness of what happens in the rest of the world because events in other countries affect their organizations. Global events will almost certainly affect managers' goals and decisions, and how they must coordinate and lead the work of other people.[6]

The opening of many world markets (for example, China), free trade agreements such as GATT, the General Agreement on Tariffs and Trade, and NAFTA, the North American Free Trade Agreement, growing economies around the world, and increases in technology that facilitate global partnerships and competition all contribute greatly to increasing globalization.[7]

Opening of markets to foreign firms coupled with economic development increases market opportunities but simultaneously leads to greater global competition. In order to compete effectively in global markets, firms have sought increasingly to outsource activities to people and firms in lower-cost countries like India and China.[8] Such actions were taken by the Junk Food Company as explained by Halvorson in the opening profile. And, the firm outsourced its manufacturing activities to overseas companies to reduce their costs, allowing Junk Food to successfully compete on price. Of course, global supply chains can also be risky because they are subject to more potential disruptions, such as host country government export and import controls and other regulations, terrorist actions, and more.[9]

Globalization promotes greater involvement in international markets. Thus, firms moving into international markets increasingly need to learn about other cultures and the institutional environments in these markets.[10] Some firms have facilitated this learning process by developing multicultural management teams. These teams have managers who speak different languages and have knowledge about the markets and environments in different regions of the world in which the firms operate.[11] Because of the complexities of operating in multiple countries and regions, some firms focus their international operations in one or a few specific regions of the world. In this way, they can develop the knowledge of the culture, markets, and institutions to operate there effectively.[12]

The changes and the complexities in the global economic environment are evident in the recent rankings of the world's most innovative companies. In the first ten years of the twenty-first century, the United States lost 2.6 million manufacturing jobs to China. In addition to the development of low technology manufacturing capabilities, several Asian countries were building the capacity to produce more sophisticated and higher technology products. Companies in these countries have also been developing their innovation capabilities. As a result, by 2010, 15 of the top 50 most innovative companies were based in Asia and a majority of the firms in the top 25 were based outside the United States. This ranking foretells of a major restructure of the global economy.[13] Entering into international markets has become a critically important growth strategy for major firms worldwide.[14] (Chapter 3 discusses, in further detail, globalization and how firms manage in a global environment.)

Wal-Mart's early entries into foreign markets such as Mexico and Japan were marked by errors suggesting the challenges of operating in foreign markets even for a highly successful and powerful company. But Wal-Mart's management team learned from these mistakes and has since built its international operations into a $100 billion business. Wal-Mart's success can be seen in its China unit. The company hires Chinese managers and sources much of its merchandise locally; still, managers have Wal-Mart values and are passionate about the company. It is expected that Wal-Mart will face additional challenges entering new foreign markets. For example, some analysts question its plans to enter the Russian market because of significant corruption. However, with Wal-Mart's financial and political power along with its managerial skills developed from operating in other foreign markets, many believe that the firm is likely to succeed.

Managing Resources

A major part of a manager's job is managing the organization's resources. The manager must ensure the efficient use of resources but also use the resources in ways that maximize achieving the organization's goals. Among the resources important to managers are financial capital, human capital, physical resources (such as buildings and equipment), and technology. Managers build and manage a portfolio of resources.[15] To build the portfolio, they must acquire and develop the resources needed to complete the organization's tasks. For example, managers need to recruit and select the best-possible employees, then continually develop their knowledge and skills.[16] As employees are developed, their value to the organization increases. This implies that managers need to be effective evaluators of people's skills in order to select the best candidates and identify the skills to be developed. Managers must also design and implement the means to promote learning in the organization.[17]

After building a portfolio of resources, managers must then allocate and coordinate these resources to accomplish the organization's tasks.[18] Managers are also responsible for developing and implementing a strategy to use the organization's capabilities to accomplish its goals.[19] A major dimension of coordination is interpersonal relationships, with other managers and with

A MANAGER'S CHALLENGE

GLOBALIZATION

Wal-Mart's Global Strategy

Wal-Mart is the largest company in the world, with slightly more than $400 billion in annual sales. It serves more than 200 million customers with over 8,000 retail units. The company has 2.1 million employees and because of joint ventures and acquisitions, it operates under 53 different names in 15 countries. There is little doubt that Wal-Mart is a major force in the global economy and has many more foreign markets to conquer with its current global strategy. Although Wal-Mart has been highly successful in the U.S. domestic market, its first forays into foreign markets were marked by mistakes and a few failures. For example, Wal-Mart's first major retail store in Mexico had a huge parking lot, similar to stores in the United States, but most customers arrived and departed by buses. And, it also had some early product failures. For example, Wal-Mart tried to sell golf balls in Mexico even though most of its customers are low-income and could not afford to play golf. Wal-Mart has had to learn about and adapt to local culture: in Japan, for example, low prices are equated with low-quality goods and few customers buy large quantities because of very small living quarters. Wal-Mart also had to close operations in Korea and Germany, two major economies.

Yet, the company has learned from early mistakes and has been more successful in its later entries into foreign markets. As an example, Wal-Mart has 260 retail outlets and almost 90,000 employees in China. All of its stores in China are operated by Chinese general managers. According to Ed Chan, Wal-Mart's China CEO, all of the management team are passionate about Wal-Mart's values, Wal-Mart in China, and about China as well. Wal-Mart sources many of its products locally within China as well, helping to keep costs low.

Wal-Mart was successful relative to most retailers during the recent recession. Overall, it experienced sales growth, and its international division was a major contributor because U.S. sales declined. Approximately 25 percent of Wal-Mart's annual sales come from its international business. In fact, if its $100 billion international business were a stand-alone company, it would be among the top five retailers in the world. Wal-Mart has plans to increase this unit by entering more markets with major operations such as India and Russia. In addition, the company plans to greatly reduce its costs by moving to global sourcing directly from the manufacturers, where possible. This move alone is expected to save the company billions of dollars. For goods unavailable in this way, it has signed a major agreement with Li & Fung to serve as a direct source for major merchandise needs. Li & Fung will focus primarily on emerging markets for the goods. Through these efforts, Wal-Mart CEO David Duke expects the company to maintain its momentum as the global economy continues to improve.

Sources: K. Talley & K. O'Keeffe, "Wal-Mart, Li & Fung Sign Sourcing Deal," *Wall Street Journal,* January 29, 2010, http://www.wsj.com; Company Web site, "Wal-Mart Leverages Global Scale to Lower Costs of Goods, Accelerate Speed to Market, Improve Quality of Products," http://www.walmart.com, accessed January 28, 2010; J. Krishna, "Bharti Wal-Mart Sets up Farm Produce Sourcing Center," *Wall Street Journal,* January 20, 2010, http://www.wsj.com; N. Majahan-Bansal, "Wal-Mart's Strategy Through the World," *Business,* October 20, 2009, http://www.business.in.com; M. Boyle, "Wal-Mart's Painful Lessons," *BusinessWeek,* October 13, 2009, http://www.businessweek.com; "China's Retail Revolution: An Interview with Wal-Mart's Ed Chan," *McKinsey Quarterly,* October 2009, http://www.mckinseyquarterly.com; S. Rosenbloom, "Wal-Mart Outlines Plans to Keep Its Momentum," *New York Times,* June 6, 2009, http://www.nytimes.com; "Case Study: Wal-Mart Stumbles in Its Global Expansion Strategy," in D. M. DePamphilis, *Mergers, Acquisitions, and Other Restructuring Activities,* http://knoll.google.com.

employees. Managers' interpersonal and communication skills are paramount in this process. We conclude that managers largely get things done with and through people in the organization. As a result, how they manage human capital is critical to their success.

Anne Mulcahy, chairman and former CEO of Xerox, is largely credited with turning around that company's performance. But Mulcahy claims Xerox employees were responsible for the turnaround. She stated that ". . . attracting them, motivating them, keeping them—making Xerox an employer of choice—is critical to our drive back to greatness."[20] These comments suggest that staffing the organization with the best human capital possible and further developing the knowledge and skills of employees is critical for the success.[21] This conclusion emphasizes the importance of managing the organization's resources (especially the people) to its ability to compete and survive in an increasingly competitive environment.[22]

Executives at Xerox know that the company is more than just its machines. Xerox's CEO, Anne Mulcahy, has emphasized that the firm's human capital (people) are critical to the company's success in the highly competitive photocopier market.

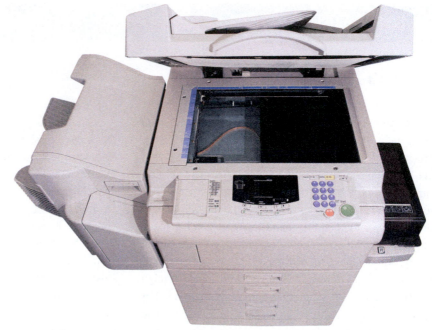

PhotoDisc/Getty Images

Managing Strategically

Managerial challenges create an incredibly complex, dynamic, and competitive landscape in which most managers must operate. To survive and perform well in such an environment, managers throughout the organization need to manage strategically.[23] Managers at the top of the organization—CEOs like Steve Jobs at Apple—establish goals and formulate a strategy for achieving those goals. To accomplish the goals, the company must effectively implement the strategy, which requires managers at all levels of the organization to set and accomplish goals that contribute to the organization's ultimate performance.

The increasing globalization and the enhanced use of technology have contributed to greater changes emphasizing the importance of knowledge to organizational success.[24] The importance placed on the intellectual capital of the organization requires managers to use their portfolio of resources effectively.[25] Of primary importance are intangible resources such as the employees and the firm's reputation. Managers are responsible for building an organization's capabilities and then leveraging them through a strategy designed to give it an advantage over its competitors.[26] They usually do this by creating more value for their customers than their competitors do.[27]

Managers are responsible for forming the strategies of the major units within the organization as well. Because people in the organization have to implement the strategy, managers must focus heavily on the human factor. As they implement their strategies, they will encounter conflicting conditions. Often this means managing multiple situations simultaneously and remaining flexible to adapt to changing conditions. In fact, when Unilever experienced problems and changed its strategy in 2005, it also found it lacked the ability to implement and execute the strategy. Therefore, to improve its performance, the company developed and implemented a process called Strategy in Action (SIA). It follows a sequence of activities to which the firm refers as think, plan, deliver and review. The managers begin by developing and testing an excellent strategy followed by planning for its implementation by management teams through the organization. Management teams mobilize to accomplish the goals established in the implementation plan, followed by a review of the results and planning for improvement. This process is based on the principle of Japanese *hoshin kanri*, or policy deployment.[28]

Additionally, achieving an organization's goals requires that managers commit themselves to always being alert to how they can improve and strengthen strategies in advancing the organization's vision. Finally, the dynamic competitive landscape entails substantial change. To adapt to this change, managers should be innovative and entrepreneurial, continuously searching for new opportunities.

Managing Entrepreneurially

Managers should regularly search for new opportunities in the current marketplace or identify ideas that could create new markets.[29] Entrepreneurship involves identifying new opportunities and exploiting them.[30] Thus, managers must be entrepreneurial. Entrepreneurial activity is not limited to new, small firms, however. Managers in large firms also must be entrepreneurial and strive to create new businesses.[31] Developing new businesses requires that the lead person, and perhaps others, take entrepreneurial actions. Given the amount of change and innovation encountered in most industries and countries, businesses cannot survive without being entrepreneurial.[32]

To be entrepreneurial, managers must develop an entrepreneurial mind-set. An entrepreneurial mind-set is a way of thinking about businesses that emphasizes actions to take advantage of uncertainty.[33] With an entrepreneurial mind-set, managers can sense opportunities and take actions to exploit them. Uncertainty in the environment tends to level the "playing field" for organizations of all sizes. Whether an organization is rich or poor in resources, uncertainty enables them to identify and exploit opportunities to achieve competitive advantage. This is how Google, in its early days, beat larger, more powerful competitors. To develop an entrepreneurial mind-set, managers must first be alert to new ideas and use them to create value for customers.[34]

Both large and small firms and new and established firms can be entrepreneurial. For reasons described earlier, they not only can be, they must be to survive. Polaroid Corporation was once an entrepreneurial company and a market leader in instant photography. But the original Polaroid organization no longer exists: it lost its entrepreneurial nature and saw market share evaporate with the introduction of digital photography technology. The firm that bought the rights to the Polaroid name struggled and went out of business, selling the assets to an entrepreneur who intends to use them to sell specialty film to artists and the few remaining owners of Polaroid cameras. As a whole, small and new firms tend to be more entrepreneurial but often lack the ability to sustain this advantage. On the other hand, large, established firms are good at using their size to gain an advantage and sustaining their positions as long as new, rival products don't enter the market. However, larger firms have a more difficult time being entrepreneurial.[35]

Polaroid, once an entrepreneurial company, and a former market leader, no longer exists because it lost its substantial market share to digital photography technology.

Historical Approaches to Management

While many think that management is a very new concept, it is not. Even ancient civilizations encountered managerial challenges and found ways to cope with them. More than 1,000 years ago, Chinese leaders searched for an effective means of governing a large organization (government) and expressed the importance of open communications and consideration of people's needs. Additionally, Chinese leaders discussed the value of specialized labor, hiring and promotions based on merit, and the need to clearly describe jobs.[36] The modern field of strategic management owes its origins to military history and an ancient Chinese warrior, Sun Tsu, and his book, *The Art of War.*[37]

Long ago, management was already being practiced in many parts of the world. The pyramids, for example, were designed and built in Egypt thousands of years ago. Completing these "wonders of the world" required a significant amount of planning, organization, and management of labor. Likewise, 2,000 years ago, the Roman Empire required effective management to build major monuments and an extensive network of roads and viaducts. Additionally, the development and growth of the Catholic church throughout the world required a significant amount of planning, organizing, and directing people's efforts and activities.

Patrick Strattner\Jupiter Images

The origins of what is often referred to as "modern management" are found in the Industrial Revolution, which began in England in the mid-eighteenth century and later spread to the United States and other regions of the world. While many have contributed to the development of management thought and practices, American engineer Frederick W. Taylor (1856–1915) is often credited as the "father of modern management." Taylor's work on linking workers' incentives to their performance provided an important base for motivation theory applied to the workplace. He argued that pay was only part of the reward and that employees should be provided regularly with feedback on their performance. His primary legacy is the principles of scientific management that form the base for many of the different functions, roles, and activities of managers explored in this book.[38] Research suggests that scientific management was a sophisticated theoretical approach that contributed to other fields as well as institutional economics.[39]

Many other people have contributed to modern management theory and practice over the course of the last two centuries. Among them are Frank and Lillian Gilbreth, who developed the beginnings of time and motion studies to determine the most efficient manner in which to complete tasks. Alfred P. Sloan (former CEO of General Motors) and Chester Barnard (an executive of AT&T) both contributed to our knowledge of how to build an efficient and effective organization. While Sloan focused on the formal aspects of organizing, such as the functions and divisions, Barnard emphasized the social characteristics of organizing, such as cooperation, building common purpose, and the importance of communication.

Mary Parker Follett and Douglas McGregor focused on the importance and value of leadership in organizations. Follett espoused principles related to the importance of integration and treating employees as partners. Similarly, McGregor is best known for promoting "Theory Y" leadership practices with positive assumptions about human nature in which positive leadership can bring forth greater efforts and levels of achievement from employees. And Abraham Maslow and Frederick Herzberg made major contributions to our knowledge of motivation that continue to be present in managerial practices today. Maslow is best known for his "hierarchy of needs" theory and Herzberg for proposing the independence of motivators and hygiene factors. Both of these individuals' ideas led to the concept of job enrichment used to design tasks that more effectively motivate employees and use more of their skills.[40]

A more detailed discussion of the history of management thought and practice is presented in the Appendix. The ideas of these management pioneers are evident in the discussion of what managers do in the following sections.

What Do Managers Do?

In the opening profile about Blaine Halvorson, we learn that management has many dimensions. Halvorson's first attempt to design and sell clothes was successful because he created a product the market desired. Yet, he was unable to satisfy that demand. He did not know how to develop and manage an organization. His description of what he did in developing and managing Junk Food to be a successful company shows a number of managerial tasks that he had to complete, which include many of the functions described in this section.

There are several ways to examine managers' jobs aside from observing what managers do. Over the years, several systems have been developed to classify (1) managerial functions, (2) the roles in which managers operate, and (3) the characteristics and dimensions of managerial jobs. These typologies can provide useful ways to examine the varied nature of managerial jobs and responsibilities. In effect, they provide a road map for understanding what management is.

One way to think about the question "What do managers do?" is to analyze their work according to the different functions that they perform. The first such classification system dates back at least 80 years and, after more than eight decades, this system remains widely used by management scholars and writers.[41] A variation of this traditional typology forms the basis for the general sequencing of the chapters in this book (as well as most other textbooks on the subject of management). The four principal managerial functions most applicable to modern organizations are planning, organizing, directing, and controlling.

Planning

Planning involves estimating future conditions and circumstances and, based on these estimations, making decisions about the work of the manager and for all employees for whom she or he is responsible. This function involves at least three distinct levels or types:

1. Strategic planning, which addresses strategic actions designed to achieve the organization's long-range goals:[42]
2. Tactical planning, which translates strategic plans into actions designed to achieve specific and shorter-term goals and objectives;[43] and
3. Operational planning, which identifies the actions needed to accomplish the goals of particular units of the organization or particular product lines in their respective markets.[44]

Planning is important in large and small organizations and in new and established companies. It may be even more important in new and small businesses because they rarely have a surplus of resources available to overcome major mistakes.[45] Firms that do not plan are frequently unprepared for the unexpected. When unexpected events occur, the firms' performance suffers, and they may have to take extraordinary actions.[46] Thus, planning is a highly important managerial function.[47]

planning
estimating future conditions and circumstances and making decisions about appropriate courses of action

Organizing

To conduct managerial work, resources must be integrated systematically, and this function is called **organizing.** It involves identifying the appropriate structure of relationships among positions, and the people occupying them, and linking that structure to the overall strategic direction of the organization.[48] Because today's world is full of uncertainties and ambiguities, organizing is a critical function of managers. At its most basic level, the purpose of this managerial function is the attempt to bring order to the organization. Without it, chaos would ensue.

organizing
systematically integrating resources to accomplish tasks

Most people think of the organization structure as represented by an organization chart. An organization chart informs others about some portions of the formal structure; yet, organizing involves much more. For example, decisions about what units should be represented on the firm's project teams are a part of organizing.[49] The degree of autonomy granted to these units is a managerial organizing decision. Often firms producing modular products also have autonomous modular organization units.[50] Such units are becoming more common when integrating units from acquired businesses and when establishing international subsidiaries.[51] As a result, the organizing function of management is complex and challenging.

Home Depot had a decentralized organizational structure prior to Bob Nardelli becoming CEO. The firm's store managers had a great deal of autonomy to select products and offer services that satisfied local customers. And, the company achieved significant success using this structure. However, because Nardelli felt the decentralized structure was costly and inefficient, he implemented a centralized structure along with a strong monitoring and control system (for example, a centralized inventory control system). While the new structure was more efficient, it also eroded the entrepreneurial spirit and customer satisfaction suffered. As a result, Home Depot lost market share to competitors and its financial performance declined. These outcomes suggest that organizational structure matters a great deal. This case example also suggests the importance of leadership in developing and implementing changes. Leadership is an important dimension of directing; the next topic to be examined.

Directing

This function has typically had a number of different labels over the years. **Directing** is the process of attempting to influence other people to attain the organization's objectives. It heavily involves leading and motivating those for whom the manager is responsible, interacting with them effectively in group and team situations, and communicating in ways that acknowledge and support their efforts to accomplish tasks and achieve organizational goals. Directing has several dimensions, including leadership, motivation, communication, and managing groups or teams.

directing
the process of attempting to influence other people to attain an organization's objectives

A MANAGER'S CHALLENGE

CHANGE

The Failure of Home Depot's Organizational Structure Changes

Home Depot was known for its entrepreneurial approach and customer service. To promote an entrepreneurial spirit and strong customer service, the company was highly decentralized, with much autonomy given to each store in serving its local community and customers. Flexibility of action was valued even at the department level within a store. As a result, Home Depot grew to be large and highly successful. Its sales grew to $45 billion in 2000 from its beginnings in 1979, earning it the title of the fastest-growing retailer in U.S. history.

In 2000 Home Depot hired a new CEO: former GE executive Bob Nardelli. Nardelli was alarmed at what he considered a lack of control and the need to reduce costs. Thus, he implemented an aggressive plan to institute controls that effectively centralized many merchandise and supply decisions. He bought self-checkout equipment and inventory control systems. The investment of almost $1 billion in new technology allowed top managers to measure better the activities at the store level and local managers were then held accountable for their numbers. Yet, while these centralized controls helped to manage the costs, morale of the many managers and employees suffered.

The management model implemented was more of a military style with a hierarchical approach to decision making, emphasizing control and efficiency—a stark contrast to the decentralized decision making and entrepreneurial culture that existed before Nardelli became CEO. In the previous environment, leaders tried to serve as mentors and coaches, enhancing morale. Store managers and unit and department managers within the stores operated in a reasonably autonomous manner and with an entrepreneurial spirit. Nardelli's approach represented a dramatic change dictated from the top.

While Nardelli's changes created greater discipline and more structure, they also led to unexpected consequences. People were unhappy with their loss of autonomy and flexibility. They disliked their inability to be entrepreneurial. Because everything was controlled according to the numbers, managers managed to the numbers. Some felt the new culture was based on fear. Morale among store managers and

Charlie Neibergall/AP Wide World Photos

CEO, Frank Blake, (Bob Nardelli's successor) refocused the business on its original structure with a more entrepreneurial spirit. Customer satisfaction once again increased, helping the firm remain financially fit.

employees declined significantly and turnover occurred. Home Depot's customer service also declined and competitors such as Lowes attained a foothold, taking market share away from Home Depot. As a result, Home Depot's stock market performance suffered. Finally, partly because of these problems and in a dispute with the board of directors, Bob Nardelli resigned.

The new CEO, Frank Blake, managed to stop the skid by closing Home Depot's specialty stores, refocusing on its prime business and eliminating expansion, especially during the recent economic recession. While the reduction in capital spending and operating costs from store closings helped Home Depot remain financially fit. Home Depot also reemphasized customer satisfaction. But, Lowes, its primary competitor is not standing still either. It has entered the Mexico and UK markets. Time will tell if these are profitable moves.

Sources: M. A. Hitt, C. Miller, and A. Collela, *Organizational Behavior* (Hoboken: John Wiley & Sons, 2011); M. Marcus, "Home Depot Rallies as Wall Street Weakens," *Forbes,* February 8, 2010, http://www.forbes.com; J. McGregor, "Smart Cost-cutting: How Home Depot Built It In," *BusinessWeek,* August 4, 2009, http://www.businessweek.com; L. Uchitelle, "Home Depot Girds for Continued Weakness," *New York Times,* May 19, 2009, http://www.nytimes.com; J. Creswell and M. Barbaro, "Home Depot Ousts Chief," *International Herald Tribune,* January 2007, http://www.iht.com.

Leaders must develop effective relationships with employees, and their actions should result in fair outcomes, often referred to as *justice*.[52] Leaders try to develop positive psychological capital in their employees, which in turn has several positive outcomes such as higher productivity and a lower probability of leaving the organization.[53] Leaders can have a significant impact on an organization's outcomes—for example, on its innovation and performance.[54] Thus, managers' leadership actions are important. Managers use leadership actions to manage change (to transform organizations and units).[55] A critical function for managers as leaders is to motivate their employees to be highly productive. To do so requires that the managers understand the individuals they manage and use the tools at their disposal to create individualized rewards tied to employees' performance.[56] Many managers focus their activities on directing teams in the current organizational environment. Thus, as leaders, they must find ways to direct the team while simultaneously motivating individuals, empowering both the team and its individual members.[57] For these reasons, directing is a challenging responsibility for managers.

Controlling

The word **controlling** sometimes has a negative connotation. Yet, *control* is a necessary and important managerial function. The essence of this function is to regulate the work of those for whom a manager is responsible.[58] Managers can accomplish control in several different ways, including setting standards of performance for employees in advance, monitoring ongoing (real-time) performance and, especially, assessing the performance of employees on completed tasks.[59] The results of these evaluations are then fed back into the manager's planning process. However, controlling employee behavior is a difficult task. If managers do not take great care in this process, they can elicit some unexpected and undesirable behaviors.[60] Therefore, managers must apply controls carefully and effectively.[61] Although they might want to avoid controls that are too tight for their employees, managers must also be careful to avoid overly loose controls. The absence of effective controls can lead to negative outcomes, such as the Enron affair and the more recent problems in several major financial services firms, such as Lehman Brothers and Goldman Sachs. Thus, managers must achieve a *balanced* set of controls.

controlling
regulating the work of those for whom a manager is responsible

It is important to consider these four managerial functions as parts of a reciprocal and recurring process, as illustrated in Exhibit 1.1.

Managerial Roles

Some years ago, the Canadian scholar Henry Mintzberg proposed another approach to understanding managerial work.[62] Mintzberg based his classification system on research regarding how managers spend their time at work, primarily with regard to the roles they play. This way of viewing managers' work activities complements the functional approach; it provides additional understanding and insights on what managers do.

Mintzberg's typology of managerial roles has three major categories—interpersonal, informational, and decisional—each of which contains specific roles. Together, there are 10 such roles in this typology, as shown in Exhibit 1.2 and described in the following sections.

Deb M. explains several interpersonal roles that she fulfilled in her managerial job (see A Week in the Managerial Life of Deb M.). Among those are the leader role and the liaison role explored next.

EXHIBIT 1.1

Managerial Functions

INTERPERSONAL ROLES Interpersonal roles are composed of three types of behavior and are derived directly from the manager's formal authority granted by the organization. They are:

1. *The Figurehead Role* This set of behaviors emphasizes ceremonial activities, such as attending a social function, welcoming a visiting dignitary, or presiding at a farewell reception for a departing employee. A familiar term

EXHIBIT 1.2

Types of Managerial Roles

for this role of representing the organization, borrowed from the military, is "showing the flag." Over time, this behavior is important and is a necessary component of a manager's job. For example, the dean of a business school often finds it necessary to participate in figurehead activities such as commencement ceremonies, which are important for the long-term benefit of the school.

2. *The Leader Role* This role involves influencing or directing others. It is the set of responsibilities people typically associate with a manager's job, as the organization gives the manager formal authority over the work of others. To the extent that managers are able to translate this authority into actual influence, they are exercising leadership behavior. A manager demonstrates leadership behavior when, for example, a newly appointed project team leader gathers her team and discusses the vision and goals for the team and how to accomplish them.[63]

3. *The Liaison Role* This role emphasizes a manager's contacts with those outside the formal chain of command. These contacts include not only other managers within the organization but also such external individuals as customers, suppliers, government officials, and managers from other organizations. It also emphasizes lateral interactions, as contrasted with vertical interpersonal interactions of a manager, and it highlights the fact that an important part of a manager's job is to serve as an integrator for his or her own unit and other units or groups.[64] The liaison role applies to the situation where a marketing manager interacts with key customers to learn about their reactions to new product ideas.

INFORMATIONAL ROLES This set of roles builds on the interpersonal relationships that a manager establishes, and it underscores the importance of the network of contacts a manager builds and maintains.[65] There are three specific informational roles:

1. *The Monitor Role* This type of behavior involves extensive information seeking in which managers engage to remain aware of crucial developments that may affect their units and their own work. Such monitoring typically deals with spoken and written information regarding "soft" as well as "hard" facts. An example of this role would be a manager attending an industry conference who spends considerable time in informal lobby and cocktail lounge conversations in order to gather data on current developments in the industry.

2. *The Disseminator Role* A manager not only receives information but also sends it. This often includes information that the receiver wants but otherwise has no easy access to without the help of the manager. A supervisor who learns about the firm's reorganization plans affecting his or her department and conveys that information to subordinates is acting in a disseminator role. For example, Deb played a disseminator

A week in the managerial life of   DEB M.

Deb M. is the director of organizational effectiveness for a Canadian oil and gas company.

Question: Describe the type and range of managerial activities in which you were involved this past week.

Last week, 70 percent of my time was spent in meetings with others. That's a bit high but not totally unusual.

One of the meetings, I organized and led. Actually, it was a two-day work meeting with HR peers in other parts of the company. We were working on coordinating our HR activities, such as recruiting and performance management, across the company. We have four separate operating units, and each has its own HR department to some extent.

One of the other meetings involved making a presentation to our corporate senior management team regarding our compensation strategy. I was explaining how changes we proposed to make would help us better attract and retain employees with key skills.

I also had a meeting with my boss to review resource needs for my team in order to manage increasing workloads. I spent several hours interviewing job candidates for a new hire to join my team.

I also conducted an orientation session with a number of our managers to explain our new job evaluation system. The rest of the time was spent working on several efforts to better integrate and harmonize certain HR practices, such as pay, across the company. This involved both working with my subordinates as well as working on my own.

Question: What do you like best about your job as a manager?

One of the things I like best about my job is that I have the opportunity to influence the decisions and actions that will have a significant impact on the success of the company. Much of our success depends on the people we attract and select into the company and the performance current employees contribute. My job in HR and the work of my subordinates contribute directly to the quality of people we have and how well they perform.

Question: In the past year or so, what is the biggest change to which you have had to respond?

We are going through a lot of changes right now. We have changed our strategy and our structure, but most of these changes were planned. The unexpected changes have involved individuals who have either deviated from the agreed-to plan and/or have not shared key pieces of information that would have caused us to plan differently. In the first case, I've had to rely on my interpersonal skills to try and get the person back on track. In the second case, I've had to incorporate the new information and adjust our plans.

---

role when she made a presentation on her company's new compensation program to the firm's senior managers.

3. ***The Spokesperson Role*** A manager is frequently called upon to represent the views of the unit for which he or she is responsible. At lower management levels, this typically involves representing the unit to other individuals or groups within the organization. At higher management levels, this typically involves an external component, presenting the organization's activities and concerns to external constituents, such as customers and suppliers.[66] For example, when the manager of the western region meets with other regional managers and presents the views of his region's sales personnel about how well a proposed new sales incentive plan is working, he is functioning in a spokesperson role.

DECISIONAL ROLES The final category in the typology of roles relates to the decision-making requirements of a manager's job. There are four such decisional roles:

1. ***The Entrepreneurial Role*** Managers not only make routine decisions in their jobs but also frequently engage in activities that explore new opportunities or start new projects. Such entrepreneurial behavior within an organization often involves a series of small

decisions that permit ongoing assessment about whether to continue or abandon new ventures.[67] Playing this role often involves some risk, but the sequence of decisions usually limits this risk. Suppose, for example, that a lower-level production manager comes up with an idea for a new organizational sales unit. She then discusses the idea with her colleagues and, based on their reactions, modifies it and presents it to upper-level management. Such a manager is playing an entrepreneurial role that goes beyond her regular responsibilities.

2. *The Disturbance Handler Role*   Managers initiate actions of their own, but they must also respond to problems or "disturbances." In this role, a manager often acts as a judge, problem solver, or conflict manager. The goal of such actions is to stop small problems from developing into larger ones. If a manager faces a situation in which employees cannot agree about who will do a particularly unpleasant but necessary task, the manager must settle the matter. In doing so, he or she is functioning as a disturbance handler. When Deb M. took action to correct an employee's deviation from the plan, she acted in the disturbance handler role.

3. *The Resource Allocator Role*   Because resources must be managed efficiently in organizations and slack rarely exists, an important responsibility of managers is deciding how to distribute resources.[68] Allocation decisions have a direct effect on a unit's performance and indirectly communicate information to employees about the relative importance of the firm's activities.[69] The manager of front desk services for a large resort hotel who decides how many and which clerks to assign to each shift is operating in a resource allocator role. Deb M.'s decisions related to her team's resource needs and their allocation represents the resource allocator role.

4. *The Negotiator Role*   Managers are often called upon to make accommodations with other units or other organizations (depending on the level of the management position). In this decisional situation, managers are responsible for knowing what resources they can or cannot commit to particular negotiated solutions. A manager who serves on a negotiating team to establish a new joint venture with another company functions in the negotiator role.

Decisional roles are particularly important in managerial responsibilities. Managers are expected to make decisions, and many of those decisions have important performance implications. For example, managers have to decide when to develop and take new products to the market, when to develop new ventures, when to hire and lay off employees, and so forth. They are expected to make these decisions efficiently, with due speed but also comprehensively.[70] Frequently, there are no clearly correct paths to follow. Rather, decisions often require that managers exercise reasonable judgment and use their education, training, and experience.[71] And, finally, managers must make decisions that leads the company to engage in ethical practices.[72]

This typology of managerial work roles emphasizes the considerable variety of behaviors required by managers. Certainly, the extent to which any particular role is important varies considerably from one managerial job to another. The front-line supervisor of a group of bank tellers is likely to have a different mix of roles than the bank's executive vice president. Nevertheless, the ten roles help to understand the total set of activities that managers usually have to perform over time.

Managerial Job Dimensions

Analyzing the dimensions of managerial jobs provides additional insight about the work. British researcher Rosemary Stewart developed one particular approach.[73] Stewart proposed that, regardless of its level and type of unit in an organization, three dimensions characterize a managerial job:

- the demands made on it;
- the constraints placed on it; and
- the choices permitted in it.

A week in the managerial life of   GREG K.

Greg K. is director of finance and accounting for a large division of a financial services firm.

Question: Describe the type and range of activities you were involved in, as a manager, this past week.

In my managerial job, I'm involved in a variety of activities, ranging from division project meetings to staff meetings to time to work on my own projects. Here is a brief overview of my activities this past week:

Monday: In the morning, I participated in a conference call with various management-level employees to discuss activity at one of our broker-dealers. The remainder of the day largely involved interacting with staff, completing my assignments, and reacting to various inquiries from other departments, divisions, and auditors.

Tuesday: On this morning I participated in a biweekly status call with our third-party administrator for one of our products. Following the conference call, I met with one of my direct reports (accounting manager) for our weekly staff meeting. We discussed the status of various department projects, staffing issues, upcoming projects, and current events affecting the division. Later that day I met with our accounting coordinator to discuss the status of a pricing project on which she was working.

Wednesday: This was a light day for meetings; however, I attended a one-hour training class regarding upcoming new product features that we will be offering. I then worked on several job-related projects.

Thursday: Thursdays are typically busy in the mornings due to two meetings I attend: a biweekly technology meeting and a weekly product meeting. When both of these meetings occur, it typically takes two or three hours of my morning. This Thursday our department head held a monthly staff meeting to discuss general events affecting the department, the division, and the company.

Friday: The morning began with a weekly investment meeting. I represent our division in this meeting, which includes other representatives from all divisions of the company. The remainder of the day was spent working on various normal tasks.

Aside from the meetings that I attend throughout the week, the remainder of my workweek typically includes other interactions with staff and completion of my other assignments (responsibilities as a "working manager"). I typically interact at least daily with our department head (the Chief Finance Officer—CFO). We discuss new requests and projects, staffing, status of current projects, and so forth. I also interact regularly throughout the day with my five direct reports to discuss projects, answer questions, and provide feedback. I also am responsible for approving all of our sales force travel and expense reports and approving sales support requests that come from our sales force.

Question: What do you like best about your job as a manager?

I need to answer this from two vantage points: one from the perspective of my direct assignments and one from a managerial perspective.

Regarding my direct assignments, the most rewarding part of my job is contributing to a division project that directly affects the division with findings and recommendations that are communicated to senior management. Feeling part of the division team is very rewarding.

As a manager, I enjoy problem solving and coaching my direct reports regarding problems they encounter and complex tasks they have to complete. My company offers several management development programs, and one that I found especially useful concerned leadership. I try to apply knowledge that I learned from the class to situations that arise in my job.

Question: In the past year or so, what is the biggest change to which you have had to respond?

From a management perspective, the most challenging change over the past year was terminating two employees (not my direct reports, but I was highly involved in the process) and adjusting accordingly on all facets of the job. I had not previously been involved in a termination, so it was challenging. The process included performance concerns, HR concerns, reallocating resources within the department to ensure that all the assignments were completed, and communication to other employees (a delicate matter).

Analyzing managerial jobs in this way not only provides further understanding of what managers do but also permits direct comparisons of different jobs, for example, how the position of "manager of information systems" compares with that of "marketing vice president" or "plant manager."

Greg K. engaged in a number of activities that reflect each of the three dimensions of managerial jobs.

DEMANDS This dimension of management refers to what the holder of a particular managerial position must do. "Demands" involve two types: activities or duties to carry out and the standards or levels of minimum performance to meet. Demands can come from several sources, such as the organization, the immediate boss, or the organization of work activities. Typical types of demands include such behavior as attending required meetings, adhering to scheduled deadlines, following certain procedures, and the like. No doubt, for example, Ursula Burns has sales and performance targets to meet in her CEO position at Xerox. Greg K. participates in several regular meetings each week, with his boss, his employees, and other department managers.

CONSTRAINTS "Constraints" are factors that limit a manager's response to various demands. One obvious constraint for any manager is the amount of time available for an activity. Other typical constraints include budgets, technology, the attitudes of subordinates, and legal regulations. All managerial jobs have constraints. Managers need to develop a good understanding of how to minimize or overcome constraints.

CHOICES This dimension underscores the fact that despite demands and constraints, managers always have the opportunity to exercise discretion. Thus, a manager regularly makes choices about what to do or not do, how to complete tasks, and which employees will participate in projects, among others. Frankly, discretion is an important part of a managerial job. How managers exercise discretion and the quality of the judgments they make largely determine their effectiveness as managers. In her present and past managerial positions, Ursula Burns has faced a multitude of choices about how to make staffing decisions, how to demonstrate leadership, how to respond to changing market conditions affecting use of technology based products, and the like.

Exhibit 1.3 illustrates these three job dimensions for two different managerial jobs, a project team manager in a manufacturing company and a manager of a medium-sized fast-food restaurant.

EXHIBIT 1.3 Two Managerial Jobs with Different Demands, Constraints, and Choices

	Job A: Project Team Manager	Job B: Fast-Food Restaurant Manager
Demands	• Develop new product with strong market appeal	• Maintain attractive appearance of restaurant
	• Hold formal weekly progress meeting with boss	• Keep employee costs as low as possible
	• Frequent travel to other company sites	• Meet standards for speed of service
Constraints	• 12-month deadline for product development	• Most employees have limited formal education
	• Project budget limit of $1 million	• Few monetary incentives to reward outstanding performance
	• No choice in selecting team members	• Federal and state health and safety regulations
Choices	• The organizational structure of the project team	• Selection of employee to promote to supervisor
	• Sequencing of project tasks	• Scheduling of shifts and assignments
	• Budget allocations	• Local advertising promotions

EXHIBIT 1.4

Manager's Skills

Technical	Interpersonal	Conceptual
• Specialized knowledge (including when and how to use the skills)	• Sensitivity • Persuasiveness • Empathy	• Logical reasoning • Judgment • Analytical ability

Although both are managerial jobs, their demands and constraints are quite different. Some of the choices permitted, however, are similar. The combination of the three dimensions determines the requirements to be a manager.

What Skills Do Managers Need?

Similar to other human activity, managing involves the exercise of skills, that is, highly developed abilities and competencies. Managers develop these skills through a combination of aptitude, education, training, and experience.[74] Three types are critical for managerial tasks, particularly for the leadership component of management: technical, interpersonal, and conceptual (see Exhibit 1.4).

Technical Skills

Technical skills involve having specialized knowledge about procedures, processes, and equipment, and include knowing how and when to use that knowledge. Research shows that these skills are especially important early in managerial careers (see Exhibit 1.5), when leading lower-level employees and gaining their respect is often part of a manager's job. In addition, technical skills seem to be particularly critical in many successful entrepreneurial start-up firms, such as those involving Steve Jobs and Steve Wozniak at Apple Computer or Bill Gates at Microsoft. Technical skills, whether in an entrepreneurial venture or in a larger organization, are frequently necessary but usually are not sufficient for managing effectively.[75] An overreliance on technical skills may actually reduce a manager's effectiveness. For example, the first Apple computer designed and built by Jobs and Wozniak required technical skills to start the fledgling company. However, as Apple grew, their technical skills became relatively less important because they employed technical specialists. However, Jobs and Wozniak were not always readily able to exchange those technical skills for other, equally impressive leadership skills. As a result, the company had to search for other managerial talent, and did so with mixed success. After gaining considerable managerial experience in other business endeavors, Jobs subsequently returned to lead Apple in the late 1990s with the assistance of other able managers. Since his return, Apple has experienced an incredible amount of success. Because of this, *Fortune* magazine recently named Jobs CEO of the Decade.[76]

Interpersonal Skills

Interpersonal skills such as sensitivity, persuasiveness, and empathy are important at all levels of management, although particularly so at lower and middle levels.[77] A longitudinal study of career advancement conducted at AT&T found evidence that such skills, measured early in careers, were

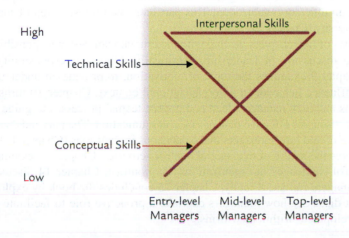

EXHIBIT 1.5

Relative Importance of Managerial Skills at Different Organizational Levels

Marcio Jose Sanchez/AP Wide World Photos

Steve Jobs, Apple Computer designer, returned to Apple in the late 90s and Apple has experienced an incredible amount of success as a result.

important in predicting advancement in managerial ranks 20 years later. However, a lack of these skills may prematurely limit managerial advancement even when other skills exist, but these skills alone are unlikely to guarantee managerial success. Exhibit 1.6 summarizes the findings of one study that investigated reasons why some fast-rising executives eventually plateau in their managerial careers, even when they appeared to start out with acceptable levels of interpersonal skills. As the management researchers suggested, "The charming but not brilliant find that the job gets too big and the problems too complex to get by on interpersonal skills [alone]."[78]

Conceptual Skills

Often called *cognitive ability* or *cognitive complexity,* conceptual skills such as logical reasoning, judgment, and analytical abilities are a relatively strong predictor of managerial effectiveness. These skills are often a major determinant of who reaches the highest management levels in the organization.[79] A clear example of someone who was selected for a CEO job precisely because of his conceptual skills is Jack Welch, former CEO at General Electric. Welch was appointed to GE's top position in 1981 and immediately set out to restructure the organization with the objective of making it more globally competitive. Over time and after several major changes in the organization, he reduced a significant amount of GE's bureaucracy and developed a more flexible organization. He also changed GE's corporate culture to one based on greater employee empowerment.

The Plan of This Book

After examining the nature of management in this chapter, we present the overall structure and plan of the remainder of the book. Following, we identify each part of the book and the chapters within it.

Part 1 provides an introduction to management and critical domains of managerial jobs. These chapters provide you with an introduction to the nature of management (Chapter 1) and its context. Two important contextual dimensions of managerial jobs are ethics and social responsibilities (Chapter 2) and international management and globalization (Chapter 3). Managers must act ethically and be sensitive to the social environment in which their organizations operate.

The rest of the book follows the functions of management. Part 2 examines the functions of planning and organizing. An important decision made by managers is the strategy the organization must follow to achieve a competitive advantage. This aspect is explored in Chapter 4. Chapter 5 discusses the process of planning designed to implement the strategy throughout the organization. Finally, Chapter 6 explains how to organize the firm in order to effectively implement the strategy and operate an efficient organization. This part ends with a discussion of managing human resources and diversity (Chapter 7).

Part 3 consists of five chapters dealing with the crucial managerial responsibility of leading. It begins with a discussion of leadership, a critically important responsibility of managers (Chapter 8). Chapter 9 examines the topic of motivation, to provide an understanding of how managers can influence behavior in an organizational context. Chapter 10 turns to the role of groups and teams and how managers lead and govern teams' processes to guide their performance. Chapter 11 discusses effective managerial communication. The part ends with a discussion of the importance of and how managers make decisions in their jobs (Chapter 12).

Part 4 explores the nature of managerial control activities. Chapter 13 examines basic evaluation and control challenges in organizations. By contrast, Chapter 14 discusses operations controls that managers can use. Finally, Chapter 15 concludes the book by exploring organizational change. It discusses how managers can take a proactive role to facilitate organizational renewal and development within their firms.

EXHIBIT 1.6 Who Succeeds? Who Doesn't?

Potential managerial leaders share traits early on:	Those who don't quite make it:	Those who succeed:
Bright, with outstanding track records	Have been successful, but generally only in one area or type of job.	Have diverse track records, demonstrated ability in many different situations, and a breadth of knowledge of the business or industry.
Have survived stressful situations	Frequently described as moody or volatile. May be able to keep their temper with superiors during crises but are hostile toward peers and subordinates.	Maintain composure in stressful situations, are predictable during crises, are regarded as calm and confident.
Have a few flaws	Cover up problems while trying to fix them. If the problem can't be hidden, they tend to go on the defensive and even blame someone else for it.	Make a few mistakes, but when they do, they admit to them and handle them with poise and grace.
Ambitious and oriented toward problem solving	May attempt to micromanage a position, ignoring future prospects; may staff with the incorrect people or neglect the talents they have; may depend too much on a single mentor, calling their own decision-making ability into question.	While focusing on problem solutions, keep their minds focused on the next position, help develop competent successors, seek advice from many sources.
Good people skills	May be viewed as charming but political or direct and tactless, cold, and arrogant. People don't like to work with them.	Can get along well with different types of people, are outspoken without being offensive, are viewed as direct and diplomatic.

Source: Adapted from M. W. McCall, Jr. and M. M. Lombardo, "Off the Track: Why and How Successful Executives Get Derailed," *Technical Report #21* (Greensboro, NC: Center for Creative Leadership, 1983), pp. 9–11. Copyright © 1983 Center for Creative Leadership. Used with permission.

Managerial Challenges from the Front Line

The Rest of the Story

We know from the opening profile that Blaine Halvorson and his partner Natalie Grof have built their company, Junk Food, into a highly successful organization. Halvorson was creative and took entrepreneurial risks but also learned, from his earlier experience, how to become an effective manager. In 2005, Delta Apparel acquired the company, making Halvorson and Grof wealthy individuals. However, part of the agreement was that Halvorson would remain with Junk Food and continue to build the business. It is his responsibility to continue taking Junk Food to new heights. For a few years Halvorson remained president and CEO, sharing the responsibilities with Grof. Then, he moved into the Chief Creative Officer position with the primary goal of building and expanding the brand. For example, he has been responsible for expanding the Junk Food's global sales and the increased market share achieved during the economic recession. He plans to extend the Junk Food brand to new products and to open Junk Food retail stores in the future.

Summary

- Management is the process of assembling and using sets of resources in a goal-directed manner to accomplish tasks in an organizational setting. It occurs in an organizational context.

- Managers face a number of significant challenges. Managerial challenges include managing change, managing resources, managing strategically, and managing entrepreneurially. Increasing technology and globalization has caused much organizational change, and companies must manage it effectively. Efficient management of resources is only part of the equation. Organizations must develop their resource portfolios and integrate resources to create capabilities that are then leveraged to achieve a competitive advantage. Managers select and implement a strategy designed to provide greater value to customers than do competitors. Finally, managers have to act entrepreneurially, even in large organizations, to identify and exploit opportunities.

- Management is an old concept dating back thousands of years; ancient Chinese rulers used management concepts of organization, specialization of labor, and strategy. The basis of modern management is traditionally thought to be scientific management proscribed by Frederick Taylor during the industrial revolution. However, a number of historical figures contributed to our knowledge of modern management. Other people have contributed to our knowledge of productivity (Frank and Lillian Gilbreth, for example), organization (Alfred Sloan and Chester Barnard), leadership (Mary Parker Follett and Douglas McGregor) and motivation (Abraham Maslow and Frederick Herzberg).

- What managers do can be understood through the functions that they perform. Among them are planning, organizing, directing, and controlling. Planning involves projecting the future conditions and tasks required to be successful in these conditions. Organizing involves identifying the appropriate structure of relationships among positions, and the people occupying them, and linking that structure to the overall strategic direction of the organization. Directing is the process of attempting to influence other people to attain organizational objectives with managerial activities such as leading, motivating, and communicating. Control is a necessary and important managerial function designed to regulate the work of those for whom a manager is responsible.

- A complementary way of viewing managerial work is through the roles they fill. Managerial roles comprise three major categories—interpersonal, informational, and decisional—each of which has specific roles. Interpersonal roles include the figurehead, leader, and liaison. Informational roles include monitor, disseminator, and spokesperson. The four decisional roles are entrepreneurial, disturbance handler, resource allocator, and negotiator.

- Managerial work can also be understood from the dimensions of managerial jobs. The dimensions include the demands and constraints placed on managers and the discretionary choices allowed by the job.

- To effectively perform the functions, fulfill the roles, and deal with the dimensions of the job, managers need several skills. Among these are technical, interpersonal, and conceptual skills. All of the skills are important, but the mix and levels of the skills required to be effective vary by type of managerial job and level in the organization.

Key Terms

controlling 13	management 4	organizing 11
directing 11	organization 4	planning 11

Review Questions

1. How is management defined, and what are its basic elements?
2. What are the four major challenges that managers face, and how do managers deal with them?
3. Who are the primary historical figures who have contributed to modern management, and what are their most important ideas?
4. What are the four primary functions of management and their contents?
5. What are the ten managerial roles and their importance to managerial work?
6. How does each of the three dimensions of managerial jobs contribute to managerial tasks?
7. What are the three primary managerial skills, and how does their importance vary with the type and level of a manager's job?

Assessing Your Capabilities

Managerial Core Values

Rank the following statements as to how important they would be to you as a manager (with 1 being most important and 16 being least important).

_____ Be professional

_____ Cooperate with others in the organization

_____ Make a profit in the short term

_____ Solve problems

_____ Achieve positive results

_____ Deliver quality outcomes

_____ Think in the long term

_____ Satisfy your client

_____ Communicate effectively with others

_____ Offer superior value to constituents

_____ Take risks in order to innovate

_____ Lead to serve others

_____ Motivate employees

_____ Enjoy your work

_____ Reach your goals

_____ Build and maintain relationships with others

There are no correct or incorrect answers, but the ranking suggests the core values that will underlie your actions as a manager. For example, if you give a high rank to cooperating with others, leading to serve others, building relationships, communicating effectively, and motivating employees, you are likely to emphasize a service role. Alternatively, if your highest rankings go to enjoying your work, making a short-term profit, and reaching your goals, your managerial activities are more likely to be opportunistic. Finally, if you highly rank solving problems, achieving positive results, delivering quality outcomes, and offering superior value, your managerial actions are likely to be results-oriented. Share rankings with a few classmates and discuss why they are different for each of you.

Source: Based on J. van Rekom, G. B. M. van Riel, and B. Wierenga, "A Methodology for Assessing Organizational Core Values," *Journal of Management Studies* 43 (2006): 176–201. Copyright © 2006. Used with permission.

Team Exercise

Form teams of three to five people.

The H. J. Heinz Company has made a number of significant changes in its operations since 2002, when it spun off several noncore businesses. Some attribute the changes to Nelson Pelz, a hedge fund manager and activist investor, who acquired over 5 percent of Heinz stock as an activist investor. Others attribute the changes and performance improvement over time to the management of Heinz CEO William Johnson.

Obtain information about the company and the changes it has made over time. The following Web sites might be useful:

www.heinz.com/heinz.aspx

http://www.heinz.com/our-company/investor-relations.aspx

For links to up-to-date information on the Heinz Company, the following Web site may be helpful: http://www.alacrastore.com/company-snapshot/H_J_Heinz_Company-1007855

Analyze the information you obtained and, as a team, answer the following questions.

1. What major challenges have Heinz managers faced over the last five years?
2. What managerial functions are evident in the actions Johnson has taken to improve his company's performance? Please link the actions and functions.
3. What managerial roles are displayed in Johnson's actions? Please relate the actions to specific roles.

Closing Case   FedEx's Successful Internationalization

Companies desiring to compete in global markets need to be flexible in how, where, and what they provide customers. As early as 1979, FedEx founder Fred Smith acknowledged that customer needs were constantly changing, and to be successful FedEx would need to implement strategies to help it become mobile and flexible and at the same time ensure strong customer satisfaction. Through a series of buyouts, FedEx implemented successful strategies in Asia. Simultaneously, the firm implemented innovative technologies, creating a seamless experience for international customers using its services.

It was no accident that FedEx became the premier carrier servicing Asia. As early as the 1980s, Smith recognized the growing market in China and knew that Asia would become an economic powerhouse. So, in 1984, FedEx launched operations in China and began the first direct express flight to the mainland in 1996. In 1989, FedEx paid $895 million to buy Tiger International Inc., a struggling hauler with rights to fly into most Asian airports and a management team familiar with the Pacific Rim. Wall Street did not like this decision because of Asia's unpredictability, but FedEx saw the potential in this region. The decision turned out to be highly profitable. FedEx's business in Asian countries has soared, with a dramatic increase in the volume of goods shipped over FedEx's international network and much of the growth coming from Asia. In January 2006, FedEx spent $400 million to buy out its partner in China, Tanjin Datian W Group, giving FedEx full control over Datian's trucking fleet and 89 distribution hubs. It also gave FedEx more control over services in secondary Chinese cities that are becoming more linked to the global economy as manufacturers shift factories further inland as they flee increasing labor costs in coastal regions. FedEx closed its Asian hub in the Philippines in 2008 and built a new $150 million super hub in the heart of Guangzhou, one of China's fastest-growing manufacturing districts. To provide seamless services, FedEx recognized the need to provide all types of services that identify communication needs and in 2004 rebranded all of its companies to make customers aware of the breadth of its services.

Implementing the proper IT system to assist FedEx with the challenges of growing internationally was equally important. FedEx managers realized that an IT system must take into account the idiosyncrasies of different countries, custom authorities, and individual needs. FedEx knew that, to provide detailed and accurate information to customs about customer shipments, it had to automate and electronically track all shipment documentation. So, FedEx installed the technology for customs authorities to review the documentation, in turn, simplifying the customs process and giving them the ability to identify and examine the inbound manifest of shipments quickly and accurately.

The IT system also gives customers seamless clearance through customs, plus visibility of their shipments and customs procedures through to a receipt. A customer can go online from anywhere to conduct a transaction or track a shipment. FedEx also administers its own IT operations and develops much of its own technology. In order to achieve this, it has a large team of developers and IT personnel.

These initiatives have helped make FedEx successful, especially in the Asian market. FedEx continues to expand its operations in Asia, opening a freight forwarding office in India in early 2010. In fact, during 2008–2010, it opened 22 freight forwarding offices in international locations such as London, Brussels and Mexico City. Additionally, in 2010, FedEx announced the start of a new international supply chain service called International DirectDistribution. The intent is to provide a single rapid, flexible solution that increases the speed to market and reduces cost. It consolidates multiple packages, bypasses distribution centers, and streamlines customs clearance, thus delivering goods quickly to their final destination. The company's managers realized that in order to be successful, they needed to respond quickly to the changes and new challenges of the "flatter" world. FedEx has been one package ahead of its competitors as a first mover in areas throughout the world.

Questions

1. Why has FedEx been so successful in Asia?
2. Can competitors imitate FedEx's approach in international markets and take market share away from the company? Why or why not?
3. Is the FedEx move to close its hub in the Philippines and build a new one in China a good decision for its Asian operations? Explain.
4. Can you identify the application of the managerial functions of planning, organizing, and controlling in FedEx activities? Explain.

Sources: "FedEx Launches New International Freight Service," *FleetOwner*, January 29, 2010, http://www.fleetowner.com/management/news/fedex-international_freight; H. Chemikoff, "Update 3-FedEx Opens First India Freight Forwarding Offices," Thomson Reuters, February 11, 2010, http://www.reuters.com/assets; J Bourke, "FedEx Opens British Freight Forwarding Offices," *RoadTransport.com*, February 18, 2010, http://www.roadtransport.com/articles; D. Goulden, "Managing IT for a Flat World," *BusinessWeek*, October 2, 2006, http://www.businessweek.com; D. Foust, "FedEx," *BusinessWeek*, April 3, 2006, http://www.businessweek.com; A. Counsell, "Doing More Faster and Better," *Financial Times*, February 14, 2006, http://www.ft.com; C. Shevlin, "Move out of Range to Think out of the Box," *Financial Times*, August 19, 2004, http://www.ft.com; S. Murray, "Putting the House in Order," *Financial Times*, November 8, 2006, http://www.ft.com; "FedEx Completes Acquisition of DTW Group," *BusinessWeek*, February 28, 2007, http://www.businessweek.com; Corporate Web site, "FedEx Reports Solid Revenue and Earnings Growth," http://www.fedex.com/us/investorrelations.com, accessed December 20, 2006.

References

1. G. Latta, "A Process Model of Organizational Change in Cultural Context (OC^3 Model)," *Journal of Leadership and Organizational Studies* 16 (2009): 19–37.

2. G. Davenport (trans. 1976), *Herakleitos and Diogenes*. Pt. 1, Fragment 23.

3. T. Reay, K. Golden-Biddle, and K. Germann, "Legitimizing a New Role: Small Wins and Microprocesses of Change," *Academy of Management Journal* 49 (2006): 977–996.

4. A. Taylor, "The Next Generation: Technology Adoption and Integration through Internal Competition in New Product Development," *Organization Science* 21, no. 1 (2010): 23–41.

5. M. A. Hitt, K. T. Haynes, and R. Serpa, "Strategic Leadership for the Twenty-first Century," *Business Horizon* (2010): in press; M. A. Hitt, B. W. Keats, and S. M. DeMarie, "Navigating in the New Competitive Landscape: Building Strategic Flexibility and Competitive Advantage in the 21st Century," *Academy of Management Executive* 12, no. 4 (1998): 22–42.

6. L. Deng and P. Gibson, "Mapping and Modeling the Capacities that Underlie Effective Cross-cultural Leadership," *Cross Cultural Management* 16, no. 4 (2009): 347–366.

7. Hitt, Haynes, and Serpa, "Strategic Leadership for the Twenty-first Century."

8. T. L. Friedman, *The World Is Flat* (New York: Farrar, Straus and Giroux, 2005).

9. C. Reuter, K. Foerstl, E. Hartmann, and C. Blome, "Sustainable Global Supplier Management: The Role of Dynamic Capabilities in Achieving Competitive Advantage," *Journal of Supply Chain Management* 46, no. 2 (2010): 45–63.

10. M. A. Hitt, V. Franklin, and H. Zhu, "Culture, Institutions and International Strategy," *Journal of International Management* 12 (2006): 222–234.

11. Y. Luo and O. Shenkar, "The Multinational Corporation as a Multilingual Community: Language and Organization in a Global Context," *Journal of International Business Studies* 37 (2006): 321–339.

12. K. Meyer, "Globalfocusing: From Domestic Conglomerates to Global Specialists," *Journal of Management Studies* 43 (2006): 1109–1144.

13. M. Arndt and B. Einhorn, "The 50 Most Innovative Companies," *Bloomberg BusinessWeek,* April 25 (2010): 35–41.

14. Y. Lu, L. Zhou, G. Bruton, and W. Li, "Capabilities as a Mediator Linking Resources and the International Performance of Entrepreneurial Firms in an Emerging Economy," *Journal of International Business Studies* 41 (2010): 419–436.

15. D. G. Sirmon, M. A. Hitt, and R. D. Ireland, "Managing Firm Resources in Dynamic Environments to Create Value: Looking Inside the Black Box," *Academy of Management Review* 32 (2007): 273–292.

16. I. Barreto, "Dynamic Capabilities: A Review of Past Research and an Agenda for the Future," *Journal of Management* 36 (2010): 256–280; S. Thornhill, "Knowledge, Innovation and Firm Performance in High- and Low-technology Regimes," *Journal of Business Venturing* 21 (2006): 687–703.

17. J. Salk and M. A. Lyles, "Gratitude, Nostalgia and What Now? Knowledge Acquisition and Learning a Decade Later," *Journal of International Business Studies* 38 (2007): 19–26.

18. D. G. Sirmon, S. Gove, and M. A. Hitt, "Resource Management in Dynamic Competitive Rivalry: The Effects of Resource Bundling and Deployment," *Academy of Management Journal* 51 (2008): 918–935; D. Tan and J. T. Mahoney, "Why a Multinational Firm Chooses Expatriates: Integrating Resource-based, Agency and Transaction Costs Perspectives," *Journal of Management Studies* 43 (2006): 457–484.

19. A. K. Gupta, K. G. Smith, and C. E. Shalley, "The Interplay Between Exploration and Exploitation," *Academy of Management Journal* 49 (2006): 693–706; D. Lavie, "Capability Reconfiguration: An Analysis of Incumbent Responses to Technological Change," *Academy of Management Review* 31 (2006): 153–174.

20. A. M. Mulcahy, "From Survival to Success: Leading in Turbulent Times," speech in the U.S. Chamber of Commerce Leadership Series, Washington, D.C., www.uschamber.com, April 2, 2003.

21. R. E. Ployhart, "Staffing in the 21st Century: New Challenges and Strategic Opportunities," *Journal of Management* 32 (2006): 868–897.

22. M. A. Hitt, L. Bierman, K. Uhlenbruck, and K. Shimizu, "The Importance of Resources in the Internationalization of Professional Service Firms: The Good, the Bad and the Ugly," *Academy of Management Journal* 49 (2006): 1137–1157.

23. M. A. Hitt, R. D. Ireland, and R. E. Hoskisson, *Strategic Management: Competitiveness and Globalization* (Cincinnati: Southwestern Publishing Co., 2011).

24. A. S. DeNisi, M. A. Hitt, and S. E. Jackson, "The Knowledge-based Approach to Sustainable Competitive Advantage," in S. E. Jackson, M. A. Hitt, and A. S. DeNisi (eds.), *Managing Knowledge for Sustained Competitive Advantage* (San Francisco: Jossey-Bass, 2003).

25. S. L. Newbert, "Empirical Research on the Resource-Based View of the Firm: An Assessment and Suggestions for Future Research," *Strategic Management Journal* 28 (2007): 121–146.

26. D. G. Sirmon and M. A. Hitt, "Contingencies within Dynamic Managerial Capabilities: Interdependent Effects of Resource Investment and Deployment on Firm Performance," *Strategic Management Journal* 30 (2009): 1375–1394.

27. Sirmon, Hitt, and Ireland, "Managing Firm Resources in Dynamic Environments to Create Value."

28. W. S. Smith, "Vitality in Business: Executing a New Strategy at Unilever," *Journal of Business Strategy* 30, no. 4 (2009): 31–41.

29. R. A. Baron, "Opportunity Recognition as Pattern Recognition: How Entrepreneurs 'Connect the Dots' to Identify New Business Opportunities," *Academy of Management Perspectives* 20 (2006): 104–119; J. M. Howell, C. M. Shea, and C. A. Higgins, "Champions of Product Innovations: Defining, Developing, and Validating a Measure of Champion Behavior," *Journal of Business Venturing* 20 (2005): 641–661.

30. J. C. Short, D. J. Ketchen, C. L. Shook, and R. D. Ireland, "The Concept of Opportunity in Entrepreneurship Research: Past Accomplishments and Future Challenges," *Journal of Management* 36 (2010): 40–65.

31. M. M. Keupp and O. Gassmann, "The Past and the Future of International Entrepreneurship: A Review and Suggestions for Developing the Field," *Journal of Management* 35 (2009): 600–633.

32. N. O'Reagan and M. Maclean, "What We Need Is an Entrepreneurial Society: An Interview with David Audretsch," *Journal of Strategy and Management* 2 (2009): 110–114; M. A. Hitt, R. D. Ireland, S. M. Camp, and D. S. Sexton, *Strategic Entrepreneurship: Creating a New Mindset* (Oxford, UK: Blackwell Publishing, 2002).

33. R. McGrath and I. MacMillan, *The Entrepreneurial Mindset* (Boston: Harvard Business School Press, 2000).

34. R. D. Ireland, M. A. Hitt, and D. G. Sirmon, "A Model of Strategic Entrepreneurship: The Construct and Its Dimensions," *Journal of Management* 29 (2003): 963–989.

35. Ibid.

36. V. P. Rindova and W. H. Starbuck, "Ancient Chinese Theories of Control," *Journal of Management Inquiry* 6 (1997): 144–159.

37. D. Ahlstrom D. Lamond, and Z. Ding, "Reexamining Some Management Lessons from Military History," *Asia Pacific Journal of Management* 26 (2009): 617–642.

38. D. A. Wren and R. G. Greenwood, *Management Innovators: The People and Ideas That Have Shaped Modern Business* (New York: Oxford University Press, 1998).

39. S. Wagner-Tsukamoto, "An Institutional Economic Reconstruction of Scientific Management: On the Lost Theoretical Logic of Taylorism," *Academy of Management Review* 32 (2007): 105–117.
40. Ibid.
41. S. J. Carroll and D. J. Gillen, "Are the Classical Management Functions Useful in Describing Managerial Work?" *Academy of Management Review* 12 (1987): 38–51.
42. V. F. Misangyi, H. Elms, T. Greckhamer, and J. A. LePine, "A New Perspective on a Fundamental Debate: A Multilevel Approach to Industry, Corporate, and Business Unit Effects," *Strategic Management Journal* 27 (2006): 571–590.
43. S. Brown and K. Blackmon, "Aligning Manufacturing Strategy and Business-level Competitive Strategy in New Competitive Environments: The Case for Strategic Resonance," *Journal of Management Studies* 42 (2005): 793–815.
44. G. Dowell, "Product Line Strategies of New Entrants in an Established Industry: Evidence from the U.S. Bicycle Industry," *Strategic Management Journal* 27 (2006): 959–979.
45. S. Shane and F. Delmar, "Planning for the Market: Business Planning Before Marketing and the Continuation of Organizing Efforts," *Journal of Business Venturing* 19 (2004): 767–785.
46. J. L. Morrow, D. G. Sirmon, M. A. Hitt, and T. R. Holcomb, "Creating Value in the Face of Declining Performance: Firm Strategies and Organizational Recovery," *Strategic Management Journal* 28 (2007): 271–283.
47. A. Burke, S. Fraser, and F. J. Greene, "The Multiple Effects of Business Planning on New Venture Performance," *Journal of Management Studies* 47 (2010): 391–415.
48. J. I. Galan and M. J. Sanchez-Bueno, "The Continuing Validity of the Strategy–structure Nexus: New Findings, 1993–2003," *Strategic Management Journal* 30 (2009): 1234–1243.
49. M. Lindgren and J. Packendorff, "What's New in New Forms of Organizing? On the Construction of Gender in Project-based Work," *Journal of Management Studies* 43 (2006): 841–866.
50. G. Hoetker, "Do Modular Products Lead to Modular Organizations?" *Strategic Management Journal* 27 (2006): 501–518.
51. S. Karim, "Modularity in Organizational Structure: The Reconfiguration of Internally Developed and Acquired Business Units," *Strategic Management Journal* 27 (2006): 799–823; A. W. Harzing, "Geographical Distance and the Role and Management of Subsidiaries: The Case of Subsidiaries Down Under," *Asia-Pacific Journal of Management* 23 (2006): 167–185.
52. B. Erdogan, R. C. Liden, and M. L. Kraimer, "Justice and Leader-Member Exchange: The Moderating Role of Organizational Culture," *Academy of Management Journal* 49 (2006): 395–406.
53. J. B. Avey, F. Luthans, and C. M. Youssef, "The Additive Value of Positive Psychological Capital in Predicting Work Attitudes and Behaviors," *Journal of Management* 36 (2010): 430–452.
54. D. S. Elenkov and I. M. Manev, "Top Management Leadership and Influence on Innovation: The Role of Sociocultural Context," *Journal of Management* 31 (2005): 381–402; R. T. Sparrowe, B. W. Soetjipto, and M. L. Kraimer, "Do Leaders' Influence Tactics Relate to Members' Helping Behaviors? It Depends on the Quality of the Relationship," *Academy of Management Journal* 49 (2006): 1194–1208.
55. F. Walter and H. Bruch, "An Affective Events Model of Charismatic Leadership Behavior: A Review, Theoretical Integration and Research Agenda," *Journal of Management,* 35 (2009): 1428–1452; R. F. Piccolo and J. A. Colquitt, "Transformational Leadership and Job Behaviors: The Mediating Role of Core Job Characteristics," *Academy of Management Journal* 49 (2006): 327–340.
56. P. Steel and C. L. Konig, "Integrating Theories of Motivation," *Academy of Management Review* 31 (2006): 889–913.
57. J. B. Wu, A. S. Tsui, and A. J. Kinicki, "Consequences of Differentiated Leadership in Groups," *Academy of Management Journal* 53 (2010): 90–106; A. Srivastava, K. M. Bartol, and E. A. Locke, "Empowering Leadership in Management Teams: Effects on Knowledge Sharing, Efficacy and Performance," *Academy of Management Journal* 49 (2006): 1239–1251.
58. T. R. Tyler and S. L. Blader, "Can Business Effectively Regulate Employee Conduct? The Antecedents of Rule Following in Work Settings," *Academy of Management Journal* 49 (2006): 1143–1158.
59. W. P. Smith and F. Tabak, "Monitoring Employee E-mails: Is There Any Room for Privacy?" *Academy of Management Perspectives* 23, no.4 (2009): 33–48.
60. Ibid.
61. B. E. Litzky, K. A. Eddleston, and D. L. Kidder, "The Good, the Bad, and the Misguided," *Academy of Management Perspectives* 20 (2006): 91–103.
62. H. Mintzberg, "The Manager's Job: Folklore and Fact," *Harvard Business Review* 5, no. 4 (1975): 49–61.
63. A. Li and R. Cropanzano, "Fairness at the Group Level: Justice Climate and Intraunit Climate," *Journal of Management* 35 (2009): 564–599.
64. W. Shi, L. Markoczy, and G. G. Dess, "The Role of Middle Management in the Strategy Process: Group Affiliation, Structural Holes and *Tertius Lungens,*" *Journal of Management* 35 (2009): 1453–1480.
65. G. K. Lee, "The Significance of Network Resources in the Race to Enter Emerging Product Markets: The Convergence of Telephony Communications and Computer Networking, 1989–2001," *Strategic Management Journal* 28 (2007): 17–37.
66. J. H. Dyer and N. W. Hatch, "Relation-specific Capabilities and Barriers to Knowledge Transfers: Creating Advantage through Network Relationships," *Strategic Management Journal* 27 (2006): 701–719.
67. D. Cumming, H. J. Sapienza, and D. S. Siegel, "International Entrepreneurship: Managerial and Policy Implications," *Strategic Entrepreneurship Journal* 3 (2009): 283–296.
68. T. R. Holcomb, R. M. Holmes, and B. L. Connelly, "Making the Most of What You Have: Managerial Ability as a Source of Resource Value Creation," *Strategic Management Journal* 30 (2009): 457–485.
69. D. G. Sirmon and M. A. Hitt, "Contingencies within Dynamic Managerial Capabilities: Interdependent Effects of Resource Investment and Deployment on Firm Performance," *Strategic Management Journal* 30 (2009): 1375–1394.
70. T. Talaulicar, J. Grundei, and A. V. Werder, "Strategic Decision Making in Start-ups: The Effect of Top Management Team Organization and Processes on Speed and Comprehensiveness," *Journal of Business Venturing* 20: 519–541.
71. E. Dane and M. G. Pratt, "Exploring Intuition and Its Role in Managerial Decision Making," *Academy of Management Review* 32 (2007): 33–54.
72. C. O. Albrecht and C. C. Albrecht, "International Ethics, Fraud, and Corruption: A Cross-Cultural Perspective," *Cross Cultural Management* 16 (2009): 237–240.
73. R. Stewart, "A Model for Understanding Managerial Jobs and Behavior," *Academy of Management Review* 7 (1982): 7–13.
74. L. Dragoni, P. E. Tesluk, J. A. Russell, and I.-S. Oh, "Understanding Managerial Development: Integrating Developmental Assignments, Learning Orientation, and Access to Developmental Opportunities in Predicting Managerial Competencies," *Academy of Management Journal* 52 (2009): 731–744.
75. K. Z. Zhou and F. Wu, "Technological Capability, Strategic Flexibility and Product Innovation," *Strategic Management Journal* 31 (2010): 547–561.
76. A. Lashinsky, "The Decade of Steve," *Fortune,* November 23, 2009, 93–100.
77. D. L. Patient and D. P. Skarlicki, "Increasing Interpersonal and Informational Justice When Communicating Negative News: The Role of the Manager's Empathic Concern and Moral Development," *Journal of Management* 36 (2009): 555–578.
78. M. W. McCall and M. M. Lombardo, *Off the Track* (Greensboro: Center for Creative Leadership, 1983).
79. M. Moldoveanu, "Thinking Strategically about Thinking Strategically: The Computational Structure and Dynamics of Managerial Problem Selection and Formulation," *Strategic Management Journal* 30 (2009): 737–763.

2

Social Responsibility and Managerial Ethics

LEARNING OBJECTIVES

After studying this chapter, you should be able to:

Describe why an understanding of basic approaches to ethical decision making and corporate social responsibility is important.

Compare and contrast the efficiency and social responsibility perspectives.

Explain the strategic corporate social responsibility approach.

Explain the basic approaches to ethical decision making.

Explain the aspects of moral intensity.

Describe the actions that can foster a high degree of ethical behavior in an organization.

Managerial Challenges from the Front Line

Half Price Books

Name: Sharon Anderson Wright

Position: CEO, Half Price Books

Outside work activities: Literacy and family literacy efforts; personally committed to Half Price Books' mission of preserving the environment by reusing and recycling.

First job out of school: Began working for Half Price Books at the age of 13, sorting and shelving paperbacks.

Management style: Collaborative

Reportedly, Sharon Anderson Wright likes finding a good deal at a thrift store. This would probably not surprise you, unless you knew that Wright is the head of Half Price Books, the largest used-book company in the country. Half Price Books was a company begun by Wright's mother, Pat Anderson along with her boyfriend, diamond salesman Ken Gjemre, in 1972. They opened their first store in a converted Dallas launderette. Anderson wanted to save trees by recycling unwanted books. "Nobody was recycling books then," says Wright. "They hated seeing all this great stuff thrown away." Over the years Half Price Books has recycled 16 million books and saved over 650,000 trees.

Today, Half Price Books has 2,500 employees and generates over $210 million in annual sales. It has nearly 100 stores in 16 states. (Most of the stores are in Texas.) It buys and sells books, magazines, and recorded material from individuals as well as leftover stock from publishers. The company sponsors literacy programs around the country and donates over 1 million books a year to schools, prisons, and hospitals all over the world. "These books are like manna from heaven to low-income families." Says Michael Hirschhorn, president of the National Alliance of Urban Literacy Coalitions. Besides donating books, the company is dedicated to recycling. Wright also encourages her employees to pursue their own philanthropic activities. "It enriches their lives," she says, "and they enrich ours."

Half Price Books' success has created its own challenges, however. On the one hand, every new store it opens employs people in the community. On the other hand, expansion has meant that the company and its managers have had to invest money in information, finance, and other systems to properly run the business. These investments coupled with rising health care costs have squeezed margins to the point where the company had to decide recently whether to continue paying health care benefits for its part-time employees. The company had always provided both its full-time and part-time employees with the benefits.

You may be wondering, "Why should I care about corporate social responsibility or managerial ethics or whether or not my employees have health care benefits? Aren't these the types of issues philosophers worry about?" To answer this question, you only need to pick up a recent newspaper or business magazine. Everything from Wall Street trading scandals to accounting frauds at AIG, Lehman Brothers, Enron, Parmalat, Satyam, WorldCom, Tyco, and Global Crossing to corporate cover-ups and massive oil spills from British Petroleum's offshore drilling rig explosion in the Gulf of Mexico seem to be in the press daily. For example, Citicorp lost billions in market value when it was revealed that a group of traders in the firm's London office had manipulated the bond market: A small set of traders disrupted the European bond market by placing 188 sell orders simultaneously (approximately $20 billion worth of bonds) on August 2, 2004 in about 18 seconds. This drove the price of bonds, in general, down dramatically. The prices continued to drop even after the Citibank traders stopped selling. Just a few minutes later, the same traders then bought the bonds back at much cheaper prices than they had been sold. This new buying triggered buying by other traders, and prices rose. In the process, Citibank traders made about $20 million in profits in under five minutes. Although the employees did not do anything illegal, their behavior was deemed unethical. In the end, Citicorp paid a $28 million fine to the Financial Service Authority for "failing to conduct its business with due skill, care and diligence, and failing to exercise proper controls over the London bond trading team."[1]

Individual or corporate decisions that are judged to be wrong, either ethically or legally, can not only hurt those directly affected by the decisions but can boomerang to generate negative publicity, hurt a company's stock price, destroy shareholder value, and, as a consequence, make it difficult for the individual to get future employment or for a firm to recruit high-quality employees. In contrast, good managerial ethics and corporate social responsibility generate significant, positive consequence for employees, customers, shareholders, and communities.

How the Ethics of Individual People Develop

At its heart, **managerial ethics** is concerned with morality and standards of business conduct, especially among individuals. Managerial ethics begins at the top of the organization.[2] For ethical decisions and practices to permeate the firm, top executives must build a culture based on those values. This includes establishing codes of ethics, implementing ethics training for employees, and rewarding ethical behaviors (as we discuss later in this chapter). Moreover, it includes top executives behaving in an ethical manner *themselves*.

managerial ethics
the study of morality and standards of business conduct

Although top managers can have an impact on the ethical (or unethical) behavior that occurs in a firm, much of what influences someone's perspective on what is or is not ethical happens long before he or she begins working. Consider your personal situation: what role have your family, friends, peers, teachers, religion, job experiences, and life experiences played in helping to shape your ethical beliefs? Think about a situation in which someone made an ethical judgment different from your own. Suppose you had been born in a different country, raised by a different family, attended a different school system, experienced different religious influences, had different friends, and held different jobs: would you hold the same ethical values you do now and make the same ethical judgments?

There is little debate that family, friends, peers, teachers, religion, job experiences, and life experiences all play a significant role in the development of an individual's ethical values and judgments.[3] What is debated is which factors play the strongest role because their influence varies from person to person.[4] This debate is unlikely to be resolved soon, nor is its resolution necessary for our purposes. The primary reason for raising the issue is to realize that in order to understand how others make decisions, you need to understand something about their backgrounds.[5]

Simply labeling other ethical judgments as wrong is likely to foster feelings of mistrust (in both directions) and hurt your working relationships. The greater the diversity in the workforce, the greater the need for tolerance and understanding. However, as a manager, tolerance does not mean simply allowing your subordinates to come to whatever ethical decisions they individually deem right. Because individual decisions can have consequences for the organization, managers often need to shape and influence their subordinates' ethical thinking, judgment, and decision making.

Consider the following real case conveyed to us recently. (We have disguised the names at the manager's request.) You are a manager in a publishing company. Your assistant manager has just recruited a new employee, Martha, from a key competitor. Martha worked for your competitor for 11 months after graduating from college. Even though Martha held a junior position at a competing company, her position provided access to key strategic plans. Given her somewhat junior position in the company, she had not been asked to sign, nor had she signed, a "noncompete" clause that would have prevented her from taking a job with a competitor for a specific time period or disclosing the strategic knowledge she had gained while working for the competing company. Your assistant manager has proposed paying Martha a $10,000 signing bonus—something unusual for a junior hire. Martha had performed well enough to earn a $10,000 bonus at the competing company but would be entitled to it only if she stayed on for a full 12 months. Given the time-sensitive nature of some of the information Martha has, you would rather have her join you now. Should you pay the signing bonus? Is it simply a legitimate replacement for the bonus Martha would have earned had she stayed on at your competitor? Or does the signing bonus constitute payment for the competitive intelligence you expect Martha to share once she joins your firm? And if it is, do you have any ethical misgivings about using a signing bonus as a means of securing competitive intelligence? Suppose your competitor pays Martha her end-of-year bonus before she completes a year of service: would that have any bearing on what you would expect her to reveal to you or whether you would still pay the signing bonus? If you were

Martha, would your ethical perspective on the money or revealing competitive intelligence change under these varying scenarios?

How should you make decisions like these? Are there ethical approaches you can look to for guidance? The answer is that there are some basic approaches, and they have been around for a long time—in part, because the challenge of ethical decision making is not something new. Having to make a choice between two competing but arguably valid options is known as an **ethical dilemma.** People have faced ethical dilemmas throughout history.

In the next section, we will describe these basic approaches for two reasons. The approaches can help you (1) understand how other people approach ethical dilemmas and (2) avoid an **ethical lapse**—that is, a decision that is contrary to one's stated beliefs and company policies.

ethical dilemma
having to make a choice between two competing but arguably valid options

ethical lapse
decision that is contrary to an individual's stated beliefs and policies of the company

Again, it is important to keep in mind that the workforce is becoming increasingly diverse. As a result, now more than ever before, you are likely to encounter people who respond to ethical dilemmas differently. Research finds significant differences among managers from different nationalities.[6] For example, one study examined the extent to which salespeople from the United States, Japan, and Korea viewed a set of actions as posing an ethical issue.[7] Koreans in the study did not think it was unethical to ask customers what price a competitor had quoted them, whereas the Americans and Japanese generally did think it was unethical. What do you think? Do you think asking a customer for information on the price submitted by your competitors is ethical or not?

From this same international study, researchers found that Korean salespeople did not think that giving free gifts constituted an ethical issue, while American salespeople did. General Motors shares this "American" view and has a policy that restricts the giving of gifts. For example when golfing with the president of the Philippines and discussing the possibility of a new GM factory in the country, the president of GM's Asia Pacific region was prohibited by company policy from paying for his guest's golf game. Do you think GM's policy is appropriate, or has it gone too far?

Even within a culture, ethical judgments vary. In one recent study, researchers found that individuals in a marketing department were less likely to judge interactions with customers as unethical as compared to peers in other functions such as HR or operations.[8]

Without understanding how or why others come to different conclusions, it is easy to criticize those who hold those beliefs as "wrong." For example, in a recent study, Chinese and Australian auditors working for the same multinational accounting firms reached different decisions about proper ethical conduct because of different cultural assumptions. Chinese auditors looked to their peers whereas Australian auditors looked to themselves for guidance in making ethical decisions. This reference point reflects the cultural group orientation of Chinese and the individual orientation of Australians.[9] If either set of auditors simply judged the other wrong without any sensitivity to how culture might influence ethical decisions, imagine how difficult it might be for them to work together on a global audit team. Research has shown that *ethnocentricity*—the view that your perspective is correct and the views of people in other cultures are inferior—tends to hurt managerial effectiveness. This is especially true in culturally diverse or international contexts.[10] So, it is important for new managers to examine the basic approaches to ethical decision making and recognize that individuals' backgrounds, including cultural values, influence their decisions and behavior.

As we stated, the second reason for examining basic approaches to ethical decision making is to avoid ethical lapses. Ethical lapses are more common than you might think. The pressures emanating from both the external environment and internal company environment often can be overwhelming. This is especially true if managers lack a systematized way of thinking through dilemmas. For example, suppose you were a sales manager about to report your current quarterly sales. You are short of your target. The policy is that you can only report sales for which a contract has been signed. You have a signed letter of intent but not a contract from a customer—a customer who has purchased from you before. The value of the deal will take you over your target and will trigger a bonus for you and the salesperson in charge of this account. The salesperson has told you that if the sale goes through, the customer will sign a contract dated prior to the close of the quarter. You barely missed your sales target last quarter. The company has a strong performance culture. In other words, if you don't perform, you don't have a career with that company. Under pressures like these, can you imagine how it might be possible to make a decision contrary to your stated beliefs?[11]

Basic Approaches to Ethical Decision Making

Several frameworks, or approaches, to making ethical decisions exist. We examine four of the most common: the utilitarian, moral rights, universalism, and justice approaches. An understanding of the basic approaches to ethical decision making will help you as a manager to examine your own personal ethics and work more effectively with employees whose ethical perspectives are different because the approach you use does have an impact on whether you judge something as ethical or unethical.[12]

The Utilitarian Approach

The utilitarian approach focuses on consequences of an action. Simplified, using a **utilitarian approach,** you try to make decisions that result "in the greatest good." For example, assume you are trying to sell grain to a developing nation, and a customs agent demands an extra fee before he will clear your shipment. From a utilitarian perspective, you would try to determine the consequences of the options available to you. For example, you could (1) pay the money, (2) not pay the money and let the grain sit there, or (3) seek intervention from a third party. Which action would result in the greatest good? If there are starving people waiting for the grain, would you argue that the "good" of saving lives outweighs the "bad" of paying an illegal bribe?

When characterizing an outcome as "good" or "bad," keep in mind that any two people may see the same outcome differently. In other words, the "goodness" or "badness" of an outcome is often subjective. Factors such as culture, economic circumstances, and religion can all affect those subjective judgments. For example, what if keeping the shipments of grain moving was needed to keep 2,000 people employed? Would you argue that the good of saving 2,000 jobs justified paying off government officials? What if unemployment were high in the region?

> **utilitarian approach**
> focuses on the consequences of an action

The Moral Rights Approach

The **moral rights approach** to ethical decisions focuses on an examination of the moral standing of actions independent of their consequences. According to this approach, some things are just "right" or "wrong," independent of consequences. When two courses of action both have moral standing, the positive and negative consequences of each should determine the more ethical course. Using this approach, you should choose the action that conforms with moral principles and provides positive consequences.

To illustrate: suppose you have an ongoing supplier relationship but no written contract. Is it ethical to cut off the supplier with no warning in order to switch to a different supplier with lower prices? From a moral rights approach, if it is wrong not to honor unwritten commitments to suppliers, it could be argued that it would be unethical to cut the supplier off with no warning. Conversely, if operating without a contract is simply a business convenience, you might easily make the case that changing suppliers is just a matter of business, not ethics.

The managerial challenge here is that the moral standing of most issues is debatable. For example, you might say it is wrong to lie. But is it wrong to make your competitors think you are about to enter one market when you are really about to enter another so as to gain a competitive advantage over them? Is it wrong to say you are not working on a new technology when you actually are in order to divert competitors from investing in the technology and thereby enjoy an advantage when you finally perfect the technology? Some would say that this is exactly what Apple did when Steve Jobs in 2003 said, "I'm not convinced people want to watch movies on a tiny little screen," while Apple was actually hard at work on its fifth-generation iPod that would include video capabilities.[13] In the same interview, Jobs also said he didn't think Apple would do well in the cell phone business: yet at that time, Apple was already at work on its smash hit, the iPhone.

> **moral rights approach**
> focuses on examination of the moral standing of actions independent of their consequences

The Universal Approach

Immanuel Kant, perhaps one of the most famous moral philosophers, articulated the best-known ethical imperative, or **universal approach.** Simplified, Kant's moral imperative was "do unto others as you would have them do unto everyone, including yourself." If you follow this

> **universal approach**
> choosing a course of action that you believe can apply to all people under all situations

approach, you should choose a course of action that you believe can apply to all people under all situations and that you would also want applied to yourself. At the heart of universalism is the issue of rights. For Kant, the basis of all rights stem from freedom and autonomy. Kant believed that actions that limit the freedom and autonomy of people generally lack moral justification. Now let's return to the customs agent and bribe scenario we just discussed. Based on the universal approach, it might be difficult to justify paying bribes to government officials. To meet the "do unto others as you would have them do unto everyone" criterion, you would have to be willing to let everyone use bribes as a means of getting the ends they desired.

The Justice Approach

justice approach
focuses on how equitably the costs and benefits of actions are distributed

The **justice approach** focuses on the equity of process and outcomes.[14] In general, costs and benefits should be equitably distributed, rules should be impartially applied, and those damaged because of inequity or discrimination should be compensated.

distributive justice
the equitable distribution of rewards and punishment, based on performance

DISTRIBUTIVE JUSTICE Managers ascribing to **distributive justice** distribute rewards and punishments equitably based on performance. This does not mean that everyone gets the same or equal rewards or punishments; rather, they receive equitable rewards and punishments as a function of how much they contribute to or detract from the organization's goals. From this perspective, it would be wrong for a manager to distribute bonuses, promotions, or benefits based on such arbitrary characteristics as age, gender, religion, or race. This is the basic rationale behind the U.S. Civil Rights Act of 1964. Under this law, even if a manager has no intention of discriminating against a particular minority group, if a minority group can demonstrate inequitable results (called *disparate impact*), legal action can be brought against the firm. For example, if 50 percent of a firm's applicants for promotion were women, but 75 percent of those receiving promotions were men, the data could be used to file a claim of discrimination based on the underlying notion of distributive justice.

procedural justice
ensuring that those affected by managerial decisions consent to the decision-making process and that the process is administered impartially

PROCEDURAL JUSTICE Managers ascribing to **procedural justice** make sure that people affected by managerial decisions consent to the decision-making process and that the process is administered impartially.[15] Consent means that people are informed about the process and have the freedom to exit the system if they choose. As with distributive justice, the decision-making process cannot systematically discriminate against people because of arbitrary characteristics, such as age, gender, religion, or race. Recent research involving employees across multiple countries consistently suggests that perceived justice relates positively to desired outcomes such as job performance, trust, job satisfaction, and organizational commitment and negatively relates to outcomes such as turnover and other counterproductive work behavior.[16] Procedural justice is generally studied and interpreted within the context of the organization. However, the findings of a recent study show that factors external to the firm can also have strong effects: In one study, violent crime rates in the community where a plant resided led researchers to correctly predict that workplace aggression in that plant would increase, whereas the plant's procedural justice climate did not.[17]

compensatory justice
if distributive and procedural justice fail, those hurt by the inequitable distribution of rewards are compensated

COMPENSATORY JUSTICE The main thesis of **compensatory justice** is that if distributive justice and procedural justice fail or are not followed as they should be, then those hurt by the inequitable distribution of rewards should be compensated. This compensation often takes the form of money, but it can take other forms. For example, compensatory justice lies at the heart of affirmative action plans. Typically, affirmative action plans ensure that groups that have been systematically disadvantaged in the past, such as women or minorities, are given every opportunity in the future. For example, special training programs could be instituted for women who were passed over for promotions in the past because they were denied access to certain experiences required for promotion.

Recent research has also focused on interpersonal and informational justice. Interpersonal justice focuses on the polite, respectful treatment of people. Informational justice focuses on the timely communication or reasonableness of explanations of organizational actions. Research suggests that employees' perceptions of interpersonal justice and informational justice in the workplace have a positive impact on such outcomes as trust in management, job satisfaction, commitment to the organization, and intent to stay with the organization.[18]

Some of the most recent research suggests that "emergent" justice rules fall outside the traditional categorizations. For example, employees may use such factors as a pleasant working environment and development opportunities in assessing the fairness in an organization or consider a supervisor's accommodating and developmental behavior in assessing the supervisor's fairness. In fact, one recent study of managers found that 76 percent utilized at least one emergent rule in ascribing fairness and only 28 percent used one of the three traditional justice rules.[19] Whatever the justice rules, people cannot be relied on to consistently hold to them. Recent research has also found that people vary by nearly 20 to 30 percent over a period as short as eight weeks.[20]

The Moral Intensity Factor

As this chapter points out, one of the challenges in managers' ethical decision making is that for many issues and consequences, people do not have identical perspectives. They differ in whether they see a situation as involving ethics and in how they would determine their course of action. So the practical question is whether managers can help people come to a common viewpoint on the "moral intensity" of issues.[21] **Moral intensity** is the degree to which people see an issue as an ethical one. Moral intensity has six components, as illustrated in Exhibit 2.1: (1) magnitude of the consequences, (2) social consensus, (3) probability of effect, (4) temporal immediacy, (5) proximity, and (6) concentration of effect.[22] In other words, the overall moral intensity of a situation is the cumulative result of all of these components. As a manager, you can use this framework both to anticipate the moral intensity of an issue and to diagnose the reasons for differing views people have about that intensity.[23]

The **magnitude of the consequences** associated with the outcome of a given action is the level of impact anticipated. This impact is independent of whether the consequences are positive or negative. For example, laying off 100 employees because of a downturn in the economy has a lower impact than if 1,000 employees were laid off. Likewise, many people would judge the consequences of a 20 percent increase in the price of lawn fertilizer to be of a lower magnitude than an explosion in the fertilizer plant as the result of poor safety procedures, in which 500 people were killed or seriously injured.

Social consensus involves the extent to which members of a society agree that an act is either good or bad. For example, in the United States, there is greater social consensus

moral intensity
the degree to which people see an issue as an ethical one

magnitude of the consequences
the anticipated level of impact of the outcome of a given action

social consensus
the extent to which members of a society agree that an act is either good or bad

EXHIBIT 2.1

Factors of Moral Intensity

concerning the wrongness of driving drunk than speeding on the highway. Recent research suggests that social consensus is potentially one of the more powerful dimensions of moral intensity.[24]

probability of effect
the moral intensity of an issue rises and falls depending on how likely people think the consequences are

Probability of effect concerns the likelihood that a given consequence will happen. For example, even if people agree that 500 people dying from a chemical explosion is a very bad consequence, the intensity of the issue rises and falls depending on the perceived likelihood of a chemical explosion. For example, one of the reasons so many countries have restricted cigarette advertising is because smoking can cause health problems, including serious ones such as lung cancer. However, cigarette ads and smoking itself have not been completely outlawed in part because the probability of health problems is not 100 percent. The higher the probability of the consequence, the more intense the sense of ethical obligation. Because people are highly likely to be injured if they are in a car accident, the intensity regarding the moral obligation of auto manufacturers to make safer cars with options such as side-impact air bags is increasing. However, because there is no certainty that you will be in an automobile accident, the law does not require many of the available safety features.

temporal immediacy
a function of the interval between the time the action occurs and the onset of its consequences

Temporal immediacy is the fourth component of moral intensity. It is a function of the interval between the time an action occurs and the onset of its consequences. The greater the interval between action and consequences, the less intensity people typically feel toward the issue. For example, even if industrial pollution were certain to lead to global warming and result in catastrophic changes to weather patterns, because the consequences are likely to happen 50 years or more from now, the moral intensity of industrial pollution is much less than if the effects were to happen next year.

proximity
the physical, psychological, and emotional closeness the decision maker feels to those affected by the decision

Proximity refers to an individual's physical and psychological closeness to the outcome. All other factors being equal, the closer the decision maker is or feels to those affected by the decision, the more the decision maker will consider the consequences of the action and feel it has ethical implications. Proximity can involve physical closeness as well as psychological and emotional closeness and identification. Consequently, an affinity between the decision maker and those affected could be a function of many factors, including people's nationality, cultural background, ethnic similarity, organizational identification, or socioeconomic similarity. For example, if you feel a psychological and emotional affinity for young people, making a decision to lay off workers based on their seniority (meaning younger workers will get laid off first) will have greater moral intensity for you. Likewise, a decision to close down a poor-performing but slightly profitable factory that could put your parents and neighbors out of work will also likely have greater moral intensity for you than would the closing of a different factory. Recent research suggests proximity may be an especially powerful dimension.[25]

concentration of effect
the extent to which consequences are focused on a few individuals or dispersed across many

The **concentration of effect** is the extent to which consequences are focused on a few individuals or dispersed across many. For example, even though laying off 100 people has a lower magnitude of effect than laying off 1,000 people, laying off 100 people in a town of 5,000 has a greater concentration of effect than laying off 1,000 people in city of 10 million.

The importance of these six facets of moral intensity is twofold. First, as a manager, you can use them to anticipate issues that are likely to be seen as significant ethical dilemmas in the workplace.[26] If you can better anticipate issues that are likely to become ethical debates, you have more time to prepare for and may be more effective at handling ethical dilemmas. Second, if you are working with a group that uses the same basic ethical approach and still can't agree on the ethical course of action, you can use these facets to determine the source of the disagreement.[27] The disagreement may stem from different perceptions of the situation on one or more of the moral intensity components.

Nike had to deal with a lot of negative media coverage regarding the alleged use of child labor in factories it did not own but that manufactured its shoes and other products (see A Manager's Challenge, "Laboring for Nike Around the World"). Nike executives were both caught off-guard by the intensity of the global and domestic public scrutiny and somewhat unprepared to respond at first. If Nike executives had used the moral intensity framework, could they have better anticipated and predicted public reaction? Would the framework have helped them make some anticipatory changes in how they managed the manufacturers around the world that make Nike's shoes?

A MANAGER'S CHALLENGE

GLOBALIZATION

Laboring for Nike Around the World

Nike has always wanted the spotlight on its products and this is one of the reasons that it has sponsored some of the most visible stars across golf, basketball, soccer, track and field, and other sports. However, in the late 1990s, when the spotlight began to focus on Nike factories and the over 400,000 workers laboring in those factories, Nike executives were not so happy with the media attention. According to critics, employees at these factories experienced substandard working conditions, such as exposure to carcinogens and other dangerous toxins, poor ventilation and/or air quality, forced overtime, sexual harassment, and corporal punishment and abuse. In addition, critics argued, workers did not receive a fair wage and many employees were too young to legally work.

Nike quickly responded by pointing out that these were contract manufacturers and that Nike did not own any of the factories or directly employ any of the workers. Groups like the Fair Labor Association, or FLA (www.fairlabor. org), however, felt that Nike's response, rather than appease the public, only demonstrated that its executives were evasive or trying to hide from the truth.

This episode marked the beginning of what chairman and founder, Phil Knight, described as four key "chapters" in Nike's efforts to improve conditions:

In the first chapter, we upgraded processes and conditions behind closed doors. The second chapter began with critics bringing working conditions in underdeveloped countries to the attention of the world. After a bumpy original response, an error for which yours truly was responsible, we focused on making working conditions better and showing that to the world.

Reflecting back on the second chapter of Nike's response, in 2009 president and CEO Mark Parker commented:

In the early 90s, we came under intense scrutiny for labor conditions in our supply chain. Our critics were smart (and right) to focus on the industry leader. Our first reaction was to defend the practices in the developing economies.... In those days the Internet was brand new, but we began to see the power of instantaneous information and new communities enabled on a global scale.... We learned to view transparency as an asset, not a risk.

Nike contracts with other companies to manufacture its sporting goods. Frequently these companies outsource the work to factories with low-cost labor in countries abroad, similar to this factory in Ho Chi Minh City, Vietnam. In recent years, numerous human rights organizations have called attention to the terrible conditions workers at these factories endure, casting Nike in a negative light. If Nike executives had used the moral intensity framework outlined in the text, could the company have averted the bad publicity?

Peter Charlesworth/OnAsia Images Pte Ltd.

The third chapter of Nike's response began in 2003 when Nike and a handful of other apparel companies allowed the FLA to post factory condition audits on the Internet. According to the FLA's 2006 annual report, 856 of Nike's factories were subject to FLA audits and the FLA made 22 independent visits. For its own internal audits, Nike employed a staff of 1,000 labor-practices managers to run a program called Safety, Health, Attitude of Management, People, and Environment (SHAPE). According to the FLA, Nike conducted 509 SHAPE assessments and gathered base-level environmental, safety, and health data on 650 factories in 52 countries. It also conducted 99 pre-sourcing evaluations. Of these, 80 factories were approved and 19 were rejected. Nike has also agreed to apply U.S. safety standards for air quality to its foreign suppliers and converted its use of toxic chemical solvents to water-based products in assembling its footwear. The firm has also increased the age requirements for its subcontractors Footwear manufacturers must employ workers who are at least 18 years old; apparel workers, at least 16 years old. These standards exceed those established by the International Labor Organization.

(continued)

Nike's fourth chapter began in earnest in 2005. CEO Mark Parker commented:

> We thought that we could be a unilateral force for systemic change. Instead, we learned that meaningful reform was not going to come from external pressure alone. Awareness and monitoring of any mandated Code of Conduct had to be embraced and enforced at the local level. And it had to be based on real business-based solutions driven by strong market signals. If we are to enable systemic change, we can't do it alone. We need partners. We need collaboration from industry, civil society and government. And we need to show the real benefits of lean manufacturing and human resource management.

Nike's fourth chapter continues today at a more collaborative level with external organizations than ever before. Still, Nike faces several practical challenges when it comes to improving contractors' factories. For example, when conditions are substandard and contract manufacturers do not improve, ultimately Nike can withdraw its contracts from noncompliant factories. However, even this is a challenge, as it found in Indonesia when it terminated a contract with a substandard supplier. All of the company's 7,000 workers lost their jobs because Nike projects constituted 100 percent of the factory's work.

CEO Mark Parker summarizes Nike's past and future this way:

> I believe our work in sustainable business and innovation has equal potential to shape our legacy. For that to happen, we have to focus on the lessons we've learned:
>
> - Transparency is an asset, not a risk.
> - Collaboration enables systemic change.
> - Every challenge and risk is an opportunity.
> - Design allows you to prototype the future, rather than retrofit the past.
> - To make real change, you have to be a catalyst.
> - There is now only one path and it leads to greater sustainability, equity, growth and prosperity.

Sources: Nike, *Corporate Responsibility Report FY 07, 08, 09*; Fair Labor Association, *2006 Annual Public Report*; Nike, *Fiscal Year 2004 Corporate Responsibility Report*; A. Maitland, "Big Brands Come Clean on Sweatshop Labor," *Financial Times*, June 10, 2003; D. Akst, "Nike in Indonesia, Through a Different Lens," *New York Times*, March 4, 2001.

Social Responsibility

Corporate social responsibility is concerned with the obligation corporations have to constituencies and the nature and extent of those obligations. Companies have a wide variety of constituencies, including current shareholders, customers, employees, specific communities, society at large, governments, and so on. These constituencies typically have expectations of companies but do not always share the same expectations. In many instances, they have competing desires. For example, shareholders may want companies to maximize their returns, whereas local communities may want companies to give something back to them. Do companies have a higher obligation to shareholders or the specific communities in which they operate? Suppose a company's trucking activities created noise pollution that bothers citizens but falls well within the legal limits. Should the company take money from shareholders by paying them lower dividends and investing that money in exhaust and muffler systems in order to reduce engine noise? Suppose the safety standards for brakes on the trucks were different in two neighboring countries. Should the firm insist on the higher of the two standards for all its trucks and as a consequence pay the extra cost? Do all their truck drivers, regardless of their nationality or employment location, have the same rights when it comes to equipment standards, such as those for brakes?

Questions such as these form the substance of social responsibility debates. Both corporate social responsibility and managerial ethics focus on the "oughts" of conducting business. Although several approaches to corporate social responsibility exist, an examination of two fundamental perspectives will help you reflect on how you personally view the issue and how you might effectively interact with others holding differing perspectives.

The Efficiency Perspective

efficiency perspective
the concept that a manager's responsibility is to maximize profits for the owners of the business

Perhaps no contemporary person presents the **efficiency perspective** of social responsibility more clearly than the late Nobel Prize-winning economist Milton Friedman.[28] Quite simply, according to Friedman, the business of business is business. In other words, a manager's responsibility is to maximize profits for the owners of the business. Adam Smith is perhaps the earliest advocate of this approach. Smith concluded nearly 200 years ago that the best way to advance the well-being of society is to place resources in the hands of individuals and allow market forces to allocate scarce resources to satisfy society's demands.[29]

MANAGERS AS OWNERS When a manager of a business is also its owner, the efficiency perspective argues that the self-interests of the owner are best achieved by serving the needs of society. If society demands that a product be made within certain environmental and safety standards, it is in the best interests of the owner to produce the product to meet those standards. Otherwise, customers will likely purchase competing product from rivals. Customers are more likely to purchase from firms that comply with widely shared and deeply held social values, so it makes sense for businesses to incorporate those values into their operations and products. To the extent that the cost of incorporating society's values is less than the price customers are willing to pay, the owner makes a profit.

Critics of the efficiency perspective, however, argue that quite often customers and society in general demand safety, environmental protection, and so on only after firms have caused significant visible damage. For example, society might hold strong values about not polluting the water and causing heath problems. However, if the consequences of polluting a river are not visible and people are not immediately hurt, social pressure might not emerge in a manner to cause the owner to align his actions with societal values until years after the fact.

MANAGERS AS AGENTS In most large organizations today, the manager is not the owner. The corporate form of organization is characterized by the separation of ownership (shareholders) and control (managers). Managers serve as the agents of the organization's owners. Within this context, Friedman argues that managers should "conduct business in accordance with [owners'] desires, which will generally be to make as much money as possible while conforming to the basic rules of society, both those embodied in law and those embodied in ethical custom."[30] From Friedman's perspective, managers have no obligation to act on behalf of society if it does not maximize value for the shareholders. For example, a company should package products in recycled paper only if doing so maximizes shareholder wealth. Whether such an action satisfies or benefits a small group of activists is irrelevant. Managers have no responsibility to carry out such a program; in fact, they have a responsibility *not* to undertake such an action if it is more costly (and therefore does not maximize shareholder wealth). Similarly, charitable donations are not the responsibility of corporations. Instead, managers should maximize the return to shareholders, and then shareholders can decide if and to which charities they want to make their contributions. Simply put, the profits are not the managers' money, and, therefore, managers have no right to decide how—or if—they should distribute the profits to charitable causes.

From the efficiency perspective, it is impossible for managers to maximize shareholders' wealth and simultaneously attempt to fulfill all of society's needs. From the efficiency perspective, it is the responsibility of government to impose taxes and determine expenditures to meet society's needs. When managers pursue actions that benefit society but not shareholders, they are exercising political power, not managerial authority. While it is hard to find any comprehensive studies detailing which companies or managers subscribe to the efficiency perspective (sometimes called the "classical view") a recent study of managers in the Middle East found that less than a quarter reported that they subscribed to the efficiency perspective.[31]

CONCERNS WITH THE EFFICIENCY PERSPECTIVE The efficiency perspective assumes that markets are competitive and that competitive forces move firms toward fulfilling societal needs as expressed by consumer demand. Firms that do not respond to consumers' demands in terms of products, price, delivery, safety, environmental impact, or any other dimension will, through competition, be forced to change or be put out of business. Societal values not expressed through market forces should be reflected in governmental laws and regulations. As with competitive forces, companies that do not abide by these laws and regulations will also find themselves out of business. Unfortunately, however, corrective action often occurs only after people are injured. The Manager's Challenge on Peanut Corporation of America (PCA) illustrates this point. In this case, the company bought inexpensive peanuts from overseas and then manufactured them into various products and ingredients for various food companies. PCA's low costs meant that they could undercut competitors and win business with major food companies. These lower costs to food companies meant that they could protect their profit margins. In the end, eight people lost their lives.

A MANAGER'S CHALLENGE

ETHICS

Poisoned Profits at Peanut Corporation of America

In January 2009, the Peanut Corporation of America (PCA) was forced to recall products after eight people died and over 19,000 fell ill across 43 states from salmonella poisoning traced to contamination at the PCA plant in Georgia. People were outraged. "Our whole family was angry," said Jeff Almer of Savage, Minn., whose 72-year-old mother, Shirley Mae, died in December after eating tainted peanut butter from the plant. "This could have been avoided." The company was a large supplier of peanut and peanut butter ingredients to such name brand companies as Jenny Craig, Kraft, Kellogg, and General Mills. A Food and Drug Administration (FDA) inspection team discovered that on 12 occasions in 2007 and 2008, PCA had found salmonella contamination in its products. However, when PCA re-conducted its tests and found no contamination, it sent the products out to customers. An outbreak in 2009 hit children especially hard: half of those stricken were under age 16, and 21 percent were under 5.

Both poor physical plant and working conditions were thought to have contributed to the problems. For example, to avoid salmonella, the physical plant must be kept bone-dry, but investigators found that the factory's roof leaked when it rained. In addition, many of the hourly workers earned only minimum wage and had gone years without a raise. Frederic McClendon, 31, a shift supervisor, reached $12 an hour last year but still could not afford health insurance for his two boys; the famliy lived in a weather-beaten trailer. "If you pay your workers, you get the best out of them," Mr. McClendon said. "If you don't, you don't."[32] In addition, PCA also used a large number of temporary workers, lowering labor costs but increasing the need to retrain as new temporary workers came on board.

Peanut Corporation of America served a wide variety of food processors from peanut butter to cookies to ice cream.

In total, more than 2,100 packaged and processed foods were affected by the recall. While big companies like Kellogg or Kraft had the experience and staff to handle the recalls, many small businesses struggled to cope. Receiving and shipping records had to be thoroughly searched and products tracked. In some cases, small business owners had to keep employees on overtime or hire additional help to handle the recall-related work. "It's not our fault this recall went through," said Tom Lundeen, who co-owns Aspen Hills Inc., in Garner, Iowa, which makes frozen cookie dough for fund-raisers. "We do everything correct and we have an incredibly high level of quality control, and we still have to pay for the mistakes of PCA." Stephanie Blackwell, co-owner of Aurora Products, an 11-year-old manufacturing and packaging company said she knew about the danger of salmonella in nuts but was not prepared for the impact of the recall. She calculated her losses at about $1 million. She said plans to hire two people were put on hold, and company efforts to help out with Habitat for Humanity were also affected.

The impact on large and small customers of PCA was significant. The impact on the 19,000 people who became ill was serious. For the eight people who died, the impact on them and their families was catastrophic. In the end, the impact from the negative publicity and lawsuits on the Peanut Corporation of America was fatal and the company had to declare bankruptcy.

Sources: Peanut Corporation of America, press release, January 13, 2009 (http://www.peanutcorp.com/pdf/Peanut%20Corporation%20of%20America%20Recall.pdf); "Peanut Corporation of America Expands Nationwide Recall of Peanut Butter," *US Recall News*, January 19, 2009 (http://www.usrecallnews.com/2009/01/fda-3224.html); Sue Kelly, "Peanut Recalls Still Trickling In," *USAToday*, March 20, 2009 (http://www.usatoday.com).

externality
an indirect or unintended consequence imposed on society that may not be understood or anticipated

The other major concern with the efficiency perspective is that corporations can impose indirect consequences that may not be completely understood or anticipated. In economic terms, such an unintended consequence is called an **externality**.[33] For example, plastic shopping bags are lightweight and convenient. On a per-bag basis, the production externalities are small, but on an aggregate basis the chemicals used to manufacture them are toxic and the pollution from delivering them are nontrivial. However, because the plastic bags are distributed at no charge in most stores, people often don't factor in these externalities. As a consequence, even though plastic bags can be recycled, only 5.2 percent were recycled in 2005 and that amount increased only to 6.7 percent by 2008.[34]

However, even when externalities can be anticipated, consumers often cannot correctly factor in the true cost or may not be willing to pay them. For example, the consequences of poor safety controls at a fertilizer plant (explosion, fire, toxic fumes, injury, and death) can be devastating.

The question is, can fertilizer consumers correctly assess the costs of a chemical disaster and how much extra they should have to pay to cover the needed safety expenditures? If the answer is "no," a plant manager will more likely skip the necessary safety practices to keep costs low and enhance profits. Only after a chemical disaster occurs will the impact of the externality (the disaster) be fully appreciated by consumers and, therefore, appropriately priced in the market.

The Social Responsibility Perspective

The social responsibility perspective argues that society grants existence to firms. Shareholders simply supply risk capital. Therefore, firms have responsibilities and obligations to society as a whole, not just to shareholders. Thus, while the efficiency perspective states that it is *socially responsible* to maximize the return to the shareholder, the social responsibility perspective states that it is *socially irresponsible* to maximize only shareholder wealth because shareholders are not the only ones responsible for the firm's existence. The most common form of corporate existence is one of *limited liability*—a privilege granted to corporations by society, not by shareholders.[35] In this form of existence, corporations' financial liability to others is limited to the company and doesn't extend to its shareholders. In other words, creditors and people seeking redress (for example, if a chemical disaster occurs) cannot go beyond the assets of the corporation and seek repayment or restitution from the assets of the owners (i.e., shareholders in a public company). Thus, the existence of the firm, in general, and the limited liability existence, in particular, are not solely a function of shareholders and, therefore, the responsibilities of the firm cannot be restricted just to shareholders.

STAKEHOLDERS From the social responsibility perspective, managers must consider the legitimate concerns of other stakeholders beyond just the firm's shareholders. A **stakeholder** is an individual or group that has an interest in and is affected by the actions of an organization. Besides an organization's shareholders, other stakeholders include current and future customers and employees; financiers; suppliers; the media; the communities in which the business operates; and society at large. A firm's customers have a special place within this set of constituencies because they pay the bills with the revenue they provide.[36] Shareholders are also given special status, but in the stakeholder approach, shareholders are viewed as the providers of "risk capital" rather than as sole owners. Consequently, shareholders are entitled to a *reasonable* return on the capital they put at risk, but they are not entitled to a *maximum* return because they are not solely responsible for the existence of the firm. To maximize the return to shareholders would take away returns owed to the other stakeholders. Thus, managers must balance the returns shareholders earn against the legitimate concerns of other stakeholders. The research evidence regarding the relationship between corporate social responsibility and financial performance is mixed, meaning that there is no definitive evidence that being more socially responsible leads to higher financial performance.[37]

stakeholder
an individual or group who has an interest in and is affected by the actions of an organization

CONCERNS WITH THE SOCIAL RESPONSIBILITY PERSPECTIVE One of the key concerns with the social responsibility perspective is that important terms such as *reasonable returns* and *legitimate concerns* cannot be defined adequately. Given that reasonable returns to shareholders and legitimate concerns of other stakeholders could conflict, not knowing exactly what is reasonable or legitimate makes it hard for managers to find the appropriate balance and act in socially responsible ways. This is why, from a practical standpoint, even if you believe in the stakeholder framework of corporate social responsibility, making decisions that balance the interests of various stakeholders is a significant challenge for which there is no magic solution. It is not only possible but quite likely that customers, employees, financiers, etc. will have conflicting and competing concerns. Moreover, it isn't clear from research whether greater corporate social responsibility leads to greater profits for firms.[38]

Consider the case of a manager in a corrugated-box factory. His customers want sturdy boxes that can be stacked several levels high. Society increasingly seems to want a higher use of recycled paper. However, boxes made of recycled paper either have higher costs for the same strength or lower strength at the same cost compared to boxes made of nonrecycled paper. Shareholders want competitive returns. In such a case, how would you determine the most socially responsible action? If customers tell you that boxes must meet a certain strength requirement regardless of whether they use recycled paper, does this outweigh the desires of other stakeholders? Should you devote more money to researching and developing stronger recycled boxes even though it takes money away from shareholders today?

A MANAGER'S CHALLENGE

ETHICS

The Eco-Cup at Starbucks

The general success of Starbucks likely needs no summary. The company sells nearly $10 billion worth of coffee and other beverages across nearly 9,000 company-operated stores and nearly 8,000 licensed operations in more than 50 countries around the world. In the process, Starbucks goes through nearly 2.3 billion cups annually. Although the company was started in 1971, it wasn't until 1996 that executives determined that they wanted to stop "double cupping"— giving customers a second cup to insulate the hot coffee in the first cup. That year Starbucks, along with Environmental Defense, held a competition for designs for a recycled cup.

This might seem like an easy target to achieve, but the design would need to meet several criteria. First, the new design would have to stand up well when filled with a hot beverage and held in a customer's hand. Second, because taste is highly influenced by smell, the new cup could not emit any odor that would compete with or detract from the beverage served. Third, the new cup would need FDA approval ensuring the safety of the recycled material for direct contact with cold or hot beverages.

The contest in 1996 resulted in no winners. Most designs were rejected because they crumpled easily, smelled bad, or both. As a consequence, in 1997 Starbucks moved to a 60 percent recycled sleeve in place of the second cup. This "saved some trees" but was not what company executives ultimately wanted. In 1999, the company tested a cup made of 50 percent post-consumer fiber but it was too flimsy and sometimes leaked.

In 2001, company executives decided to start over and work directly with a group of partners. They selected pulp maker Mississippi River Corp., paper mill MeadWestvaco, and cup manufacturer Solo Cup to help them create an eco-friendly cup. The team's new design and product received FDA approval in 2004 and was launched at selected locations in January 2006.

Although the eco-cup is made up of just 10 percent postconsumer fiber, it will conserve 5 million pounds of

Don Ryan/AP Wide World Photos

As early as 1996, Starbucks wanted to stop using a second container as insulation for its coffee servings. Hence began the company's quest to develop an "eco-cup" made out of recycled material. After much trial and error, in 2006, the company began successfully rolling out such a cup to its stores around the world, saving five million pounds of paper, or approximately 78,000 trees, a year.

paper per year. According to Starbucks' director of environmental affairs Ben Packard, "We had our eyes on the prize of an earth-friendly cup. Ten percent is just the first step. Increasing the recycled fiber in any paper product for environmental reasons must be balanced with product durability and safety considerations. In the future, we will look for ways to increase the percentage of post-consumer recycled fiber contained in our cups, but first we want to be assured of the quality, safety and durability of these new cups. In the meantime, we are actively exploring additional innovations to reduce the environmental impacts of our paper cups and other packaging." The Environmental Defense Fund estimates that Starbucks' eco-cup saves nearly 80,000 trees, enough energy to power 640 homes annually, and 47 million gallons of waste water each year.

Sources: Starbucks's *Corporate Social Responsibility 2005 Annual Report*; "Creating the Eco-Cup," *Fortune*, October 2006, 42; http://www.edf.org/page.cfm?tagID=2155, updated September 14, 2009, accessed March 24, 2010; *Starbucks's Annual Report, 2009.*

Even when you try to balance the concerns of competing stakeholders, it isn't easy, as Starbucks found out (and as illustrated in A Manager's Challenge, "The Eco-Cup at Starbucks"). Starbucks's quest to create a coffee cup made of recycled paper took 10 years, and in the end yielded a cup made with just 10 percent recycled paper. After reading the Challenge, do you think Starbucks achieved the right balance among different stakeholders? If you were a shareholder, what would be your perspective? As a customer, how would you view the effort and results? If you were an employee, how would you view these efforts? Would they make any difference to you?

EXHIBIT 2.2

Comparing Efficiency and Social Responsibility Perspectives

Comparing the Efficiency and Stakeholder Perspectives

The efficiency and social responsibility perspectives differ mainly in terms of the constituencies to which organizations have responsibilities. However, the two perspectives differ little in terms of how they evaluate actions that either harm or benefit both shareholders and society (see Exhibit 2.2). When actions benefit both shareholders and other stakeholders from both perspectives, managers should undertake these actions. For example, in January 2010, the Walt Disney Company drained its "Rivers of America" amusement at Disneyland in Anaheim, Calif., in order to restore it with clean water and to perform maintenance on systems normally submerged. In the past, Disney typically drained the 5 million gallons of water directly to the ocean. This time, however, the company worked with the local water district to drain it through the water district, which purified it and added it to county storage. When park officials refilled the river, they used the same amount of water they had banked with the water district. This approach didn't cost them any more than the previous approach, but it helped conserve water in drought-prone southern California.

The efficiency and stakeholder evaluations differ most markedly when actions help one group and harm the other. Actions that benefit shareholders but harm the other stakeholders would be viewed as managerially responsible from the efficiency perspective but socially irresponsible from the social responsibility perspective. Actions that harm shareholders but benefit other legitimate stakeholders would be viewed as managerially irresponsible from the efficiency perspective but socially responsible from the social responsibility perspective.

How Corporations Respond to the Efficiency and Stakeholder Perspectives

How corporations react to the various pressures and constituencies connected to the topic of social responsibility varies widely. These reactions can be simplified and laid out on a continuum that ranges from defensive to proactive, as illustrated in Exhibit 2.3.

DEFENDERS Companies that might be classified as defenders tend to fight efforts that they see as resulting in greater restriction and regulation of their ability to maximize profits. These firms often operate at the edge of the law and actively seek legal loopholes in conducting their business. Typically, they change only when legally compelled to do so.

ACCOMMODATERS These companies are less aggressive in fighting restrictions and regulations, but they too change only when legally compelled to do so. This type of firm tends to obey the letter of the law but does not make changes that might restrict profits unless they are required to.

REACTORS Reactor firms make changes when they feel that pressure from constituencies is sufficient such that nonresponsiveness could have a negative economic impact on the firm. For example, the firm might change to recycled paper for boxes only when pressure from customers becomes strong enough that nonresponsiveness would lead customers to boycott their products or to simply choose products from a competitor that uses recycled paper.

EXHIBIT 2.3 Corporate Responses

	Defenders	Accommodaters	Reactors	Anticipators
Belief:	We must fight against efforts to restrict or regulate our activities and profit-making potential.	We will change when legally compelled to do so.	We should respond to significant pressure even if we are not legally required to.	We owe it to society to anticipate and avoid actions with potentially harmful consequences, even if we are not pressured or legally required to do so.
Focus:	Maximize profits. Find legal loopholes. Fight new restrictions and regulations.	Maximize profits. Abide by the letter of the law. Change when legally compelled to do so.	Protect profits. Abide by the law. React to pressure that could affect business results.	Obtain profits. Abide by the law. Anticipate harmful consequences independent of pressures and laws.

ANTICIPATORS Firms in this category tend to believe that they are obligated to a variety of stakeholders—customers, employees, shareholders, general citizens, and so on—not to harm them independent of laws or pressures that restrict or regulate their actions. Firms in this category not only abide by the law, but might also take action to avoid harming constituencies, even when the constituencies might not be aware of the potential danger. For example, a firm might take steps to protect employees from harmful chemicals within the workplace even before employees suffered negative side effects sufficient for them to demand work environment changes or before safety laws are passed.

Though we might imagine that firms adopting the efficiency perspective are more likely to be defenders, accommodaters, and reactors while firms adopting the stakeholder perspective are more likely to be anticipators, we know of no research that has examined this specific association. The accompanying "Manager's Challenge" helps illustrate some of these corporate responses in the face of advancing technology. A Manager's Challenge, "Cleaning Up Dirty Little Engines" focuses on how firms making two-stroke engines for handheld power tools are responding to the emissions and pollution these engines create. As you read the feature, ask yourself what the motivation seems to be for each firm mentioned to explore new combustion technology. For even the anticipators, are they motivated primarily to try and help the environment and reduce air pollution or are they motivated because they believe meeting or beating the proposed regulations with new technology could enhance their competitive position? What would you do if meeting or exceeding environmental or other societal goods potentially hurt your business? For example, what would you do if the technology for exceeding environmental standards for two-stroke engines resulted in engines that were 30 percent more expensive and at the same time weighed 20 percent more? What would you do if your market research suggested that commercial users of handheld tools (for example, trimmers or leaf blowers) were unlikely to pay the premium price or want the extra weight? After all, it is one thing for a consumer to deal with the extra weight for an hour or so once a week, but it is quite another thing for a small landscaping and yard work company to ask its employees to pack around 20 percent more weight six to eight hours a day, five days a week. What would you do if commercial sales accounted for half of your company's total sales?

The Strategic Corporate Social Responsibility Perspective

strategic corporate social responsibility perspective a three-criteria model that can help managers focus on social areas where there is the highest possibility of creating shared value for the business and society

A more recent approach to corporate social responsibility tries to address the balancing act managers must engage in when responding to the concerns of all their stakeholders.[39] Called the **strategic corporate social responsibility perspective,** it argues that three fundamental criteria can guide managers.

The first criterion takes an "inside-out" approach. In other words, managers can look inside the company at issues that are more rather than less important as a function of the company's strategy and business activities. For example, if you are a manager at Wal-Mart, the labor-intensive

A MANAGER'S CHALLENGE

TECHNOLOGY

Cleaning Up Dirty Little Engines: Dealing with Technology

The whine of a two-stroke engine powering a leaf blower, chainsaw, or trimmer; the puff of blue smoke it emits; and the pungent smell of its oil and gas mixture are as common as a warm day in summer. Whether you are walking through a residential neighborhood or driving by the tidy landscape of an office building, you see, hear, and smell this $15 billion-dollar-a-year industry. At least 30 million of these handheld products are currently in use in the United States. Two million blowers, 2.5 million chainsaws, and 6 million trimmers are sold each year. About two-thirds of the sales are to consumers. The rest involve more heavy-duty products for commercial users. The Environmental Protection Agency (EPA) estimates that blowers, trimmers, and the like contribute 5 percent of the total nonfactory hydrocarbon and oxides of nitrogen (NOx) emissions. (Manufacturers contend the number is closer to 2 percent to 3 percent.)

Two-stroke engines are so popular because they are extremely reliable, lightweight yet powerful, and fairly inexpensive. However, they are also dirty because, unlike four-stroke engines, there is no separate intake and exhaust stroke, and, as a consequence, 30 percent of the gas-oil mix escapes unburned.

In 1990, the California Air Resources Board (CARB) began a three-phase emissions initiative, with Phase I requiring emissions from handheld engines to be reduced by 30 percent by 1995. Phase II required a reduction of 80 percent from Phase I levels by 1999. Phase III required a further 40 percent reduction by 2007. Fred Whyte, president of Stihl, one of the largest manufacturers of two-stroke handheld engines, echoed the sentiments of many manufacturers: "Is this the greatest challenge ever faced by handheld engine manufacturers? No question." Larry Will, vice president of engineering at Echo, stated even more bluntly: "Meeting the regulations is one thing; meeting them and surviving is another."

Companies like Echo, McCulloch, Stihl, and other members of the Outdoor Power Equipment Institute enlisted powerful lobbyists to lower and delay the emission reductions. Representatives argued that the regulations would "virtually eliminate" all two-stroke engines and impose unreasonable cost burdens on consumers. Even if the standards could technically be met, the engines would cost 15 percent to 30 percent more. Given consumers' price sensitivity and the fact that "big-box" retailers like Home Depot, Wal-Mart, and Lowes control about two-thirds of consumer sales, no one wanted to be the first company to invest in the new technology and introduce the higher-priced products.

By 1995 virtually all the manufacturers were able to meet CARB's Phase I standards simply by capturing more hydrocarbons in the exhaust system, a further 80 percent reduction looked technically impossible. So in the mid-1990s, the manufacturers' association again took up the fight against the regulations.

However, three manufacturers broke ranks. RedMax (a subsidiary of Japan's Komatsu), Tanaka, and Deere & Co. (the $13 billion-a-year farm machinery giant) tried to be anticipators. Both RedMax and Tanaka created new technology for injecting a shot of pure air between exhaust gases and fuel intake that significantly reduced emissions in two-stroke engines beyond the Phase II standards. Although Deere had originally opposed the California standards, it subsequently lobbied both CARB and the EPA to *not* lower standards or delay their implementation. Deere had perfected a new technological design called "compression wave" for its Homelite brand that was similar to RedMax's solution. However, after big-box retailers pressured Deere to lower its prices on the higher-cost, lower-emission engines, its Homelite division lost $100 million over the next 21 months. Subsequently, Deere sold Homelite to TechTronics Industries of Hong Kong.

To meet the CARB standards and deadlines, virtually all the other manufacturers trying to sell the engines in California had to buy engines from RedMax and Tanaka; Stihl, for example, bought 60,000 engines from RedMax. To meet the EPA standards set to take effect nationally in 2007, manufacturers such as Stihl, Echo, and Briggs and Stratton finally launched their own attempts at technological breakthroughs. For example, Stihl moved from being a defender to an accommodater, and then to a reactor. At a cost of $12 million, Stihl developed an engine that acts like a four-stroke engine but is lubricated like a two-stroke engine and weighs only 10 percent more.

By 2009, advances in reducing emissions in two-stroke engines and advances in power and reductions in weight of four-stroke engines (which have significantly lower emissions than two-stroke engines) had pushed nearly every

(continued)

major manufacturer out of the Defender role. The result is that today these once "dirty little engines" have gotten a lot cleaner. Over the last 10 years, improvements in outdoor power equipment design have resulted in the reduction of exhaust emissions by over 70 percent according to the Outdoor Power Equipment Institute.

Source: Outdoor Power Equipment Institute, www.opei.org, accessed March 24, 2010; "U.S. Power and Hand Tools Demand to Reach $15.5 Billion in 2009," *Grounds Maintenance*, http://grounds-mag.com/news/tools_demand_051705/index.html, accessed February 23, 2009; E. Chapman, "Handheld Lawn and Garden Products," *Grounds Maintenance*, July 2003, 12; M. Boyle, "Dirty Little Engines Get Cleaner," *Fortune*, May 13, 2002, I146[B–L].

nature of your business places a heavy emphasis on workers. In contrast, the capital-intensive nature of Boeing places a heavy emphasis on technology.

The second criterion takes an "outside-in" approach. In other words, managers can look outside the company at issues the company can influence. For example, suppose you are a Wal-Mart manager in charge of the energy costs consumed by all the company's stores. As such, not only would you have a significant impact on the stores' energy consumption and greenhouse gas emissions, you would also be able to influence the power companies that produce electricity for your stores. For example, you might be able to get those companies to use alternative fuels that would enable the production of energy with lower greenhouse gas emissions.

The third criterion takes an "outside-out" approach. In other words, managers look at social issues in general terms of the extent to which they are problematic. Clearly, there are nearly an unlimited number of social issues to consider—everything from poverty to literacy to sanitation and more. However, the strategic social responsibility approach does not advocate looking at all social issues, rather assessing those that come into focus as a function of the first two criteria.

Taken together, the three criteria form a three-dimensional matrix that can help managers focus on those social areas with the highest possibility of creating shared value for society *and* the business. Exhibit 2.4 illustrates this matrix. Marriott provides an illustration of the framework in action. It is critical that Marriott, as a labor-intensive business, maintains a substantial supply of workers to do relatively low-tech jobs, such as housekeeping. Most of the company's larger, upscale hotels are in big cities like New York, where chronic unemployment is a problem, particularly among poorly educated individuals with fewer skills. Chronic unemployment leads to a number of socially undesirable consequences including homelessness and drug abuse. As a large employer of low-skilled labor, Marriott's social outreach efforts targeting chronically unemployed workers in large cities like New York create the opportunity for shared value creation for employees, communities, shareholders, and customers.

EXHIBIT 2.4

Strategic Corporate Social Responsibility: A Criteria Matrix

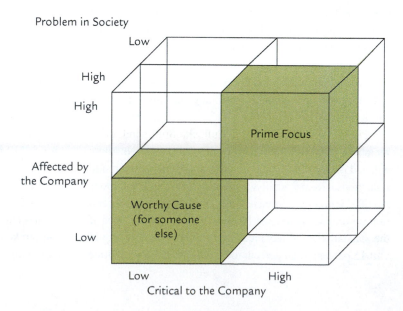

Marriott provides 180 hours of paid classroom and on-the-job training for chronically unemployed individuals. More than 90 percent complete the program and are hired by Marriott. After one year, more than 65 percent are still in their jobs—a high retention rate for the industry in general and a much, much higher rate for the chronically unemployed. In the end, Marriott, its newly trained employees, and their communities all benefit.

Suppose you were a manager in the human resource department at Marriott and someone suggested that the company should also get involved in another inner-city problem: HIV/AIDS. Should you recommend that the company invest time and resources in this issue? Although it's an important issue, the problem is that HIV/AIDS does not seem to affect the company's key activities, such as recruiting. Furthermore, because Marriott is a small employer in the scheme of this set of individuals, it seems unlikely that the company's actions could have a significant impact on the issue. The company lacks the potential to create shared value for society and the business. However, if you are a Marriott human resource manager in Bangkok, Thailand, or Johannesburg, South Africa—where HIV/AIDS seriously compromises the supply of low-skilled workers—the same analysis might yield different conclusions. Low-skilled workers constitute a critical group for the company's operations, and Marriott is a large employer in the two cities. For these reasons, its approach to preventive health care could have a significant impact on the incidence of HIV/AIDS in each city. As a consequence, what potentially is for Marriott in New York a "worthy cause for someone else" may be a "strategic corporate social responsibility issue" for Marriott in Bangkok and Johannesburg.

How People and Firms Can Make Better Ethical Decisions

While the media helps uncover the ethical misconduct of high-profile people, such as CEOs of major companies, there is some evidence that ethical misconduct at all levels is rising.[40] If this is the case, a significant challenge remains to you as a manager: How can you foster and encourage ethical decisions?

The Manager

As mentioned at the outset of the chapter, part of the reason for exploring various approaches to ethical decision making is to help you refine your own approach so that when pressures arise, you can make decisions consistent with your ethical framework and avoid ethical lapses. To this end, there is perhaps no substitute for taking personal responsibility for your decisions.

Even after you have become more comfortable and explicit about how you would resolve ethical dilemmas, the question still remains: How much should you change your approach to fit in with others or try to change their approaches? If you were at Nike, how hard should you work to change the public's perception, persuading them to see the positive benefits workers in their factories enjoy and what their lives would be like without jobs making Nike products? It is probably impossible to argue that one of this chapter's approaches is best. However, applied consistently, each approach will result in a consistent pattern of ethical decision making. Even if people don't always agree with your decisions, they will appreciate the fact that you are consistent.[41]

The Organization

Just as managers try to foster ethical decisions, organizations have a significant impact on ethical decision making. A company's overall culture plays a significant role. For example, the emphasis on generating revenues and keeping clients happy seemed to contribute to a number of rather lax audits of companies like Enron and WorldCom by accounting firm Arthur Andersen. Andersen subsequently went out of business. In contrast, firms can also have a positive impact on ethical decision making and behavior. In many firms, senior managers go out of their way to encourage managers to behave ethically. Codes of ethics and whistle-blowing systems are perhaps two of the more visible efforts.

CODES OF ETHICS Many firms have adopted codes of ethics to guide their managers' decision making. A **code of ethical conduct** is typically a formal one- to three-page statement outlining the types of behavior that are and are not acceptable. Exhibit 2.5 displays the Johnson & Johnson credo, one of the oldest among U.S. corporations. The credo was first adopted in 1945 and has been revised four times.

code of ethical conduct
a formal settlement that outlines types of behavior that are and are not acceptable

EXHIBIT 2.5

Johnson & Johnson Credo

We believe our first responsibility is to the doctors, nurses, and patients, to mothers and fathers and all others who use our products and services. In meeting their needs everything we do must be of high quality. We must constantly strive to reduce our costs in order to maintain reasonable prices. Customers' orders must be serviced promptly and accurately. Our suppliers and distributors must have an opportunity to make a fair profit.

We are responsible to our employees: the men and women who work with us throughout the world. Everyone must be considered as an individual. We must respect their dignity and recognize their merit. They must have a sense of security in their jobs. Compensation must be fair and adequate, and working conditions clean, orderly, and safe. Employees must feel free to make suggestions and complaints. There must be equal opportunity for employment, development, and advancement for those qualified. We must provide competent management, and their actions must be just and ethical.

We are responsible to the communities in which we live and work and to the world community as well.

We must be good citizens—support good works and charities and bear our fair share of taxes. We must encourage civic improvements and better health and education.

We must maintain in good order the property we are privileged to use, protecting the environment and natural resources.

Our final responsibility is to our stockholders. Business must make a sound profit. We must experiment with new ideas. Research must be carried on, innovative programs developed, and mistakes paid for. New equipment must be purchased, new facilities provided, and new products launched. Reserves must be created to provide for adverse times.

When we operate according to these principles, the stockholders should realize a fair return.

An examination of 84 codes of ethics in U.S. firms found three specific clusters of issues addressed in these statements.[42] The first main cluster includes items that focus on being a good "organizational citizen." The second cluster includes items that guide employees to restrain from unlawful or improper acts that would harm the organization. The third cluster includes items that address directives to be good to customers. Each of these clusters was further divided into subcategories.

A study of codes of ethics for firms in the United Kingdom, France, and Germany found that a higher percentage of German firms had codes of ethics than do British or French firms (see Exhibit 2.6).[43] Although only about one-third of the European firms in this study had codes of ethics, approximately 85 percent of U.S. firms have formal codes.

In a separate study, researchers found that important differences in codes of conduct exist among U.S., Canadian, and Australian firms.[44] For example, ethics codes differ substantially in terms of explicitly defining acceptable ethical conduct on such issues as gifts, meals, and entertainment for domestic government officials (87 percent of U.S. firms, 59 percent of Canadian, and 24 percent of Australian firms include this information).

Exhibit 2.7 provides information about the content of the codes of ethics for the firms that had formal codes. While 100 percent of the European firms' codes cover issues of acceptable and unacceptable employee behavior, only 55 percent of U.S. firms address these issues. By contrast, only 15 percent of the European firms covered issues of political interests (that is, business-government relations) and 96 percent of U.S. firms covered these issues in their codes.

Research indicates that executives believe codes of conduct are the most effective way of encouraging employees' ethical behavior.[45] Unfortunately, the

EXHIBIT 2.6

Adoption of Codes of Ethics

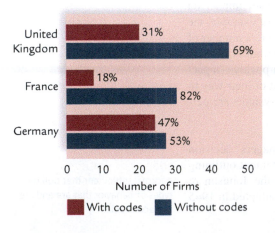

	With codes	Without codes
United Kingdom	31%	69%
France	18%	82%
Germany	47%	53%

Number of Firms

EXHIBIT 2.7 Subjects Addressed in Corporate Codes of Ethics

Subjects	UNITED KINGDOM N = 33		FRANCE N = 15		GERMANY N = 30		TOTAL EUROPEAN COUNTRIES		UNITED STATES N = 118		SIGNIFICANCE
	Number of Firms	%	Number of Firms	%	Number of Firms	%	Number of Firms	%	Number of Firms	%	Europe vs. U.S.
Employee conduct	33	100	15	100	30	100	78	100	47	55	SIG
Community and environment	21	64	11	73	19	63	51	85	50	42	NS
Customers	18	39	14	93	20	67	52	87	96	81	SIG
Shareholders	13	39	11	73	18	60	42	64	NA	NA	NA
Suppliers and contractors	7	21	2	13	6	20	15	19	101	86	SIG
Political interests	4	12	3	20	5	17	12	15	113	96	SIG
Innovation and technology	2	6	3	20	18	60	26	33	18	15	SIG

NS = Not significant   NA = No comparable data available   SIG = Significantly different

research does not support a strong link between codes of ethics and actual employee behavior. Firms without formal codes seem to have no higher or lower incidents of unethical behavior than those with formal codes.[46] This may be because simply having a formal, documented statement is not sufficient. For example, although nearly all *Fortune* 500 firms in the United States have codes of ethics, only about one-third have training programs and ethics officers, and only half have distributed formal codes to all their employees.[47]

SUCCESSFULLY IMPLEMENTING CODES OF ETHICS Actions speak much louder than words; employees are unlikely to conform to the formal code unless other actions taken by the organization reinforce the code and communicate that the company is serious about compliance.[48] Some companies have instituted "ethics officers" or ombudsmen: individuals responsible for communicating ethics information and policies to employees and ensuring that their concerns and observations of misconduct are reported to senior managers so corrective actions can be taken.

Communication For maximum impact, communicating a company's ethical standards must take a variety of forms and be repeated. It is not enough to simply disseminate a one-time memo. Rather, the company must repeatedly communicate the code in memos, company newsletters, videos, and speeches by senior executives over a period of time if people are to embrace and internalize the message.

Training For the code of ethical conduct to be effective, people will likely need training.[49] For maximum impact, training must be engaging. For example, Motorola developed approximately 80 different short cases. Each case presents a situation requiring a manager to make a decision. Trainees are asked to individually and collectively decide what they would do in similar situations. They then compared their decisions to those of senior executives, including Motorola's CEO, to examine what these executives believe is in keeping with the firm's code of ethics.

Lockheed Martin also has taken an engaging approach to ethics training—with an interesting and innovative twist. In the late 1990s, the company developed a board game based on Scott Adam's "Dilbert" character. The game features 50 ethical dilemmas for players (employees) to consider. Participants found this approach to be more satisfying than traditional ethics training.

They also seemed to recall the learning points more effectively. After the Dilbert craze wore off, Lockheed Martin used real business ethics problems as a basis for discussion. The company also maintains an ethics hotline employees can call for advice if they are experiencing a business dilemma.[50]

Sometimes, the need for training emerges because of embarrassing problems. For example, in early 2010 AstraZeneca PLC paid a $250 million fine for promoting its drug Seroquel for conditions other than those approved by the FDA. Marketing and promoting a drug for "off-label" uses is illegal. As a result, AstraZeneca increased its ethics training for employees. According to a company spokeswoman, "Last year, AstraZeneca took a number of steps to strengthen its ethics training for employees, including introducing a new 'openness' program designed to encourage staff to report alleged ethics violations."[51]

Although officials at organizations often think that ethics training programs are effective, current research is less conclusive. What we can say based on research is that the greater employees' psychological and emotional involvement in the training, the greater their retention of the learning points. This may explain Lockheed Martin's positive experience with ethics training.

Reward and Recognition In addition to communicating the code to employees and training them, it is critical to make sure that compliance is recognized and rewarded. Otherwise, employees will simply view the code as the "formal rhetoric but not the real deal." ExxonMobil regularly celebrates individuals who honor the company's code of conduct, even when doing so might have cost the company money. For example, when a government official in a developing company solicited a bribe from one of ExxonMobil's drilling teams in exchange for permission to drill there, the team manager refused to pay. The drilling team and their expensive equipment sat idle for more than a week at a cost of over $1 million. Finally, the government official admitted that all the paperwork and permits were in order and the team was allowed to proceed. ExxonMobil described this incident in its employee newsletter to reinforce that the company takes its code of ethical conduct seriously and rewards people who honor it, even when doing so may be costly for the organization.

whistle-blower

an employee who discloses illegal or unethical conduct on the part of others in the organization

Whistle-Blowing A **whistle-blower** is an employee who discloses illegal or unethical conduct on the part of others in the organization. Although some firms have implemented programs to encourage whistle-blowing, most have not.[52] As a group, whistle-blowers tend *not* to be disgruntled employees but conscientious, high-performing employees. In general, whistle-blowers report these incidents not for personal fame but because they believe the wrongdoings are so grave that they must be exposed.[53] For example, nuclear power-plant supervisor Randy Robarge never intended to be a whistle-blower. In his mind, raising concerns about the improper storage of radioactive material at ComEd's Zion power plant on Lake Michigan was just part of doing a good job.[54]

Research suggests that the more employees know about internal channels for whistle-blowing and the stronger the protection of past whistle-blowers, the more likely they are to initially use internal rather than external channels, such as the media, to call attention to problems.[55] IBM receives up to 18,000 letters a year from employees making confidential complaints through IBM's "Speak Up" program. Firms such as Hughes Tool Co., General Motors, and Bloomingdale's offer financial rewards to employees who report valid claims.[56] In general, research suggests the following steps can be effective in encouraging valid whistle-blowing:[57]

- Clearly communicate whistle-blowing procedures to all employees.
- Allow for reporting channels in addition to the chain of command or reporting incidents to one's boss.
- Thoroughly investigate all claims based on a consistent procedure.
- Protect whistle-blowers who make valid claims.
- Provide moderate financial incentives or rewards for valid claims.
- Publicly celebrate employees who make valid claims.

Examples Set by Top Managers The examples top managers set—both in terms of how they behave personally and how they reward, punish, or ignore the actions of others—probably has the biggest impact on ethical conduct.[58] Managers' behavior can severely damage the best intentions and implementation of any corporate ethics program. Middle managers are rarely persuaded by top executives to "do as I say not as I do."

Leaders at Enron, such as Ken Lay and Jeff Skilling, set an example of reporting growth at any price. Standard accounting rules were ignored so that higher revenues and profits could be recorded immediately. Once one rule, law, or policy is ignored by senior officers, who is to say that others shouldn't be? This pattern of illegal and unethical conduct was not confined to Enron but was complemented by the behavior of senior partners in the accounting firm engaged to monitor and certify Enron's accounting practices: Arthur Andersen. In an effort to retain Enron's auditing business and its more lucrative consulting engagements, leaders at Arthur Andersen ignored Enron's accounting irregularities despite their legal and ethical obligation to report them. In the end, leaders even instructed subordinates to destroy and shred documents (against company policy and legal statutes) in an effort to hide wrongdoing on both sides.

By following the steps outlined earlier, managers can catch problems before they become national media events and seriously damage the firm's reputation. In addition, new laws in the United States both protect and reward whistle-blowers. Employers cannot discharge, threaten, or otherwise discriminate against employees because they report a suspected violation of the law. Employees who blow the whistle on companies with federal government contracts can actually receive a small portion of the judgment if the company is found guilty. Jane Akre was one of the first to receive such a reward. Akre received $425,000 when she blew the whistle on her employer, a TV station, that deliberately distorted the news.[59] However, an award of $52 million to three men who blew the whistle on pharmaceuticals giant SmithKline Beecham really grabbed people's attention.[60] And an even bigger eye-opener occurred when Jim Alderson and John Schilling helped disclose Medicare fraud on the part of HCA, the nation's largest hospital chain. Alderson and Schilling shared a $100 million whistle-blower award granted on a $1.7 billion fine levied on HCA.

Scott J. Ferrell/Congressional Quarterly/Alamy Images

Joseph F. Berardino, managing partner and CEO of Arthur Andersen testifies during the House Capital Markets Insurance and Government Sponsored Enterprises Subcommittee hearing on the collapse of Enron and the unethical accounting practices of Arthur Andersen that hid Enron's accounting irregularities.

How Governments Can Foster Ethical Behavior

The governments of the United States and many other countries have also tried to foster ethical behavior. For example, the U.S. government has enacted a number of laws and regulations designed to achieve this objective. Perhaps the most discussed, given today's global environment, is the Foreign Corrupt Practices Act.

Few issues of ethical behavior have received more attention than questionable payments or bribes. For American managers, this is the heart of the **Foreign Corrupt Practices Act (FCPA).** The act was passed in 1977 primarily because U.S. firms were making payments to foreign government officials to win government contracts and receive preferential treatment.

One of the key incidents that sparked the FCPA was the revelation that Lockheed Martin had made over $12 million in payments to Japanese business executives and government officials in order to sell commercial aircraft in that country. Subsequent discoveries showed that nearly 500 U.S. companies had made similar payments around the world, totaling over $300 million.

Lockheed's chairman at the time, Carl Kotchian, argued that the payments represented less than 3 percent of the revenue gained from the sale of aircraft to Japan. Kotchian also claimed the sales had a positive effect on the salaries and job security of Lockheed workers, with beneficial spillover effects for their dependents, communities, and shareholders. He said he was "between a rock and a hard spot": If he made the payments, people would say they were unethical; if he did not make the payments, a competitor would, and some Lockheed workers would lose their jobs. Do you agree with Kotchian? Whether you do or not, can you figure out which

Foreign Corrupt Practices Act (FCPA)
a law prohibiting employees of U.S. firms from corrupting the actions of foreign officials, politicians, or candidates for office

Managerial Challenges from the Front Line

The Rest of the Story

After her mother died of lung disease in 1995, Sharon Anderson Wright became the CEO of Half Price Books. "I think we've grown more than she could have imagined," said Wright about her mom. In fact, even though the company now has about double the number of stores it did in 1995, it has never taken a lot of debt. Nonetheless, the growth of the business forced the firm to become more organized, which has involved investing additional finances in things like computer and inventory systems. The expansion also made it too costly to maintain full health care benefits for part-time workers, a decision that Wright said she made "not lightly."

Wright still lives in her childhood Dallas home with her children and husband Ken (who also works for the company). She pays herself a relatively small five-figure salary. Employees are also paid modestly but receive shares in the company. Wright says that she and her sister, Ellen O'Neal, executive vice president of Half Price Books, have turned down many buyout offers from competitors and venture-capital firms. "We could have been rich many times over," she says. "But my mom made a commitment to do the right thing, and it's my job to uphold it."

Sources: H. Landy, "Founder's Daughters Write Their Own Chapter," *Fort Worth Star-Telegram,* May 12, 2007, 1C, 6C; "Strong Results Fuel Chain's Decision to Add Stores," *Fort Worth Star-Telegram,* January 9, 2007; J. Lynch and G. Cosgriff, "Shelf Help," *People,* May 20, 2003, 127, 2p, 3c.

ethical approach he seems to be following? Is it a moral right approach, justice approach, or utilitarian approach?

Until the passage of the FCPA, these dilemmas were purely ethical ones. Upon its passage, they became legal ones: The FCPA made it illegal for employees of U.S. firms to corrupt the actions of foreign officials, politicians, or candidates for office. The act also outlaws an employee from making payments to *any* person when the employee has "reason to know" that the payments might be used to corrupt the behavior of officials. The act also requires that firms take steps to provide "reasonable assurance" that their transactions are in compliance with the law and to keep detailed records of them.

The FCPA does not cover payments made to business executives, though. For American managers, payments made to executives are ethical decisions, not legal ones. The FCPA also does not prohibit payments to low-level government employees to perform their duties in a more timely manner—duties they normally would have performed anyway. These types of payments are typically called *facilitating payments.* For example, a payment of $100 to a customs inspector not to delay the inspection of an imported product would not violate the FCPA because the payment simply facilitates something that the customs inspector would do anyway. However, the payment of $100 to pass a product *without* inspecting it would be a violation of the FCPA because the payment would entice the customs agent to do something he or she is not supposed to do.

Companies can be fined up to $1 million for violating the FCPA. Individuals face a $10,000 fine and up to *five years in prison.* Clearly, a $1 million fine is not a deterrent when deals can be worth $100 million. Rather, the prison terms for individuals are the real teeth in the law.

The general debates concerning ethics and social responsibility have raged for generations. The purpose of this chapter has not been to resolve the debate but rather to examine the assumptions and rationales of fundamental perspectives. If there were a magic formula for meeting these challenges, there would likely be little need for bright, capable people as managers wrestling with these issues (we could just turn the problem over to computer algorithms). Nor would there be much excitement in being a manager. We hope this examination enables you to evaluate your own views so that you will be prepared when situations arise concerning ethics or social responsibility. Perhaps then the pressure of the moment will be less likely to cause you to take actions that you might later regret. Understanding the general frameworks also helps you to better appreciate others who have differing perspectives and, thereby, interact more effectively with them.

Summary

- The four basic approaches to ethical decision making include utilitarian, moral rights, universal, and justice approaches. The utilitarian approach is based on the premise that the right thing to do is that which brings about the greatest good. The moral rights approach assumes that actions should be consistent with existing principles with moral standing. The universal approach is based on the notion that actions should be guided by principles that you believe should be universally applied, including to yourself. The justice approach is predicated on the notion that costs and benefits should be equitably distributed, rules should be impartially applied, and those damaged because of inequity or discrimination should be compensated.
- Moral intensity is the degree to which people see an issue as an ethical one. It is influenced by six factors: (1) the magnitude of the consequences, (2) social consensus, (3) the probability of effect, (4) temporal immediacy, (5) proximity, and (6) the concentration of effect.
- Poor judgments regarding social responsibility and lapses in ethical decision making can inflict irreparable damage to a firm's value. As a consequence, as a manager, you need to be able to make sound, ethical decisions and encourage your subordinates to do likewise.
- The efficiency perspective argues that "the business of business is business." Therefore, a manager's obligation is to maximize shareholders' returns. The values of society should only be reflected in a manager's decisions insofar as those values are codified by law.
- The social responsibility perspective argues that corporations owe their existence not just to shareholders, who provide risk capital, but to society at large. As a consequence, managers should provide a reasonable return to shareholders while also meeting the legitimate concerns of society.
- The strategic corporate social responsibility approach argues that the best social responsibility is that which creates shared value for society and the business. Determining which issues have the highest probability of fulfilling this objective comes from assessing the activities that are key to the business, issues that the company affects, and issues that are of concern to society.
- When it comes to fostering ethical decisions and behavior throughout an organization, few things are more important than the example set by senior executives. Codes of conduct, communication, training, and rewards (and punishments) are all additional steps that can have an effect on the decisions and behavior of employees.

Key Terms

code of ethical conduct   45
compensatory justice   32
concentration of
    effect   34
distributive justice   32
efficiency perspective   36
ethical dilemma   30
ethical lapse   30
externality   38

Foreign Corrupt Practices
    Act   49
justice approach   32
magnitude of the consequences   33
managerial ethics   29
moral intensity   33
moral rights approach   31
probability of effect   34
procedural justice   32

proximity   34
social consensus   33
stakeholder   39
strategic corporate social
    responsibility perspective   42
temporal immediacy   34
universal approach   31
utilitarian approach   31
whistle-blower   48

Review Questions

1. What is the major premise of the efficiency perspective regarding corporate social responsibility?
2. What are the key concerns with the efficiency perspective of social responsibility?
3. What is the fundamental objective of the strategic social responsibility approach?
4. What are the key differences between managerial ethics and corporate social responsibility?
5. Contrast and compare the utilitarian approach, moral rights approach, universal approach, and justice approach.
6. What six factors influence moral intensity?
7. What are five powerful means of enhancing the influence of formal codes of conduct on actual employee behavior?
8. What is a whistle-blower?
9. What is the Foreign Corrupt Practices Act?

Assessing Your Capabilities

An Honesty Test

Have you ever cheated on a test? What about calling in sick at work when you weren't ill? Have you ever downloaded music from an Internet site and not paid for it? To get a quick idea of how you stack up against in terms of your honesty, go to http://www.cbsnews.com/stories/2002/11/08/48hours/main528 761.shtml.

Team Exercise

The Limits of Privacy

Divide into teams of three. One person will play the role of the employee. One person will play the role of the supervisor. The third person will observe the encounter and provide a summary. Each person should read the following scenario. The individuals playing the roles of the employee and boss should then engage in a five- to ten-minute conversation to try and resolve the issue. The questions at the end of the scenario will stimulate your thinking and prepare you for the conversation.

Your firm has a stated policy that e-mails constitute company correspondence and, therefore, are subject to screening. Although the company includes the policy explanation in the thick orientation document that every new employee receives, most employees aren't aware of the policy. Most of those who are aware of it do not believe that the company reviews their e-mail or other Internet activities.

Your boss comes to you with the password to all your subordinates' e-mail accounts and asks you to review them. He has some concern but no hard evidence that one of your subordinates either may be talking with a competitor about coming to work for them or may even be leaking sensitive marketing information to them. He instructs you to not be fooled by what appears in the subject line of the e-mails because anyone with any smarts would not put the real nature of the e-mail there if he or she were up to something unethical. Therefore, he wants you to read through all the employees' e-mails over the last four weeks and monitor them over the next few weeks until the allegation is proven to be true or groundless. He has transferred a small project from you to ensure that you have the time to complete this review over the next week.

1. What would you do? Would you take the assignment?
2. If so, why? If not, why not?
3. If you didn't want to take the assignment, how could you turn it down without hurting your relationship with your boss or potentially damaging your career?
4. Is it ethical to read employees' e-mail that they may consider private?
5. Is it ethical to not inform employees of what you are about to do?

Nicolo Pignatelli, president of Gulf Italia (a subsidiary of Gulf Oil), stared at the notice from the Italian government. "How could this be possible?" he thought. The government had given Pignatelli permission to build an oil refinery with a capacity of almost 6 million tons. He had just completed it at a cost of several hundred million dollars. Now the Italian government was telling him that he could only operate at slightly more than 50 percent capacity (3.9 million tons of the total 6 million ton capacity). On top of that, the notice from the government also said that not only would he need to get "production permission" to go from 3.9 million to 6.0 million tons in actual production, he would also need a *separate* "implementation permission" to put into effect the "production permission."

Pignatelli didn't know whether to be intimidated or infuriated. The government had given him permission to build a 6 million ton facility. However, they were now allowing him to operate at only 3.9 million tons. Because of the plant's high fixed cost, it needed to operate near capacity to make money. Operating at 3.9 million tons would lose millions of dollars and was out of the question. Shutting down the plant completely would also cost money.

Pignatelli was understandably upset—he had spent seven long years implementing a strategy to take the company from one of the small fries in the Italian oil and gasoline industry to one of the major players. When Pignatelli took over, Gulf gas stations were located in northern Italy. To build a national presence, Pignatelli acquired 700 gasoline stations, primarily in central and southern Italy, from Marathon Oil. This purchase allowed Gulf to have gas stations throughout Italy. Gulf also had crude oil operations in southern Italy and in the nearby Middle East, which it could use to supply crude oil to Italy. What Gulf lacked was the middle part of the chain—a refinery. Without it, Pignatelli was dependent on competitors for a refined gasoline supply and had to take whatever wholesale prices they dictated. Pignatelli felt Gulf needed its own refinery to complete the chain from the wellhead to the gas pump and thereby control its own destiny.

Building a refinery in Italy was a long and expensive task. Even after receiving permission to build the refinery in northern Italy, local community opposition resulted in five location changes before construction could finally start. These location changes alone cost Gulf an additional $16 million. To ensure that the smoke and fumes would not contribute to city smog, Pignatelli spent extra money on a 450-foot smokestack (twice as tall as normal). Pignatelli also installed a special combustion chamber so that flare towers (used to burn off waste gas) and the loud noise and noxious fumes associated with them weren't necessary. He also added a state-of-the-art water purification system. Pignatelli demonstrated the quality of the system by personally drinking the waste water. These environmental additions added several million dollars to the project.

So that the refinery would be profitable, Pignatelli wanted to assure strong demand for the supply created by the refinery. In addition to the internal demand from Gulf gas stations, Pignatelli arranged a joint venture with Mobil Oil. Mobil had many service stations in northern Italy where Gulf's refinery was located but no refinery of its own. This would secure demand for the refinery's products, and the money Mobil was to invest for its equity share would reduce Gulf's financial burden in building the refinery. However, Mobil had the option of pulling out of the deal if Gulf's refinery could not operate at capacity because in that case, the refined gas would be too expensive for Mobil to buy.

It had taken seven years for the refinery to be approved and built. Hundreds of millions of dollars were on the line. On top of this, Pignatelli personally had sold the expansion strategy (both the acquisition of the retail stations and the building of the refinery) to senior executives at Gulf's global headquarters. As a consequence, his personal reputation was also on the line. Trying to obtain approval to operate at capacity and a separate authorization to implement that approval might take many more months, if not years. Pignatelli wondered if he was being purposely set up by government officials.

Four options occurred to Pignatelli:

1. He could play it straight and try to gain government authorization.
2. He could ask his more-influential partners (for example, Mobil) to pressure government officials to quickly grant the two needed permissions.
3. He could pay a large sum of money ($1 million deposited to a Swiss bank account) to a "consultant" who had "debottlenecked" problems like this before and who promised Pignatelli that he could fix the situation quickly.
4. He could pay money "under the table" directly to government officials to obtain the permissions needed to run the refinery economically.

Pignatelli considered each option. Playing it straight would likely take several months and possibly years before government authorization could be obtained. In the meantime, the refinery would not operate, or would operate at such a low capacity that it would lose millions of dollars. Pignatelli was not certain that pressure from his partners would influence government officials. He wondered about the effect of going to the media. Given the current cost of the project, the thousands of jobs that depended on an operating refinery, and time pressures, $1 million seemed like a small price to pay to a consultant to get things de-bottlenecked. He might be able to gain approval for even less money if he went directly to government officials.

Questions

1. What should Pignatelli do? What would you do and why?
2. Pignatelli seems to be leaning in the direction of hiring a consultant who might use part of the money for bribes. If Pignatelli does not pay the bribes directly, does this absolve him of responsibility?
3. Bribes are illegal in Italy. Even if bribes were common practice there, would this justify paying them?
4. Does Pignatelli have a responsibility to Italian citizens to build an environmentally friendly refinery above and beyond what the law requires? Is it appropriate for Gulf to spend this extra money and essentially take it away from shareholders?
5. How would you feel if you were a lower-level employee in the company and learned that Pignatelli intended to pay bribes to get things "debottlenecked"? What would your ethical obligations be? Should you ignore the situation or confront Pignatelli? Should you inform your direct boss or go to the media?

Source: Personal conversations with Nicolo Pignatelli.

References

1. P. Hosking, "Citigroup Agree to Pay," *Timesonline,* June 29, 2005.
2. M. A. Hitt, R. D. Ireland, and R. E. Hoskisson, *Strategic Management: Competitiveness and Globalization* (Cincinnati, OH: South-Western Publishing, 2005).
3. J. B. Cullen, K. Parboteeah, and M. Hoegl, "Cross-National Differences in Managers' Willingness to Justify Ethically Suspect Behaviors: A Test of Institutional Anomie Theory," *Academy of Management Journal* 47, no. 3 (2004): 411–421.
4. D. Peterson, A. Rhoads, and B. C. Vaught, "Ethical Beliefs of Business Professionals: A Study of Gender, Age, and External Factors," *Journal of Business Ethics* 31, no. 3 (2001): 225–232; E. Marnburg, "The Questionable Use of Moral Development Theory in Studies of Business Ethics: Discussion and Empirical Findings," *Journal of Business Ethics* 32, no. 4 (2001): 275–283.
5. J. Tsalikis, B. Seaton, and P. Tomaras, "A New Perspective on Cross-Cultural Ethical Evaluations: The Use of Conjoint Analysis," *Journal of Business Ethics* 35, no. 4 (February 2002): 281–292; L. Thorne and S. B. Saunders, "The Socio-Cultural Embeddedness of Individuals' Ethical Reasoning in Organizations (Cross-Cultural Ethics)," *Journal of Business Ethics* 35, no. 1 (February 2002): 1–14; J. B. Hamilton III and S. B. Knouse, "Multinational Enterprise Decision Principles for Dealing with Cross-Cultural Ethical Conflicts," *Journal of Business Ethics* 31, no. 1 (May 2001): 77–94; C. J. Robertson and W. F. Crittenden, "Mapping Moral Philosophies: Strategic Implications for Multinational Firms," *Strategic Management Journal* 24, no. 4 (2003): 385–392.
6. Cullen, Parboteeah, and Hoegl, "Cross-National Differences in Managers' Willingness to Justify Ethically Suspect Behaviors: A Test of Institutional Anomie Theory"; Thorne and Saunders, "The Socio-Cultural Embeddedness of Individuals' Ethical Reasoning in Organizations (Cross-Cultural Ethics)"; A. J. Dubinsky, M. A. Jolson, M. Kotabe, and C. U. Lim, "A Cross-National Investigation of Industrial Salespeople's Ethical Perceptions," *Journal of International Business Studies* (Fourth Quarter 1991): 651–669; J. K. Giacobbe-Miller, D. J. Miller, W. Zhang, and V. I. Victorov, "Country and Organization-level Adaptation to Foreign Workplace Ideologies: A Comparative Study of Distributive Justice Values in China, Russia and the United States," *Journal of International Business Studies* 34, no. 4 (2003): 389–406.
7. A. J. Dubinsky, M. A. Jolson, M. Kotabe, and C. U. Lim, "A Cross-National Investigation of Industrial Salespeople's Ethical Perceptions," *Journal of International Business Studies* 4 (1991): 651–669.
8. D. M. Wasielski and J. Weber, "Does Job Function Influence Ethical Reasoning?" *Journal of Business Ethics* 85 (2008): 187–189
9. A. Kolk and R. Van Tulder, "Ethics in International Business," *Journal of World Business* (February 2004): 49–61; J. Tsui and C. Windsor, "Some Cross-Cultural Evidence of Ethical Reasoning," *Journal of Business Ethics* 31 (2001): 143–150; Robertson and Crittenden, "Mapping Moral Philosophies: Strategic Implications for Multinational Firms."
10. L. Stroh, M. E. Mendenhall, J. S. Black, and H. B. Gregersen, *International Assignments: An Integration of Research and Practice* (Hillsdale, NJ: Erlbaum, 2005).
11. C. Hess and K. Hey, "Good Doesn't Always Mean Right," *Across the Board* 38, no. 4 (2001): 61–64; A. Chia and L. S. Mee, "The Effects of Issue Characteristics on the Recognition of Moral Issues," *Journal of Business Ethics* 27 (2000): 255–269; A. Gaudine and L. Thorne, "Emotion and Ethical Decision Making in Organizations," *Journal of Business Ethics* 31, no. 2 (2001): 175–187.
12. R. W. McGee, "Analyzing Insider Trading from the Perspective of Utilitarian Ethics and Rights Theory," *Journal of Business Ethics* 91 (2009): 65–85.
13. B. Chaffin, "Steve Jobs: No Tablet, No PDA, No Cell Phone, Lots Of iPods," *Mac Observer,* June 4, 2003 at 3:00 PM, http://www.macobserver.com/tmo/article/Steve_Jobs_No_Tablet_No_PDA_No_Cell_Phone_Lots_Of_iPods/
14. J. Rawls, *A Theory of Justice* (Cambridge, MA: Harvard University Press, 1971); J. Greenberg, "A Taxonomy of Organizational Justice Theories," *Academy of Management Review* 12 (1987): 9–22; Colquitt, J. A., Conlon, D. E., Wesson, W. J., Porter, C. O. L. H., and Ng, K. Y. "Justice At The Millennium: A Meta-Analytic Review Of 25 Years Of Organizational Justice Research," *Journal of Applied Psychology* 86 (2001): 425–445; Colquitt, J. A. "On The Dimensionality Of Organizational Justice: A Construct

Validation Of A Measure," *Journal of Applied Psychology* 86 (2001): 386–400.

15. T. Donaldson and T. W. Dunfee, "Toward a Unified Conception of Business Ethics," *Academy of Management Review* 19 (1994): 252–84; J. A. Colquitt, R. Noe, and C. L. Jackson, "Justice in Teams: Antecedents and Consequences of Procedural Justice Climate," *Personnel Psychology* 55, no. 1 (2002): 83–109.

16. R. Pillai, E. Williams, and J. J. Tan, "Are the Scales Tipped in Favor of Procedural or Distributive Justice? An Investigation of the U.S., India, Germany, and Hong Kong (China)," *International Journal of Conflict Management* 12, no. 4 (2001): 312–332; D. Fields, M. Pang, and C. Chiu, "Distributive and Procedural Justice as Predictors of Employee Outcomes in Hong Kong," *Journal of Organizational Behavior* 21, no. 5 (2000): 547–562; Y. Cohen-Charash and E. Spector, "The Role of Justice in Organizations: A Meta-Analysis," *Organizational Behavior and Human Decision Processes* 86, no. 2 (2001): 278–321; J. A. Colquitt, D. E. Conlon, M. J. Wesson, C. Porter, and Y. K. Ng, "Justice at the Millennium: A Meta-Analytic Review of 25 Years of Organizational Justice Research," *Journal of Applied Psychology* 86, no. 3 (2001): 424–445; S. L. Blader, C. C. Chang, and T. R. Tyler, "Procedural Justice and Retaliation in Organizations: Comparing Cross-Nationally the Importance of Fair Group Processes," *International Journal of Conflict Management* 12, no. 4 (2001): 295–311; J. Greenberg, "Who Stole the Money, and When? Individual and Situational Determinants of Employee Theft," *Organizational Behavior and Human Decision Processes* 89, no. 1 (2002): 985–1003; B. J. Tepper and E. C. Taylor, "Relationships Among Supervisors' and Subordinates' Procedural Justice Perceptions and Organizational Citizenship Behaviors," *Academy of Management Journal* 46, no. 1 (2003): 97–105.

17. J. Dietz, S. L. Robinson, R. Folger, R. A. Baron, and M. Schultz, "The Impact of Community Violence and an Organization's Procedural Justice Climate on Workplace Aggression," *Academy of Management Journal* 46, no. 3 (2003): 317–326.

18. Kernan, M. C. and Hanges, P. J. "Survivor Reactions to Regorganization: The Consequences of Procedural, Interpersonal and Informational Justice," *Journal of Applied Psychology* 87 (2002): 916–928.

19. Hollensbe, E. C., Khazanchi, S., and Masterson, S. S., "How Do I Assess If My Supervisor And Organization Are Fair? Identifying The Rules Underlying Entity-Based Justice Perceptions," *Academy of Management Journal* 51 (2008): 1099–1116.

20. Holtz, B. and Harold, C. M. "Fair Today? Fair Tomorrow? A Longitudinal Investigation Of Overall Justice Perceptions," *Journal of Applied Psychology* 94 (2009): 1185–1199.

21. Carlson, D. S., Kacmar, K. M., and Wadsworth, L. L. "The Impact Of Moral Intensity Dimensions On Ethical Decision-Making: Assessing The Relevance Of Orientation." *Journal of Managerial Issues* 21 (2009): 534–551; J. M. Jones, "Ethical Decision Making by Individuals in Organizations: An Issue-Contingent Model," *Academy of Management Review* 16 (1991): 366–395.

22. M. Jones, "Ethical Decision Making by Individuals in Organizations: An Issue-Contingent Model," *Academy of Management Review* 16 (1991): 366–395.

23. J. Paolillo and S. J. Vitell, "An Empirical Investigation of the Influence of Selected Personal, Organizational and Moral Intensity Factors on Ethical Decision Making," *Journal of Business Ethics* 35, no. 1 (2002): 65–74.

24. Jones, D. A. "Getting Even With One's Supervisor And One's Organization: Relationships Among Types Of Injustice, Desires Or Revenge, and Counterproductive Work Behaviors," *Journal of Organizational Behavior* 30 (2009): 525–542

25. Carlson, D. S., Kacmar, K. M., and Wadsworth, L. L. "The Impact Of Moral Intensity Dimensions On Ethical

Decision-Making: Assessing The Relevance Of Orientation." *Journal of Managerial Issues* 21 (2009): 534–551.

26. A. Chia and L. S. Mee, "The Effects of Issue Characteristics on the Recognition of Moral Issues," *Journal of Business Ethics* 27, no. 3 (2000): 255–269.

27. D. Carlson, K. M. Kacmar, and L. L. Wadsworth, "The Impact of Moral Intensity Dimensions on Ethical Decision Making: Assessing the Relevance of Orientation," *Journal of Managerial Issues* 14, no. 1 (2002): 15–30; J. M. Dukerich, M. J. Waller, E. George, and G. Huber, "Moral Intensity and Managerial Problem Solving," *Journal of Business Ethics* 24, no. 1 (2000): 29–38.

28. M. Friedman, "The Social Responsibility of Business Is to Increase Its Profits," *New York Magazine,* September 13, 1970, 32–33, 122, 126.

29. A. Smith, *An Inquiry into the Nature and Causes of the Wealth of Nations,* ed. R H. Campbell and A. S. Skinner (Oxford, UK: Clarendon Press, 1976).

30. Friedman, "The Social Responsibility of Business Is to Increase Its Profits," 32; C. E. Bagley, "The Ethical Leader's Decision Tree," *Harvard Business Review* 81, no. 2 (2003): 18–19.

31. D. Jamali and Y. Sidani, "Classical vs. Modern Managerial CSR Perspectives," *Business and Society Review* 113 (2008): 329–346.

32. M. Moss, "Peanut Case Shows Holes in Safety Net," *New York Times,* February 9, 2009, A1.

33. S. K. May, G. Cheney, and J. Roper, eds., *The Debate over Corporate Social Responsibility* (Oxford University Press, 2007); P. Kotler and N. Lee, *Corporate Social Responsibility* (Hoboken, NJ: John Wiley & Sons, 2005).

34. http://www.plasticbageconomics.com/index.php?option= com_content&task=view&id=15&Itemid=28, Accessed 4/25/10; Post-consumer film recycling hit record high in 2008. Environmental Leader: Energy and Environmental News for Business. http://www.environmentalleader.com/2010/03/17/ post-consumer-film-recycling-hit-record-high-in-2008/, Accessed 4/25/10; http://www .plasticbagrecycling.org/ plasticbag/index.html, Accessed 4/25/10

35. J. Joha, L. Serbet, and A. Sundaram, "Cross-Border Liability of Multinational Enterprises: Border Taxes and Capital Structure," *Financial Management* (Winter 1991): 54–67; C. Handy, "What's a Business For?" *Harvard Business Review* 80, no. 12 (2003): 49–55.

36. Joha, Serbet, and Sundaram, "Cross-Border Liability of Multinational Enterprises: Border Taxes and Capital Structure."

37. A. McWilliams and D. Siegel, "Corporate Social Responsibility and Financial Performance: Correlation or Misspecification?" *Strategic Management Journal* 21 (2000): 603–609; B. Ruf, K. Muralidhar, R. Brown, J. Janney, and K. Paul, "An Empirical Investigation of the Relationship Between Change in Corporate Social Performance and Financial Performance: A Stakeholder Theory Perspective," *Journal of Business Ethics* 32, no. 2 (2001): 143–156; C. Sanchez, "Value Shift: Why Companies Must Merge Social and Financial Imperatives to Achieve Superior Performance," *Academy of Management Executive* 17, no. 2 (2000): 142–144; J. Griffin and J. F. Mahon, "The Corporate Social Performance and Corporate Financial Performance Debate: Twenty-five Years of Incomparable Research," *Business and Society* 36 (1997): 5–31; T. M. Devinney, "Is the Socially Responsible Corporation a Myth? The Good, the Bad, and the Ugly of Corporate Social Responsibility," *Academy of Management Perspectives* 23, no. 2 (2010): 44–56.

38. McWilliams and Siegel, "Corporate Social Responsibility and Financial Performance: Correlation or Misspecification?"; B. Ruf, K. Muralidhar, R. Brown, J. Janney, and K. Paul, "An Empirical Investigation of the Relationship Between Change in Corporate Social Performance and Financial Performance: A Stakeholder Theory Perspective"; Sanchez, "Value Shift: Why

Companies Must Merge Social and Financial Imperatives to Achieve Superior Performance"; Griffin and Mahon, "The Corporate Social Performance and Corporate Financial Performance Debate: Twenty-five Years of Incomparable Research."

39. M. E. Porter and M. R. Kramer, "Strategy and Society: The Link Between Competitive Advantage and Corporate Social Responsibility," *Harvard Business Review* (December 2006): 78–93; M. E. Porter and M. R. Kramer, "The Competitive Advantage and Corporate Philanthropy," *Harvard Business Review* (December 2002); D. Grayson and A. Hodges, *Corporate Social Opportunity* (Austin, TX: Greenleaf, 2004).

40. J. Katz, "Study: Ethical Misconduct Rising," *Industry Week,* October 20, 2005.

41. S. Ring and A. Van De Ven, "Developmental Process of Cooperative Interorganizational Relationships," *Academy of Management Review* 19 (1994): 90–118.

42. D. Robin, M. Giallourakis, F. R. David, and T. Moritz, "A Different Look at Codes of Ethics," *Business Horizons* (January–February 1989): 66–73.

43. C. C. Langlois and B. B. Schlegelmilch, "Do Corporate Codes of Ethics Reflect National Character? Evidence from Europe and the United States," *Journal of International Business Studies* (Fourth Quarter 1991): 519–539.

44. G. Wood, "A Cross-Cultural Comparison of the Content of Codes of Ethics: USA, Canada, and Australia," *Journal of Business Ethics* 25, no. 4 (2000): 281–298.

45. Robin, et al., "A Different Look at Codes of Ethics."

46. Rodriguez-Dominguea, L., Gallego-Alvarez, I., and Garcia-Sanchez, I. M. "Corporate Governance And Codes Of Ethics," *Journal of Business Ethics* 90 (2009): 187–202; McKinney, J. A., and Moore, C. W. "International Bribery: Does A Written Code Of Ethics Make A Difference In Perceptions Of Business Professionals?" *Journal of Business Ethics* 79 (2008): 103–111.

47. B. Ettorre, "Ethics Inc.: The Buck Stops Here," *HR Focus* (June 1992): 11.

48. L. White and L. W. Lam, "A Proposed Infrastructural Model for the Establishment of Organizational Ethical Systems," *Journal of Business Ethics* 28, no. 1 (2000): 35–42; S. A. DiPiazza, "Ethics in Action," *Executive Excellence* 19, no. 1 (2002): 15–16.

49. C. Verschoor, "To Talk About Ethics, We Must Train on Ethics," *Strategic Finance* 81, no. 10 (2000): 24, 26; T. Donaldson, "Editor's Comments: Taking Ethics Seriously—A Mission Now More Possible," *Academy of Management Review* 28, no. 3 (2003): 363–366.

50. "Stronger Than Ever," *LM Today* (January 2004): 8; K. Shelton, "The Dilbert Dilemma," *Executive Excellence* (November 2003): 2; R. Carey, "The Ethics Challenge," *Successful Meetings* 47, no. 5 (1998): 57–58.

51. Whalen, J. "AstraZeneca Sharpens Focus on Drug Ethics," *Wall Street Journal* 254, no. 148 (2009): 82.

52. A. Pomeroy, "Whistleblowing: When It Works—and Why," *Academy of Management Perspectives* 20, no. 3 (2006): 128–130; M. McClearn, "A Snitch in Time," *Canadian Business,* June 18, 2004, 60–67; M. Miceli and J. Near, *Blowing the Whistle* (Lexington, MA: Lexington Books, 1992).

53. Miceli and Near, *Blowing the Whistle.*

54. C. Daniels, "It's a Living Hell," *Fortune,* April 15, 2002, 367–368.

55. M. Miceli and J. Near, "The Relationships Among Beliefs, Organizational Position, and Whistle Blowing Status: A Discriminant Analysis," *Academy of Management Journal* 27 (1984): 687–705.

56. M. Miceli and J. Near, "Whistle Blowing: Reaping the Benefits," *Academy of Management Executive* 8 (1994): 65–71.

57. Miceli and Near, *Blowing the Whistle.*

58. R. Sims and J. Brinkmann, "Leaders as Moral Role Models: The Case of John Gutfreund at Salomon Brothers," *Journal of Business Ethics* 35, no. 4 (2002): 327–339; R. Galford and A. S. Drapeau, "The Enemies of Trust," *Harvard Business Review* 81, no. 2 (2003): 88–95; L. R. Offermann and A. B. Malamut, "When Leaders Harass: The Impact of Target Perceptions of Organizational Leadership and Climate on Harassment Reporting and Outcomes," *Journal of Applied Psychology* 87, no. 5 (2002): 885–893.

59. *Columbia Journalism Review* 39, no. 4 (November–December 2000): 13.

60. M. Zuckerman, "Policing the Corporate Suites," *U.S. News & World Report*, January 19, 2004, 72; *Modern Healthcare* 28, no. 16 (April 20, 1998): 54–56.

International Management and Globalization

3

LEARNING OBJECTIVES

After studying this chapter, you should be able to:

Explain what globalization is and how it affects firms and countries.

Identify and differentiate the two major elements of the global environment.

Name and explain the three major institutions of a country's institutional environment.

Define the term *culture* and identify four primary cultural dimensions.

Describe the five international market entry strategies and explain when to use each strategy.

Explain the three types of international organization focus.

Discuss the benefits and challenges of managing across cultures.

Describe how to effectively manage multicultural teams.

Define the term *global mind-set* and explain its importance for managers.

Courtesy of Chetan Choudhury

Name: Chetan Choudhury

Position: Manager, Strategy & Operations

Alma mater: St. Xavier's College, Calcutta University (Bachelor of Commerce), Institute of Chartered Accountants (Associate Chartered Accountant), Arizona State University (Master of Science and Master of Business Administration)

Outside work activities: Reading, watching movies, trivia

Book reading now: *The Bhagavad Gita*

Person(s) most admired: Krishna (from the epic "The Mahabharata") and Steve Jobs (Apple)

Motto to live by: Do unto others as you would have others do unto you

Management style: Hands-on approach that is both collegial and collaborative, keeping team members informed and involved, trusting them and allowing them to work independently

Chetan Choudhury was originally hired by Deloitte as a summer intern while working on his MBA at Arizona State. After completing his MBA, he accepted a job with Deloitte located in one of its major offices in California. He primarily worked on large-scale implementation projects in the public sector. In 2006, Choudhury left Deloitte to start a new company in India. He gained valuable experience from this entrepreneurial venture. He and his partners worked on the development of sustainable models to improve the quality of education for the less fortunate (those at the "bottom of the pyramid").

In 2008, Choudhury sold the company and rejoined Deloitte to work in its strategy practice in Ottawa, Canada. He currently manages Deloitte's strategy and operations consulting unit in Ottawa. He spends most of his time on consulting work in business process improvement, operations excellence, citizen service, and technology strategy for public-sector organizations. Because Deloitte is a global organization, Choudhury's work takes him to many places

overseas; for example, he recently worked on a major project in the Middle East. Having studied and worked in both India and the United States, Choudhury has a basic understanding of cultural differences and the importance of adapting to the local culture when operating in that environment. Yet, he explains a challenge that he and his colleagues encountered while working on a complex but interesting business transformation project for a public-sector client in Asia. They experienced general working conditions that differed from their norm. For example, there was a strict dress code and standing meetings were commonly cancelled while impromptu meetings were called with little notice. It was not uncommon for clients to come late to meetings and for them to converse with each other in their native language during meetings. Furthermore, client meetings rarely had an agenda and included little or no introductions. Clients did not like to communicate through e-mails, preferring phone conversations or text messages. Clients rarely examined and responded in a timely manner to the materials and recommendations provided by the consulting teams. Because of these conditions, the Deloitte team suffered from low morale and some left the project, causing further problems in the client relationship.

Choudhury and his colleagues were concerned about the potential for losing the account and felt a need to act. They analyzed the situation carefully and decided that the basic problem was related to cultural differences. Therefore, they set out to correct the problems and adapt to the local culture to better respond to and satisfy the client's needs. In this chapter, we examine the issues addressed by Choudhury and his colleagues working to provide effective advice and service to their Asian client. We begin discussing globalization and its effects on markets and businesses. We then examine the different institutional and cultural environments of countries and the strategies firms use to enter international markets, the reasons firms use each strategy, and the risks that they pose. We also discuss how to manage people and teams across cultures, an issue of importance in the situation described by Choudhury. We examine both as they have become highly important in our global economy and with multinational companies such as Deloitte. Finally, we discuss what's called a "global mind-set," what it is, and the importance for managers to have one.

Globalization

Globalization refers to the flow of goods and services, capital (money), and knowledge across country borders. Globalization enhances the economic interdependence among countries and organizations across countries.[1] According to Thomas Friedman, author of the popular book, *The World Is Flat,* we are in the third stage of globalization, with the first involving internationalization of countries, the second involving companies moving into international markets, and the current and third stage involving individuals collaborating (and competing) on a global basis.[2] The increasing interdependence among countries, companies, and even individuals across country borders has reduced the influence that a national government can have on its economy.[3] The interdependency of country economies across the globe became exceedingly clear in the most recent financial and economic crisis. The crisis began in the United States and spread to many other countries.

globalization
the flow of goods and services, capital (money), and knowledge across country borders

In recent years, increasing globalization has dramatically changed the competitive landscape for everyone. For example, when coupled with new technology, especially in information systems, small firms now have access to markets and resources in other countries. This has allowed them to compete effectively with larger and often more established firms. Additionally, even firms from less-developed economies can better compete in international markets.[4]

According to Thomas Friedman, globalization has gone beyond the point where small and large companies have moved into international markets. Today, even individuals are collaborating (and competing) on a global basis.[5] Friedman suggests that, regardless of our country of origin, increased globalization has made all of us "next-door neighbors"—and competitors.[6] This is exemplified by the foreign sales of Orb Audio and Air Transport described in A Manager's Challenge. In fact, Air Transport—located in a small rural town in West Texas—is an unlikely competitor of companies based in Europe and Latin America, which manufacture and market similar types of aircraft.

In the professional services area, many functions have shifted to countries like China and India because their workers have the ability to do a quality job at a much lower cost. Many U.S. firms are outsourcing services such as software development and tax-return preparation to India. Some U.S. companies are sending their U.S. employees to India for surgery because it is less expensive there, and the quality of care is excellent.

India and China are expected to be major players in the global economy over the next 30 to 40 years. Some have argued that, by the year 2040, the combined economies of Brazil, China, India, and Russia are likely to outstrip the total economies of what are currently the six largest economies: Canada, France, Germany, Japan, the United Kingdom, and the United States.[7]

The reach of globalization has become longer through the use of technology that allows a person in a tiny country like Bhutan in the Himalayas to become an international celebrity through a photo posted on Facebook. And, partly because of the changes in the world, Bhutan has also undergone major changes in the first decade of the twenty-first century. For example, it introduced a new constitution in 2005 and had its first parliamentary voting in 2008. In addition, it has its first Miss Bhutan, 25-year old Tsokye Tsomo Karchung, the object of a Facebook posting and an international following.[8] Undoubtedly, globalization has both positive and negative effects on most countries, as suggested in Friedman's *The World Is Flat.* It provides opportunities for companies to expand and grow by entering new foreign markets. It can also improve a country's economic development. Yet, competition from foreign firms entering a country's home market can harm local companies. Some of the questions about China relate to its effect on U.S.–based firms and their U.S.–based employees. For example, competition in United States markets from Chinese firms has seriously harmed U.S. furniture and textile firms. Government officials have to weigh the benefits of globalization against the costs. Often, these officials are under significant pressure by different constituencies to institute trade barriers that make it more difficult for foreign firms to compete effectively in their home markets.

Understanding a Country's Environment

Wal-Mart, the world's largest company, had total sales of more than $400 billion in 2010. The company serves approximately 200 million customers per week from its 8,400 stores in 15 countries.[9] To continue to grow and be profitable, it is important for Wal-Mart to know which markets to enter and how to compete in them. And, to this end, managers need to understand two major aspects of a country's environment: institutions and culture.

A MANAGER'S CHALLENGE

GLOBALIZATION

Small Business: Going Global

Because of increasing opportunities in international markets, many businesses have entered new foreign markets in recent years. In fact, some firms were able to offset domestic sales reductions related to the economic recession with increased international sales. For example, Orb Audio, a small manufacturer of high-end home theatre systems, has increased its foreign sales from 10 percent to 35 percent of annual sales, which recently totaled more than $5 million. During that same period, the company experienced a 10 percent decline in its U.S. domestic sales due to the recession. The company is making sales in developed markets such as Australia and Great Britain and also in developing countries such as Zimbabwe and Nigeria. And 10 percent of its total sales are now in Finland. Likewise, Air Tractor, the Olney, Texas–based manufacturer of crop dusters and other aircraft used for agricultural purposes, has been able to avoid sales declines related to the recession by selling in other parts of the world. The U.S. Export-Import Bank has helped Air Tractor sell in foreign markets. This bank helps ensure that small businesses are paid for goods and services exported to foreign markets. In a recent year, the bank provided $4.36 billion to support 2,540 transactions involving exports into international markets.

Real estate developer Gale International largely focused on building office parks in the United States until 2001 when it was approached by the government of South Korea to build a completely new city, Songdo. Korea's banks helped finance the project with $35 billion in loans to Gale. Although the new city will not be finished until 2015, Gale is making good progress. In 2010, it completed Songdo's 100-acre Central Park, modeled after the park by the same name in New York City. Songdo is to be fully wired with the latest technology—this part of the project is being managed by Cisco. Based on its experience in South Korea, Gale has partnered with Cisco, 3M, United Technologies, and architectural firm Kohn Pedersen Fox to build new cities in other countries. For example, Gale recently announced that this consortium will build 20 new cities in China and India using Songdo as the model. With China projected to need at least 500 new cities the size of Songdo, Gale's new global business could be very lucrative indeed.

These examples suggest that international markets provide significant opportunities for growth in both large businesses, such as Cisco, and small businesses like Orb Audio. The U.S. Commercial Service helps businesses expand overseas. Funded by the U.S. government, the organization can be particularly helpful to small firms because it provides free consulting services on many topics, including cultural sensitivity and developing effective business plans. Such services could be useful for such companies as EQ Smart Energy, which manufactures and distributes an energy drink. The company recently announced approval for its first attempt to enter foreign markets. It announced plans to export its effervescent tablets used to create the energy drink to Mexico and Brazil. Likewise, Dickinson Brands Inc., in East Hampton, Connecticut, distributes its witch hazel products globally, allowing it to balance sales across economic surges and declines in various countries. Globalization has been a boon to many businesses but has also made the management of those companies much more complex and challenging.

Sources: E. Maltby, "Three Best Ways to Expand Overseas," *Wall Street Journal*, May 28, 2010, http://www.wsj.com; "EQ Smart Energy Brand Goes International," *Business Wire*, May 28, 2010, http://www.businesswire.com; I. Mount, "Tips for Increasing Sales in International Markets," *New York Times*, April 21, 2010, http://www.nytimes.com; G. Linsday, "Cisco's Big Bet on New Songdo: Creating Cities from Scratch," *Fast Company*, February 1, 2010, http://www.fastcompany.com; E. Olson, "Some Small Businesses That Grew in 2009," *New York Times*, December 31, 2009, http://www.nytimes.com.

The Country's Institutional Environment

institutional environment
the country's rules, policies, and enforcement processes that influence individuals' and organizations' behaviors that operate within the country boundaries

Each country has a distinct institutional environment composed of multiple institutions, including economic development, political-legal, and physical infrastructure. Institutional environments are often complex, having many important institutions that interact to create unique effects in each country.[10] The **institutional environment** consists of the country's rules, policies, and enforcement processes. This, in turn, influences the behavior of the individuals and organizations that operate within the country.[11]

THE ECONOMIC DEVELOPMENT INSTITUTION Countries vary in their level of economic development. Economic development and growth is vital to most countries because it contributes to better living standards and citizens' health and welfare.[12] Economic development is important to local and foreign firms as well because it opens up greater market opportunities.

Country economies may be classified into developed, emerging, and developing economies. Some countries, such as the United States and Japan have highly developed economies. Others such as Sudan and El Salvador have less-developed economies. Still others, like China and India have economies that are not highly developed but are growing rapidly. These economies are classified as emerging.[13] Countries in Western Europe have developed economies, whereas most of the countries in Eastern Europe are considered to be emerging economies.

Developed economies tend to be larger than less-developed or emerging economies. They also tend to have more effective capital markets. In effective capital markets, people and businesses are readily able to borrow money from banks and other financial institutions or raise it by selling shares in stock markets. Developed economies tend to be larger than those in other countries. Emerging economy countries such as China often have rapidly growing economies and their capital markets tend to be young and underdeveloped. Finally, the weakest economies exist in developing economies.

THE POLITICAL-LEGAL INSTITUTION This dimension of the institutional environment refers to a country's political risks, regulations, and laws, and their enforcement. Governments develop laws and policies to govern the behavior of their citizens and organizations operating within the country's boundaries.[14] Regulations can have a major influence on a country's economy for countries can institute regulatory changes to encourage more entrepreneurship. The level of entrepreneurship has a strong influence on a country's economic growth.[15] Among the important regulations that affect businesses are those related to the way foreign firms operate. These regulations include laws that impose tariffs and quotas on imported goods, laws that dictate the way employees are treated, and laws dictating how publicly traded firms listed on major stock exchanges in the country must behave.

For example, after China began to relax its markets (partially at least), all foreign firms entering the country were required to form joint ventures with Chinese firms. Foreign firms' behavior was also regulated in order to protect local firms that often lacked the necessary resources and capabilities to compete with firms from developed countries.[16] the Sarbanes-Oxley Act (often

Workers ride tricycles past the first Wal-Mart store in Shanghai as preparations are made for the grand opening of China's 48th store. Wal-Mart is the biggest company on the planet, employing more than a halfmillion people in 2,700-plus stores worldwide.

Getty Images, Inc.

referred to as SOX), enacted by the United States in 2002, was designed to curtail scandals like the ones at Enron and WorldCom. Both domestic and foreign firms registered on U.S. stock exchanges must adhere to the provisions in SOX. For example, all CEOs and CFOs must certify that their firms' financial statements published by the firm are accurate and satisfy the rules set forth by standards in the industry and legal requirements. Also legal rights given to shareholders can influence the strategies used by firms. For example, firms based in countries with strong shareholder rights are better able to restructure assets of acquired firms based in another country because of the supporting laws and regulations.[17] Primarily, the rules established by the law are intended to make the management of public firms more transparent. Yet, the rules can be excessive and discourage investment from abroad. Furthermore, an increasing amount of companies are going private (buying back their publicly traded stock) in order to avoid having to deal with the costly reporting rules required by the law. Laws such as SOX play an important role in countries' institutional environments.

Among the important laws are those regarding intellectual property rights. When laws related to enforcement of intellectual property rights (e.g., patents) are weak, firms with valuable technologies are reluctant to bring them into the country; And, if they do enter the country's markets, they may not use the valuable technology in that market or will disallow their local partners from accessing it. However, when barriers to such knowledge exist, they reduce the value of a joint venture, especially to the local partner. Local partners in developing and emerging markets often seek to gain technological and managerial capability from their more capable foreign partners.[18]

THE PHYSICAL INFRASTRUCTURE INSTITUTION Institutional infrastructure is critical to the operation of businesses within a country because it facilitates business communications and the movement of goods from their source to the ultimate consumer. Physical infrastructure includes such aspects as the amount and quality of roads and highways, number of telephone lines per capita, and the number of airports. The availability of physical infrastructure often plays an important role in decisions to enter a new international market by a foreign firm because it tends to perform more poorly in countries with underdeveloped infrastructure.[19] Therefore, countries that wish to attract foreign investment must try to develop their physical infrastructure.[20]

Without a good physical infrastructure, it is difficult for firms to distribute their products to potential customers. Thus, they either have to sell to smaller markets because they are unable to reach as many potential customers, or they have to distribute their products in much more costly ways. In either case, the firm earns lower profits than it would if the country's physical infrastructure was well developed.

Table 3.1 depicts clusters of selected country institutional environments. As shown, developing countries e.g., Nigeria and Brazil, with relatively weak economies and central regulations (largely government control/low political rights), form the first cluster. Emerging market countries form the second cluster. These countries are experiencing generally strong economic growth and are beginning to develop the other institutions needed for further economic growth (e.g., enhanced transportation, new laws and regulations such as intellectual property rights). The third cluster of countries has relatively advanced institutional environments exemplified by Western European countries. Finally, the most advanced institutional environments are in Japan and the United States.[21]

IMPORTANCE OF THE INSTITUTIONAL ENVIRONMENT Economic growth is vital to most countries because it contributes to the standards of living, health, and welfare of their citizens.[22] Economic growth is important to local and foreign firms as well. Higher rates of economic growth suggest greater market opportunities for all firms and attract new business development and foreign investments in the country's economy.

Beyond the attractiveness of a country's economic development and health, its laws, regulations, political stability, and physical infrastructure play an important role in firms' behaviors.[23] In particular, multinational firms seeking to invest in new international markets need to understand these elements of a country's institutional environment. These institutional dimensions can greatly affect a firm's willingness to make direct investments in a country's markets. Furthermore, recent research shows that the large presence of multinational firms in a country strongly influences the development of the country's institutional environment. For example, the greater number of multinational corporations in a country, the greater the pressure on government to develop and enforce legislation to reduce corruption.[24] The influences are partly because of these firms' effects on the country's economic development and growth. Corruption

TABLE 3.1 Country Institutional Environment Clusters

Cluster 1: This cluster largely consists of developing and transition economies. These countries are high in regulatory control and low in political rights.

Examples: Brazil, Russia, and Nigeria

Cluster 2: This cluster largely consists of emerging market countries that are more advanced than Cluster 1 countries but still need greater development of institutional dimensions. These countries score a little higher on political rights but the lowest on monetary policy and second highest on investment restrictions.

Examples: China, India, the Netherlands, and Singapore

Cluster 3: These countries have the second highest regulatory controls but also score high on political rights. They also have strong physical infrastructures.

Examples: Countries in Western Europe to include Finland, France, Germany, Portugal, and Sweden

Cluster 4: This cluster of countries has the most developed institutional infrastructure overall, with balanced regulatory controls and political rights; strong economic and physical infrastructure institutional dimensions

Only two countries are in this cluster, Japan and the United States

Source: M. A. Hitt, R. M. Holmes, T. Miller, and M. P. Salmador, "Modeling Country Institutional Profiles: The Dynamics of Institutional Environments" paper presented at the Strategic Management Society Conference, Vienna, November 2006.

also discourages foreign companies from making major investments in a country.[25] As explained later in this chapter, institutional environments have a major effect on firms' international strategies and especially affect which countries firms enter.

While institutional forces play an important role in determining firms' behaviors within a country, societal culture plays an equally strong role. Culture's effects may be more pervasive because of its influence on human behavior.

Culture

Although institutional forces play an important role in terms of how and where businesses globalize, a society's culture is critical. **Culture** is a learned set of assumptions, values, and beliefs that have been accepted by members of a group and that affect human behavior.[26] Some scholars refer to culture as a collective programming of the mind that has a powerful effect on individual behavior.[27] Although a culture can exist among any group of people, our focus is on national cultures.

Understanding culture is critical because it can dramatically influence how people observe and interpret the business world around them—for example, whether they see situations as opportunities or threats. A person's culture likely affects his or her opinion about the "right" managerial behavior. For example, only 10 percent of Swedish managers believe they should have precise answers to most questions subordinates ask them, whereas 78 percent of Japanese managers think they should.[28] As this example illustrates, culture can contribute to preexisting ways of interpreting events, evaluating them, and determining a course of action. And, national culture exerts a strong influence on the nature of a country's institutions.[29]

CULTURAL DIMENSIONS The two most prominent studies of culture were conducted by Dutch scholar Geert Hofstede and by a large number of researchers led by Robert House referred to as GLOBE.[30] Both of these complex studies identified at least four prominent dimensions of national culture: power distance, uncertainty avoidance, individualism versus collectivism, and gender focus.

Power distance is the extent to which people accept power and authority differences among people. Power distance is not a measure of the extent to which a group has power and status differences; most countries have richer and poorer citizens, and more and less powerful citizens. Power distance does not suggest whether status and power differentials exist in a country, rather, the extent to which people in the country accept those differences. In Hofstede's study, people from the Philippines, Venezuela, and Mexico had the highest levels of acceptance of power differences. In contrast, Austria, Israel, and Denmark had the lowest levels of acceptance.

Cultures differ in the extent to which they need clarity or can tolerate ambiguity. This dimension of culture has been labeled **uncertainty avoidance.** Citizens in nations high in uncertainty avoidance prefer clear norms (rules that govern behavior). Groups high in uncertainty

culture
a learned set of assumptions, values, and beliefs that members of a group have accepted and that affect human behavior

power distance
the extent to which people accept power and authority differences among people

uncertainty avoidance
when cultures differ in the extent to which they need things to be clear or ambiguous

individualism

the extent to which people's identities are self-oriented and people are expected to take care of themselves and their immediate families

collectivism

the extent to which identity is a function of the group(s) to which an individual belongs (e.g., families, firm members, community members, etc.) and the extent to which group members are expected to look after each other

gender focus

the extent to which people in a country value masculine or feminine traits

avoidance create structures and institutions to reduce uncertainty. By contrast, groups that are low in uncertainty avoidance prefer to have fewer rules and tend to be more comfortable in ambiguous situations. For example, managers from Sweden, the Netherlands, and the United States are most comfortable with uncertainty; managers from Indonesia and Japan are least comfortable with high uncertainty.

Individualism is the extent to which people's identities are self-oriented and people are expected to take care of themselves and their immediate families. People from the United States and Great Britain often score high on individual orientations. Individuals from these countries exhibit high emotional independence from organizations and institutions and tend to emphasize and reward individual achievement and value individual decisions.[31] Alternatively, **collectivism** is the extent to which a person's identity is a function of the group(s) to which the person belongs (his or her family, firm, community, and so forth) and the extent to which group members are expected to look after each other. People from China, Venezuela, and Pakistan have high collective orientations. People from these countries tend to exhibit emotional dependence on organizations and institutions to which they belong, emphasize group membership, and value collective decisions.[32]

Gender focus represents the extent to which people in a country value masculine or feminine traits. Countries emphasizing masculine traits value activities that lead to success, money, and possessions. Alternatively, those emphasizing feminine traits value activities that show caring for others and enhance the quality of life.

Countries such as the United States tend to emphasize masculine traits. In the United States, people often work many hours a week (over 60 hours is not uncommon), and take shorter vacations. In countries that do not emphasize masculine traits, work often has lower value. Table 3.2 presents the culture scores of selected countries.

Understanding cultures can be valuable for a number of reasons. For example, cultural characteristics can predict how managers will respond to socially responsible actions. Research has shown that managers in cultures that emphasize collectivism and are low in power distance engage in greater amounts of socially responsible activities than cultures with high individualism and high power distance.[33]

Globalization has greatly enhanced the extent to which cultural diversity plays a role in business. As companies globalize and expand their operations around the world, they create an increased opportunity and demand for people from different cultures to effectively interact

TABLE 3.2 Cultural Values and Scores (for Select Countries)

	Power Distance[a]	Uncertainty Avoidance[b]	Individualism/ Collectivism[c]	Gender Focus[d]
Brazil	5.33	3.60	3.83	3.31
Canada	4.82	4.58	4.38	3.70
China	5.04	4.94	4.77	3.05
England	5.15	4.65	4.27	3.67
France	5.28	4.43	3.93	3.64
India	5.47	4.15	4.38	2.90
Japan	5.11	4.07	5.19	3.19
Mexico	5.22	4.18	4.06	3.64
Netherlands	4.11	4.70	4.46	3.50
Poland	5.10	3.62	4.53	4.02
Russia	5.52	2.88	4.50	4.07
United States	4.88	4.15	4.20	3.34

[a]Higher scores indicate higher power distance.
[b]Higher scores suggest more uncertainty avoidance.
[c]Higher scores indicate greater collectivism.
[d]Higher scores suggest greater gender equality whereas lower scores indicate male domination.

Source: Based on data from R. J. House *et. al.,* eds., *Culture, Leadership and Organizations: The GLOBE Study of 62 Countries* (Thousand Oaks: Sage Publications, 2004).

together. Managers must interact and deal with suppliers, customers, and partners from different cultures. We discuss the management of cultural diversity within companies and relationships across cultures later in this chapter.

Knowing and understanding different institutional environments and cultures is important if managers are to make good strategic decisions about which foreign markets to enter and how to manage operations established in these markets. We examine these strategies next and discuss how different institutional and cultural environments affect the strategies chosen and how to implement and manage them.

International Market-Entry Strategies

Choosing which international markets to enter and how to enter them has become critically important to many small, medium, and large firms. With increasing globalization discussed at the beginning of this chapter, a large number of firms are servicing international markets at their birth. International markets are attractive to firms for several reasons. They increase the size of a firm's potential markets and sales revenue. When they sell more products abroad, these firms gain greater economies of scale which, in turn, increases potential profit. Firms can also gain access to special resources (e.g., lower-cost labor, valuable raw materials) in some international locations that can help them become more competitive in global markets. These are referred to as location advantages.[34]

The previous information suggests that firms have considerable motivation to enter international markets. Yet, all international markets are not created equal. As stated earlier, countries vary in their institutional environments and cultures. Thus, the attractiveness of countries' markets also varies. First, early in their internationalization efforts, firms prefer to enter markets with institutional environments and cultures similar to their own. Typically, they have a better understanding of these environments and therefore entry seems less risky. This is important, especially for small firms with less capital, because entering international markets requires resources and learning about the new market and environment rapidly.[35] For these reasons and to reduce potential costs, firms often cluster their international operations in one or a few geographic regions.[36] As firms gain more experience entering and operating in international markets, they are willing to enter markets where the differences in institutional environments and cultures are greater. Yet, the institutional environments and cultural differences also influence the means by which firms enter new international markets.[37]

Firms can enter new foreign markets in a variety of ways. Each poses different risks and requires different levels and types of resources. Among the ways to enter a new market are by exporting products to the market, licensing products to firms there, either acquiring or creating strategic alliances with local firms, or establishing your own operations in the country.

Exporting

The most common way to enter an international market is by exporting goods. This is especially true for smaller firms and for firms initially entering into foreign markets. **Exporting** involves manufacturing products in a firm's home country and shipping them to a foreign market. It is a popular entry strategy because of its lower risks and capital requirements. Because exporting does not require establishing operations in the country, firms avoid making a large capital investment. However, the exporting firm must establish a means of marketing and distributing its goods within the country.[38] Thus, exporters may have to combine exporting and strategic alliances with local firms in order to distribute their goods to customers. As a result, the costs of transportation and sharing profits with a local firm can reduce a firm's net gain from the international market. Therefore, although an export strategy is less risky, it is unlikely to provide big returns because of the associated costs. If the exporting firm's transportation costs are high, for example, it might be limited to exporting only to countries in close proximity of its home base of operations. Exports are also particularly sensitive to fluctuations in exchange rates.[39]

Licensing

Licensing arrangements allow a local firm in the new market to manufacture and distribute its product. Usually, the licensing contract provides the specifications necessary to maintain quality

exporting
manufacturing products in a firm's home country and shipping them to a foreign market

licensing
arrangements establishing how to allow a local firm in the new market to manufacture and distribute its product

and for the quantities to produce and sell along with the royalty percentages on the sales. In these cases, the licensor has low costs and takes little risk; the licensee assumes the major risks. Yet, licensing is unlikely to produce major returns for the licensor unless the potential sales in the new market are large.[40]

The Altria Group, owner of Philip Morris brand cigarettes, is losing sales in the United States due to declining cigarette use. Thus, Altria licenses its products for sale in 160 countries. For example, it has a licensing agreement with two Chinese firms to manufacture and market cigarettes in China under the Marlboro brand. This arrangement is lucrative for the Altria Group because the market for cigarettes in China is large and growing.[41]

Although licensing has advantages, it also has disadvantages. The primary disadvantage is that the licensing firm has little control over its product and the use of its brand in the new market. This underscores how important it is for a firm's licensing contracts to be clear and enforceable. Unfortunately, contracts with Chinese firms often are difficult to enforce. As suggested earlier, most of China's legal and regulatory institutions are relatively new. Thus, the Altria Group could experience problems if it doesn't like how China is marketing the Marlboro brand. Similar to exporting, licensing is also unlikely to produce big returns for a firm unless sales in the new market are large.

Creating Strategic Alliances

The most popular strategy for international expansion has become strategic alliances. A **strategic alliance** is a cooperative arrangement between two firms in which they agree to share resources to accomplish a mutually desirable goal. Strategic alliances allow firms to share the costs and risks of entering new markets, and they provide the opportunity for firms to access resources they do not have. As such, it also allows them to sometimes learn new capabilities from their partners.[42] In this way, alliances can contribute to a firm's ability to maintain or increase its competitiveness in global markets.

Strategic alliances allow firms to outsource functions that they completed in-house previously. The "A Manager's Challenge" "Outsourcing and Offshoring," explains the advantages and disadvantages of outsourcing. In general, outsourcing allows firms to gain access to better and often cheaper performance of functions. In this way, firms can compete better in international markets and even to enter and compete in some markets where they could not compete previously. The vignette also suggests that outsourcing alliances benefit large and small firms alike. The top outsourcing countries are India, China, and Malaysia, with much of the outsourcing to India focused on information technology and services while manufacturing is the primary emphasis in China.

Not all strategic alliances are successful; a large number of them fail. Yet equity-based alliances, such as joint ventures whereby companies share risks and rewards, tend to be more successful because the firm has more voice in and control of the activities completed by the alliance or venture. Trust also seems to be an important factor in the success of an alliance.[43] So is the way in which firms manage alliances. As such, many firms are establishing alliance management functions to increase the success because of the large number of strategic alliances firms are forming.[44]

A country's institutional environment affects the decision to enter its markets and the means chosen to enter. In addition to the particular institutions in place, the stability of the institutions is of interest to foreign firms. Uncertainty in the institutional environment can stunt economic growth, making markets less desirable.[45] At the very least, firms entering uncertain institutional environments need to do so in ways that lower their risk. Forming strategic alliances to share resources and risks is one way of doing so.[46] Uncertainty in the country's institutional environment also affects the type of alliance formed and the type of partner desired. For example, in uncertain environments, firms look for short-term partners. In more stable institutional environments, firms select alliance partners with whom they can work over the long term. In other words, they seek long-term returns from their alliance partnerships.[47]

strategic alliance
a cooperative arrangement between two firms in which they agree to share resources to accomplish a mutually desirable goal

A MANAGER'S CHALLENGE

CHANGE

Small Business: Outsourcing and Offshoring

Outsourcing has been popular for several years but its use dipped during the economic recession in 2008-2010. However, in 2010, outsourcing began to increase again, driven primarily by lower costs (because of the economic decline). Yet, although lower cost is often a benefit of outsourcing, perhaps a more important benefit is that the outsourced activities can be performed by those with high-quality specialized capabilities. Thus, tasks are accomplished more effectively.

The top three countries in receipt of outsourcing are India, China, and Malaysia, respectively. In particular, India and the Philippines account for 50 percent of business process outsourcing but India holds a large lead. India's quality technical capabilities, low costs, and use of the English language facilitate continued growth as the leading recipient of outsourcing activities. However, China has major goals to lead these rankings. For example, the Chinese government recently provided $1 billion in subsidies, incentives, and training to garner more outsourced activities. It has a goal of increasing the number of vendors to 1,000, attracting 100 additional foreign customers and developing ten hubs of outsourcing in the country, creating 1.2 million jobs by 2013. Currently, China's largest outsourcing company has $540 million in annual revenues, with 15,000 employees and 8,000 corporate customers.

Many companies and countries are getting into the act. For example, Xerox recently acquired Affiliated Computer Services (ACS), the leading business process outsourcing company, for $6.4 billion. Snapple has outsourced much of its information technology services to Noida in India. And the *San Francisco Chronicle* quit printing its own newspaper in favor of outsourcing all printing to Transcontinental Printing, a Canadian-based company.

Alternatively, some firms have reduced or eliminated their outsourcing activities, instead favoring offshoring. Offshoring involves firms establishing their own operations in another country. In this way, the firm can save money (e.g., access to lower labor costs) and also gain the help of those with special capabilities. Banks have increased their offshoring activities because of concerns about the financial crisis and the need to control the quality of the tasks performed. Importantly, banks are concerned about fraud and even inadvertent errors in outsourcing over which they do not have control. A benefit for small businesses is that outsourcing can help give them access to the same economies of scale, efficiency, and expertise that large companies enjoy. Outsourcing providers also assume and manage a certain amount of risk for their companies. This can be beneficial because markets, competition, government regulations, and technology abroad often quickly change.

Sources: G. Colvin, "Ursula Burns Launches Xerox into the Future," *Fortune*, April 22, 2010, http://www.money.cnn.com; R. Fannin, "China: $1 Billion and Ambition," *Forbes*, March 10, 2010, http://www.forbes.com; G. Dennis, "The True Benefits of Outsourcing," *Fast Company*, March 16, 2010, http://www.fastcompany.com; E. Sperling, "Outsourcing Makes a Comeback," *Forbes*, January 25, 2010, http://www.forbes.com; R. Perez-Pena, "*San Francisco Chronicle* Outsources Its Printing," *New York Times*, July 13, 2009, http://www.nytimes.com; N. Heath, "Banks: Offshoring, Not Outsourcing," *BusinessWeek*, March 10, 2009, http://www.businessweek.com; N. Shivapriya, "India Remains World's Top Outsourcing Destination," *BusinessWeek*, July 10, 2010, http://www.businessweek.com; H. Timmons, "Snapple Deal to Outsource May Add Jobs in America," *New York Times*, July 1, 2009, http://www.nytimes.com.

Acquisitions

The purchase of a local firm made by a foreign firm to enter a new international market is referred to as a **cross-border acquisition.** The number of cross-border acquisitions has increased in recent years. Such acquisitions are more common among non-U.S. firms. For example, the number of cross-border acquisitions by European firms has grown dramatically in recent years; in fact, in a recent year they exceeded those made by U.S. firms for the first time in history.[48] Even firms from emerging market countries have used this strategy, as exemplified by the Chinese firm Lenova's acquisition of IBM's laptop computer business.

In recent years, approximately 40 percent to 50 percent of acquisitions made worldwide are cross-border acquisitions.[49] Acquisitions of a local firm in order to enter a new foreign market have several advantages. For one, it provides a fast way to enter a market. Operations in the new market are immediate with the acquired firm's customers, facilities, and relationships (e.g., with suppliers, government units, etc.). It generally represents the largest new market entry of the

cross-border acquisition
acquisitions of local firms made by foreign firms to enter a new international market

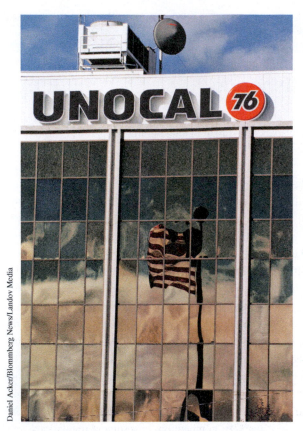

Globalization is fraught with difficulties. A Chinese firm found out as much when it tried to acquire Unocal, a large U.S.-based oil company. But U.S. citizens and Congress objected strenuously to the deal, effectively killing it.

different alternatives. With the recent acquisition of Kuwaiti telecommunications firm Zain, India's Bharti Airtel became the fifth-largest mobile phone operator in the world.[50] Cross-border acquisitions are sometimes controversial with the local public or government. Such was true when CNOOC, the large Chinese petroleum company, attempted to acquire Unocal, a large U.S.-based oil company. CNOOC withdrew its bid because of objections from many in the U.S. Congress. Thus, there are disadvantages to cross-border acquisitions as well.

Cross-border acquisitions usually entail many of the potential advantages of acquisitions made within a firm's home country, but problems with a cross-border acquisition can be severe. For example, a common problem in acquisitions is the challenge of integrating two previously independent companies. Differences in the corporate cultures between the acquiring and acquired firms make integration difficult. Yet, cross-border acquisitions face a double-layered cultural integration problem.[51] Integration requires overcoming differences in corporate culture and national culture. Outside of selecting the right target, integration is the largest reason for the failure of acquisitions.[52]

Costs are another major disadvantage of cross-border acquisitions. It has become common for acquiring firms to pay a premium (that is, more than market value) for target firms. Yet, premiums may be a larger problem in cross-border acquisitions because the acquiring firms frequently have less information on the target than in domestic acquisitions. And, research has shown that premiums are highest in host countries known for having a large amount of corruption.[53] Additionally, greater differences in the institutional environments of the home countries of the acquirer and target firms increase the challenges of making the acquisition successful.[54]

When an acquiring firm makes the correct choice of target and does not overpay for the acquisition, entering a new foreign market can be a positive opportunity. Yet, the acquiring firm still must achieve integration, and that is likely to present a challenge.

Establishing New, Wholly Owned Subsidiaries

wholly owned subsidiary
a direct investment to establish a business in a foreign market in which the local firm owns and controls 100 percent of the business

Some firms prefer to establish a new, wholly owned subsidiary to enter a new international market. When a company creates a **wholly owned subsidiary** in a foreign country, it makes a direct investment to establish a business that it solely owns and controls. Such a subsidiary is often called a *Greenfield venture.*

Greenfield ventures afford a firm maximum control over the operations. Firms such as Starbucks—those with strong intangible resources including a good brand name, human capital, and so forth—may prefer to enter international markets through Greenfield ventures because it allows them to buffer these assets from current and potential competitors in the new market.[55]

Greenfield ventures are often complex and expensive to launch, however. To maintain control requires that not only must the firm build its own facilities, it must also establish relationships with suppliers, build distribution networks within the foreign country, and foster a positive relationship with potential consumers. Thus, the new business must attract customers from existing competitors or convince new customers to buy its product. Firms establishing Greenfield ventures must learn about the national culture and institutional environment—on their own. If the cultural or institutional distance between home and host countries is high, a firm may experience difficulties establishing a new wholly owned subsidiary or making it successful. Therefore, the risks of establishing these subsidiaries can be quite high.[56]

With the development of China's economy and the significant amount of cross-border trade between Western and Chinese firms, UPS established a new wholly owned subsidiary in Shanghai and FedEx did the same in Guangzhou. The firms entered the markets with Greenfield investments because they needed to ensure fast and reliable service and desired to maintain control over their logistics operations.[57]

While wholly owned subsidiaries are valuable and allow firms to control their operations, they are risky and not always successful. In 2002, eBay entered the China market with a partial acquisition of Eachnet.com, and fully acquired the company the following year for $180 million. In 2005, eBay invested over $100 million in marketing for its wholly owned Chinese subsidiary. Even with the acquisition, eBay was unable to manage the Chinese marketplace and fend off competition. Its primary competitor in China, Taobao, took market share from eBay's subsidiary. In December 2006, eBay announced it was shutting down its main Web site in China and forming a joint venture with Tom Online, Inc., to operate in the Chinese market. Analysts said eBay lost market share because not only did it not understand the Chinese market and culture, it did not move quickly to counter Taobao's challenge.[58] The decisions regarding what foreign markets to enter and how to enter them are very important. Yet, the management of international operations also affects their success. In the following sections, we explore the management of international operations, examining the corporate approach used and how to manage across cultures, with an emphasis on managing cross-cultural teams.

Managing International Operations

Companies must choose the manner in which they manage their international subsidiaries. These choices carry important meaning for the management and flow of resources and information throughout a company's international operations. Of critical importance is the degree of autonomy granted to individual subsidiaries to develop and implement their own strategies. The home office can choose from three different approaches: a global focus, a region/country focus, or a transnational focus.

Adrian Sherratt/Alamy Images

A worker helps load product at a Cemex dock in England. Cemex, a company headquartered in Mexico, has operations in Europe, North America, South America, and Asia. Because the company sells a largely standardized project—ready mix cement—it's been able to take a more centralized approach to globalization and achieve economies of scale as a result.

Taking a Global Focus

In a **globally focused organization,** the firm's home office makes major strategic decisions. Thus, the global organization has centralized authority, and international subsidiaries usually follow the same or similar strategy in each of their markets. These organizations normally attempt to market a relatively standardized product across geographic markets. Such an approach provides economies of scale and helps to manage costs and thereby enhance profits. Thus, it helps firms to gain returns on innovative products developed in the home country market, especially firms that compete in markets where price is a critical competitive concern. In a globally focused organization, subsidiaries often share resources, allowing the most efficient allocation of resources throughout the company.

globally focused organization
an organization that invests the primary authority for major strategic decisions in the home office

While a global focus offers several advantages as noted previously, it also presents some disadvantages. Because it does not allow the international subsidiary the flexibility to decide how to compete, it may be unable to take advantage of market opportunities when they occur. Furthermore an international subsidiary operating in a globally focused organization does not have the flexibility to react quickly to competitors' strategic moves. As such, they are vulnerable to competitors taking strategic actions with the intent of "stealing" market share in the local market. These international subsidiaries cannot respond easily to changes in customers' needs in the local market. When Vodaphone used a global focus, it was unable to respond to local customers' needs in Japan and lost market share. On the other hand, Cemex, the world's third-largest cement company, uses a global focus successfully. In this case, the type of product sold (ready-mix cement) can largely be standardized. Cemex, headquartered in Mexico, has operations in North America, South America, Asia, and Europe. The centralized approach used by Cemex provides economies of scale and higher returns.[59]

Taking a Region–Country Focus

In an organization using a **region–country focus,** the primary authority to determine competitive strategy rests with the managers of its international subsidiary based in a region of the world or a specific country.[60] In this way, the region or country managers can tailor their strategies to local market conditions and demands. For example, subsidiaries can design, manufacture, and sell products that best satisfy local market customers. In this sense, subsidiaries can customize

region–country focus
a situation in which primary authority for determining competitive strategy rests with the management of the international subsidiary based in a region of the world or a specific country

products for the local customers as opposed to the home office dictating product features. Thus, this type of organization is highly decentralized. The advantage of this approach is that it is flexible and allows a subsidiary to react quickly to changes in the marketplace. It can respond rapidly to competitors' strategic moves and can also respond quickly to take advantage of new market opportunities identified. It is most effective when the firm's subsidiaries operate in widely different markets indicated by countries with different cultures and different institutional environments. However, such an approach can be expensive for the company because it cannot achieve economies of scale. Furthermore, the diversity of strategies across markets may be difficult to oversee and govern from the home office. In particular, it may be difficult for home-office managers to evaluate the performance of subsidiary managers, especially if it requires assessing the value of the strategy chosen by that manager.

European multinational firms commonly use the region–country focused approach because they operate in multiple countries with different institutional environments across Europe.[61] Unilever, a well-known European consumer products company, has traditionally used a decentralized approach to manage its international operations.[62]

Taking a Transnational Focus

transnational organization
an organization that strives to be simultaneously centralized and decentralized

Two well-known scholars and management consultants, Christopher Bartlett and Sumantra Ghoshal, developed the idea of a transnational organization. They suggest that a **transnational organization** is one that strives to be simultaneously centralized and decentralized. As such, its goal is to achieve global efficiency while maintaining local market responsiveness. In these organizations, strategic decisions are decentralized. Nonetheless, the organizations usually try to achieve global efficiency by having their subsidiaries share resources. Shared values, trusting relationships, and incentive systems that reward subsidiary managers for the firm's overall performance help facilitate this cooperation.

Effectively managed, this type of an organization often outperforms either of the other two types of organizations. Although it's easier to achieve either global efficiency or local responsiveness than it is to achieve both simultaneously, a company can do it. For example, Nissan CEO Carlos Ghosn used a transnational focus to turn around that automaker's performance. The different business units worked to achieve global efficiency while also maintaining responsiveness to regional markets. Thanks partly to the transnational focus, Nissan is now one of the top performers in the global automobile industry.[63]

While overall focus, amount of authority delegated to subsidiary managers, and degree of resource sharing across international subsidiaries are all important, managing diverse units across cultures and multicultural teams is critical to the firm's performance.

Managing Across Cultures

In multinational firms with subsidiaries operating in multiple international markets, managers must often oversee, direct, and evaluate employees and other managers from different cultures and institutional environments. Managing people from a single country is a significant challenge; managing people operating in different cultures and institutional environments is often an extreme challenge—one that is very complex.[64] It requires managers to understand cultural differences and how these differences affect employees' attitudes and behaviors.

cultural context
the degree to which a situation influences behavior or perception of the appropriateness of behaviors

high-context culture
a culture in which people pay close attention to the situation and its various elements

low-context culture
a culture in which contextual variables have much less impact on the determination of appropriate behaviors

Perhaps one of the most useful concepts for examining and understanding different countries' cultures is cultural context.[65] **Cultural context** is the degree to which a situation influences behavior or perception of the appropriateness of behaviors. In a **high-context culture,** people pay close attention to the situation and its various elements. Key contextual variables determine appropriate and inappropriate behavior. In a **low-context culture,** contextual variables have much less impact on the determination of appropriate behaviors. In other words, in low-context cultures, the situation may or may not affect what is considered appropriate behavior, but in high-context cultures, the context has a significant influence on this judgment.

For example, in Japan there are five different words for the pronoun *you*. The context determines what form of the pronoun *you* is appropriate for addressing different people. If you are talking to a customer holding a significantly higher title than yours, who works in a large company such as Matsushita and is several years older, you would be expected to use the term *otaku* when addressing the customer. If you were talking to a subordinate several years

TABLE 3.3 Low-Context and High-Context Cultures

Low-Context Cultures	High-Context Cultures
American	Vietnamese
Canadian	Chinese
German	Japanese
Swiss	Korean
Scandinavian	Arab
English	Greek

Source: Adapted from E. Hall, *Beyond Culture* (Garden City: Doubleday, 1976); S. Rosen and O. Shenkar, "Clustering Countries on Attitudinal Dimensions: A Review and Synthesis," *Academy of Management Review* 10, no. 3 (1985): 449.

younger, *kimi* is the appropriate pronoun. Table 3.3 provides a list of some low-context and high-context cultures.

With this in mind, consider some of the issues related to managing both people who come from low-context and high-context cultures. For example, imagine a team composed of one person each from the United States, Australia, Korea, and Japan. The team meets to discuss a global production problem and report to a senior executive from a client company. For the two people from low-context cultures (the United States and Australia), the phrase "Say what you mean, and mean what you say" would not only be familiar to them but appropriate. Consequently, if the senior executive asked if the team could complete a specific task and the team had already discussed the impossibility of the task, the two team members from low-context cultures would most likely say "no." To say "yes" when you mean "no" would not be appropriate regardless of the fact that the senior executive from a client is in the room. These two people would likely view someone who said "yes" when he or she meant "no" with suspicion and perhaps even as untruthful.

But for the two team members from high-context cultures, the fact that the senior executive from a client is in the room asking the questions influences their perception of the appropriate response. For them, in this situation, saying "yes" when they meant "no" would be entirely appropriate. To say "no" without considering the context would be considered unsophisticated, self-centered, or simply immature.

Imagine, then, the manager's problem if the American replies that what the client is asking for is not possible while the Korean member of the team says it is. Not only will this confuse the client, but imagine the attributions that the American and Australian are likely to make about their Japanese and Korean team members, and, in turn, what the Korean and Japanese team members probably think of the other two. Without understanding the influence of culture context, the team trust and effectiveness could suffer.

The key issue for managers leading multicultural teams is to recognize that neither high-context nor low-context cultures are correct or incorrect; rather, they are quite different. These differences influence the effectiveness of a manager's behaviors, including their communication, negotiation, decision making, and leadership skills. The previous case helps illustrate the concept and some of its implications. It points out that a lack of awareness of this fundamental dimension of cultural differences can lead to misinterpretations, mistaken attributions, mistrust, and ineffectiveness. Multicultural teams effectively allows for greater creativity because of the heterogeneity. Alternatively, the differences in cultures can lead to conflict and lower cohesiveness in the team if not carefully managed.[66]

However, managing people working in different countries, cultures, and institutional environments is not the only complex situation managers face in multinational enterprises. Even within countries, local workforces are becoming more culturally diverse. This is certainly true in the United States, which is considered a "melting pot" of many cultures. As globalization continues at a rapid pace, it is also becoming increasingly the case in many other countries. Many people of European descent, Asian ethnicities (e.g., Chinese, Korean, Japanese, Vietnamese), African ethnicity, Hispanic ethnicity, etc., coexist, living and working together in the same organizations and in similar jobs. Therefore, managers often have to manage multicultural teams within one organization in one location.

Managing Multicultural Teams

The first type of multicultural team is geographically dispersed across country borders. Although geographically dispersed, they often focus on regular business tasks such as developing new marketing programs and products. Yet, the team interacts somewhat differently than a more traditional team. Instead of face-to-face meetings, members frequently depend on technologically mediated communications, such as e-mail, Internet chat rooms, company intranets, teleconferencing, video-conferencing, and so forth.[67] Often a group of this type is called a **virtual team** because of its reliance on electronic communication.

virtual team
a team that relies on electronically mediated communication

The forms of communication vary in their richness, leaving open the possibility that messages will be misperceived or misunderstood especially because the communications must cross cultures. Problems such as this can disrupt the team's ability to complete tasks. If misunderstandings occur early in the development team's formation, members may not develop trust: a characteristic critical to the team's efficient functioning. Trust is especially important for geographically dispersed multicultural teams because they often lack traditional direct supervision, must work more autonomously, and cannot coordinate with other team members as easily as more traditional teams.[68]

swift trust
the rapid development of trust in teams with positive and reciprocal communications about the team's task activities

In these international teams, significant responsibility rests with the team manager to ensure effective functioning. Early in the team's development, the manager must build trust rapidly. Building trust rapidly is sometimes referred to as swift trust. **Swift trust** is the rapid development of trust in teams with positive and reciprocal communications about the team's task activities.[69] To build swift trust, the team manager must help members communicate with one another in a positive way, coordinate their efforts, and quickly eliminate any misunderstandings. To do this, the manager must have significant cultural knowledge and sensitivity in addition to effective managerial skills. The manager builds a unified vision and emphasizes collaborative outcomes with international teams for greatest success.[70]

Developing a Global Mind-set

With the opening of world markets, firms from all over the world are formulating strategies to increase their presence in international markets. As such, these strategies and managers' abilities to manage diverse country operations and people from multiple cultures are critical to firm performance.[71] Because of this global evolution, the competitive terrain is changing in many international markets, especially with the increasing competitive capabilities of firms from large emerging economy countries such as Brazil, Russia, India and China.[72] Competing in international markets, managing international operations, and managing multicultural teams requires managers to develop a global mind-set. A **global mind-set** is a set of cognitive attributes that allows an individual (such as a manager) to influence individuals, groups, and organizations from diverse sociocultural and institutional environments.[73] A team's composition can influence such a mind-set. A. G. Lafley, former CEO of Procter & Gamble, reformulated his top management team so that at least 50 percent of its members came from outside the United States. Lafley's goal was to help his top managers adopt a global mind-set.[74]

global mind-set
a set of cognitive attributes that allows an individual (e.g., manager) to influence individuals, groups, and organizations from diverse sociocultural and institutional environments

While a global mind-set is important for operating multinational enterprises, cultural intelligence is becoming a necessity because of globalization. As described in "A Manager's Challenge," managers must develop cultural intelligence in order to manage effectively in a multicultural organization. Toyota's problems provide an example of why this is important. Obviously, other Japanese companies such as Nippon Sheet Glass have already made moves to become more multicultural. Firms and managers that understand the value of unique cultures and institutions can adapt to and use cultural differences to their advantage. A global mind-set helps them do that.

Jagdish Sheth a well-known scholar and consultant on international trends, argues that we can expect cultural integration over time—not cultural clashes. Sheth believes that Western cultures will not dominate the globe as some people fear. Rather, he believes Western societies such as the United States will adopt Asian cultural values because of the increase in economic power and influence of China and India and the greater acceptance and willingness by Westerners to assimilate diverse cultures. The United States and Canada, for example, are already multicultural with large minority populations, including ethnic Chinese and Indians. This cultural integration will lead to increased diversity within cultures and geographic regions.[75] As a result, the ability to manage multicultural workforces and serve multicultural consumer markets will continue to be more highly valued. These trends heighten why it's important for managers to develop a global mind-set.

A MANAGER'S CHALLENGE

GLOBALIZATION

Multicultural Organizations in a Globalized Economy

Multicultural organizations are necessary to compete effectively in a global economy. A prime example is found in the problems experienced by Toyota. By 2008, the company had become the world's largest automaker, only to experience severe problems in 2009 because of quality control problems with autos sold in the United States. Toyota has had an insular corporate culture typical of many Japanese firms. Although it sells autos all over the world, the top management structure is wholly Japanese and little input is provided to top executives by country managers, even those in the United States, which is the largest country auto market in the world. Akio Toyoda, the company's current CEO, has promised to change this insularity to allow more information to flow across the management teams in the two countries. Yet, this change is a long way from a multicultural organization.

Toyota could learn from the recent changes made by Nippon Sheet Glass Company, a Japanese company that hired an American CEO, includes four foreign members on its board of directors, and made English the official language of its business. Nippon has done so because it recognizes it is competing in the global market. For example, 40 percent of its sales are in European countries. The new CEO hired a Brazilian to head the Human Resources unit and plans to hire more foreign-born executives, hoping to create the diversity that allows heterogeneous thinking and ideas needed to better compete in global markets. Nippon Sheet glass has followed other Japanese companies that hired foreign CEOs, such as Sony's Howard Stringer and Nissan's Carlos Ghosn.

Because of the need to better understand many cultures and to include more different cultures among the management teams in organizations, managers in general and top managers specifically need to have *cultural intelligence*. A person with cultural intelligence is able to operate effectively in a variety of national, ethnic, and organizational cultures. For example, such managers can help their organization adapt their products and services to the tastes of culturally diverse markets while simultaneously maintaining the company's brand identity. Culturally sensitive managers can more effectively deal with the requirements of different religious faiths (for example, Christian, Jewish, Muslim, etc.) and with different ethnic and cultural norms in the workplace.

Jose Gil/Shutterstock

Toyota is one of the largest automakers in the world; however due to its insular corporate culture typical of many Japanese firms, it experienced severe problems in 2009.

To be culturally intelligent, managers need to understand characteristics such as the importance of building relationships in other cultures (for example, *guanxi* in China), the importance of dress, and what types of gifts to give and when in meetings they should be offered.

Technology now makes it much easier to communicate with colleagues in other countries, be they internal team members, customers, suppliers, or other important stakeholders. Videoconferencing and Skype have facilitated meetings of geographically diverse participants. However, Cisco has developed a new technology, called Cisco Telepresence, that represents a major advance over the older technologies. It integrates audio, ultra-definition video, and other advanced technologies to create the feeling that people are present in the room while participating in the meeting. Global consultant Simma Lieberman suggests that Cisco Telepresence has elevated global business and global relationships to a whole other level. There is no doubt that the future is multicultural for business and many other types of organizations.

Sources: M. Sanchanta, "Cultivating Multiculturalism," *Wall Street Journal*, June 7, 2010, http://www.wsj.com; M. Maynard, "At Toyota, A Cultural Shift," *New York Times*, June 2, 2010, http://www.nytimes.com; M. Sanchanta, "Nippon Sheet CEO Vows to Continue Culture Shift," *Wall Street Journal*, May 19, 2010, http://www.wsj.com; S. Lieberman, "How Cisco Took Me Where No One Has Gone Before," *Fast Company*, April 15, 2010, http://www.fastcompany.com; R. Tulshyan, "Quirkiest Cultural Practices from Around the World," *Forbes*, March 18, 2010, http://www.forbes.com; D. Livermore, "CQ: The Test of Your Potential for Cross-Cultural Success," *Forbes*, January 6, 2010, http://www.forbes.com.

Managerial Challenges from the Front Line

The Rest of the Story

As noted in the opening profile, Chetan Choudhury has considerable experience working and living in diverse cultures. He obtained his education in India and the United States. He worked with a home base in the United States and now in Canada. Projects on which he has worked have been in multiple countries and in different locations around the world, including Asia, Europe and the Middle East. Yet, Choudhury worked as a part of a team whose members all experienced problems adapting to a unique culture. But, in his case, he and his colleagues wanted this project to be successful, so they stepped back and analyzed the situation. They wanted to do an excellent job on the project but had to understand what to do in order to make the client successful. They decided that most of the problems experienced were due to cultural differences. Choudhury then reached out to local people he knew well to help him better understand the culture. Based on what he learned about the local culture, the team changed how they worked with the client. In short, his team adapted to the client. They were more relaxed about the timing of meetings and tried to better manage the client's expectations. They worked to develop a better relationship with the client, including social discussions in the meetings (for example, small talk about their families). They quit using e-mails for communication and instead substituted text messages and other means of communication. They had to invest more time and work longer hours to adapt in this way, but they and their client gained mutual respect for each other. Most importantly, the project was a success.

Choudhury believes his work is very important. Governments play an increasingly important role in the lives of many people, especially in a global economy. So, actions taken by governments in Asia, Europe, and other parts of the world affect everyone in all countries. Therefore, it is important for them to function effectively. Choudhury's work advising them and helping them to be more innovative and effective, then, is good for all of us.

Summary

- Globalization refers to the flow of goods and services, capital, and knowledge across country borders. Globalization enhances the economic interdependence among countries and organizations across countries. In general, globalization has heightened the economic development and welfare of many countries but also created concerns about the homogenization of cultures.

- Two major elements of global environments are institutions and cultures. A nation's institutional environment consists of the country's rules, policies, and enforcement processes that influence the behavior of individuals and organizations that operate there. By contrast, national culture is a learned set of assumptions, values, and beliefs that members of a group have accepted and that affect human behavior.

- Each country has a distinct institutional environment composed of economic development, political-legal, and physical infrastructure dimensions. Countries vary in their level of economic development. Country economies can be classified into developed, emerging, and developing economies. The political-legal dimension of the institutional environment includes the degree of regulation of economic factors, political behavior, political risk, and laws and their enforcement. Institutional infrastructure is critical to the operation of businesses within a country because they facilitate business communications and the movement of goods from their source to the ultimate consumer. Physical infrastructure includes such elements as the amount and quality of roads and highways, the number of telephone lines per capita, and the number of airports.

- Culture is a learned set of assumptions, values, and beliefs that members of a group have accepted and that affect human behavior. Some refer to culture as a collective programming of the mind with a profound effect on behavior. There are four prominent dimensions of national culture: power distance, uncertainty avoidance, individualism versus collectivism, and gender focus.

■ Firms can enter new foreign markets in a variety of ways. Each has different risks and requires different levels and types of resources. Among the entry strategies are exports, licensing, strategic alliances, and acquiring or establishing new wholly owned subsidiaries abroad. Companies must choose how they manage their international subsidiaries, especially the degree of autonomy granted to the individual subsidiaries to develop and implement their own strategies.

■ One of three different approaches reflects the focus of the home office: a global focus, a region–country focus, or a transnational focus. A globally focused organization has international subsidiaries that usually follow the same or a similar, strategy one which the firm develops centrally.

■ In organizations with a region–country focus, authority is decentralized, and region or country managers can tailor their strategies to local market conditions and demands. An organization that follows a transnational approach strives to be simultaneously centralized and decentralized in order to achieve both global efficiency and local market responsiveness.

■ Managing people operating in different cultures and institutional environments is often a challenging task. It requires managers to understand cultural differences and how those differences affect employees' attitudes and behaviors. For example, in geographically dispersed multicultural teams, rarely can managers schedule face-to-face meetings. They frequently depend on technologically mediated communications, such as e-mail, Internet chat rooms, company intranets, teleconferencing, and videoconferencing. Such teams are often called virtual teams because of their reliance on electronically mediated communication. In international teams, significant responsibility rests with the team manager to ensure effective functioning. These managers need to build trust early in the formation of these teams.

■ A global mind-set is a set of cognitive attributes that allows managers to influence individuals, groups, and organizations from diverse cultural and institutional environments. The globalization trend heightens the importance of managers building a global mind-set in order to effectively manage a multicultural workforce and serve multicultural consumer markets.

Key Terms

collectivism   64
cross-border acquisition   67
cultural context   70
culture   63
exporting   65
gender focus   64
global mind-set   72
globalization   59

globally focused
   organization   69
high-context culture   70
individualism   64
institutional environment   60
licensing   65
low-context culture   70
power distance   63

region–country
   focus   69
strategic alliance   66
swift trust   72
transnational organization   70
uncertainty avoidance   63
virtual team   72
wholly owned subsidiary   68

Review Questions

1. What is globalization, and how does it affect different countries?
2. What are the two major elements of the global environment, and why are they important?
3. What are the three major institutions of a country's institutional environment and how do they differ?
4. What is culture and its four primary dimensions?
5. How are the five international strategies used to enter new foreign markets and when is each most useful?

6. What are the three types of international organization focus and how would you describe each?
7. Why do managers need to understand how to manage across cultures?
8. What are the primary factors with which managers must deal in managing multicultural teams?
9. What is a global mind-set and why is it important?

Assessing Your Capabilities

Evaluating Your Global Skills

List different products you use on a regular basis, such as your alarm clock, camera, car, coffeemaker, computer, telephone, television, DVD player—perhaps even your favorite CD, shirt, fruit juice, or footwear. Determine which firms made these items. After you have developed your list, search the Internet for answers to the following questions:

1. In which country is the firm headquartered?
2. What percentage of the firm's annual sales comes from its home market? What percentage comes from other countries?
3. Where was the item most likely manufactured?
4. Why do you think it was manufactured there?

Based on this chapter, answers you found to the questions listed above and your own knowledge, please answer the following questions:

1. What do you believe are the 10 most common products the average college student might use?
2. What is the relative impact of international business on your daily life?
3. Which of the products is likely made by foreign firms?
4. Do you think some of the 10 products listed include components that are both domestically made and foreign made?
5. On a scale of 1–10 (10 is the highest), how would you rate your "global skills"?

Based on: R. Griffin & M. Pustay, 2010, *International Business*, Upper Saddle River, NJ: Pearson Prentice Hall, p. 19.

Team Exercise

1. Form teams of three to five people, and then examine the information presented in Tables 3.1 and 3.2 in this chapter.
2. As a team, develop written descriptions of the institutional environments and cultures of Brazil, China, France, and Japan. (Feel free to refer to the Internet or other sources to confirm the accuracy of your descriptions.)

3. Using these descriptions, develop a list of at least three important points regarding "ways of doing business" in each country that businesspeople from outside that country should understand.

When Ronald Ostertag took over the management of General Semiconductor, he realized quickly that he would have to change the $500 million company's culture for the firm to survive. The first step Ostertag took toward changing General Semiconductor's corporate culture was to replace nearly every member of the company's senior management team. Job insecurity rapidly spread throughout the ranks. "I realized we needed to do something to develop a sense of teamwork," says Ostertag suggesting that laying people off was not enough. "We needed to develop a culture of mutual respect that fostered cooperation and innovation."

However, changing General Semiconductor's culture was a significant challenge because the New York-based manufacturer of electronics parts had 60,000 workers around the world who spoke five different languages. Only 200 of those workers were employed in the United States. Its facilities outside the United States were in China, France, Germany, Ireland, and Taiwan.

After taking over as CEO, Ostertag decided to schedule a team-building meeting in which the new management team would decide on the company's guiding principles. "Our task," he says in retrospect, "was to put down on paper what our core values were and then make sure everyone was on the same page." A cohesive mission statement and a list of eight company values, which are called General Semiconductor's "culture points," came out of that meeting and were centered around goals like "quality," "integrity," "good customer service," and "on-time delivery."

Soon, everyone in the company knew the culture points and even carried them around on small cards. "They knew when they saw me coming, whether it was in the factory in Taiwan or Ireland or here, that I might come up to anyone and ask them to rattle off four or five of those values," says Ostertag. "I didn't mean it as a test, but more to show that that is what everyone here is striving for."

Unfortunately, Ostertag's changes did not occur quickly enough for General Semiconductor to fend off a hostile takeover. Believing that more improvements could be made and greater value extracted from General Semiconductor, Vishay Intertechnology purchased the company in 2001. Today, General Semiconductor is a subsidiary of the Pennsylvania-based firm. Vishay Intertechnology has grown considerably and broadened its product line through acquisitions. It also has a global presence with manufacturing facilities in six Asian countries, including China; Europe; Israel; and the United States; and sales offices in many other countries around the globe. Vishay uses the international expertise in developing new technologies. This is exemplified in the continued success of the subsidiary now named Vishay General Semiconductor LLC which had two patents issued in May. These new technologies were developed by researchers working in the unit's R&D labs in Tianjin, China and Taipei, Taiwan.

Questions

1. In your opinion, what actions taken by Ostertag stood the most chance of changing General Semiconductor's culture?
2. Do you think requiring everyone in a multinational firm to carry around a card with the firm's core values on it can change a company's culture? Why or why not?
3. In your opinion, was Ostertag managing the cross-cultural operations effectively in the process of trying to change the firm's culture? Explain.
4. Did Ostertag appear to have a global mind-set? Why or why not?

Sources: S. Chin, "Vishay Finally Gets General Semi," *EBN*, August 6, 2001, 1c; C. L. Cole, "Optimas 2001—Global Outlook Eight Values Bring Unity to a Worldwide Company," *Workforce*, March 2001, 44–45; Company Web site, http://www.vishay.com, accessed May 20, 2010; "Patent No. 7,719,096 Issued on May 18, Assigned to Vishay General Semiconductor for Semiconductor Device, Manufacturing Method," U.S. Federal News Service, May 20, 2010, http://www.highbeam.com; "Patent No. D616,387 Issued on May 25, Assigned to Vishay General Semiconductor, Ornamental Design for Bridge Rectifier Package," U.S. Federal News Service, May 26, 2010, http://www.highbeam.com.

References

1. M. A. Hitt, R. D. Ireland, and R. E. Hoskisson, *Strategic Management: Competitiveness and Globalization* (Cincinnati: Thomson/South-Western Publishing, 2011).

2. T. L. Friedman, *The World Is Flat* (New York: Farrar, Straus and Giroux, 2005).

3. M. Mandel, "Can Anyone Steer This Economy?" *BusinessWeek*, November 20, 2006, 56–62.

4. R. D. Cremer and B. Ramasamy, "Engaging China: Strategies for the Small Internationalizing Firm," *Journal of Business Strategy* 30 (6) (2009): 15–26; M. A. Hitt, H. Li, and W. Worthington, "Emerging Markets as Learning Laboratories: Learning Behaviors of Local Firms and Foreign Entrants in Different Institutional Contexts," *Management and Organization Review* 1 (2005): 353–380.

5. Friedman, *The World Is Flat.*

6. Ibid.

7. M. A. Hitt and X. He, "Firm Strategies in a Changing Global Competitive Landscape," *Business Horizons* 51 (2008): 363–369.

8. S. Dhume, "The Meaning of Miss Bhutan," *Wall Street Journal*, http://online.wsj.edu, May 26, 2010.

9. Company Web site, *WalMart Annual Report, 2010*, http://walmartstores.com, accessed May 28, 2010.

10. B. Batjargal, "The Effects of Network's Structural Holes: Polycentric Institutions, Product Portfolio, and New Venture Growth in China and Russia," *Strategic Entrepreneurship Journal* 4 (2010): 146–163.

11. G. D. Bruton, D. Ahlstrom and T. Puky, "Institutional Differences and the Development of Entrepreneurial Ventures: A Comparison of the Venture Capital Industries in Latin America and Asia," *Journal of International Business Studies* 40: 762–778.

12. S. Chetty, K. Eriksson, and J. Lindbergh, "The Effect of Specificity of Experience on a Firm's Perceived Importance of Institutional Knowledge in an Ongoing Business," *Journal of International Business Studies* 37 (2006): 699–712.

13. R. Hoskisson, L. Eden, C. M. Lau, and M. Wright, "Strategy in Emerging Economies," *Academy of Management Journal* (Special Research Forum on Strategies in Emerging Economies) 433 (2000): 249–267.

14. J. Dunning, "Reevaluating the Benefits of Foreign Direct Investment," *Transnational Corporations* 34 (1994): 23–51.

15. D. Cumming, H. J. Sapienza, D. S. Siegel and M. Wright, "International Entrepreneurship: Managerial and Policy Implications," *Strategic Entrepreneurship Journal* 3 (2009): 283–296.

16. G. Redding and M. A. Witt, "China's Business System and Its Future Trajectory," *Asia Pacific Journal of Management* 26 (2009): 381–399.

17. L. Capron and M. Guillen, "National Corporate Governance: Institutions and Post-acquisition Target Reorganization, *Strategic Management Journal* 30 (2009): 803–833.

18. M. A. Hitt, M. T. Dacin, E. Levitas, J.-L. Arregle, and A. Borza, "Partner Selection in Developed and Emerging Market Contexts: Resource-based and Organizational Learning Perspectives," *Academy of Management Journal* 434 (2000): 4349–4467.

19. T. Isobe, S. Makino, and D. B. Montgomery, "Resource Commitment, Entry Timing, and Market Performance of Foreign Direct Investments in Emerging Economies: The Case of Japanese International Joint Ventures in China," *Academy of Management Journal* 43 (2000): 468–484.

20. S. M. Lee, "South Korea: From the Land of Morning Calm to ICT Hotbed," *Academy of Management Executive* 17 (2003): 7–18.

21. M. A. Hitt, R. M. Holmes, T. Miller, and M. P. Salmador, "Modeling Country Institutional Profiles: The Dynamics of Institutional Environments," paper presented at the Strategic Management Society Conference, Vienna, November 2006.

22. Chetty, Eriksson, and Lindbergh, "The Effect of Specificity."

23. M. Farashahi and T. Hafsi, "Strategy of Firms in Unstable Institutional Environments," *Asia Pacific Journal of Management* 26 (2009): 643–666.

24. C. C. Kwok and S. Tadesse, "The MNC as an Agent of Change for Host-Country Institutions: FDI and Corruption," *Journal of International Business Studies* 37 (2006): 767–785.

25. A. Cuervo-Cazurra, "Who Cares About Corruption?" *Journal of International Business Studies* 37 (2006): 807–822.

26. K. Leung, R. S. Bhagat, N. R. Buchan, M. Erez, and C. B. Gibson, "Culture and International Business: Recent Advances and Their Implications for the Future," *Journal of International Business Studies* 36 (2005): 357–378.

27. P. C. Earley, "Leading Cultural Research in the Future: A Matter of Paradigms and Taste," *Journal of International Business Studies* 37 (2006): 922–931.

28. R. Steers and J. S. Black, *Organization Behavior* (New York: HarperCollins, 1994).

29. M. A. Witt and G. Redding, "Culture, Meaning, and Institutions: Executive Rationale in Germany and Japan," *Journal of International Business Studies* 40 (2009): 859–885.

30. G. Hofstede, *Culture's Consequences* (Beverly Hills: Sage, 1980); G. Hofstede, *Cultures and Organizations* (Berkshire, UK: McGraw-Hill, 1994); R. J. House, P. J. Hanges et al., *Culture, Leadership and Organizations: The Globe Study of 62 Societies* (Thousand Oaks: Sage, 2004).

31. A. Li and R. Cropanzano, "Do East Asians Respond More/Less Strongly to Organizational Justice Than North Americans: A Meta-Analysis," *Journal of Management Studies* 46 (2009): 787–805.

32. I. O. Williamson, M. F. Burnett, and K. M. Bartol, "The Interactive Effect of Collectivism and Organizational Rewards on Affective Organizational Commitment," *Cross Cultural Management* 16 (2009): 28–43.

33. D. A. Waldman, A. S. de Luque, N. Washburn, R. J. House et al., "Cultural and Leadership Predictors of Corporate Social Responsibility Values of Top Management: A GLOBE Study of 15 Countries," *Journal of International Business Studies* 37 (2006): 823–837.

34. Hitt, Ireland, and Hoskisson, *Strategic Management.*

35. H. J. Sapienza, E. Autio, G. George, and S. Zahra, "A Capabilities Perspective on the Effects of Early Internationalization on Firm Survival and Growth," *Academy of Management Review* 31 (2006): 914–933.

36. E. Maitland, E. L. Rose, and S. Nicholas, "How Firms Grow: Clustering as a Dynamic Model of Internationalization," *Journal of International Business Studies* 36 (2005): 435–451.

37. S. E. Feinberg and A. R. Gupta, "MNC Subsidiaries and Country Risk: Internalization as a Safeguard Against Weak External Institutions," *Academy of Management Journal* 52 (2009): 381–399.

38. I. Filatotchev, X. Lui, T. Buck, and M. Wright, "The Export Orientation and Export Performance of High-technology SMEs in Emerging Markets: The Effects of Knowledge Transfer by Returnee Entrepreneurs," *Journal of International Business Studies* 40 (2009): 1005–1021.

39. Hitt, Ireland, and Hoskisson, *Strategic Management.*

40. M. S. Jiang, P. S. Aulakh, and Y. Pan, "Licensing Duration in Foreign Markets: A Real Options Perspective," *Journal of International Business Studies* 40 (2009): 559–577.

41. "Philip Morris International," Answers.com, http://www.ansswers.com/topic/philip-morris-international, accessed June 18, 2010; N. Zamiska and V. O'Connell, "Philip Morris in Talks to Make Marlboro in China," *Wall Street Journal,* April 21, 2005, B1–B2.

42. B. B. Neilsen and S. Neilsen, "Learning and Innovation in International Strategic Alliances: An Empirical Test of the Role of Trust and Tacitness," *Journal of Management Studies* 46 (2009): 1031–1056; J. S. Harrison, M. A. Hitt, R. E. Hoskisson, and R. D. Ireland, "Resource Complementarity in Business Combinations: Extending the Logic to Organizational Alliances," *Journal of Management* 27 (2001): 679–690.

43. J. J. Reuer and M. Zollo, "Termination Outcomes of Research Alliances," *Research Policy* 34 (1) (2005): 101–115.

44. R. D. Ireland, M. A. Hitt, and D. Vaidyanath, "Alliance Management as a Source of Competitive Advantage," *Journal of Management* 28 (2002): 413–446.

45. Chetty, Eriksson, and Lindbergh, "The Effect of Specificity."

46. T. Jandik and R. Kali, "Legal Systems, Information Asymmetry, and Firm Boundaries: Cross-border Choices to Diversify Through Mergers, Joint Ventures, or Strategic Alliances," *Journal of International Business Studies* 40 (2009): 578–599; Hitt, Dacin, Levitas, Arregle, and Borza, "Partner Selection in Developed and Emerging Market Contexts."

47. J.-P. Roy and C. Oliver, "International Joint Venture Partner Selection: The Role of the Host-country Legal Environment," *Journal of International Business Studies* 40 (2009): 779–801; M. A. Hitt, D. Ahlstrom, M. T. Dacin, E. Levitas, and L. Svobodina, "The Institutional Effects on Strategic Alliance Partner Selection in Transition Economies: China Versus Russia," *Organization Science* 15 (2004): 173–185.

48. C. Moschieri and M. Campu, "The European M&A Industry: A Market in the Process of Construction," *Academy of Management Perspectives* 23 (4) (2009): 71–87.

49. K. Shimizu, M. A. Hitt, D. Vaidyanath, and V. Pisano, "Theoretical Foundations of Cross-border Mergers and Acquisitions: A Review of Current Research and Recommendations for the Future," *Journal of International Management* 10 (2004): 307–353.

50. S. Wagstyl, "A Change in Gear," *Financial Times,* May 12, 2010, http://www.ft.com.

51. R. Chakrabarti, S. Gupta-Mukherjee, and N. Jayaraman, "Mars–Venus Marriages: Culture and Cross-border M&A," *Journal of International Business Studies* 40 (2009): 216–236; H. G. Barkema, J. H. J. Bell, and J. M. Pennings, "Foreign Entry, Cultural Barriers, and Learning," *Strategic Management Journal* 17 (1996): 151–166.

52. M. A. Hitt, V. Franklin, and H. Zhu, "Culture, Institutions, and International Strategy," *Journal of International Management* 12 (2006): 222–234.

53. U. Weitzel and S. Berns, "Cross-border Takeovers, Corruption, and Related Aspects of Governance," *Journal of International Business Studies* 37 (2006): 786–806.

54. D. Dikova, P. R. Sahib, and A. van Witteloostuijn, "Cross-border Acquisition Abandonment and Completion: The Effect of Institutional Differences and Organizational Learning in the International Business Service Industry, 1981–2001," *Journal of International Business Studies* 41 (2010): 223–245.

55. D. Tan, "Foreign Market Entry Strategies and Post-entry Growth: Acquisitions Versus Greenfield Investments," *Journal of International Business Studies* 40 (2009): 1046–1061.

56. B. Elango, "The Influence of Plant Characteristics on the Entry Mode Choice of Overseas Firms," *Journal of Operations Management* 23 (2005): 65–79.

57. B. Stanley, "United Parcel Service to Open a Hub in Shanghai," *Wall Street Journal,* July 8, 2005, B2; B. Stanley, "FedEx Plans Hub in Guangzhou: Facility to Begin Operation in 2008 as Cargo Industry Tries to Claim Turf in Asia," *Asian Wall Street Journal,* July 14, 2005, A3.

58. D. Lee, "EBay to Enlist a Partner in China," *Los Angeles Times,* December 20, 2006, http://www.latimes.com; K. Hafner and B. Stone, "EBay Is Expected to Close Its Auction Site in China," *New York Times,* December 19, 2006, http://www.nytimes.com.

59. Hitt, Ireland, and Hoskisson, *Strategic Management.*

60. J.-L. Arregle, P. Beamish, and L. Hebert, "The Regional Dimension of MNEs' Foreign Subsidiary Localization," *Journal of International Business Studies* 40 (2009): 86–107.

61. A.-W. Harzing and A. Sorge, "The Relative Impact of Country of Origin and Universal Contingencies in Internationalization Strategies and Corporate Control in Multinational Enterprises: Worldwide and European Perspectives," *Organization Studies* 24 (2003): 187–214.

62. G. Jones, "Control, Performance and Knowledge Transfers in Large Multinationals: Unilever in the United States, 1945–1980," *Business History Review* 76 (2002): 435–478.

63. J. P. Millikin and D. Fu, "The Global Leadership of Carlos Ghosn at Nissan," *Thunderbird International Business Review* 47, no. 1 (2005): 121–137.

64. S. Teng, T. W. Tong, G. Chen, and H. Kim, "Expatriate Utilization and Foreign Direct Investment Performance: The Mediating Role of Knowledge Transfer," *Journal of Management,* 35 (2009): 1181–1206.

65. E. Hall, *Beyond Culture* (Garden City: Doubleday, 1976); S. A. Zahra, R. D. Ireland, and M. A. Hitt, "International Expansion by New Venture Firms: International Diversity, Mode of Entry, Technological Learning, and Performance," *Academy of Management Journal* 43 (2000): 925–950.

66. G. K. Stahl, M. L. Maznevski, A. Voigt, and K. Jonsen, "Unraveling the Effects of Cultural Diversity in Teams: A Meta-analysis of Research on Multicultural Work Groups," *Journal of International Business Studies* 41 (2010): 690–709.

67. D. L. Shapiro, S. A. Furst, G. M. Spreitzer, and M. A. Von Glinow, "Transnational Teams in the Electronic Age: Are Team Identity and High Performance at Risk?" *Journal of Organizational Behavior* 23 (2002): 455–467.

68. Y. Shin, "A Person–Environment Fit Model for Virtual Organizations," *Journal of Management,* 30 (2004): 725–743.

69. S. L. Jarvenpaa and D. E. Leidner, "Communication and Trust in Virtual Teams," *Organization Science,* 10 (1999): 791–815.

70. M. A. Hitt, C. C. Miller, and A. Colella, *Organizational Behavior* (Hoboken: John Wiley & Sons, 2011).

71. M. A. Hitt, L. Tihanyi, T. Miller, and B. Connelly, "International Diversification: Antecedents, Outcomes, and Moderators," *Journal of Management* 32 (2006): 831–867.

72. J. Bell, "BRICOland Brands: The Rise of the New Multinationals," *Journal of Business Strategy* 30 (6) (2009): 27–35.

73. M. Javidan, R. M. Steers, and M. A. Hitt (eds.), *The Global Mindset. Advances in International Management,* vol. 19 (Amsterdam: Elsevier Science, 2007).

74. G. Colvin, "Lafley and Immelt: In Search of Billions," *Fortune,* December 11, 2006, 70–72.

75. J. Sheth, "Clash of Cultures or Fusion of Cultures? Implications for International Business," *Journal of International Management* 12 (2006): 218–221.

Part Two
Planning and Organizing

Strategic Management

LEARNING OBJECTIVES

After studying this chapter, you should be able to:

Explain what a competitive advantage is and identify its components.

Describe the strategic management process.

Explain the role an environmental analysis plays in strategy formulation.

List and describe the five dimensions of the general environment.

Explain the five forces in the industry and competitor environments.

Discuss how to conduct an internal analysis of a firm's resources using value chain analysis.

Utilize SWOT analysis to describe how to evaluate the organization's conditions and select the best strategy.

Identify and explain business-level, generic strategies.

Describe strategic actions used in strategy implementation such as acquisitions and strategic alliances.

Courtesy of William F. Prichett

Name: William F. "Rick" Prichett

Position: Regional President, Houston North Markets Spirit of Texas Bank

Alma maters: Texas Tech University (BBA); Texas A&M University (MBA)

Outside work activities: Golf, running, supporting the Houston Astros, typical grandfather activities, and travel

Business book I recommend: *Have a Little Faith.* The book tells the stories of two men, one a rabbi and the other an African American nondenominational preacher. Both come from extraordinarily different backgrounds but suggest similar principles about life. They tell the story of the importance of purpose, the similar source of purpose for all of us, and the need to give of one's self.

Someone I admire: My father—He taught me the importance of pride; not false pride, but true pride, and the absolute necessity to have well founded principles. He constantly gave his best regardless of the job at hand, and exhibited "emotional intelligence" before anyone heard of the term. He showed how to love family and country, as well as exemplified the art of aging with grace and vitality.

Motto I live by: "Don't Blink"—We frequently have to make adjustments because things do not turn out as we expect. However, one should never lose sight of their goals and dreams. One should re-evaluate their situation when necessary, but never take their eyes off the target. Stare down your challenges; be thankful for them, but if you blink, you lose.

Management style: Treat people fairly and be tolerant as long as they are trying. Try to set high standards and ensure they are well trained as they will be happier, loyal, and productive. Delegate responsibility and allow them the flexibility to do the job. Get the right people on the bus (Jim Collins'

philosophy). You should trust others but verify and create an environment where people can have fun while they achieve.

After completing his MBA (an executive MBA program while working full-time), Rick Prichett decided he wanted to start his own bank. He evaluated the area banking landscape and determined the market was prime to establish a community bank because there were few of them at the time and the banking community was dominated by very large banks, such as Citibank and Bank of America. Thus, he identified a community north of Houston where no locally owned community banks were headquartered, and those that were serving the market were doing so rather ineffectively.

Prichett put together an excellent strong team of investors and an experienced management team for the new bank. They then made application with the Texas Department of Banking and the FDIC regional office in Dallas. During this time, according to Prichett, the "perfect storm" occurred. The year the application was filed, 176 charters were issued in the United States for de novo banks (new and locally owned). However, the federal regulators had their hands full with the banking crisis and were tightening all banking activities.

One result of this increased scrutiny was the granting of only 12 new charters across the entire country in 2009. A year after Prichett's team submitted the application, the regulators suggested they try to buy an existing bank rather than continue to acquire a de novo charter.

Based upon this recommendation, Prichett and his ownership team evaluated the financials of many financial institutions, and ultimately executed an agreement to make a purchase.

All they needed was approval.

Ultimately, $15 million in capital was raised to make the purchase, but regulatory approval was never granted. The turmoil that was affecting the entire financial industry in the United States eventually caused multiple delays with the application, and ultimately resulted in the Bank4Texas organizing group pursuing an alternative path. Subsequently, the opportunity arose for Prichett and his investors to redirect their efforts/investment to a new and dynamic bank group, Spirit of Texas Bank.

As suggested in the opening profile, the external environment has a major effect on the strategy employed by business leaders to develop and implement a strategy. Certainly, the banking industry has been highly chaotic in recent times and placing significant pressure on the institutions intended to provide oversight for the industry and also pressures on all banking organizations.[1] Prichett and his major organizers experienced a "perfect storm" in his words. As such, they had to be flexible and adapt to the environment. Because of the ability exhibited by Prichett and those supporting his efforts, to adapt to the environmental demands, they eventually established a community bank in the market desired. Prichett's bank is competing in this market primarily with larger national banks and thus it experiences serious competition, but his bank is differentiated in strategy by emphasizing community relationships and support for businesses and individuals in the community.

The domestic automobile market provides another illustration of chaotic conditions and substantial competition. As recently as 25 years ago, three major manufacturers—General Motors, Ford, and Chrysler—dominated the largest automobile market in the world, the United States. Then, Chrysler was acquired by DaimlerBenz of Germany, which was acquired by a private equity company that in turn filed for bankruptcy. Thereafter, the Chrysler assets were acquired by Italian automaker Fiat. Additionally, the market shares of both GM and Ford have lost significant market share over the years as foreign competitors, including BMW, Daewoo, Fiat, Honda, Hyundai, Isuzu, Kia, Nissan, Renault, Subaru, Suzuki, Toyota, and others, captured market share. In fact, GM received major monies from the U.S. government and eventually filed for bankruptcy. It recently came out of bankruptcy.

Although Toyota eventually gained the largest market share in the United States and became the largest auto manufacturer in the world, it also has suffered significant problems with declining sales because of the recession and widely reported quality control problems.

This industry exemplifies how globalization has become a powerful force behind competition and market shares. Communication and transportation technology only add to the competitive intensity in major markets.

Never has the need been greater to understand how to develop and implement effective strategies. Andrew Grove, former Intel CEO, observed that only the "paranoid" firms survive, primarily because they continuously analyze their external environments and competition, but also because they continuously innovate. Managers who help their firms gain competitive advantage recognize that it is only temporary; they must be ready to change their strategy at any time based on their analysis of the competition and changes in their environments.[2]

Although the principles of strategic management are critical for top managers of a company, the principles also are applicable for managers at various levels of the organization. For example, a senior manager like Rick Prichett might be responsible for a regional organization with several units at different locations, each having a separate manager. To some degree, the products and service may vary by region, tailored to regional market needs. You can apply the principles presented in this chapter to create a strategy for a regional subsidiary, a product line, or an entire company. In addition, even though top executives largely develop a company's strategy, the organization's other managers and employees must then implement the strategy throughout the organization. Managers at all levels can do a better job of helping implement a strategy if they understand the strategic management process, how the strategy was developed, and its intended targets.[3] These topics are the focus of this chapter.

What Is a Competitive Advantage?

Fundamentally, the objective of strategic management is to determine, create, and maintain competitive advantage. At its essence, the concept of **competitive advantage** is a firm's ability to provide value to customers that exceeds what competitors can provide.[4] In a for-profit organization, having a competitive advantage contributes to consistently higher profits than its competitors.

A competitive advantage is created by having and managing resources to provide goods and services that meet the following criteria: (1) they provide superior value, (2) they are rare—competitors do not provide similar products and services in quality and quantity, (3) they are difficult to imitate, and (4) they are nonsubstitutable.[5] Hewlett-Packard (HP) is the market leader in printers. Clearly, this indicates that HP has a competitive advantage in this market. HP's products and services in the printer market meet the four criteria. Recently, HP acquired Palm for $1.2 billion trying to enhance its competitiveness in the smart-phone market.[6] But, it has struggled in the smart-phone market; its products in this market to date do not meet the four criteria. Next, we explore each of the four criteria that lead to competitive advantage.

competitive advantage
the ability of a firm to win consistently over the long term in a competitive situation

Superior Value

The essence of **superior value** as an aspect of competitive advantage is straightforward. Does the firm provide a product or service which provides value to customers that is greater than that of a competitor's product or service? FedEx was one of the first companies to introduce package tracking capability. It created a system for tracking a package all along its route. The system

superior value
products and services that produce value for customers that is superior to the value provided by competitor's

enabled FedEx to locate a customer's package at any point along the delivery route more effectively than its primary competitor, UPS. Of course, UPS soon implemented its own tracking system, trying to reach parity in the value it provides customers. As a student, you chose the particular school that you attend because of the special value it provides you. For example, it may provide a superior education in the major of your choice. It also may provide a superior location or special place where you prefer to live. In recent years, Apple has introduced several superior products such as the iPad. Thus, Apple has a competitive advantage because it sells audio, video, and other visual products that provide superior value to customers. This is sometimes referred to as a *comparative advantage* because, compared to others, the firm provides superior value. It is also sometimes referred to as a *distinctive competence* because the superior product or service is the result of a competence that is distinctive.

Rarity

For a company to hold a competitive advantage, no other firms can have the capabilities needed to provide the quality and quantity of products and services it produces. If even one other firm has similar capabilities, it can then provide the customers products and services of equal value. You may ask the question, "How many other firms hold similar capabilities?" If the answer is none and the capabilities held by the firm produce superior value for the customers, the firm clearly will hold a competitive advantage. Yet most competitive advantages are temporary because competitors are constantly trying to wrest an advantage from the market leader.[7] In particular, competitors often try to imitate market leaders.

Difficult to Imitate

Having capabilities that provide superior value for customers and that are rare will produce only a temporary advantage. Firms must try to avoid competitor imitation of these capabilities and must create barriers that make it difficult for others to imitate these capabilities to produce a competitive advantage.[8] These barriers can involve a variety of obstacles from tangible ones, such as size, to more intangible ones, such as a company's culture and corporate reputation.[9]

Disney's theme parks have been praised for having a comparative advantage in friendly employees. While Disney may provide superior value to customers with its friendly employees, you may ask the question, "Is it easy for other firms to replicate this attribute?" If friendly employees represent a major contributor to offering superior value, Disney's advantage would likely disappear. But how easy is it to recruit, hire, train, and retain employees who can and are

Disney's characters—Mickey Mouse, Goofy, Pluto, and so forth—are well known and renowned the world over. As such, they give Disney a competitive advantage. So do the companies well-trained, friendly employees.

© imagebroker/Alamy

willing to be very friendly to all customers over a long period of time? The harder it is for other firms with theme parks to hire, develop, and retain friendly employees, the longer Disney will enjoy comparative advantage.

Friendly employees clearly contribute to Disney's advantage, but other attributes also contribute to it. For example, the well-known and loved Disney characters (such as, Mickey Mouse, Goofy, Pluto) also contribute to Disney's advantage. Therefore, a competitive advantage may result from the combination of several factors, making it more difficult for competitors to imitate.

Additionally, some advantages are more durable than others. Legal protection, such as patents, can prolong their existence. Many scientific patents are awarded for durations of 17 to 20 years. Advantages like brand recognition can last a long time and may take years to deteriorate. The Disney brand has endured in the minds of children and their parents for more than 60 years.[10]

Nonsubstitutability

In addition to the qualities identified previously, for a competitive advantage to be sustainable over time requires a low possibility of substitution.[11] **Substitution** refers to the ability to fulfill a customer's need by alternative means. Let's differentiate substitution and imitation with an example: Godiva chocolates are famous for their quality and unique flavor. They have an advantage with regard to taste and smoothness other companies' chocolates don't have. Godiva's specialized knowledge, which helped it to create this unique and highly valued flavor, makes it difficult for other firms to replicate, or imitate, the taste and texture of Godiva chocolates. However, if Godiva is to sustain its competitive advantage, customers must find it difficult to find a substitute that equally satisfies their desire for the sweet taste and smooth texture obtained from the Godiva chocolates. To reach more customers available to competitors, Godiva now distributes selected products through supermarkets.[12]

substitution
the ability to fulfill a customer's need by alternative means

Turning a Competitive Advantage into Profits

Firms must manage their resources in such a way as to capture profits from their competitive advantage.[13] **Above-average returns** are the profits greater than the average for a comparable set of firms (usually compared by industry and size).[14] These above-average profits are primarily a function of larger-than-average cost-price margins. For example, if, on average, a 750- megabyte USB drive costs $5 for firms in the hardware industry to produce, and, on average, the sales price within the industry is $20, the average profit margin is $15. More than $15 in profit on all such USB drives sold would represent an above-average return. Importantly, customers must perceive that they receive value. If they do and the firm can earn above-average returns, the firm is creating value for its shareholders and usually for all of its stakeholders.

above-average returns
profits that are above the average for a comparable set of firms

The following sections examine specific aspects of the strategic management process, including the formulation and implementation of strategy. Strategy is developed and implemented with one basic objective—achieving a competitive advantage.

The Strategic Management Process: Setting Direction

Strategic management is a type of planning process in which managers (1) establish the organization's general direction and objectives, (2) formulate a specific strategy, (3) plan and carry out the strategy's implementation, and (4) monitor results and make necessary adjustments. To understand what this means, we examine each step in the process (see Exhibit 4.1).

Determining the Firm's Strategic Vision

The first step in the strategic management process is the determination of the firm's strategic vision. The **strategic vision** provides a view of the firm over the long term and what it should achieve in the future.[15] For example, the strategic vision for Xerox Corporation is to be "the World's Document Company." Kellogg's strategic vision is to have Kellogg's Products on Every Table in the World. As these examples illustrate, a firm's vision captures its general identity, direction, and level of aspirations. The strategic vision is the heart of the strategy and strategic plan.[16] In practice, an effective statement of strategic vision is short and compelling, and provides a general understanding of the organization's aspirations while engendering passion among managers and other organization members. The vision and mission are closely integrated.

strategic vision
a view of the firm over the long term that describes what it should achieve in the future

EXHIBIT 4.1

Strategic Management Process

Formulating the Firm's Mission Statement

mission statement

a statement that articulates the fundamental purpose of the organization; often contains several components

Although statements of strategic intent are typically only a sentence in length, mission statements are usually much longer. A **mission statement** articulates the fundamental purpose of the organization and often contains several components, among them:

- Company philosophy
- Company identity or self-concept
- Principal products or services
- Customers and markets
- Geographic focus
- Obligations to shareholders
- Commitment to employees[17]

An example of a mission statement is provided in Exhibit 4.2. As the example illustrates, mission statements describe an organization's purpose and should support and be consistent with its strategic vision. One of the major differences between statements of strategic vision and mission statements is that mission statements tend to be much more specific in terms of the values and the primary focus of the organization.

To determine what strategy to pursue requires an analysis of both the firm's external environment and internal resources and capabilities. Kenneth Andrews probably first advanced this view, in the early 1970s.[18] The results of an assessment of both needs to be integrated to determine the appropriate objectives and to formulate the strategy necessary to achieve them.

Conducting an External Environmental Analysis

Firms must thoroughly analyze the external general environment and the industry and competitor environment because each can significantly affect the strategy a firm might develop, as well as whether the firm is likely to succeed or fail.[19] Although the effects of the general environment

EXHIBIT 4.2

Mission Statement for the Internal Revenue Service

> ✤ *IRS Mission Statement* ✤
>
> The IRS mission is to "provide America's taxpayers top quality service by helping them understand and meet their tax responsibilities and by applying the tax law with integrity and fairness to all."

are often indirect, they can be critical in formulating an effective strategy. Certainly, the forces in an industry and those associated with competitors are of particular importance in developing a company's strategy.[20]

The General Environment

A variety of forces in the **general environment** can influence the effectiveness of an organization's strategy include sociocultural, technological, economic, political-legal, and global forces.

SOCIOCULTURAL FORCES **Sociocultural forces** consist primarily of the demographics and the cultural characteristics of the societies in which an organization operates. Demographics are essentially the descriptive characteristics of people in the society, such as average age, birth rate, level of education, literacy rate, and so on. For example, in 1920 the average life expectancy was 53.6 years in the United States, and by 2009 it was 78.1 years.[21]

Demographics can significantly affect both organizational inputs and outcomes. For example, the average level of education and the birth rate in the United States combined can have a significant impact on the supply of workers with a given level of education and training. Specifically, a low birth rate and a modestly increasing level of education could result in a slow-growing or even declining number of technical workers. For example, in the 1990s and for most of the first decade of the twenty-first century, demand for workers with strong technical capabilities, such as software programmers, far outstripped supply in the United States.

Japan's population declined for the first time in 2005. By 2007, the number of people over 65 years of age more than doubled from 10 percent of the population to 21 percent in less than a generation. With one of the world's longest life expectancies (82.1 years in 2009), fewer workers will be supporting Japan's retirees than at any time in the country's history, and many of Japan's retirees will live so long that they are likely to use up their retirement savings before they die if they retire at age 65.[22] This may mean that younger workers will face higher government taxes to support social security systems for senior citizens.

Although demographics provide important data about the population, societal values help to translate those data into business implications.[23] Societal values are commonly shared desired "end states." In practical terms, societal values determine the extent to which an organization's products or services have a market. For example, consider the earlier controversy surrounding sport utility vehicles (SUVs) in North America. Throughout the 1990s, SUVs, such as the Ford Explorer, Dodge Durango, and Chevy Suburban were the fastest-selling automobiles. However, as concerns about the impact of pollution on global warming increased and the prices of gasoline increased, some consumers developed a negative sentiment toward SUVs and pressured car companies to make "hybrid" cars. Instead of an SUV's 12 miles to the gallon, hybrids get 50 or 60 miles to the gallon.

general environment
sociocultural, technological, economic, political-legal, and global forces that can influence the effectiveness of an organization's strategy

sociocultural forces
forces consisting primarily of the demographics or cultural characteristics of the societies in which an organization operates

Parents in SUVs line the parking lot at a Dallas Christian school while they wait to pick up their children. But "Would Jesus drive an SUV?" That's what some people began asking after concerns about the environment heightened people's awareness about the vehicles' CO_2 emissions. Changing societal values such as this are constantly changing the products people demand—changes astute managers need to be aware of.

Richard Michael Pruitt/Dallas Morning News/CORBIS-NY

Astute managers need the ability to combine demographics and societal values in order to determine important implications for their organizations.[24]

TECHNOLOGICAL FORCES Technology is another external environment force that can critically affect organizations.[25] A specific technological innovation can spell the birth and growth of one firm and the decline and death of another. Although the technological environment can be quite complicated, managers especially need to focus on two basic dimensions of the technology environment—product and process changes.

Product technological changes are those that lead to new features and capabilities in existing products or to completely new products. Managers need to know what product technology changes are occurring, especially in their industries. Because firms increasingly win or lose as a function of their technological advantages and disadvantages, an awareness of technological advances at home and abroad is critical.

Process technological changes typically relate to alterations in how to make products or how to manage enterprises. For example, management information system (MIS) technology, such as that used by Wal-Mart (the largest retailer in the world with over $400 billion in annual sales), allows managers to track merchandise on a daily or hourly basis and thereby know which products are selling and which are not. The tracking, in turn, allows them to effectively order merchandise so that they do not run out of hot-selling items (and miss out on the sales revenues) and avoid overstocking poor-selling items (tying up valuable cash in inventory).[26]

Many North American steel manufacturers were driven into bankruptcy because virtually all of the largest firms were slow to adopt an important new process technology, the electric arch furnace. Most large (or what are called "integrated") steel companies made steel by starting with raw iron ore and melting and converting it to large steel slabs that were further rolled and refined. Electric arch furnaces allowed so-called "mini-mills" to start with scrap metal, melt it, and make it into steel products. Starting with scrap metal was significantly cheaper than starting with iron ore. Although the metal made in mini-mills cannot be made into such things as beams for skyscrapers, it can be made into sheet metal for making car exteriors, washing machines, toasters, and so on. ArcelorMittal Dofasco of Hamilton, Canada, was the first—and, at the time, the only—integrated steel company to add this technology to its traditional steel-making processes. However, although the company now enjoys the benefits of the new electric arch furnace technology, it still took it nearly ten years to adopt the technology after it was introduced.[27]

ECONOMIC FORCES A variety of economic forces in the external environment can also significantly influence organizations. Not all economic forces affect all organizations equally, however. The exact nature of the business and industry determines the specific factors that have the strongest influence on an organization.

Current economic conditions clearly can affect the demand for products and the costs of producing them. For example, the level of inflation can directly affect how quickly costs increase, which in turn might reduce profits. The current level of unemployment can directly influence how easy or difficult it is to find the type of employees needed. Current interest rates can determine how expensive it is to borrow money or even how much money the firm can borrow to finance activities and expansions. When interest rates are low, home builders and mortgage loan providers generally experience higher demand for their services.

But economic activity is not static.[28] Economic activity tends to move in cycles. Although it is difficult to predict exactly when an upturn or downturn in economic conditions will occur, understanding that cycles exist and the key factors that move them is critical for managerial activities, such as planning. It is also important to understand that specific industry cycles can be more or less pronounced than the general economic cycle of the country. For example, the construction industry tends to have higher peaks and lower valleys than the overall national economy.

Perhaps the most difficult thing to determine about economic conditions is whether changes in the economy are temporary or whether they represent longer-term, structural changes. Structural changes significantly affect the current and future dynamics of economic activity. For example, the shift from an agrarian (agricultural) economy to an industrial one and the shift from an industrial to a service economy were structural changes that took place in the United States. They affected where people worked, what work they did, and the education level they needed to do the work. In many service companies, such as engineering, consulting, and law firms, the company's primary assets are its people. The knowledge held by these people represents intangible assets.[29] This is in contrast to industrial companies, such as car manufacturers, which have millions of dollars in tangible assets like plants and equipment. As a consequence, while a car manufacturer may be able to replace a worker who leaves the assembly line with relative ease and feel only small effects of employee turnover, the same is not true for service companies. For example, when a star consultant leaves her firm, she takes most of her value with her. Her understanding of clients' problems and solutions leaves with her. In some cases, the value is so closely tied to the individual that clients leave the company with a person's departure and redirect their business to wherever the star consultant works.

POLITICAL AND LEGAL FORCES Political and legal forces can have important effects on organizations. Laws frame what organizations can and cannot do and, as a consequence, create both challenges and opportunities. For example, new pollution laws significantly increased the operating costs of coal-burning power plants. At the same time, these laws created new business opportunities for firms such as Corning, which developed and sold new filter systems to coal-burning power plants.[30] Alternatively, regulations sometimes based on laws and sometimes the result of government policies can have a major influence on business strategies. Uncertainty of regulations can have a major influence because it causes firms to withhold critical investments that could be affected by potential new regulations.[31]

Perhaps one of the most important political aspects of the external general environment is federal government spending. On one hand, changes in government spending can have a significant impact on the overall economy. Total government spending at the local, state, and national levels accounts for about 20 percent of gross domestic product (the total dollar value of final goods and services produced by businesses within a nation's borders). More complicated, but perhaps even more important, is whether government spending increases or reduces the deficit. When federal spending increases the federal deficit, interest rates sometimes increase. As interest rates increase, money becomes more expensive for firms to borrow and, as a consequence, they typically borrow less. As firms borrow less, they expand their business activities at a slower pace or even contract their overall activity. These actions contribute to unemployment, which in turn reduces consumer spending. In combination, these conditions can create an economic downturn.

GLOBAL FORCES Although all managers should pay attention to the global environment, its importance depends on the organization's size and scope of business. When the percentage of international sales increases as part of total sales, the global environment becomes more important.[32] For example, 70 percent of Coca-Cola's income comes from international sales in over 200 countries; consequently, the global environment is critical to the company's performance. Managers of multinational firms that operate in multiple countries must try to integrate those operations into an almost borderless enterprise. As Wal-Mart has grown internationally, it has had to become sensitive to the global forces in the general environment. Global forces affect each of the other four general environmental forces.

When analyzing a foreign country, there are two additional dimensions of the external environment that are typically examined in the context of a foreign country—institutional and physical environmental forces. They are often included in analyses of foreign countries primarily because of the vast differences among them in terms of institutions and physical characteristics.[33]

As explained in Chapter 3, **institutional forces** include the rules, policies, and enforcement processes that influence individuals' and organizations' behaviors within a country's borders.[34] The institutions that should be assessed include a country's government, labor unions, religious institutions, and business institutions because they can be (and often are) dramatically different from those "at home." These institutions also include the laws and regulations and economic factors as described in Chapter 3. **Physical forces** involve a country's infrastructure, such as roads, telecommunications, air links, arable land, deepwater harbors, mineral resources, forests, and climate, all of which can affect existing and potential business operations in a country. For example, China has vast coal resources deep in its interior, but they are not an attractive business opportunity because of the poor rail and road infrastructure in those regions.

Exhibit 4.3 summarizes the analyses of the general environment for Coca-Cola. The socio-cultural information suggests that managers at Coca-Cola may desire to increase their marketing efforts to reach out to ethnic groups from countries and cultures in which drinking soft drinks, especially with carbonation, is not common. The information captured in the global dimension of the general external environment showed that managers at Coca-Cola should increase their efforts in emerging foreign markets with large populations, such as China.

institutional forces
the country's rules, policies, and enforcement processes that influence individuals' and organizations' behaviors that operate within a country's borders

physical forces
involve infrastructure that can affect existing and potential business operations in a country such as roads, telecommunications, air links, deepwater harbors, etc.

EXHIBIT 4.3

Description of the General Environment of Coca-Cola

Sociocultural

- Demographics
  Baby boomers drinking less soft drinks as they age.
  U.S. population growth is slowing and much of the growth comes from immigrants who generally drink less soft drinks.
- Values
  Society is increasingly concerned about pollution and recycling.
  Increasing focus on health and the negative aspects of caffeine, carbonation, and sugar.

Technological

- New "canning" technology makes using recycled aluminum easier and cheaper.
- Internet opens up a new means of running promotion contests and activities.

Economic

- Slow economy reduces per-person consumption primarily due to fewer social occasions (parties) at which soft drinks might be served.
- Nearing end of economic downturn and prospects of economic recovery.
- Stricter liability for illness caused by beverage contamination.

Global

- Gradual increase in acceptance of carbonated soft drinks in other countries, such as India and China.
- Widely available electricity and increased ability to afford refrigerators in emerging countries and economies.

A Manager's Challenge, "Google Retreats on Its China Strategy," suggests that managers for the company did a poor job of analyzing China's general environment. In particular, Google did not seem to understand well China's institutional environment. And, it underestimated Baidu, its primary competitor in the Chinese markets. Thus, the managers evidently did a poor job of analyzing the competitor environment in China as well. These failures cost Google hundreds of millions of dollars in investments made to enter and stay in the Chinese market. Google did not earn above-average returns in China.

The Firm's Industry and Competitor Environment

Michael Porter developed perhaps the most well-known model for analyzing a firm's industry and competitor environment.[35] This framework, known as Porter's Five Forces, focuses on five **industry and competitor forces** that can significantly influence a company's performance within an industry (see Exhibit 4.4). Porter's original research was designed to explain why some industries were more profitable as a whole than others and why some companies within industries were more profitable than others in the same industry. In general, research has supported the validity of this model.[36] Three of the five forces (the nature of rivalry, new entrants, and substitutes) involve competitors and the other two forces are customers and suppliers.

industry and competitor forces

five environmental forces (Porter's Five Forces) that can significantly influence the performance of organizations in an industry

EXHIBIT 4.4

Profits and Industry Forces

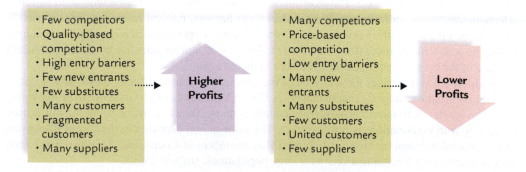

A MANAGER'S CHALLENGE

GLOBALIZATION

Google Retreats on Its China Strategy

Google voiced strong concerns that it was subjected to a cyber attack in which intellectual property was stolen and human-rights activists' accounts were accessed by hackers. Until this time, Google seemed to go along with the Chinese government's policies that forbid access to sites it deemed undesirable by the national government. Many felt that Google was compromising its values to access the major markets in China. At the time, Google had about 35.6 percent of the Chinese search market with its chief competitor, Baidu, having a sizable lead in the market. Although this is sizable, it is small by comparison to the market shares that Google commands in many other countries.

Even though Google tried to practice censorship, it could never satisfy the Chinese government. Google announced it was moving the search business in China to Hong Kong and then announced it was closing its China search business. Some analysts believe that this is a good move for Google overall because it bases its strategic actions in the firm's core values. Research by Harvard professors John Kotter and John Heskett found that firms operating on a strong set of core values tended to outperform by a large margin firms that did not operate in this manner. And, when Google quit doing business in China, only about 2.5 percent of its sales were derived from the country.

The Google example highlights the risks of foreign businesses investing and operating in Chinese markets. For example, China has been trying to emphasize its own technology industries and firms. Therefore, it creates an unfavorable environment for foreign businesses, especially those in high-technology industries. Some foreign

Google's managers did a poor job of analyzing the competitor environment in China, costing Google hundreds of millions of dollars in investments made to enter the Chinese market.

businesses in other industries have begun to express concerns as well. They note that China props up home businesses through access to financial capital, tax breaks, and more onerous policies towards outsiders. Yet, these types of actions are not uncommon in other countries as well, including the United States. However, some foreign businesses have been seeking to invest in other Asian markets where they feel more welcome.

Sources: S. Sundeep, "Risks of Investing in China Exposed," *Financial Times,* May 13, 2010, http://www.ft.com; L. Nirel, "The Impact of Google's 'China Syndrome' on Your Business Strategy," *Fast Company,* March 28, 2010, http://www.fastcompany.com; J. Boudreau, "Doing Business in China Getting Tougher for U.S. Companies," *The Mercury News,* March 27, 2010, http://www.mercurynews.com; F. Balfour, "Google Exit Reminds Companies Asia Strategy Is Not Just China," *BusinessWeek,* March 23, 2010, http://www.businessweek.com; B. Einhorn, "In China, Google Declares War on Censorship," *BusinessWeek,* January 13, 2010, http://www.businessweek.com.

The first dimension of this environment is the nature of rivalry among competitors. For example, it is important to understand the strength of competitors relative to your firm. If competitors are stronger, they are likely to take actions to gain market share from your firm. Thus, it might be important to focus on market segments that competitors avoid to build the strengths of your firm. In the analysis, it is important to learn competitors' weaknesses. Their weaknesses may represent opportunities that can be exploited. The number of direct competitors also provides information on the nature of potential rivalry.

Large industries, such as automobile manufacturing, quite often include different segments and the nature of rivalry can differ by segment. For example, in the subcompact segment of the auto industry, competition is largely based on price. However, in the luxury automobile segment, competition is primarily based on quality and differentiated features.

Issues of safety, engineering, and comfort dominate the ads for Mercedes, Lexus, BMW, and Infiniti.

The second dimension of the industry and competitor environment is the amount of difficulty firms encounter upon entering the industry. In general, new entrants will increase competition. Increased competition usually produces lower profit margins because customers have more choices. Unless it is difficult and expensive for customers to switch from one company to another (this is typically called a *switching cost*), companies are forced to provide greater value to customers. American Airlines invented the frequent-flier program, to increase the switching costs. If customers decided to fly on a different airline, they lost the advantage of the upgrades or free flights offered by American Airlines. Where switching costs are low, competitors must offer greater value to attract and retain customers. This greater customer value commonly is traded for lowering profits.

entry barriers
obstacles that makes it difficult for firms to enter a particular type of business (industry).

Entry barriers are obstacles that make it difficult for firms to enter a particular type of business. The larger the barriers, the more difficult it is to enter the business. So, larger barriers lead to fewer new entrants. For example, the barriers to enter the restaurant business are quite low. As a result, there are often many new restaurants opening each year (and many that fail, as well). However, the barriers to enter the semiconductor business are high because a fabrication plant costs $6 billion or more to build.

A third environmental dimension is the potential for substitutes. This dimension focuses on the extent to which alternative products or services can substitute for existing products or services. Substitution is different from competition. It involves an alternative means of satisfying a customer's need. Generally, fewer available substitutes lead to greater profits. Different forms of transportation are substitutes (for example, bus, train, airplane). People usually decide on which means of transportation based on the time required and cost.

CUSTOMERS Customers represent a critical component of an external environment. Organizations exist largely to serve customers and, thus, managers focus their efforts on satisfying customer needs. As explained earlier in this chapter, when they provide customers value that is superior to the value provided by competitors, they achieve a competitive advantage. To the extent that there are relatively few customers and these customers are united, they have more power to demand lower prices, customized products or services, attractive financing terms from producers, and so on. When customers have more power, they can extract greater value. When customers are powerful, the firm is in a poor bargaining position, and its profits may suffer. When one customer buys a large amount of a firm's output, that customer also usually has power even if the firm has many other customers. For example, Wal-Mart usually is in a powerful position with its suppliers because it purchases very large quanitities. It has power even with very large companies, such as Procter & Gamble, because of the amount it orders. Managers want to serve the firm's customers, providing them superior value without allowing them to gain too much power.[37] The balance of power between the firm and its customers affects its ability to compete effectively and to earn above-average returns.

SUPPLIERS Managers must try to achieve a power balance with the firm's suppliers as well. If one or a few suppliers control a valuable good necessary for the products or services provided by the firm, the supplier will have considerable power.[38] Such a supplier likely can command a premium price or even limit access to the good. In this case, it may be difficult for the firm to earn an above-average return because of the high cost of the supplies. Regardless of the power of suppliers, it is important to build and maintain good relationships with them. Suppliers can contribute value to the products and services firms offer by customizing their processes and providing help in other ways that increase quality, improve the firm's marketing to its customers, lower its costs, and provide the supplies in a timely manner. Many firms have developed in-house units responsible for managing their strategic alliances with their partners, such as suppliers.[39]

In summary, firms must carefully analyze their external environment. They cannot afford "blind spots" in the knowledge of current and potential competitors.[40] If they overlook a competitor, they could end up fighting for survival. For example, Apple's competitors failed to foresee and predict the potential success of the iPhone and the iPod, which dramatically changed two different industries. The company may do the same in another industry with the iPad.[41]

Exhibit 4.5 presents a description of the industry and competitive environment for JetBlue. This exhibit provides examples of the different segments of this environment that you can analyze.

Internal Analysis

An analysis of the organization's internal capabilities is equally important to an analysis of its external environment. Of the various tools or frameworks for this purpose, the "value chain" approach proposed by Michael Porter is one of the most widely used.[42] The **value chain** consists of a set of key activities that directly produce or support the production of a firm's products and services offered to customers. Porter separates the internal components of a firm into five primary activities and four support activities (see Exhibit 4.5). The **primary activities** are those that are directly involved in the creation of a product or service, and distributing it to the customer. As the label suggests, **support activities** facilitate the creation of the product or service and its transfer to the customer. Managers should assess the value these activities add to the product or service to gain an understanding of the firm's ability to compete. The absolute value of a product or service is a function of how many customers are willing to purchase the product or service and how much they are willing to pay for it. A firm makes a profit if it can provide a product or service whose value exceeds its costs. To determine where value is added in the firm's internal value chains, managers need to understand each of the nine activities in the chain, which we discuss next.

value chain
the set of key activities that directly produce or support the production of a firm's products and service offered to customers.

primary activities
Activities that are directly involved in the creation of a product or service, and distributing it to the customer.

support activities
activities that facilitate the creation of a product or service and its transfer to the customer

INBOUND LOGISTICS This component of the value chain consists of activities that are designed to receive, store, and then disseminate various inputs related to the firm's products or services. Inbound logistics commonly includes raw materials, receiving, transportation, inventory, and information. In the beer industry, inbound logistics involve getting hops, barley, and malt to the various brewing sites. The use of information technology is important for most value chain activities but it is of special importance in the management of inbound logistics.[43]

OPERATIONS The operations component of the value chain includes a variety of activities that transform inputs into the products and services of the firm. In addition, the operations segment of the value chain also includes activities (such as maintenance) that keep machines in working order. In the beer example, the firm's operational activities might involve producing the beer for different markets as well as the process of bottling and labeling the products.

OUTBOUND LOGISTICS Outbound logistics include activities that move the product or service from the firm to the customers. The beer producer needs to warehouse the finished product,

EXHIBIT 4.5

A Description of the Industry and Competitive Environment of JetBlue

Competitors
- Rivalry
  Primarily based on price, which generally hurts performance.
  Many established and big players including profitable ones such as Southwest.
- New Entrants
  With $35 million anyone can start an airline; however, the frequency of past failure makes it less likely for new entrants.
- Substitutes
  As video conferencing gets better with faster connections, it may substitute for some face-to-face business meetings. It is less likely to substitute for leisure, tourist, or personal visit travel.

Customers
- Business travelers who want convenience.
- Leisure travelers who want low price.

Suppliers
- Airbus supplies all of JetBlue's planes (all are Airbus 320s).
- Many jet fuel suppliers, such as ExxonMobil.

process the orders, schedule delivery trucks, and distribute its products (either directly or through distributors) to stores, bars, ballparks, restaurants, and other places where it can be sold.

MARKETING AND SALES Marketing and sales activities are designed to inform potential customers about the products and services the firm has available and entice them to purchase them. The beer manufacturer, thus, advertises, promotes its products, and sells them.

SERVICE Service activities are designed to do what is necessary to ensure that the product satisfies the customer after the purchase and to increase the probability of a repeat purchase. Service activities may involve repair, supply of parts, installation, or product adjustments. They can also help the customer learn how to best use the product.

Each of these primary activities has associated costs. When done well, they enhance the firm's industry position and profitability if a customer is willing to pay more for them than they cost. The importance of the various activities changes depending on customer preferences. For example, in the fashion industry, customers often want the latest styles, colors, and fabrics soon after they are introduced. This places a premium on both inbound and outbound logistics to ensure that products can be delivered quickly to customers.

In addition to the five primary activities, there are four support activities. As illustrated in Exhibit 4.6, these activities cut across all five of the primary activities; that is, elements of a given support activity facilitate each of the five primary activities.

PROCUREMENT The activity of procuring usable and consumable assets is found in each of the primary activities. For example, not only must raw materials used in products be purchased in the inbound logistics activities, but also delivery trucks and scheduling software for the fleet must be purchased so that those materials can arrive for processing. The purchases of machinery and replacement parts are examples of specific procurement activities within operations. Firms often have purchasing departments, but various people ranging from purchasing agents to secretaries may handle procurement. Procurement is a critical in the process to ensure quality and timeliness of the raw materials needed.[44] Suppliers play a key role here as well. They influence the quality, cost and timeliness of raw materials delivered to the firm.[45] Suppliers also often participate in the innovation process through direct involvement in new product development or in providing new information relevant to the development process.[46]

TECHNOLOGY DEVELOPMENT Technology development revolves around expertise and the tools or equipment used in the exercise of that expertise.[47] The technology may be as simple or complicated as a supercomputer and related software. Although technology development concentrates on product development or process innovation, technology and the means by which a company applies it to tasks also has an effect on all five primary activities.[48] Thus, technological capabilities play a key role in the value chain.[49]

HUMAN RESOURCE MANAGEMENT Given that no activity is completely removed from humans (humans even design and implement automatic processes and equipment), the process of acquiring, training, evaluating, compensating, and developing human resources is present in all

EXHIBIT 4.6

The Value Chain

Source: Based on The Free Press, a Division of Simon & Schuster Adult Publishing Group, from *COMPETITIVE ADVANTAGE: Creating and Sustaining Superior Performance* by Michael E. Porter. Copyright © 1985, 1998 by Michael E. Porter. All rights reserved; Robert M. Grant, *Contemporary Strategy Analysis.* (Oxford, UK: Blackwell, 2002); R.E. Hoskisson, M.A. Hitt & R.D. Ireland, *Competing for Advantage* (Mason, OH, Thomson-Southwestern, 2008).

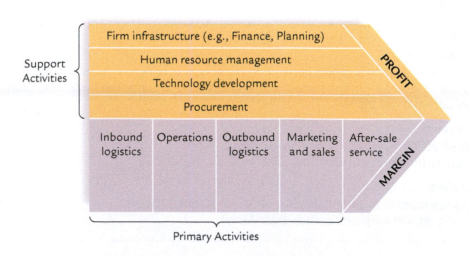

five primary activities. Capable and motivated people can have a profound impact on all the activities of a firm so human resource management is a critical support activity. In service firms such as banks, law, consulting, or accounting firms, the quality of the people is especially critical.[50] Their expertise is the basis of the service provided. Therefore, this component of the value chain is critical to a service firm's fortune or failure.

FIRM INFRASTRUCTURE Although infrastructure usually brings plant, utilities, and equipment to mind, a firm's infrastructure has less to do with brick and mortar than with the administrative functions that support its primary activities. A firm's infrastructure consists of its planning, finance, accounting, legal, government relations, and other activities supplied by its various primary activities. For example, a firm is likely to need legal information on worker-safety standards for its operations department and legal information about "truth in advertising" for its marketing and sales departments.

Support activities enhance the firm's market position and profitability to the extent that they assist primary activities and contribute to the final products or services that customers value.[51] The importance of the support activities also changes depending on customer preferences. For example, in the fashion industry, customers' preferences for the latest styles, colors, and fabrics may increase the importance of planning information in the value chain. Planning information related to forecasting trends, buying seasons, purchasing cycles, and customer preferences would be valuable, in this case. Customers' preferences might also increase the importance of the firm's technology-development support activity. For example, technology that allows yarn to be dyed *after* it has been knit into sweaters (rather than before) adds value. Benetton of Italy developed such a process to incorporate the latest color trends demanded by consumers as late in the manufacturing process as possible.

The value chain framework facilitates evaluation of the resources held and their ability to deliver value to the customer. The value chain framework enables a systematic and comprehensive analysis of the firm's activities.

LEVERAGING THE VALUE CHAIN The first step in managing the value chain for greater profits and performance is to determine where in the value chain there is potential to add the *greatest* value.

Returning to the beer example, many German customers value a rich-tasting beer and are relatively less sensitive to price. If the quality of a beer's ingredients determines its flavor, procuring the highest-quality ingredients is critical. Identifying high-quality ingredients is primarily a function of experienced buyers. Thus, the firm's human resource management systems of recruiting, selecting, and training these ingredient buyers must be superior. The power of the value chain model is that by segmenting the firm's business activities, managers can better understand the important linkages among them. However, managers must perform an analysis to identify which activities add the most value, and which linkages are the most important.

Recent research has suggested that to fully understand a firm's competitive position and advantage, not only do you need to analyze the firm's value chain but also how suppliers, distributors, and other business partners fit into a "value net."[52] Because of today's increasingly tight connections among firms and suppliers, distributors, and other business partners, the strengths and weaknesses of one's partners throughout the entire value network affect a firm's competitive position and advantage.[53]

EVALUATING THE MANAGEMENT OF RESOURCES Analyzing the firm's resources and capabilities places emphasis on building and exploiting the internal strengths of the company.[54] So, managers should develop valuable capabilities and use them to provide products and services to customers that are superior in value. These capabilities might be in technology, marketing, or another area of importance in the industry. Critical issues regard how managers obtain and bundle resources to develop capabilities, and how they then leverage those capabilities.[55] This suggests that managers should invest in strategic resources that have special value.[56] For example, in professional service firms, such as law and accounting firms, managers should acquire the very best lawyers and accountants available in the labor market.[57] Managers have to deploy the resources in the firm's resource portfolio.[58] Usually managers have to combine different resources to create a capability. For example, a capability to manufacture a product combines physical resources, such as plant and equipment, technology, and human capital.

Resources must be in a continual state of development. Some refer to this as *dynamic capabilities.*[59] As a final step, managers need to leverage the capabilities that they build in order to use the strategy formulated to earn above-average returns.[60] Some of the capabilities developed may become core competencies for the company.

A **core competence** is an interrelated set of activities that can deliver competitive advantage, both short-term and long-term. Competencies are "core" when they (1) provide access to a wide variety of markets, (2) significantly contribute to perceived customer benefits of the end products or services, and (3) are difficult for competitors to imitate.[61] As an example, Honda believes that one of its core competencies is the technology behind its manufacture of combustion engines. First, combustion engines have the potential to apply to a wide variety of markets and products. Honda uses its technology in producing motorcycles, cars, scooters, lawn mowers, snow blowers, small electric generators, and other items. Second, customers value the performance of the combustion engines in these products. For example, better combustion can result in significantly better acceleration in cars and motorcycles. Third, combustion technology is hard to imitate. This is partly why Honda moved its engines into various car racing leagues such as Indy and even Formula One.

Integrating Internal and External Analyses

Although a variety of tools and techniques can help integrate the internal and external analyses, we focus on one of the most well-known and enduring approaches, SWOT analysis.

A **SWOT analysis** approach to integrate the separate analyses requires managers to consider their firm's strengths (S), and weaknesses (W), along with opportunities (O), and threats (T) for its continued operation. SWOT analysis is a basic framework for integrating the results of the analyses that guide the formulation of an appropriate strategy. In conducting a SWOT analysis, the firm should identify and evaluate its strengths and weaknesses. In doing so, understanding how to manage resources and core competencies can be of great help. Alternatively, managers can use the value chain framework previously discussed to analyze the firm's strengths and weaknesses. For example, what parts of the value chain does the firm do well, such as sourcing and marketing? What does it perform poorly, such as customer service or public relations?

The next step in the SWOT analysis focuses on the external environment. First, identifying the opportunities for the firm is important. For example, what products or businesses are about to enter the growth stage? What countries have conditions conducive to the growth of particular products or businesses? Are there new products that could become substitutes for the firm's products or new entrants into the market that could constitute serious threats?

The important insights of a SWOT analysis come after comparing and matching the organization's strengths and weaknesses and the environment's opportunities and threats. For example, Wal-Mart currently has many international opportunities. Wal-Mart's strengths include the ability to acquire, distribute, and sell large volumes of products to customers at low prices. However, as a result of its strong focus on the U.S. market, very few Wal-Mart managers have experience or knowledge of foreign markets. Fortunately for Wal-Mart, few competitors can capture immediately the new international opportunities that exist; however. Wal-Mart must pursue international expansion opportunities because French discount retailer Carrefour and major U.K-based retailer Marks & Spencer are also expanding internationally. Wal-Mart has responded to international opportunities. In 2010, Wal-Mart had more than 8,400 stores in 15 countries serving approximately 200 million customers per week. Wal-Mart knows that if an opportunity to make money exists in these foreign markets, a competitor will seek it out. To effectively respond, Wal-Mart has used partners with knowledge of specific international markets, developed managers internally, hired people who can help it expand internationally, and sometimes acquired existing operations in various countries.

Setting Strategic Objectives

Unless an organization translates its strategic intent and mission into specific performance goals, they will remain statements of good intentions and unrealized achievements. Furthermore, an analysis of the environment is an academic exercise unless the implications find their way into strategic objectives. **Strategic objectives** translate the strategic intent and mission of the firm into concrete and measurable goals. Setting strategic objectives is a critical step in the strategic management

core competence
an interrelated set of activities that can deliver competitive advantage in the short term and into the future

SWOT analysis
an analysis of the firm's strengths, weaknesses, opportunities, and threats (SWOT) to its continued operation

strategic objectives
objectives that turn the strategic intent and mission of a firm into concrete and measurable goals

process because it facilitates a firm's ability to (1) allocate resources appropriately, (2) reach a shared understanding of priorities, (3) delegate responsibilities, and (4) hold people accountable for results.[62] Specifically, strategic objectives might address any of the following issues:

- Revenue growth
- Profitability
- Customer satisfaction
- Market share
- Financial returns (for example, return on equity, return on assets)
- Technological leadership
- Cash flow
- Operating efficiency (for example, costs per unit, expense per employee)

It is important to note that strategic objectives differ from other performance objectives in one fundamental way: Strategic objectives are longer-term in nature,. They are not yearly objectives or goals. They represent targets the company aims for over the long term (typically five years or more). Although setting strategic objectives is critical, much of the time managers actually spend on strategic management is taken up in the subsequent steps of the process. These involve analyzing the organization's internal environment, formulating a strategy, developing an implementation plan, and monitoring the results.

The Strategic Management Process: Formulating a Strategy

There are at least three levels of strategy—corporate, business-level or competitive strategy, and functional or unit strategy.[63] The corporate-level strategy determines what business or businesses the firm wishes to operate. In other words, this level of strategy determines the markets in which the firm will compete.[64] The business-level strategy determines how a firm will compete in each of these markets.[65] Unit-level strategies focus on the operations of each function or unit and their contribution to help the firm achieve a competitive advantage. While all levels of strategy are important, the most important for achieving a competitive advantage is the business-level strategy.[66] This is the focus of our analysis.

In many ways, the essence of formulating a competitive strategy is determining how the company is going to compete and achieve its strategic objectives, its mission, and ultimately its strategic vision. Next, we explain a set of generic strategies for achieving a competitive advantage.

Generic Strategies for Obtaining a Competitive Advantage

The two most-discussed generic strategies pertain to cost leadership and differentiation.[67]

COST LEADERSHIP STRATEGY In the **cost leadership strategy,** a firm competes by striving to be the lowest-cost provider of a product or service. Usually firms using this strategy charge slightly less than industry-average prices. To the extent a firm has lower costs than its competitors (for example, cost leadership) and can command prices similar to its competitors, it can achieve above-average profits.

For a USB drive manufacturer to obtain above-average returns using a cost leadership strategy requires that it have lower costs than the industry average (for example, $10 per unit versus the industry average of $15) and provide the quality product that allows the firm to charge near the industry average price (for example, $20). In this case, the firm would make a profit of $10 instead of the industry average of $5. It is important to understand that the cost leadership strategy does not necessarily imply price *leadership,* that is, offering the lowest price. For example, if the cost leader had costs of $10 per disk but also charged the lowest price ($15), it would earn average returns (that is, the industry average of $5) per product sold. However, if its product quality was equal to competitors' products, it would likely sell many more products at that price and gain a large market share. Thus, the profit margin on each product does not fully project the value of a particular strategy.

There are a variety of means to achieve cost leadership. The use of special technology has become a common means. For example, managers might invest in the latest technology to

cost leadership strategy
a strategy that involves being the lowest-cost producer of a product or provider of a service while charging only slightly less than industry average prices

reduce defects and increase the production "yield" (percentage of good chips manufactured), thereby reducing the average cost per chip. Managers can also gain cost leadership through economies of scale. For example, increasing overall output across the firm's factories can reduce cost per unit manufactured. Amazon.com has tried to achieve economies of scale (with better financial results more recently than at first) by selling more products through its existing sales channel, its Web site.

The Mexican company Cemex has used technology in a traditionally low-tech business to help it achieve a cost leadership position at home and in international markets as well. Executives at Cemex use information technology to improve efficiency and performance. To both reduce costs and use their assets more efficiently and effectively, executives use computers and global positioning system receivers in every cement truck to achieve more efficient routing and more precise delivery times. Previously, any number of problems, including bad weather and traffic, could delay deliveries. Combining precise information about the trucks' locations with plant output and customer orders, managers can calculate more precisely which truck it should use and how to reroute trucks if necessary. The system allows Cemex's managers to accurately direct trucks to be within 20 minutes of their delivery time instead of the more typical three hours.

The firm's advanced internal information systems have allowed Cemex to expand beyond the borders of Mexico. For example, Cemex operates in more than 50 countries worldwide. And, the company produces approximately 97 million metric tons of concrete annually.[68]

differentiation strategy
a strategy to gain competitive advantage by making a product or service different from those of its competitors

DIFFERENTIATION STRATEGY Managers pursuing a **differentiation strategy** seek to make their product or service different from those of competitors on dimensions their customers value. Achieving differentiation allows them to command a premium price.[69] If managers can also keep costs at approximately the industry average, the premium price will allow the firm to earn above-average profits. For example, assume that a USB drive manufacturer was able to offer greater memory without substantially increasing the costs of manufacturing the disks and, as a consequence, could command a premium price (say, $22.50 instead of $20) but keep its costs near the industry average of $15. In this case, the firm would make a profit of $7.50 per disk instead of the industry average of $5. Any number of characteristics might provide the basis for differentiation.

There are a variety of ways to differentiate products and services—style, quality, reliability, speed, fashion, durability, and so on. The key is to add differentiation that customers (or, at least, an important segment of customers) value at a cost that produces a superior margin. In other words, the cost increase to add the differentiation has to be less than the price premium customers will pay for the differentiation. If it costs 20 percent more to make a product more reliable, but customers will only pay 20 percent more for this differentiation, it will not generate above-average profits.

Starbucks is known for charging a premium price for its coffee. To do so, it has special means of differentiating the product it provides customers. In particular, it differentiates the flavor of its coffee by buying premium coffee beans and using a specially formulated roasting process. In this way, it differentiates the product through specific characteristics of the product. Yet, Starbucks also differentiates what it provides to the customer in other ways. Starbucks's executives refer to it as the "experience." The intent is to provide excellent service to customers. So, it trains service providers well and rewards them for providing high-quality service. Finally, because of the quality coffee, excellent service, and pleasant atmosphere in Starbucks' stores, Starbucks' brand has value as well. So, Starbucks differentiates through its product, service, experience, and brand reputation.[70] Some of the differentiation comes from product characteristics (the flavor of the coffee), and other dimensions of the differentiation come from related but less direct factors (the Starbucks experience and its brand reputation).

Firms seeking to differentiate their products often invest in research and develop and emphasize the importance of learning new capabilities in order to stay ahead of their competition. However, the firms must also have the capability to exploit the knowledge they gained and the innovative products they developed. Thus, they have to distribute their products effectively and convince customers of the valuable characteristics of new products introduced to the market.[71] Yet, firms known for differentiating their products tend to attract competitors trying to imitate, or differentiate, their own products in similar locations.[72] Because of this fact, firms must not only "run harder and differently than their competitors, they must also run smarter."[73]

To be successful with a differentiation strategy, firms must continuously search for market opportunities and develop new products to exploit those opportunities.[74] To do so often requires firms to be bold and innovative in all areas of their business.[75] That is, they must simultaneously search for new opportunities and take actions (innovate) to gain and sustain competitive advantages.[76]

STRATEGIC SCOPE A firm can limit the scope of its strategy (its **strategic scope**) by focusing on a specific segment of customers. Although the restriction reduces the total volume and revenue the firm can obtain from a product, it does not necessarily affect its ability to earn above-average returns. For example, Ferrari differentiates its product based on style and performance and focuses on a very narrow segment of customers (not many people can afford a car that costs more than $300,000). A narrow scope strategy can also be applied to cost leadership. To the extent that the cost leader can provide products or services sufficiently valuable to command prices near the industry average for some targeted segment of customers, it can achieve above-average profits. Thus, firms can follow a *focused differentiation strategy* or a *focused cost leadership strategy.*

To succeed when pursuing a **focus strategy,** there must be significant differences among the firm's targeted customers or among geographical segments of its customers. A **customer segment** is essentially a group of customers who share similar preferences or place a similar value on product features. For example, in selling cars, clear segments exist. Some people value gas mileage while others value performance. Thus, manufacturers of a high-performance sports car focus on a different segment of customers from those who prefer small economy cars. Geographical segments may also be a factor. For example, customers in different locations may prefer different product features: In southern locales, people demand more cars with air conditioning. In northern locales, they demand more four-wheel drive vehicles to cope with snow. Customers in hot and humid climates prefer clothes made with cotton while those in drier and cooler climates prefer clothes made with wool.

Commonly, firms that follow a focus strategy are more likely to make only incremental improvements in their products over time.[77] But, managers pursuing any one of the four generic strategies must understand that a current competitive advantage may be obsolete in the near future. Firms that offer more products in a particular market segment have higher survival rates. They reduce their risks by offering more product variations.[78] Regardless, to have a sustainable competitive advantage, managers must continually build a series of temporary competitive advantages, replacing old ones with new ones.

Many industries require differentiation for a firm to be a major competitor as explained in A Manager's Challenge, "Differentiation Is a Continuous Strategy." If firms do not continue to differentiate their products in ways that consumers value, they will lose market share and experience many resulting problems. This is shown in the dramatic decline of Blockbuster, the problems currently being experienced by Campbell Soup, and the general demise of the airline industry. In an effort to stay ahead of competition and maintain its competitive advantage in its special market niche, Ferrari is changing how it designs its luxury autos. We will have to evaluate Ferrari in a few years to judge the success of its efforts. It appears to be successful, though. However, we will need to observe Merck over the long term to see if its strategies are sustainable.

Other Generic Strategies

There are at least two other important "generic" strategies that managers can use to gain a competitive advantage—an integrated differentiation-cost leadership strategy and a multipoint competition strategy. We examine each in turn.

INTEGRATED DIFFERENTIATION-COST LEADERSHIP STRATEGY An **integrated differentiation-cost leadership strategy** consists of a set of actions designed to differentiate the product in the marketplace while simultaneously maintaining a low-cost position relative to competitors. This strategy is difficult to develop and implement effectively because some of the objectives of both strategies often conflict with one another. For example, achieving differentiation may require substantial investments in R&D to develop innovative products and in advertising to inform the market of the benefits of new products. It is difficult to achieve economies of scale when continuously introducing new products to the market. Additionally, a cost leadership strategy often emphasizes efficient manufacturing, making retooling to produce new products a challenge.

---

strategic scope
the scope of a firm's strategy or breadth of focus

focus strategy
a strategy that targets a particular market segment. The strategy may be a focused cost leadership strategy or a focused differentiation strategy

customer segment
a group of customers who have similar preferences or place similar value on product features

integrated differentiation-cost leadership strategy
a set of actions designed to differentiate the firm's product in the marketplace while simultaneously maintaining a low-cost position relative to its competitors

A MANAGER'S CHALLENGE

CHANGE

Differentiation Is a Continuous Strategy

Firms that follow any strategy must continuously update or change it in order to maintain a competitive advantage. Consider Blockbuster, for example. Blockbuster is in a fight to survive in 2010, and many analysts predict it will fail. What happened to the former industry leader of movie rentals? We can answer this question with another question. Why would anyone want to go to a store to rent a movie, drive home and watch it and then, within the next few days, return the movie to the store? The answer is "almost no one," when they can sit at home and order movies through the mail or order electronically through their cable or satellite systems. In other words, how did Blockbuster ignore Netflix and video-on-demand?

Campbell Soup was the market leader in the U.S. soup market for many years. But, its sales of soup have suffered in recent years. And, analysts predict that the company's sales will grow only two percent in 2010 and three percent in 2011. In the recession in 2009, it suffered a decline in sales even though industry sales grew by five percent during the same period. What happened? Essentially, the company managers were asleep at the wheel. For example, Campbell's began development to make its soups more nutritious. These efforts extended to its line of Chunky soups, which had not been changed in ten years. The firm is following a wiser strategy to enter the Chinese and Russian markets in an effective way. For example, it has done considerable market research in Russia and based on it, Campbell's developed a broth product that Russians could use as a base in making their own soups. Major portions of soup are consumed in China and Russian but most of the soup is made at home. In 2011, Campbell's intends to introduce 14 different soups available in the Russian markets. Campbell's sales in international markets are increasing but they represent only 20 percent of the company's sales. Campbell's must move quickly or analysts predict that it may become extinct.

Ferrari, the ultimate in luxury automobiles, is concerned about maintaining its special differentiation and competitive advantage in its niche market. It has always relied on the highly respected design firm, Pininfarina, to design its new autos. However, in 2010, Ferrari appointed an internal chief of design. The intent of the company is to ensure its market leadership with the special designed autos. These autos have to be special for individuals to pay more than $300,000 for one.

Finally, the airline industry has been suffering for years. Very few airlines have found a way to differentiate

Campbell's soup was the market leader in the United States for many years, but analysts predict that the company will experience slow growth for the foreseeable future.

the service they provide to customers. Southwest Airlines and JetBlue provide low-price service but also add unique forms of service that most customers like. But airlines such as United, Delta, American, and Continental are rarely able to differentiate their services and few of them are profitable, especially in recessionary economies. After suffering from major net losses for several years, Continental agreed to be acquired by United. It is unlikely that the new merged airline to be named United will be more successful. In fact, their stated purpose for the merger is to gain economies of scope. This might lower the new airline's costs a little but it will do little to differentiate the service provided to consumers.

We conclude that many firms fail to differentiate their products and services. And, even many of those who successfully differentiate often quit developing new and differentiated products and services. Thus, they eventually decline and may even go out of existence as competitors take their market share away with new differentiated and valuable products for the consumers.

Sources: J. Jannarone, "Change Stirring at Campbell Soup," *Wall Street Journal,* May 17, 2010, http://online.wsj.com; "Continental Name Change: So Long, Proud Bird," *Wall Street Journal,* May 3, 2010, http://blog.wsj.com; M. Boyle, "Campbell's: Not About to Let the Soup Cool," *BusinessWeek,* April 26, 2010, http://www.businessweek.com; D. Gardner, "Avoiding Corporate Death Spirals in a Sea of Change," *Fast Company,* March 22, 2010, http://www.fastcompany.com; P. Patton, "New Design Chief Hire May Signal Change for Ferrari," *New York Times,* January 14, 2010, http://wheelas.blogs.nytimes.com.

Michael Porter once recommended against such a strategy, referring to it as "stuck in the middle"—firms trying to achieve both are likely to do neither and become stuck in the middle. Yet the globally competitive landscape increasingly requires that firms build high-quality and unique products of value and do so with an efficient cost structure. In some industries, firms are unable to survive without doing so. Having access to global markets and using sophisticated information technology can help firms achieve economies of scale and recoup major R&D investments, making this strategy feasible. Target uses this strategy by building a strong, distinctive brand for quality goods while competing with other retailers, such as Wal-Mart, that focus on low costs.[79]

MULTIPOINT COMPETITION STRATEGY A **multipoint competition strategy** involves competing with firms across markets by using strengths in one market to overcome weaknesses in another.[80] The competition can occur across product markets, geographic markets, or both. For example, at one time UPS was the market leader in ground shipping and delivery whereas FedEx was the market leader in overnight delivery. However, UPS entered the overnight delivery market, and FedEx bought trucks and other ground shipping assets to compete in that market. Thus, they compete with each other in both markets and also compete in many geographic markets, domestic and international. Recently, they have engaged in fierce competition in China in both service markets. UPS has also been gaining market share by becoming a logistics company and making value chain activities, particularly for small- and medium-sized businesses operating in foreign markets.[81] Yet, multimarket competition can be fierce and harm the competitive outcomes of firms. For example, research has shown that competing against firms in multiple markets causes firms harm in the quality of services offered to customers. Such firms are in danger of losing their competitive advantage.[82]

> **multipoint competition strategy**
> a strategy that involves competing with firms across markets by using strengths in one market to overcome weaknesses in another market.

The Strategic Management Process: Strategy Implementation

After formulating a strategy, a manager must effectively implement it for the desired results to materialize. Some evidence indicates that an average strategy superbly implemented is better than a great strategy poorly implemented.[83] Consequently, strategy implementation is at least as important as strategy formulation.

One strategy implementation framework popular in past years was developed by a well-known strategy consulting firms, McKinsey Consulting. The framework is called the Seven S approach. About 20 years ago, McKinsey discovered that when many of its clients implemented the strategic plans that it recommended, clients' performance often declined. Essentially, McKinsey discovered that the reason clients were doing worse when they implemented the new strategies was because their clients implemented the strategies within old structures, cultures, skills, styles, and staff. These old activities and context of the organization were inconsistent with the new strategy. So, the new strategy often was ineffective. The key to successful strategy implementation is having an internal organization that is consistent with and supportive of the strategy.[84]

If the strategy calls for entering new product or geographic markets, firms can choose to do so organically, through acquisitions, or by using strategic alliances. Organic entries involve developing the new products internally (this requires a strong R&D unit) or establishing operations in new locations, often referred to as Greenfield ventures. But, in some markets, acquisitions may be more attractive as a means of entry.[85] For example, even Wal-Mart has used acquisitions to enter or expand in some foreign markets. Acquisitions not only provide immediate access to new markets, they also provide instant knowledge about these markets.[86] Perhaps one of the most popular and common approaches to entering new markets (and obtaining reliable sources of supplies) is strategic alliances. Although popular, alliances are not easy to manage and are not always successful.[87] However, they can be successful when balanced with the firm's own internal development and an alliance partner from which the firm can learn or gain access to valuable resources.[88]

In A Manager's Challenge, "A New Strategy at Home Depot," it explains how Bob Nardelli attempted to change the firm's strategy from differentiation to an integrated differentiation-cost leadership strategy. However, neither was accomplished effectively so Home Depot appeared to be "stuck in the middle." Nardelli emphasized managing costs through centralizing decision making

A MANAGER'S CHALLENGE

CHANGE

A New Strategy at Home Depot: Trying to Recapture a Competitive Advantage

In recent years, Home Depot has made several strategic changes. In 2007, it also changed its executive leadership. The company and CEO Bob Nardelli "mutually" agreed that he would resign. Institutional shareholders called for Home Depot's top executives and board members to be held accountable for manipulating stock options and for the sluggish stock price in an otherwise positive stock market. Nardelli's resignation from Home Depot highlighted the company's failure to properly manage the dissatisfaction of shareholders.

Under Nardelli's leadership, Home Depot had developed a strategic plan to improve the firm's financial performance following a slowdown in sales and a slump in the company's stock price. Some of the initiatives of the plan included reorganizing management so that Nardelli had more direct involvement in the company's retail business. A layer of management was removed that previously had distanced him from the day-to-day operations. Nardelli also eliminated a sizable number of full-time positions and replaced them with part-time staff to help reduce costs.

Nardelli also took major actions to increase the efficiency of Home Depot's operations. For example, he invested $1 billion to centralize the control of Home Depot's information technology. To help generate the desired data, it implemented self-checkout aisles and inventory management systems. He implemented a military management model, which was a key part of the move to reshape Home Depot into a more centralized organization. Unfortunately, the organization never fully embraced Nardelli's leadership style. Many Home Depot employees could not embrace his military-style leadership and resented the replacement of many thousands of full-time store workers with legions of part-time employees. Some of their managers describe a demoralized staff and say a "culture of fear" caused customer services to wane. As a result, Home Depot lost its former entrepreneurial culture along with its focus on the customer.

The new management team at Home Depot has made major changes. Leaders kept many of Nardelli's changes to improve efficiency but tried to reenergize the culture and focus on the customer. They sold off the wholesale supply business and implemented additional efficiency moves, such as the actions taken to reduce energy use. The goal is to reduce energy usage by 20 percent. They have already reduced it by 16 percent in the last six years. The reductions to date have saved the company money and reduced an amount of energy used equal to that needed to operate 203,000 homes for one year. The Home Depot managerial team also implemented a new supply chain system that increased efficiency while simultaneously helping the firm increase sales.

Perhaps the most important moves are those designed to improve customer satisfaction. Under Nardelli's leadership, customer satisfaction was the lowest of all competitors, allowing Lowes, its chief competitor, to gain market share at Home Depot's expense. Marvin Ellison, who was appointed Home Depot's executive vice president of U.S. stores, said store managers now focus on three goals: clean warehouses, well-stocked shelves, and the highest customer service. CFO Carol Tom says Home Depot's major goal is providing everyday value to customers. This value includes having the right products at the right price and providing exceptional service to the customer in the sales process. These changes have improved customer satisfaction, sales, and Home Depot's stock price. Its sales are projected to increase in 2010 at a rate of 4 percent over 2009. A recent customer commented that her experience found sales associates to be friendly, helpful, and available when needed. As a result of these changes, Home Depot's stock price increased by 56 percent from 2009 to 2010.

Sources: M. Lindner, "Home Depot Is Still A Fixer Upper," *CNNMoney,* May 21, 2010, http://www.cnnmoney.com; M. Hincha-Ownby, "Home Depot Shrinks Its Energy Bill," *Forbes,* March 11, 2010, http://www.forbes.com; G. Colvin, "Renovating Home Depot," *CNNMoney,* August 20, 2009, http://www.cnnmoney.com; J. McGregor, "Marvin Ellison: Home Depot's Mr. Fixit?" *BusinessWeek,* May 7, 2009, http://www.businessweek.com; A. Wardin, "Home Depot Unveils Shake-Up," *Financial Times,* October 13, 2006, http://www.ft.com,; J. Politi, "Company Failed to Quell Shareholder Anger," *Financial Times,* January 3, 2007, http://www.ft.com; B. Grow, "Out at Home Depot," *BusinessWeek,* January 15, 2007, http://www.businessweek.com; J. Creswell and M. Barbaro, "Home Depot Ousts Chief," *International Herald Tribune,* January 4, 2007, http://www.iht.com.

Managerial Challenges from the Front Line

The Rest of the Story

Rick Prichett continued to pursue his goal and eventually succeeded. Although he was not able to found an independent new community bank, he became the regional president of Houston North Markets Spirit of Texas Bank. Through the agreement his investors also realized their financial goals. This bank also has several branch bank operations in other communities in the region. So, it represents a major effort and the response to the new community bank by customers in the community has been very positive.

Prichett's original strategy had to change because of institutions in the external environment of banks (federal regulators). Prichett adapted by making at least two major changes in his strategy. Because of his strategic flexibility and his capability to navigate in a challenging environment, Prichett was successful. In fact, Prichett applied his motto of "don't blink". He also used the knowledge he had gained from his education, prior business experience in banking, and life experiences to accomplish his goal. As a result, he now leads a successful regional community bank and applies his management philosophy. Prichett's experience suggests how managers can succeed even in very challenging environments.

and replacing full-time staff in the stores with part-time employees. But, these actions reduced the entrepreneurial actions and, thus, decreased the differentiation. They also lost the customer focus. As such, these actions allowed competitors such as Lowe's to increase their share of the market at Home Depot's expense. The new leaders of Home Depot who replaced Nardelli and his management team made several changes. Importantly, they increased the consumer focus and with a strong store management system began to regain some market share. They continue to increase efficiencies and thus control costs. But, Home Depot is now winning back customers.

Monitoring and Evaluating the Strategy's Implementation

The final step in the strategic management process is evaluation. Evaluation and feedback can improve the performance of individuals and also enhance the organization's performance. When a small number of managers are responsible for the organization's strategic, tactical, or operational objectives, their individual performance evaluations can often provide a rough indication of how the organization is doing. If the individual's personal objectives are tied directly to the firm's operational objectives, and he or she is meeting or exceeding all goals, the organization as a whole is likely meeting its operational objectives.

Most organizations carry out annual or even quarterly organizational performance evaluations. Typically, the strategic results of these evaluations are given to the more senior executives, and the operational results are disseminated principally to lower-level managers. Similar to individual feedback, a company performs an organizational performance evaluation to reinforce efforts that have contributed to the desired results and to correct those that have not.

Summary

- Fundamentally, the objective of strategic management is to determine, create, and maintain competitive advantage. A competitive advantage is the ability of a firm to provide value to customers that exceeds what competitors can provide. It is created by having and managing resources to provide goods and services that provide superior value, and that are rare, difficult to imitate, and nonsubstitutable.
- The strategic management process begins with the development of the strategic vision and mission for the organization. After establishing these, the organization should analyze its external environment and internal resources. The results of these analyses help to identify the organization's strengths and weaknesses and the opportunities and threats in the external

environment. The strategic objectives are developed and the strategy is formulated to achieve the objectives. Finally, the strategy is implemented.

■ Analyzing the firm's external environment includes examining the general environment and the company's industry and competitor environment. The general environment consists of sociocultural, technological, economic, political-legal, and global forces. Analyzing the industry and competitor environment focuses on the five forces identified by Michael Porter. Three of the five forces (the nature of rivalry, new entrants, and substitutes) involve competitors; the other two forces are customers and suppliers.

■ A comprehensive internal analysis of the firm's resources can be accomplished using the value chain. The value chain consists of a set of key activities that directly produce or support the production of a firm's products and service offered to customers. Porter separates the internal components of a firm into five primary activities and four support activities. The primary activities are those directly involved in the creation of a product or service and distributing it to the customer. By contrast, support activities facilitate the creation of the product or service and its transfer to the customer.

■ A SWOT analysis (with *SWOT* standing for strengths, weaknesses, opportunities, and threats) can be used to integrate and interpret the results of the internal and external analyses. The SWOT analysis leads to the establishment of the firm's strategic objectives and the formulation of its strategy.

■ Setting strategic objectives is a critical step in the strategic management process because it facilitates a firm's ability to (1) allocate resources appropriately, (2) reach a shared understanding of priorities, (3) delegate responsibilities, and (4) hold people accountable for results.

■ The business-level strategies, from which the firm can select include cost leadership, differentiation, focused cost leadership, focused differentiation, integrated differentiation-cost leadership, and a multipoint competitive strategy. The choice of strategy depends on market opportunities, competitors' actions, and the firm's resources and capabilities. The integrated strategy has been facilitated by globalization and technology and simultaneously sometimes necessitated by global competition. The multipoint strategy allows firms to compete with others across product and geographic markets.

■ After formulating a strategy, managers must effectively implement it for the desired results to materialize. Oftentimes, in addition to organic growth, firms use strategic alliances and acquisitions to enter new markets. After implementation, managers need to monitor the outcomes to see if adjustments are necessary in the strategy or its implementation.

Key Terms

above-average returns   85
competitive advantage   83
core competence   96
cost leadership strategy   97
customer segment   99
entry barriers   92
differentiation strategy   98
focus strategy   99
general environment   87

industry and competitor forces   90
institutional forces   89
integrated differentiation-cost
   leadership strategy   99
mission statement   86
multipoint competition
   strategy   101
physical forces   89
primary activities   93

sociocultural forces   87
strategic objectives   96
strategic scope   99
strategic vision   85
substitution   85
superior value   83
support activities   93
SWOT analysis   96
value chain   93

Review Questions

1. What is a competitive advantage, and what are the characteristics of a sustainable advantage?

2. What is the strategic management process? What are its major components?

3. How is an environmental analysis used to formulate a strategy?

4. What are the five dimensions of the general environment? Please explain each.

5. How do each of Porter's "five forces" affect the industry and competitor environment?
6. How can you use a value chain analysis to analyze the firm's internal resources? What are primary and secondary activities?
7. What is a SWOT analysis and how does it facilitate selecting the best strategy?
8. When is each generic business-level strategy most appropriate for use?
9. What are the strategic actions useful for implementing a strategy? Please explain each.

Assessing Your Capabilities

1. Think about, collect information on, and identify your college's primary strengths and weaknesses, then identify the major opportunities and threats related to its external environment.
2. Select a classmate and compare your lists. How are they different? If there are differences, why did they occur? You should also check to see if your school has a strategic plan online. If so, in your opinion, does the strategy match well with the strengths, weaknesses, opportunities, and threats your college faces?
3. What did you learn by trying to identify your college's strengths, weaknesses, opportunities, and threats? What would you do differently the next time you conduct such an analysis?

Team Exercise

After forming teams of three to five people, analyze the following information and answer the questions at the end.

You are the top management team of senior managers in a small company that provides software and technical training to the employees of larger companies. Your firm has not really had a formal strategy (let alone a statement of strategic vision or a mission statement). The company started when a group of friends who did freelance training decided to pool their company contacts and hire some additional help to meet the demand for their services, which exceeded their collective productivity. The company is now three years old and has a total of 35 employees, most of whom are trainers.

The management team meets to discuss the firm's future and strategy. You suggest that the team conduct a simple SWOT analysis to inform the discussions. The following is the collective group's assessment:

Strengths

- The management team has done a good job of hiring people who have both solid technical capabilities and good teaching skills.
- There is a good pool of technical talent from the local university.
- The firm has a strong relationship with a few of the larger companies in the area.

Weaknesses

- There has been some inconsistent pricing of training for clients based on case-by-case negotiations and relationships. Some contracts have high profit margins and some have low profit margins.
- Employees do not fully understand how the value provided to customers by the company compares to the value provided by competitors.
- The firm does not have a strategy for competing in the market and capturing future market share.

Opportunities

- Demand seems to be reasonably strong and growing.
- There is potential for expanding geographically because some current customers have offices in other cities and have inquired about providing training in those locations. However, they do not want to pay the travel and lodging costs associated with sending trainers to those sites.

Threats

- Some of the large "temp" agencies, like Manpower and Kelly, which do a lot of training of their temps, are beginning to market their training capabilities to their clients. The prices these firms are quoting are about 15 percent higher than your firm's prices. Customers are somewhat price-sensitive.
- The type of training your firm provides is difficult to differentiate from that provided by competitors. The real difference is not in the content of the training (everyone covers the same topics) but in how well trainers do the job and how much the students enjoy the experience and remember what they learned.

Your team should answer the following questions and be prepared to defend its answers.

1. Based on this SWOT analysis, what is your assessment of how the firm can provide superior value to customers and achieve a competitive advantage?
2. What additional internal or external assessment does the company need to identify the best strategy of these additional assessments? What are the top two priorities and why?
3. What should the firm's strategy be? Should it try to expand geographically?

After years of successful growth, Blockbuster, the world's largest video rental chain, separated from its parent company, Viacom. Video and DVD rental sales have decreased markedly, and new technology, including digital movies on demand, threatens Blockbuster's original core business. To survive, Blockbuster needs a new strategy.

David P. Cook, a young entrepreneur, created the first Blockbuster video rental store. To capitalize on customer dissatisfaction with mom-and-pop video rental stores, which offered a limited selection of titles, short hours, and minimal customer service, Cook created the now-familiar video superstore: the large, brightly lit Blockbuster stores. He provided an environment where customers could browse through thousands of titles including classics, foreign films, musicals, westerns, dramas, and animated films. Blockbuster expanded rapidly and broadly through acquisitions and by opening new stores. Eventually, almost 50 percent of its stores were franchised.

Blockbuster had tremendous success, for several years but changes in the entertainment industry and new technology led to increased competition (such as satellite TV and digital-on-demand technology). Products such as TiVo and Replay TV made recording and watching your own choice of movies at home an attractive option for consumers. Firms like Netflix also created strong competition. Netflix doesn't charge late fees but rather has a monthly subscriber fee and customers can check out as many movies as they want. To counter Netflix, Blockbuster started its own online service and a flat-fee subscription service. Unlike Netflix, though, the company had the overhead costs associated with 8,700 brick-and-mortar stores.

Blockbuster is currently in significant trouble. Netflix's stock price hovers around $70 per share and Blockbuster's is 30 cents per share. Blockbuster lost a total of $932 million in 2008 and 2009 and continued to lose money subsequently. Many analysts predict it will have to file for bankruptcy in the near future.

Although its recent actions may be too late, the company has made several moves to respond to competition in an attempt to recapture lost market share. For example, it signed an agreement with TiVo to bring its online OnDemand service to customers through the TiVo set-top boxes. Blockbuster has signed an agreement with major movie studios for access to popular movies for in-store and online rentals. Finally, Blockbuster is offering to rent movies on SD cards. The desire here is to compete with the popular RedBox movie kiosks.

Will Blockbuster be successful in avoiding bankruptcy and turning around its performance? It is unclear at this point. To some, it is the classic case of Schumpeter's creative destruction. Several competitors designed better systems, some using unique and new technology to better satisfy customer needs. Netflix was the original "disruptor" but a number of other competitors, such as Redbox, followed with additional new ideas and Blockbuster was very slow to respond.

Questions

1. How successful do you predict that Blockbuster's recent moves (agreements with TiVo and major movie studios) will be? Please explain.
2. Can Blockbuster avoid bankruptcy and survive? Justify your response.
3. Should Blockbuster increase its entry into international markets where digital-on-demand technology is not yet available?
4. In what other ways can Blockbuster try to redefine its core business and pursue other options in entertainment or home electronics? What strategy would you recommend to save the business?

Sources: R. Grover, "The Last Picture Show at Blockbuster?" *BusinessWeek,* April 26, 2010, http://www.businessweek.com; "Blockbuster Makes Payment Deals with Movie Studios," *Forbes,* April 7, 2010, http://www.forbes.com; K. Eaton, "Blockbuster Goes Online with TiVo, Apple to Save Its Business," *Fast Company,* March 26, 2010, http://www.fastcompany.com; J. Tamny, "What Blockbuster Video Can Teach Us About Economics," *Forbes,* March 22, 2010, http://www.forbes.com; C. Dannen, "Blockbuster to Rent Movies on SD Cards, But Why?" *Fast Company,* November 9, 2009, http://www.fastcompany.com; S. G. Beatty, "Viacom's Blockbuster Rethinks Strategy," *Wall Street Journal,* November 20, 1995, A1; C. Taylor, "The Movie Is in the Mail," *Time Canada,* March 18, 2002, 40; S. Diaz, "Digital Video Recorders Challenge Television-Advertisement Makers," *San Jose Mercury News,* June 13, 2002; R. A. Munarriz, "Date Netflix, Marry Amazon, Kill Blockbuster," *The Motley Fool,* February 14, 2007, http://www.fool.com;

References

1. M. A. Hitt, K. Haynes, and R. Serpa, "Strategic Leadership in the 21st Century," *Business Horizons* 53 (2010): in press.

2. M. A. Hitt, R. D. Ireland, and R. E. Hoskisson, *Strategic Management: Competitiveness and Globalization* (Cincinnati: South-Western Publishing Company, 2011).

3. M. A. Hitt, C. C. Miller, and A. Colella, *Organizational Behavior: A Strategic Approach* (Hoboken: John Wiley & Sons, 2011).

4. Hitt, Ireland, and Hoskisson, *Strategic Management*; J. Granovac and D. J. Miller, "Competitive Advantage and Performance: The Impact of Value Creation and Costliness of Imitation," *Strategic Management Journal* 30 (2009): 1192–1212.

5. H. C. Wang, J. He, and J. T. Mahoney, "Firm-specific Knowledge Resources and Competitive Advantage: The Roles of Economic- and Relationship-based Employee Governance Mechanisms," *Strategic Management Journal* 30 (2009): 1265–1285; S. L. Newbert, "Empirical Research on the Resource-based View of the Firm: An Assessment and Suggestions for Future Research," *Strategic Management Journal* 28 (2007): 121–146; D. G. Sirmon, M. A. Hitt, and R. D. Ireland, "Managing Firm Resources in Dynamic Environments to Create Value: Looking Inside the Black Box," *Academy of Management Review* 32 (2007): 273–292.

6. A. Vance and J. Wortham, "H.P. to pay $1.2 billion for Palm," *New York Times,* http://www.nytimes.com, April 29, 2010.

7. Hitt, Ireland, and Hoskisson, *Strategic Management*.

8. M. B. Lieberman and N. S. Asaba, "Why Do Firms Imitate Each Other?" *Academy of Management Review* 31 (2006): 368–385; D. M. De Carolis, "Competencies and Imitability in the Pharmaceutical Industry: An Analysis of Their Relationship with Firm Performance," *Journal of Management* 29 (2003): 27–50.

9. S. K. Ethiraj and D. H. Zhu, "Performance Effects of Imitative Entry," *Strategic Management Journal* 29 (2008): 797–817; S. K. McEvily and B. Chakravarthy, "The Persistence of Knowledge-based Advantage: An Empirical Test for Product Performance and Technological Knowledge," *Strategic Management Journal* 23 (2002): 285–305.

10. D. J. Collis and C. A. Montgomery, "Competing on Resources: Strategy in the 1990s," *Harvard Business Review* (July–August 1995): 119–128.

11. A. Enders, A. Konig, H. Hungenberg, and T. Engelbertz, "Towards an Integrated Perspective of Strategy," *Journal of Strategy and Management,* 2 (2009): 76–96.

12. V. Wong, "Godiva Goes to the Supermarket," *BusinessWeek,* October 14, 2009, http://www.businessweek.com.

13. D. Lehmberg, W. G. Rowe, R. E. White, and J. R. Phillips, "The GE Paradox: Competitive Advantage through Fungible Non-firm Specific Investment," *Journal of Managemen,* 35 (2009): 1129–1153; Sirmon, Hitt, and Ireland, "Managing Resources in Dynamic Environments to Create Value."

14. J. Kraaijenbrink, J.-C. Spender, and A. J. Groen, "The Resource-based View: A Review and Assessment of Its Critiques," *Journal of Management* 36 (2010): 349–372.

15. Hitt, Haynes, and Serpa, "Strategic Leadership"; M. A. Hitt, R. D. Ireland, and R. E. Hoskisson, *Understanding Business Strategy* (Cincinnati: Thomson South-Western, 2006).

16. R. Emmerich, "What's in a Vision?" *CMA Management* 75, no. 8 (2001): 10.

17. J. Collins and J. Porras, "Building Your Company's Vision," *Harvard Business Review* 74, no. 5 (1996): 65–77; C. Rarick and J. Vitton, "Mission Statements Make Sense," *Journal of Business Strategy* 16, no. 1 (1995): 11–12.

18. K. Andrews, *The Concept of Corporate Strategy* (Homewood: Richard Irwin, 1971); S. A. Zahra and A. P. Nielsen, "Sources of Capabilities Integration and Technology Commercialization," *Strategic Management Journal* 23 (2002): 377–398; V. K. Garg,

B. K. Walters, and R. I. Priem, "Chief Executive Scanning Emphases Environmental Dynamism and Manufacturing Firm Performance," *Strategic Management Journal* 24 (2003): 725–744.

19. E. Zajac, M. S. Kraatz, and R. Bresser, "Modeling the Dynamics of Strategic Fit: A Normative Approach to Strategic Change," *Strategic Management Journal* 21 (2000): 429–453.

20. M. E. Porter, *Competitive Advantage* (New York: Free Press, 1985).

21. "Life Expectancy for Countries, 2009," Infoplease.com, http://www.infoplease.com, accessed May 25, 2010; M. Moynihan, *Global Consumer Demographics* (New York: Business International, 1991).

22. "Life Expectancy for Countries, 2009," Infoplease.com; *Statistical Handbook of Japan*, Statistics Bureau and Statistical Research and Training Institute, www.stat.go.jp/english/data/handbook, accessed February 11, 2006; S. Moffett, "For Ailing Japan, Longevity Takes Bite Out of Economy," *Wall Street Journal,* February 11, 2003, 1.

23. A. Sagie and Z. Aycan, "A Cross-cultural Analysis of Participative Decision-making in Organizations," *Human Relations* 56 (2003): 453–473.

24. S. P. Seithi and P. Steidlmeier, "The Evolution of Business' Role in Society," *Business and Society Review* 94 (Summer 1995): 9–12; L. L. Martins, K. A. Eddleston, and J. E. Veiga, "Moderators of the Relationship between Work-Family Conflict and Career Satisfaction," *Academy of Management Journal* 45 (2002): 399–409.

25. D. Lederman, "An International Multilevel Analysis of Product Innovation," *Journal of International Business Studies* 41 (2010): 606–619.

26. Company Web site, *WalMart Annual Report, 2010,* http://www.walmartstores.com, accessed May 28, 2010; A. Serwer, "The Next #1," *Fortune*, April 4, 2002.

27. ArcelorMittal Dofasco, "History," http://www.dofasco.ca, accessed May 27, 2010; personal communication with Dofasco senior management, 2003.

28. M. Farashahi and T. Hafsi, "Strategy of Firms in Unstable Institutional Environments," *Asia Pacific Journal of Management* 26 (2009):641–666.

29. T. R. Holcomb, R. M. Holmes, and B. L. Connelly, "Making the Most of What You Have: Managerial Ability as a Source of Resource Value Creation," *Strategic Management Journal* 30 (2009): 457–485.

30. "Glass Fibers Make Smokestacks Cleaner," *Machine Design* 67, no. 18 (1995): 123.

31. V. H. Hoffmann, T. Trautmann, and J. Hamprecht, "Regulatory Uncertainty: A Reason to Postpone Investments? Not Necessarily," *Journal of Management Studies* 46 (2009): 1227–1253.

32. S.-H. Lee and M. Makhija, "The Effect of Domestic Uncertainty on the Real Options Value of International Investments," *Journal of International Business Studies* 40 (2009): 405–420; L. E. Lopez, S. K. Kundu, and L. Ciravegna, "Born Global or Born Regional? Evidence from an Exploratory Study in the Costa Rican Software Industry," *Journal of International Business Studies* 40 (2009): 1228–1238.

33. J. E. Oxley and B. Yeung, "E-Commerce Readiness: Institutional Environment and International Competitiveness," *Journal of International Business Studies* 32 (2001): 705–723.

34. M. W. Peng, S. L. Sun, B. Pinkham, and H. Chen, "The Institution-based View as a Third Leg for a Strategy Tripod," *Academy of Management Perspectives* 23, no. 3 (August 2009): 63–81; C. M. Lau, D. K. Tse, and N. Zhou, "Institutional Forces and Organizational Culture in China: Effects on Change Schemas, Firm Commitment, and Job Satisfaction," *Journal of International Business Studies* 33 (2002): 533–550.

35. M. Porter, *Competitive Strategy: Techniques for Analyzing Industries and Competitors* (New York: Free Press, 1980).
36. W. S. DeSarbo, R. Grewal, and J. Wind, "Who Competes Against Whom? A Demand-based Perspective for Identifying and Representing Asymmetric Competition," *Strategic Management Journal,* 27 (2006): 101–129; S. Slater and E. Olson. "A Fresh Look at Industry and Market Analysis," *Business Horizons* 45, no. 1 (2002): 15–22.
37. R. L. Priem, "A Consumer View of Value Creation," *Academy of Management Review,* 32 (2007): 219–235.
38. C. C. de Fontenay and J. S. Gans, "A Bargaining Perspective on Strategic Outsourcing and Supply Competition," *Strategic Management Journal* 27 (2006): 819–839.
39. R. D. Ireland, M. A. Hitt, and D. Vaidyanath, "Alliance Management as a Source of Competitive Advantage," *Journal of Management* 28 (2002): 413–446.
40. D. Ng, R. Westgren, and S. Sonka, "Competitive Blind Spots in an Institutional Field," *Strategic Management Journal* 21 (2009): 349–369.
41. A. Lashinsky, "The Decade of Steve: How Apple's Impervious, Brilliant CEO Transformed American Business," *Fortune,* November 23, 2009: 93–100.
42. Porter, *Competitive Advantage.*
43. Y. Yao, M. Dresner, and J. W. Palmer, "Impact of Boundary Spanning Information Technology Position in Chain on Firm Performance," *Journal of Supply Chain Management* 45, 3 (2009): 3–17.
44. D. R. Krause, S. Vachon, and R. D. Klassen, "Special Topic Forum on Sustainable Supply Chain Management: Introduction and Reflections on the Role of Purchasing Management," *Journal of Supply Chain Management* 45, no. 4 (2009): 18–25.
45. D.-J. Kamann and V. Van Nieulande, "A Four-filter Method for Outsourcing to Low-cost Countries," *Journal of Supply Chain Management* 46, no. 2 (2010): 64–79; B. T. McCann and T. B. Folta, "Demand- and Supply-side Agglomerations: Distinguishing between Fundamentally Different Manifestations of Geographic Concentration," *Journal of Management Studies* 46 (2009): 362–392.
46. G. D. Markman, P. T. Gianiodis, and P. H. Phan, "Supply-side Innovation and Technology Commercialization," *Journal of Management Studies* 46 (2009): 625–649.
47. D. Tzabbar, "When Does Scientist Recruitment Affect Techno-logical Repositioning," *Academy of Management Journal* 52 (2009): 873–896.
48. K. Z. Zhou and F. Wu, "Technological Capability, Strategic Flexibility, and Product Innovation," *Strategic Management Journal* 31 (2010): 547–561.
49. M. Makri, M. A. Hitt, and P. J. Lane, "Complementary Technologies, Knowledge Relatedness, and Invention Outcomes in High Technology Mergers and Acquisitions," *Strategic Management Journal* 31 (2010): 602–628.
50. D. G. Sirmon and M. A. Hitt, "Contingencies within Dynamic Managerial Capabilities: Interdependent Effects of Resource Investment and Deployment on Firm Performance," *Strategic Management Journal* 30 (2009): 1375–1394.
51. Y.-S. Su, E. W. K. Tsang, and M. W. Peng, "How Do Internal Capabilities and External Partnerships Affect Innovativeness?" *Asia Pacific Journal of Management* 26 (2009): 309–331.
52. D. Bovet and J. Martha, "From Supply Chain to Value Net," *Journal of Business Strategy* 21, no. 4 (2000): 24–28; D. Bovet and J. Martha, "Value Nets: Reinventing the Rusty Supply Chain for Competitive Advantage," *Strategy and Leadership* 28, no. 4 (2000): 21–26; A. Afuah, "How Much Do Your Competitors' Capabilities Matter in the Face of Technological Change?" *Strategic Management Journal* 21, (2000): 387–404.
53. J. S. Harrison, D. A. Bosse, and Robert A. Phillips, "Managing for Stakeholders, Stakeholders Utility Functions and

54. Competitive Advantage," *Strategic Management Journal* 31 (2010): 58–74.
54. J. Barney, "Looking Inside for Competitive Advantage," *Academy of Management Executive* 9, no. 4 (1995): 49–61; B. S. Teng and J. L. Cummings, "Trade-offs in Managing Resources and Capabilities," *Academy of Management Executive* 16, no. 2 (2002): 81–91; D. G. Hoopes, T. L. Madsen, and G. Walker, "Guest Editors' Introduction to the Special Issue: Why Is There a Resource-based View? Toward a Theory of Competitive Heterogeneity," *Strategic Management Journal* 24, (2003): 889–902.
55. Sirmon, Hitt, and Ireland, "Managing Resources in Dynamic Environments to Create Value."
56. D. M. De Carolis, Y. Yang, D. L. Deeds, and E. Nelling, "Weathering the Storm: The Benefit of Resources to High-technology Venture Navigating Adverse Events," *Strategic Entrepreneurship Journal* 3 (2009): 147–160.
57. M. A. Hitt, L. Bierman, K. Uhlenbruck, and K. Shimizu, "The Importance of Resources in the Internationalization of Professional Service Firms: The Good, the Bad and the Ugly," *Academy of Management Journal* 49 (2006): 1137–1157; M. A. Hitt, L. Bierman, K. Shimizu, and R. Kochhar, "Direct and Moderating Effects of Human Capital on Strategy and Performance in Human Service Firms: A Resource-based Perspective," *Academy of Management Journal* 44 (2001): 13–28.
58. D. Tan and J. T. Mahoney, "Why a Multinational Firm Chooses Expatriates: Integrating Resource-based, Agency, and Transaction Costs Perspectives," *Journal of Management Studies* 43 (2006): 457–484.
59. O. R. Malik and M. Kotabe, "Dynamic Capabilities, Government Policies, and Performance in Firms from Emerging Economies: Evidence from India and Pakistan," *Journal of Management Studies* 46 (2009): 421–450; R. Adner and C. E. Helfat, "Corporate Effects and Dynamic Managerial Capabilities," *Strategic Management Journal* 24 (2003): 1011–1025; K. Eisenhardt and J. Martin, "Dynamic Capabilities: What Are They?" *Strategic Management Journal* 21, (2000): 1105–1121.
60. H. J. Sapienza, "A Capabilities Perspective on the Effects of Early Internationalization on Firm Survival and Growth," *Academy of Management Review* 31 (2006): 914–933.
61. C. K. Prahalad and G. Hamel, "The Core Competence of the Corporation," *Harvard Business Review* 68, no. 3 (1990): 79–91.
62. P. Jarzabkowski and J. Balogun, "The Practice and Process of Delivering Integration through Strategic Planning," *Journal of Management Studies* 46 (2009): 1255–1288.
63. S. C. Abraham, *Strategic Planning: a Practical Guide for Competitive Success* (Cincinnati: Thomson South-Western, 2007).
64. Hitt, Ireland, and Hoskisson, *Strategic Management.*
65. S. Brown and K. Blackmon, "Aligning Manufacturing Strategy and Business-level Competitive Strategy in New Competitive Environments: The Case for Strategic Resonance," *Journal of Management Studies* 42 (2005): 793–815.
66. V. F. Misangyi, H. Elms, T. Greckhamer, and J. A. LePine, "A New Perspective on a Fundamental Debate: A Multilevel Approach to Industry, Corporate and Business Unit Effects," *Strategic Management Journal* 27 (2006): 571–590.
67. Porter, *Competitive Advantage*; M. Partridge and L. Perren, "Developing Strategic Direction: Can Generic Strategies Help?" *Management Accounting-London* 72, no. 5 (1994): 28–29.
68. Company Web site, *Cemex 2009 Annual Report,* http://www .cemex.com, accessed May 30 2010.
69. D. W. Voorhies, R. E. Morgan, and C. D. Autry, "Product-market Strategy and the Marketing Capabilities of the Firm: Impact on Market Effectiveness and Cash Flow Performance," *Strategic Management Journal* 30 (2009): 1310–1334.
70. Hitt, Miller, and Colella, *Organizational Behavior.*

71. A. K. Gupta, K. G. Smith, and C. E. Shalley, "The Interplay Between Exploration and Exploitation," *Academy of Management Journal* 49 (2006): 693–706.

72. L. Nachum and C. Wymbs, "Product Differentiation, External Economies, and MNE Locations Choices: M&As in Global Cities," *Journal of International Business Studies* 36 (2005): 415–434.

73. S. Voelpel, M. Leibold, E. Tekie, and G. von Krogh, "Escaping the Red Queen Effect in Competitive Strategy: Sense-testing Business Models," *European Management Journal* 23 (2005): 37–49.

74. J. A. Pearce, "How Companies Can Preserve Market Dominance After Patents Expire," *Long Range Planning* 39 (2006): 71–87.

75. G. Hamel, "Innovate Now!" *Fast Company,* December 2002, http://www.fastcompany.com.

76. M. A. Hitt, R. D. Ireland, S. M. Camp, and D. L. Sexton, *Strategic Entrepreneurship: Integrating a New Mindset* (Oxford, UK: Blackwell Publishing, 2003).

77. O. Sorenson, S. McEvily, C. R. Ren, and R. Roy, "Niche Width Revisited: Organizational Scope Behavior and Performance," *Strategic Management Journal* 27 (2006): 915–936.

78. G. Dowell, "Product Line Strategies of New Entrants in an Established Industry: Evidence from the U.S. Bicycle Industry," *Strategic Management Journal* 27 (2006): 959–979.

79. Hitt, Ireland, and Hoskisson, *Strategic Management.*

80. J. Anand, L. F. Mesquita, and R. S. Vassolo, "The Dynamics of Multimarket Competition in Exploration and Exploitation Activities," *Academy of Management Journal* 52 (2009): 802–821; L. Fuentelsaz and J. Gomez, "Multipoint Competition, Strategic Similarity, and Entry into Geographic Markets," *Strategic Management Journal* 27 (2006): 477–499.

81. T. L. Friedman, *The World Is Flat* (New York: Farrar, Straus & Giroux, 2005).

82. J. T. Prince and D. H. Simon, "Multimarket Contact and Service Quality: Evidence from On-time Performance in the U.S. Airline Industry," *Academy of Management Journal* 52 (2009): 336–354.

83. B. Quinn, *Intelligent Enterprise* (New York: Free Press, 1992); C. B. Dobni and G. Luffman, "Determining the Scope and Impact of Market Orientation Profiles on Strategy Implementation and Performance," *Strategic Management Journal* 24 (2003): 577–585; L. G. Love, R. L. Priem, and G. T. Lumpkin, "Explicitly Articulated Strategy and Firm Performance Under Alternative Levels of Centralization," *Journal of Management* 28 (2002): 611–627.

84. J. I. Galan and M. J. Sanchez-Bueno, "The Continuing Validity of the Strategy–Structure Nexus: New Findings, 1993–2003," *Strategic Management Journal* 30 (2009): 1234–1243.

85. U. Weitzel and S. Berns, "Cross-border Takeovers, Corruption, and Related Aspects of Governance," *Journal of International Business Studies* 37 (2006): 786–806.

86. K. Uhlenbruck, M. A. Hitt, and M. Semadeni, "Market Value Effects of Acquisitions Involving Internet Firms: A Resource-based Analysis," *Strategic Management Journal* 27 (2006): 899–913; M. B. Heeley, D. R. King, and J. G. Covin, "Effects of Firm R&D Investment and Environment on Acquisition Likelihood," *Journal of Management Studies* 43 (2006): 1513–1535.

87. J. J. Reuer and R. Ragozzino, "Agency Hazards and Alliance Portfolios," *Strategic Management Journal* 27 (2006): 27–43.

88. J. H. Dyer and N. W. Hatch, "Relations-specific Capabilities and Barriers to Knowledge Transfers: Creating Advantage Through Network Relationships," *Strategic Management Journal* 27 (2006): 701–719; R. J. Arend, "SME-Supplier Alliance Activity in Manufacturing: Contingent Benefits and Perceptions," *Strategic Management Journal* 27 (2006): 741–763; F. T. Rothaermel, M. A. Hitt, and L. A. Jobe, "Balancing Vertical Integration and Strategic Outsourcing: Effects on Product Portfolio, Product Success, and Firm Performance," *Strategic Management Journal* 27 (2006): 1033–1056.

5

Planning

LEARNING OBJECTIVES

After studying this chapter, you should be able to:

Define *planning* and explain its purpose.

Differentiate between strategic, tactical, and operational plans.

Describe the interrelationship between an organization's types of plans and the levels at which they are developed.

Explain the planning process.

Discuss budgeting as a planning tool.

List and explain the five characteristics of effective goals.

Courtesy of Matt Kincaid

Name: Matt Kincaid

Position: Former restaurant owner and manager and former management consultant; currently a Ph.D. student and instructor

Alma mater: Gonzaga University (BBA, MBA)

Outside work activities: Basketball, guitar, and spending time with my fiancée

First job out of school: Sold CUTCO knives for Vector Marketing Corporation

Recommended business book for reading: *Crucial Conversations*

What drives me: The idea that I can make a positive difference in the world and improve a person's life, or perhaps and hopefully, many peoples' lives.

Management style: I truly desire to be a servant leader.

Matt Kincaid grew up understanding the value of hard work—his mother had a saying painted on a rock in their home stating that "he who rolls up his sleeves seldom loses his shirt." The saying became important to Kincaid's professional success as an owner of two restaurants and in his consulting position. The company that sold Kincaid the franchise charges a franchise fee and provides market projections, marketing plans, and training to owners as to how to operate their restaurants. Kincaid depended heavily on the information the corporation gave him. Yet, the information and plans were not effective for him, requiring significant actions on his part.

Kincaid had to build brand recognition for both restaurants, requiring that he understood the markets his restaurants served, and develop aggressive marketing plans to reach his potential customers. He worked long hours (almost 100 hours a week) but was successful in both ventures. He sold his restaurant in West Lafayette, Indiana and moved back to the state of Washington where he developed his new restaurant and bar. After about a year and a half with the new venture in Washington, he was approached by a buyer and he sold the restaurant.

Kincaid then accepted a job as a consultant working for New Edge Consulting, a relatively small firm that did work for a number of *Fortune* 500 companies. The firm focused primarily on innovation and business strategy. Kincaid worked on several projects in his two years with New Edge, on topics ranging from consumer packaging to energy management. His work on these projects carried him to distant locations such as Australia, the United Kingdom, and The Netherlands.

Kincaid's work at New Edge offered a wonderful learning opportunity but there was considerable turnover among the professionals on the staff, making his time there more challenging and frustrating at times. Additionally, while he had some wonderful experiences, he still felt a little unfulfilled. He wanted to take a more holistic perspective on business and find a way to achieve his goals, one of which is to make a positive difference in many people's lives. To do so, he decided to go back to school and earn a Ph.D. Thus, he entered the doctoral program at Gonzaga University and serves as an instructor at a community college in the local area.

Kincaid estimated that he worked about 100 hours a week trying to make his businesses a success. He says he learned that he had to do his own analyses of the market and develop plans for serving it to get more customers into his restaurants. In his consulting work, he helped others learn to do the type of analyses and planning needed to be successful. Therefore, his experience as a business owner and manager helped him be a more effective consultant to other managers.

The challenge Matt Kincaid faced clearly illustrates the importance of fully analyzing your firm's market and formulating a plan to compete effectively in it. But, Kincaid had gained a significant amount of business-operation knowledge through his education, which he applied, along with hard work, to make his businesses successful. And, the experience and knowledge he gained from managing his businesses contributed to his ability as a consultant to other managers, helping them develop effective plans. Kincaid's example shows the importance of following the planning process. Planning is especially critical in highly competitive markets. It helps firms to achieve and maintain an advantage over their competitors.[1]

On one hand, if the managers of an organization or business unit fail to plan and, as a consequence, drift off-course or lose momentum, strong competitors are likely to overtake it. On the other hand, the speed of change and rapid flow of information increasingly require business plans that are flexible and dynamic. In today's world, a rigid plan can be as fatal as no plan at all. Increasingly, as a manager, you must not only be aware of local competitors but also of competitors based in other parts of the world.

Effective planning at all organizational levels can have a significant impact on the firm's performance. Without effective planning, Procter & Gamble (P&G) might have failed in its efforts to enter and compete successfully in eastern Europe and China. But, the company's activities in these markets turned out to be successful, in part, because the company's managers had a plan and regularly reevaluated and changed it. Managers need to continuously analyze and understand their external markets, and adjust their plans accordingly. Today, the instantaneous availability of information, rapid changes in economies, markets, and the political environments of countries in which firms do business affect planning efforts. Managers need to be prepared to adapt to changes that occur rapidly, no matter what their plans are.

This ability to adapt rapidly requires managers to accurately analyze their internal resources. For example, current research suggests that an organization's human capital is absolutely critical to the successful implementation of a firm's strategic plans.[2] So, managers must have the necessary human resources available in order for the firm to be successful. Certainly, the link between human capital and a firm's performance is evident at both P&G and General Electric (GE). These two companies are known for having excellent leadership development programs, such that China chose GE to help train 25 top Chinese executives each year.[3] Both companies have been high performers with GE ranked fifth and P&G ranked number 22 in the 2010 *Fortune* 500.[4]

An analysis of the organization's internal resources and external environment helps a manager determine the company's strengths, especially the organization's core competencies, along with its weaknesses and how they might affect its future plans.[5] This analysis can also identify the other resources managers will need to implement their plans and ultimately achieve their goals. Research has shown that effective analyses and planning are important to success in large firms[6] and in small- and medium-sized firms as well.[7] Says Jeff Immelt, General Electric: "Most people just assume that big companies are slow and lethargic. But if you get good processes, you can make size an advantage."[8] GE has developed an effective strategy and an excellent planning process to help implement the strategy. This chapter examines types and levels of planning along with the planning process that firms should use.

General Electric (GE) has one of the best leadership development programs of any company in the world. People from different companies around the globe go through GE's prestigious programs to learn the fine art of corporate planning and improve their managerial skills. Former GE managers are also highly sought-after in the marketplace.

An Overview of Planning

Few activities are more basic to management than deciding where the company is going and how it will get there. An organization creates **objectives** to serve as a future "end states" targeted by its managers, whereas **plans** are the means by which managers achieve the objective. **Planning,** then, is essentially a process to determine and implement actions to achieve organizational objectives. From this perspective, setting organizational objectives has to precede the development of organizational plans. Without objectives or targets, plans are of little value. Objectives help set direction, focus effort, guide behaviors, and evaluate progress.[9] We now explore the types of plans that exist, the basic planning process, and the methods for implementing plans effectively.

Types of Plans

Most organizations of any size offer more than one product or service. As a consequence, they cannot develop a single plan to cover all organizational activities; they must develop plans for multiple levels.[10] To understand the planning process for complex organizations, we need to differentiate among three types of plans (see Exhibit 5.1).[11]

STRATEGIC PLANS **Strategic plans** focus on the broad future of the organization. Incorporating both external information gathered by analyzing the company's competitive environment and the firm's internal resources, managers determine the scope of the business (products and services the firm provides) to achieve the organization's long-term objectives.[12] Research shows that the rigorous use of strategic plans is associated with superior financial performance.[13] As we explained in the previous chapter, strategic plans cover the major aspects of the organization, including its products, services, finances, technology, and human resources. Most strategic plans focus on how to achieve goals three to five years into the future.

TACTICAL PLANS **Tactical plans** translate strategic plans into specific goals for specific parts of the organization. Consequently, tactical plans often have a shorter time frame and are narrower in scope. Instead of focusing on the entire corporation, tactical plans typically affect a single business within an organization and its product lines (one or more related product lines).[14] Although tactical plans should complement the organization's overall strategic plan, they are often somewhat independent of other tactical plans. Tactical plans are developed for GE's jet engine business, for example.

OPERATIONAL PLANS **Operational plans** translate tactical plans into specific goals and actions for small units of the organization. Operational plans typically focus on the short term, usually 12 months or less. These plans are the least complex of the three and rarely have a direct effect on other plans outside of the department or unit for which the plan was developed. For example, in GE's jet engine business, the purchasing group create an operational plan calling for the purchase of several parts that are used in the manufacture of the engines. Research has shown that the formal plans for units or teams have effects on the long-range success of these groups. Therefore, while short-term and less complex, they remain highly important.[15]

As summarized in Exhibit 5.1, strategic, tactical, and operational plans differ from each other on five important dimensions: time horizon, scope, complexity, impact, and interdependence.[16] Although these differences matter, the three types of plans should align and integrate with one another. Each type of plan generally aligns with a different level in the organization.

The Organizational Levels at Which Plans Are Developed

In addition to plans that address strategic, tactical, and operational issues of the organization, managers at different levels of the company face different planning challenges. Exhibit 5.2 provides a graphical representation of the three primary levels of a corporation. Managers at each level attempt to address somewhat different questions.

CORPORATE LEVEL Most corporations of even moderate size have a corporate headquarters. However, complex and large organizations often divide the various businesses of the company into large groups. The heads of these groups are typically part of the group of senior executives at

---

objectives
the end states or targets that a company's managers aim to achieve

plans
the means by which managers hope to achieve the desired targets

planning
a decision-making process that focuses on the future of an organization and how it will achieve its goals

strategic plans
plans that focus on the broad future of the organization and incorporate both external environmental demands and internal resources into managers' actions

tactical plans
plans that translate strategic plans into specific goals for specific parts of the organization

operational plans
plans that translate tactical plans into specific goals and actions for small units of the organization and focus on the near term

EXHIBIT 5.1 Types of Plans: Key Differences

	Strategic Plans	Tactical Plans	Operational Plans
Time Horizon	Typically 3–5 years	Often focused on 1–2 years in the future	Usually focused on the next 12 months or less
Scope	Broadest; the original plans with a view of the entire organization	Normally focused on a strategic business unit	Most narrow; usually centered on departments or smaller units of the organization
Complexity	The most complex and general because of the different industries and business potentially covered	Complex but more specific, with a more limited domain of application	The least complex, because they usually focus on small, homogenous units
Impact	Have the potential to have a dramatic impact, both positively and negatively, on the survival and success of the organization	Affect specific business units, but the effect on the entire organization is measured	Impact is usually restricted to a specific department or organization unit
Interdependence	High interdependence; must take into account the resources and capabilities of the entire organization and its external environments	Moderate interdependence; must take into account the resources and capabilities of several units within a business	Low interdependence; the plans may be linked to higher-level tactical and strategic plans but are less interdependent on these plans

the corporate headquarters. Executives at the corporate level in large firms include both those in the headquarters and those heading up the large corporate groups such as finance, human resources, legal, and so on. These corporate-level executives primarily focus on questions such as the following:

- What industries should we get into or out of?
- What markets should the firm be in? For example, is it time to move aggressively into China? If so, what businesses should move first?
- In which businesses should the corporation invest money?
- What resources should be allocated to each of the businesses?

In the current times, these executives are also concerned about the corporate reputation.[17] Thus, the corporate executives at Best Buy were pleased to be honored for the company's ethical standards and business practices by being named to Ethisphere's 2010 list of the World's Most Ethical Companies.[18] Best Buy, a *Fortune* 100 company, has over 1000 retail operations selling electronic and technical products and services in the United States and in several foreign countries. Best Buy retail stores often contain products and services from several of its different business units, including Five-Star Appliance, Future Shop, The Geek Squad, Magnolia Audio Video, and Pacific Sales Kitchens and Bath Centers. The corporate office decides where and in what stores to emphasize the various products and services and allocates the resources accordingly.[19]

BUSINESS LEVEL The next level is sometimes referred to as the strategic business unit (SBU) level. At this level, managers focus on determining how they are going to compete effectively in the market. For example, within Best Buy, The Geek Squad and Magnolia Audio Video (home theater installment) operate as business units. In such business units, managers attempt to address questions such as the following:

- Who are our direct competitors?
- What are their strengths and weaknesses?
- What are our strengths and weaknesses?

- What do customers value in the products or services we offer?
- What advantages do we have over competitors?

This chapter examines some of the tools business-level managers can use to answer these questions. However, these planning questions, which business-level managers must answer, focus more on how to compete effectively in the specific market. If coordination across different departments (finance, marketing, product development, and so on) or units within the business is required, managers are responsible for recognizing and ensuring that the coordination occurs.

A MANAGER'S CHALLENGE

CHANGE

Cisco Develops Plans to Prepare for the Future

Cisco has had to deal with two major recessions in the first decade of the twenty-first century. But, Cisco has developed aggressive plans to capture the new market share as the economy improves. For example, in the midst of the 2009 recession, Cisco completed two major acquisitions in the same months. It acquired Starent and Tandberg, the fifth and sixth largest acquisitions made by Cisco, for about $5.9 billion. Starent, produces software and hardware to support the management of data traffic for wireless devices. Cisco makes and markets related products and thus hopes to sell more products to both Starent and Cisco customers. In recent times, Cisco has also purchased companies that produce and sell video conferencing and web security products. Cisco is making these acquisitions to increase its reach into new markets.

In addition, Cisco desires to internally develop new products for existing and new markets. They develop teams of managers and employees working together and with other teams to develop new products and to exploit new market opportunities. To facilitate their efforts, Cisco has decentralized to the teams the authority to commit resources and to take actions necessary to accomplish their goals.

In other plans to prepare for the future, Cisco is implementing actions that demonstrate the firm's sensitivity to the environment. For example, it has been implementing plans to reduce the company's carbon emissions during 2007–2012. In fact, Greenpeace ranked Cisco number 1 among information technology companies for these efforts. Cisco has also reduced water use at its San Jose, California campus, with such actions as the elimination of external water fountains, using drought-resistant plants in the landscaping, and installing waterless urinals, among others. These efforts save 42 million gallons of water annually: enough to serve 2,000 homes per year. These actions are good business because they fulfill the expectations of society and customers, but they also

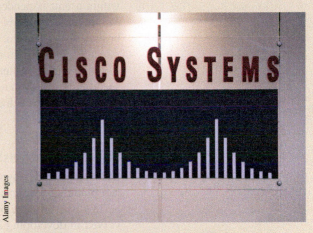

Alamy Images

Part of Cisco's plans for the future includes implementing actions that demonstrate the firm's sensitivity to the environment. Thus, Cisco plans to reduce the company's carbon emissions and was ranked number 1 among information technology companies for these efforts by Greenpeace.

produce financial savings. In this case, the reduced water usage saves Cisco about $135,000 annually.

The plans and implementation of these plans is preparing Cisco for substantial growth over the next decade. Cisco's projections of growth are much higher than the average for high-technology companies in the next few years.

Sources: D. Kahn, "Climate Policies Earn Cisco Top Spot in Greenpeace IT Rankings," *New York Times*, April 29, 2010, http://www.nytimes.com; O. J. Chiang, "Re-Routing Water at Cisco," *Forbes*, March 22, 2010, http://www.forbes.com; M. Marcus, "Cisco Signals Recovery," *Forbes*, February 4, 2010, http://www.forbes.com; C. Nuttall, "Cisco Data Signal 'Second Phase of Recovery'," *Financial Times*, February 4, 2010, http://www.ft.com; R. Cyran & L. S. Laughlin, "Assessing Cisco's Growth Strategy," *New York Times*, October 14, 2009, http://www.nytimes.com; A. Greenberg, "Cisco Aims Telepresence at Consumers' TVs," *Forbes*, January 6, 2010, http://www.forbes.com; D. Clark, "Tech Firms Jockey Ahead of Recovery," *Wall Street Journal*, December 31, 2009, http://online.wsj.com; J. Fortt, "Cisco: We're a Growth Machine," *Fortune*, December 9, 2009, http://www.fortune.com.

FUNCTIONAL LEVEL At the functional level, managers focus on how they can facilitate the achievement of the competitive plan of the business. These managers are often heads of departments such as finance, marketing, human resources, or product development. Depending on the firm's structure, this can include managers responsible for the business within a specific geographic region or managers responsible for specific retail stores. Generally, these functional managers attempt to address questions such as the following:

■ What activities does my unit need to perform well in order to meet customer expectations?
■ What information about competitors does my unit need in order to help the business compete effectively?
■ What are our unit's strengths and weaknesses?

The main focus of functional managers' planning activities is on how they can support the business and corporate plans. Functional-level managers are responsible for recognizing and ensuring effective and efficient operations. For example, if coordination between individuals within a unit is needed, it is their responsibility for facilitating it to enhance unit productivity. Middle and first-level managers will play a key role in the integration of Starent and Tandberg businesses into Cisco. In addition, these managers will be responsible for implementing environmentally sensitive programs in each location and units in the company. Functional unit managers (those in charge of finance, human resources, and so forth) are responsible for implementing the specific programs to reduce carbon emissions and to reduce water use; some of those plans must be tailored to each location (because of the special landscaping needed, amount of motorized vehicles used).

The Interrelationship between Plan Types and Levels

Strategic plans are typically developed at the corporate level. Strategic planning is arguably the key planning responsibility of corporate managers. Corporate managers, however, tend not to be involved in developing tactical or operational plans. Business-level managers may be involved in developing strategic plans for their business units and are usually involved in developing tactical plans for their businesses. However, business-level managers typically are not involved in developing operational plans. In contrast, functional-level managers are not often involved in developing either strategic or tactical plans. Instead, their planning responsibilities largely focus on the development of operational plans. Exhibit 5.2 illustrates the general pattern of planning responsibility by organizational level. Keep in mind, however, that the specific pattern in any given organization could be different. For example, the size of the organization could affect the pattern. In small organizations, the top managers often are involved in developing strategic, tactical, and operational plans. This was true when Matt Kincaid owned and managed each of the two restaurants.

The Planning Process

The planning process has six key elements: environmental analysis, resources, objectives, actions, implementation, and outcomes (see Exhibit 5.3). In this section, we examine each of these elements and the role they play in the overall planning process.

The first two of the simultaneous stages of the planning process include an assessment of the external environment and internal resources. Managers who formulate or implement plans in the absence of any assessment of the environment and resources may be unable to produce the

EXHIBIT 5.2

Interaction Between Plans and Levels

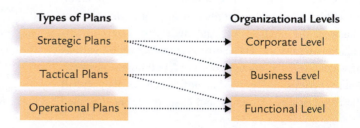

EXHIBIT 5.3

Planning Process

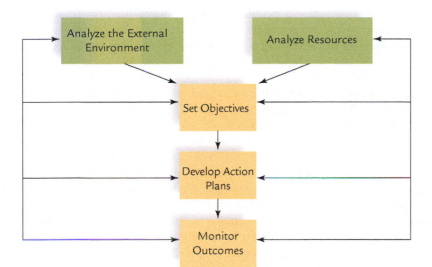

desired results. In contrast, managers who carefully scan the environment, understand their organizations' resources and capabilities, and incorporate the information gathered into the planning process can enjoy greater success from the plans they formulate and implement.[20] We discussed environmental analyses and analyzing internal resources and capabilities in Chapter 4. Here, we focus on the processes of analysis and how to incorporate them into the planning process.

Analyzing the Firm's External Environment

Forecasts are challenging, critical tools for analyzing the environment and perhaps even more critical in highly uncertain environments. Benchmarking is another useful tool in assessing competitors. Next, we discuss each.

FORECASTS One of the principal tools managers use to assess the business environment is a forecast. Forecasts are or can be made about virtually all critical elements in the environment that are likely to affect the organization or the manager's area of responsibility.[21] For example, if you were in the residential construction business, business cycle and interest-rate forecasts would be important to you. Generally, as interest rates go up and borrowing money becomes more expensive, or as economic expansions begin to slow down (or a recession begins causing fears of job loss), fewer people purchase new homes.[22] Those who still purchase new homes may necessarily have to purchase less expensive homes than they might when interest rates were lower or when the economy was healthier. The interest-rate forecast would influence the plan for the number of houses to build in the coming year, as a consequence.

Forecasts have a "cascading" effect. For example, if a manager forecasts that her firm will build 1,000 homes instead of 1,500 homes over the next year because interest rates are expected to increase from 6 percent to 7 percent, she will also likely forecast a decline in annual revenues. This may lead the purchasing manager to plan for smaller purchases of lumber and cause the human resource manager to plan for a smaller number of construction workers. The key point for managers is that it's vital to make and understand key forecasts and to keep track of any changes to develop appropriate objectives and action plans to compete effectively within the projected environment.

Environmental Uncertainty Forecasting environmental uncertainty accurately is difficult. It is even more challenging in dynamic environments.[23] Turbulent and uncertain environments are common in certain industries and in some countries. For example, in high-technology industries, such as the computer hardware and software industries, new technological developments are introduced regularly and can rapidly change the competitive landscape. Likewise, large economic changes can occur in developing and emerging economies sometimes because of unstable governments or major government policy changes (e.g., in some Latin American countries).[24] Firms must incorporate this uncertainty into their planning process.[25] This information is important because it might affect a plan to enter a particular market or how much to invest in the subsidiary operations across several markets, such as subsidiaries in Brazil, China, and Poland.[26]

A key issue for managers and their planning activities is that the greater the environmental uncertainty, the more flexible their plans need to be. In some cases, managers may even develop contingency plans. A **contingency plan** typically identifies key factors that could affect the desired results and specifies what different actions will be taken if changes in key events occur.[27] For example, suppose you were a manager at KB Home, the fourth-largest residential construction company in the United States.[28] Clearly, forecasts of future interest rates and changes in the business cycle are important to the operation of the company. The forecast might call for interest rates and economy activity to remain unchanged for the next year. But rather than rely solely on the forecast, it might be better to develop contingency plans. For instance, if interest rates go up one percentage point, people likely will buy fewer houses or less-expensive houses. Your contingency plan might include offering reduced financing charges if customers choose certain upgrades in their homes, such as granite countertops. You could perhaps afford to offer buyers this incentive because the profits from the upgrades might be greater than the costs of the finance subsidies. By having this contingency plan in place before the change in interest rates, you are more prepared to respond, if it occurs.

BENCHMARKING Another popular tool for assessing the environment is benchmarking. **Benchmarking** can lead to strong positive results.[29] It involves investigating the best practices used by competitors and noncompetitors in order to identify and imitate those that can be done in the firm.[30] In terms of results, managers might assess competitors with the highest revenue-to-employee ratio as a means of assessing productivity. Managers would then compare their own revenue-to-employee ratio to identify how they compared to competitors in the industry.[31] An important part of this assessment, however, is identifying the practices that contribute to the high revenue-to-employee ratios. For example, they might find that the firms with the highest ratios have fewer levels of managers because they delegate decision-making authority to lower levels in the organization, thus, emphasizing participative management and employee involvement.

These same types of assessments might also be made of noncompetitors. The inclusion of noncompetitors has potential pitfalls and benefits that are different from benchmarking competitors. Clearly, noncompetitors face different business conditions that make appropriate comparisons difficult. For example, a telemarketing company that sells relatively inexpensive items over the phone will have a much lower revenue-to-employee ratio than a manufacturer of supercomputers. The telemarketing firm has a relatively labor-intensive business, whereas the supercomputer manufacturer has a technology-intensive business. Likewise, the inventory practices of a service firm will be difficult to apply directly to a manufacturing firm. However, by looking outside your set of competitors, sometimes you can find unique and significantly better ways of doing things. For example, benchmarking TQM practices in noncompetitors may help to identify some unique practices that could be used to improve the firm's quality control processes.[32]

Consider the case of Outback Steakhouse. Even though the steel industry is totally different from the chain-restaurant industry, Outback Steakhouse has incorporated, with great success, a motivational practice used by several steel "mini-mills." Outback's success depends on the performance of its restaurants, and the people most responsible for that performance are local restaurant managers. In particular, managers must hire the right people and motivate them effectively to ensure that they provide good food and customer service. Thus, Outback needs highly motivated restaurant managers. The "best practice" that Outback adopted was giving the restaurant managers some ownership in the restaurants they managed. Therefore, if a restaurant made money, so did the manager. The manager felt more like an owner and less like an employee. The adoption of this best practice has helped Outback Steakhouse achieve significant success. Thus, even though benchmarking noncompetitors requires some judgment as to the relevant or appropriateness of practices, it can produce ways to gain a competitive advantage.

contingency plan
a plan that identifies key factors that could affect the desired results and specifies what actions will be taken if key events change

benchmarking
identifying the best practices by your competitors and noncompetitors and the results that they produced

Assessing the Firm's Internal Resources

Another element in the planning process is an assessment of the required resources and the resources available to you. Managers should conduct this assessment simultaneously with the analysis of the external environment.

RESOURCES AVAILABLE You should identify the resources that are available to your firm because they affect what objectives you should establish and what plans you should formulate.[33] Clearly, for a plan to be effective it must not only be well formulated but feasible to implement. If the resources required significantly exceed those available, you either must acquire new resources or design different actions.[34] In assessing resources available, managers must ask themselves questions such as the following:

- What human capital do we have currently?[35]
- Can people work on new and additional projects or will we need new people?
- Can we develop or acquire additional human capital if needed for new projects?[36]
- What financial resources do we have available? Can we obtain additional funding from the debt or equity markets if needed?
- Do we have the cutting-edge technology or can we gain access to it at a cost-effective price?

Although these are certainly not the only questions managers would need to ask, they are typical of the questions managers need to ask to determine the portfolio of resource capabilities available in the organization.

It is especially important to analyze the knowledge held in the firm because of its importance for gaining and maintaining a competitive advantage.[37] Tacit knowledge that is unique to the firm and held by employees can be especially valuable.[38] Such knowledge should be identified, and diffused where possible. For example, top performers can be observed and interviewed to obtain information that identifies the knowledge they hold that helps them to be top performers.[39] To build composite knowledge stocks, firms could identify such knowledge for a complete function in order to understand its capabilities in key areas (e.g., marketing capabilities).[40]

Setting Objectives

After the external and internal analyses, the next element in the planning process is setting objectives. To design and implement specific actions requires knowing what you expect them to achieve.

PRIORITIES AND MULTIPLE OBJECTIVES One of the first challenges for managers as they set objectives is to determine priorities.[41] Not all objectives are of equal importance or value. Furthermore, some objectives might be important now and less important later. Without a clear understanding of which objectives are most important and temporal priorities, employees may be working at odds with each other or it might create unnecessary conflicts as well.[42]

Consider your own university. Most universities have multiple and sometimes conflicting objectives. For example, students feel they pay tuition in order to learn leading-edge content from the best professors the school has to offer. Universities cannot ignore the expectations of this important set of constituents. At the same time, to generate leading-edge knowledge, universities must hire top researchers and fund their research. Without a clear idea of the university's priorities, department heads may find it difficult to determine how best to allocate their budgets to teaching and to research. How much of the budget should go toward activities that help develop the teaching skills of the faculty? How much should go toward funding research?

Temporal priorities among objectives can also exist. For example, suppose you are launching a new product in an established market with well-positioned competitors. You might decide that your current objective is to gain market share and thereby establish a presence in the market. You tell your salespeople to go after 10 percent market share and to offer discounts of up to 20 percent when needed to get the sale. However, after the product has a 10 percent market share, you might want the sales representatives to focus more on profitability objectives than gaining additional market share. Without a clear understanding of this sequence in priorities, your salespeople would be less able to help you achieve these objectives. If objectives are sequential, identifying that fact in advance helps subordinates better understand what is expected of them.

MEASURING OBJECTIVES After the organization's objectives are clear to everyone, managers need to establish how to measure their achievement. For example, a manager might determine that the organization's financial performance is the top objective. However, financial performance can be measured in a variety of ways.[43] For example, it can be measured in terms of profits relative to sales or profits relative to the company's assets. Nordstrom measures clerks' performance in terms of sales per hour. This is in contrast to many other retailers that only measure net sales. The difference in approach is important if salespeople are measured on net sales, they will likely be motivated to work the greatest number of hours they can (to produce more sales). In contrast, Nordstrom's sales-per-hour objective causes clerks to focus on "sales efficiency," or selling the most in every hour they work. And, the best way to improve sales per hour is to sell to repeat customers because clerks know the types of things they like, how much they are likely to spend, and so on. Specific measures are important. Even slight differences, such as net sales versus sales per hour, can significantly influence employee behavior.[44]

The case of IDEO is an interesting one as described in A Manager's Challenge. It is difficult to measure the success of a design until some time has passed. Yet, IDEO has had many successes because of the very thorough approach it uses to develop a design for its clients. The brainstorming, prototype testing, and exhaustive search for information increase its rate of success. All companies must manage their costs. However, overemphasizing costs can cause the firm to overlook other important market criteria. In this case, reducing costs might actually harm the success of a new design. Firms may be tempted to cut short the prototype and information search steps to reduce costs. Such actions are likely to lead to a poor design, however. IDEO does not take such shortcuts.

You can't manage what you can't measure. That's why Nordstrom records the sales of its clerks on an hour-by-hour basis. The company found out that even slight differences in hourly sales can have a big impact on the motivation of clerks—assuming they know what those sales are. That's why Nordstrom makes the sales numbers available to everyone.

A MANAGER'S CHALLENGE

IDEO Helps Other Companies Achieve Their Objectives

IDEO is a highly successful design firm used by many companies to help design new products and service. It has won numerous awards and is commonly recognized as one of the most innovative companies. It has helped Ford design its new hybrid automobile; it has worked with Shimano, a Japanese company, on designing an innovative new bicycle; and it partnered with Bank of America to design its "Keep the Change" savings account.

Ford established an objective to develop a new dashboard to use for all of its automobiles. Ford vice president of product development Derrick Kuzak suggested that the company wanted the system to represent a new product that would be as revolutionary for the auto industry as the mouse was to the PC industry. It hired IDEO to help it design this new dashboard. The new dashboard represents an internal communications and entertainment system. The challenges are dramatic because of the different levels of technological expertise of the drivers (from different generations). The intent was to design a sophisticated system that was easy to use and to eliminate the clutter of buttons and other pieces of equipment, such as the gearshift, providing a more visually appealing and efficient system for driving and managing the auto. For example, the gearshift appears on a touchtone screen. The bicycle IDEO designed for Shimano is called "coasting." The bike was developed for people who only ride a bicycle occasionally. For example, they may ride a bicycle to the store every few weeks (or even months). IDEO developed a form of open-source design using inputs from bicycle advocacy groups, local government units, and major bicycle manufacturers that allows riders to experience the enjoyment of coasting on a bike.

IDEO also develops plans and objectives for its own company and processes. Some might argue that it plans for failure in the sense that it builds redundancy into its design processes. For example, IDEO teams engage in exhaustive information searches even from unlikely sources such as local government units in the design of the new type of bicycle. These teams engage in brainstorming on every design project developing a large number of ideas. This is necessary because many ideas will not succeed. For example, only 12 out of every 4,000 ideas for new toys are successful. IDEO uses structure brainstorming, rapid prototyping, and field research before and after developing new designs to develop and test new concepts, eventually leading to successful projects. IDEO also engages in the development of a vision for its future and the plans needed to achieve that vision. It calls on all of its employees to provide new ideas for the company on a regular basis. Are there new fields it should consider? What are the next big projects in which it should engage?

Sources: H. Walters, "Ford and IDEO Redesign the Dashboard," *BusinessWeek*, January 7, 2010, http://www.businessweek.com; Company Web site, "Hybrid Vehicle Dashboard Interaction for Ford Motor Company," http://www.ideo.com, accessed December 29, 2009; A. Bryant, "He Prizes Questions More Than Answers," *New York Times*, October 25, 2009, http://www.nytimes.com; T. Brown, "Change by Design," *BusinessWeek*, September 24, 2009, http://www.businessweek.com; A. Chen, "Built to Fail: How Companies like Google, IDEO and 37 Signals Build Failure-tolerant Systems for Anything," July 7, 2009, andrewchenblog.com; T. Weiss, "Designing a Better World," *Forbes*, December 21, 2006, http://www.forbes.com.

Developing Action Plans

The next element in the planning process is the development of specific action plans. The action plans describe what the organization will do to accomplish the objectives it has established.

SEQUENCE AND TIMING A characteristic of an effective action plan is the sequence and timing of the specific steps or actions that must be taken.[45] One of the common tools used to graphically display the sequence and timing of the specific actions is a Gantt Chart (see Exhibit 5.4). Time typically appears on the horizontal axis of the chart, and the tasks to be done appear on the vertical axis. The chart shows when actions are to start and how long they require for completion. It shows the sequence in which to complete the actions, whether a preceding action must be completed before a subsequent one can start, and the expected overlap in the timing of specific actions if any exists.

In addition to the planned sequence and timing of events, managers can also plot the firm's actual progress on the Gantt chart. This allows managers to assess their progress against the plan and potentially make adjustments if needed. Today, sophisticated computer programs can assist managers in formulating and implementing plans involving literally hundreds of raw materials

EXHIBIT 5.4

Gantt Chart

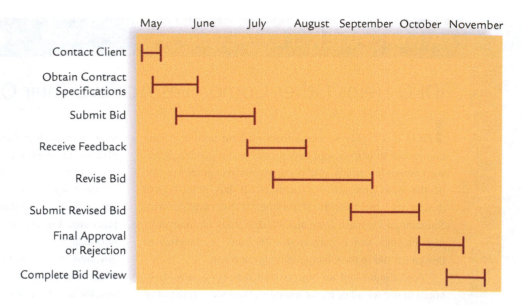

and components that must be brought together in the right amounts and sequences for the cost-effective production of finished goods.[46]

ACCOUNTABILITY The second key aspect of effective action plans is establishing who is accountable for the specific actions identified. Knowing who is responsible for specific actions facilitates coordination, especially if multiple people are involved in the execution of the plan. Accountability also increases the likelihood that the actions will be taken as planned in both quality and timing. Assigning accountability is especially important if managers need to change action plans during the course of their implementation (discussed next).[47]

Dell Computer developed a team approach whereby every member of the team believes in a shared accountability for implementing action plans and achieving the firm's objectives. Such an approach can be positive if it is complemented with the appropriate objectives and measures of success.[48] The team approach clearly has been successful at IDEO.

Implementing Plans

Action plans must be implemented. In addition to the quality of the plan, the effectiveness of the plan's implementation influences the results achieved.[49] Plans often fail in the implementation stage because of the inadequate assessment of resources required or the lack of accountability assigned to individuals for implementation. Yet, critically, the means of implementation must be carefully matched with the objectives to be achieved and the action plans designed.[50]

In the opening profile, we noted that Matt Kincaid had to build the brand image of his restaurants to increase the number of customers for them. For example, for his first restaurant, he had T-shirts printed with the restaurant's logo and distributed flyers and discount coupons to attract more customers. Kincaid also ensured that his employees were well trained and motivated to prepare quality food and deliver high-quality service. Managing all of these diverse efforts required a significant amount of time on Kincaid's part. As he explained, he worked sometimes as many as 100 hours per week.

No matter how carefully the implementation is designed, managers still need to monitor and adjust implementation efforts when unanticipated events occur.

MONITORING THE IMPLEMENTATION Even if the previous steps in the planning process are done well, there is no guarantee that the plan will be successfully implemented. This is why it is essential for you to monitor the implementation of the plan. In particular, you need to monitor three critical factors.

First, it is important to monitor the progress of the plan and its implementation. Are those responsible for taking specific actions well aware of their responsibilities and the timing of their expected actions? Are they adequately motivated and prepared to implement their portion of the plan? Are the necessary actions being taken at the right time? Are they being done at the desired or necessary level of quality? These are the types of questions that a manager needs to ask in order to monitor the progress of the implementation. Quite often plans include "milestones" that mark the progress of the implementation.

Second, the manager needs to monitor the level of support that the plan receives as it is being implemented.[51] This support might take the form of encouragement, money, or coaching. Few plans of any complexity or duration can be effectively implemented without continuous support. Are the other key supporters providing the encouragement needed? Kincaid found support from his corporate franchisor to be lacking. As a result, he developed his own plan and implemented it on his own. He also provided this type of support to other companies when he worked as a management consultant.

Third, the manager needs to monitor the level of resistance. Many plans and their implementation involve change. To the extent that they do, resistance to the plan's implementation can occur. One of the general causes of resistance is people anticipate performing poorly when first doing new tasks. Even if they see that the change is good, they resist it because they fear failure at first. In these cases, managers may need to provide extra encouragement or provide training to ensure that employees succeed.

MAKING REAL-TIME ADJUSTMENTS As discussed in previous chapters, organizations exist in a dynamic environment; thus, most plans likely will need to be adjusted. As the environment changes, a perfectly acceptable objective when it was formed can become unrealistic or too easily achieved, and therefore, may need to be changed. Likewise, what were perfectly reasonable time frames at one point may become unreasonable because of changes in the sociocultural, technological, economic, or political-legal environment. Events occur that cannot always be anticipated, requiring a change in the plans or their implementation.

One of the key principles is redundancy. If a catastrophic event occurs that knocks out some of a company's equipment, having a backup to the original equipment is necessary because obtaining replacement equipment quickly is difficult. As such, Google has thousands of servers because if any one of them fails, others are available to carry the load.

Managers need to help employees recognize and accept the need to adapt plans in real time. To do so, managers likely should build capabilities that enable them to adapt effectively. These capabilities might include skills such as good environmental scanning and quick requirement and resource assessment. Thus, in today's dynamic environment, a fixed and rigid plan can be as dangerous as having no plan at all.

Monitoring Outcomes

The final element in the planning process involves monitoring outcomes. If the organization's objectives have been well defined from the outset of the planning process, there should be little question as to what outcomes to monitor or how to measure them. If the plan was expected to improve the firm's financial performance and to measure them in terms of increased sales, the outcome should be easy to gauge.

However, most plans also produce negative or positive unanticipated consequences.[52] Both can be valuable sources of learning. To monitor outcomes may require the use of specially designed information systems to capture and report these consequences on a real-time basis. Such systems can be particularly important for large, complex organizations. For example, most large firms carefully monitor the financial performance of their major business units. However, other types of information may be needed, too. For example, monitoring the success of all products provided to the market by the firm may be necessary.[53] If one product is not selling well, a company needs to identify the reasons for it. Therefore, managers should capture as much information as possible when monitoring outcomes. There also needs to be a feedback loop so that the company can use what they've learned to modify and improve the planning process.

Many companies have developed aggressive plans to become more environmentally conscious. As such, the market for green products and technologies has created significant market opportunities resulting in high demand for Texas Carpet Recycling, Eco-Products, Enel Green Power, and Liberty Tire Recycling, as described in A Manager's Challenge. In fact, many businesses have developed very specific, measurable, and time-bound goals. For example, Wal-Mart has a goal to increase the fuel efficiency of its trucking fleet by 25 percent over a three-year period.

A MANAGER'S CHALLENGE

ETHICS

Small Business: There Is Gold in Green: Carpet, Food Containers, Power, and Tires

Texas Carpet Recycling was selected in 2009 by the State of Texas Alliance for Recycling to receive its STAR award for outstanding leadership in debris reuses/recycling. Texas Carpet Recycling is the only full-service landfill alternative for commercial carpet. The firm processes approximately 2,000 tons of carpet annually. After grinding down the used carpet, the firm ships it to Georgia to be recycled into carpet again.

Eco-Products, Inc., is a privately held firm based in Boulder, Colorado that produces cups, cutlery, and food containers that largely disintegrate in landfills within 120 days leaving no toxic residue. Eco-Products experienced substantial growth in 2009 growing at an annual rate of 428.5 percent to total sales of $11.4 million. And, its growth is likely to continue at a high rate. To date, it has largely sold its products to food service companies. However, a major supermarket chain, King Soopers, began carrying Eco-Products' GreenStrip products in its stores.

Enel Green Power is a renewable power subsidiary of the Italian utility firm, Enel. Enel is planning an initial public offering (IPO) for a stake in this subsidiary and hoping to receive more than $5 billion. Enel Green Power has been highly successful. For example, the company received $61 million in U.S. stimulus money to build two geothermal plants in Nevada. It also plans to obtain more money for wind, solar, and geothermal projects in the United States. The company benefits greatly from regulatory rules allowing companies to charge above-market prices for energy produced from renewable sources. A major impetus for the strong market for its renewable energy is national governments around the world that are targeting monies for renewable energy projects.

Liberty Tire Recycling is based in Pittsburgh, Pennsylvania and is the top tire recycler in the United States. In fact, the company has kept 100 million tires out of landfills which is approximately 25 percent of the tires scrapped in the United States annually. The recycled rubber from the tires is used in the production of artificial turf, playground surfaces, doormats, and similar products. Liberty's CEO Dick Guest is co-chairman of the Environmental Advisory Council of the Tire Industry Association.

All of these companies have taken advantage of the rapidly increasing market for environmentally sensitive products. In fact, many governments have been providing special incentives for businesses to produce green products and to be more environmentally sensitive. These types of actions are being highly valued across the world to include such countries as China, the United States those in Europe as well, among others.

Sources: M. Scott and A. Morales, "A Gold Rush in Green Technology," *Business Week*, April 15, 2010, http://www.businessweek.com; "Liberty Tire Recycling's Dick Guest Appointed to Environmental Advisory Council," *Earthtimes,* February 2, 2010, http://www.earthtimes.com; K. Galbraith, "Companies Call Government Incentives the Key to Green," *New York Times*, November 19, 2009, http://www.nytimes.com; "Texas Carpet Recycling Wins 2009 'Star' Award," *Floorbiz*, October 16, 2009, http://www.floorbiz.com; "The 2009 *Inc.* 500: The Top Green Companies," *Inc.*, October 2009, http://www.inc.com; company Web site, "The Fruitguys Makes the San Francisco Business Times Fast 100 Five Years Running," www.fruitguys.com, accessed November 1, 2009; A. Wallace, "Eco-Products Names New Ceo," *Daily Camera*, July 14, 2009, http://www.dailycamera.com.

---

budget
a tool used to quantify and allocate resources to specific activities

capital expenditure budget
a tool that specifies the amount of money to spend on specific items that have long-term use and require significant amounts of money

expense budget
a budget that includes all primary activities on which a unit or organization plans to spend money and the amount allocated for the upcoming year

Planning Tools

Managers use a variety of planning tools. In this section, we discuss two tools that managers widely use: budgets and goal setting.

Budgets

Managers use a **budget** to quantify and allocate resources to specific activities. Most organizations propose and set budgets on an annual basis, and they address a variety of issues. For example, a **capital expenditure budget** specifies the amount of money a company plans to spend on specific items that have long-term use and require significant financial investments. These items might include things such as manufacturing equipment, land, and buildings.

Another common budget is an expense budget. An **expense budget,** typically includes all primary activities on which the unit or organization plans to spend money and the amount allocated for each item during the year. Most profit and nonprofit organizations of a moderate or larger size use expense budgets, both for planning and for control purposes.

And most organizations have a two-phased process relative to budgets. The first consists of managers looking ahead and planning their needs. Thereafter, the organization develops a budget that specifies expected major expenditures or expenses. This **proposed budget** provides a plan of how much money the organization needs, and it is submitted to a superior or budget review committee. After the proposed budget is reviewed, often in the context of other proposed budgets, it receives approval (or requests for revisions and resubmission). An **approved budget** specifies the amount of money the manager is authorized to spend and what items can be purchased or expenses are allowed.

Two main approaches to the budgeting process are common. The first approach is typically called the **incremental budgeting approach.**[54] With this approach, managers use their approved budgets from the previous year as a starting point for developing the current year's budget. They then present arguments for why the upcoming budget should be more or less than the previous year's budget. Incremental budgeting is efficient because managers do not need to spend a significant amount of time justifying allocating money toward the same types of purchases or recurring expenses each year. The principal negative consequence of incremental budgeting is that it can result in "budget momentum." This means that money may be allocated to a unit in the future merely because the unit had been allocated money in the past. Consider the true case of a small town in North Carolina. Every year around Christmas, all the parking meters on the main street are turned off and people park free. Most of the city residents think that this is the city's way of giving folks a nice Christmas gift. Actually, it is the city council's way of maintaining its budget level given the incremental approach the mayor takes to budgeting. The council calculates the town's budget surplus toward the end of the year and computes how many days of free parking the city will need to use up the surplus. It then allocates that many days of free parking to maintain the same level of funding for the next year. As in this case, incremental budgeting can lead to the inefficient use of valuable resources.

The **zero-based budgeting approach** assumes that all funding allocations must be justified, starting at zero each year.[55] The benefit of this approach is that items that cannot be justified on their current merits (regardless of their past merits and budgets) will not be allocated money. In general, this approach can lead to a more effective allocation of the organization's financial resources. However, zero-based budgeting requires an investment of time because each item must be justified each year.

With either approach, managers typically use budgets as planning tools to determine priorities, required resources, and keys to implementation. In particular, because financial resources are usually scarce in most organizations, there is rarely as much money available as there are requests for its use. Allocating money among various activities forces managers to discuss the relative priority of the firm's activities. This is true at all three organization levels. For example, department managers are likely to find they have more demand for money than they have the resources to allocate. Similarly, corporate officers are likely to find departments and business units requesting more money than the organization has available to allocate. This leads to a determination of which units and related activities are of highest priority and should receive budget approval.

In this sense, budgets can be an effective means of integrating and quantifying many aspects of the firm's corporate-, business-, and functional-level plans. Although the budgeting process does not guarantee that managers will make good decisions about the integration and coordination process nor that they will make good decisions about priorities, it does increase the likelihood of these key items being discussed and decisions made.

Goal Setting Criteria

Goal setting is a specific planning process for managing performance. Normally, goal setting is used at the individual level, although the principles are applicable to setting goals for teams, units, and organizations. The research suggests that effective goals can have a significant and positive effect on performance. The research also suggests that effective goals have five characteristics.[56]

SPECIFIC To be most effective, the goals for the firm, its units, and subordinates, should be specific. For example, a goal "to achieve the highest performance possible" is too vague. Rather, state the goal in specific terms, such as "to achieve a 10 percent return on assets during the next year" or "to gain a 15 percent increase in market share in the next six months." These statements are specific and detail which actual performance can be measured and compared.

proposed budget
a budget that outlines how much money an organization needs; submitted to a superior or budget review committee

approved budget
a budget that specifies what the manager is actually authorized to spend money on and how much

incremental budgeting approach
a budgeting approach whereby managers use the approved budget of the previous year and then present arguments for why the upcoming year's budget should be more or less

zero-based budgeting approach
a budgeting approach that assumes that all funding allocations must be justified from zero each year

MEASURABLE One way to determine if a goal is specific enough is by whether its achievement can be measured. For example, it would be highly difficult to measure the achievement of a goal "to reach the highest performance possible," What is "the highest performance possible"? How could a firm know when it is achieved? Yet, a goal to achieve a 10 percent return on assets," or an increase of 15 percent in market share can be measured. These are specific and measurable goals. In addition, you need to actually measure progress toward the goal.

Goal setting is most effective when progress toward the goal is measured on a regular basis. The frequency of the measurement should depend upon the nature of the activities associated with the goal and its timing. For example, if the goal is to achieve a 10 percent return on assets over the next year, the goal can easily be assessed on a quarterly basis. Most companies develop and report their earnings each quarter. However, a goal to increase market share by 15 percent in the next six months would be better evaluated on a monthly basis. The interim measures allow managers to know how the achievement of the goal is progressing and if any corrective actions are needed to ensure the achievement of the goal.

COMMITMENT Even if a goal is specific and measurable, those involved in its achievement must agree and be committed to it for the goal to be achieved.[57] Thus, for organizational goals, this means that a substantial portion of employees must agree to them and be committed to their achievement. To achieve a 10 percent return on the firm's assets, many employees will have to do their jobs exceptionally well and take actions to minimize costs or to enhance revenues (or both). For unit goals, those in the unit must accept and be committed to the achievement of the goal.

Managers should be careful when securing employee commitment. Because managers are in a position of power, their subordinates often say what they believe their managers want to hear—even when it is not what the subordinates really think. For example, sales representatives may "agree" to the goal of increasing market share by 15 percent, but they may not believe they can do it. If so, they are unlikely to commit to the goal, and they will probably not achieve it. Thus, managers do not want superficial agreement to the goal but instead want a deep commitment to it. The research shows that one way to gain commitment to a goal is to allow employees to discuss and participate in the development of the goal. In doing so, the employees have a feeling of ownership.[58]

REALISTIC For people to be committed to the achievement of goals, they must be realistic.[59] Research has shown that unrealistic goals (goals that are perceived to be unachievable) can produce several reactions from those charged with the achievement of them, none of which are good. First, some employees will ignore an unrealistic goal and set their own goals, which the organization may or may not desire. Other employees may become discouraged and their motivation to perform well will suffer. So, if sales representatives perceive that a goal of increasing market share by 15 percent in the next six months is not achievable, they are unlikely to work toward the goal.

Alternatively, goals that are too easy are not effective, they are not effective for at least two reasons: On the one hand, they do not inspire motivation. As such, people are likely to perform below their capabilities. On the other hand, easy goals are not effective because they do not deliver substantial results. Even if they are achieved, easy goals will not have a large effect on the results achieved at the organizational, unit, subordinate, or personal level.

TIME BOUND Even specific, measured, and realistic goals to which people are committed need to be time-bound in order to be effective. Thus, goals need a specific time span within which they are to be achieved. Some goals will take a substantial time to achieve (for example, a year or more), whereas others will require shorter time intervals. For example, the goal of achieving a 10 percent return on assets was stated earlier in terms of a one-year time frame. Consequently, milestones should be set, and the goal measured on shorter time frames, such as every three months. By contrast, progress toward the goal of increasing market share by 15 percent in a six-month time frame should probably be measured every month. Having a time frame for goals is necessary in order to evaluate their success, and it also affects the realism of the goals. Perhaps it is unrealistic to expect large increases in market share in only six months, but such increases might be achievable in 12 to 18 months. Therefore, the time frame plays an important role in the goal-setting process.[60]

Managerial Challenges from the Front Line

The Rest of the Story

With a lot of hard work and using his knowledge gained from his business education, Matt Kincaid achieved success. His efforts helped build positive brand recognition for his restaurant in Indiana, and he was subsequently able to sell the business for a profit. Thereafter, Kincaid purchased a restaurant and a bar in Spokane, Washington and subsequently sold it as well. Despite the successful outcome of his two ventures, he says that he has learned some valuable lessons—the most important of which is to do your own research and develop your own plans before embarking upon a major business project. He used this knowledge gained from his experience to good advantage in his time as a consultant. He now uses these experiences as examples in teaching students.

Summary

- Few activities are more basic to management than deciding where the company is going and how it will get there. Organizational objectives are the future end states targeted by managers, while plans are the means by which managers achieve the objectives. Planning, then, is essentially a process to determine and implement actions to achieve organizational objectives. This process includes an assessment of the organization's external environment and internal resources.

- Most companies of any size develop three different types of interrelated plans, strategic, tactical, and operational. Strategic plans focus on the broad future of the organization. Incorporating external information gathered by analyzing the company's competitive environment and the firm's internal resources, managers determine the scope of the business (products and services the firm will provide) to achieve the organization's long-term objectives. Tactical plans translate strategic plans into specific goals for specific parts of the organization. Consequently, they often have shorter time frames and are narrower in scope. Instead of focusing on the entire corporation, tactical plans typically affect a single business within an organization and its product lines (one or more related product lines). Operational plans translate tactical plans into specific goals and actions for small units of the organization. They typically focus on the short term, usually 12 months or less. These plans are the least complex of the three and rarely have a direct effect on other plans outside of the department or unit for which the plan was developed.

- In addition to plans that address strategic, tactical, and operational issues of the organization, managers at different levels of the company face different planning challenges. Managers at each level attempt to address somewhat different questions. Strategic plans are typically developed at the corporate level. Strategic planning is arguably the key planning responsibility of corporate managers. Business-level managers may be involved in developing strategic plans for their business units and are usually involved in developing tactical plans for their business. Functional-level managers largely focus on the development of operational plans.

- The planning process has six key elements: environmental analysis, resources, objectives, actions, implementation, and outcomes. Forecasts and benchmarking can be helpful in analyzing the organization's external environment. However, the uncertainty in this environment often makes analyzing it a significant challenge. Firms must currently have the resources or the ability to acquire them to implement the plans developed. Thus, analysis of the internal resources is necessary to establish realistic objectives. Next, the organization designs and implements the plan's action steps.

- Budgets are used to quantify and allocate resources to specific activities. Most organizations propose and set budgets on an annual basis. A capital expenditure budget specifies the amount of money an organization plans to spend on specific items that have long-term use and require significant financial investments. Another common budget is an expense budget. An expense budget typically includes all primary activities on which the unit or organization plans to spend money and the amount allocated to each during the year.

■ Goal setting is a specific planning process for managing performance. The principles are applicable to setting goals not only for individual employees but for teams, units, and organizations. The research suggests that effective goals can have a significant and positive effect on performance, and five characteristics distinguish them: They are specific, measurable, realistic, time-bound, and have the commitment of those charged with the responsibility of achieving them.

Key Terms

approved budget   125
benchmarking   118
budget   124
capital expenditure budget   124
contingency plan   118

expense budget   124
incremental budgeting approach   125
objectives   113
operational plans   113
planning   113

plans   113
proposed budget   125
strategic plans   113
tactical plans   113
zero-based budgeting approach   125

Review Questions

1. What is planning and what is its purpose?
2. How are strategic, tactical, and operational plans different?
3. What are the three organizational levels and how do they interrelate with the three types of plans?

4. What is the planning process? Briefly explain each step in the process.
5. How is budgeting used in the planning process?
6. What are the five characteristics of effective goals, and why are they important for implementing action plans?

Assessing Your Capabilities

Predicting the Prime Interest Rate

Each quarter, members of the Federal Open Market Committee of the U.S. Federal Reserve meet to examine the economy and decide whether it needs to be stimulated to encourage economic growth or whether the "brakes" need to be applied to slow down economic growth. The chairman of the Federal Reserve (currently Ben S. Bernanke) chairs the meeting. While the committee examines a significant amount of data and reports on the economy, the goal is to balance the need for economic growth with the intent to keep inflation low. So, the committee examines data on changes in the country's gross domestic product (GDP) and other economic indicators (e.g., unemployment rate), along with data on the rate of inflation. The committee then makes a decision about the "federal funds rate" charged to banks. If the rate is increased, banks almost automatically change the prime interest by the same degree of change in the rate charged to them by the Federal Reserve.

1. Your task is to review carefully data on the economic growth in the United States since the last announcement

from the Federal Open Market Committee regarding the federal funds rate. (a) Based on your evaluation of the data, make a prediction as to whether or not the Federal Reserve will increase, decrease, or leave unchanged the federal funds rate the next time the committee meets. (b) Also, predict the amount the rate will change (if it changes at all). (c) Write down the reasons for your predictions.

2. After the next meeting of the Federal Reserve Open Market Committee, obtain information on its announcement regarding the federal funds rate. How accurate was your prediction? Were your analyses in line with those explained in the announcement supporting the decision of the committee?

For more information, see http://www.federalreserve.gov.

Source: J. Havemann, "Fed Chief Bernanke Wins High Marks for First Year," *Los Angeles Times,* January 31, 2007, http://www.latimes.com.

Team Exercise

Form teams of three to five people. Reread the segment in this chapter about changes to prepare for growth and to be more environmentally sensitive. Next, visit Cisco's Web site (http://www.cisco.com) and read some recent articles on the company. In particular, read articles on Cisco's recent performance and other changes.

Analyze Cisco's external environment and its recent action plans. Based on your analyses, answer the following questions:

1. What are the greatest threats in Cisco's environment?
2. Will the plans and desired outcomes described in the segment in the chapter help Cisco to increase its competitive advantage and help it continue to grow? Why or why not?
3. Are there additional objectives that you would recommend to improve Cisco's future opportunities?

"Pam" (a disguised name but a real person) was director of training at a large, Midwestern training company—Leadership Development Center (LDC). One of Pam's responsibilities was to plan the launch of LDC's new training programs. The company had a reputation for excellent programs targeted at mid-level managers. However, LDC's top executives felt that the company should offer more training programs for senior executives, arguing that if senior executives personally experienced the quality of the firm's training, they would be more likely to recommend and approve training requests for their mid-level managers.

Pam discussed the program objectives for the new Senior Executive Leadership Program with her boss and her peers. Some thought the program should be a "loss leader" or in other words, that it should lose money but pay for itself by generating more participants for LDC's mid-level managerial programs. Others thought that the new program should break even financially. Everyone agreed, however, that the program should be of sufficient quality that participants would have a very favorable impression of LDC. As a result, they would be more likely to encourage their employees to attend LDC programs and approve their requests to do so.

Pam determined that the program's success would be measured in three ways. First, the number of participants taking the first program would be monitored. Pam calculated it would take about 18 participants for the program to break even financially. Second, she would survey all participants regarding their satisfaction with the program, its content, materials, facilities, administration, and instructors. Finally, LDC would track the number of mid-level managers from the companies of those attending the senior executive program to determine if there was an increased participation level over time.

In launching the program, Pam examined the past marketing costs of other new programs. Previous new launches had cost about $30,000 in brochure and mailing expenses. She expected that an extra $5,000 ought to be enough to launch the new senior executive program.

The current budget did not anticipate the launch of the senior executive program, but another program in marketing had been cancelled. Consequently, $20,000 remained in the budget for that program, which Pam thought she could spend on the new senior executive program. In addition, she thought she could access $15,000 from the general contingency budget of $30,000.

One of the first things she needed to do was to talk to LDC's possible instructors and select a "faculty director."

This person would design the specific content of the program and coordinate the other instructors along with the content of their training efforts. After the faculty director was chosen, the program would need to be designed and, based on the design, a brochure created. She estimated that the program design would require about three weeks and that the development of the brochures would take an additional two weeks. Printing the brochures would require four days, and assembling them for mailing would take another three days. Delivery of the mailed brochures would take about a week. Normally, LDC allowed about 12 weeks between the time people received brochures and the due date for their program applications. In general, program applications were due (along with the program fees) three weeks before the start of the program. Two weeks before the program starts, all materials (handouts, notebooks, etc.) would need to be assembled.

Pam had two people who reported directly to her and could assist in the implementation of the plan. Tammy would be responsible for contacting the brochure design firm and the printing company and ensuring that the brochure would be ready on time. In addition, she would secure the mailing list and arrange for an outside contractor to stuff the envelopes with brochures for mailing. Dan would be responsible for venue details. LDC had its own training facilities and had contracts with several nearby hotels for lodging arrangements. Dan would also be responsible for the assembly of all training materials, which required obtaining the handouts and other materials from the instructors on time.

As the plan was put into action, everything seemed to go fine. A faculty member was selected to be the faculty director, and the program design and content were ready in two rather than the anticipated three weeks. The outside design firm quickly produced a brochure that with a few modifications was ready for mailing. Tammy obtained several mailing lists that had the names of senior executives in medium-to-large companies. The mailing was sent out about five days early.

Inquiries regarding the program were 100 percent higher than those for other new programs LDC had launched in the past. However, as the program's start date drew nearer, the ratio of inquiries to registrations was not good. Traditionally, one in ten people who contacted LDC for further information regarding a particular program ended up registering for it. However, eight weeks before the program's start, the inquiry to registration ratio was 100 to 1 (not 10 to 1). Four weeks before the start of the program, only ten had signed up. Pam was stressed about what she should do.

Questions

1. What adjustments would you make at this point? Would you cancel the program or run it at a loss?
2. Draw a Gantt chart of the sequence and timing of key activities. What insights does this give you regarding the plan and its implementation?
3. What do you think went wrong? What do you see as the strengths and weaknesses of the planning process used in this case?
4. LDC seemed to follow a planning process that had worked well for its mid-level managerial programs. Are there differences between senior executives and mid-level managers that might explain why the plan did not seem as successful as anticipated? Could these differences have been anticipated? Should they have been?

References

1. R. Adner and P. Zemsky, "A Demand-based Perspective on Sustainable Competitive Advantage," *Strategic Management Journal* 27 (2006): 215–239; J. A. Pearce III, "How Companies Can Preserve Market Dominance after Patents Expire," *Long Range Planning* 39 (2006): 71–87.

2. M. A. Hitt, L. Bierman, K. Uhlenbruck, and K. Shimizu, "The Importance of Resources in the Internationalization of Professional Service Firms: The Good, the Bad and the Ugly," *Academy of Management Journal* 49 (2006): 1137–1157; M. A. Hitt, L. Bierman, K. Shimizu, and R. Kochhar, "Direct and Moderating Effects of Human Capital on Strategy and Performance in Human Service Firms: A Resource-based Perspective," *Academy of Management Journal* 44 (2001): 13–28.

3. M. Forsythe, "How GE Helps China Build Business Leaders." *BusinessWeek,* May 16. 2010, 24–25.

4. "Largest U.S. Corporations." *Fortune,* May 3, 2010, F-1–F-27.

5. M. A. Hitt, R. D. Ireland, and R. E. Hoskisson, *Strategic Management: Competitiveness and Globalization* (Cincinnati: South-Western Publishing Co., 2011).

6. G. S. Yip, A. M. Rugman, and A. Kudina, "International Success of British Companies," *Long Range Planning* 39 (2006): 241–264.

7. H. E. Hodges and T. W. Kent, "Impact of Planning and Control Sophistication in Small Business," *Journal of Small Business Strategy* 17 (2006/2007): 75–87.

8. G. Colvin, "On the Hot Seat," *Fortune,* December 11, 2006, 75–82.

9. A. Burke, S. Fraser, and F. J. Greene, "The Multiple Effects of Business Planning on New Venture Performance." *Journal of Management Studies* 47 (2010): 391–415.

10. V. F. Misangyi, H. Elms, T. Greckhamer, and J. A. LePine, "A New Perspective on a Fundamental Debate: A Multilevel Approach to Industry, Corporate, and Business Unit Effects," *Strategic Management Journal* 27 (2006): 571–590.

11. R. Van Wingerden, "Managing Change," *International Journal of Technology Management* 21, nos. 5, 6 (2001): 487–95.

12. O. Sorenson, S. McEvily, C. R. Ren, and R. Roy, "Niche Width Revisited: Organizational Scope, Behavior, and Performance," *Strategic Management Journal* 27 (2006): 915–936.

13. P. Jarzabkowski and J. Balogun, "The Practice and Process of Delivering Integration through Strategic Planning," *Journal of Management Studies* 46 (2009):1255–1288; D. Rheault, "Freshening Up Strategic Planning: More than Fill-in-the-Blanks," *Journal of Business Strategy* 24, no. 6 (2003): 33–38.

14. G. Dowell, "Product Line Strategies of New Entrants in an Established Industry: Evidence from the U.S. Bicycle Industry," *Strategic Management Journal* 27 (2006): 959–979.

15. J. E. Mathieu and W. Schulze, "The Influence of Team Knowledge and Formal Plans on Episodic Team Process-Performance Relationships," *Academy of Management Journal* 49 (2006): 605–619.

16. J. Carnillus, "Reinventing Strategic Planning," *Strategy and Leadership* (May–June 1996): 6–12.

17. J. Block, "Family Management, Family Ownership and Downsizing: Evidence from S&P 500 Firms," *Family Business Review* 23 (2010): 109–130.

18. Company Web site, "Ethisphere Names Best Buy to 2010 List of World's Most Ethical Companies," http://www.bestbuy.com, accessed March 24, 2010.

19. "Best Buy," Wikipedia, http://en.wikipedia.org/wiki/Best_Buy, May 19, 2010.

20. M. A. Peteraf and M. E. Bergen, "Scanning Dynamic Competitive Landscapes: A Market-based and Resource-based Framework," *Strategic Management Journal* 24 (2003): 1027–1041; M. D. Watkins and M. H. Bazerman, "Predictable Surprises: The Disasters You Should Have Seen Coming," *Harvard Business Review* 81, no. 3 (2003): 72–80.

21. E. A. Boyd and I. O. Bilegan, "Revenue Management and E-commerce," *Management Science* 49 (2003): 1363–1386; M. Spann and B. Skiera, "Internet-based Virtual Stock Markets for Business Forecasting," *Management Science* 49 (2003): 1310–1326.

22. P. Navarro and P. Bromiley, "Business Cycle Management and Firm Performance," *Journal of Strategy and Management* 3 (2010): 50–71.

23. U. Lichtenthaler, "Absorptive Capacity, Environmental Turbulence, and the Complementarity of Organizational Learning Processes," *Academy of Management Journal* 52(2009): 822–846.

24. V. H. Hoffman, T. Trautmannand, and J. Hamprecht, "Regulatory Uncertainty: A Reason to Postpone Investments? Not Necessarily," *Journal of Management Studies* 46 (2009): 1224–1253; E. M. Reid and M. W. Toffel, "Responding to Public and Private Politics: Corporate Disclosure of Climate Change Strategies," *Strategic Management Journal* 30 (2009): 1157–1178.

25. J. A. Zuniga-Vicente and J. D. Vicente-Lorente, "Strategic Moves and Organizational Survival in Turbulent Environments: The Case of Spanish Banks (1983–1997)," *Journal of Management Studies* 43 (2006): 485–519.

26. A. S. Cui, D. A. Griffith, S. T. Cavusgil, and M. Dabic, "The Influence of Market and Cultural Environmental Factors on Technology Transfer between Foreign MNCs and Local Subsidiaries: A Croatian Illustration," *Journal of World Business* 41 (2006): 100–111.

27. M. Hileman, "Future Operations Planning Will Measure Plan Achievability," *Oil and Gas Journal,* March 18, 2002, 84–87.

28. D. Cameron, "KB Home in Stock-options Investigation," *Financial Times*, January 29, 2007.

29. "Benchmarking Strategies," *Brand Strategy* (December/January 2004): 3; D. J. Smith, Y. Hwang, B. K. W. Pei, and J. H. Reneau, "The Performance Effects of Congruence Between Product Competitive Strategies and Purchasing Management Design," *Management Science* 48 (2002): 866–885.

30. S. A. Fernhaber and D. Li, "The Impact of Interorganizational Imitation on New Venture International Entry and Performance," *Entrepreneurship Theory & Practice* 34 (2010): 1–30.

31. N. Balabramanian and M. B. Lieberman, "Industry Learning Environments and the Heterogeneity of Firm Performance," *Strategic Management Journal* 31 (2010): 390–412.

32. M. T. Kennedy and P. C. Fiss, "Institutionalization, Framing, and Diffusion: The Logic of TQM Adoption and Implementation Decisions Among U.S. Hospitals," *Academy of Management Journal* 52 (2009): 897–916.

33. I. Barreto, "Dynamic Capabilities: A Review of Past Research and an Agenda for the Future," *Journal of Management* 36 (2110): 256–280.

34. E. Doving and P. N. Gooderham, "Dynamic Capabilities as Antecedents of the Scope of Related Diversification: The Case of the Small Firm Accountancy Practices," *Strategic Management Journal* 29 (2008): 841–857.

35. T. R. Holcomb, R. M. Holmes, and B. L. Connelly, "Making the Most of What You Have: Managerial Ability as a Source of Resource Value Creation," *Strategic Management Journal* 30 (2009): 457–485.

36. D. G. Sirmon and M. A. Hitt, "Contingencies within Dynamic Managerial Capabilities: Interdependent Effects of Resource Investment and Deployment on Firm Performance," *Strategic Management Journal* 30 (2009): 1375–1394.

37. V. Ambrosini, N. Collier, and M. Jenkins, "A Configurational Approach to the Dynamics of Firm Level Knowledge," *Journal of Strategy and Management* 2 (2009): 4–30.

38. H. C. Wang, J. He, and J. T. Mahoney, "Firm-specific Knowledge Resources and Competitive Advantage: The Roles of Economic- and Relationship-based Employee Governance Mechanisms," *Strategic Management Journal* 30 (2009): 1265–1285.

39. D. A. Peliso, "Preserving Employee Know-how: Retain and Transfer the Knowledge of Departing Top Performers Using Cognitive Task Analysis," *HR Magazine,* May 2010, 99.

40. N. A. Morgan, D. W. Vorhies, and C. H. Mason, "Market Orientation, Marketing Capabilities and Firm Performance," *Strategic Management Journal* 30 (2009): 909–920.

41. C. Barker, C. Thunhurst, and D. Ross, "An Approach to Setting Priorities in Health Planning," *Journal of Management in Medicine* 12, no. 2 (1998): 92.

42. A. Locke and G. P. Latharn, *A Theory of Goal Setting and Task Performance* (Upper Saddle River: Prentice Hall, 1990); A. Lederer and A. Mendelow, "Information Systems Planning and the Challenge of Shifting Priorities," *Information and Management* 24, no. 6 (1993): 319–328.

43. J. Barney, *Gaining and Sustaining a Competitive Advantage* (Upper Saddle River: Pearson Prentice Hall, 2007).

44. I. Morgan and J. Rao, "Aligning Service Strategy Through Super-measure Management," *Academy of Management Executive* 16, no. 4 (2002): 121–131; L. G. Love, R. L. Priem, and G. T. Lumpkin, "Explicitly Articulated Strategy and Firm Performance Under Alternative Levels of Centralization," *Journal of Management* 28 (2002): 611–627.

45. I. Rivenbark and M. Frost, "Strategic Planning for Success," *HR Magazine*, July 2003, 120–121.

46. S. Mallya, S. Banerjee, and W. G. Bistline, "A Decision Support System for Production/Distribution Planning in Continuous Manufacturing," *Decision Sciences* 32 (2001): 545–556; P. Cowling and M. Johansson, "Using Real Time Information for Effective Dynamic Scheduling," *European Journal of Operational Research* 139 (2002): 230–244.

47. R. Wiltbank, N. Dew, S. Read, and S. D. Saravathy, "What to Do Next? The Case for Non-predictive Strategy," *Strategic Management Journal* 27 (2006): 981–998.

48. M. A. Hitt, C. C. Miller, and A. Colella, *Organizational Behavior: A Strategic Approach* (Hoboken: John Wiley & Sons, 2011).

49. W. S. Smith, "Vitality in Business: Executing a New Strategy at Unilever," *Journal of Business Strategy* 30 (2009): 31–41.

50. C. S. Katsikeas, S. Samiee, and M. Theodosiou, "Strategy Fit and Performance: Consequences of International Marketing Standardization," *Strategic Management Journal* 27 (2006): 867–890.

51. W. R. Guffey and B. J. Nienhaus, "Determinants of Employee Support for the Strategic Plan of a Business Unit," *S.A.M. Advanced Management Journal* (Spring 2002): 23–30.

52. J. Balogun, "Managing Change: Steering a Course Between Intended Strategies and Unanticipated Outcomes," *Long Range Planning* 39 (2006): 29–49.

53. F. T. Rothaermel, M. A. Hitt, and L. A. Jobe, "Balancing Vertical Integration and Strategic Outsourcing: Effects on Product Portfolio, Product Success, and Firm Performance," *Strategic Management Journal* 27 (2006): 1033–1056.

54. J. White, "Almost Nothing New Under the Sun: Why the Work of Budgeting Remains Incremental," *Public Budgeting and Finance* 14, no. 1 (1994): 113–134.

55. W. Llewellyn, "A Review of the Budgeting System," *Assessment* 1, no. 5 (1994): 47–50.

56. Hitt, Miller, and Colella, *Organizational Behavior;* Locke and Latham, "A Theory of Goal Setting and Task Performance."

57. S.W.M. Elias, "Employee Commitment in Times of Change: Assessing the Importance of Attitudes toward Organizational Change," *Journal of Management* 35 (2009): 37–55.

58. Hitt, Miller, and Colella, *Organizational Behavior.*

59. M. W. Gerhardt and R. A. Luzadis, "The Importance of Task Difficulty in Goal Orientation—Assigned Goal Alignment," *Journal of Leadership & Organizational Studies* 16 (2009): 167–174.

60. G. P. Latham, *Work Motivation: History, Theory, Research and Practice* (Thousand Oaks: Sage Publications, 2006).

6

Organizational Structure and Design

LEARNING OBJECTIVES

After studying this chapter, you should be able to:

Explain the concepts of organizational structure and design.

Discuss the concepts of differentiation and integration and their role in organizational structure and design.

Describe the concepts of formalization, informalization, centralization and decentralization, and discuss their interrelationships.

Identify the common structures used by organizations and describe the strengths and weaknesses of each of these structures.

Understand how network structures help firms manage their value chain activities and contribute to achieving a competitive advantage.

Describe how environmental factors and the organization's strategy influence organizational structure.

Explain the types of organizational structure important for firms to use when operating in international markets.

Managerial Challenges from the Front Line

Courtesy of Luiz Freire

Name: Luiz Freire

Position: Angola Country Vice President, Halliburton

Alma mater: University of Phoenix (BA); Texas A&M University (MBA)

Outside work activities: Spending time with my family; sailing on the ocean

First job out of school: Owned and operated a landscaping firm

Hero: Bill Gates, who started and built a multibillion-dollar company and now shares his wealth through the Gates Foundation to support quality secondary education and fight AIDS across the world, among other social needs.

Motto to live by: Be an example for my children and others

What drives me: To be a successful manager with principles

Management style: Lead by example

Pet peeve: Being stuck in heavy traffic

For over 19 years, Luiz Freire has worked at Halliburton, one of the world's largest engineering-construction and oilfield services companies. Halliburton is known for using innovative technology and for providing high-quality service to its customers. Freire is currently the Angola Country Vice President for Halliburton. Halliburton is a market leader in providing well-site services, and is a large multinational company.

Freire is responsible for all company activities in Angola, including business development, operations, and the overall representation of Halliburton in the country. In business development, he is responsible for the overall strategic positioning and the presence of the company in Angola. With all Halliburton's product service lines (PSL's) deployed to Angola, part of his job is to ensure the correct structure to support this activity and deliver top-quality services to clients. Freire also serves as a liaison with local authorities to convey Halliburton's commitments to the country. Halliburton uses a matrix organization structure in all of its operations so Freire shares project responsibility with the company's regional managers and team managers, who are responsible for technical excellence.

All projects are evaluated after their completion using Halliburton's "Done Right" index, under which projects are rated on such criteria as meeting the project's objectives, incurring no accidents, finishing on time, and achieving customer satisfaction. Each year managers are expected to achieve a high standard: at least a 96 percent rating across all of the company's projects. This requires the various managers in the matrix organization to cooperate and work closely together in order to meet this standard.

Freire recounts a recent challenge he faced in Angola: The economic crisis had a major negative impact in Angola. Halliburton's clients reduced their activities and sought discounts on the company's services. This happened in the worse time possible, when some 80 percent of all the contracts were in development stage which means the prices were open for negotiation before contracts could be signed. The price concessions reduced Halliburton's profits on the services provided and, thus, the company's overall bottom line. As a result, Freire's unit was forced to implement a strong cost reduction campaign (which is very difficult to do in Angola, reportedly the most expensive country in the world) while simultaneously maintaining or increasing the quality of the service they provided. Other side effects of the change in the business conditions were in the areas of inventory management and accounts receivable.

Freire says the company has successfully completed its tender campaign and is ready to begin delivering on new contracts. Ultimately, he says, Halliburton was able to maintain and in some cases expand its presence in Angola.

The managerial profile on Luiz Freire shows the complex environment in which firms such as Halliburton must operate today. Consider, for example, the fact that Freire manages many people throughout the country of Angola. He must deal with local government officials as well as regional managers. Before he took over his current job, he was a regional manager in Latin America that covered eight countries, which meant dealing with the governments and unique rules and regulations of eight different countries. This experience likely helped prepare him to work with government officials in Angola. However, he had to adapt to a different culture and institutional environment, and manage a large, diverse group of managers and employees. Halliburton's structure is very important when it comes to managing the firm's operations and diverse staff members. Although the structure has advantages and disadvantages, if managers like Freire establish good working relationships with their regional and team managers, they will better deal with the challenge from a competitor that he and Halliburton encounters in Angola.

Firms should be structured effectively to survive and prosper. A firm's structure can determine the success or failure of its strategy and its overall performance. Recent research shows that for a firm to perform at its optimal level, its structure needs to closely fit the environment in which it must operate. For example, a firm operating in a dynamic environment like those in most African countries requires a structure that allows flexibility to deal with unexpected challenges—challenges such as those Freire describes in his experience with Halliburton. Usually, for greater efficiency, a firm operating in less dynamic economic environments can and should be more formally structured.[1]

As discussed in previous chapters, a firm's strategy must be carefully implemented to be successful. How the strategy gets implemented is largely a question of how managers organize the firm and its activities, in other words, what they determine to be the firm's structure.[2] Additionally, the centralization or decentralization of a firm's structure also affects the implementation of divisional and overall strategies. Sometimes a firm's structure affects the very strategy it should choose.[3]

An increasingly common structure used by organizations today is a network structure (discussed in more detail later in this chapter). An example is when a firm decides to outsource its manufacturing operations, as Nike and many other athletic shoemakers do, and it must establish a network structure allowing it to maintain close contact with the firms to which it is outsourcing the work. The company also might need to maintain close relationships with a number of suppliers to ensure the quality and timely supply of goods. Because organizations often have many alliances, a network structure becomes important for implementing this type of cooperative strategy.[4]

It is important for current and future managers to understand the fundamentals of organizational design and structure so that they can better prepare for implementing structures to make them effective. There are usually multiple structural options. Consequently, it is important for them to understand common organizational structures and the general advantages and disadvantages of each. This includes the principles linking particular structures, organizational strategy, and the external environment and the key factors that determine a good fit among these elements. Finally, managers must be able to apply this knowledge in planning and implementing appropriate organizational structures.

Principles of Organizational Structure

A firm's **organizational structure** can be defined as the sum of the ways an organization divides its labor into distinct tasks and then coordinates them.[5] The structure provides the blueprint for the reporting relationships, controls, authority and decision making within an organization.[6] **Organizational design** is the process of assessing the organization's strategy and environmental demands and determining the appropriate organizational structure.

Often, organizational structure is discussed in terms of organizational charts. An **organizational chart** illustrates relationships among units and lines of authority among supervisors and subordinates through the use of labeled boxes and connecting lines. For example, Exhibit 6.1 shows the organizational chart of Suncor Energy. Although organizational charts provide a view of an organization's structure, it does not show the complete organizational structure. An organization's structure is more complex than what a chart can depict. Understanding

organizational structure
the sum of the ways an organization divides its labor into distinct tasks and then coordinates them

organizational design
the process of assessing an organization's strategy and environmental demands and then determining the appropriate organizational structures

organizational chart
a graphic illustration of the relationships among a firm's units and the lines of authority among supervisors and subordinates

EXHIBIT 6.1

Suncor Energy Organizational Structure

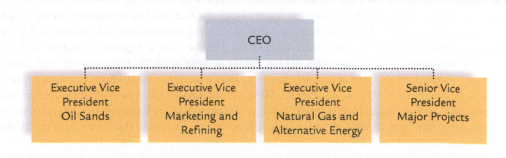

the principles of organizational structure and design is the key to correctly interpreting organizational charts while simultaneously being aware of an organization's other structural characteristics, which are less visible but are still important.

The base of an organization's structure and design includes people and activities.[7] On the one hand, all but the smallest of organizations have people performing different tasks. Even a small organization requires some differentiation and specialization to get tasks accomplished. On the other hand, each of the people performing different tasks must be integrated to meet the needs of the customers and the objectives of the organization. Balancing people and tasks and integrating them represent the primary challenges of organizational structure and design.[8] Fundamentally, the "right" structure that achieves the "right" balance between differentiation and integration is a function of the demands in the environment and the organization's strategy.

To focus on this basic challenge of organizational structure and design, we first examine some of the core elements of organizing and then explore the most common organizational structures. Finally, we discuss the challenge of designing structures that can fit the changing demands of the environment and the organization's strategy.

Differentiation

An important dimension of the organizing process is differentiation. **Differentiation** is the extent to which tasks are divided into subtasks and performed by individuals with specialized skills.[9] The main benefit of differentiation is greater specialization of knowledge and skills. For example, because of the complexity of building a commercial jetliner, Boeing has engineers who specialize in designing wings and others who design airplane doors. Even among those who design airplane doors, some focus primarily on designing the door hinges, whereas others focus on designing the locking mechanisms that keep the doors sealed at 35,000 feet. This differentiation by task is typically referred to as **task differentiation**.

The nature of differentiation is not limited only to the tasks people perform, but can also involve the way employees think. This is called **cognitive differentiation.** Cognitive differentiation is the extent to which people in different units within the organization think about things in different ways and the extent to which people think about similar things differently.[10] For example, accountants typically think about assets and liabilities, whereas marketing managers focus on brand image and market share. However, these two groups might also think about the same thing in different ways. Accountants might think about the organization's performance in terms of financial results, whereas marketers might think about the organization's performance in terms of customer satisfaction and number of products sold.

Differentiation is important for several reasons. First, to serve its customers, the firm must complete many specialized tasks. Moreover, the company wants these tasks performed especially well to serve the customer better than its competitors do in order to achieve a competitive advantage. Specialization also allows people to develop high levels of expertise in specific tasks in order to perform them especially well. In addition, research has shown that differentiation and the expertise developed from specialization helps firms to learn and use unique concepts that in turn help them develop more innovative products and services to satisfy their customers.[11]

While differentiation brings greater specialization, often it also presents a challenge in integrating the various specialized capabilities to deliver a product or service to the customer.[12] Suppose both design engineers and manufacturing personnel at Boeing need to work together to ensure that a newly designed 777 door operates properly. Greater specialization makes this coordination more difficult because designers might think about door performance in terms of design sophistication, whereas manufacturing managers might think about door performance in terms of the ease of making and installing the door on the plane. If Boeing has a door that is well designed but difficult and expensive to install, it may suffer potential undesirable consequences. It may end up with an expensive door that reduces profits because it is costly to install. Or, it might end up with a door that doesn't operate properly because of mismatches between design and assembly. This example suggests the importance of integration.

Integration

Integration is the extent to which various parts of the organization interact, coordinate, and cooperate with each other.[13] The primary benefit of integration is the coordinated actions of

differentiation
the extent to which tasks are divided into subtasks and performed by individuals with specialized skills

task differentiation
differentiation by what employees do

cognitive differentiation
the extent to which people in different units within an organization think about different things or about similar things differently

integration
the extent to which various parts of an organization cooperate and interact with each other

people and activities to achieve a desired organizational objective. To develop innovation from the differentiation discussed in the previous section requires effective coordination to achieve integration of the multiple people and activities.[14] Often, to achieve a high level of coordination requires a *boundary spanner,* a person who is either formally or informally designated to coordinate the activities across units or even sometimes across organizations. The role of the boundary spanner is to build effective relationships between the groups involved.[15] One of the driving forces of integration is interdependence. **Interdependence** is the degree to which each unit or person depends on other units or people to accomplish a required task.[16]

There are three types of interdependence.[17] **Pooled interdependence** occurs when several groups are largely independent in their functions but collectively contribute to a common output. For example, two independent product divisions in the same company might each sell products to the same hospital to meet the customer's overall needs. **Sequential interdependence** exists when the outputs of one group become the inputs of another group. For example, at Boeing the raw materials of aluminum provided by the firm's purchasing department become the inputs of the firm's pressing department. That department then shapes the aluminum sheets for doors and its outputs become the inputs of the door assembly department. **Reciprocal interdependence** exists when two or more groups depend on one another for inputs. For example, at Boeing the new-product development department relies on the marketing research department for product ideas to investigate, and marketing research relies on new-product development for new products to test on customers. In principle, the greater the interdependence, the greater the need for cooperation and, thus, the more important it is to achieve integration. Middle managers often play a key role in building and maintaining coordination across units in the organization.[18] And, they may play an even larger role in the coordination between internal and external units in a global supply chain. Such coordination is critical for firms to integrate the suppliers' activities with the firm and to meet customers' needs.[19]

Another factor that can influence the need for integration is uncertainty. For a firm, **uncertainty** refers to the extent to which it cannot forecast accurately future input, process, and output factors. The more difficult it is to accurately forecast these factors, the greater the uncertainty a firm faces. Greater uncertainty inspires a greater need for integration and coordination because as events unfold, individuals and organizational units have to coordinate in real time their responses to the events.

Integration and coordination can be achieved through a variety of mechanisms.[20] The appropriateness of each mechanism relates to the level and type of interdependence and the extent of uncertainty in the environment. Among these mechanisms are rules, goals, and values.

RULES Rules establish guidelines for behavior and consequences under specific conditions. Basically, rules are the standard operating procedures (SOP) for the organization. In general, the more task independence that exists within the organization, the more useful rules are as an integration mechanism. In contrast, the more task interdependence and uncertainty that exist, the less useful rules are as an integration mechanism. For example, a manager in the promotion department of a record company would find it difficult to use rules for coordination and integration to implement concert cancellations due to weather, travel problems for the band, or any number of other unpredictable factors. Rules might work well in the accounting department of the record company, where the environment is stable and the requirements are largely standard but would likely be less effective in the dynamic environment and requirements of the advertising and promotion department.

GOALS As task uncertainty and interdependence increase, preset rules become less effective for coordinating tasks. Consequently under these conditions, goals are a more effective coordination mechanism than rules. Instead of specifying what individuals should do, goals specify what outcomes individuals should achieve. Effective goals define measurable outcomes and often require high levels of effort to achieve. Specifying the outcomes but not the process gives employees greater flexibility to determine how they will accomplish their tasks. It also facilitates integration by ensuring that people are working toward the same outcomes. For example, university professors encounter students with a wide variety of needs and situations. Rather than impose strict rules on professors, a university typically sets forth goals in terms of student proficiency. These goals ensure that professors are working toward the same outcome but have the flexibility to respond to different needs and situations faced by individual students.

VALUES In conditions of high task uncertainty and interdependence, values become an important coordinating mechanism. The **values** in an organization identify fundamentally important behaviors, activities, and outcomes, such as customer satisfaction. But unlike goals, values do not necessarily represent measurable outcomes. Thus, values are a better integrating mechanism than goals when there is high uncertainty and high interdependence. Shared values facilitate coordination under these conditions because those holding the same values all work toward the same outcomes while maintaining flexibility in the process of how they are accomplished.

Exhibit 6.2 helps illustrate the level of appropriateness of rules, goals, and values in conditions of low to high levels of uncertainty. The exhibit also helps illustrate the partial overlap among them. As a matter of practice, it is impossible to specify the line where rules are no longer effective and goals should be used. Likewise, an exact boundary between the use of goals and values cannot be specified. Managers need to understand the relationship of rules, goals, and values with different levels of uncertainty and to use judgment in applying them.

values
fundamentally important behaviors, activities, and outcomes

Formalization

One way to balance both differentiating (separating) and integrating people and activities is through formalization. **Formalization** consists of the defined structures and systems related to decision making, communication, and control in the organization. These mechanisms usually explicitly define where and how people and activities are independent along with how they are integrated.[21] While all organizations have to manage differentiation and integration, they vary substantially in how much formalization they use to accomplish this.

Officially designating the line of authority within an organization is a common way of achieving formalization. A firm's **line of authority** specifies who reports to whom. It is often called line of authority because in organizational charts a line is typically drawn between subordinates and their bosses. Although it is important to follow the line of authority in many situations, in some cases managers and employees go outside of the line of authority to seek special expertise needed to resolve a problem.

More formal organizations also tend to stress unity of command. **Unity of command** suggests that an employee should have only one boss. Thus, people working in a highly formal organization with a strong orientation to unity of command are likely to have one boss who directs their work and evaluates their performance. As we explain later, the matrix structure used by Luiz Freire's company, Halliburton, violates the unity of command principle. Yet, such a structure has advantages that frequently offset the problems caused by people having two or more bosses.

More formal systems also often limit a supervisor's span of control. **Span of control** refers to the number of employees reporting to a given supervisor. More formal organizations tend to have a narrow rather than a wide span of control. The logic for this is that normally the fewer people a manager has to supervise, the more closely the manager can oversee and control them. However, several factors can influence the effectiveness of span of control. First, the nature of

formalization
the official and defined structures and systems related to decision making, communication, and control in an organization

line of authority
specifies who reports to whom

unity of command
the notion that an employee should have one and only one boss

span of control
the number of employees reporting to a given supervisor

EXHIBIT 6.2

Appropriateness of Rules, Goals, Values

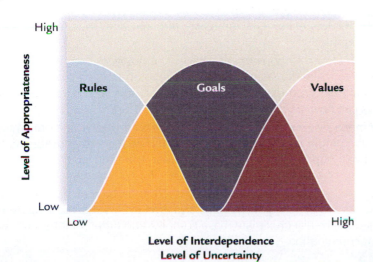

the task is an important factor. Usually, the more routine subordinates' tasks, the wider the effective span of control can be; managers can effectively supervise more subordinates if they have predictable and routine tasks. Another factor influencing effective span of control is subordinates' capabilities. Generally, the stronger the subordinates' capabilities, the less close supervision they require—thus, a larger span of control can be effective. Also, managerial capabilities influence effective span of control. The greater the manager's capabilities are, the wider the span of control that a manager can handle effectively. Integrating these three factors, we can see that if a manager is highly capable and his or her subordinates highly skilled, a wider span of control is possible. Exhibit 6.3 provides a brief summary of key factors that influence the effective span of control.[22]

Consistent patterns of span of control can affect the overall "shape" of the organization. Narrow spans of control throughout the entire organization tend to result in a **tall organization structure,** or one that has multiple layers with significant vertical differentiation. Wide span of control throughout the organization will generally lead to a more **flat organization structure.** Given similar number of employees, a flat organization will have fewer layers in its hierarchy than a tall organization. Exhibit 6.4 shows examples of tall and flat organizational structures, as well as span of control.

The external environment largely affects the appropriateness of a tall or flat organization. Tall and formal organizations tend to be slower at making decisions and responding to changes in the business environment. As a result, tall and formal organizations tend to be best suited to stable external environments.[23] Because many organizational environments have become more dynamic, managers often respond by trying to "flatten" their organizational structures—often removing whole levels of hierarchy and people in the process (often referred to as *downsizing*). They do this so that information does not have to travel as far (from the bottom to the top) for decisions to be made, and as a consequence they can make and implement them faster.[24]

tall organization structure
a structure that has multiple layers or is high in terms of vertical differentiation

flat organization structure
a structure that has fewer layers in its hierarchy than a tall organization

EXHIBIT 6.3

Factors that Influence the Span of Control

- *Job complexity*—Jobs that are complicated require more managerial input and involvement and, thus, the span of control tends to be narrower.
- *Job similarity*—If one manages a group of employees performing similar jobs, the span of control can be considerably wider than if the jobs of subordinates are substantially different.
- *Geographic proximity of supervised employees*—Because the employees who work in one location are more easily supervised than employees in dispersed locations, physical proximity to employees tends to allow a wider span of control.
- *Amount of coordination*—A narrower span of control is advisable in firms where management expends much time coordinating tasks performed by subordinates.
- *Abilities of employees*—Supervisors who manage employees who are more knowledgeable and capable can have a wider span of control than supervisors managing less knowledgeable and capable employees. The greater the abilities of employees, the less managerial inputs are required and, thus, a wider span of control is possible.
- *Degree of employee empowerment*—Because employees who are trusted and empowered to make decisions need less supervision than employees with less autonomy and decision-making discretion, supervisors who empower their employees can have a wider span of control.
- *Ability of management*—More capable managers can manage more employees than less competent managers. The abilities of managers to educate employees and effectively respond to their questions lessen the need for a narrow span of control.
- *Technology*—Communication technology, such as mobile phones, fax, e-mail, workshare software, can allow managers to effectively supervise employees who are not geographically proximate, have complex and different jobs, and require significant coordination.

EXHIBIT 6.4 Tall and Flat Organization Structures

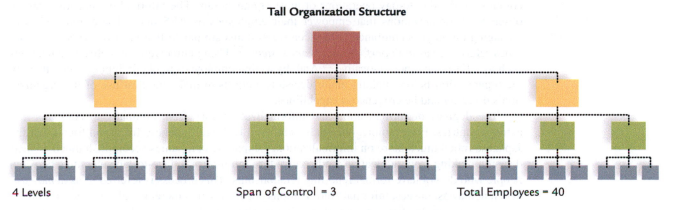

Tall Organization Structure

4 Levels   Span of Control = 3   Total Employees = 40

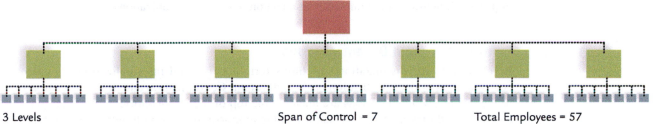

Flat Organization Structure

3 Levels   Span of Control = 7   Total Employees = 57

Nonetheless, implementing and managing flat structures can be a challenge. As environmental uncertainty increases for many organizations, managers often design flatter structures so that information can flow faster and decisions can be made more quickly. However, the environmental uncertainty also tends to result in more nonroutine tasks, which often require more narrow spans of control, creating taller, rather than flatter, organizations. Thus, flatter organizations and wider spans of control with more nonroutine tasks are possible only if subordinates and managers have stronger capabilities. Technology can arguably help companies remain flat by influencing the effective span of control.

In summary, formalization mechanisms, such as span of control, line of authority, and chain of command, work to both differentiate and integrate people and their activities. They do so in an explicit and official way.

In A Manager's Challenge, "AES Gives Power to the People," electric-power producer AES's structure empowers lower-level employees to make major decisions. To ensure accountability and increase the probability of success, AES also provides its employees incentive compensation based on the company's performance. Thus, they will be motivated to help the company perform well. For many years, AES also operated a more informal organization with no human resources, operations, purchasing, or legal affairs departments. But, for legal and other reasons, it has developed a few departments (such as finance and human resources) and centralized decisions in those functions. But the firm continues to empower its employees and encourages them to seek advice from one another and from managers in different parts of the company before making major decisions. This process fosters informal communication across the company's units and levels. AES's organizational structure and approach have been very successful.

Informalization

While virtually all organizations have some degree of formalization, even the most formal organizations also have some degree of informalization. The **informal organization** consists of the unofficial but influential means of communication, decision making, and control that are part of the habitual way things get done in the organization. Informal structures for decision making,

informal organization
the unofficial but influential means of communication, decision making, and control that are part of the habitual way things get done in an organization

communication, and control usually are not represented in organizational charts, yet they are common in the day-to-day operations of most organizations. The informal organization can be observed in organizations that empower their employees as AES does. These approaches to managing employees combined with incentive systems similar to that used by AES are sometimes referred to as *high performance work systems*.[25] Using empowerment helps organizations such as AES to be more innovative.[26] And, by asking employees to obtain inputs from others in the organization before making major decisions help them make the best use of the organization's diversity and heterogeneous capabilities.[27]

The degrees of formalization and informalization vary from company to company and across countries. For example, one study compared U.S. and Japanese firms and found that the Japanese relied much more on informalization.[28] Japanese companies accomplish much of their decision making, communication, and control through informal, face-to-face meetings between people who do not have formal reporting relationships. This process is referred to as *nemawasi*. When nemawasi ensues, informal conversations occur in which incremental decisions are made. Consequently, by the time an official meeting is held to make the formal decision, the decision has already been made informally. In China, much is accomplished through relationships referred to as *guanxi*. Guanxi is developed over time. Basically, trust evolves between two people who take actions that benefit one another. In other words, reciprocity is expected. Guanxi is an important dimension of the informal organization in Chinese organizations.[29]

Centralization and Decentralization

In addition to the organization structure's formalization and informalization, its extent of centralization or decentralization is also important. Centralization and decentralization refer to the level at which decisions are made, at the top of the organization or at lower levels. In a **centralized organization,** decision-making authority resides with only a few individuals, usually at the top of the organization. In contrast, a **decentralized organization** pushes decision-making authority down to the lowest-possible level. For instance, European multinational organizations tend to be decentralized and allow units in different countries to make decisions according to local conditions. Often this enables them to adapt to government demands and different consumer preferences.[30]

For many years, Philips, a large multinational electronics firm headquartered in the Netherlands, exemplified a decentralized international organization. Philips operated in over 60 countries around the world, and many of the larger-country units enjoyed considerable freedom and autonomy. For example, even though the V2000 videocassette recorder (the first VCR) was developed at the company's headquarters, the North American division of Philips refused to purchase and sell the product in the United States and Canada. Instead, North American Philips purchased a VCR made by a Japanese rival and resold it in the United States and Canada under the Philips brand name.

Japanese firms, on the other hand, exhibit a stronger degree of centralization and tend not to delegate decisions as frequently as either European or American firms.[31] Most Japanese multinational firms operate like centralized hubs into which information flows, and from which decisions are announced to foreign subsidiaries. Japanese firms have encountered increasing complaints from host nationals in local subsidiaries about a "bamboo ceiling"—the fact that host nationals are sometimes excluded from strategic decision making because Japanese expatriates sent by headquarters to ensure more centralized control occupy nearly all key positions in the subsidiary.[32] Toyota's recent quality control problems with autos sold in the United States have been partially attributed to the central control from the home office managers in Japan and the unwillingness to share information with managers of Toyota's operations in the United States. A major "bamboo ceiling" was broken in 2005 when Sony named Howard Stringer, a citizen of Great Britain, as the company CEO. At the time, Sony's performance was suffering, and Stringer was charged with the task of turning it around. Some may perceive that formalization and centralization are largely the same, and that informalization and decentralization are also synonymous. This is not the case (see Exhibit 6.5). A highly formal organization may be centralized, but a formal organization can also be fairly decentralized. For example, as illustrated previously, Philips is a fairly decentralized company in that

centralized organization
organizations that restrict decision making to fewer individuals, usually at the top of the organization

decentralized organization
organizations that tend to push decision-making authority down to the lowest-possible level

A MANAGER'S CHALLENGE

DIVERSITY

AES Gives Power to the People

AES, one of the world's largest electric-power producers, has been able to achieve a remarkable level of success through its informal organization and empowerment of its employees. In addition, employees in the field make many decisions. The company has been successful partly because its local units are empowered to make decisions yet are held accountable for their profitability.

Many AES managers and employees see this empowerment as beneficial because it gives them a great deal of flexibility and freedom. It's as if they are running their own business versus working for other people. They also feel more creative and motivated. As a result, turnover is lower. AES even allows lower-level employees to make critical decisions. The system works because prior to making a decision, AES employees are expected to ask for advice (often by e-mail) from other people in the company, including senior managers.

Another reason for AES's success is due to the way the company is structured—its organization is very flat. For many years, the company did not establish separate corporate departments for its human resources, operations, purchasing, or legal affairs functions. Multiple teams work under a single level of management so bottom-up decision making is the norm. Fewer levels of management and shorter lines of communication accelerates decision making. Consequently, the company is nimble and can quickly respond strategically to changes in the marketplace. In more recent years, AES has had to develop some separate departments. For example, because of the Sarbanes-Oxley law, the firm centralized financial decisions in a finance unit headed by the CFO. He also created a human resources department. Yet, AES still provides employees freedom to experiment to identify the best way to complete tasks thereby trying to maintain its entrepreneurial culture.

Employee incentives programs have also contributed to AES's success. For example, the company gives an employee the option of earning a salary plus bonus (incentive) compensation in lieu of hourly and overtime pay. About 90 percent of AES's employees have chosen the salary-plus-bonus option. It is important to note that when standards and incentives are in place, employees are less likely to need intervention from "centralized" managers. AES feels that by giving the employees the power to make decisions, they will be more prone to support the company and will be more successful, which in turn will make the company more profitable. The culture thrives on individual empowerment, developing more capable employees, and holding them accountable for company performance with compensation through stock options. The firm's approach to managing its people and the changes recently implemented (e.g., new departments of finance and human resources) have helped the company overcome the problems of the two major recessions in the first ten years of the twenty-first century. Also, AES has enjoyed a balance of its revenues across many countries. For example in 2009, only 21 percent of the firm's revenue was from the United States. And, its international presence has allowed it broader access to global capital markets. In 2009, AES received a $2 billion capital injection from the China Investment Corporation. Overall, analysts project a very bright future for AES growth and financial vitality.

Sources: D. Bogoslaw, "AES: Ready for a Recharge," *Bloomberg BusinessWeek,* June 3, 2010, http://www.businessweek.com; S. Geidi, "AES Getting $2 Billion from China Sovereign Fund," *MarketWatch,* November 6, 2009, http://www.marketwatch.com; M. Gunther, "AES's Powerful Comeback," *CNNMoney.com,* October 19, 2009, http://www.cnnmoney.com; G. Lee, "AES Corporation: Rewriting the Rules of Management," *Ray Shan's Journal,* December 6, 2005, http://www.rayshan.com; T. W. Malone, "Pioneers That Cultivate a New Model of Work," *Financial Times,* August 11, 2004, http://www.ft.com; H. Wee, "A Nasty Short-Circuit at AES," *BusinessWeek*, October 4, 2001, "A Worldwide Power Play," *BusinessWeek*, November 27, 2000, http://www.businessweek.com.

decisions are pushed down into the organization. At the same time, however, Philips is also relatively formalized. Lines of authority, chain of command, official policies, and so on are prevalent. In contrast, the U.S. military is both formal and centralized.

Similarly, a highly informal organization can be either decentralized or highly centralized. For example, on average, Japanese firms are relatively centralized but at the same time function through a high degree of informalization. Likewise, it is quite common for family-owned businesses to be both centralized and informal. That is, the owner makes most of the decisions, but

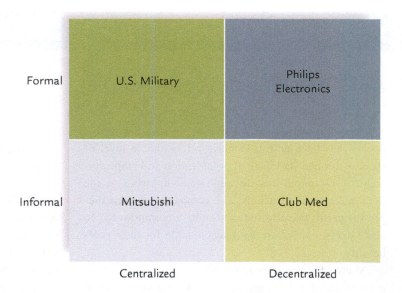

using informal connections, communication, and control rather than formal structures or rules to accomplish tasks. In contrast, Club Med is fairly decentralized and informal. Each resort's general manager is relatively free to make decisions that meet the needs of his or her unique market. Club Med achieves coordination through an array of informal relationships among general managers and corporate managers.

Some research suggests that the strategic use of decentralized structures allows units to adopt important new procedures to fit their needs and environment. Thus firms use decentralization to allow their subsidiaries and divisions to adopt new programs such as quality management standards and approaches.[33] Additional research shows that decentralized structures facilitate a more entrepreneurial approach among units of a firm leading to the development of more innovation.[34]

Matsushita broke with tradition and decentralized decision-making authority to its various divisions and departments. Today, it is largely decentralized, with centralized R&D operations to eliminate the duplicate products developed by divisions within the company trying to compete against each other. Thus, Matsushita was simultaneously decentralized and centralized (in different areas). The outcomes of the change in structure were dramatic and positive. The company is now positioned well for the future with its international sales base growing, especially in Europe.

Common Organizational Structures

While a variety of organizational structures exist, six structures represent the most common forms. We examine each of these basic structures although there are hybrids that combine more than one structural form. In reality, most organizations do not have pure forms but rather have hybrids. After we review these basic organizational structures and briefly examine their general strengths and weaknesses, we present a discussion of the conditions that determine which type of structure a manager should adopt.

Functional Structure

Perhaps the simplest structure is the functional structure (Exhibit 6.6). The functional structure is used to organize the firm around traditional functional areas, such as accounting, finance, marketing, operations, and so on.[35] This structure is one of the most common types because it separates the specialized knowledge of each functional area through horizontal differentiation and can direct that knowledge toward the firm's key products or services.

Firms with operations outside their domestic borders might also adopt a functional structure. The key difference between a purely domestic organization and a multinational organization with a functional structure is the scope of the responsibilities functional heads in the multinational firm bear. In a multinational, each department has global responsibilities. Although each subsidiary

A MANAGER'S CHALLENGE

CHANGE

Matsushita Finds a New Way to Electrify Its Profits

In 1994, Matsushita's then-CEO Teruo Tanni resigned abruptly from the firm, saying his departure was due to the company's sagging fortunes, for which he took responsibility. Tanni's sudden departure shocked many in Japan's corporate world because CEO ousters are almost unheard of there. It seemed especially odd for Matsushita, which had commonly adhered to traditional Japanese-style management. Subsequent to Tanni's resignation, Chairman Matsushita asked the most junior of Matsushita's executive vice presidents to manage the company. His selection sent a strong message that the company wanted to change how it managed the business. This was reinforced when the company failed to keep ex-CEO Tanni on its board of directors.

Matsushita wasted no time reorganizing following Tanni's departure. The company hired a new CEO, Kunio Nakamura, who played a pivotal role turning the company around. A three-year strategic plan was developed in which its approach was referred to as "Four-S Management" (with the four S's being "simple," "small," "speedy," and "strategic"). The company's new management team wanted to simplify the company's managerial approach and make it less hierarchical.

Decentralizing decision authority to Matsushita's lower-level managers was essential to this plan. In so doing, the company removed an entire layer of management at headquarters, and the heads of the operating divisions were given full responsibility for product development as well as production and finance. Basically, each division had the autonomy to operate its own business, with Matsushita acting as the "shareholder" of each division.

Such decentralization and focus on individual responsibility is unusual in Japan, where group-oriented decision making is the norm and centralized authority is common. However, the change positively affected the heads of divisions, encouraging them to be more entrepreneurial. In addition, all managers from the lowest to the highest levels were required to provide Nakamura with a personal, three-year "revival" plan for each of their divisions or departments.

By centralizing the company's research and development operations, each individual then had authority and responsibility directly provided by the CEO, which, in turn, created a flat organizational structure. Nakamura also ended the internal rivalries that led some divisions to develop identical products by centralizing the R&D operations.

Ultimately, the restructuring of Matsushita led to the recovery of the company. With the reduction in management levels and reorganization of 30 divisions into four groups with shared R&D facilities, the company was able to reduce costs by operating much more efficiently thereby enhancing its profits. Today, the $77.2 billion company is one of the largest consumer electronics makers in the world and is receiving the benefits of the changes. Matsushita has experienced small sales declines in the recession in 2008–2009 but it is strong and doing much better than many of its competitors and other Japanese companies. The company is well-positioned for the future. Although it has a wide range of consumer electronics products, its core business is in flat-screen TVs. In fact, the company has made significant advances in the technology, greatly improving the efficiency such that the 42-inch screens are much brighter but use less electricity than a 100-watt light bulb. And, the company has expanded its sales across the globe with special inroads to the European markets. Interestingly, 25 percent of its international sales are in European markets and 25 percent are in the United States. Matsushita will continue to be one of the global leaders in consumer electronics products.

Sources: Company Web site, "Panasonic Sponsors Sustainable Brands 2010 Conference in Monterey, California," http://www.panasonic.com, accessed June 18, 2010; "Panasonic Corporation," *Answers.com,* www.answers.com/topic/masushita-electric-industrial-co, accessed June 10, 2010; Y. I. Kane, H. Kachi and J. Osawa, "Matsushita Electric's Profit Growth Is Driven by Its Flat-panel Unit," *Wall Street Journal,* July 30, 2008, http://online.wsj.com; "Matsushita Shifts Strategy to Succeed in Europe," *Wall Street Journal,* July 10, 2008, http://online.wsj.com; K. Hall, "Matsushita's Transformer Steps Down," *BusinessWeek,* June 30, 2006, http://www.businessweek.com; M. Nakamoto, "Reforms Drive Up Profits at Matsushita," *Financial Times,* February 5, 2005; "Management Tradition Be Damned," *BusinessWeek,* October 31, 1994, http://www.businessweek.com/archives.

might have a local human resource manager, the top human resource manager in the company (usually in the home office) is responsible for directing worldwide human resource activities, such as hiring, training, appraising, and rewarding employees. This structure is most commonly used when the technology and products of the firm are similar throughout the world.

EXHIBIT 6.6

Functional Structure

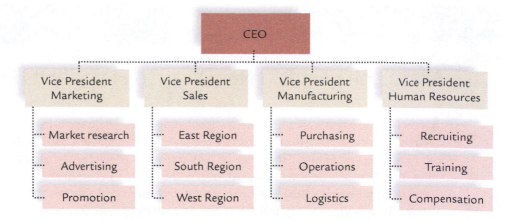

Following are some major advantages of this structure:

1. It is well suited for small and medium-sized firms with limited product diversification.
2. It facilitates specialization of the firm's functional knowledge.
3. It reduces the duplication of the firm's functional resources.
4. It facilitates coordination within the firm's functional areas.

A global functional structure can also reduce headquarters–subsidiary conflicts because it integrates operations throughout the world into their functional areas and charges functional department executives with global responsibility. This, in turn, enhances the overall international orientation of managers. For example, the higher a marketing manager rises in the marketing department, the more that manager needs to think about and understand the firm's global marketing issues.

The primary weaknesses of this structure include the following:

1. It often creates problems of coordination across the firm's functional groups.
2. It leads to a narrow view of the organization's overall goals.
3. It can limit the attention paid to customers as functional groups focus on their specific areas.
4. It can result in the organization responding more slowly to market changes.
5. It often burdens chief executives with decisions that involve multiple functions.

In an international setting, a functional structure can be disadvantageous when the firm has a wide variety of products and these products have different environmental demands, such as different government restrictions or standards, customer preferences, or performance requirements. This weakness is exacerbated when different functional departments experience different demands across geographic areas. For example, if accounting practices are similar between the United Kingdom and France but advertising approaches differ between the two countries, the accounting and marketing departments are likely to experience coordination difficulties.

Product Structure

In a product structure as shown in Exhibit 6.7, the firm is organized around specific products (or services) or related sets of products (or services). Typically, each product group contains all the traditional departments a functional structure has, such as finance, marketing, operations, human resource management departments, and so on. Each product is generally treated as a **profit center.** That is, the expenses related to a product are subtracted from the revenues generated by the product's sales. Most commonly, the heads of the product or services units are located in the headquarters of the company. However, this is not necessarily the case. For example, the headquarters for Honeywell's commercial and residential control product group is in Minnesota, whereas the headquarters for its commercial flight instruments product group is in Arizona.

The principal advantages of a product structure include the following:

1. Individuals in different functional areas within the product group focus more on the specific products and customers.
2. The performance of the firm's products (profits and losses) is typically easier to evaluate.

profit center

a unit or product line whose related expenses are deducted from the revenue it generates

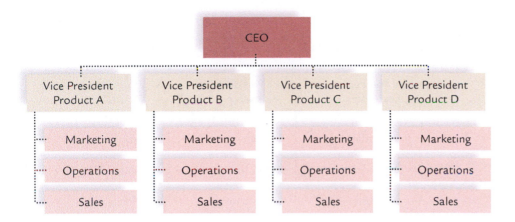

EXHIBIT 6.7

Product Structure

3. There is usually greater product responsiveness to market changes.
4. It often reduces the operating decision-making burden of the top executive.

The major disadvantages of the product structure include the following:

1. Duplication and lack of economies of scale for functional areas (for example, IT, finance, human resources, and so on).
2. It can create problems for customers who purchase products across multiple product groups.
3. Sometimes there are conflicts between the firm's corporate objectives and the objectives of its product groups.
4. There is an increased likelihood of conflict between different product groups and greater difficulty coordinating across product groups.

Multinational firms also use global product structures. This typically occurs when customer needs for a given product are similar throughout the international markets in which the firm participates. After Becton Dickinson adopted a global product structure, the head of the biosciences unit became responsible for global strategy formulation and implementation of those products.

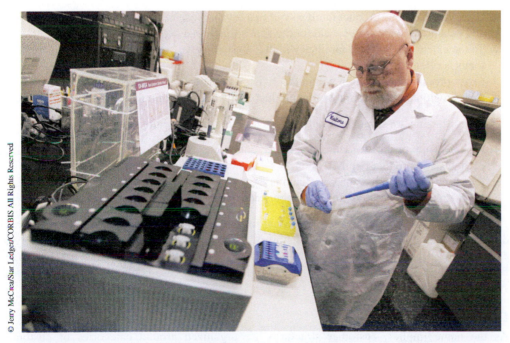

Multinational firms, such as Becton Dickinson, a medical products firm, based in Franklin Lakes, New Jersey, frequently use global product structures. They typically do so when their customers' needs for a given product are similar throughout the international markets in which the firm participates.

EXHIBIT 6.8

Division Structure

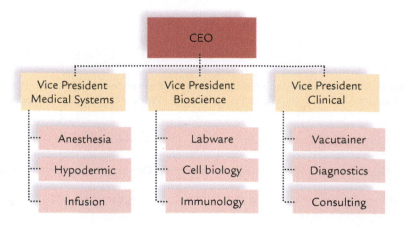

Division Structure

The division structure can be viewed as an extension of a product structure. Exhibit 6.8 provides a partial organizational chart of the division structure of Becton Dickinson, a medical products company. Divisions typically consist of multiple products within a generally related area, though specific products may not necessarily be closely related. General Electric (GE) has over 11 different business units, organizing a diversified portfolio of products including financial services, transportation, energy, insurance, medical systems, and entertainment products.

Within each unit, there are broad arrays of product groups and specific products. For example, the Medical Systems Division within GE consists of 12 different product groups, such as cardiology, radiology, emergency room equipment, and products related to orthopedics and sports medicine. Within each of these groups are many more specific products. Clearly, a significant size and diversity of products are needed to justify the creation of a division structure. A division structure also facilitates the use of modular products each of which is different but which contain some of the same parts. Thus, modular parts are produced and assembled in different ways to produce several different products.[36] Typically, in a division structure, all functional activities are located within each division.

The following are common strengths of a division structure:

1. Organizing various product families within a division can reduce functional duplication and enhance economies of scale for the firm's functional activities.
2. To the extent that product families within a division serve common customers, customer focus is often stronger.
3. Cross-product coordination within the division is easier.
4. Cross-regional coordination within product families and within the division is often easier.

The following are common disadvantages of a division structure:

1. Primarily appropriate for large, diversified companies with significant numbers of specific products and product families.
2. It can inhibit cross-division coordination.
3. It can create coordination difficulties between corporate and division objectives.

Similar to domestic firms, multinational firms often use this structure. In this case, each division is charged with global responsibility. Because a division structure is generally an extension of a product structure, it has many of the same advantages and disadvantages. For large, diversified multinational firms, the division structure is one of the more common structures used.

Customer Structure

As the name implies, customer structures are organized around categories of customers (Exhibit 6.9). Typically, this structure is used when different categories of customers have independent, differing needs. For example, industrial customers might purchase a different set of products than retail customers.

EXHIBIT 6.9

Customer Structure

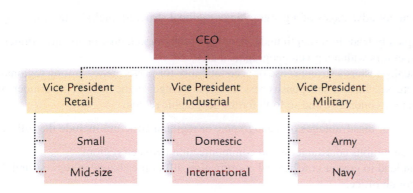

The primary strengths of this structure include the following:

1. It facilitates in-depth understanding of specific customers.
2. It increases the firm's responsiveness to changes in customer preferences and needs as well as the firm's responsiveness to actions taken by competitors to better serve customers.

The primary weaknesses of this structure include the following:

1. It typically creates duplication of functional resources in each of the customer units.
2. It often makes it difficult to coordinate between customer units and corporate objectives.
3. It can fail to leverage technology or other strengths of one unit across other units.

Many multinational firms find this type of structure difficult to implement because customers differ across regions and countries. For example, even though IBM initially had a consulting unit focused on government customers, it was difficult to organize the unit on a global basis because different governments had different needs and requirements for selecting computing-solution providers. Thus, while government customers in the United States were significantly different in their needs from other IBM customers, the advantage gained by focusing on this customer segment was not possible across the rest of the world.

Geographic or Regional Structure

As Exhibit 6.10 shows, firms can develop an organizational structure based on various geographical areas or regions in which it has operations. Within this type of structure, regional executives are generally responsible for all functional activities and products in their regions. For example, a Western regional vice president might be responsible for all key business activities in the states of Washington, Oregon, California, Nevada, Montana, Utah, Idaho, Wyoming, Colorado, Arizona, and New Mexico. The individual regions are often treated as profit centers. Thus, each region's profitability is measured against the revenues it generates and the expenses it incurs.

EXHIBIT 6.10

Geographical/Regional Structure

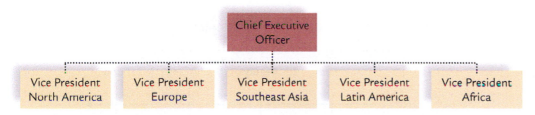

Strengths:
- Facilitates local responsiveness
- Develops in-depth knowledge of specific regions or countries
- Creates accountability by region
- Facilitates cross-functional coordination within regions

Weaknesses:
- Often creates cross-regional coordination difficulties
- Can inhibit ability to capture global scale economies
- Duplicates resources and functions across regions

The major advantages of a geographic or regional structure include the following:

1. It typically leads to in-depth understanding of the market, customers, governments, and competitors within a given geographical area.
2. It usually fosters a strong sense of accountability for performance among regional managers.
3. It increases the firm's responsiveness to unique changes in the market, government regulations, economic conditions, and so forth for the geographic region.

The major disadvantages of a geographic or regional structure include the following:

1. It often inhibits coordination and communication between regions.
2. It can lead to greater conflict and coordination difficulties between regions and the firm's corporate office.
3. It normally produces duplication of functional resources across regions.
4. Separating production facilities across multiple regions reduce the opportunity to gain economies of scale.
5. It can foster competitive behavior among regions, which is particularly frustrating for customers who have operations across multiple regions.

Multinational firms commonly employ geographic or regional structures.[37] This is primarily because customers' demands, government regulations, competitive conditions, the availability of suppliers, and other factors vary significantly from one region of the world to another. The size or scope of the region is typically a function of the volume of business. For example, in consumer products companies, the Middle East and Africa are often included in the European region because the volume of sales in these areas is too small to justify separate regions (EMEA—Europe, Middle East, and Africa). On the other hand, for most oil and gas companies with a geographic structure, the Middle East is a separate region because of its importance as a source of oil.

Matrix Structure

A matrix structure, such as the one shown in Exhibit 6.11, consists of two organizational structures superimposed on each other. As a consequence, there are dual reporting relationships. That is, one person essentially reports to two bosses. These two structures can be a combination of the general forms already discussed. For example, the matrix structure might consist of product divisions intersecting with functional departments or geographical regions intersecting with product divisions. This is the structure used by Halliburton as described in the opening profile. As we explained, Luiz Freire is a country manager. He coordinates with regional managers and oversees product or project managers. The two overlapping structures used are often based on the two dominant aspects of an organization's environment.

The major strengths of a matrix structure include the following:

1. It typically facilitates information flow throughout the organization.
2. It can enhance decision-making quality because the organization considers both intersecting perspectives in making key decisions.
3. It is best suited to a changing and complicated business environment.
4. It can facilitate the flexible use of human resources.

EXHIBIT 6.11

Matrix Structure

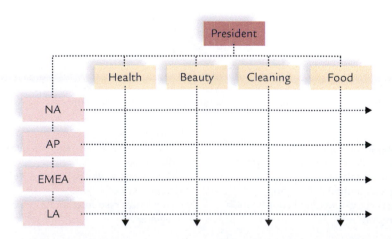

The major disadvantages of a matrix structure include the following:

1. It often makes performance evaluations more complex because employees usually have two bosses.
2. It can inhibit the organization's ability to respond to changing conditions quickly.
3. It can diffuse accountability.
4. Conflicts can occur when the firm attempts to integrate the differing perspectives and objectives of intersecting units.

Multinational companies frequently use matrix organization structures, as exemplified by Halliburton. They are used often because although economies of scale for global product, division, or even customer structures are compelling, regional differences relative to governments, cultures, languages, and economies are also strong. However, matrix structures are especially difficult to manage in multinational companies. ABB, a large industrial company based in Switzerland, for many years had a regional division matrix structure. However, in the late 1990s, senior executives at ABB determined that the conflicts and difficulties of managing the matrix outweighed the benefits so they changed to a global division structure. Even though such changes are positive, they also are difficult to design and implement. Thus, it requires much planning for major changes in structure.[38]

Mixed Organizational Structures

As mentioned earlier, although there are pure structural forms, any combination of the basic organizational structures is possible. The typical objective of a mixed, or a hybrid, organizational structure is to gain the advantages of one structure and reduce its disadvantages by incorporating the strengths of different structures. Exhibit 6.12 provides an example of a hybrid

EXHIBIT 6.12 Hybrid Structure

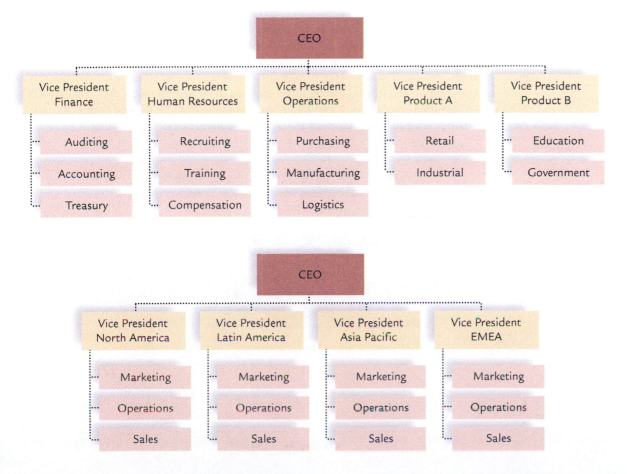

functional-product-customer structure. Because many of these hybrid structures are reflected in contemporary organizational forms, we explore this issue in more depth in the next section;

Network Organizational Structures

There are a variety of contemporary organizational structures. Many of them do not have common labels or names. This is, in part, because many of them have their essence in the configuration of organizational units and activities and organizational charts cannot easily depict them. One way of addressing these forms is to use the value chain concept introduced in Chapter 5. A major part of creating a contemporary structure involves reconfiguring the firm's value chain in an effort to gain cost savings and specialization benefits and improve integration and coordination.

Often these contemporary structures are referred to as *network structures.* There are several versions of network structures, ranging on a continuum from "low networked" to "high networked." In a low-networked structure, the quantity and magnitude of externally networked activities is limited. That is, a firm owns and executes most of its primary and support value chain activities and networks, and outside organizations are used for only a limited number of more minor value chain activities. In contrast, the high-networked structures include a larger quantity and magnitude of externally networked activities. In these structures, the number of externally networked value chain activities often exceeds those owned and executed internally by the firm.

One of the most common ways of networking with an external organization is to outsource a value chain activity. Outsourcing is the practice of taking a significant activity within the organization and contracting that activity out to an independent party. For example, the European Space Agency originally contracted with EDS to perform virtually all the agency's IT functions.[39] EDS was acquired by Hewlett Packard and is now a part of HP's Enterprise Services unit. A major portion of that unit's revenues comes from performing IT functions for a variety of customers (see Exhibit 6.13).

Nike outsources nearly all its shoe manufacturing, essentially the operations segment of the primary activities in its value chain. It is networked with its many contract manufacturers. Nike is so tightly networked that it can design a shoe at its Beaverton, Oregon, headquarters, send the blueprints via satellite to one of its contractors, and receive back by FedEx a prototype shoe from the contract factory all within a week. Increasingly, activities that executives once believed could be performed only internally—such as IT, human resource administration, design, manufacturing, sales, and customer support—are now being outsourced. Technology has made it possible to integrate activities performed in a network of separate organizations and retain reliability as well as lower costs. Much of the current outsourcing is directed to companies in another country. All of Nike's manufacturing contractors, for example, are located outside the United States. Many outsourced activities are going to companies in India, particularly in IT.[40] The available technology

EXHIBIT 6.13

Outsourced Structure

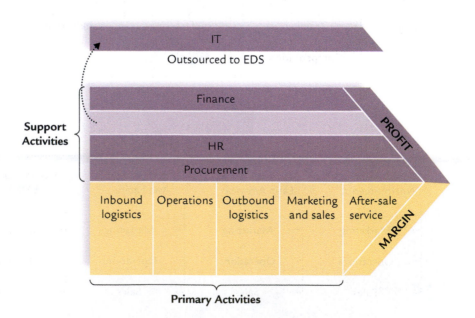

allowing communication and coordination to occur between distant locations and among multiple people on a real-time basis facilitates network-type structures. Some refer to this context as the digital era. Technology allows people to coordinate and to integrate their activities even though a formal organization does not bind them together.[41] Use of this new technology to "network" (coordinate and integrate) diverse people, activities, and organizations creates new and sometimes significant challenges for managers. As noted previously, managers must ensure that all activities are completed effectively—not an easy task if people are only loosely related to their organization.

In high-networked structures, firms have more value chain activities networked to external organizations than owned and executed internally. Assume a clothing design company formulated a strategy to compete by having superior design, world-class raw materials, and close relationships with retailers. Based on this strategy, the firm may own and control only a few elements of the entire value chain, such as design, procurement, and sales, but virtually nothing else. The firm could network with a company such as Ryder to perform its inbound logistics. It could network with various contractors in Asia to manufacture the clothes as designed. The firm could contract with UPS to perform all the outbound logistics. It could outsource to Avaya to handle its customer services. IBM or HP could operate the IT functions. Ernst & Young could manage the HR, finance, and tax functions. In this way, managers of the company could focus their energies on the critical dimensions of the value chain, such as design, procurement, and sales, that are the most likely to provide a competitive advantage (see Exhibit 6.14).

Similar to the more traditional structures, a **network structure** has both advantages and disadvantages. One of the most compelling advantages is that networking allows managers to focus on core competencies or the activities that are most likely to yield competitive advantage. By concentrating on core activities, managers can ensure that they are performed effectively. However, the "noncore" activities that are networked must also be performed well. It takes time, attention, energy, and skill to manage these relationships with external organizations. Simplified, network structures can provide greater focus and specialization on specific value chain activities, and such structures also require oversight, coordination with the organizations that are performing the networked activities, and the integration of their outputs into the firm.

network structure
the formal or informal relationships among units or organizations (for example, along the firm's value chain)

EXHIBIT 6.14

Network Structure

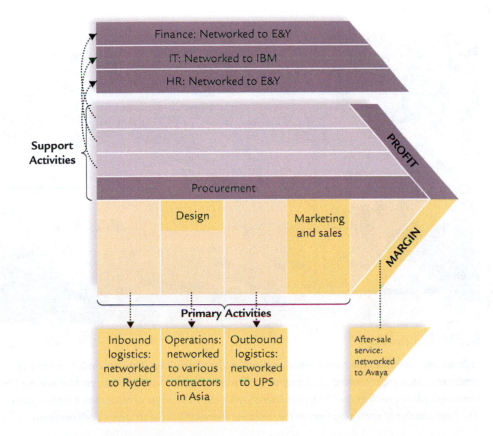

Designing Organizations

Fundamentally, in designing organizations managers face the challenge of capturing both specialization and integration advantages while minimizing the often mirror-image disadvantages. So then, "How should the managers decide to actually structure an organization?" The two main determinants of this decision are the external environment and the strategy of the company.

The External Environment

A key factor in determining the match between the environment and organizational structure is environmental uncertainty.[42] We offered a relatively simple description of environmental uncertainty earlier in this chapter. Next, we expand this view with two related but separate constructs: the extent to which the environment is (a) complex and (b) dynamic.

environmental complexity
the breadth and depth of differences and similarities in an organization's external environment

ENVIRONMENTAL COMPLEXITY **Environmental complexity** is fundamentally the breadth and depth of differences and similarities in an organization's external environment. Complex environments have greater breadth and depth of differences than simple environments. The differences and similarities can be assessed along many dimensions, but there are several core categories. These core categories include products, customers, technology, competitors, suppliers, and geography.

The complexity relative to products can vary widely from firm to firm. For example, a BIC pen consists of approximately seven parts. Each part is produced with relatively low technology, and the assembly of the parts into the final product also requires relatively low technology. At the other end of the continuum, when Boeing assembles a 777 jet, it has a huge breadth of over 1 million parts to integrate. The depths of these components range from a simple metal bolt to a panel composed of rare composite materials. Thus, Boeing has a highly complex product environment, especially relative to the BIC pen's environment.

Customers constitute another important dimension of environmental complexity. For example, McDonald's serves hamburgers to millions of customers each day, but the difference among these customers is relatively small compared to the group's overall size. In contrast, Toyota serves millions of customers each year, but their needs are sufficiently different that key aspects of Toyota cars, such as the suspension and emissions systems, vary greatly from one region of the world to another.

John Froschauer/AP Wide World Photos

A firm's environmental complexity relates not only to the competition that surrounds it but also its products, customers, technology, and geography. In terms of product complexity, consider Boeing: The company's planes, such as the 787 Dreamliner shown here, can consist of more than a million parts. The huge number of parts alone makes the operation more difficult to structure and coordinate.

Technology is another important dimension of environmental complexity. Technological complexity includes both the diversity of the technology required and the level of its sophistication. For example, Alcatel-Lucent Technologies uses analog, digital, and photonic technologies in its telephone and communication products. But the technology involved in both the manufacturing of its photonic switches for transmission of data along fiber optic lines and in the actual products Alcatel-Lucent makes is of a depth that many people with PhDs in physics have difficulty understanding it.

Competitors constitute an important dimension of environmental complexity. A larger number and greater diversity of competitors produce more complex environments. For example, in the design and manufacture of commercial aircraft, Boeing has a fairly complex product environment, but it simultaneously has a much simpler competitor environment. Basically, its only direct competitor is Airbus. Although competing against Airbus is not easy, Boeing's competitor environment is simpler than the environment of The GAP. The GAP competes with thousands of clothing manufacturers and labels for the same customers.

Suppliers are an additional dimension of environmental complexity. The greater number and diversity of suppliers lead to more complex environments. For example, despite having a simpler competitor environment, Boeing has a complex supplier environment. While Boeing designs most of the commercial aircraft it produces, it also uses hundreds of suppliers, some making such large components as the entire tail sections of Boeing's planes.

The final dimension, geographic complexity, is included because it tends to have a significant effect on all of the dimensions previously mentioned. This is principally because the more geographic regions covered, the greater the probability of differences across the other categories. For example, the greater the number of countries in which a firm operates, the greater the probability that dissimilarities will exist between the countries (for example, in their regulations, laws, customer preferences, and language). These differences are likely to increase the breadth and depth of differences relative to products, customers, technology, competitors, and suppliers. Consequently, greater geographic scope increases the complexity of the environment.

ENVIRONMENTAL DYNAMISM The second element contributing to the overall uncertainty of the environment is the extent to which the environment is static or dynamic.[43] Static environments may have few or many factors, but these factors tend to remain stable over time. For example, the manufacturing technology for pens and the component parts has changed little in the last 30 years. In contrast, factors in dynamic environments change rapidly. For example, advancements in composite materials and electronics have changed significantly for commercial aircraft manufacturers over the last 30 years. The fashion industry operates in an even more dynamic external environment. Benetton faces an environment in which colors, fabric, and styles change not just year to year but season to season. Firms operating in dynamic environments often describe them as "white water" environments in reference to the challenges of navigating a raft down the changing rapids of a river. A rapidly changing external environment typically requires quick internal organizational changes. While we note the effects of change in several chapters, we discuss at length, in Chapter 15, why organizational change is difficult, and systematic methods for enhancing its success.

Combining the dimensions of simple-complex and static-dynamic creates a four-cell matrix that provides a broad backdrop against which organizational design structures can be placed (see Exhibit 6.15). In general, the more complex and dynamic the environment is, the more the organizational structure needs to coordinate different groups' efforts and the greater the speed with which this coordination needs to occur. This means that the more complex and dynamic the firm's environment, the more the structure will need to make use of mechanisms that facilitate coordination and integration, such as values, teams, and liaisons.

The Organization's Strategy

The second major element that managers must consider in designing their organization's structure is the company's strategy.[44] Unfortunately, there are no simple rules to use to match a particular structure to a company's strategy.

However, a few principles can help explain the relationship between strategy and structure. For example, the structure should complement and leverage the strategy. But, it is difficult to determine if a given structure complements or leverages the strategy. However, we can gain

EXHIBIT 6.15

Matrix of Organizational Uncertainty

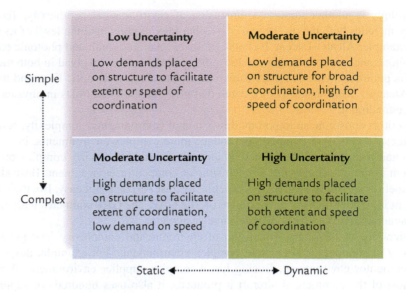

important insights into this principle by examining one of the most common strategy formulation approaches.[45] As discussed in Chapter 5 on strategy, one of the common concerns of formulating strategy is to determine the company's core competencies or resources, which are hard to imitate and are scarce, that produce value for customers. By focusing on these identified competencies or resources, we can more easily evaluate the fit or misfit of a proposed structure with the strategy.

Additionally, companies commonly use a division structure to complement a multiproduct strategy. Firms with such a strategy seek to operate in diverse product markets.[46] GE uses this strategy to manufacture and sell household electronic products and jet airplane engines and to provide financial and entertainment services. For each product or service market, it has a separate division.

The structure a firm uses can influence the specific strategic actions it takes, such as the formation of strategic alliances to collaborate on the development of new technologies.[47] To be able to respond to a dynamic environment with the development of innovative technologies may require that firms maintain strategic flexibility, at least in specific actions they might use in developing new technologies. The diverse actions could include acquisitions to buy a firm with new technologies, strategic alliances to access resources for internal development, or joint ventures to partner with others in the development among other alternative strategic moves.[48]

Organizational Structures in an International Context

So far, this chapter has focused on basic organizational structures in both domestic and international contexts. Now, we examine organizational structure in an international context. Although more firms today are international in focus from the time they are started because of the technological reach, some are moving into international markets after they gain a level of maturity and needed managerial capabilities. Most start in one country and for a period of time focus on the customers within that country. Although international organizations would be easier to understand if they evolved steadily and systematically, they do not do so. However, there is a general relationship between the nature of the firm and its structure. This relationship was first proposed over 30 years ago and has generally been supported, including in recent times.[49] Exhibit 6.16 summarizes this theory and its findings.

The first dimension of the matrix is the extent of foreign sales. For example, 97 percent of Nokia's sales come from outside its home country of Finland. The second dimension of the matrix is the extent of product diversification. Product diversification is the extent to which the firm has many different products across many different segments and even industries.[50] For example, Nokia sells primarily mobile phones and network equipment for mobile phone systems. This represents fairly low product diversification. In contrast, GE has many different products across such diversified industries as jet engines, lighting, medical equipment, television and

EXHIBIT 6.16

International Strategy and Structure

	Low International Product Diversity	High International Product Diversity
High Foreign Sales	Geographic Structure	Matrix Structure
Low Foreign Sales	International Division	Worldwide Product Division

broadcasting, plastics, and power plants. Firms with low foreign sales and low product diversification generally form an international division to manage their international sales. Because there is not much in foreign sales to manage and because the products are relatively similar, it is more efficient to manage the international sales of all products in a single unit—the international division.

Firms having low product diversification with high foreign sales usually employ a geographic structure. This was the case with Nokia for a number of years. It was divided into four major geographic regions: Europe and the Middle East and Africa (EMEA), North America, Latin America, and Asia Pacific.

Firms with low foreign sales but high product diversification typically use global product divisions because the foreign sales are more effectively managed in units aligned with each product. Alternatively, firms with high foreign sales and high product diversification frequently use a matrix structure. This was the case for ABB. Similar to GE, ABB is a large industrial company with a highly diversified set of products ranging from train locomotives to power

Firms such as Nokia, with low product diversification and high foreign sales, usually employ a geographic structure.

transmission. Because these products are significantly different, ABB needed to manage each independently. However, because international sales are a large percentage of overall sales, the company also needed a geographic structure. In combination, this formed a product-geography matrix structure.

Thus, while there are some associations between strategy and structure in international firms, the development of international organizations can be divided into two basic states: initial international structures and advanced international structures. Although most international organizations rarely use advanced international structures early, there is no consistent sequence that companies follow. Rather, the size of the organization's international sales, product diversity, size of foreign R&D, and foreign manufacturing determine the advanced global structures.[51]

A DOMESTIC ORGANIZATION WITH AN EXPORT DEPARTMENT As firms venture into foreign markets, they usually begin with a limited number of products. Typically, the products to be sold in foreign markets are designed and produced in the domestic market. Consequently, the primary international task is exporting the products to foreign markets. To manage these foreign sales, most firms simply add an export department to their existing structure to handle specialized tasks, such as international shipping and customs regulations.

A DOMESTIC ORGANIZATION WITH AN INTERNATIONAL DIVISION When the volume of exports exceeds the capabilities of a few specialists, firms commonly establish an international division. International divisions typically are responsible for all functional activities relative to international markets. The international division often has its own small departments for accounting, finance, marketing, and sales. However, production activities are not usually part of the international division. Products are produced within the normal domestic organizational structure and modified as needed for the international division. Consequently, the products sold by the international division typically have broad appeal, and there are relatively few customer differences across countries.

Adding an international division has a number of advantages. First, it is an efficient means of dealing with the international market when a firm has limited experience. The focus on international activities and issues within the division can foster a strong professional identity and career path for its members. It also allows for specialization and training in international activities, which can be valuable when the firm moves more heavily into the international marketplace and needs employees with global market knowledge. The focus on international markets, competitors, and environments can also facilitate the development of a more effective global strategy. Furthermore, because the top officer of the international division often reports to the firm's CEO (or another senior executive), international concerns often receive a high level of corporate support with this structure.

However, international divisions are sometimes vulnerable because they depend so heavily on other divisions for products and support. Because domestic sales of a particular product are often the largest percentage of a product's overall sales, lower priority may be given to providing the supply of products needed for international sales. Other parts of the firm that supply products and services to the international division may be unwilling to make modifications that cost them time and money, even if the changes could produce higher international sales.

ADVANCED GLOBAL STRUCTURES When international sales as a percentage of the firm's overall sales increase, and as the organization expands into a larger number of countries, it becomes increasingly difficult to maximize the benefits of an international division and minimize its weaknesses. When the organization outgrows its initial international structure, it can choose from among six advanced global structures. As mentioned, there is no particular sequence from one structure to another. The six advanced global structures correspond to the basic functional, geographic or regional, product, division, customer, and matrix structures already discussed, except that they have a global rather than a domestic scope.

Increasing globalization is contributing to a number of the changes in the organizational structures used by domestic and multinational firms. As we explain in the following "Manager's Challenge," globalization has contributed to increasing **outsourcing** (networked structures), flatter organization structures, more flexible structures and increasing integration (strategic alliances, for example). Thus, over time, many firms are using more advanced global structures, and these structures are common across country boundaries and cultures.

outsourcing
the practice of contracting out a significant activity within the organization to an independent party

Organizing to Think Globally and Act Locally

Given the increasingly international environment in which organizations compete, it is important to examine one other factor that managers must consider when designing organizational structures—whether the organization satisfies global or local demands.[52] A **global approach** involves the integration of activities on a coordinated, worldwide basis. Firms are likely to use a global approach when the benefits gained from worldwide volumes, efficiencies, or economies of scale are significant. These benefits include economies of scale for production, greater leverage of high-cost distribution networks, and higher leverage of expensive R&D activities. In a variety of industries, the minimally efficient production scale is beyond what a single market could support. For example, Boeing's break-even point for a new commercial aircraft is approximately 300 airplanes, with each airplane costing in excess of $100 million. This requires total sales of $30 billion. To achieve an acceptable return on its investment, Boeing must try to develop airplanes that will have global appeal because the U.S. market alone is not large enough to absorb the sales needed for a reasonable return. The high levels of R&D and scale economies require that firms centralize activities such as product development and manufacturing.

global approach
integrating the firm's activities on a coordinated, worldwide basis

A MANAGER'S CHALLENGE

CHANGE

Globalization and Organizational Structures

Because businesses are increasing their sales, manufacturing, research, and management internationally, they are also changing how they do business. Globalization has changed labor markets, created flexible work settings, flattened organizational structures, and increased the ability of firms to network across nations. In addition, globalization is linking markets and governments, creating more opportunities and exposures for people and firms.

Outsourcing

IT companies have led the way in terms of global sourcing. These firms discovered over 30 years ago that IT functions could be performed at lower costs abroad. Outsourcing to firms located in other countries is done largely because of lower costs. India and China, two of the largest recipients of outsourcing, have much lower wages for well-trained professionals and blue-collar employees than in the United States, for example. And, in fact, recent studies suggest that 80 percent of the companies using IT outsourcing plan to increase it or keep it at the same level. The three largest Indian IT companies recently added almost 17,000 new employees in anticipation of increased demand for their services. As a result, electronics companies such as Motorola, Texas Instruments, and Intel began sending manufacturing operations abroad to reduce their operating costs and speed product development by taking advantage of time zone differences and lower wages. Many other firms have followed their lead by outsourcing work ranging from software development to HR administration and even accounting and finance functions.

Flexibility

Organizational systems, processes, and people are working with fewer detailed rules, procedures, and levels of management. Instead, they are being given greater autonomy and are being empowered to be creative and take initiative. Partly because of globalization, businesses are also beginning to customize their employment contracts with workers, who are increasingly engaging in telecommuting and job sharing. In addition, employees are being empowered to make decisions with fewer levels of management. For example, 93 percent of Deloitte's employees and 85 percent of Cisco's employees regularly telecommute for up to 20 percent of their work time. This approach gives employees more flexibility and empowerment in doing their jobs.

Flat Organizational Structures

Many companies expanding their business globally often decentralize the employee benefits function. Instead, they are using local managers to create employment plans and job designs, develop financial strategies, and select insurance carriers in each country. Companies are also using global approaches by benchmarking local country designs, incorporating strategic plans that meet local compliance measures, and ensuring that local insurance carriers meet minimum-security standards and evaluate catastrophic exposures. Employees are learning new skills and taking on more challenging assignments to earn pay increases because there are fewer vertical positions for domestic promotions. IT advances are allowing

(continued)

employees to communicate directly across the globe, thereby decreasing the need for middle managers to control communications. In other words, employees are less likely to be required to communicate through the "chain of command." And, frankly, this approach is necessary because of the growing demand for more skilled workers and the reduced availability of workers with the necessary skills. One contributor to this problem is the aging of the work forces particularly in western countries.

Integration

Many characterize the 1980s as an era of quality, the 1990s as an era of reengineering, and the twenty-first century as an era of integration. Integration has allowed companies to network with other companies, enhancing their competitiveness by giving them access to complementary resources.

Studies have shown that with globalization, the gross domestic product is growing for most countries participating in the global economy (except during global recessions such as that experienced by many countries in 2008-2010). Alternatively, the wealth of countries with trade barriers and protectionism is declining. Thus, globalization has increased opportunities, but governments must open their markets to take advantage of these opportunities. Yet, there are disadvantages as well with some fears that local cultures and traditions may be lost over time.

Sources: M. A. Costonis and R. Salkowitz, "The Tough Match of Young Workers and Insurance," *New York Times,* June 11, 2010, http://www.nytimes.com; "Statistics Related to Offshore Outsourcing," RTTS, March 24, 2010, http://www.rttsweb.com; "Best Benefits: Telecommuting," *CNNMoney,* February 8, 2010, http://money.cnn.com; G. Hamel and A. Blitz, "Unshackling Employees," *Wall Street Journal,* August 7, 2009, http:/blogs.wsj.com; R. Garnick, "Globalization's Gloomy Guses Must Adapt," *BusinessWeek,* March 21, 2006, http://www.businessweek.com; R. Hof, "Web 2.0 Has Corporate America Spinning," *BusinessWeek,* June 5, 2006, http://www.businessweek.com; S. Borgatti, "21st Century Organizational Trends," Analytic Technologies, http://www.analytictech.com, February 5, 2001; B. Fung, "Technology Advances and Globalization Are Changing the Face of Risk," *Aon Focus,* February 20, 2006, http://www.aon.com.

local approach

differentiating the firm's activities country by country

In contrast, differences among countries and customer preferences are two key factors that drive companies toward a local approach. A **local approach** involves differentiating activities in each country served. Firms often use a local approach when the benefits from location-specific differentiation and adaptation are significant and factors such as economies of scale are small. Procter & Gamble (P&G) was forced to use a local approach for a laundry detergent it developed. Initially, P&G wanted to develop one detergent, Visor, for all European countries served to capture the efficiencies of a single development, manufacturing, and marketing effort. However, it found significant differences between countries. Germans, for example, prefer front-loading washers whereas the French prefer top-loading washers. This created a problem because detergent was not distributed as well among the clothes when poured into a front-loading washer. P&G solved the problem by developing a plastic ball into which detergent could be poured and that then could be thrown in with the clothes in a front-loading machine. The plastic ball was designed to dispense the detergent gradually though small holes as the ball bounced around in the clothes while they were being washed. Thus, P&G had adapted the product to fit customers' needs in the German market.

As the P&G example illustrates, the greater the differences between countries and the more significant these differences are for a product or service, the greater the need is for a local approach. However, forces can simultaneously push toward global and local emphases, requiring firms to be globally integrated and locally responsive.[53] In the case of P&G, the manufacturing process was globally integrated because making detergent is basically continuous; that is, like many chemical products, the final product is delivered after a long process of mixing various chemicals in different states and temperatures until the desired chemical reactions create the final product. Thus, the process cannot be stopped at discrete points and finished elsewhere, nor is it economical to alter the process to create different detergents. Both of these factors necessitated a global approach concentrating the manufacturing activities without many modifications being made for local markets. On the other hand, the significant differences in washing machines between Germany and France required attention to local needs.

In general, firms heavily involved in international business face strong pressures for both integration and differentiation. They need specialists for certain functions, such as marketing to Germans, dealing with French government officials, and complying with U.S. accounting rules. However, they also face greater needs for integration. Using one or more of the following structural mechanisms—direct contact, liaisons, and teams—can meet these increased integration needs.

DIRECT CONTACT Often, direct contact is an important means of integration by sharing information. One of the largest firms in the world, Matsushita, has an interesting way of accomplishing this. Because R&D is vitally important in the consumer electronics industry, Matsushita has a large central research and development lab, as explained earlier in the chapter. To ensure that managers are informed about lab activities and to ensure that lab scientists understand emerging market needs around the globe, Matsushita holds an annual, worldwide, internal trade show. Senior managers throughout Matsushita's worldwide operations gather and examine research results and potential new products. Managers also provide to R&D scientists information about market differences, customer preferences, and competitor positioning. The result is a massive sharing of information through direct contact that has helped Matsushita maintain its competitive advantage.

LIAISONS A **liaison** is an individual or unit designated to act as a "bridge" or connection between two or more areas of a company. Liaison roles are designed to enhance the links, and, therefore, information flows, between groups, including teams, departments, divisions, and subsidiaries. Part of Matsushita's success in the videocassette recorder (VCR) market was due to a purposeful liaison: The vice president in charge of Matsushita's U.S. subsidiary was also a member of the senior management committee of the Japanese parent company and spent about a third of his time in Japan. This facilitated the link between headquarters and the United States, which was the company's most important consumer market for VCRs. In addition, the general manager of the U.S. subsidiary's video department had previously worked for many years in the video product division of the production and domestic marketing organization in Japan. This created a strong link between the product division in Japan and the U.S. subsidiary. Also, the assistant product manager of the U.S. subsidiary had spent five years in Matsushita's central VCR manufacturing plant in Japan. Through these three individuals, Matsushita ensured the existence of vital links at the corporate, product, and factory levels between Japan and the United States.

liaison
an individual designated to act as a "bridge" or connection between two or more areas of a company

TEAMS When integration needs arise across an array of functional areas, teams can serve as an effective integration mechanism. Philips uses teams as an integrative mechanism. For example, Philips has long had an office of the president, as opposed to a single CEO. The office of the president consists of technical, commercial, and financial executives. Each product has a team of junior managers from the firm's commercial and technical functions. These teams integrate various perspectives and information on a single product to ensure that they resolve interfunctional differences early and that they integrate necessary design, manufacturing, and marketing needs and concerns from the outset in an effort to increase the success of a product.

Managerial Challenges from the Front Line

The Rest of the Story

While a matrix structure often slows some response activities because of the need to make joint decisions and coordinate actions prior to implementing them, in Halliburton's case, the structure worked very well. The challenges presented by the economic downturn and the need to ensure high-quality service required a coordinated response. The matrix structure facilitated this response because managers already had established working relationships and coordinated their efforts on a regular basis. Thus, Luiz Freire worked with his team of managers and each product line manager to ensure the commitment to and to deliver high quality service, even with a much tighter budget. He then turned his attention to financial matters and inventory management. Collaborating with a team of managers, they were able to reduce costs, manage their inventory levels, and collect the monies due on the outstanding payments on accounts receivable. Therefore with hard work as a team of managers representing various perspectives and functional areas, Freire and his team successfully overcame the challenges they faced.

Summary

- A firm's organization structure can be defined as the sum of the ways in which it divides its labor into distinct tasks and then coordinates them. The structure provides the blueprint for reporting relationships, controls, authority, and decision making in the organization. Organizational design is the process of assessing the firm's strategy and environmental demands and determining the appropriate organizational structure. Often, organizational structure is presented in the form of an organizational chart. Organizational charts illustrate relationships among units and lines of authority among supervisors and subordinates through the use of labeled boxes and connecting lines.

- Important dimensions of the organizing process include differentiation and integration. Differentiation is the extent to which tasks in the organization are divided into subtasks and performed by individuals with specialized skills. The main benefit of differentiation is greater specialization of knowledge and skills. Integration is the extent to which various parts of the organization interact, coordinate, and cooperate with each other. The primary benefit of integration is the coordinated actions of different people and activities to achieve a desired organizational objective.

- Formalization, informalization, centralization, and decentralization are structural dimensions that balance and help to manage differentiation and integration. Formalization is represented by the defined structures and systems in decision making, communication, and control in the organization. These mechanisms usually explicitly define where and how people and activities are independent along with how they are integrated. The informal organization consists of the unofficial but influential means of communication, decision making, and control that are part of the habitual way things get done in the organization. Centralization and decentralization refer to the level at which decisions are made—at the top of the organization or at lower levels. Centralized organizations largely restrict decision making to a few individuals, usually at the top of the organization. In contrast, decentralized organizations tend to push decision-making authority down to lower levels in the organization.

- Six common organization structures include functional, product, division, customer, geographic or region, and matrix. The functional structure is used to organize the firm around traditional functional areas, such as accounting, finance, marketing, operations, and so on. In a product structure, the firm is organized around specific products or related sets of products. Divisions typically consist of multiple products within a generally related area, though specific products may not necessarily be closely related. Customer structures are organized around categories of customers. Firms can develop a structure around various geographical areas or regions. A matrix structure consists of two organization structures superimposed on each other. As a consequence, there are dual reporting relationships.

- One of the most contemporary structures is the network structure. A common network structure results from outsourcing. Often, firms outsource noncore activities of their value chain so that they can focus on core activities that give them a competitive advantage.

- Designing organizations must be done within the context of the organization's external environment and its strategy. The environment's complexity and dynamism are important in designing organizations. Environmental complexity is fundamentally the breadth and depth of differences and similarities in an organization's external environment. Static environments may have few or many factors, but these factors tend to remain stable over time. Dynamic environments change constantly. The structure should complement and leverage the strategy. A division structure is commonly used to complement a multiproduct strategy. In dynamic environments a flexible strategy may be needed and thus the structure should facilitate changing the strategy when it is necessary to do so.

- Firms usually begin with simple structures, such as an international department or an international division, as they venture into international markets. However, their international structures grow more complex over time as they enter more countries. The structures chosen usually depend on the amount of the firm's foreign sales and degree of product diversification.

Key Terms

centralized organization   140
cognitive differentiation   135
decentralized organization   140
differentiation   135
environmental complexity   152
flat organization structure   138
formalization   137
global approach   157
informal organization   139
integration   135

interdependence   136
liaison   159
line of authority   137
local approach   158
network structure   151
organizational chart   134
organizational design   134
organizational structure   134
outsourcing   156
pooled interdependence   136

profit center   144
reciprocal interdependence   136
sequential interdependence   136
span of control   137
tall organization
    structure   138
task differentiation   135
uncertainty   136
unity of command   137
values   137

Review Questions

1. What are the concepts of organization structure and organization design, and how do they differ?
2. What are differentiation and integration, and what is the role of each in organization structure?
3. How are formalization, informalization, centralization, and decentralization interrelated, and how can organizations use them to balance differentiation and integration?
4. What are six common organization structures and the strengths and weaknesses of each?

5. How does a network structure facilitate managing activities and help a company achieve competitive advantage?
6. How do environmental factors and the organization's strategy affect the type of structure it should adopt?
7. What organization structures are most effective for organizations operating in international markets? Explain why.

Assessing Your Capabilities

Risk-taking Orientation

Answer the following questions using the scale below:

	Strongly Disagree	Disagree	Neutral	Agree	Strongly Agree
1. I prefer to think of opportunities in the future as opposed to focusing on past outcomes or even current tasks.	1	2	3	4	5
2. If I had $100 to invest, I prefer to do so in a way that ensures a return (e.g., 5 percent CD) and no loss of the original amount invested, rather than one in which I could potentially earn as much as a 20 percent return on my investment but with a reasonably high risk of earning no return and potentially losing a portion of the original investment.	1	2	3	4	5
3. I like to work with new ideas and undertake new tasks because they motivate me.	1	2	3	4	5
4. I dislike regular change, preferring instead a steady work environment in which my tasks are predictable.	1	2	3	4	5
5. When I am given a task to accomplish, I prefer autonomy to complete it in the way I desire.	1	2	3	4	5
6. Rules and established procedures are very helpful in getting a job done.	1	2	3	4	5
7. When given a new task to do, I find the careful directions and oversight of a supervisor to be helpful and comforting.	1	2	3	4	5
8. I believe in being aggressive (as opposed to passive) in accomplishing tasks that I am assigned.	1	2	3	4	5

9. In most situations, I feel most comfortable when people undertake traditional roles (e.g., traditional gender roles).	1	2	3	4	5
10. When considering complex decisions with uncertain outcomes, I prefer to make the decision alone because I can do it faster than working in a group.	1	2	3	4	5

Scoring Your Answers:

Add the numbers you assigned as responses to questions 1, 3, 5, 8, and 10 (Set 1) and those assigned to questions 2, 4, 6, 7, and 9 (Set 2). Subtract the total score for Set 2 from the score for Set 1.

If the resulting score is positive, you prefer to take risks and feel comfortable operating in ambiguous and uncertain situations. The highest positive score you could obtain is +20.

If the resulting score is negative, you prefer a more certain and structured environment with less risk. The lowest negative score you could obtain is –20.

Team Exercise

Form a team of three to five people.

Your team has been hired as a consultant to help a manager form and structure a new department. Please read the following explanation of the manager's situation. Then, your team must make recommendations to the manager. You'll make your recommendations through your team's answers to the questions at the end of this piece.

The new manager has been offered the position of brand manager for a new sports drink produced by a large food and beverage company. Her manager has asked her how she wants to structure her unit. Specifically, how many people will she need in her department and how should their jobs be structured.

Most new managers at this level have about four to six subordinates. The new manager indicates that she could have as few as three and as many as 13, depending on what she requests and her rationale for the request. Prior to this promotion, the new manager worked on a brand team for three years and acted as the informal team leader for the last 14 months. She was told that part of the reason she was given the promotion was because of how well she managed her team, which consisted of three other employees who were all doing primarily market research work.

The new sports drink has been on the market for six months and has enjoyed a successful launch in the United States and Asia. Continued expansion in Europe and Latin America is expected. Below is a brief profile of the 13 potential subordinates prepared by the new manager.

Market Researcher: Three people are currently doing marketing research on the product. Much of their work was done prior to the launch, and now they focus on customer satisfaction and the competitive response to the product. Two of the people work in the United States (one on the East Coast and one on the West Coast), and the other works in Japan.

Statistician: There are two statisticians. One currently is based in the firm's corporate headquarters on the East Coast, and the other is based in the European regional headquarters in London. Both do a similar job of analyzing data to identify statistical relationships between customer characteristics, product characteristics, marketing and promotion activities, and buying patterns.

Advertising Specialist: There are three advertising specialists. One deals primarily with print media; one focuses on broadcast media (principally radio and TV); the third specializes in "alternative advertising," which includes everything from promotional contests to the Internet. The print ad and broadcast staff are based in the company's East Coast office, whereas the alternative advertising person telecommutes from his home in San Diego. The company's West Coast office closest to San Diego is in Los Angeles.

Administrative Assistant: There is one administrative assistant, who works for the brand manager who launched the sports drink. This individual acts as secretary, organizer, and general assistant to the brand manager.

Marketing Specialist: There are four marketing specialists, each one residing in a different region (United States, Asia, Europe, and Latin America). These people are primarily responsible for creating the marketing strategy for their regions. Given that the product has not yet been launched in Europe and Latin America, the two individuals in those regions are currently working on other products and task forces.

Based on this information, reading of the chapter material, and external search for information (if needed), your team should formulate its advice to the new manager by providing answers to the following questions.

1. How many total subordinates should she request? What should be her span of control?
2. Are all the jobs listed necessary? Please explain. How many subordinates should she request in each job and why?
3. Are there other jobs that you recommend she should include? Should all people report directly to her or should there be one or more supervisors? Please be specific.
4. How much formalization should the new manager develop? How much autonomy should she provide employees in each job category?

Restructuring the Organizational Structure at Kimberly-Clark

In 2003, Kimberly-Clark, the maker of paper products including Kleenex, Huggies, and Depends, announced it was creating a radical new structure to shore up parts of its business that were performing poorly by restructuring its products into three categories. The categories were "grow," "sustain," and "fix"—somewhat unconventional categories. They weren't devised based on product type, customers, or the geographic locations in which Kimberly-Clark sold goods, but instead on the perceived strength of the products themselves.

Background

Kimberly, Clark and Company was established in 1872 by four young businessmen, John A. Kimberly, Havilah Babcock, Charles B. Clark, and Frank C. Shattuck. Based in Neenah, Wisconsin, the company initially manufactured paper, but over the years it began to branch out, broadening into the personal hygiene consumer products area to compete with companies like Procter & Gamble.

In 1978, Kimberly-Clark introduced what would become its top seller: Huggies disposable diapers. Huggies were an instant hit and soon became the nation's number-one diaper brand. Over the course of the next two decades, Kimberly-Clark introduced Depends for adults and training pants for toddlers, and acquired its competitor Scott Paper, a leading maker of toilet paper and paper towels. Today, the merged company sells its products in over 150 countries around the world. In 80 of those countries, it holds the number-one or number-two spot in the marketplace. It has physical operations in 38 countries and employs more than 55,000 employees.

Restructuring Problems

Like many corporate mergers, the merger between Kimberly-Clark and Scott Paper in 1995 didn't roll out smoothly. Most of Scott's senior management team left after the merger, and Kimberly-Clark experienced problems integrating the two companies. The following year, operating income and sales dropped.

By the late 1990s, the company's senior managers had finally worked through the integration challenges of the merger. But the dawn of the twenty-first century brought new challenges. Chief among these was the lack of growth in developed countries for Kimberly-Clark products due to market saturation. To continue to grow, the company had to look to new markets. The company was also losing market share to its fiercest rival, P&G. By introducing a high-end line of Pampers in 2002, P&G had been able to capture market share from Huggies.

Given the tough competition in the disposable diapers industry, Kimberly-Clark tried to diversify by producing a related product: disposable baby wipes. But these growth plans were upset when Johnson & Johnson, the prominent maker of baby shampoo, launched its own line of baby wipes.

It was within the context of these competitive dynamics that Kimberly-Clark's senior managers announced their radical reorganization plan in 2003. The "grow" category (brands and sectors growing the fastest) included products such as training pants, household towels and wipes, and Kleenex. The "sustain" category (brands generating solid returns) included U.S. infant care products and other facial tissue lines. Whereas the "fix" category included products related to European personal care along with the U.S. professional washroom business. Sales of these products were relatively flat. And although they accounted for about 20 percent of the firm's total sales, they contributed only 10 percent of the profits.

Kimberly-Clark's senior managers argued that reorganization would help increase the company's speed to market, streamline its decision making regarding allocating capital, and deliver cost reductions on a sustainable basis. However, simultaneous to the reorganization announcement, Kimberly-Clark announced it had revised its forecasts for sales increases down from 6 percent to 8 percent annually to 3 percent to 5 percent. Predictably, shareholders reacted negatively, and Kimberly-Clark's stock price closed down immediately after the announcements. Thus, executives began to reconsider the planned changes.

Kimberly-Clark eventually presented a new and different organizational structure in early 2004. Rather than organize products by the "grow, sustain, and fix" categories, management announced that it would organize around personal care, washroom products, and emerging markets. Specifically, management planned to combine the company's North American and European personal care groups under one organizational unit. The same would happen for products related to the washroom business. In addition, management planned to create an "emerging markets" business unit to maximize the growth of all Kimberly-Clark's products in Asia, Latin America, and Eastern Europe. As an example of this growth, in 2010 the company announced its first plant in Russia to manufacture Huggies diapers.

By 2010, Kimberly Clark's changes reshaped the company into a consumer product health and hygiene firm. Analysts have reacted well to these changes. In addition, the company announced that its efforts to reduce costs are likely to exceed its initial estimates. The management projected that cost savings could be as high as $450 million by the end of 2010. And, management also announced a new plan to reduce up to $500 million more by 2013. Finally, the company is searching for good acquisitions in the health care industry.

Questions

1. Why would Kimberly-Clark executives restructure the company based on "grow, sustain, and fix" categories? What disadvantages might result from such a structure?

2. Was the organizational structure presented by Kimberly-Clark executives in 2004 better than the first structure proposed? Why or why not?

3. Are the company's changes to reshape its identity as a consumer product health care and hygiene company and its cost reduction efforts likely to improve its competitive position relative to P&G? Please explain your answer.

Sources: "Kimberly-Clark Opens First Plant in Russia," *Bloomberg BusinessWeek,* June 2, 2010, http://www.businessweek.com; M. Clothier, "Kimberly-Clark CEO Sees Acquisitions up to $1 Billion," *Bloomberg BusinessWeek,* March 23, 2010, http://www.businessweek .com; M. Lindner, "Kimberly-Clark Kicks Higher on Cost Savings," *Forbes,* March 22, 2010, http://www.forbes.com; Company Web site, "Kimberly-Clark Reviews Global Business Plan Progress and Long-term Objectives through 2015 at Investor Meeting,", http://www.investor.kimberly-clark.com, accessed March 22, 2010; Company Web site, http://www.kimberly-clark.com, accessed March 5, 2007; J. Neff, "K-C Huggies Plans Baby Wipe, Wash Line," *Advertising Age,* December 8, 2003, 49–50; S. Solley, "Kimberly-Clark Rejigs to 'Repair' Weak Brands," *Marketing* (UK), July 31, 2003, 3; "Kimberly-Clark Earnings Fall in 2Q," *Associated Press,* July 24, 2003; S. A. Forest and H. Dawly, "Pulp Fiction at Kimberly-Clark," *BusinessWeek,* February 23, 1998.

References

1. W. D. Sine, H. Mitsuhashi, and D. A. Kirsch, "Revisiting Burns and Stalker: Formal Structure and New Venture Performance in Emerging Economic Sectors," *Academy of Management Journal* 49 (2006): 121–132.

2. C. W. L. Hill, M. A. Hitt, and R. E. Hoskisson, "Cooperative Versus Competitive Structures in Related and Unrelated Diversified Firms," *Organization Science* 3 (1992): 501–521.

3. J. I. Galan and M. J. Sanchez-Bueno, "The Continuing Validity of the Strategy-Structure Nexus: New Findings, 1993–2003." *Strategic Management Journal* 30 (2009): 1234-1243.

4. M. A. Hitt, R. D. Ireland, and R. E. Hoskisson, *Strategic Management: Competitiveness and Globalization* (Cincinnati: South-Western Publishing Co., 2011).

5. H. Mintzberg, *The Structuring of Organizations* (Upper Saddle River: Prentice Hall, 1979).

6. B. Keats and H. O'Neill, "Organizational Structure: Looking through a Strategy Lens," in *Handbook of Strategic Management,* eds. M. A. Hitt, R. E. Freeman, and J. S. Harrison, (Oxford, UK: Blackwell Publishers, 2001), 520–542.

7. P. Lawrence and J. W. Lorsch, *Organization and Environment* (Boston: Harvard University Press, 1967); J. R. Galbraith, *Designing Complex Organizations* (Reading: Addison Wesley, 1977).

8. N. Malhotra and T. Morris, "Heterogeneity in Professional Service Firms," *Journal of Management Studies* 46 (2009): 895–922.

9. Lawrence and Lorsch, *Organization and Environment.*

10. D. Miller and C. Droge, "Psychological and Traditional Determinants of Structure," *Administrative Science Quarterly* 31 (1986): 539–560; L. L. Levesque, J. Wilson, and R. Douglas, "Cognitive Divergence and Shared Mental Models in Software Development Project Teams," *Journal of Organizational Behavior* 22 (2001): 135–144.

11. C. Fang, J. Lee, and M. A. Schilling, "Balancing Exploration and Exploitation through Structural Design: The Isolation of Subgroups and Organizational Learning," *Organization Science* 21 (2010): 625–642; P. Puranam, H. Singh, and M. Zollo, "Organizing for Innovation: Managing the Coordination–Autonomy Dilemma in Technology Acquisitions," *Academy of Management Journal* 49 (2006): 263–280.

12. J. A. Martin and K. M. Eisenhardt, "Rewiring: Cross-Business-Unit Collaborations in Multibusiness Organizations," *Academy of Management Journal* 53 (2010): 265–301.

13. Lawrence and Lorsch, *Organization and Environment*; Galbraith, *Designing Complex Organizations*; M. A. Schilling and H. K. Steensma, "The Use of Modular Organizational Forms: An Industry-level Analysis," *Academy of Management Journal* 44 (2001): 1149–1168; O. Sorenson, "Interdependence and Adaptability: Organizational Learning and the Long term Effect of Integration," *Management Science* 49 (2003): 446–463.

14. Puranam, Singh, and Zollo, "Organizing for Innovation."

15. A. W. Richter, M. A. West, and R. van Dick, "Boundary Spanners' Identification, Intergroup Contact, and Effective Intergroup Relations," *Academy of Management Journal* 49 (2006): 1252–1269.

16. J. D. Sherman and R. T. Keller, "Suboptimal Assessment of Interunit Task Interdependence: Modes of Integration and Information Processing for Coordination Performance," *Organization Science* 21 (2010): in press.

17. R. Steers and J. S. Black, *Organizational Behavior* (New York: HarperCollins, 1993); R. H. Hall, *Organizations: Structures, Process, and Outcomes,* 5th ed. (Upper Saddle River: Prentice Hall, 1991); Sorenson, "Interdependence and Adaptability," 446–463.

18. W. Shi, L. Markoczy, and G. G. Dess, "The Role of Middle Management in the Strategy Process: Group Affiliation, Structural Holes, and Tertius Lungus," *Journal of Management* 35 (2009): 1453–1480.

19. J.-K Thun, "Angles of Integration: An Empirical Analysis of the Alignment of Internet- based Information Technology and Global Supply Chain Integration," *Journal of Supply Chain Management* 46, no. 2 (2010):30–44.

20. R. Cyert and J. March, *The Behavioral Theory of the Firm* (Upper Saddle River: Prentice Hall, 1963); J. R. Galbraith, "Organization Design: An Information Processing View," *Interfaces* 4, no. 3 (1974): 28–36; Hall, *Organizations*; J. Birkinshaw, R. Nobel, and J. Ridderstrale, "Knowledge as a Contingency Variable: Do the Characteristics of Knowledge Predict Organization Structure?" *Organization Science* 13 (2002): 274–289; R. J. Trent and R. M. Monczka, "Pursuing

Competitive Advantage Through Integrated Global Sourcing," *Academy of Management Executive* 16, no. 2 (2002): 66–80.

21. J. S. Bunderson and P. Boumgarden, "Structure and Learning in Self-managed Teams: Why "Bureaucratic" Teams Can Be Better Learners," *Organization Science* 21 (2010): in press.

22. E. E. Klein, "Using Information Technology to Eliminate Layers of Bureaucracy," *National Public Accountant* 46 (June 2001): 46–48.

23. Sine, Mitsuhashi, and Kirsch, "Revisiting Burns and Stalker."

24. D. Nadler and M. Tushman, *Competing by Design: The Power of Organizational Architecture* (New York: Oxford University Press, 1997).

25. P.-C. Wu and S. Chaturvedi, "The Role of Procedural Justice and Power Distance in the Relationship between High Performance Work Systems and Employee Attitudes: A Multilevel Perspective," *Journal of Management* 35 (2009): 1228–1247.

26. X. Zhang and K. M. Bartol, "Linking Empowering Leadership and Employee Creativity: The Influence of Psychological Empowerment, Intrinsic Motivation, and Creative Process Engagement," *Academy of Management Journal* 53 (2010): 107–128.

27. E. Kearney, D. Gebert, and S. C. Voepel, "When and How Diversity Benefits Teams: The Importance of Team Members Need," *Academy of Management Journal* 52 (2009): 581–598.

28. Y. Rhy-song and T. Sagafi-nejad, "Organizational Characteristics of American and Japanese Firms in Taiwan," *Academy of Management Proceedings* (1987): 111–115.

29. S. H. Park and Y. Luo, "Guanxi and Organizational Dynamics: Organizational Networking in Chinese Firms," *Strategic Management Journal* 22 (2001): 455–477.

30. C. A. Bartlett and S. Ghoshal, "Organizing for Worldwide Effectiveness: The Transnational Solution," *California Management Review* 29 (Fall 1988): 54–74; D. H. Doty, W. H. Glick, and G. P. Huber, "Fit, Effectiveness, and Equifinality: A Test of Two Configurational Theories," *Academy of Management Journal* 36 (1993): 1196–1250.

31. J. R. Lincoln, M. Hanada, and K. McBride, "Organizational Structures in Japanese and U.S. Manufacturing," *Administrative Science Quarterly* 31 (1986): 338–364.

32. J. Schachter, "When Hope Turns to Frustration: The Americanization of Mitsubishi Has Had Little Success," *Los Angeles Times*, July 10, 1988, 1.

33. A. A. King, M. J. Lenox, and A. Terlaak, "The Strategic Use of Decentralized Institutions: Exploring Certification with the ISO 14001 Management Standard," *Academy of Management Journal* 48 (2005): 1091–1106.

34. A. Leiponen and C. E. Helfat, "Location, Decentralization, and Knowledge Sources for Innovation," *Organization Science* 21 (2010): in press; O. Jones and H. Crompton, "Enterprise Logic and Small Firms: A Model of Authentic Entrepreneurial Leadership," *Journal of Strategy and Management* 2 (2009): 329–351.

35. S. C. Abraham, *Strategic Planning: A Practical Guide for Competitive Success* (Cincinnati: Thomson South-Western, 2006).

36. G. Hoetker, "Do Modular Products Lead to Modular Organizations?" *Strategic Management Journal* 27 (2006): 501–518.

37. A.-W. Harzing, "Geographical Distance and the Role and Management of Subsidiaries: The Case of Subsidiaries Down-Under," *Asia-Pacific Journal of Management* 23 (2006): 167–185.

38. S. Karim, "Modularity in Organizational Structure: The Reconfiguration of Internally Developed and Acquired Business Units," *Strategic Management Journal* 27 (2006): 799–823.

39. Company Web site, Recent Contract Awards, http://www.eds.com, accessed March 3, 2007.

40. J. Sandberg, "How Long Can India Keep Office Politics Out of Outsourcing?" *Wall Street Journal*, February 27, 2007, http://online.wsj.com.

41. A. Deutschman, "Open Wide: The Traditional Business Organization Meets Democracy," *Fast Company*, March 2007, 40–41.

42. D. G. Sirmon, M. A. Hitt, and R. D. Ireland, "Managing Firm Resources in Dynamic Environments to Create Value: Looking Inside the Black Box," *Academy of Management Review* 32 (2007): 273–292; Y. Luo, "Market-seeking MNEs in an Emerging Market: How Parent–Subsidiary Links Shape Overseas Success," *Journal of International Business Studies* 34 (2003): 290–309.

43. J, Haleblian, C. E. Devers, G. McNamara, M.A. Carpenter, and R. B. Davison, "Taking Stock of What We Know About Mergers and Acquisitions: A Review and Research Agenda," *Journal of Management* 35 (2009): 469–502; V. K. Garg, B. A. Walters, and R. L. Priem, "Chief Executive Scanning Emphases, Environmental Dynamism, and Manufacturing Firm Performance," *Strategic Management Journal* 24 (2003): 725–744

44. D. E. W. Marginson, "Management Control Systems and Their Effects on Strategy Formation at Middle Management Levels: Evidence from a U.K. Organization," *Strategic Management Journal* 23 (2002): 1019–1031; J. Smith David, Y. Hwang, B. K. W. Pei, and J. H. Reneau, "The Performance Effects of Congruence Between Product Competitive Strategies and Purchasing Management Design," *Management Science* 48 (2002): 866–885; M. Goold and A. Campbell, "Do You Have a Well-designed Organization?" *Harvard Business Review* 80, no. 3 (2002): 117–124.

45. S. F. Slater, E. M. Olson, and G. T. M. Hult, "The Moderating Influence of Strategic Orientation on the Strategy Formation Capability–Performance Relationship," *Strategic Management Journal* 27 (2006): 1221–1231.

46. Hitt, Ireland, and Hoskisson, *Strategic Management.*

47. J. Zhang and C. Baden-Fuller, "The Influence of Technological Knowledge Base and Organizational Structure on Technology Collaboration.," *Journal of Management Studies* 47 (2010): 679–704.

48. K. Z. Zhou and F. Wu, "Technological Capability, Strategic Flexibility and Product Innovation," *Strategic Management Journal* 31 (2010): 547–561.

49. J. Stopford and L. Wells, *Managing the Multination Enterprise* (New York: Basic Books, 1972); J. Daniels, R. Pitts, and M. Tretter, "Strategy and Structure of U.S. Multinationals: An Exploratory Study," *Academy of Management Journal* 27 (1984): 292–307; J. Wolf and W. Egelhoff, "Reexamination and Extension of International Strategy–Structure Theory," *Strategic Management Journal* 23 (2002): 181–189.

50. M. A. Hitt, L. Tihanyi, T. Miller, and B. Connelly, "International Diversification: Antecedents, Outcomes, and Moderators," *Journal of Management* 32 (2006): 831–867; M. W. Peng and A. Delios, "What Determines the Scope of the Firm over Time and Around the World? An Asia Pacific Perspective," *Asia Pacific Journal of Management* 23 (2006): 385–405.

51. N. Malhotra and C. R. Hinings, "An Organizational Model for Understanding Internationalization Processes," *Journal of International Business Studies* 41 (2010): 330–349; Wolf and Egelhoff, "Reexamination and Extension of International Strategy–Structure Theory."

52. J. Anderson, "Expanding Globally with a Local Vision: Foreign Market Entry and the Value Chain," *Journal of Business Strategy* 30, no. 5 (2009): 32–39; C. Bartlett and S. Ghoshal, *Managing Across Borders* (Boston: Harvard Business School Press, 1989); P. Ghemawat, "The Forgotten Strategy," *Harvard Business Review* 81, no. 11 (2003): 76–84.

53. S. J. Gould and A. F. Grein, "Think Glocally, Act Glocally: A Culture-centric Comment on Leung, Bhagat, Buchan, Erez and Gibson (2005)," *Journal of International Business Studies* 40 (2009): 237–254.

7

Managing Diverse Human Resources

LEARNING OBJECTIVES

After studying this chapter, you should be able to:

Explain why maximizing the potential of the firm's human resources is important for both a company's human resource department and all managers.

Explain how a firm's human resource capabilities affect its strategy.

Highlight the key aspects of getting the right people in the right jobs

Outline the effective methods for selecting job candidates.

Highlight the keys to effective socialization and training.

Describe various methods for providing employees feedback on their performance.

Discuss the various compensation and reward systems commonly used by firms.

Discuss why managing diversity is increasingly important in the light of globalization.

Jean-Jacques Beaussart

Name: Jean-Jacques Beaussart

Position: Chief Procurement Officer, Key Bank

Alma mater: Columbia University

Outside work activities: Travel, reading, hiking, and gardening

First job out of school: Engineer

Business book reading now: *Good to Great* and *Think Outside the Box*

Hero: Bill Gates

What drives me: Excellence

Management style: Tough but fair; I always strive for excellence and demand it of those around me.

Jean-Jacques Beaussart was born and raised in France but lived in Morocco and Latin America before moving to the United States and attending Columbia University, graduating with a master's degree in engineering. Later, Beaussart received an Executive MBA from Fairleigh Dickinson University in New Jersey. Beaussart is the chief procurement officer for Key Bank, a Cleveland-based bank, with assets of approximately $95 billion providing investment management, retail and commercial banking, consumer finance, and investment banking products and services to individuals and companies throughout the United States through over 1,000 branch offices in 14 states. Currently, Beaussart oversees more than

$2 billion in annual purchases and a team that manages various aspects of this function.

Not long ago, Beaussart encountered a delicate human resource issue. Believing the overall performance of his team could be better, he raised the group's performance targets.

One of Beaussart's key subordinates had been with the bank for several years and was now nearing retirement age. Although his past performance ratings had been good, after several months Beaussart felt the employee was not meeting the new performance standards. Beaussart spoke with the individual and communicated the gap he perceived between his actual performance and the target. Six months later, the employee's performance still fell short of the target.

Beaussart faced a difficult challenge. On one hand, data demonstrated that the employee had failed to meet his goals. As a manager, Beaussart could work with the bank's Human Resources department to terminate the employee. This presented a problem, however: the individual might claim he had been discriminated against because of his age, particularly if he were let go and replaced by a younger worker (which, given the employee's age, would most likely be the case). Still, Beaussart believed the hard facts supported his contention that if the individual were terminated, poor performance, not discrimination, would be the reason.

On the other hand, the individual had amassed a great deal of knowledge over the course of his 30 years with the bank. Beaussart believed it would be a shame to lose this knowledge. In addition, it was clear the employee had other strengths and skills. How, as a manager, could Beaussart resolve the situation?

As the opening case illustrates, as managers we have to think carefully about how we manage people—human resources. On one hand, allowing poor performance to persist will hurt a unit's overall performance, as Jean-Jacques Beaussart was acutely aware. On the other hand, losing the knowledge, experience, and other assets employees have to offer if they can be retained and managed effectively hurts a unit too.

Although people have always been integral to business, they are even more important these days. Why do we say this? As we move more deeply into a service and information economy, it is *people* rather than *plant and equipment* that constitute a greater proportion of competitive advantage. For example, when fixed, tangible assets, such as plant and equipment, contribute a lion's share of a company's output, it is easier to replace a departed employee with a new hire without significant negative impact on overall performance. However, when a business depends largely on the quality of service and information, the more the critical assets of the company are not tangible but rather intangible.[1] These assets include such elements as the company's culture, brand, leadership, customer service, and knowledge. In most cases, people either are the essence of these intangible assets or directly affect them. As a consequence, the key assets of the company are essentially "walking out the door" each evening and back in the door (hopefully) the next morning.

Nordstrom is a highly regarded national retailer that sells top-quality merchandise—apparel for men, women, and children—in beautifully appointed stores. However, Nordstrom's success lies much more in its service reputation than in these tangible aspects of the company. Its superior customer service is not embedded in some piece of equipment or display unit somewhere. It is inculcated in its people and embodied in its culture. If you take people out of a service culture, what do you have left? Clearly, the answer is, "Not much." This is why we say that human resources and their effective management is increasingly a critical factor in an organization's success.

This points to two key managerial implications:

1. Managers' ability to attract, develop, leverage, and retain superior human resources will increasingly have a direct effect on the organization's success.[2]
2. As a manager, your career success or failure will increasingly depend on how well you manage the human resources for which you are responsible.[3]

However, not only are human resources and their effective management in general more critical than ever before, but so is the diversity of employees and, therefore, a manager's ability to work with a wide variety of people.

As a result of changes in the nature of our economy and competition, human resource management has evolved in recent years, particularly the strategic aspects of it.[4] In this chapter, we underscore the importance of this link. We also stress the need for individual managers to enhance their ability at identifying and selecting employees who have the knowledge, skills, and capabilities the organization needs to compete and fostering and retaining those employees with good development, compensation, and reward systems.

The traditional view of human resource management (HRM) activities focuses on planning for staffing needs, recruiting and selecting employees, orienting and training staff, appraising their performance, providing compensation and benefits, and managing their career movement and development. In most organizations, the human resources department has a special and specific role relative to these activities. However, the reality is that while the human resources department plays an important role, managers implement and execute these activities. For example, although a firm's HR department likely sets the policies and practices for hiring people, managers typically interview and select the candidates. Similarly, although the HR department is likely to create employee performance appraisal forms and processes, managers are the ones who actually assess employee performance. Thus, although it is important for you to understand the role a company's human resource department plays, it is even more important for you as a future manager to understand how to manage human resources well. How can you manage your human resources effectively? In general, you need the following capabilities:

- To *recruit* and *select* the right people
- To effectively *socialize* and *train* people in your unit
- To effectively *evaluate* employees' performance
- To determine *reward* systems that will motivate employees to perform at a high level
- To know what additional experience or education your subordinates need to *develop* to advance in their careers

One of the most enlightening studies on the importance of effective HRM and career success looked at cases of career derailment. The study found that the number-one reason for managerial career derailment—that is, why managers lost their way along an upwardly mobile career path—was the inability to successfully implement activities associated with human resource management.[5] More recent research finds that managerial capabilities in executing key human resource practices has a positive impact on firm performance.[6] Consequently, managers with better human resource skills place themselves squarely in a superior position for upward movement and greater opportunities and responsibilities.

The Strategic Role of Human Resource Management

As discussed in Chapter 4, a firm obtains a competitive advantage by creating and leveraging products and services that provide value to customers but are hard for competitors to copy. For example, Southwest Airlines has been one of the few airlines to consistently deliver profits since deregulation in 1978 in the United States. Why? Is it Southwest's unique planes? No. The company operates only Boeing 737s, but anyone can buy these planes from Boeing. Is Southwest competitive because of its reservation system? No. Until the Internet made it easy for many people to go online to make reservations, Southwest was not part of the major reservation systems that most travel agents used to book flights. This actually put the airline at a competitive disadvantage because travel agents had to call the company rather than look to their computer screens—as they could do for United, American, Delta, and other airlines—to find ticket prices and availability and book a reservation. So, what explains Southwest's competitive success? By their own account, Southwest's executives believe it is their people and the way they manage their human resources that has been and continues to be the key to the company's success.[7]

Human Resources and Strategy Formulation

Traditionally, people have looked at human resources as a department not involved in strategy formulation. However, this perspective is changing.[8] Increasingly, executives are looking at their people and their present and future capabilities to determine what the company's competitive strategy ought to be.[9] As one executive put it, "In football, if you have a quarterback with a great throwing arm, does it make sense to design an offense built upon the run?" Recall from our discussion in Chapter 4 that a competitive advantage comes largely from creating value for customers through resources that are hard for competitors to copy. The capabilities employees possess are often hard for competitors to copy. To the extent that these capabilities also create value for customers, they become a source of competitive advantage and, therefore, can play a role in what the company's competitive strategy ought to be.

This is part of Southwest Airlines' success. Even though United and other airlines can buy identical Boeing 737s, they have difficulty attracting, selecting, training, and retaining employees who consistently serve customers with a smile. Yet, many customers value the smiles and friendly service they get from Southwest Airlines employees compared to the condescending or rude service they often get from employees on other airlines. The fact that the Southwest Airlines' business model has existed for 30 years and very few, if any, other airlines have been able to copy it—especially the intangible aspects associated with its people—shows how hard copying the aspects of human resources can be and what a powerful competitive advantage a company's workforce can provide.

Human Resources and Strategy Implementation

Clearly, a firm's human resources should not drive every strategy. However, it is hard to think of any strategy that a firm can effectively implement without the proper management of its human resources. For example, earlier in this text we introduced Nordstrom and how it

Phil Huber/Black Star

Having earned a profit for more than 30 years straight, Southwest Airlines is a success story in the beleaguered airlines industry. The company's executives say they believe it's Southwest's employees who give the firm a competitive advantage.

EXHIBIT 7.1

General Framework of HRM

competed, in part, through superior service. This superior service comes largely from Nordstrom employees, not the retailer's technology, the physical structure of its stores, or other company resources. If Nordstrom's managers do not select employees with a customer-service mentality, if they do not train employees in the specific techniques and practices of customer service, and compensate and reward them for superior customer service, the superior customer service that is a core element of the company's strategy will fail to materialize. Consequently, both executives in charge of the HR function and managers throughout an organization need to manage the firm's human resources in a way that supports and helps implement the company's strategy.[10]

Exhibit 7.1 incorporates these various perspectives into a strategic framework of HRM. As the figure illustrates, specific human resource activities (planning, job analysis, recruiting, selecting, socialization and training, job design, performance appraisal, compensation, and development) exist within the context of the firm's strategy and environment. The fit of these human resource activities with the firm's strategy and environment leads to competitive advantage for the organization and for the individual manager.[11]

Human Resource Management Activities That Get the Right People

To this point, we have explored the link between competitive advantage and HRM and have also briefly examined the importance of the fit between HRM practices and the firm's strategy. We now outline the key HRM activities listed in Exhibit 7.1.

Simplified, there are two main HRM goals: (1) getting the right people and (2) maximizing their performance and potential. Although many activities are related to these two general categories, all managers need to get the right people into the right place at the right time and then help them maximize their performance and future potential. However, it is important to appreciate that someone who is right for one organization might not be right for another. For example, a brilliantly creative person might be right for a firm like Google and Apple, which compete by creating innovative products and services. However, that same person might be the wrong fit for an organization that competes through cost leadership and low prices, such as Wal-Mart.

You cannot hire the right people without an understanding of a firm's HRM activities and aligning them with its corporate strategy.[12] While each of these activities is discussed separately, it is important to remember that they are related and that success or failure in one activity can significantly influence the success or failure of another. For example, Disney's ability to select "cast members" (employees) with a happy disposition to work in its theme parks enhances the effectiveness of the "friendly service" training they receive. These two activities combined help keep millions of guests pouring through the gates into the parks each year.

Planning

Human resource planning involves assessing the firm's future human resource needs (demand), determining the availability of the type of people needed (supply), and creating a plan for meeting those needs (fulfillment). At the organizational level, human resource planning is sometimes a shared responsibility among human resource specialists and executives in other functional areas of the firm, such as accounting, finance, marketing, and operations.

FORECASTING DEMAND   Forecasting demand involves determining how many and what type of employees the firm will need at some future point (for example, in one or five years). This is done considering the firm's strategy and the general business and economic environment. For example, going into the recent economic recession, Netflix (the by-mail and video-streaming movie rental company) realized that demand for its services would actually increase as people stayed home and rented movies as a less costly form of entertainment. This meant Netflix would likely need to hire more people.[13]

ASSESSING SUPPLY   At the time, the supply of various types of employees, including engineers, was good as many firms experienced decline as a result of the recession and had to lay off employees. However, laid-off employees are generally not the top performers, and it was the top performers that Netflix really wanted to tap into.

FORMULATING FULFILLMENT PLANS   Netflix wanted to recruit and hire the best talent away from other firms and not just pick up laid-off employees. To do this, recruits would have to perceive Netflix's employment value proposition as greater than what they currently enjoyed. In addition, Netflix believed that to attract and retain such employees, new hires would have to perceive the value proposition as not just better at the moment but better over the longer term. Therefore, the company decided to emphasize their culture and not just money. Specifically, Netflix described its culture as one that focused on "what people get done, not on how many hours they worked."

Even though the HR department might be specially charged with looking at human resource planning, individual managers must also be skilled planners as well. As a manager, you will want to be able to determine the number and types of employees you will need in your units, assess the supply in the marketplace, and develop a plan to get the right people. Just as with the organization, as a manager, you cannot distinguish between a "right" and "wrong" employee without considering your firm's strategy. For example, after his first departure from Apple, Steven Jobs started a company called NeXT to compete in the high-end computer and work station market. Within just a few years, Jobs decided to shift the firm's strategic orientation from hardware to software. For managers in product development, this meant they needed more software programmers and fewer hardware engineers and, initially, fewer employees overall. Because the market for software programmers was tight, NeXT managers focused their efforts on attracting dissatisfied programmers at other companies by highlighting the exciting things going on at NeXT. This shift was what fundamentally set the stage for NeXT to be acquired by Apple and formed the foundation of the new Apple OS X operating system.

To fulfill your employment needs, you may need to consider the use of part-time or temporary employees who can provide the flexibility to meet temporary increases in demand for your product or service. It also allows you to reduce your workforce more easily if demand falls as well as to try out employees before hiring them permanently if demand remains strong.

Alternately, you might decide to outsource specific workforce demands.[14] For example, many U.S. companies outsource their customer service and telemarketing jobs to companies abroad. In a sense, this offloads the fluctuations in demand for call center representatives to another company that specializes in these tasks and has concentrated capabilities in hiring and training people for these jobs.

To match a company's needs with talent supply often requires searching for talent in places a firm hasn't looked before. This was the case for Wal-Mart in the Manger's Challenge "Wal-Mart Suits Up in the War for Talent."

Job Analysis

Job analysis is a critical but often overlooked human resource activity. **Job analysis** is a process that determines the scope and depth of a job and the required skills, abilities, and knowledge that people need to do the job. For example, when Motorola decided to shift its strategic orientation

job analysis
determination of the scope and depth of jobs and the requisite skills, abilities, and knowledge that people need to perform their jobs successfully

A MANAGER'S CHALLENGE

DIVERSITY

Wal-Mart Suits Up in the War for Talent

Given the high unemployment as a result of the recent devastating recession, you wouldn't think that Wal-Mart, or any other company, would be worried about a talent shortage. But with the company scheduled to post $30 billion in new revenue in 2010 (about the total revenue of a company like Coca-Cola), primarily through the opening of new stores, Wal-Mart is desperately short of store and department managers. Traditionally, the firm has focused on promoting managers from within and tended not to recruit managers from the outside. In that sense, it was not only possible but quite normal for someone to start as a stockroom clerk or cashier and then, over time, work up to being a department or store manager. However, managerial capabilities cannot be developed overnight. As a consequence, Wal-Mart needed a variety of people and backgrounds to fill its managerial needs and needed to diversify and expand the pool of talent from which they drew their managers.

Fortunately for the company, a trend of junior military officers (JMOs) leaving the military at the end of their first obligation was bringing a new supply of battle-tested managers. JMOs tend to be in their 20s and 30s, almost all have college degrees, and have managed teams numbering between 6 and 200. Soon after September 11, 2001, the rate of Army officers leaving active duty at their first opportunity dropped by more than 30 percent to a low of just over 6 percent. But as the patriotism of that period began to wane and the wars in Iraq and Afghanistan wore on, the trend reversed itself, beginning in about 2004. As a consequence, significant numbers of JMOs were leaving the military at their first opportunity in search of higher pay and a better quality of life, especially more time with their families.

Although some companies such as GE had been actively recruiting JMOs for years, Wal-Mart got started in 2008. At that time, Wal-Mart COO Bill Simon, a 25-year veteran of the Navy and Naval Reserves, proposed that Wal-Mart actively recruit JMOs. According to Jennifer Seidner, a senior recruiting manager at Wal-Mart, "The thinking was that we could bring in world-class leadership talent that was already trained and ready to go and then we could teach them retail." Once the program was put in place, Wal-Mart recruited about 150 JMOs in about four months. At that point, they were so satisfied with the results that they recruited Gary Profit, a retired brigadier general, to expand their recruiting efforts.

While recruiting combat veterans is a tricky business given the physical, emotional, and psychological scars war can cause, Wal-Mart has found that JMOs have formal education and on-the-ground leadership experience under stress and tough performance conditions that far exceed those of their nonmilitary peers.

According to Professor Noel Tichy of the University of Michigan, "There's a big pool of these officers who have the kind of under-fire judgment experience that makes them really valuable. Whoever has the best screening and development is going to get some great leaders."

Sources: B. O'Keefe, "How a Decade of War Has Created a New Generation of Elite Business Leaders," *Fortune*, March 22, 2010, http://www.fortune.com; T. Shanker, "Young Officers Leaving the Army at a High Rate," *New York Times*, April 10, 2006, http://www.nytimes.com.

away from simply filling customer orders to creating world-class quality products, its managers analyzed the nature of the firm's factory jobs in light of the new strategy. Based on the new quality initiatives and associated tools and techniques, Motorola found many of its existing employees were underqualified. Managers had to decide whether to try to train the existing employees and get them to the level required or whether to terminate them and replace them with more capable employees who could handle the new systems and procedures.[15] In the end, Motorola did both, but focused heavily on training existing employees.

The data and insights that come from a job analysis are typically used to create a *job description,* a list of duties and capabilities required for the job. Typically, this leads to a *job specification*, or a statement that describes the skills, experience, and education that a candidate should have to perform the job.

Recruiting

Recruiting is primarily concerned with determining which candidates you want to attract and undertaking activities to entice them to apply for specific positions within the organization.[16] As with the other activities already discussed, the desired pool of candidates depends on the firm's strategy. Whether you can get the type of person you want is a different story. To some degree, it depends on what you, as compared to your competitors, have to offer.

Let's assume you have candidates in mind and now want to attract them to your company. The key here is knowing what your "target" recruits want. Consider the case of UPS in Germany. When UPS expanded into Germany, managers had a difficult time selecting good drivers because they simply were not attracting high-quality applicants. Several factors contributed to this, most notably the fact that the brown UPS uniforms were the same color that Nazi youth groups wore during World War II. UPS was not offering what high-quality, prospective drivers wanted and was, in fact, offering something they did not want (brown uniforms).

Let's assume that you now have attracted the right people. Next, you need to ensure that what you offer is more attractive to your target candidates than what they already have or might receive from a competing offer. People will always care about money, but if you emphasize money exclusively, money will be the only element on which you can compete for talent. In the case of UPS in Germany, the company discovered that the freedom to determine their own routes appealed to the professional nature of their targeted drivers. This in turn differentiated UPS's employment offering from those of other firms.

Once you have identified what your targeted candidates would find attractive in an employment offering and believe you have a compelling proposition, you need to generate actual job candidates. There are a variety of methods for this. Each method has its strengths and weaknesses and, as a consequence, you should use them as the situation dictates.

David R. Frazier Photolibrary, Inc.\Alamy Images

When UPS expanded to Germany, the company discovered that the freedom they gave employees to determine their own routes appealed to the professional nature of their targeted drivers.

JOB POSTING Job posting is a popular internal recruiting method in which a job, its pay, level, description, and qualifications are posted or announced to all current employees. Increasingly, companies post their jobs electronically through e-mail or on the company's Web site. Job postings help ensure that all qualified employees have an opportunity to apply for a particular job. Job posting can also help current employees get a better idea of the types of jobs available to them and the qualifications needed to be successful in those jobs. This can allow them to plan their careers. On the negative side, job postings can generate responses from unqualified applicants who need to receive explanations about why they were unqualified and did not get the job. Without adequate explanation, they are likely to wonder whether the job was really "open" when it was posted. If employees begin to doubt the process of posting jobs, it can generate skepticism, limit the pool of candidates, or even generate lawsuits. For example, the District of Columbia Department of Consumer Affairs was recently sued by a female employee who applied for a supervisor position each of the five times it was posted after she learned that a less qualified male applicant was hired after the fifth posting.[17]

job posting

an internal recruiting method in which a job, its pay, level, description, and qualifications are posted or announced to all current employees

ADVERTISEMENTS Advertisements in general or in specialized publications can also be an effective means of generating job candidates. National business newspapers such as the *Wall Street Journal* cast a wide net. Professional magazines such as *HR Magazine* cast a very specialized net. Regional or local publications, such as your city newspaper, focus on the local labor pool. Increasingly, companies are using the Internet to advertise job openings. As the Internet matures, regional and industrial segments are likely to develop, facilitating more targeted advertising of jobs.[18]

EMPLOYMENT AGENCIES In some fields, employment agencies can also be effective in generating job candidates. The agency's effectiveness is largely a function of how well it understands your organization and a job's requirements. Agencies tend to be expensive and usually are not cost-effective for low-level and low-paying jobs. In contrast, most openings at the senior management level use executive search firms as part of their recruiting efforts. For example, the hospitality division of Force Temporary Services understands the tourism industry in Puerto Rico and the Caribbean and places managers and executives in leading hospitality firms in the region.[19] As their fee for finding an acceptable candidate, these firms typically charge at least one-third of the successful candidate's first-year compensation.

EMPLOYEE REFERRALS Managers often find current employees a great source for job candidates.[20] Current employees with tenure in the organization understand the organization, its culture, and often the particular job that needs to be filled. They usually know something about an applicant as well: work history, educational background, skills and abilities, personal characteristics, and so on. Given that, to some degree, their recommendation puts their own reputation on the line, current employees tend to recommend individuals who they believe will do well. Their personal relationship with the recommended candidate allows employees not to just sell the company on the individual but to sell the individual on the company. In general, research suggests that employee referrals are one of the most effective recruiting methods. Employee referrals are less effective when the firm is looking for a different type of employee than they currently have. Current employees tend to recommend people like themselves. As a result, a company pushing into international activities or new technology may find their employees don't know people in these new areas to refer.

SCHOOL PLACEMENT CENTERS School placement centers are also a popular source of job candidates. Placement center offices can range from those found in high schools, technical schools, and junior colleges to universities and advanced degree programs. Given an adequate amount of time and clear job specifications and requirements, school placement centers can do much of the prescreening for an employer, filtering out unqualified candidates. This can save the firm time and money in the recruiting process.

Schools are also increasingly using video conferencing capabilities to set up "virtual" interviews and online job fairs. Technology helps firms broaden their candidate search, reaching places to which they may not be able to travel physically. The weakness of school placement centers is that they often deal with so many companies and students that they might not know enough about either to conduct ideal screening.

THE INTERNET Companies are discovering that the Internet is a powerful recruiting tool. Most major companies use their corporate Web sites to list jobs and attract candidates. In addition to using their own sites to attract candidates, companies are increasingly using sites such as Monster.com. Monster.com now has over 41 million résumés in its database and is the number-one online job search site. Companies also frequently post ads to two other popular sites, Careerbuilder.com and Yahoo!'s Hotjobs.com. These and other sites now have the ability to screen résumés for companies, freeing up the human resources staff from this task. Companies like Virgin Atlantic are also using professional networking sites, such as LinkedIn, to find new employees. And given the cuts forced by the downturn in the air transport industry, Virgin also is using the site as a way to stay in touch with former employees with an eye to rehiring them once economic conditions improve.

Today's high-tech world offers some interesting new ways of finding the right recruits. For example, Elance.com, highlighted in A Manager's Challenge, "Elance.com Survives and Thrives," functions a bit like a cyberspace matchmaker of freelance workers and the firms that employ them. What do you think of this sort of high-tech approach? As an employer, how likely would you be to search for talent via this sort of mechanism? What types of jobs would fit this and what type of jobs would not? Conversely, would you likely seek out employment this way? If yes, can you see yourself doing it for a long period of time or would it only be as a temporary means of supplementing your income?

Selecting

Successful selection is a function of effective planning, analyzing, and recruiting as well as applying appropriate selection techniques.[21] Even with a good set of candidates, managers must also determine which one is best for the job. For example, international banks like Goldman Sachs or JP Morgan have no trouble attracting people to overseas positions because international experience is important in the increasingly global banking industry. However, managers selected for overseas assignments sometimes fail and have to return home early at a cost of about $150,000 per employee. This is costly for employers, but it can also hurt an employee's career. These failures are partly a function of poor identification of the characteristics that lead to success in an overseas assignment and also a function of limited use of effective selection techniques to identify the right candidate.[22]

A MANAGER'S CHALLENGE

TECHNOLOGY

Elance.com Survives and Thrives

The term *freelance* comes from the Middle Ages: Knights would put themselves up for hire because they were not beholden to a specific king. Therefore, they were free to fight and use their lances for any noble who would pay them. Now, fast-forward to the twenty-first century: With the explosion of broadband Internet connections and cheap telecommunication, the world of virtual employees who freelance for a while or for their entire careers has arrived. Freelancers like the arrangement because they can work for different companies without having to relocate, and they can move from one interesting project to another. Freelancers offer employers flexibility to move "headcount" up or down quickly—something that simply isn't possible with permanent workers. Using freelancers, employers can more easily move the headcount up or down as demand dictates. They are also able to choose from an almost unlimited number of skill sets for each specific project they want to assign.

There are scores of freelancer sites on the Web designed to bring "knight" and "noble" together. One of the oldest is Elance.com. Founded in 1998, the privately held company recently announced that nearly 104,000 employers had posted nearly 320,000 jobs on its site in the last 12 months. It had nearly 107,000 registered professional freelancers who specialize in professional categories, including everything from Web site design, programming, graphic design, and business consulting to administrative support. Since its inception, Elance.com posted total earnings of $206 million. However, the company reported that $20 million in projects transpired in just the first quarter of 2010, which was a 40 percent increase over the same quarter the previous year.

In the IT category, the company reported that PHP (Hypertext Preprocessor, a widely used scripting language designed for web development to produce dynamic web pages) remained the number-one job posting. However, iPhone development had moved up three spots into the top 10 of its job postings. The top five countries providing talent in winning the IT job postings were India, Ukraine, Pakistan, the United States, and Russia, respectively.

In the "creative" category, job postings increased 31 percent in 2010 over 2009 and earning increased 37 percent. The top two requests remained graphic design and article writing. The top five countries providing talent in winning the creative job postings were the United States, India, UK, Canada, and Argentina, respectively.

Prospective employees, known as "providers," set up an account by completing standard skill and experience templates and adding other descriptions of their capabilities. They can then establish alerts to notify them when new jobs are posted. They can also search the entire database by category, budget, time, and whether the job is paid hourly or by project fee. At the end of the day, technology can bring together "employers" and "employees" from anywhere on the planet who otherwise would likely have need to be physically much closer to each other in days past.

Elance has a 7-step process for using its services:

1. *Finding Providers and Posting a Job*: If you are an employer, you can either post a public job and begin receiving proposals from any Elance service provider or search for specific providers and privately invite them to submit a proposal to you.

2. *Reviewing Proposals and Choosing a Provider*: Employers then review proposals and evaluate candidates (their profiles, portfolios, tested skills, credentials, and feedback on Elance). Often there is an online interview. Once satisfied, the employer makes his or her selection by clicking the "Award" button next to the provider's name. Once a job is awarded, a Workroom is created and all communications from the proposal review phase are transferred over automatically. All future communications, files, status reports, and milestones will be managed from within the Workroom.

3. *Defining the Business Terms*: The employer then establishes key milestones and dates of delivery, including interim payments made for meeting milestones.

4. *Starting the Work*: Once both parties accept the terms, the employer is notified that it's time to fund the first milestone for the work to begin. Payments are handled through Elance Escrow.

5. *Managing the Work*: Providers and their clients use the Workroom to communicate and collaborate on the work in progress. Files are shared, comments are made, and live communication is facilitated through messaging and even live chat. All communications are stored to ensure that both parties can review all comments at any time. Every week, the provider is prompted to submit a Status Report, outlining what was done that week, how much time was spent, and tracking progress toward established milestones. If there are changes during the course of a

(continued)

job, at any time either the employer or the provider can update the Terms by going to the job Workroom. Once any changes are submitted, the other party can choose to accept, modify or decline the updates.

6. *Receiving Results and Releasing Payment*: As a milestone is met and accepted, the funds for that milestone are released and transferred to the provider's account. At this point, the next milestone gets funded, and work continues.

7. *Leave Feedback*. Once the job is complete and the final milestone payment is released, both the employer and provider can leave feedback about their experience.

Sources: Company Web site, http://www.elance.com, accessed May 4, 2010; C. Barbierri, "Elance report: Free lance is the new full time." *VentureBeat*, April 12, 2010 http://venturebeat.com/2010/04/12/elance-report-freelance-is-the-new-full-time/.

---

valid selection technique

a screening process that differentiates those who would be successful in a job from those who would not

One of the key points to keep in mind about any selection technique is that if legally challenged, the organization must be able to demonstrate that the selection technique is valid. A **valid selection technique** is one that can differentiate between those who would be more successful in the job and those who would be less successful. For example, educational background is often used in selecting new hires because knowledge typically has a proven relationship with job performance. That is, it is hard to perform well in a job for which you do not have the requisite education and knowledge. There are a variety of selection techniques; each has its own strengths and weaknesses.

INTERVIEWS The most widely used selection technique is the interview.[23] In most cases, the interview is unstructured. An unstructured interview is one in which interviewers have a general idea of the types of questions they might ask but do not have a standard set of questions. As a consequence, interviewers might ask different candidates different questions. With different questions and responses, comparing candidates can be like comparing apples and oranges. Not surprisingly, a major weakness of unstructured interviews is that they tend to have low levels of validity.[24] In contrast, in a **structured interview,** interviewers ask a standard set of questions of all candidates about their qualifications and capabilities, can be quite valid.[25] Carefully recording interviewees' responses on a standardized form and taking approximately the same time to interview each candidate can further enhance validity. Exhibit 7.2 provides tips for interviewers, and Exhibit 7.3 provides tips for interviewees.[26] However, some questions in the United States, by law, cannot be asked. For example, prospective employers cannot ask if a candidate is married or plans to have children. Employers also cannot ask about race, religion, birthplace, national origin, or age.

structured interview

one in which interviewers ask a standard set of questions of all candidates about qualifications and capabilities related to job performance

---

EXHIBIT 7.2

Tips for Interviewers

1. Plan the interview by reviewing the candidate's resume and the job specifications.
2. Establish rapport with a friendly greeting and start the interview with a nonjob question.
3. Follow a structured set of questions.
4. Avoid questions that require or solicit a simple *yes* or *no* response.
5. Try not to telegraph, or give cues for, the desired answer.
6. Make sure the candidate has plenty of time to answer—do not monopolize the conversation.
7. Listen carefully and paraphrase key candidate answers to be sure you understand what the individual meant to say.
8. Ask for specific, not general, examples of the candidate's experience and accomplishments.
9. Leave time at the end of the interview to answer questions from the candidate.
10. At the close, make sure the candidate knows what the next steps are and approximate timing.
11. After the candidate leaves, review your notes and highlight important points while they are fresh in your mind.

EXHIBIT 7.3

Tips for Interviewees

1. Prepare for the interview by researching the company through articles and its own Web site.
2. Smile and provide a warm greeting and firm handshake if the interviewer extends his or her hand.
3. Make sure that your overall appearance (hair style, clothing, makeup, and so on) match the nature of the business and culture of the company.
4. Watch your nonverbal behavior to ensure that you maintain good eye contact and convey enthusiasm without being overly expressive with your hands or other body movements.
5. Try to solicit the interviewer's needs early in the interview.
6. Early in the interview, be sure to get a complete picture of the job through such questions as, "Can you tell about what has led people to succeed in this job in the past?"
7. Explicitly relate yourself and capabilities to the interviewer's needs through statements such as, "You mentioned that one of the keys to this position is the ability to motivate others. In my experience at XYZ. . . ."
8. Take your time before answering; you do not need to begin talking the instant the interviewer finishes asking a question.
9. Conclude the interview by thanking the person for the opportunity and expressing your interest in the company and the position.

WORK SAMPLING A variety of techniques can be classified as work sampling. Essentially, these techniques attempt to simulate or exactly duplicate the job the person would be doing if hired. The underlying rationale is straightforward: If you perform poorly or well in the work sample, you will likely perform similarly in the real job. In general, the main strength of work sampling techniques is that they make a reasonably accurate prediction of how a candidate will do in a job. The main drawback is they tend to be time- and cost-intensive.

WORK SIMULATIONS Work simulations typically involve situations in which job candidates perform work that they would do if hired or work that closely simulates the tasks they would perform. For example, when Nissan set up its new assembly plant in Tennessee to assess applicants' manual dexterity skills, a key requirement for assembly line workers, the company required them to assemble flashlights. At Motorola, technical writing job candidates are given a piece of equipment, shown how to use it, given time to practice using it, and then are required to write a technical description of the equipment and an operation manual. This gives Motorola a clear idea of those who can write technical material well.

ASSESSMENT CENTERS Assessment centers typically use any number of selection tools, including work sampling and simulation techniques, in order to get a broader and richer sense of the fit of the employee to the job. Typically, candidates are required to go through a number of exercises, and each exercise is designed to capture one or more key aspects of the job. For example, a supervisor's job might require good prioritization skills. To assess this skill, the assessment center might set up an "in-basket" exercise. The exercise consists of an in-basket filled with letters, memos, and reports that the candidate must read and then prioritize. This activity demonstrates the individual's ability to recognize and respond to high-priority items. In general, research shows that assessment centers are an effective selection method.[27] However, using an assessment center to screen candidates is typically time and resource intensive.[28]

WRITTEN TESTS Written tests are also widely used. This is due to the fact that employers can administer the tests cost-effectively to a large number of job candidates. Cognitive ability and intelligence tests measure an individual's general cognitive complexity and intellectual ability. Although the validity of these tests has been mixed, they do seem to be acceptable predictors for supervisory and management jobs. Personality tests are more controversial. Although they can be reasonably good predictors of people's ability to work well with other particular personalities, they have not been good overall predictors of job performance.[29] Integrity tests are a more recent development. These tests try to assess the general level of a person's honesty. In general, they seem to be of debatable validity.[30] Written tests have the advantage of generally being inexpensive to administer, but the results are more valid regarding how applicants will perform in general rather than in a specific job.

BACKGROUND AND REFERENCE CHECKS Employers perform background checks to verify factual information provided by the applicants they have interest in hiring.[31] Between 10 percent and 15 percent of applicants either lie about or exaggerate factual information.[32] As a consequence, it can be valuable to check to make sure applicants graduated with the degrees they claim, from the schools they cite, and held the jobs with the responsibilities they describe. The objective of reference checks is to get candid evaluations from those who have worked with the job candidate. However, recent legal judgments against past employers that made negative statements about their former employees have led employers to provide only factual information, such as title, years employed, and so on. On the other hand, court rulings have suggested that employers can be held liable for not conducting adequate checks. For example, financial service firms need to ensure that individuals involved in security transactions have not been convicted of a felony in the past.

PHYSICAL EXAMINATIONS Companies that require a physical examination as part of the selection process typically do so because the job has high physical demands. In addition to helping an employer select physically qualified candidates, physical exams also protect the firm. First, the information from the physical exam may help firms reduce insurance claims. Second, the physical exam may help protect the firm from lawsuits by identifying high-risk applicants, such as someone who might experience a heart attack from the physical strains of the job. However, given recent legislation in the United States, managers must be careful to ensure that the physical requirements being screened in the examination relate to job performance and are not sources for discrimination.[33] For example, BNSF Railway required some of its employees to take a medical examination to prevent on-the-job injuries. At one point, the company included testing a genetic factor only for employees claiming work-related carpal tunnel syndrome. Subsequently, a court ordered BNSF to stop testing employees because the test had nothing to do with an employee's current degree of carpal tunnel syndrome. Drug testing is another screening mechanism companies use to ensure that employees' judgment and capabilities are not impaired while on the job.

Up to this point we have covered a large number of specific techniques so it may be helpful to review the basics as illustrated in Exhibit 7.4. Planning for the employees you need is the first major task. You need to establish what the demand and supply balance for employees looks like in your industry in order to determine how you will fulfill your needs. The organization's strategy and an analysis of the firm's jobs clearly affect these activities. Once the major planning is done, it is a matter of recruiting and attracting the desired candidates. The last step is to select the best people to hire.

Human Resource Management Activities That Maximize Performance

Once the right people are in the right positions, managers need to ensure that employees perform well. What constitutes maximum performance and potential is largely a function of the organization's strategy. For example, Google chooses to compete on new product innovation and strives to have the majority of its revenue come from products that are less than three years old. It,

EXHIBIT 7.4

Key Aspects of Getting the Right People

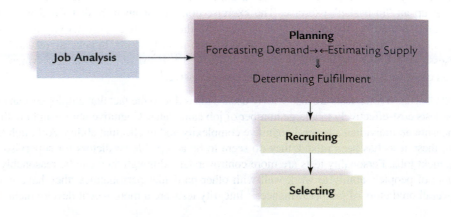

therefore, needs employees who can think of and test new ideas. For Google, maximum performance and potential are largely defined in terms of employee innovations. Based on this, Google undertakes a variety of activities to maximize employees' creativity. Five specific categories of activities can significantly influence employee performance and potential.

Socialization and Training

Just as early life experiences can shape a person's general character, personality, and behavior, so too can early training and socialization experiences shape important aspects of employees' performance.[34] For example, early training and socialization each affects (1) the probability that new hires will stay with the firm, (2) the extent to which they will perform well, and (3) the degree to which they will develop to their full potential.[35]

Managers can use a variety of training methods to enhance the performance and potential of employees. We cover several here. Although early career training is important, in today's changing environment, training and learning are likely to become career-long necessities.

ORIENTATION The orientation period is one of the first opportunities for an organization to shape the expectations and behavior of new employees.[36] Typically, orientation programs provide a broad overview of the industry, the company and its business activities; its key competitors; and general information about working for the company (such as key policies, pay procedures, and fringe benefits). Work-unit orientation sessions are typically narrower and are generally designed to help the new employee get up to speed on the new job, co-workers, the work-unit's policies, procedures, and expectations. To maximize the effectiveness of orientation programs, managers should consider doing the following:[37]

- Keep paperwork to a minimum to avoid information overload. Do include paperwork that must be completed immediately.
- Include an informal meeting with the individual's immediate supervisor.
- Alternate heavy information, such as that related to benefits and insurance, with lighter live or video presentations from corporate officers.
- Provide a glossary of terms unique to the organization.
- Match each new employee with a "buddy" (that is, an experienced worker) based more on personality compatibility than similarity of jobs.

ON-THE-JOB TRAINING TECHNIQUES On-the-job training (OJT) is the most widely used training technique in organizations. As Exhibit 7.5 illustrates, there are a wide variety of techniques that a manager can use to train employees. Over your career, you will likely be exposed to most, if not all, of these approaches.

OFF-THE-JOB TRAINING TECHNIQUES The most common off-the-job training occurs in a classroom. The training program may be only an hour or several weeks in length. In-house experts (employees of the company) or outside experts from industry or education fields, such as a university professor, may conduct the training program. The program may involve lectures, case studies, discussions, videos, simulations, or computer-based training. Many computer-based training programs now adjust the program's content and difficulty level based on how well the individual is doing. Formal correspondence courses and online learning are sometimes used for off-the-job training.

TECHNICAL, INTERPERSONAL, AND CONCEPTUAL TRAINING Orientation and training programs can have a variety of objectives. However, at a fundamental level, these programs are intended to address employees' technical, interpersonal, or conceptual abilities. An employee's technical skills can range from being able to read and perform simple math to being able to program a supercomputer. As mentioned earlier, when Motorola made a strategic commitment to quality, it discovered that over a third of its employees could not read, write, or do math at the level the new quality control program required. This discovery led to a massive technical training effort.

Because very few employees work in isolation, improved interpersonal abilities are the target of a wide variety of training programs. Programs such as these might address skills such as effective listening, conflict resolution, negotiation, and coaching. Over the last several years, executives have cited poor interpersonal skills as one of the biggest problems associated with new college or MBA graduates.[38]

EXHIBIT 7.5

On-the-Job Training Techniques

1. *Expanded Responsibilities.* This training technique expands an individual's job duties, assignments, and responsibilities.
2. *Job Rotation.* Also called *cross-training*, this practice moves individuals to various types of jobs within the organization at the same level or next-immediate-higher level for periods of time from an hour or two to as long as a year.
3. *Staff Development Meetings.* Meetings are usually held offsite to discuss facts of each individual's job and to develop ideas for improving job performance.
4. *"Assistant to" Positions.* Promising employees serve as staff assistants to higher-skill-level jobs for a specified period of time (often one to three months) to become more familiar with the higher-skilled positions in the organization.
5. *Problem-Solving Conferences.* Conferences are held to solve a specific problem being experienced by a group or the organization as whole. It involves brainstorming and other creative means to come up with solutions to the basic problems.
6. *Mentoring.* A guide or knowledgeable person higher up in the organization helps a new employee "learn the ropes" of the organization and provides other advice.
7. *Special Assignments.* Special tasks or responsibilities are given to an individual for a specified period of time. The assignment may be writing up a report; investigating the feasibility for a new project, process, service, or product; preparing a newsletter; or evaluating a company policy or procedure.
8. *Company Trainers.* Special programs can cover such topics as safety, new personnel procedures, new product or services, affirmative action, and technical programs.
9. *Outside Consultants.* Recognized experts are brought to the company to conduct training on such topics as goal setting, communications, assessment techniques, safety, and other current topics of importance. They often supplement training done by company trainers.
10. *Consultant Advisory Reviews.* Experts in specialized fields meet with various managers and employee groups to investigate and help solve particular problems. The emphasis is on problem solving rather than training.
11. *Reading Matter.* A formal program is created to circulate books, journals, selected articles, new business material, and other materials to selected employees. An effective program also includes periodic scheduled meetings to discuss the material.
12. *Apprenticeship.* Training is provided through working under a journeyman or master in a craft. The apprentice works alongside a person skilled in the craft and is taught by that person. Apprenticeship programs also often include some classroom work.

Source: Adapted from W. P. Anthony, D. L. Perrewé, and K. M. Kacmar, *Strategic Human Resource Management* (Fort Worth: Harcourt Brace Jovanovich, 1993).

The final category is conceptual abilities. This category includes a variety of skills and abilities, such as problem solving, decision making, planning, and organizing. A given training program might be designed to address just one, two, or all three of these categories.

Regardless of the category the program is designed to target, most successful programs provide participants with several things:

- An understanding of what the correct employee behavior is and is not
- A clear knowledge of why certain behaviors are correct or incorrect
- Sufficient opportunities to practice the desired behaviors
- Feedback on their performance with further opportunities to practice and improve

An important part of training is evaluating its effectiveness.[39] The simplest way to do this is by using the "smile index"—that is, by gauging the satisfaction of the participants who received the training. This is often gathered by administering a questionnaire to participants just after the training is finished. Participants who do not like the training they receive are unlikely to retain it and use it to their benefit. However, just because participants enjoyed the training or thought it was useful does not guarantee it will be useful. A more rigorous assessment of training would involve a pre-training and post-training assessment. This would involve assessing participants' knowledge and skills before the training and at some point afterward. If the training is intended to improve on-the-job performance, such as quality, managers could assess its impact by comparing important metrics. For example, a manufacturing company might measure defects per 1,000 units assembled before and after the training. However, while a reduction in defects might reveal whether the training had the intended effect, it will not demonstrate that the training was cost-effective. Determining cost-effectiveness is much more complicated. In general, both the direct and indirect costs of training would need to be assessed. Next, the costs would need to be compared to the benefits, such as the savings from having fewer defective products returned. However, one key challenge is determining the period over which to add up the benefits. For example, if higher quality saves a firm $100 per day in returns, should the firm estimate the total value of these savings over the course of a week, a month, a year, or several years? An organization's decision will dramatically affect the calculations—and, therefore, whether the training was worth it.

Job Design

Job design focuses on the structuring or restructuring of key components of a job.[40] A job design typically includes the job's responsibilities. Thus, while job analysis focuses on a job's components, job design is the process of determining which components ought to be put together and how they should be arranged to enhance performance.[41] For example, does an assembly line worker work in isolation and repetitively attach a given part to a product, or does he work in a team with others building an entire unit? Dell is one company whose assembly line workers work in teams building entire computer units. In some texts, job design would be much earlier in the sequence than we have placed it. In general, for a brand new job that has never been filled before, job design does take place early in the sequence. Also, traditionally jobs were designed and then appropriate people were selected to fit into the jobs. The reality of today's dynamic environment has changed that approach. In some cases, it is possible and appropriate to design jobs and then try to match people to them, but in other cases, jobs might need to be designed or redesigned to fit the available people. There are also situations that require a combination of both fitting the person to the job and fitting the job to the person. For example, **job sharing** involves two people working part-time in the same job. Effective job sharing requires two individuals who can coordinate well and have similar capabilities. Job sharing has become popular with working mothers who must balance family and professional demands. Increasingly, technology is allowing managers to design and redesign jobs in ways that make them more flexible, productive, and satisfying to employees. For example, JetBlue, a relatively new airline and one of the most profitable, saved money by having its reservation agents work from home instead of putting money into large call centers. Improved communications technology has been one way to provide that flexibility.

During the early and mid-1990s, reengineering became a popular concept regarding the design or redesign of work. **Reengineering** involves rethinking and radically redesigning business processes to achieve dramatic improvements in performance, such as cost, quality, service, or speed.[42] Computer and information technology today have allowed organizations to design more enriched, satisfying, and productive jobs. Increasingly, organizations are looking at ways to give employees more flexibility in the way they accomplish their work. For example, before a major reengineering project at IBM, customer financing approvals involved four different people performing very specific, narrow, and repetitive jobs. One person reviewed the customer's financial strength by accessing a standardized database. Another reviewed the company's past payment history with IBM. A third examined whether the financing request was within or outside prescribed norms IBM had established. And one person then compared the contract to the standards IBM had established. Redesigning the job for one person to do all four steps and supporting that with needed technology produced important results. First, employee satisfaction with the job went up because it was much more interesting to employees, and productivity went up as well by nearly 1000 percent. Maximizing subordinates' performance and your unit's performance is your goal as a manager regarding effective job design.

Evaluating Employees' Performance

Before organizations or managers can encourage or correct the actions of employees, they must know how the employees are doing.[43] The performance appraisal process should (1) establish

job design
the structuring or restructuring of key job components

job sharing
situation in which two people share the same job by each working part-time

reengineering
fundamental rethinking and radical redesign of business processes to achieve dramatic improvements in critical, contemporary measures of performance, such as cost, quality, service, or speed

performance objectives and standards, (2) measure the performance of employees against those standards, and (3) give employees feedback about that measurement and evaluation.[44] As we stated before, the strategy of the firm must drive the objectives of a job and its associated performance standards. When Motorola decided to compete on quality, it set "six sigma" as its standard. A six-sigma quality standard allows for only 3.4 defects per 1 million opportunities. For Motorola, this had wide-ranging implications from the factory floor to the corporate kitchen. On the floor, this meant that only 3.4 products per million produced could have a defect. For the kitchen, it meant that only 3.4 muffins for every million baked could be burnt. Although six sigma was not immediately achievable for Motorola, it did have a significant impact on the performance of the company's employees.

For most managers, the performance appraisal is perhaps the most important, yet most difficult, human resource activity. Sometimes employees do not quite measure up to the firm's standards and must be told as much; however, few people like to give or receive negative feedback. Still, without such feedback, neither employees nor organizations can maximize their performance. As a consequence, all managers need to understand the key factors that drive effective performance appraisal systems and be skilled at implementing them.

GRAPHIC RATING SCALES Perhaps the most popular method of providing performance feedback is through graphic rating scales (see Exhibit 7.6). A graphic rating scale typically lists a set of qualities upon which to evaluate the employee. The employee's level of performance on each of these items is then rated in terms of a graduated scale typically ranging from 1 to 5. The degree of specificity concerning the definition of each point on the scale can range from one-word descriptors (for example, 1 = poor) to complete sentences (for example, 1 = Does not meet the minimum standards).

Graphic ratings are popular for two main reasons. First, they are relatively quick and easy for managers to complete. Given that most managers must evaluate many employees and are typically not rewarded for writing up high-quality evaluations, they have a natural incentive to complete the evaluations as quickly as possible. Second, it is easy to quantify the results and compare employees' performance ratings.

However, there are two key limitations that as a manager you should keep in mind relative to graphic rating scales. First, the characteristics being evaluated may not be clearly defined; thus, they are left to individual interpretation. Consequently, one manager might focus her interpretation of "interpersonal skills" on conflict resolution abilities, while another manager might focus his interpretation on listening skills. Given the two different interpretations, it is difficult to compare the employees evaluated by the two different managers. Furthermore, the two different managers might have different interpretations of the rating scale. One manager might only allow the top 5 percent of employees to receive a high rating of "5 = excellent." Another manager might interpret a "5" as applicable to the top 20 percent of employees. Once again, the different interpretations would make comparing employees rated by different managers difficult.[45] This incomparability is important because over 85 percent of firms use performance appraisals to determine merit increases, bonuses, and promotions.

EXHIBIT 7.6

Graphic Rating Scale

Employee name: _____ Dept. _____					
	Excellent	Good	Average	Fair	Poor
1. Quality of work	☐	☐	☐	☐	☐
2. Quantity of work	☐	☐	☐	☐	☐
3. Cooperation	☐	☐	☐	☐	☐
4. Dependability	☐	☐	☐	☐	☐
5. Initiative	☐	☐	☐	☐	☐
6. Job knowledge	☐	☐	☐	☐	☐
7. Attitude	☐	☐	☐	☐	☐

BEHAVIORALLY ANCHORED RATING SCALES Behaviorally anchored rating scales (BARS) are designed to reduce the disadvantages associated with graphic rating scales. The two scales are similar in that managers rate employee characteristics using a quantitative scale. However, with behaviorally anchored rating scales, the characteristics are specified in greater detail and described in terms of behaviors rather than abstract qualities (see Exhibit 7.7). The greater specificity and link to behaviors reduces, but does not eliminate, the potential for different raters to evaluate employees differently.[46] Some potential for bias remains.[47]

360-DEGREE FEEDBACK The rationale behind a 360-degree feedback appraisal system is that a person's performance should be viewed from multiple perspectives.[48] Most **360-degree feedback** systems involve collecting appraisal evaluations from an employee's boss, peers, subordinates, and even the employee. In some companies, evaluations are also collected from suppliers and

behaviorally anchored rating scales (BARS)
a performance appraisal system in which the rater places detailed employee characteristics on a rating scale

360-degree feedback
performance appraisal system in which information is gathered from supervisors, co-workers, subordinates, and sometimes suppliers and customers

EXHIBIT 7.7 **Behaviorally Anchored Rating Scale**

| Position: _____ |
| Job dimensions: _____ |

Plans work and organizes time carefully so as to maximize resources and meet commitments.	**9**	
	8	Even though this associate has a report due on another project, he or she would be well prepared for the assigned discussion on your project.
	7	This associate would keep a calendar or schedule on which deadlines and activities are carefully noted, and which would be consulted before making new commitments.
	6	As program chief, this associate would manage arrangements for enlisting resources for a special project reasonably well, but would probably omit one or two details that would have to be handled by improvisation.
Plans and organizes time and effort primarily for large segments of a task. Usually meets commitments, but may overlook what are considered secondary details.	**5**	This associate would meet a deadline in handing in a report, but the report might be below usual standard if other deadlines occur on the same day the report is due.
	4	This associate's evaluations are likely not to reflect abilities because of overcommitments in other activities.
	3	This associate would plan more by enthusiasm than by timetable and frequently have to work late the night before an assignment is due, although it would be completed on time.
	2	This associate would often be late for meetings, although others in similar circumstances do not seem to find it difficult to be on time.
Appears to do little planning. May perform effectively, despite what seems to be a disorganized approach, by concerted effort, although deadlines may be missed.	**1**	This associate never makes a deadline, even with sufficient notice.

Source: Table from William P. Anthony, Pamela L. Perrewé, and K. Michele Kacmar, *Strategic Human Resource Management*, p. 456. © 1993. Reprinted by permission of William P. Anthony.

customers, depending on the nature of interaction the employee has with these constituencies or groups of people. The positive aspect of 360-degree feedback is that because data are gathered from multiple sources, employees are encouraged to focus on all of the firm's key constituencies. This reduces the incentive, for example, for employees to simply cozy up to the boss but work poorly with their peers or subordinates. The major drawback is the time and energy it takes to collect, process, and effectively feed the data back to the individual. In addition, a recent study shows that 360-degree feedback might not have the validity attributed to it that it should.[49]

EFFECTIVE PERFORMANCE FEEDBACK Regardless of the appraisal system used, the results of the evaluation need to be fed back effectively to employees to make a positive difference in their performance. First, if the employer's expectations concerning unacceptable, acceptable, or superior performance were not clear to the employee prior to the appraisal, a negative evaluation is not likely to motivate the employee or improve his or her performance. Consequently, the performance expectations must be clear and acceptable to the employee from the outset. Second, if the employee believes that, as the manager, you are biased in your observations, your assessment will not have the effect you desire. This is why it is important to record critical incidents. A **critical incident** is any important, specific event in which the employee's behavior and performance were above or below expectations. This record enables managers to recall all events with regard to an employee, not just the most recent ones. It also facilitates your ability to talk about specifics in the appraisal interview.[50] This brings us to a brief list of recommendations for an effective performance appraisal interview:

critical incident
a specific incident in which the employee's behavior and performance were above or below expectations

1. Review the key work objectives, goals, or standards against which the employee's performance is measured.
2. Summarize the employee's overall performance by reviewing specific positive and negative incidents.
3. Discuss causes of weak performance and listen carefully to the employee's explanation.
4. Discuss different ways to improve the employee's future performance and encourage the person's input.
5. Establish an agreed-upon approach, timetable, and review process for future improvement.
6. Establish key objectives, timetables, and standards for the upcoming performance period.
7. Leave the meeting on an encouraging and positive note.

These may seem like simple steps. Nonetheless, they can go a long way toward improving how well you handle one of the most difficult yet important challenges you will face as a manager. However, even when following these steps, differences in generational expectations can frustrate the effort. For example, Brian Castro, a baby-boomer and manager of a help desk staffed by 23 employees, reported that he was stunned when one of his Millennial generation (born 1980-1999) subordinates came into his office to tell him Friday would be his last day. While Castro thought he was providing plenty of "constructive" feedback to keep the employee on the right track, the employee was looking for appreciative feedback on what he was doing well. According to Castro, the generational expectations on the nature and frequency of feedback were simply different and there is some research to support this.[51]

Compensation

Although rewards and compensation can be instrumental in getting the right people, their primary function is retaining and maximizing the performance of employees once they have entered the organization. Rewards by their nature are designed to encourage desired behaviors. As already discussed, desired behaviors must be linked to the firm's strategy. Thus, reward systems also must be linked to the firm's strategy.

pay structure
a range of pay for a particular position or classification of positions

broadband system
a pay structure in which the range of pay is large and covers a wide variety of jobs

PAY Most firms establish a pay structure based on the level in the company and type of position. A **pay structure** establishes a range of pay for a particular position or classification of positions. The most common element of any pay structure is the wage. Wages tend to be structured on an hourly basis or as a fixed amount by calendar year. When structured by calendar year, the wage is typically referred to as a salary, and the most common calendar division is annual, although payment of the salary is typically divided and made monthly.

Traditionally, salary structures have been hierarchical and segmented. Most companies are now moving to what is called a **broadband system,** in which the range of pay is large and covers a wide variety of jobs.[52] Exhibit 7.8 provides a graphic illustration of a traditional pay structure and a more modern broadband system. The major advantage to a broadband system is the greater flexibility it gives organizations to match an employee's pay to his or her individual value and changing labor market conditions.

Another important pay trend is the movement away from an individual's total compensation package being primarily composed of salary and toward a greater portion of compensation being at risk.[53] **At-risk compensation** (sometimes referred to as *variable compensation*) is simply pay that varies depending on specified conditions. These conditions might include the general profitability of the company; hitting particular budget, revenue, or cost savings targets for a unit; or meeting specific individual performance targets. Increasingly, companies are placing a higher portion of employees' total compensation "at risk." This is primarily because if total compensation is made up of salary and if salaries are raised at a level comparable to inflation, inflation and subsequent salary increases can add significantly to company costs. On the other hand, if a higher percentage of compensation is tied to performance, higher compensation costs only occur with higher performance. Consequently, the concept of an **incentive plan,** or a system that ties some compensation to performance, is increasingly being used throughout organizations where once they were reserved for only the most senior managers.

BENEFITS Traditional benefit plans include items such as medical, dental, and life insurance. In some cases, certain benefits are mandated by law at the state or national level. Companies operating internationally find that the laws regarding mandated benefits differ substantially from one country to another. In the past, companies used to compete for employees and retain them in part through offering attractive benefit plans. However, as companies added more features to the plans to make them attractive to a broader base of employees with differing needs, companies

at-risk compensation
pay that varies depending on specified conditions, including the profitability of the company; hitting particular budget, revenue, or cost savings targets for a unit; or meeting specified individual performance targets

incentive plan
a system that ties some compensation to performance

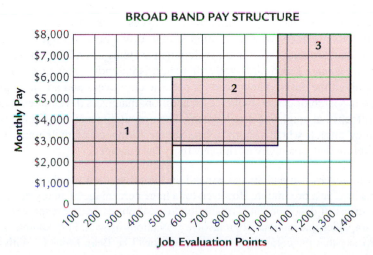

EXHIBIT 7.8

Traditional and Contemporary Pay Structures

found themselves paying 20 percent to 40 percent of salary in benefits. To reduce the soaring benefit costs and still meet differing employee needs, companies began to offer what is called a **cafeteria-style plan,** in which employees receive a set number of "benefit dollars" that they can use to purchase the specific benefits that fit their particular needs.

cafeteria-style plan
a benefit plan in which employees receive a set number of "benefit dollars" that they can use to purchase benefits that fit their particular needs

REWARDS AND MOTIVATION Although the human resources department holds much of the responsibility for reward and compensation systems, effective rewards are more than the dollars paid out in salaries and bonuses or the dollars tied up in health care and other benefits. Although individual managers can influence pay increases and the like, they also have the greatest control over equally powerful rewards such as recognition and praise. Consequently, it is important for you to understand the broad range of rewards and how they influence the performance of your employees, discussed at greater length in Chapter 10. Still, it is important to point out here that employees are often rewarded for doing one thing and yet expected to do another. For example, as Motorola began to shift from simply shipping products to producing world-class quality products, employees continued to be rewarded for timely shipments (with quality levels well below six sigma). Furthermore, employees were punished if shipments were late, even if the quality levels of the late shipments approached six-sigma. Because rewards were not aligned with the firm's new strategy, results of the six-sigma effort at Motorola were less than what senior executives expected. As another example, most stockbrokers at retail brokerage firms are rewarded with bonuses based on the volume of transactions they complete. This leads many brokers to "churn" individual investors' accounts. That is, brokers buy and sell shares in order to generate commissions even though the investment objectives of the investors did not justify such frequent transactions. As a consequence of this churning and the associated fees charged to customers, investors often take their accounts to competing brokerage firms. In the end, the reward structures encourage churning, but churning ultimately hurts firm revenue and broker commissions because customers defect.

Employee Development

One of the most powerful motivators for people to join a firm and perform well is the opportunity to grow and develop.[54] Career and employee development systems are designed to respond to that particular motivation and to ensure that the human capabilities needed in the organization are being developed. Depending on the organization's strategy, it may want an employee to embark on a **career path**—that is, a set and sequence of positions and experiences—to prepare for certain responsibilities. For example, Shell operates in over 120 countries around the world. Part of its strategy involves taking on large and complex projects that only a few other companies could tackle. As a consequence, it needs managers who have good cross-cultural skills and can work with a variety of people all over the world and who can manage large and complex projects that often involve tens of billions of dollars. These complex capabilities are not developed overnight, so Shell has a career path that typically involves working in several countries and on increasing levels of complex projects so that they have the right number of people with the right level of capabilities to manage its big projects wherever in the world they might occur. The company also utilizes integrated teams—that is, employees from various functional areas such as market research, engineering, sales, and finance—who work together to deliver complex projects. Shell, therefore, places a premium on employees working in several functional areas over the course of their careers, or what is referred to as **cross-functional job rotation.**

career path
a set and sequence of positions and experiences

cross-functional job rotation
an arrangement in which an employee has an opportunity to work in different functional areas and gain additional expertise

As we have said, creating career and development systems often falls upon the shoulders of the firm's human resource function. Usually, though, it is individual managers who are the most knowledgeable about the development needs of specific employees and are often those to whom these people go in search of career guidance. In addition, managers develop reputations as being effective or ineffective at employee development. Their reputations often affect the quality of the subordinates they attract, which in turn affects the performance of their units. Consequently, career-path development is actually a critical activity for managers.

PROMOTION Employees can and should expand and improve their capabilities on the job. This need not always involve a promotion. However, for a large percentage of an organization's employees, part of the driver of development is promotion to positions of greater responsibility and pay.

In large companies, promotions often involve relocations as well. For example, many employees within IBM say that the company's initials stand for "I've Been Moved." With an increasing percentage of couples who both work, these relocations, especially international relocations, can be challenging.[55] For a **dual-career couple,** finding a job for the employee's partner, especially in a foreign country, can be a serious obstacle to the person accepting a promotion and transfer. Even if a transfer or interim job can be located for the spouse, work visa restrictions can prevent the person from working in a foreign country. To cope with this challenge, companies are expanding their spouse relocation assistance programs and are also forming informal associations so employees interested in relocating, and employees who have already relocated, can exchange information about job opportunities and other aspects of accepting international assignments.[56]

dual-career couple
a couple in which both partners work full-time in professional, managerial, or administrative jobs

TERMINATION. Despite your best efforts to recruit, hire, train, compensate, and manage the performance of your employees, you may find that you have to terminate, or fire, an employee. Firing for cause usually involves the termination of an employee for criminal behavior, such as theft of company property, or for violating the company's policies, such as sharing confidential information with its competitors. Most companies have detailed and written policies about the criteria for "cause terminations" and the steps that a manager must follow to fire an employee who meets these conditions. An employee can also be fired for failing to perform. Again, most companies have detailed policies about what must be done first before an employee can be fired for a poor performance. Often these policies involve the following:

1. Informing the employee of the performance standards
2. Formally and specifically documenting incidents of poor performance
3. Informing the employee of these performance failures, reiterating the job's standards, and outlining timeframes and actions for improvement
4. Formally informing the employee of the consequences of failing to meet the standards within the timeframe established

If the employee's performance does not improve sufficiently subsequently to taking these measures, many companies require his or her manager to work with a specialist in the human resources department to actually fire the employee.

Layoffs Layoffs involve the termination of groups of employees because of economic or business reasons. Research has demonstrated that companies that do not conduct layoffs in a *reasonable* manner are less able to attract and retain good employees in the future.[57] In many cases by contract or law, companies have to provide a certain amount of advance notice before they can conduct a sizable layoff. Clearly, "reasonable" is open to interpretation, but practices that are reasonable include outplacement aids such as résumé-writing assistance, career counseling, office space access, secretarial help, and job-hunting assistance. Often companies outsource these activities to other companies that specialize in helping laid off workers find employment.

Labor Relations

Labor relations come into play when formal unions represent employees for the collective bargaining of their wages, benefits, and other terms of their employment. Unions represent a large proportion of employees in some industries, such as the automobile manufacturing and airline industries. For example, in the airline industry, not only are many lower-paid employees, such as baggage handlers, unionized, but so are highly paid employees, such as pilots.

Although the percentage of U.S. employees represented by unions has declined over the course of the last 50 years, good labor relations remain critical for many companies.[58] Managers walk a fine line between meeting the needs of unionized employees and meeting the needs of their employers.

Managing a Diverse Workforce

When we use the term *diversity,* we are talking about differences among people, including their age, gender, race, religion, cultural background, education, mental and physical disabilities, sexual orientation, and other dimensions. Clearly, the U.S. workforce is in the midst of a sweeping demographic transformation. For example, from 1980 to 2020, the white working-age population is projected to decline from 82 percent to 63 percent (see Exhibit 7.9). During the same period, the minority portion of the workforce is projected to double (from 18 percent to 37 percent), and the Hispanic or Latino portion is projected to almost triple (from 6 percent to 17 percent).

EXHIBIT 7.9

U.S. Workforce Demographic Changes, 1980–2020

Notes: Population projections are based on historical rates of change for immigration, birth, and death. Pacific Islanders are included with Asian Americans. Alaska Natives are included with Native Americans. Projections for Native Americans are based on the 1990 Census. The Census category "other races" is not included.

Sources: U.S. Census Bureau, 5% Public Use Microdata Samples (based on 1980, 1990, and 2000 Census) and U.S. Population Projections (based on the 2000 Census).

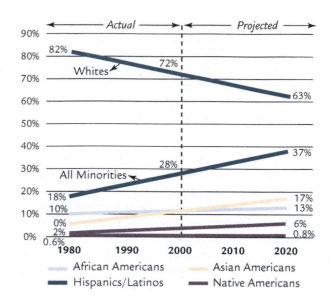

This demographic shift is a function of two primary drivers. First, a larger number of younger Americans (from birth to age 44) are ethnic minorities. Second, an increasing number of white workers are reaching retirement age and leaving the workforce. These are the "baby boomers"—people born from 1946 to 1964. Between 2000 to 2015, the largest increase in the younger U.S. population is projected to be among people of Hispanic or Latino descent (see Exhibit 7.10).

Executives at Marriott International recognize and embrace this change. In the "A Manager's Challenge" on the next page, we highlight some of the key actions the company has take to leverage the diversity of existing and potential employees. What do you think of what the company is doing?

Gender and Diversity

Along with ethnic dimensions of diversity, gender is another important aspect. Women constitute 46 percent of the U.S. labor force.[59] More than 59 percent of U.S. women are employed outside the home, 75 percent of whom work full-time. In 2008, the largest percentage of employed women (39 percent) worked in management, professional, and related occupations; 33 percent worked in sales and office occupations; 21 percent worked in service occupations; 6 percent worked in production, transportation, and material moving occupations; and 1 percent worked in natural resources, construction, and maintenance occupations. Women outnumbered men in such occupations as public relations managers; financial managers; human resource managers;

EXHIBIT 7.10

Projected Changes in the U.S. Population by Age and Ethnicity, 2000–2020

Notes: Population projections are based on historical rates of change for immigration, birth, and death. Pacific Islanders are included with Asian Americans. Projections based on the 2000 Census are not available for Native Americans.

Source: U.S. Census Bureau, 5% Public Use Microdata Samples (based on the 2000 Census).

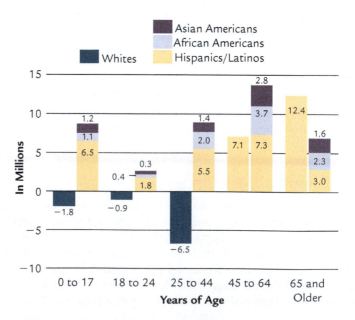

A MANAGER'S CHALLENGE

DIVERSITY

Marriott Embraces and Leverages Diversity

Among Marriott's over 124,000 employees in the United States, 61 percent are minorities and 55 percent are women. In all, these employees speak over 50 languages. The majority of Marriott employees work in entry-level jobs from housecleaning to laundry and food services. Given the changing demographics of today's employees, Marriott's managers must find a way to seek out and leverage an increasingly diverse workforce. However, for Marriott it is not enough to simply get warm bodies in the door to work. Because Marriott competes on its service reputation, managers need workers who will not just do their jobs but will do them in a way that makes customers feel great. In addition, because the company promotes from within (more than a third of its managers start out in entry-level positions), Marriott's managers need to attract and retain the best of its entry-level employees.

Among Marriott's entry-level employees, many lack good work habits, have difficulty managing money, experience domestic abuse, or have inadequate child-care arrangements. In addition, many entry-level workers are immigrants

Jeff Zaruba/Zaruba Photography

To attract, motivate, and retain the entry-level, hourly workers upon which it relies, Marriott has developed landmark programs such as social-services referrals, parenting classes, and childcare facilities. Responding to the needs of its employees has helped the company keep its turnover rates low and sustained its reputation for exceptional service.

who speak limited or no English or have limited education and skills. "It's critical that we become more skilled at managing this workforce," states Donna Klein, who directs Marriott's "work-life" programs.

To find out more about its unskilled workforce, Marriott managers conducted a study and learned that its workers faced various challenges. For example, it found that its existing child-care program barely scratched the surface of this group's needs. The study also found that about one-quarter of the workers had literacy problems. In response, Marriott initiated an on-site English as a second language (ESL) program during work hours.

Despite these efforts, managers were still busy offering advice about family conflicts and child-care solutions, and sometimes loaning money to employees for urgent bills. Instead of attending to the needs of its customers, notes Clifford J. Erlich, Marriott's senior vice president for human resources, "Many managers spent 15 percent of their time doing social work [with employees]."

As a result, Marriott managers changed their human resource program, adding such items as social services referrals, parenting classes, and child-care facilities to attract and motivate hourly workers—and keep turnover lower than that of competitors.

After a number of changes were made to U.S. welfare programs, Marriott's management instituted a program called "Pathways to Independence" to help welfare recipients become productive Marriott workers. As part of the program, participants learn business skills like work punctuality as well as life skills like money management. For a $5,500 per-person investment (half funded by government subsidies), more than 3,000 former welfare recipients now work for Marriott—a new labor pool that, importantly, has a below-average turnover rate.

Critics say Marriott's managers are too paternalistic. But the company's success stories show how these alternative approaches have added value. For example, Thong Lee has worked for Marriott for 16 years. A bartender in the Seattle Marriott, Lee learned English through the hotel's classes and used his Marriott stock and pay to buy rental properties. Lee also remembers when his boss shut down the hotel laundry for a day so the staff could attend the funeral of Lee's mother.

Responding to the changing composition of the U.S. workforce and needs of its entry-level employees has helped

(continued)

sustain Marriott's competitive position and its reputation for exceptional service. Moreover, the company's continued growth has created even more opportunities for the personal and professional development of its employees—a fact that managers highlight to attract and retain workers. It also doesn't hurt that Marriott is 1 of only 22 companies to consistently make *Fortune's* "100 Best Places to Work" list—an accomplishment that further enhances managers' ability to recruit and retain good employees.

Sources: "100 Best Companies to Work For," *Fortune*, January 2009; "Marriott Makes Major Strides Toward Diversity Goals, Setting Industry Standards," Hospitalitynet.org, July 21, 2006; A. Wheat, "The Anatomy of a Great Workplace," *Fortune*, February 4, 2002, 75+; J. Hickman, "America's 50 Best Companies for Minorities," *Fortune*, July 8, 2002, 110.

education administrators; medical and health services managers; accountants and auditors; budget analysts; biological scientists; preschool, kindergarten, elementary, middle, and secondary school teachers; physical therapists; writers and authors; and registered nurses. Approximately 4 million women were self-employed in nonagricultural industries. These self-employed women represented 5 percent of all employed women.

glass ceiling
an invisible barrier that prevents women from promotion to the highest executive ranks

Despite their high participation rate in the workforce overall and in business in particular, women have been underrepresented in managerial positions. Some people refer to this phenomenon as hitting the "**glass ceiling,**" meaning that women can "see" into the executive ranks, but an invisible barrier prevents them from being promoted in proportion to their representation in the workforce. Although the glass-ceiling phenomenon is changing, it is changing slowly. For example, in 1998, 11.2 percent of all *Fortune* 500 corporate officer positions were held by women, compared to 15.7 percent by 2008.[60]

As business globalizes, the glass-ceiling phenomenon gets even more complicated.[61] One would naturally expect that, with globalization, international work experience would become more important, at least for an executive's career. To ensure that equal opportunity was afforded all citizens regardless of gender, race, or other difference, the Civil Rights Act of 1991 requires U.S. firms to abide by the same nondiscrimination laws relative to their U.S. personnel overseas as their U.S. employees residing in the United States.[62] One of the specific implications of this law is that unless a particular host country prohibits women from occupying managerial positions, a U.S. firm cannot discriminate against a woman candidate being sent overseas on assignment even if the norms and values of the host country would make it difficult for a woman to be effective.

When the Civil Rights Act of 1991 was passed, only 3 percent of U.S. expatriate employees—employees sent overseas on temporary assignments for three to five years—were women. This occurred despite the fact that 41 percent of all U.S. managers were female. This suggests that there may have been some gender bias in the selection of U.S. expatriate managers. If U.S. firms increasingly require an international assignment as part of a person's development for top management positions, given that only 3 percent of those receiving this opportunity were women, they may find the glass-ceiling problem even more challenging in the future.

The specific countries to which managers might be sent for development opportunities only complicate the situation. For example, because Japan is the United States' second-largest trading partner, U.S. firms are likely to send employees to operations in Japan. However, in Japan, less than 1 percent of all managers are women. This may suggest that in that traditionally male-dominated society, female expatriate managers from the United States might have difficulty being successful. Yet, the Civil Rights Act of 1991 mandates that the gender of a U.S. candidate cannot be a factor in the selection decision. It is interesting to note that despite initial inclinations to think that women expatriates would have a more difficult time in Japan than male expatriates, research actually suggests that women expatriates do just as well as men in Japan.[63]

The increase in women employed is also reflected in the increase in dual-career couples.[64] According to one study, women in dual-income couples contribute an average 44 percent to family income, up from 39 percent in 1997. Men and women are both less likely to embrace traditional gender roles; the number of men who think it's better if they earn the money and the woman cares for home and children dropped from 74 percent in 1977 to 42 percent by 2008. Nearly a third of women say their spouses or partners are taking at least equal responsibility for the care of their children (up from 21 percent in 1992). And men's work-life conflict has gone up commensurately, increasing from 34 percent in 1977 to 45 percent in 2008.

Sexual Harassment

Over the last ten years, sexual harassment has become a major workforce issue, especially given the significant financial penalties that can be levied on organizations where it occurs. Sexual harassment takes two basic forms. The first is sometimes termed *quid pro quo*. It involves requests or implied suggestions that sexual relations are required in exchange for continued employment or benefits, such as a promotion. The second form involves actions that create a "hostile environment." A hostile environment can be created through jokes, touching, comments, pictures, and other means of communicating unwanted sexual innuendos. Sexual harassment suits have increased dramatically over the last several years. As a consequence of the judgments (which are often several hundred thousand dollars), companies are increasingly offering training programs to try to help managers understand the law and avoid such incidents.

Laws and Regulations Affecting Human Resource Management

Because peoples' good intentions to treat everyone fairly regardless of gender, race, ethnicity, age, and other differences are not always demonstrated in their actions, an important set of established laws and regulations have been put in place. Many of these have a significant impact on the management of human resources. For example, a group of flight attendants for Delta Airlines filed suit because Delta had weight limits for flight attendants. The attendants claimed they experienced discrimination because although weight limits were applied to all flight attendants, both male and female, there were no similar standards applied to pilots. Delta first argued that the weight limits were legal because certain size limitations were necessary for flight attendants to perform their jobs in the limited space on planes. Despite this argument, Delta later dropped the weight requirements for all flight attendants.[65]

Exhibit 7.11 provides a summary of the laws enacted in the United States that have had a significant impact on human resource practices and policies. The basic intent of most of this legislation has been to ensure that equal opportunity is provided for both job applicants and current employees. Because the laws were intended to correct past inequalities, many organizations have either voluntarily implemented or been pressured by employees and other constituencies to implement an **affirmative action program** to ensure that organizational changes are made. These programs may involve such things as taking extra effort to inform minority candidates about job opportunities, providing special training programs for disadvantaged candidates, or paying special attention to the racial or gender mix of employees who are promoted.

Keep in mind that the intent of most of the legislation and regulation in the United States is designed to provide equal opportunity. This, however, does not prevent organizations from using certain criteria that might be regarded as discriminatory, as long as the firm can demonstrate that the criterion in question is a **bona fide occupational qualification (BFOQ),** or a qualification that has a direct and material impact on job performance and outcomes.[66] For example, you might think that refusing to hire male employees who have a mustache or beard (or requiring them to shave them before being hired) would constitute discrimination. However, Disney has such a policy for its theme park workers and has prevailed when taken to court. Disney was able to retain the policy despite legal challenges because the company was able to demonstrate statistically that customers reacted better to and were more satisfied with clean-shaven park employees than those with beards and mustaches. In Disney's case, being clean-shaven is a BFOQ.

affirmative action program
a hiring and training program intended to correct past inequalities for certain categories of people based on gender, race and ethnicity, age, or religion

bona fide occupational qualification (BFOQ)
a qualification that has a direct and material impact on job performance and outcomes

Diversity and the Firm's Performance

At this point, more than 20 years of research has been conducted on diversity and its relationship to the performance of small groups and larger organizations.[67] The results of these studies are mixed. Some studies have found a positive relationship between the level of a firm's diversity and performance, whereas other studies have found a negative relationship. More recent studies have found that there is not a simple, linear relationship.[68]

In general, managers can think of diverse groups as presenting both assets and liabilities. All of the differences among group members can potentially constitute assets for the group. These include their different perspectives, knowledge, experiences, education, values, orientation, and

EXHIBIT 7.11 Major U.S. Federal Laws and Regulations Related to Human Resource Management

Act	Requirements	Covers	Enforcement Agency
Thirteenth Amendment	Abolished slavery	All individuals	Court system
Fourteenth Amendment	Provides equal protection for all citizens and requires due process in state action	State actions (e.g., decisions of governmental organizations)	Court system
Civil Rights Acts of 1866 and 1871 (as amended)	Grant all citizens the right to make, perform, modify, and terminate contracts and enjoy all benefits, terms, and conditions of the contractual relationship	All individuals	Court system
Equal Pay Act of 1963	Requires that men and women performing equal jobs receive equal pay	Employers engaged in interstate commerce	EEOC
Title VII of CRA	Forbids discrimination based on race, color, religion, sex, or national origin	Employers with 15 or more employees working 20 or more weeks per year; labor unions; employment agencies	EEOC
Age Discrimination in Employment Act of 1967	Prohibits discrimination in employment against individuals age 40 or older	Employers with 15 or more employees working 20 or more weeks per year; labor unions; employment agencies; federal government	EEOC
Rehabilitation Act of 1973	Requires affirmative action in the employment of individuals with disabilities	Government agencies; federal contractors and subcontractors with contracts greater than $2,500	OFCCP
Americans with Disabilities Act of 1990	Prohibits discrimination against individuals with disabilities	Employers with more than 15 employees	EEOC
Executive Order 11246	Requires affirmative action in hiring women and minorities	Federal contractors and subcontractors with contracts greater than $10,000	OFCCP
Civil Rights Act of 1991	Prohibits discrimination (same as Title VII)	Same as Title VII, plus applies Section 1981 to employment discrimination cases	EEOC
Family and Medical Leave Act of 1993	Requires employers to provide 12 weeks of unpaid leave for family and medical emergencies	Employers with more than 50 employees	Department of Labor

so on. They allow the group as a whole to see and consider more angles than a more homogeneous set of individuals and perspectives likely would have. This can be particularly valuable in situations where an organization needs innovation and new ideas.

However, these differences can also become liabilities. This is because all the points of diversity that provide different perspectives can be potential sources of friction. Diverse work groups often encounter the following problems:

- Communication problems and misunderstandings
- Mistrust
- Conflict and incompatible approaches to resolving the conflict
- Lower group cohesiveness and greater subgroup formation based on elements of diversity such as language, race, or gender

In practice, diversity is a two-edge sword. Diversity can lead to new ideas, innovation, and higher performance but it does not happen automatically. To the extent that the differences lead to conflict and to the extent that the conflict is not managed well, the group's performance will suffer.

Leveraging the Diversity of Your Firm's Workforce

With this in mind, the practical question for a practicing manager is, "How can I limit the liabilities and leverage the assets of diversity?" One of the first things to consider is the complexity of the problems or opportunities you face. If, on one hand, the situation is rather simple and straightforward, a highly diverse team or workforce might not outperform a more homogeneous one with equal job capabilities. If, on the other hand, the situation is complex and multifaceted, the multiple perspectives of members of a diverse group can add value. In this situation, assuming the potential liabilities, such as conflict, are well managed, diversity does seem to lead to a higher performance.

In addition to paying attention to the situations in which a diverse group of employees might excel, there are several other actions you as a manager can take to leverage the assets of diversity and limit the liabilities:

- *Know yourself.*   How much exposure have you had to people with different ethnic, racial, religious, educational, or cultural backgrounds? How tolerant and understanding of those differences have you been? How comfortable were you? How curious were you?
- *Prepare yourself and your employees.*   How skilled are you and your employees at listening, communicating, negotiating, and resolving conflicts?
- *Provide support.*   Are there support groups for minority employees to keep them from feeling unappreciated and wanting to leave the organization? To what extent do minority employees have mentors who can help them understand and become an effective part of the organization?
- *Guide behavior.*   Do you monitor the behavior of your subordinates and peers? Do you consistently and positively reinforce behaviors that foster tolerance and the effective use of diversity? To what extent do you privately provide negative feedback to employees who display intolerance or other problem behaviors?

From both a domestic and international perspective, workforce diversity will only increase. One of the ways you can distinguish yourself from others and add value to your organization is by working effectively with your subordinates, peers, customers, and suppliers with diverse backgrounds.

How Globalization Is Affecting Diversity

Not only is the U.S. workforce becoming increasingly diverse, but globalization is increasingly causing multinational companies to hire a more diverse set of employees. Many people argue that the world is getting smaller. However, from a human resources perspective, the world is getting larger! If you look at the history of most multinational corporations, upon their founding they operated primarily in one or a very limited number of countries. However, as the firms grew, they expanded into more and more countries. Telecommunication and transportation technologies in particular have facilitated this expansion. Now, companies like Marriott, Philips, and Citicorp operate in over 60 countries around the world. For them, that translates into employees speaking over 40 different languages, dealing with 60 different governments, interacting with people from ten different major religions, and coping with hundreds of different customs, holidays, and traditions. As companies expand into new countries and cultures, the world for them gets larger and more complicated.

EXHIBIT 7.12

Where the Workers Are

Source: U.S. Department of Labor, 1997.

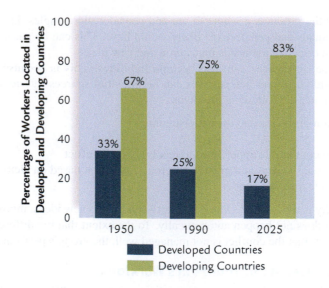

Most firms cannot simply avoid expanding overseas. Consider where the world's workers will be in the future compared with where they are now: Exhibit 7.12 indicates that most of them will be in developing countries. Given that most of the large multinationals are headquartered in developed countries and most of the workers in the future will be in developing countries, continued expansion abroad seems inevitable.

As firms continue to expand outside their home countries, they will continue to confront a variety of diversity-management challenges. For example, do the selection techniques that work in one country also work in another? Can one performance appraisal form apply to all operations around the globe? Must a company adapt or change its reward systems from one country to the next? If it must adapt, how can a firm avoid the risk of employees perceiving these differences as inequitable? What must a firm do to ensure that it provides developmental opportunities for employees in all its operations? For example, recently a Korean multinational firm was seeking to fill its top global marketing position. Is the best person for the job Korean? How does a global firm ensure that it finds and develops the best possible talent wherever in its worldwide operations that talent might be located? When a firm needs to send employees abroad, how does it select these individuals? How should it train these employees prior to their international assignments? And how should they evaluate these employees when real changes in exchange rates, government price controls, and other external factors affect the bottom-line results of an overseas operation? These are just a few of the human resource questions managers will have to try to answer in today's increasingly global and diverse environment.

Managerial Challenges from the Front Line

The Rest of the Story

After careful consideration, Jean-Jacques Beaussart decided that the best thing to do during his subordinate's end-of-year performance appraisal was to tell him that his performance that year had been unacceptable. However, Beaussart saw value and strengths in the individual and wanted to construct a set of responsibilities that put those strengths to their best use. Specifically, the individual was good at managing contracts, negotiations, and working with suppliers, many of whom he had dealt with for years. After some discussions, the two men agreed to change the subordinate's job to one that focused on managing the company's outsourcing and offshoring activities—an important new task for the company. The new job design was a great fit with the subordinate's capabilities, and his resulting performance the following year was good. Thus, Beaussart was able to turn a bad situation into a win-win arrangement for both his procurement team and the long-time employee.

Summary

The capabilities of a firm's employees will influence both the company's strategy (formulation) and how well it is executed (implementation). Because human resource capabilities are hard for competitors to copy, they can be a source of competitive advantage for firms.

- Getting the right people in the right jobs has four fundamental components. First, managers must plan for their human resource needs. This consists of three related activities: (a) forecasting their human resource demand, (b) estimating supply, and (c) determining fulfillment. Second, managers must perform a job analysis to determine the nature of the firm's jobs and their requirements. Third, managers must attract the right people to the company and its job opportunities (recruit them). Fourth, managers must select the right people for the jobs.

- Unstructured interviews are most commonly used to select employees, but they are less valid than structured interviews. Methods such as work sampling, whereby candidates perform tasks identical or similar to the work they would be doing if hired, tend to be more valid indicators of who would be a better employee.

- Effective socialization and orientation should be done very early in the employee's tenure with the company. Paperwork and information should be kept to only what is required to avoid overload. Employees should meet their supervisors early in the process. Pairing a new hire with a "buddy" (a more experienced employee) can also be helpful.

- Effective training can involve both formal (classroom or computer-based) training as well as on-the-job training. In both cases, effective training requires (1) a clear understanding of what is and is not correct or desired behavior and why that is the case, (2) sufficient opportunities to practice the behavior, and (3) feedback on the person's performance with further opportunity for them to practice and improve.

- Because it is simple and efficient, a graphic rating scale is a commonly used method of assessing the performance of employees. Behaviorally anchored rating scales are also common and provide richer descriptions of levels of performance. During a 360-degree feedback appraisal, multiple people assess the employee's performance.

- Most compensation systems consist of wages or salaries, at-risk pay, and benefits. At-risk compensation is typically tied to performance results and, therefore, moves up or down with performance. Benefits, such as health care, typically have a monetary value of 20 percent to 40 percent of an employee's wages or salary.

- A well-managed, diverse workforce can exceed, in many cases, the performance of a homogeneous workforce. Managing a diverse workforce will become even more important in the future as firms continue to globalize and search for tomorrow's employees in developing countries.

Key Terms

360-degree feedback 183	cafeteria-style plan 186	job analysis 171
affirmative action program 191	career path 186	job design 181
at-risk compensation 185	critical incident 184	job posting 173
behaviorally anchored rating scales	cross-functional job	job sharing 181
(BARS) 183	rotation 186	pay structure 184
bona fide occupational qualification	dual-career couple 187	reengineering 181
(BFOQ) 191	glass ceiling 190	structured interview 176
broadband system 184	incentive plan 185	valid selection technique 176

Review Questions

1. Why is it important to keep the firm's strategy in mind when engaged in human resource activities such as selection?

2. What are the principal aspects of job analysis?

3. What does it mean for a selection technique to be valid?

4. How are structured interviews different from unstructured interviews?

5. Identify three written tests used in employee selection and describe their validity.

6. List the five things that organizations can do to make orientation programs more effective.

7. What are the key differences between graphic rating scales and behaviorally anchored rating scales?
8. List seven steps that an organization can take to make performance appraisal sessions more effective.
9. Why are organizations moving away from traditional pay structures to broadband pay structures?

10. What is the purpose of affirmative action programs?
11. What is the difference between quid pro quo and a hostile environment in cases of sexual harassment?
12. Describe three things you can do to improve your capability to manage greater diversity in the workforce.

Assessing Your Capabilities

Indicate the extent to which you agree or disagree with the following statements. Be as candid as you can.

	Strongly Disagree	Somewhat Disagree	Neutral	Somewhat Agree	Strongly Agree
1. I sympathize with the homeless.	1	2	3l	4	5
2. I acknowledge others' accomplishments.	1	2	3	4	5
3. I am wary of others.	1	2	3	4	5
4. I distrust people.	1	2	3	4	5
5. I believe in an "eye for an eye."	1	2	3	4	5
6. I find it hard to forgive others.	1	2	3	4	5
7. I put down others' proposals.	1	2	3	4	5
8. I look down on any weakness.	1	2	3	4	5
9. I treat people as inferiors.	1	2	3	4	5
10. I accept people as they are.	1	2	3	4	5
11. I respect others.	1	2	3	4	5
12. I believe there are many sides to most issues.	1	2	3	4	5
13. I believe that others have good intentions.	1	2	3	4	5
14. I can accept a lot from others.	1	2	3	4	5
15. I am a bad loser.	1	2	3	4	5
16. I get irritated easily.	1	2	3	4	5
17. I lay down the law to others.	1	2	3	4	5
18. I am quick to judge others.	1	2	3	4	5
19. I am annoyed by others' mistakes.	1	2	3	4	5
20. I understand people who think differently.	1	2	3	4	5

Source: International Personality Item Pool: A Scientific Collaboratory for the Development of Advanced Measures of Personality Traits and Other Individual Differences http://ipip.ori.org.

Scoring

For items 1, 2, 10, 11, 12, 13, 14, and 20, take the number you circled and subtract it from 6. (Example, if on item 1 you circled 5, then your score would be 1 [6 − 5 = 1]). Add up all the computed scores for items 1, 2, 10, 11, 12, 13, 14, and 20, and the actual score for all other items. The higher your score, the less tolerant of differences you tend to be. The lower your score, the more tolerant of differences you tend to be. How might these scores be relevant in the management of diversity?

Team Exercise

Divide into teams of four and read the following short scenario. Assign one person to play the role of the female firefighter who finds the firehouse's sexually hostile environment disturbing and another should play the role of the firehouse captain. One person should play the role of the other female firefighter and one person should play the role of the fire department's human resources manager.

A female firefighter complaining about the sexually hostile environment has asked for another meeting to hear what the captain plans to do about the situation. The captain must make a decision and then explain it. The questions at the end of the exercise are designed to stimulate thinking and suggest potential courses of action.

You are the captain of a firefighting squad consisting of 12 firefighters, two of whom are women. Your squad is on duty for 24 hours and then off duty for 24 hours at a time. When on duty, you all live together in the firehouse where you eat, sleep, train, relax, and hang out together. Some days are so intense with emergency calls that you do not have time for anything else. Other days are quite slow.

Good firefighting skills are vital to your team. A significant amount of trust is also important. For example, if you were injured in a burning building, you would want to know that your team members would be able to get you out.

In most firehouses, including yours, the addition of women has happened only recently. All women firefighters have to pass the same physical and skill tests that men do. However, male-oriented conversation, humor, and activities, such as weightlifting, have traditionally helped squad members bond with one another.

One of your newest female recruits has complained to you that the firehouse is a sexually hostile work environment. She says that the jokes she overhears are full of offensive humor and that several of the guys have offensive pictures inside their lockers. She is physically as strong as a couple of the guys and has performed well. Because the firehouse is an older one, there are no separate locker rooms or showers. Although separate shower times have been scheduled, the recruit also complained that some of the guys had "accidentally" walked in when she was showering because they "forgot" the schedule.

You have talked about the complaints to the other female member of your squad, who has been in your unit for nearly a year. She disagrees that the firehouse's environment is sexually hostile but will not go into any details. Her performance has been okay but not high.

1. What actions would you take as the captain?
2. What would satisfy you as the individual lodging the complaint?
3. What should the human resources manager do about this situation? How much of the decision should be left to the discretion of the firehouse captain?
4. Suppose that other squad members tell you that a couple of the younger, single male firefighters might act a bit "macho" when they talk among themselves. If you confront these men about the problem, what will you do if they allege that the new female recruit is wrongly eavesdropping on their private conversations?

Alliant Energy Puts Spark into Diversity

Alliant Energy provides electrical power and natural gas to approximately 1 million customers in Illinois, Iowa, Minnesota, and Wisconsin. It's a medium-sized organization with about $3.3 billion in revenues. Relative to other domestic utility companies, Alliant places a significant emphasis on diversity. As one of its core values, the company states that it "is committed to creating a workplace that welcomes an individual's talents, ideas, and perspectives. Our goal is to create and maintain a diverse workforce and supplier base, so we can better understand the marketplace and maximize our capabilities to succeed."

Consistent with this statement, over the last few years Alliant Energy has sought to expand the diversity base of its suppliers. William D. Harvey, Chairman and CEO of Alliant Energy, commented, "Alliant Energy supports the growth and development of minority- and women-owned businesses. We are equally committed to helping them sustain and grow their businesses through mentoring and supplier development activities. We have a responsibility to implement procurement processes and procedures that will enhance opportunities with minority- and women-owned businesses."

When asked why Alliant has made such a commitment to diversity relative to its suppliers, Jamie Toledo, the head of the company's supplier diversity program, cited three key reasons:

1. It makes good business sense to explore numerous sources of supply when making a purchasing decision for the company. By encouraging diverse suppliers to compete for our business, we benefit from the creativity and new perspectives they have to offer.
2. Working with diverse suppliers is an investment in our local communities.
3. Promoting opportunities for diverse businesses ensures that they have fair opportunities in the marketplace.

In terms of workforce diversity, Alliant's managers define diversity as differences in gender, race, age, physical and mental abilities, lifestyles, cultures, education, ideas, and background. The company expects all its employees to appreciate and seek out the different perspectives associated with diversity and reject behaviors that conflict with its mission of nurturing a diverse workforce. Alliant's first diversity-related step was to create a "Diversity Steering Team" consisting of 15 diverse employees representing each level in the organization. Using a company-wide survey, the team set out to gauge employees' perceptions of diversity issues such as

affirmative action, job satisfaction, interpersonal relationships, and work attitudes. After analyzing the results, team members concluded that employees were confused about Alliant's definition of diversity and management's expectations regarding diversity. In response, they recommended that all employees receive diversity awareness training to better understand the range of perspectives offered by a diverse workforce and the benefits of diversity.

To communicate senior management's commitment to diversity, an Alliant vice president or department manager introduced each eight-hour workshop. Then, a facilitator took over to explain the benefits of diversity, outline Alliant's expectations, and discuss behaviors that are consistent and inconsistent with diversity. The highlight of the workshops, however, came when employees participated in two exercises designed to help them think through the issues. In the first exercise, each employee was asked to identify specific actions he or she would take to support diversity. In the second, employees worked in groups to create a list of diversity ground rules. For example, one group created the rule that "all offensive jokes and language should be eliminated from the workplace." Another group created a rule they initially worded as "respect the ideas of others" and later revised to "accept, understand, respect, and celebrate our differences." This active participation helped employees carry the momentum back to their own work areas.

All new employees go through the training before completing their first year of employment. Most employees seem to believe that the training has helped them support diversity in their own work groups.

To continue supporting diversity throughout the organization, Alliant's top managers recently created an internal diversity council. The council recommends and drives the implementation of new policies and programs to promote diversity. Managers have also initiated new programs to attract and retain a more diverse workforce. The purpose is to encourage ethnic diversity and bring women into nontraditional positions within the organization.

The steps that Alliant's managers have taken to promote diversity are innovative in two ways. First, rather than make the human resources department solely responsible for diversity, senior managers have demonstrated their active support and involvement. Second, the diverse composition of the steering team and diversity council helped these groups address diversity on a larger scale.

The expanded set of ongoing diversity initiatives include the following:

- Employee Resource Groups—These groups serve as a resource for employees and provide an opportunity to participate in diversity initiatives across the company. Existing affinity groups include the "Multicultural Business Council," the "Women's Network," and the "Alliant Pride Network."

■ Diversity and inclusion awareness training for all employees.
■ Diversity recruiting initiatives in key business units.
■ Supplier diversity and development program.
■ Community networking, support, and involvement.
■ International days and "holidays around the world" celebrations.
■ A printed diversity calendar distributed to all employees.
■ Ongoing employee engagement surveys regarding the firm's organizational culture and diversity awareness.

Questions

1. Why is Alliant so committed to workforce diversity? How will this benefit the company?
2. Alliant Energy does not publicly report the results of its supplier-diversity initiatives. Do you think it should? What measures should be used to determine if its supplier-diversity initiatives are effective?
3. Do you believe the company is forcing the issue of diversity? Is it necessary to make diversity training mandatory for all employees? Explain your answer.
4. Independent surveys suggest that companies cannot easily quantify the effects of diversity. How would you suggest that Alliant measure the costs and benefits of having a diverse workforce?

Sources: "Alliant Energy 2006 Proxy Statement," *Alliant Energy 2005 Annual Report*; "Alliant Energy Corp.," *Business Record* (Des Moines), June 11, 2001, 18+; N. Mueller, "Wisconsin Power & Light's Model Diversity Program," *Training & Development* (March 1996): 57–61; and Alliant Web site, www.alliantenergy.com.

References

1. D. Ulrich and W. Brockbank, *HR Value Proposition* (Boston: Harvard Business School Press, 2005).
2. S. A. Snell, M. A. Shadur, and P. M. Wright, "Human Resources Strategy: The Era of Our Ways," in *Handbook of Strategic Management,* eds. M. A. Hitt, R. E. Freeman, and J. S. Harrison (Oxford, UK: Blackwell Publishing, 2001).
3. M. A. Hitt and R. D. Ireland, "The Essence of Strategic Leadership: Managing Human and Social Capital," *Journal of Leadership & Organization Studies* 9 (2002): 3–14.
4. K. Moore and R. Furlong, "Human Resources as a Profitability Factor." *Human Resources* 15, no. 1 (2010): 14–15; M. L. L Lengnick-Hall, C. A. Lengnick-Hall, L. S. Andrade, and B. Drake, "Strategic Human Resource Management: The Evolution of the Field" *Human Resource Management Review* 19 (2009): 64–85; D. Ulrich and W. Brockbank, *HR Value Proposition* (Boston: Harvard Business School Press, 2005); P. M. Wright, B. B. Dunford, and S. A. Snell, "Human Resources and the Resource–based View of the Firm," *Journal of Management* 27 (2001): 701–721.
5. M. W. McCall and M. M. Lombardo, *Off the Track: Why and How Successful Executives Get Derailed* (Greensboro: Center for Creative Leadership, 1983).
6. Y. Gong, K. Law, S. Chang, and K. R. Xin, "Human Resources Management and Firm Performance: The Differential Role of Managerial Affective and Continuance Commitment," *Journal of Applied Psychology* 94 (2009): 263–275.
7. J. H. Gittell, *The Southwest Airlines Way* (New York: McGraw–Hill, 2003).
8. K. Moore and R. Furlong, "Human Resources as a Profitability Factor." *Human Resources* 15, no. 1 (2010): 14–15; M. L. L Lengnick-Hall, C. A. Lengnick-Hall, L. S. Andrade, and B. Drake, "Strategic Human Resource Management: The Evolution of the Field" *Human Resource Management Review* 19 (2009): 64–85; D. Ulrich and W. Brockbank, *HR Value Proposition*; D. Ulrich, *Human Resource Champions* (Boston: Harvard Business School Press, 1997).
9. A. Clardy, "The Strategic Role of Human Resource Development in Managing Core Competencies," *Human Resource Development International* 11 (2008): 183–197; S. C. Kang, S. S. Morris, and S. A. Snell, "Relational Archetypes, Organizational Learning, and Value Creation: Extending the Human Resource Architecture," *Academy of Management Review* 32, no. 1 (2007): 236–256; R. W. Rowden, "Potential Roles of the Human Resource Management Professional in the Strategic Planning Process," *S.A.M. Advanced Management Journal* 64, no. 3 (1999): 22–27.
10. H. Y. Ngo, C. M. Lau, and S. Foley, "Strategic Human Resource Management, Firm Performance, and Employee Relations Climate in China," *Human Resource Management* 47 (2008): 73–90; K. Birdi, C. Clegg, M. Patterson, A. Robinson, C. B. Stride, T. D. Wall, and S. J. Wood, "The Impact of Human Resource and Operational Management Practices on Company Productivity: A Longitudinal Study," *Personnel Psychology* 61 (2008): 467–501; C. J. Collins and K. G. Smith, "Knowledge Exchange and Combination: The Role of Human Resource Practices in the Performance of High-technology Firms," *Academy of Management Journal* 49, no. 3 (2006): 544–560; M. A. Huselid, S. Jackson, and R. Schuler, "Technical and Strategic Human Resource Management Effectiveness as Determinants of Firm Performance," *Academy of Management Journal* 40 (1997): 171–188; S. L. Rynes, K. G. Brown, and A. E. Colbert, "Seven Common Misconceptions About Human Resource Practices: Research Findings Versus Practitioner Beliefs," *The Academy of Management Executive* 16, no. 3 (2002): 92–102; R. Batt, "Managing Customer Services: Human Resource Practices, QUIT Rates, and Sales Growth," *Academy of Management Journal* 45, no. 3 (2002): 587–597.
11. M. Subramaniam and M. A. Youndt, "The Influence of Intellectual Capital on the Types of Innovative Capabilities," *Academy of Management Journal* 48, no. 3 (2005): 450–463; J. Pfeffer, *Competitive Advantage Through People: Unleashing the Power of the Workforce* (Boston: Harvard Business School Press, 1994).

12. I. H. S. Chow and S. S. Liu, "The Effect of Aligning Organizational Culture and Business Strategy with HR Systems on Firm Performance in Chinese Enterprises," *International Journal of Human Resource Management* 20 (2009): 2292–2310; R. E. Ployhart, "Staffing in the 21st Century: New Challenges and Strategic Opportunities," *Journal of Management* 32, no. 6 (2006): 868–897.

13. R. J. Grossman, "Tough Love at Netflix." *HRMagazine* 55, no. 4 (2010): 36–41.

14. O. Williamson, "Outsourcing: Transaction Cost Economics and Supply Chain Management," *Journal of Supply Chain Management* 44, no. 2 (2008): 5–16; D. P. Lepak and S. A. Snell, "Examining the Human Resource Architecture: The Relationships Among Human Capital, Employment, and Human Resource Configurations," *Journal of Management* 28, no. 4 (2002): 517–543.

15. W. Wiggenhorn, "Motorola U: When Training Becomes an Education," *Harvard Business Review* (July–August 1990): 71–83; Lepak and Snell, "Examining the Human Resource Architecture."

16. J. A. Breaugh, "Employee Recruitment: Current Knowledge and Important Areas for Future Research," *Human Resource Management Review* 18, no. 3 (2008): 103–118.

17. M. Chapman, "The Legal Danger of Playing 'Peek-A-Boo' with Job Postings." *HR Specialist.* 40, no. 2 (2010): 6.

18. M. O'Daniel, "Online Assistance for Job Seekers," *New Strait Times,* November 11, 2003; L. Goff, "Job Surfing," *ComputerWorld* 30, no. 36 (1996): 81; M. K. McGee, "Job Hunting on the Internet," *Informationweek* 576 (1996): 98.

19. "Staffing Firm Focuses on Two New Divisions: Executive Placement and Hospitality," *Caribbean Business* 37, no. 38 (2009): S15.

20. G. Van Hoye and F. Lievens, "Tapping the Grapevine: A Closer Look at Word-of-Mouth as a Recruitment Source," *Journal of Applied Psychology* 24 (2009): 341–352; J. A. Breaugh and M. Starke, "Research on Employee Recruitment: So Many Studies, So Many Remaining Questions," *Journal of Management* 26, no. 3 (2000): 405–434.

21. J. L. Farr and N. T. Tippins, *Handbook on Employee Selection* (New York: Routledge, 2010); L. M. Berry, *Employee Selection* (New York: Wadsworth Publishing Company, 2002); D. Terpstra, "The Search for Effective Methods," *HR Focus* 73, no. 5 (1996): 16–17.

22. L. Stroh, M. E. Mendenhall, J. Stewart Black, and H. B. Gregersen, *International Assignments: An Integration of Research and Practice* (Hillsdale: Lawrence Erlbaum, 2005); J. S. Black, H. B. Gregersen, M. E. Mendenhall, and L. Stroh, *Global People Through International Assignments* (Reading: Addison–Wesley, 1999).

23. M. C. Marchese, "The Validity of the Employment Interview: A Meta-analysis," *International Journal of Selection and Assessment* 1 (2007): 18–26.

24. J. Conway, R. Jako, and D. Goodman, "A Meta-analysis of Interrater and Internal Consistency Reliability of Selection Interviews," *Journal of Applied Psychology* 80, no. 5 (1995): 565–579; M. McDaniel, D. Whetzel, F. Schmidt, and S. Maurer, "The Validity of Employment Interviews: A Comprehensive Review and Meta-analysis," *Journal of Applied Psychology* 79, no. 4 (1994): 599–616.

25. M. C. Marchese, "The Validity of the Employment Interview: A Meta-analysis," *International Journal of Selection and Assessment* 1 (2007): 18–26.

26. G. Dessler, *Human Resource Management*, 8th ed. (Upper Saddle River: Prentice Hall, 2000), Chapter 6.

27. J. P. Meriac, B. J. Hoffman, D. J. Woehr, and M. S. Fleisher, "Further Evidence for the Validity of Assessment Center Dimensions: A Meta-analysis of the Incremental Criterion-related Validity of Dimension Ratings," *Journal of Applied Psychology* 93 (2008): 1042–1052; S. Delchirt and D. S. Ones, "Assessment Center Dimensions: Individual Differences Correlates and Meta-analytic Incremental Validity," *International Journal of Selection and Assessment* 17 (2009): 254–270.

28. F. Lievens, "Trying to Understand the Different Pieces of the Construct Validity Puzzle of Assessment Centers: An Examination of Assessor and Assessee Effects," *Journal of Applied Psychology* 87, no. 4 (2002): 675–686; W. Arthur Jr., E. A. Day, T. L. McNelly, and P. S. Edens, "A Meta-analysis of the Criterion–related Validity of Assessment Center Dimensions," *Personnel Psychology* 56, no. 1 (2003):125–154; P. Lowry, "The Assessment Center: Effects of Varying Consensus Procedures," *Public Personnel Management* 21, no. 2 (1992): 171–183; T. Payne, N. Anderson, and T. Smith, "Assessment Centres: Selection Systems and Cost-effectiveness," *Personnel Review* 21, no. 4 (1992): 48–56; D. J. Schleicher, D. V. Day, B. Mayes, and R. E. Riggio, "A New Frame for Frame-of-reference Training: Enhancing the Construct Validity of Assessment Centers," *Journal of Applied Psychology* 87, no. 4 (2002): 735–746; D. J. Woehr and W. Arthur Jr., "The Construct-related Validity of Assessment Center Ratings: A Review and Meta-analysis of the Role of Methodological Factors," *Journal of Management* 29, no. 2 (2003): 231; K. Dayan, R. Kasten, and S. Fox, "Entry-level Police Candidate Assessment Center: An Efficient Tool for a Hammer to Kill a Fly?" *Personnel Psychology* 55, no. 4 (2002): 827–849.

29. M. P. Frederick, M. A. Campion, R. L. Dipboye, J. R. Hollenbeck, K. Murphy, and N. Schmitt, "Are We Getting Fooled Again? Coming to Terms with Limitations in the Use of Personality Tests for Personnel Selection," *Personnel Psychology* 60, (2007): 1029–1049; S. Adler, "Personality Tests for Salesforce Selection," *Review of Business* 16, no. 1 (1994): 27–31.

30. M. McCullough, "Can Integrity Testing Improve Market Conduct?" *LIMRA's Marketfacts* 15, no. 2 (1996): 15–16; H. J. Bernardin and D. Cooke, "Validity of an Honesty Test in Predicting Theft Among Convenience Store Employees," *Academy of Management Journal* 36, no. 50 (1993): 1097.

31. J. Levashina and M. A. Campion, "Expected Practices in Background Checking: Review of the Human Resource Management Literature," *Employee Responsibilities and Rights Journal,* 21 (2009): 231–249.

32. J. L. Wood, J. M. Schmidtke, and D. L. Decker, "Lying on Job Applications: The Effects of Job Relevance, Commission, and Human Resource Management Experience," *Journal of Business and Psychology* 22 (2007): 1–9.

33. S. Hunt, *Hiring Success: The Art and Science of Staffing Assessment and Employee Selection* (Hoboken: Pfeiffer, 2007), Chapter 3, 41–51; B. Murphy, W. Barlow, and D. Hatch, "Employer-mandated Physicals for Over-70 Employees Violate the ADEA," *Personnel Journal* 72, no. 6 (1993): 24; R. Ledman and D. Brown, "The Americans with Disabilities Act," *SAM Advanced Management Journal* 58, no. 2 (1993): 17–20.

34. T. N. Bauer, T. Bodner, B. Erdogan, D. M. Truxillo, and J. S. Tucker, "Newcomer Adjustment During Organizational

Socialization: A Meta-analytic Review of Antecedents, Outcomes, and Methods," *Journal of Applied Psychology* 92 (2007): 707–721; C. Fisher, "Organizational Socialization: An Integrative Review," in K. Rowland and J. Ferris (eds.), *Research in Personnel and Human Resource Management* 4 (1986): 101–145.

35. T. J. Fogarty. "Socialization and Organizational Outcomes in Large Public Accounting Firms," *Journal of Managerial Issues* 12, no. 1 (2000): 13–33; M. K. Ahuja and J. E. Galvin, "Socialization in Virtual Groups," *Journal of Management* 29, no. 2 (2003): 161; E. W. Morrison, "Newcomers' Relationships: The Role of Social Network Ties During Socialization," *Academy of Management Journal* 45, no. 6 (2002): 1149–1160.

36. B. Jacobson and B. Kaye, "Service Means Success," *Training and Development* 45, no. 5 (1991): 53–58; J. Brechlin and A. Rossett, "Orienting New Employees," *Training* 28, no. 4 (1991): 45–51.

37. W. P. Anthony, P. L. Perrewe, and K. M. Kacmar, *Strategic Human Resource Management* (Fort Worth: Harcourt Brace Jovanovich, 1993).

38. L. W. Porter and L. E. McKibbin, *Management Education and Development* (New York: McGraw-Hill, 1988); A. Kristof-Brown, M. R. Barrick, and M. Franke, "Applicant Impression Management: Dispositional Influences and Consequences for Recruiter Perceptions of Fit and Similarity," *Journal of Management* 28, no. 1 (2002): 27–46.

39. J. De Kok, "The Impact of Firm-provided Training on Production," *International Small Business Journal* 20, no. 3 (2002): 271–295.

40. M. Kilduff and D. J. Brass, "Job Design: A Social Network Perspective," *Journal of Organizational Behavior* 31 (2010) 309–318.

41. J. K. Eskildsen and J. J. Dahlgaard. "A Causal Model for Employee Satisfaction," *Total Quality Management* 11, no. 8 (2000): 1081–1094; J. L. Pierce, "Employee Affective Responses to Work Unit Structure and Job Design: A Test of an Intervening Variable," *Journal of Management* 5 (1979): 193–211.

42. M. Hammer and J. Champy, *Reengineering the Corporation* (New York: HarperCollins, 1993); D. A. Buchanan, "Demands, Instabilities, Manipulations, Careers: The Lived Experience of Driving Change," *Human Relations* 56, no. 6 (2003): 663.

43. J. D. Elicker, P. E. Levy, and R. J. Hall, "The Role of Leader-Member Exchange in the Performance Appraisal Process," *Journal of Management* 32 (2006): 531–551; R. D. Bretz Jr., G. T. Milkovich, and W. Read, "The Current State of Performance Appraisal Research and Practice: Concerns, Directions, and Implications," *Journal of Management* 18 (1992): 321–352.

44. S. L. Rynes, K. G. Brown, and A. E. Colbert, "Seven Common Misconceptions About Human Resource Practices: Research Findings Versus Practitioner Beliefs," *Academy of Management Executive* 16, no. 3 (2002): 92–103; T. Redman, E. Snape, and G. McElwee, "Appraising Employee Performance: A Vital Organizational Activity?" *Education and Training* 35, no. 2 (1993): 3–10.

45. R. Cardy and G. Dobbins. *Performance Appraisal* (Cincinnati: South-Western Publishing, 1994).

46. J. Greenberg, C. E. Ashton-James, and N. M. Ashkanasy, "Social Comparison Processes in Organizations," *Organizational Behavior and Human Decision Processes* 102, no. 1 (2007): 22–41; L. Gomez-Mejia, "Evaluating Employee Performance: Does the Appraisal Instrument Make a

Difference?" *Journal of Organizational Behavior Management* 9, no. 2 (1988): 155–172.

47. M. Hosoda, E. F. Stone-Romero, and G. Coats, "The Effects of Physical Attractiveness on Job-related Outcomes: A Meta-analysis of Experimental Studies," *Personnel Psychology* 56, no. 2 (2003): 431; T. J. Watson, "Ethical Choice in Managerial Work: The Scope for Moral Choices in an Ethically Irrational World," *Human Relations* 56, no. 2 (2003): 167–185; C. Rarick and G. Baxter, "Behaviorally Anchored Rating Scales: An Effective Performance Appraisal Approach," *Advanced Management Journal* 51, no. 1 (1986): 36–39.

48. R. Lepsinger and A. D. Lucia, *The Art and Science of 360 Degree Feedback* (Hoboken: Pfeiffer, 2009); D. Bohl, "Minisurvey: 360-Degree Appraisals Yield Superior Results," *Compensation and Benefits Review* 28, no. 5 (1996): 16–19; M. Vinson, "The Pros and Cons of 360-Degree Feedback," *Training and Development* 50, no. 4 (1996): 11–12.

49. F. Shipper, R. C. Hoffman, and D. M. Rotondo, "Does the 360 Feedback Process Create Actionable Knowledge Equally Across Cultures?" *Academy of Management Learning & Education* 6, no.1 (2007): 33–50; L. K. Johnson "The Ratings Game: Retooling 360s for Better Performance," *Harvard Management Update* 8, no. 1 (January 2004); M. S. Brutus and M. Derayeh, "Multisource Assessment Programs in Organizations: An Insider's Perspective," *Human Resource Development Quarterly* 13, no. 2 (2002): 187–202.

50. V. Marshall and R. E. Wood, "The Dynamics of Effective Performance Appraisal: An Integrated Model," *Asia Pacific Journal of Human Resources* 38, no. 3 (2000) 62–90; J. Lawrie, "Steps Toward an Objective Appraisal," *Supervisory Management* 34, no. 5 (1989): 17–24.

51. J. G. Sujansky and J. Gerri-Reed, "Don't Be So Touchy!" *Supervision* 70, no. 12 (2009), 7–9.

52. "Changing with the Times," *IRS Employment Review,* February 21, 2003, issue 770, 14–17; J. Kanin-Lovers and M. Cameron, "Broadbanding—A Step Forward or a Step Backward?" *Journal of Compensation and Benefits* 9, no. 5 (1994): 39–42.

53. K. M. Kuhn and M. D. Yockey, "Variable Pay as a Risky Choice: Determinants of the Relative Attractiveness of Incentive Plans," *Organizational Behavior and Human Decision Processes* 90, no. 2 (2003): 323–341; L. Stroh, J. Brett, J. Baumann, and A. Reilly, "Agency Theory and Variable Pay Compensation Strategies," *Academy of Management Journal* 39, no. 3 (1996): 51–67.

54. J. Herman, "Beating the Midlife Career Crisis," *Fortune* 128, no. 5 (1993): 52–62.

55. L. Stroh, M. E. Mendenhall, J. S. Black, and H. B. Gregersen, *International Assignments: An Integration of Research and Practice* (Hillsdale: Lawrence Erlbaum, 2005); S. Werner, "Recent Developments in International Management Research: A Review of 20 Top Management Journals," *Journal of Management* 28, no. 3 (2002): 277–305.

56. J. S. Black and H. B. Gregersen, *So You're Going Overseas: A Handbook for Personal and Professional Success* (San Diego: Global Business Publishers, 1999).

57. J. Brockner, G. Spreitzer, A. Mishra, and W. Hochwarter, "Perceived Control as an Antidote to the Negative Effects of Layoffs on Survivors' Organizational Commitment and Job Performance," *Administrative Science Quarterly* 49 (2004): 75–100; W. F. Cascio, "Downsizing: What Do We Know? What Have We Learned?" *Academy of Management Executive* 3, no. 1(1997): 95–104.

58. H. S. Farber and B. Western. "Accounting for the Decline of Unions in the Private Sector, 1973–1998," *Journal of Labor Research* 22, no. 3 (2001): 459–485.

59. U.S. Department of Labor, www.dol.gov/wb/stats, accessed May 18, 2010.

60. http://www.infoplease.com/spot/womenceo1.html, accessed May 20, 2010.

61. G. S. Insch, N. McIntyre, and N. Napier, "The Expatriate Glass Ceiling: The Second Layer of Glass," *Journal of Business Ethics* 83 (2008): 19–28.

62. P. Feltes, R. K. Robinson, and R L. Fink, "American Female Expatriate and the Civil Rights Act of 1991: Balancing Legal and Business Interests," *Business Horizons* (March–April 1993): 82–86.

63. N. Adler, "Expecting International Success: Female Managers Overseas," *Columbia Journal of World Business* 19 (1987): 79–85.

64. *Work-life Newsbrief & Trend Report*. Families and Work Institute, May 2009.

65. Personal communication with human resource executive at Delta Airlines.

66. E. P. Gray, "The National Origin of BFOQ Under Title VII," *Employee Relations Law Journal* 11, no. 2 (1985): 311–321.

67. A. A. Cannela, J. H. Park, and H. U. Lee, "Top Management Team Functional Background Diversity and Firm Performance: Examining the Roles of Team Member Co-location and Environmental Uncertainty," *Academy of Management Journal* 51 (2008): 768–784; M. A. Neale, G. B. Northcraft, and K. N. Jehn, "Exploring Pandora's Box; The Impact of Diversity and Conflict on Work Group Performance," *Performance Improvement Quarterly* 12 (2008): 113–126; K. Williams and C. O'Reilly, "Forty Years of Diversity Research: A Review," in *Research in Organizational Behavior*, ed. B. M. Staw and L. L. Cummings (Greenwich: JAI, 1981), 77–140; D. Van Knippenberg, C. De Dreu, and A. C. Homan, "Work Group Diversity and Group Performance: An Integrative Model and Research Agenda," *Journal of Applied Psychology* 89, no. 6 (2004): 1008–1022; L. H. Pelled, K. M. Eisenhardt, and K. R. Xin, "Exploring the Black Box: An Analysis of Work Group Diversity, Conflict, and Performance," *Administrative Science Quarterly* 44, (1999): 1–28.

68. O. C. Richard, T. Barnet, S. Dwyer, and K. Cadwick, "Cultural Diversity in Management, Firm Performance, and the Moderating Role of Entrepreneurial Orientation Dimensions," *Academy of Management Journal* 47 (2004): 255–265.

Part Three

Leading

8

Leadership

LEARNING OBJECTIVES
After studying this chapter, you should be able to:

Define *leadership* and be able to discuss its significance in organizations.

Compare managing and leading and differentiate between them.

Analyze a leader's sources of power and issues in using power effectively.

Describe and contrast the roles of the leader, followers, and the situation in the overall leadership process.

Discuss the extent to which national cultures create differences in effective leadership behaviors from one country to another.

Explain the conditions that can substitute for, or neutralize, effective leadership.

Plan how to improve your own leadership capabilities.

Courtesy of Taylor Ridout, The Shoppes at Brownstone Village

Name: Taylor Ridout Gray

Position: Owner and Operator, The Shoppes at Brownstone Village, Arlington, Texas

Alma mater: University of Texas at Austin (BA in Advertising)

Outside work activities: Swimming as a family

First job out of school: Events coordinator for a trading-card company

Hero: My parents

Motto to live by: Several, including: "trust your instincts"; "think, execute, and balance"; and "do the right thing"

Management style: Firm, but friendly

When she was growing up in Arlington, Texas, a city between Dallas and Fort Worth, Taylor Ridout Gray used to go to a nearby skating rink. Over the years, though, she stopped going there because it had become somewhat dilapidated and rundown. However, a few years later, after graduating from college, and with the help of her father, a developer, she bought the rink!

By her late twenties Gray had totally remodeled the structure and turned it into a retail complex of boutiques and restaurants called The Shoppes at Brownstone Village. Developing and marketing the site haven't been major hurdles for Gray, given her educational and family background. In fact, that was almost easy compared to the challenge of developing an appropriate leadership style to manage the complex's hundred or so employees and vendors.

In her first job out of college, Gray obtained plenty of marketing savvy and experience by coordinating events at the Super Bowl and World Series for her employer, a trading-card company. She found the job really interesting, and even exciting, but after her first child was born, she realized she needed to reduce the extensive travel involved in her event-coordinating job and find something closer to home that did not require frequent out-of-town trips. That's when she decided to follow her father's footsteps and try her hand at developing a piece of property and then operating and managing the newly formed entity.

The Shoppes at Brownstone Village opened in November 2004 and immediately became—and continues to be—a popular local shopping destination. Customers flocked to the stores and even created a typical good news/bad news problem: Too many cars, too few parking places. But that problem was not as difficult for Gray to solve as figuring out how to lead the employees and vendors who worked for and with her. As she says, her natural tendency is to "want everybody to be friends." That philosophy of congeniality guided her leadership approach in the early months following the Shoppes' opening. However, she soon found this approach didn't work very well and many employees were performing in a rather indifferent and laid-back manner.

As Taylor Ridout Gray had to learn at the beginning of her managerial career, leadership is an undeniably critical part of the overall management process. It lies at the very heart of that part of managing that deals with "Leading" (the title of this part of the book). Without leadership, organizational performance would be minimal. Indeed, it would be difficult if not impossible to talk about the accomplishments of twenty-first-century organizations of all types—whether in business, government, education, or other settings—without referring to the role that leadership played in those successes. Clearly, leadership is important to organizations, and to society at large. What is not so clear is how to increase its presence in organizations and its effectiveness. That is the managerial challenge—the one faced by Taylor Ridout Gray. But she is no exception.

Leadership is, above all, a process of influence. As such, it is not a set of behaviors limited to the chief executive officer, the executive vice president, the director of manufacturing, the regional marketing manager or, for that matter, a sports team's coach or captain. It is a process that almost anyone can exhibit, *potentially anywhere* in an organization.

However, although acts of leadership in an organization can be widespread and commonplace, often they are not. The central issue, then, both for organizations and for individual managers, is to turn leadership potential into reality. The very fact that so many articles and books have been, and continue to be, written on the topic of leadership is a good indication that this challenge is not being met well by either the typical organization or the practicing manager.

This chapter addresses three age-old questions: What is leadership? Are leading and managing the same? Does leadership differ across national cultures? Next, it explores the relationship between leadership and its close cousins, influence and power. Following this, the chapter identifies different sources and types of power and analyzes issues in how to use power effectively. This provides a background for examining the basic elements of the leadership-influence process: the leader, the followers, and the situation. Throughout this discussion of the process of leadership, we explain different theoretical approaches at the place where they are most relevant to a particular part of the process. The chapter concludes by examining whether there are effective substitutes for leadership.

What Is Leadership?

Although *leadership* is a familiar everyday term, it's nevertheless far more complex than one might assume. That's what makes it such an interesting and intriguing subject. Let's look at how organizational scientists have defined the term *leadership*. Unfortunately, there is no clear consensus because, as one prominent scholar observed some years ago, "There are almost as many definitions of leadership as there are persons who have attempted to define the concept."[1] Consistent with most definitions, however, we define **organizational leadership** as an interpersonal process that involves attempts to influence other people to attain a goal.

> **organizational leadership**
> an interpersonal process that involves attempts to influence other people in attaining organizational goals

While there is general agreement that leadership is an influence process, there is less agreement on (1) whether the definition must refer only to influence used by those occupying a designated leadership position (a "manager," "president," "chairperson," "coach," and so forth), (2) whether the influence must be exercised deliberately and for the specific attainment of the group's or organization's goals, and (3) whether the compliance of others must be voluntary. Our view on each of these issues follows.

As we explained at the outset of this chapter, *anyone can exhibit* acts of leadership behavior in an organization, and those acts are not limited only to persons holding designated leadership positions. (In recent years, some have termed this way of looking at leadership as "distributed leadership.")[2] In particular, this means that leadership should not be thought of as occurring only, or even mostly, at the top of the organization. Leadership can also be seen in the actions of the first-line supervisor who inspires her subordinates to increase their attention to safety procedures to avoid production downtime. The group member who champions his team's new product and convinces others of its potential demonstrates leadership. The human resources manager who makes sure—without being ordered to—that those in the human resources division treat all applicants for positions with the company respectfully and equitably shows leadership. Workers who set an example for their coworkers by continually seeking ways to improve processes and working conditions exhibit leadership.

Ordinarily, however, people in positions that are labeled managerial or supervisory have more opportunities to exert leadership. Also, leadership behavior is expected more frequently from supervisors and managers than from other types of employees. Such expectations often profoundly affect the behavior of both those who hold leadership positions and those around them. Expectations count! For instance, pharmaceutical giant Johnson & Johnson (J&J) prides itself on its dedication to ethics in management and, as such, J&J employees expect their managers to demonstrate such standards—to lead by example, in other words. A manager who does not abide by the ethical principles of the company, or who is even perceived as not adhering to them, is likely to lose first the trust of employees, followed by the ability to lead them effectively.[3] A very recent example of J&J's leadership expectations occurred when a problem developed with product contamination from manufacturing process lapses and subsequent efforts by marketing managers to minimize official recalls of the product. The company promptly demoted six "key executives" who had responsibility for production and over-the-counter-sales.[4]

A MANAGER'S CHALLENGE

DIVERSITY

Leading at the Top—While Still Under 30

Elsewhere in this chapter we will talk about the role that leadership-type experiences play in developing future top executives. Ordinarily, in past years, in organizations larger than several hundred employees, senior executives would have acquired those experiences at lower levels before ascending to leadership positions at or near the top. More importantly, by the time in their careers that they arrived at those lofty echelons they would be in their forties or fifties (Bill Gates in the 1980s being a notable exception, of course). These days, however, as part of a greater overall trend of diversity in composition of organizations, there are an increasing number of significant firms in the business world who are led by chief executives who have *never* had this kind of background and who are not yet even 30 years old! Why? In most cases it's because they are (like Bill Gates was) the founders or co-founders of their companies.

One of the poster boys, so to speak, for this phenomenon is Mark Zuckerberg, the founder of Facebook, the world's largest social network. Starting from a dorm room at Harvard in 2004, Zuckerberg rapidly implemented an internet version of a paper Facebook student directory with pictures that had been popular at his high school, Phillips Exeter Academy. Within two weeks after Zuckerberg launched his Harvard effort, half of the colleges in the Boston area were clamoring for a Facebook network. Only four months later, with the help of two close friends, Zuckerberg's Facebook had expanded to include over 30 college networks, and he was already turning down an offer of $10 million for the company.

Skip ahead six years to 2010. By that time, Facebook had over 400 million active users, more than 1,000 employees and revenue (in fiscal 2009) of over $50 million, and Zuckerberg (now all of 25 years old) had several years before turned down an offer of $1 billion for the company. For now (in 2010) at least, he clearly seems to want to remain leader of his company. With a reputation as a demanding boss, he is highly task-focused. As one employee said, "[When] working with Zuck [don't] expect acknowledgment for your role in moving the discussion forward—getting the product right should be its own reward."

Running a company growing at warp speed has not been easy. Zuckerberg added an experienced executive from Google as second in command and has put several other senior executives from other companies on Facebook's Board of Directors. Even so, there have been problems. For example, in late 2009 Facebook received considerable criticism for a redesign of its privacy controls that resulted in some account data of users becoming public; because of this backlash, the company altered some of its previously instituted changes. This is just one illustration that starting an organization with an innovative idea is one thing; leading it as it grows and evolves is something different. In the view of Yale management expert Jeffrey Sonnenfeld: "Facebook is in the phase where some founders get themselves in trouble by being too sure of themselves. [Facebook] is at a crossroads where we have to see if Mark can build a team strong enough to challenge him." Perhaps it is worth noting that in early 2009 Zuckerberg had changed his business attire from T-shirt, jeans, and sandals to a buttoned-down shirt and tie. "This is a serious year," he explained.

Of course, Mark Zuckerberg is just one example of current top leaders under the age of 30. Others would include Chase Mattioli who, at 20, was vice president for Mattioli Racing; Michael Seibel, CEO of Justin TV; and Nathaniel Broughten who, by age 27, has already been involved with five start-ups. Whether ten years from now any or all of these and other similar under-30 early leaders of firms will still be managing and leading organizations effectively is an open question. At the least, their career trajectories and accomplishments should provide additional evidence on the issue of how necessary, or not, experience in leadership positions at lower levels of organizations is for leading at the top.

Sources: FaceBook. Company website. FactSheet. http://www.facebook.com/home.php#!/press/info.php?factsheet. Accessed 6/4/2010; Milani, J. (2009) Literally "driving" a new business, Chase Mattioli. *Under 30 CEO: Live the Dream.* http://under30ceo.com/literally-driving-a-new-business-chase-mattioli/ Accessed 5/29/2010; Anon. (2/23/10) Skip class, Make money: CEO Nathaniel Broughton. *Under 30 CEO: Live the Dream.* http://under30ceo.com/skip-class-make-money-ceo-nathaniel-broughton/ Accessed 5/29/2010; Fenn. D. 10/1/09. Getting by with a little help from their friends. *Inc.com* http://www.inc.com/30under30/2009/articles/getting-by-with-a-little-help-from-their-friends.html Accessed 5/29/2010; McGirt, E. (5/1/2007). Facebook's Mark Zuckerberg: Hacker, Dropout, CEO. Fast Company.com. Accessed at http://www.fastcompany.com/magazine/115/open_features-hacker-dropout-ceo.html. Date accessed 5/21/2010; Vascellaro, J. E. (3/3/2010), Facebook CEO in no rush to 'Friend' Wall Street. Wall Street Journal Online. Accessed at http://online.wsj.com/article/SB10001424052748703787304575075942803630712.html?KEYWORDS=Facebook+CEO+in+no+rush+to+%27friend%27+wall+street Accessed on 5/21/2010.

People act as leaders for many reasons, and their efforts are not necessarily aimed solely at attaining a group's or organization's goals. In other words, leaders' motives can be directed at multiple objectives, including their own objectives, instead of the organization's. People's motives are seldom single-focused. However, for the sake of our discussion, in this chapter we will assume that leaders are seeking the attainment of the organization's goals, regardless of their personal objectives. The accompanying A Manager's Challenge Box on "Leading at the Top—While Still Under 30" provides a good example of young leaders intent on pursuing goals of the organization – especially of one that they have created.

The use of coercion to gain compliance (for example, threats such as "do this or you will be fired") is not typically considered leadership. However, the dividing line between what is and is not coercion is often very difficult to determine. Probably the safest generalization is this: the greater the degree of purely voluntary actions by followers toward the leader's intended direction, the more effective the leadership.

effective leadership

influence that assists a group or organization to perform successfully and meet its goals and objectives

The preceding discussion raises a further key issue: What is **effective leadership**? Put most simply, it is influence that assists a group or an organization to meet its goals and objectives and perform successfully. This implies that effective leadership is "enabling" behavior—that is, it is behavior that helps other people accomplish more than if there had been no such influence.[5]

By their actions, those who exhibit effective leadership add an extra ingredient to the sum of the efforts of many people and thereby help them to achieve together more than they would have otherwise. Effective leadership unlocks the potential that resides in other people.

Leading and Managing: The Same or Different?

Leading and managing are two terms often used interchangeably. But are they really the same? In recent years, some scholars have argued that the terms are different—that leadership involves creating a vision for organizations or units: setting, communicating, and promoting new directional goals and procedures, and inspiring subordinates.[6] These activities can be contrasted with more mundane, task-oriented "managerial" functions, such as dealing with interpersonal conflicts, planning and organizing and, in general, implementing the goals set by others (the organization's leaders).

When leading and managing are defined in these ways, then, of course, they are different. However, if we consider managing from a broader perspective, as it is throughout this book, the two activities do not differ as much as might appear on the surface. That is, managing *ought* to involve most of the kinds of activities that are included in the leader's role. Removing such "leading" activities from managing makes an artificial distinction between the two and relegates managing to a routine, almost trivial activity—which it is not.

The relationship between leading and managing can be illustrated using a Venn diagram, similar to those encountered in mathematics classes. The diagrams consist of circles that are completely independent of each other, circles that overlap one another completely, or circles that partially overlap. Imagine all the leaders from one organization in one circle and all the managers from that same organization in another. The two circles are likely to be partially, but not totally, separate, as shown in Exhibit 8.1. Some people can be leaders, and some people can be managers; but many people can be *both* leaders *and* managers. Bluntly, leadership is a very important component of management, but management is more than just leadership. It includes other tasks that don't directly involve influencing people.

Thus, although not all leaders are managers, and not all managers are leaders, modern organizations need most of their managers to engage in leadership behaviors such as those that foster innovation and creativity, inspire other people, and improve their organization's performance. Consequently, in this chapter and in this book, we view organizational leadership as a process that should be included as a significant part of the managerial role, but it is definitely not the total role.

EXHIBIT 8.1

The Overlapping Roles of Leaders and Managers

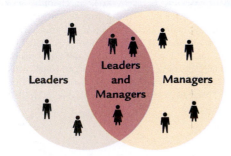

Does Leadership Differ Across National Cultures?

Does leadership differ fundamentally from country to country? Nobody knows for sure, although researchers are attempting to find out.[7] As some observers point out: "*Leadership* is a fairly modern concept. It did not appear in English-language usage

Examples of Leader Attributes Universally Viewed as *Positive* +	Examples of Leader Attributes Universally Viewed as *Negative* –	Examples of Leader Attributes Viewed as *Positive* or *Negative* Depending on the Culture +/–
+ Trustworthy	– Noncooperative	+/– Ambitious
+ Encouraging	– Irritable	+/– Individualistic
+ Honest	– Dictatorial	+/– Cunning
+ Decisive	– Ruthless	+/– Cautious
+ Communicative	– Egocentric	+/– Class Conscious
+ Dependable	– Asocial	+/– Evasive

Source: P. Dorfman, P. J. Hanges, and F. C. Brodbeck, "Leadership and Cultural Variation: The Identification of Culturally Endorsed Leadership Profiles," In R. J. House, P. J. Hanges, M. Javidan, P. Dorfman, and V. Gupta (eds.), *Leadership, Culture, and Organizations: The GLOBE Study of 62 Societies* (Thousand Oaks: Sage Publications, Inc., 2004) 667–718.

until the first half of the 19th century and has been primarily the concern of Anglo-Saxon influenced countries. Prior to that, and in other countries, the notion of *headship* has been more prominent, as in the head of state, chief, or other *ruling* [italics added] position."[8] Or, as another scholar put it, "The universality of leadership [as a part of the managerial role] does not…imply a similarity of leadership style throughout the world."[9]

Experts on Southeast Asia, for example, point out two essential cultural features of leadership there: the requirement for order and compliance and the requirement for harmony.[10] The "order" requirement involves traditional values that support the acceptance of hierarchies, conformity, and deference to authority. The "harmony" requirement involves not only the obligations of the subordinate to the superior but also the obligations of the superior to respect the subordinate and care for his or her welfare. This style can be summarized by the word *paternalism,* whereby a leader is regarded as the provider, or "father," who will take care of the subordinate in return for responsible behavior and performance. In addition to Asia, it is a style often found in Central and South American countries where there is a strong emphasis on collective values as opposed to individual values.[11]

Despite such differences, some similarities in leadership practices—such as giving subordinates more participation in the decision-making process—are beginning to appear with increasing regularity around the world.[12] The results from the GLOBE project, the most recent and comprehensive international study of leadership, appear consistent with this conclusion as Exhibit 8.2 shows.[13] According to the data collected for this study, certain leader attributes, such as "trustworthy" and "decisive," are viewed as positive across all cultures. Likewise, other attributes, such as "dictatorial" and "asocial" are universally viewed as negative. However, how other attributes, such as "cautious" and "ambitious," are viewed depends heavily on a particular culture and its values. Some cultures view them positively, but other cultures view them negatively.

Because of expanding industrialization, the need for effective leadership has become a worldwide phenomenon. Precisely *how* that need is being met in specific organizations and countries, however, still appears to be influenced by cultural circumstances and traditions. Nevertheless, the picture of particular leadership styles and practices around the world at the beginning of the twenty-first century could change dramatically during the next few decades. It already is in some places, as exemplified by Yifei Li, former head of Viacom's China MTV and now head of Publicis Groupe's Vivake in China.[14] Yifei Li has been leading youth-oriented firms operating in the mostly older, male-entrenched regulatory bureaucracy of China. She is normally confident, brash and upfront, but when interacting with the authorities she modifies her style somewhat. A century ago, or even a decade ago, her natural leadership style would unlikely to have been tolerated, let alone accepted, in that kind of setting.

Kistone Photography

Yifei Li is a high-level executive with Publicis Groupe in China. Formerly she was the Managing Director of MTV Greater China, Executive Vice President of MTV Networks Asia, and the Chief Representative of Viacom China. Smart, confident, and female, Yifei Li has had to take a different approach to dealing with male business people in that country. "Particularly as a woman in China, you have to be a little bit softer, and humble," she has said. Yifei Li made The Asian Wall Street Journal's *"Ten Women to Watch in Asia" list in 2005 and 2006.*

Leadership and the Use of Power

power
the capacity or ability to influence

It is virtually impossible to study leadership as a type of social influence without also taking into account the idea of power. **Power** is typically thought of as the capacity or ability to influence. Thus, the greater a person's power, the greater the potential for influencing others. Power can be used "to change the course of events, to overcome resistance, and to get people to do things that they would not otherwise do."[15] However, the fact that a leader, or anyone else, has power does not guarantee that he or she will use it—or use it well. Possession and use are two different matters.

Whether a leader will use power depends on many factors. One principal reason leaders resist using their power, even when they can, is because they believe doing so will generate negative reactions. As has been said, "For many people, power is a four-letter word."[16] The famous, but somewhat exaggerated, statement of this view of power was made more than a century ago in Britain, when Lord Acton wrote to Bishop Mandell Creighton that "power tends to corrupt [and], absolute power corrupts absolutely."[17]

It is not too difficult to think of an organization where a would-be leader used power inappropriately. This was illustrated some years ago when a chief executive officer of a consumer products manufacturer was removed from office, even though he had presided over a major turnaround that had brought the company out of bankruptcy. The reason he was dismissed was because of the way he used his power to intimidate subordinates. On occasion, he even threw objects at them when he was angry. His actions so severely damaged morale at the company that the board of directors had no other option but to find a new CEO.[18]

It would be quite misleading, however, to regard power only from the perspective of the damage it can do. In many circumstances, a leader's skillful use of power can produce positive outcomes. Frequently, though, the problem in organizations is not that leaders use too much power but rather that they fail to use the power available to them.[19] This was noted by two behavioral scientists who have studied leadership extensively when they said: "These days power is conspicuous by its absence. Powerlessness in the face of crisis. Powerlessness in the face of complexity. . . ."[20]

Types and Sources of Power

Power, however used, does not arise spontaneously or mysteriously. Rather, it comes from specific and identifiable sources. The two major types of power, based on their sources, are position powers and personal powers.[21] **Position power** is based on a manager's rank in an organization. **Personal power** is based on a person's individual characteristics.

Clearly, someone who wants to be a leader could have large amounts of both types of power, which should facilitate the exercise of influence. For example, think about whether Taylor Ridout Gray, featured in the opening profile, had access to both types of power and whether this helped her to exercise influence. There are also circumstances where a would-be leader might be low on both types of power, in which case the task of leading obviously would be more difficult. For instance, a lower-level manager who lacks the initiative to develop new products or programs and who is a poor communicator would find it difficult to inspire subordinates to put out extra effort to make changes and reach new goals. This manager lacks personal power and would be unlikely to be promoted—thus, also failing to increase his position power.

In many situations, though, a potential leader who is low in one type of power—for example, a person occupying a relatively junior-status position—can compensate for that by having very strong personal leadership characteristics that are recognized by other people, regardless of the person's formal status in the organization.

To help us better understand the nature of power in organizations, it is helpful to think about several subtypes of position power and personal power (see Exhibit 8.3).[22]

POSITION POWERS The powers associated with a position, include legitimate power, reward power, and coercive power.

Legitimate Power **Legitimate power** is a type of position power granted to a person—for example, a manager—by the organization. It is sometimes called *formal authority*. In the work setting, legitimate power is intended to give a manager the right to expect compliance by his or her employees. It allows the manager to initiate or stop actions.[23]

In today's organizations, however, with increasing levels of education of the workforce and changing societal norms about what is "legitimate" authority, the effectiveness of this type of power has distinct limits. (The Manager's Challenge box "Leadership Experience Counts" describes one set of leaders who have learned how to exercise this type of power but also understand something about those limits.) Often, subordinates will disagree about the scope of a manager's authority; that is, they question the boundaries regarding "appropriate" requests. For example, in the past, many managers expected their secretary or assistant to make personal appointments for them and perform other nonwork-related services. Today, the relationship between a manager and his or her assistant has changed, and these types of requests are generally not considered legitimate.

The precise scope of legitimate authority in today's complex organizations is ambiguous, and the resulting agreement between manager and subordinate can typically be more implicit than explicit, leaving room for potential conflict. In addition, the extent of a manager's formal authority is bounded by subordinates' perceptions of that person's credentials. If the basis of a person's selection for a managerial position is questioned, the leverage of

position power
power based on a person's position and rank in an organization

personal power
power based on a person's individual characteristics

legitimate power (also known as *formal authority*)
a type of position power granted to a person by the organization

Position Powers	Personal Powers
Legitimate—How much authority does the organization give to your position?	**Expert**—Do you have knowledge that others need?
Reward—Are you able to give others the rewards they want?	**Referent**—Do others respect you and want to be like you?
Coercive—Are you able to punish others or withhold rewards?	

EXHIBIT 8.3

Types of Power

A MANAGER'S CHALLENGE

CHANGE

Leadership Experience Counts—Especially Coping Experience

In almost any human endeavor that requires the exercise of skill, experience can be a potentially great asset. This is especially so when the activity of leadership is involved. But, not all types of experience are equally valuable when it comes to leading people in organizational settings. One type of experience that *does* seem to be highly valuable, however, is learning to cope with ambiguity, change, and the unexpected. One set of potential leaders in organizations who are particularly likely to have developed good coping skills are military veterans, especially officers who have had experience in leading subordinates in combat-type situations. Furthermore, not only do military officers have opportunities to learn lessons from their experiences in the field, but they also have had extensive prior training that helps prepare them to learn effectively from those experiences.

In the immediate decades following World War II, many executives had had this kind of experience. For example, even in 1980, 59 percent of CEOs of large U.S. companies had had such experience. However, by the year 2006, that percentage had shrunk to only 8 percent. Subsequent to that year, though, due to the number of recent deployments to conflicts in various parts of the world, returning veterans are again becoming a promising source of managers with already-developed leadership skills and extensive coping experiences.

What is it about their experiences that make these former military officers especially credible as potential leaders in civilian organizations? In the words of U.S. Army General David Petraeus, "These are pretty formative experiences. It's a bit of a crucible-like experience that they go through." Another knowledgeable observer, a former British army officer concurs: "[Military officers] can analyze problems and produce solutions in a very short time. [They] make tough

choices every day." Or, as Noel Tichy, noted management professor at the University of Michigan, puts it: "There's a pool of these officers who have had the kind of under-fire judgment experience that makes them really valuable."

The fact that military officers who have completed their service in recent years are especially well equipped for leadership roles is no accident. In 2001, a special panel, convened by the U.S. Army, issued a report based on a year-long study of the qualities that officers would need in the changing set of circumstances in the post-Cold War era. It concluded that "self-awareness" and "adaptability" were the two most-needed attributes in today's officer. In the view of one former officer, "The Army has accepted that the future is uncertain and learned to embrace risk." Similarly, GE CEO Jeffrey Immelt, in response to a question about what impressed him most about those with recent military experience, said: "Dealing with ambiguity." Other pluses that observers have noted are "cultural sensitivity and ability to build new relationships" and "a highly tuned awareness of resources: budgets, equipment, and people."

Not everyone can have—and many certainly would never want to have—the experience of leading others in combat or similar dangerous situations, but everyone can learn something from their variety of experiences that helps them learn to cope better with rapid changes and unexpected events. Military experience just happens to be one type that can especially accelerate such leadership relevant learning.

Sources: McCall, M. W., Lombardo, M. M. and Morison, A. M.., "Lessons of experience: How successful executives develop on the job" (New York: Free Press, 1988); B. O'Keefe, "Battle-tested: How a Decade of War Has Created a New Generation of Elite Business Leaders," *Fortune* 161 (4): 107–108; N. Haston (2/26/09), "Military veterans: Ready to serve in the workplace," BusinessWeek Online, Accessed at: http://www.businessweek.com/bwdaily/dnflash/content/feb2009/db2009 90225_702876.htm Accessed on: 5/29/2010.

legitimate power is somewhat reduced. For example, take a medium-sized firm where the CEO decides to appoint a close relative with little knowledge of the business to an executive-level position that in the past was filled by employees who worked their way up through the ranks. In this case, subordinates may not acknowledge that the relative has a right to the formal power that would normally be associated with the position, and thus they might not respond to requests rapidly and enthusiastically. This would probably be especially the case in many Western work situations, but perhaps not as much so in Asian cultures, where family connections are viewed as more appropriate for determining who should occupy high-level positions. In essence, though, in most organizational settings, formal authority represents power, but it definitely is not unlimited power.

Reward Power One of the strongest sources of position power for any manager is **reward power,** that is, the authority to distribute rewards, especially differing amounts of highly valued rewards to different people. In any hierarchy, this power can have significant effects on others' behavior because it involves dispensing relatively scarce, but desired, resources. Only a few people, at most, can receive plum assignments; only one or two subordinates usually can be given the largest yearly performance bonus; only one person can be awarded the promotion. One positive aspect of rewards is that they have a "signaling" effect. They let subordinates know, for example, where they "stand" with the boss and give them an idea of what they must do to improve their standing. On the negative side, rewards can sometimes "demotivate" those who do not receive them or receive what they believe to be insufficient amounts of them. Because the use of reward power can have potentially important consequences, both good and bad, managers need to use rewards carefully and skillfully and be very alert to how subordinates perceive the administration of them.

> **reward power**
> a type of position power based on a person's authority to distribute rewards

Coercive Power **Coercive power** is the power to administer punishments, either by withholding something desired, like a raise, or by giving out something that is not desired, such as a letter of reprimand. In typical organizations, such power is used sparingly these days, at least directly and overtly. However, coercive power is sometimes used indirectly in the form of implied threats. A manager, for instance, can let her employees know that noncompliance with her requests will result in an assignment to the least-desired projects or committees. A manager in charge of assigning shift work could subtly influence subordinates by assigning those who do not agree with his policies to a series of inconvenient split shifts.

> **coercive power**
> a type of position power based on a person's authority to administer punishments, either by withholding something that is desired or by giving out something that is not desired

A major problem with the use of coercive power is that it can cause recipients to avoid being detected by disguising their objectionable behavior, rather than motivating them to perform in the desired manner. Furthermore, the use of coercion can generate retaliation. Threatening employees with reduced hours or a pay cut if they don't take on more duties or accept a less than generous incentive plan might result in work slowdowns, an increased number of faulty parts, or complaints to government regulators. Any of these actions clearly would be counterproductive.

It should also be noted that although people with higher-level positions have greater ability to apply coercive power, its use is not confined to managers and supervisors. Potentially, anyone has coercive power. For example, a lower-level employee can harm someone higher by withholding valuable information or making a situation more difficult than it might otherwise be. This use of coercive power by subordinates may be subtle, but in some cases it may actually be quite effective for that reason.

PERSONAL POWERS Personal powers are attached to a person and stay with that individual regardless of the position or the organization. For those who want to be leaders, personal powers are especially valuable because they do not depend directly or only on the actions of others or of the organization. In effect, they enhance the ability of the manager to use persuasion. The two major types are expert power and referent power.

Expert Power **Expert power** is based on specialized knowledge not readily available to many people. It is a potential source of power because other people depend on, or need advice from, those who have that expertise. The best example of expert power in everyday life is the physician–patient relationship. Most people follow their doctor's directives not because of any formal position power but because of the potential negative consequences of ignoring their expertise. Given today's increased percentage of knowledge workers (those who have special expertise) and the increased use of highly sophisticated knowledge in many types of contemporary organizations, it is becoming imperative for most managers to have some type of expertise. Having expertise may not necessarily set a manager apart from his or her subordinates, but not having it may greatly diminish the effectiveness of various forms of position power.

> **expert power**
> a type of personal power based on specialized knowledge not readily available to many people

Expert power is not confined to higher organizational levels. Lower-level employees can possess some of the most specialized, and yet most needed, knowledge in an organization.[24] One only needs to observe a boss trying to find a particular document in a file to appreciate the expert power that an administrative assistant often has in certain situations; or to watch the high-level executive waiting impatiently while the technician makes repairs on a computer or fax machine. These examples illustrate the fact that dependencies create an opportunity for expertise to become power, whatever the position a person holds.

A decade or so ago, Jack Welch, former CEO of General Electric, used this principle deliberately by introducing the idea of "mentoring up" into the organization. He started by requesting that several hundred of his worldwide executives reach down in the ranks and pick younger, "Webified" subordinates to teach them the intricacies of the Net. Based on this experience, the upper-level executives indicated that they had become more receptive to receiving input from those in lower-power positions.[25]

referent power
a type of personal power gained when people are attracted to, or identify with, that person

Referent Power When people are attracted to, or identify with, someone, that person acquires what is called **referent power.** This power is gained because other people "refer" to that person. They want to please that person or in some way receive acceptance. Referent power often can be recognized by its subtle occurrences. A subordinate, for example, may begin using gestures similar to those of his superior or even imitating certain aspects of his speech patterns. Or, the subordinate might find his opinions on important work issues becoming similar to those of his boss.

For anyone in a leadership position in a work setting, being able to generate referent power is clearly a great asset. It is a cost-free way to influence other people. Referent power makes it possible to lead by example rather than by giving orders. A manager can use her referent power to change work habits, for example. If she comes in early, stays late, takes shorter breaks, and finishes her work rather than putting it off until the next day, her subordinates may model themselves on her behavior and change their own work habits as well.

A problem with referent power, however, is that it is not obvious how such power can be deliberately and easily developed. There is no formula for how to increase your referent power, and attempting to get others to like or admire you can frequently cause the opposite reaction. Certain personal attributes, such as honesty and integrity, obviously help. Also, experience and a demonstrated record of success certainly help. The basic lesson seems to be that the referent power of a potential leader is built up over time by consistent actions and behavior that cause others to develop admiration for them.

Using Power Effectively

There are at least four key issues for managers to think about in relation to the use of power (as shown in Exhibit 8.4):

- How much power should be used in a given situation?
- Which types of power should be used?
- How can power be put to use?
- Should power be shared?

HOW MUCH POWER TO USE? The answer to this question seems to be: Use enough to achieve objectives but avoid using excessive power. Using too little power in organizational settings can lead to inaction, and this is especially the case when change is needed but strong resistance exists or is anticipated. Often, managers seem reluctant to wield power because of anticipated opposition. Yet, the use of power is sometimes the only way to accomplish significant change. As management author Jeffrey Pfeffer said, "Managing with power means understanding that to get things done, you need power—more power than those whose opposition you must overcome."[26]

Using too much power, though, also can be a problem. When more power is used than is necessary, people's behavior may change, but resentments and reactions often are self-defeating

EXHIBIT 8.4

Four Key Issues in Using Power

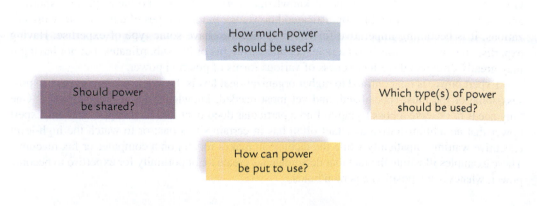

to the power user in the long run. In many organizational situations, people have a sense of what is an appropriate amount of power. If that sense is violated, a manager may actually undermine his power for the future. Excessive use of power in work organizations, like excessive use of police force in civil disturbances, can result in potentially severe negative reactions.

WHICH TYPES OF POWER TO USE? Answers to this question depend on characteristics of the situation and circumstances: What has happened before, what type of change is needed, what amount of resistance is expected, where is opposition located, and the like. Each type of power, whether a position power or personal power, has a particular impact. Some types of power, especially referent and expertise, have relatively low costs. That is, their use generates little direct opposition. Thus, they would seem to be the powers to use whenever possible. The problem, however, is that they may not be strong enough to have an impact. If a manager has very little referent power, then trying to use that method is not likely to accomplish much. Similarly, if subordinates do not perceive the expertise of the manager as high, regardless of the actual degree of expertise, then the manager is unlikely to be able to motivate them to change. In such cases, the use of a form of position power, such as formal authority or reward power, might be necessary. However, the risks of creating a negative reaction are increased, thereby lessening the effects of such power.

HOW CAN POWER BE PUT TO USE? Power, in its various forms, provides the basis for influence. However, power must be converted into actual leader behaviors. The skillful use of different types of power is a type of expertise that anyone can develop. This means that the total amount of power available to you as a manager is not a fixed quantity but rather a resource that can expand or shrink over time.

To put power to use involves influence tactics. An **influence tactic** is a specific behavior that can affect the behavior and attitudes of other people. Exhibit 8.5 shows a representative sample of tactics that can be employed.[27] Different types of power match up with some tactics

influence tactic
a specific behavior used to affect the behavior and attitudes of other people

EXHIBIT 8.5

Types of Influence Tactics

Rational Persuasion: The agent uses logical arguments and factual evidence to show a proposal or request is feasible and relevant for attaining important task objectives.

Apprising: The agent explains how carrying out a request or supporting a proposal will benefit the target personally or help advance the target person's career.

Inspirational Appeals: The agent makes an appeal to values and ideals or seeks to arouse the target person's emotions to gain commitment for a request or proposal.

Consultation: The agent encourages the target to suggest improvements in a proposal or to help plan an activity or change for which the target person's support and assistance are desired.

Exchange: The agent offers an incentive, suggests an exchange of favors, or indicates willingness to reciprocate at a later time if the target will do what the agent requests.

Collaboration: The agent offers to provide relevant resources and assistance if the target will carry out a request or approve a proposed change.

Personal Appeals: The agent asks the target to carry out a request or support a proposal out of friendship, or asks for a personal favor before saying what it is.

Ingratiation: The agent uses praise and flattery before or during an influence attempt or expresses confidence in the target's ability to carry out a difficult request.

Legitimating Tactics: The agent seeks to establish the legitimacy of a request or to verify authority to make it by referring to rules, formal policies, or official documents.

Pressure: The agent uses demands, threats, frequent checking, or persistent reminders to influence the target person.

Coalition Tactics: The agent seeks the aid of others to persuade the target to do something or uses the support of others as a reason for the target to agree.

Source: Yukl, Gary, *Leadership In Organizations*, 7th, © 2010. Printed and Electronically reproduced by permission of Pearson Education, Inc., Upper Saddle River, New Jersey.

more than others. For example, a high degree of expertise would support the use of rational persuasion. Someone possessing a great deal of referent power could more effectively use inspirational appeals than could someone with less referent power. A leader with little position power would have trouble using legitimating tactics.

The other major factor affecting the use of specific influence tactics is the circumstances of the situation, particularly with regard to the people targeted. Thus, if the target of influence is a person higher up in the organization, pressure would likely be an inappropriate and ineffective tactic. Likewise, exchange might work very well with a peer but perhaps be unnecessary in a typical situation involving subordinates. On the other hand, rational persuasion could be a potentially useful tactic in a wide variety of situations, whether with one's superiors, peers, or subordinates.

SHOULD POWER BE SHARED? In recent years, the concept of empowerment has become prominent in management literature.[28] In its broadest sense, **empowerment** simply means the sharing of power with others, particularly those with more power sharing it with those who have less, especially with regard to decision making. This can be done on a firmwide basis, but an individual manager or leader also can do it. A well-regarded company that strongly embraces empowerment is Novo Nordisk, a Danish pharmaceutical company. The manager of one of its clinical units, for example, describes the organization as "a debating and arguing culture." However, he also points out that once a decision has been made, "externally, we show extreme loyalty to the company . . . grumbling after the fact isn't tolerated here."[29]

Those who advocate empowerment suggest that it is a key leadership practice for helping organizations perform at high levels and cope successfully with major changes.[30] Empowerment can also facilitate organizational commitment, learning, and innovation. However, for empowerment to take place, managers cannot simply declare that those below them have more power. They must provide the necessary means, such as, for example, delegating more formal authority to make specified decisions, offering increased training opportunities to develop expertise and self-confidence, providing more resources and access to information to implement effective decisions, and not rescinding the shared power at the first sign of trouble.

The Leadership Process: Leaders

In this and the following two major sections, we examine leadership as a process. As pointed out earlier, this process—within organizational settings—has three fundamental components: leaders, followers, and situations. All three components need to be considered to gain a comprehensive understanding of how the process unfolds. As shown in Exhibit 8.6, what has been termed the "locus of leadership" is the intersection of these three variables: where and when the leader with a particular set of characteristics and behaviors interacts with a specific set of followers in a situation with certain identifiable characteristics.[31] Each component influences, and is influenced by, the other two, and a change in any one will alter how the other two interact.

We will discuss the impact of each of these three variables on the basic leadership process in this and the two sections that follow. In this first section on the leadership process, the focus will be on the leader: specifically, leaders' traits, skills and competencies, and behaviors.

Leaders' Traits

A critical component of what leaders in managerial roles bring to the work setting is their traits. A **trait** is a relatively enduring characteristic of a person. The scientific study of the role of leaders' traits has had a somewhat rollercoaster history: At the beginning of the twentieth century, the "great man" view of leadership was in vogue. Note that in that era it was not the "great person." Leaders were thought of, almost always, as men, and were assumed to have inherited combinations of traits that distinguished them from followers. The notion, then, was that those destined to be leaders were "born," not made. As years passed, however, this theory faded away because of the difficulty in proving that such traits were inherited. Instead, the focus shifted in the 1920s and 1930s to a search for specific traits or characteristics—such as verbal fluency, physical size, dominance, and self-esteem—that would unambiguously separate leaders from nonleaders.

empowerment
the sharing of power with others, particularly those with more power sharing it with those who have less

trait
any relatively enduring characteristic of a person

EXHIBIT 8.6

Locus of Leadership: Intersection of the Basic Components of the Leadership Process

The current view is that although specific traits do not invariably determine a leader's effectiveness, they can increase its likelihood (at least in Western-oriented work environments).[32] As shown in Exhibit 8.7, among the traits that research has indicated are most apt to predict effective leadership are drive, the motivation to lead, honesty/integrity, self-confidence, and emotional maturity.[33]

- *Drive:* A high level of energy, effort, and persistence in the pursuit of objectives.
- *Motivation to Lead:* A strong desire to influence others, to "be in charge." Such a person is comfortable with the use of power in relating to other people.[34]
- *Honesty/Integrity:* Trustworthiness. Someone with this trait is a person whose word can be relied on consistently and who is highly likely to do what he or she says.[35]
- *Self-confidence:* A strong belief in one's own capabilities.[36] People with this trait set high expectations for themselves and others, and they tend to be optimistic rather than pessimistic about overcoming obstacles and achieving objectives.[37] In contrast to honesty/integrity, self-confidence is a trait that in the extreme can be a negative. It can result in a sense of infallibility and in an attitude of arrogance that can alienate potential followers. In other words, too much self-confidence can lead to what has been called "the shadow side of success."[38] That is, too much leadership success, paradoxically, can sow the seeds for later leadership problems. Moreover, no matter how much confidence managers have in themselves, their staffs, and their employees, nothing substitutes for preparation. The manager who relies on self-confidence at the expense of planning is setting the scene for potential disaster.
- *Emotional Maturity:* Remaining even-tempered and calm in the face of stress and pressure. People with maturity tend to accurately assess their own strengths and weaknesses; moreover, they are less likely to be self-centered and unduly defensive in the face of criticism.[39]

It is important to reemphasize that these traits do not guarantee that a person will become a leader or will necessarily lead effectively. Very few people possess exceptionally high levels of each and every trait. However, if a person has one or more of these relatively enduring characteristics, it increases his or her chances of being a successful leader. Traits provide potential, but other factors such as skills, attitudes, experience, and opportunities determine whether that potential will be realized.

Finally, it must be stressed that most of the research on the relationship between personal traits and leadership effectiveness has not considered the impact of culture and has focused primarily on Western, mostly American, work environments. Whether traits can universally predict successful leadership is still an open question (see the discussion of the GLOBE research project later in this chapter). It may be that in at least some other cultures, different traits would be equally or more influential. The very notion that specific personal qualities or leadership traits are critical to successful influence is itself open to question in many non-Western cultures. In countries such as Korea or Malaysia, for example, a person often assumes a leadership position by virtue of ownership or family position; others show respect for that reason rather than because of certain personality features.[40]

EXHIBIT 8.7

Leaders' Traits

Source: Adapted from S. A. Kirkpatrick and E. A. Locke, "Leadership: Do Traits Matter?" *Academy of Management Executive* 5, no. 2 (1991), 48–60.

From her humble beginnings in rural Mississippi, Oprah Winfrey has become one of the most charismatic and influential leaders of our time. As the chairman of Harpo, Inc., Winfrey manages employees as she has done over the years with audiences—with emotion and empathy.

charismatic leader

one who has influence over others based on the individual's inspirational qualities rather than formal power or position

THE SPECIAL CASE OF CHARISMA Charisma constitutes a set of traits that can produce an especially strong form of referent power. The term *charisma* has a theological origin and comes from the Greek word for "gift." It literally means "divinely conferred gift." Its relevance to organizational settings was first highlighted in the early decades of the twentieth century by the sociologist Max Weber.[41] Weber described the **charismatic leader** as one who has influence over others based on the individual's inspirational qualities rather than formal power or position. Thus, followers or subordinates are assumed to identify with that person because of those exceptional qualities. Many people would like to think they are endowed with charisma, but only relatively few people have these special powers. If they were common, they wouldn't be exceptional.

The term *charisma* has been used particularly in the political sphere to describe those who are especially influential with large numbers of people. Examples include historical figures such as Mahatma Gandhi, Nelson Mandela, Winston Churchill, Mother Teresa, Martin Luther King Jr., and John F. Kennedy. In the business world, such people as Steve Jobs, Sam Walton, and Richard Branson come to mind.

Only in the last couple of decades has charisma been examined by scholars of organizational leadership. However, the topic has steadily received increased attention since then.[42] One of the first studies conducted found that charismatic leaders have traits such as:

- A strong need for power
- High levels of self-confidence
- A strong belief in their own ideas[43]

With these kinds of traits, charismatic leaders, more than other types of leaders, are especially likely to:

- Model desired behavior[44]
- Communicate high expectations for followers' performance
- Be concerned with, and try to influence, the impressions of others
- Emphasize ideals, values, and lofty goals

The views of Southwest Airlines founder Herb Kelleher, a business executive often described as charismatic, exemplify the last two points. Kelleher would always tell new employees: "I want you to be able to tell them [the employees' children] that being connected to Southwest Airlines ennobled and enriched your life—it made you bigger and stronger than you ever could have been alone."[45]

Based on several scholarly analyses, Exhibit 8.8 presents a summary set of attributes of charismatic leaders.

Since charisma is a type of "special power" possessed by relatively few people, can a typical manager or leader try to increase his or her charisma? It is clear that no one can create this type of power simply by assuming they have it, or by asking for or demanding it. It must be generated or conferred in some fashion. Although relatively few managers have the personality traits to produce easily or spontaneously the levels of charisma that certain renowned business and political leaders have achieved, most persons in leadership positions can increase the chances that their subordinates will be motivated to follow them and work with and for them.[46] The kinds of behavior, summarized in Exhibit 8.8, are ones that can be developed.

One final point should be raised about charisma: its potential downside. A highly charismatic and overpowering leader does not always suit the requirements of the situation. Take, for example, the case of Christos Cotsakos, former CEO of online brokerage company E*Trade and widely viewed as charismatic. Among his other traits, Cotsakos moved extremely fast. He modeled that behavior for his subordinates, even going so far as to sponsor a day of Formula One racing for his top aides. (He spent his "spare time" working on his PhD in economics at the University of London!) Cotsakos also was not shy about espousing company values and setting high goals: "At E*Trade, we're an attacker, we're predatory . . ."; "(Our culture) is all about

EXHIBIT 8.8

Attributes of the
Charismatic Leader

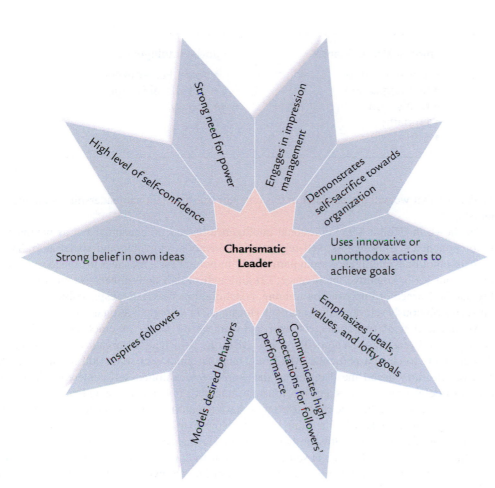

getting people excited about how they can make a difference as a person and as a team…”; “(We have) a lust for being different…”.[47] Cotsakos led E*Trade during the height of the dot-com boom. When circumstances changed and the external environment became more competitively complex for dot-com firms, the company's directors released him as CEO and turned to someone with an apparently different style to guide the organization.

It should also be obvious that charisma can be used for harmful ends as well as good. Society and the world at large are all too familiar with how certain "leaders"—such as Adolf Hitler in Nazi Germany before and during World War II—used an apparently extreme level of charisma with disastrous consequences. Charisma represents a set of traits that confer special power, but that does not guarantee that it will always be used for worthy goals.

Leaders' Skills and Competencies

In Chapter 1 we discussed three types of skills that are important for anyone in a managerial position: technical skills, interpersonal skills, and conceptual skills. As we pointed out in that chapter, early in a managerial career the first two categories of skills—technical and interpersonal—loom especially large in determining whether someone will advance to higher organizational levels. As a person moves up in the organization, the relative importance of technical skills decreases, the importance of interpersonal skills continues to remain strong, and the importance of conceptual skills becomes increasingly critical.

In the last 15 years or so, two other sets of skills or competencies have become increasingly prominent in research relating to influence processes: "emotional intelligence" and "social intelligence." The first of these, **emotional intelligence,** has probably received the most attention to date.[48] One of its chief proponents has even gone so far as to say it is "the *sine qua non* [indispensable ingredient] of leadership."[49] The essence of emotional intelligence, as the name implies, is an awareness of others' feelings and a sensitivity to one's own emotions and the ability to control them. These features are especially prominent in two major contemporary approaches

emotional intelligence
an awareness of others' feelings and a sensitivity to one's own emotions and the ability to control them

EXHIBIT 8.9

Components of Emotional and Social Intelligence

Emotional Intelligence	Social Intelligence
• Self-Awareness	• Social Perceptiveness
• Self-Regulation	• Behavioral Flexibility
• Motivation	• "Savvy"
• Empathy	
• Social Skill	

to leadership that we will discuss later in this chapter: transformational leadership and authentic leadership.[50]

As shown in Exhibit 8.9,[51] emotional intelligence has been conceptualized as having five key components: self-awareness, self-regulation, motivation, empathy, and social skill. Three aspects of emotional intelligence seem particularly important for a manager to consider: (1) it is distinct from IQ or cognitive intelligence; (2) although in part determined genetically, it probably can be learned or improved by training, coaching, practice, and—especially—effort; and (3) it seems obviously relevant to a leader's performance in an organizational setting.

An illustration of two managers who had contrasting levels of emotional intelligence occurred several years ago at a news division of BBC, the British media organization. A decision had been made to close a particular BBC unit, one that employed some 200 journalists. The executive who announced the decision to the employees exhibited self-centered behavior in addition to delivering the message in a brusque, uncaring manner. It created such a negative reaction that it appeared that the executive might have to call in company security. The next day, a different executive spoke with the same set of employees in a calm and understanding manner and with a high degree of empathy for their situation. He was actually cheered.[52]

Although social intelligence is somewhat similar to emotional intelligence, the two also differ. Whereas major components of emotional intelligence involve self-awareness and self-regulation, **social intelligence** focuses more on being able to "read" other people and their intentions. (See Exhibit 8.9.) Social perceptiveness is a principal ingredient. However, so is what has been called "behavioral flexibility," or the ability and motivation to modify your own behavior in response to what you perceive socially. Thus, like emotional intelligence, social intelligence puts a premium on being able to monitor your own behavior and adjust that behavior according to assessment of the social context and circumstances. A person who is socially intelligent is someone who has considerable tacit knowledge—knowledge that is not always directly made explicit—or, to use a more everyday term, is *savvy*. Again, as with emotional intelligence, social intelligence is both desirable and important for leadership and is something that a person can work on and presumably improve.[53]

social intelligence
the ability to "read" other people and their intentions and adjust one's own behavior in response

Leaders' Behaviors

For leadership to occur, a leader must transform traits and skills into behaviors. Thus, considerable research has focused on leaders' behaviors and their impact on subordinates and followers. As far back as the 1950s, researchers zeroed in on two fundamental types of leader behaviors: those involving assistance in the direct performance of the task, and those involving the interpersonal relationships necessary to support task performance. These two types of behavior have been called by various names over the years, but probably the easiest terms to remember are *task behaviors* and *people behaviors*. Exhibit 8.10 shows examples of both.

TASK BEHAVIORS   The key aspects of task behaviors, also termed *initiating structure* behaviors, center on specifying and identifying the roles and tasks of the leaders and their subordinates. Such behaviors involve planning assignments, scheduling work, setting standards of performance, and devising the procedures to carry out the tasks.

PEOPLE BEHAVIORS   This dimension of leader behaviors has also been termed *consideration-* or *relationship-oriented*. Essentially, people behaviors include being friendly and supportive, showing trust and confidence in your subordinates, being concerned about their welfare, and recognizing them for their accomplishments.

EXHIBIT 8.10

Leaders' Behaviors

Task Behaviors (Initiating Structure)	People Behaviors (Consideration)
• Specifies roles and tasks • Plans assignments • Schedules work • Sets performance standards • Develops procedures	• Is friendly • Is supportive • Shows trust and confidence in subordinates • Shows concern for subordinates' welfare • Gives recognition to subordinates for their accomplishments

These two dimensions of leadership behavior have been identified in a wide variety of research studies over the years. Thus, you might expect that the most effective leaders would rate high on both dimensions—that is, be both strongly task-oriented and strongly people-oriented.[54] This has not been conclusively demonstrated, however, although it has been fairly consistently found that leaders who score highest on people behaviors tend to have the most satisfied subordinates.

Do female leaders demonstrate different behaviors than male leaders? Some research shows that women are more likely than men to exhibit high levels of people skills. However, conflicting evidence and considerable controversy surrounds this issue.[55] What seems clear is that the *individual* differences among women and among men, and the specifics of a given organizational context, are probably more important than any relatively small overall average difference between the two gender groups as a whole.[56]

In terms of the behaviors of leaders, five decades of research seem to boil down to this: Effective leaders need to focus on *both* structuring the work (task behaviors) *and* supporting and developing good interpersonal relationships with and among subordinates (people behaviors). Looking at leadership in this way can help you assess your own leadership behaviors. Periodically ask yourself: "How am I doing on task behaviors, and how am I doing on people behaviors?"

APPROACHES TO LEADERSHIP THAT EMPHASIZE LEADERS' BEHAVIORS Among the major conceptual approaches, or theories, that have been proposed over the years to understand leadership in action, several have focused on leaders' behaviors.

Blake and Mouton's Managerial Grid Several decades ago, an approach to improving leadership effectiveness was developed by psychologists Robert Blake and Jane Mouton that focused specifically on the two types of leader behavior discussed previously: orientation to tasks and orientation to people.[57] They coined the term *Managerial Grid* because it was proposed that each of these two dimensions could be thought of as going from a low score to a high score and the scores plotted on a graph. The central theme of this approach was that the best managers would be those highest on both dimensions—in effect, a high task-oriented and a high people-oriented leader. Those who were high on one dimension but low on the other were viewed as lacking in one or the other of the two critical skills needed for leadership success. Those who were in the middle on both dimensions were regarded as average or mediocre leaders.

This approach to leadership puts heavy emphasis on the leader, and gives relatively little attention to the attributes of the followers and, especially, the characteristics of the situation. A high-high leader was thought to be the best kind of leader, irrespective of who the followers were and what kinds of situations confronted the leader. The "managerial grid" approach could be thought of as a "universal" leadership theory—that is, one that says that there is one absolute best type of leader—one who is high on both types of behavior—under *all* conditions. Although this approach helped to highlight two dimensions of leader behavior that are clearly important, it ignores many important situational variables that affect both how leaders behave and how followers react. As noted previously, research has not confirmed that one type of leadership style, whether the so-called high-high style, or any other style, is universally appropriate and effective.

Transformational Leadership Within the past couple of decades, many scholars who write about leadership have been advocating an approach that emphasizes a particular set of leader behaviors: those that inspire followers to make major changes or to achieve at very high levels. That

transformational leadership

leadership that motivates followers to ignore self-interests and work for the larger good of the organization to achieve significant accomplishments; emphasizes articulating a vision that will convince subordinates to make major changes

approach is called **transformational leadership.** The original concept of transformational leadership, authored by a political scientist, James M. Burns, described it as a process in which "leaders and followers raise one another to higher levels of morality and motivation."[58] Later refinements of this approach—by social scientists specifically addressing organizational contexts—emphasized that leaders are transformational even if they don't necessarily appeal to "higher levels of morality and motivation," as long as they motivate followers to ignore their own self-interests and instead to work for the larger good of the organization.[59]

Like charismatic leaders, transformational leaders inspire their followers. However, they do this not only because followers identify with them (as is the case with charismatic leaders) but also by empowering and coaching them. In other words, followers are not required to be highly dependent on transformational leaders like they are on charismatic leaders.[60] Also, whereas instances of charismatic leadership are rare, transformational leadership behavior is assumed to be potentially possible and even capable of being developed and increased almost anywhere throughout the organization.[61]

transactional leadership

leadership that focuses on motivating followers' self-interests by exchanging rewards for their compliance; emphasizes having subordinates implement procedures correctly and make needed, but relatively routine, changes

Those who advocate greater transformational leadership in organizations typically contrast it with so-called **transactional leadership,**[62] as shown in Exhibit 8.11. The latter is regarded as leadership that is more passive. It emphasizes the exchange of rewards for followers' compliance. Whereas transformational leaders appeal to followers' organizational or "common good" interests, transactional leaders rely more on followers' pursuit of self-interests to motivate their performance. In many respects, however, this distinction is artificial since individuals often act for both their own interests *and* organizational interests, and transactional actions by leaders can sometimes even augment the positive effects of their transformational behavior.[63]

Another distinction drawn between transformational and transactional leadership by some experts is that the former involves motivating subordinates to make fundamental and creative changes, while the latter involves the implementation of routine changes and procedures. Again, this distinction is not always clear-cut in many organizational situations. In any event, a transformational perspective does focus on motivating people to make highly significant, or even unusual, achievements and accomplishments. Several studies have explored how transformational leaders influence their followers to achieve such exceptional results. One study of 12 CEOs, for example, found that transformational leaders (1) recognized the need for major changes, (2) helped subordinates prepare for and accept such changes, and, especially, (3) were particularly skillful in persuading subordinates to accept a new way of doing things. That is, they communicated a new vision within the organization. The study indicated that transformational leaders

- Viewed themselves as agents of change
- Were thoughtful risk takers
- Were sensitive to people's needs
- Stated a set of core values to rally around
- Were flexible and open to learning
- Had good analytical skills
- Had considerable confidence in their vision for the organization[64]

Another study of 90 leaders in both the corporate world and the public sector came to similar conclusions:

[Transformational leaders] paid attention to what was going on, they determined what parts of events at hand would be important for the future of the organization, they set a

EXHIBIT 8.11

Transformational Versus Transactional Leadership

	Transformational Leadership	Transactional Leadership
Leader gains subordinates' compliance by:	Inspiring, empowering, and coaching followers	Exchange of rewards and benefits
Appeals focus on:	Organizational and "common good" interests	Self-interest
Type of planned change:	Major organizational change	Routine changes

EXHIBIT 8.12

Guidelines for Transformational Leadership

Those Who Want to Be Transformational Leaders Should:

Develop a clear and appealing vision
Develop a strategy for attaining the vision
Articulate and promote the vision
Act confident and optimistic
Express confidence in followers
Use early success in small steps to build confidence
Celebrate successes
Use dramatic, symbolic actions to emphasize key values
Lead by example

Source: Adapted from G. Yukl, *Leadership in Organizations*, 3d ed. (Upper Saddle River: Prentice Hall, 1994).

new direction, and they concentrated the attention of everyone in the organization on (that new future). This was . . . as true for orchestra conductors, army generals, football coaches, and school superintendents as for corporate leaders.[65]

Exhibit 8.12 summarizes a set of guidelines for those who aspire to transform their organizations or parts of their organizations.[66]

Authentic Leadership A recent and somewhat similar approach to leadership that focuses on leaders' behavior has been called *authentic leadership development theory*.[67] Two contemporary factors have contributed to the interest in this approach: a spate of ethical lapses by some managers and companies in the past decade or so, and the development of an area of psychological theory and research called "positive psychology."[68] According to the proponents of this leadership approach, those who earn the designation from others as "authentic leaders" have high levels of self-awareness and self-regulation. In other words, they know themselves well, and they behave in ways that are consistent with their own basic characteristics. Put another way, they do not try to come across as somebody they are not, and this, in turn, should help to develop followers' trust in their behaviors.[69] In effect, they model self-awareness and regulation for their followers and, according to the theory, motivate them to act more authentically too. Examples from the world of business who are frequently mentioned as authentic leaders include Warren Buffett of Berkshire Hathaway, and Ratan Tata of the Tata Group in India.[70] This approach to conceptualizing leadership is too new to know how influential it will become. Nevertheless, it is consistent with recent trends in organizations to place more emphasis on positive types of behavior by all members, leaders and followers alike.

The Leadership Process: Followers

We now turn our attention to the second key component of the leadership process: those who *receive* the leadership and influence, namely, followers or subordinates. The amount of research on followers has been considerably less than that on leaders. The fact is, however, that followers often impact a leader's success to a great degree.[71]

Like leaders, followers have personality traits, past experiences, beliefs and attitudes, and skills and abilities. What may be different about them, though, are the amount and nature of these characteristics in relation to the leader's. Rarely would they be exactly the same. Also, in a work setting, followers typically have lower position power than the leader. However, in increasingly flatter and less hierarchical contemporary work organizations, that difference is not likely to be as great as in the past. The greater access to information by subordinates due to Internet technology, for example, is decreasing the difference in power. Such a decrease in the difference between followers' and leaders' formal authority is changing the very nature of the leadership process in today's organizations and thus presents new challenges to would-be leaders. In contemporary organizations, leaders cannot assume that they possess more expertise and knowledge than those in a subordinate position.

Not to be overlooked, moreover, is the fact that—in organizations—almost every leader is also a follower of someone else. Thus, most people in organizations have to learn how to become good followers as well as good leaders. The U.S. Military Academy at West Point

Joseph Sohm/Alamy Images

The first year at the U.S. Military Academy at West Point is used to teach cadets to be good followers and in so doing to demonstrate to them what makes an effective leader.

recognizes this point by using cadets' first year to instruct them in the basics of followership. As a former West Point instructor stated: "[New] cadets don't know how to lead soldiers well. They don't know how to motivate or train or reward or discipline effectively." Consequently, the first year is used to teach them to be good followers and in so doing to demonstrate to them what makes an effective leader.[72] As a knowledgeable observer has pointed out: "Organizations stand or fall partly on the basis of how well their leaders lead, but partly also on the basis of how well their followers follow."[73] Learning how to be effective in a follower role can be a significant ingredient in becoming an effective leader, but this is not the same thing as saying that all followers can or will become good leaders.

How the Behaviors of Followers Affect the Leadership Process

Leaders influence followers, but the reverse is also true: Leaders act, followers respond, and leaders react to those responses. Especially important in these evolving interactions are the followers' perceptions of the leaders—that is, how followers view the leader's characteristics and behaviors versus what they think those should be.[74] In effect, followers tend to judge a leader's actions against particular standards or expectations they have in mind.[75] When expectations aren't met, followers may blame leaders for a group's or organization's failures; likewise, when expectations are met, leaders typically get the credit.

Some theorists argue that leaders in organizations, just like certain stars of athletic teams, frequently get excessive—and sometimes undeserved—credit or blame for outcomes.[76] For example, for many years it seemed that no story concerning Microsoft could be written without mentioning Bill Gates. Rightly or wrongly, he became the icon of the company. Articles commending or criticizing some new software product of the company seemed to place all the praise or blame squarely on the leader at the top: Bill Gates. It is likely, however, that others in his organization should have received a relatively greater share of the attention.

APPROACH TO LEADERSHIP THAT EMPHASIZES FOLLOWERS' BEHAVIORS Although all theories or approaches to understanding leadership emphasize the importance of the role of the leader, one places particular attention on the followers: **Hersey and Blanchard's situational leadership model.** It is one of the earliest models of leadership and pays particular attention to followers. Although labeled a "situational" approach, it focuses primarily on a single aspect of the situation: followers' "readiness" to engage in learning new tasks.[77] Subordinates' readiness consists of two parts: their ability, and their willingness to undertake the task. The model advocates that certain types of leader behaviors are best, depending upon subordinates' readiness levels.

Despite some positive features of this model, research support for it is at best weak, and there are some fairly obvious problems with its implementation.[78] Subordinate readiness levels, for example, typically do not come in simple high and low combinations. More often, the combinations of ability and willingness cluster around the middle. Probably the most critical deficiency of the model, however, is that it considers only subordinate readiness as a feature of the task and organizational environment. It essentially ignores other possible major elements of the context, such as the amount and type of interaction subordinates have with other individuals or units in the organization, the culture of the group or organization, the history of past events, and the like.

Hersey and Blanchard's situational leadership model
a model that proposes that different types of appropriate leadership are contingent on some other variable, in this case, followers' readiness to learn new tasks

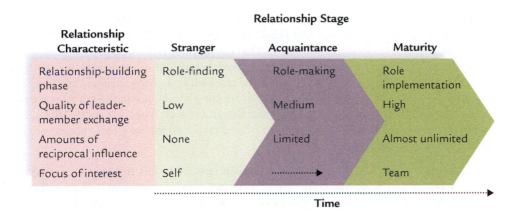

Relationship Characteristic	Relationship Stage		
	Stranger	**Acquaintance**	**Maturity**
Relationship-building phase	Role-finding	Role-making	Role implementation
Quality of leader-member exchange	Low	Medium	High
Amounts of reciprocal influence	None	Limited	Almost unlimited
Focus of interest	Self	------>	Team

Time

EXHIBIT 8.13

Development of Leader-Member Relationships over Time

Source: Adapted from G. B. Graen and M. Uhl-Bien, "Relationship-Based Approach to Leadership: Development of Leader-Member Exchange (LMX) Theory of Leadership over 25 Years: Applying a Multi-level Multi-domain Perspective," *Leadership Quarterly* 6, no. 2, Special Issue: "Leadership," (1995), pp. 219–47.

The Leader–Follower Relationship

As we have stressed, in organizational work settings leaders and followers engage in reciprocal relationships: The behavior of each affects the behavior of the other. In cases where a leader has direct contact with a group of followers, such as in a work unit, two-person leader–follower relationships are built between a supervisor and each subordinate. Research shows that these relationships may vary considerably.[79] In other words, how a supervisor relates to his or her subordinates can be quite different from one subordinate to another.

APPROACH TO LEADERSHIP THAT EMPHASIZES THE LEADER–FOLLOWER RELATIONSHIP The importance of this relationship has led to the development of the **leader–member exchange (LMX) theory**.[80] Research based on this theory appears to suggest that the quality of such two-person relationships can strongly influence the effort and behavior of subordinates.[81] LMX theory focuses on the types of relationships that develop between a leader and a follower, rather than on only the behavior of the leader or the follower. According to the theory, the leader's central task is to build strong, mutually respectful, and satisfying relationships. However, the degree to which such relationships progress depends as much on the behavior and performance of the follower as on the actions of the leader.[82] Also, developing such deep relationships is not always easy, so this approach can be time-consuming. In later versions of the LMX theory like the one shown in Exhibit 8.13, the leader–member relationship is viewed as taking time to develop across different stages—for example, from that of a "stranger" interaction, to an "acquaintance" relationship and, ultimately, to a "mature partnership."[83]

The proponents of LMX theory stress though that not all leader–follower relationships develop into the partnership phase, and some may not even get to the acquaintance stage. However, if the mature relationship phase can be reached, each party can exercise sizable influence over the other for the benefit of both themselves and the organization. For example, there is evidence to show that strong leader–follower relationships help to reduce the typically higher levels of turnover in groups composed of diverse members.[84] What is significant about the LMX approach is that it places particular emphasis on how individualized leader–follower relationships develop and on the potentially important consequences that can flow from high-quality relationships.[85]

leader–member exchange (LMX) theory
a belief proposing that leaders develop different levels of relationships with different subordinates, and that the quality of these individual relationships affects the subordinate's behavior

The Leadership Process: Situations

The third key element in the analysis of the leadership process is the situation surrounding the process. In addition to followers, the two most important categories of situational variables are the tasks to be performed and the organizational context.

Types of Situations Affecting the Leadership Process

TASKS The nature of the work to be performed provides a critical component of the situation facing leaders. Change the task, and the leadership process is highly likely to be changed. Research shows that two of the dimensions of tasks that affect the leadership process include whether the tasks are relatively structured or unstructured and whether they involve high or low levels of worker discretion.[86] For example, a manager of a group of newly trained but relatively inexperienced tax preparers at a firm like H&R Block would probably need to use a fairly high degree of task-oriented leadership to be sure that the tax preparers followed precise guidelines in analyzing clients' returns. Alternatively, a project leader in charge of reviewing the work of a group of highly educated scientists doing advanced research in a pharmaceutical company such as Merck would probably be more concerned with ensuring a continuous flow of new scientific information and obtaining additional funding for the group even when it appears they are not producing immediately useful results. Therefore, this manager might use a more person-oriented, less directive form of leadership.

ORGANIZATIONAL CONTEXT The term *organizational context* in this instance means both the immediate work group (those who come in direct contact with a leader) and the larger organization (composed of all individuals and groups who do not usually have frequent, direct personal contact with a leader). A number of features of the organizational context can affect the leadership process.[87] Of particular importance is the fundamental culture of the organization—that is, its history, traditions, and norms. Someone formerly employed by a large and comparatively slow-moving company, for example, probably would find that the style of leadership he had used effectively there would not be equally effective in a fast-changing start-up entrepreneurial firm. The reverse also would be equally true: A leadership style consistent with the fun, informal culture at Ben & Jerry's Ice Cream would not necessarily work at a larger and more traditional firm, such as Bank of America. These may be extreme cases, but they illustrate that an organization's culture is highly likely to determine what forms of leadership will succeed. In addition to culture, other important aspects of the organizational context affecting leadership include its structure (Chapter 6), its human resource policies (Chapter 7), and its pattern of controls (Chapter 14). Certainly, an example of a leader operating in a unique organizational context is Bill Green, CEO of global management consulting firm Accenture, as described in the accompanying A Manager's Challenge, "Leading Accenture When It Is Anywhere and Everywhere."

Leadership Approaches Emphasizing Situational Contingencies

FIEDLER'S LEADERSHIP CONTINGENCY THEORY This theory, developed several decades ago by psychologist Fred Fiedler, grew out of a program of research that centered on leaders' attitudes toward their co-workers. Like some other leadership models, this approach emphasized the degree to which a leader was especially task oriented or person oriented. Fiedler's theory was that leadership effectiveness would be contingent on a combination of the type of leader (relative task or person oriented) *and* the relative degree of favorability of the situation for the leader.[88] According to the theory, a favorable situation for the leader exists when three conditions are present:

- when relations with subordinates are good,
- when the task is highly structured, and
- when the leader has considerable position power.

An unfavorable situation would be when none of these conditions exist. For example, a vice president of finance who has been assigned the task of preparing the company's annual report, who will be able to work with the same team that produced the previous year's report, and who also is regarded as excellent by top management would be in a highly favorable situation. In contrast, the leadership situation would be less favorable for a senior manager asked to develop a new product in conjunction with a subordinate who had hoped to be promoted into the position now held by the new manager. The theory predicts that task-oriented leaders are most effective in highly favorable *or* highly unfavorable situations. On the other hand, high relationship-oriented leaders will do best in moderately favorable or moderately unfavorable situations. The reasoning, according to the theory, is that task-oriented leaders do not need to be especially sensitive to interpersonal relations in very favorable situations, but that in very unfavorable situations a strong task orientation by the leader is the only approach that will work. Conversely, when situations are neither especially favorable nor unfavorable, the theory presumes that leaders more attuned to other people's feelings will do best.

Probably the chief value of this leadership theory is that it highlights the importance of the nature of the situations leaders face, and it suggests how those situational conditions could make

A MANAGER'S CHALLENGE

GLOBALIZATION

Leading Accenture When It Is Anywhere and Everywhere

Revenue of over $21 billion in a recent year. More than 180,000 employees. Offices in 200 cities—in over 50 countries. By almost any measure, the global management consulting and technology service company Accenture is big. It consists of a large percentage of highly educated professionals. But size is not what distinguishes Accenture from other professional services firms. Rather, it is the fact that Accenture has no operational headquarters. In that sense, it could be considered almost a "virtual" organization. Just a few years ago, Accenture CEO Bill Green was based in Boston, but the firm's chief financial officer was located in Silicon Valley in California. The head technology officer lived in Germany. The executive in charge of human resources was based in Chicago. The leadership challenges for Green, who in a recent year flew more than 165,000 miles, are obvious.

Accenture was founded in 1989 when the partners in the management consulting part of the Arthur Andersen accounting firm split off to form their own independent company called Andersen Consulting. (The name was changed to Accenture in 2000.) At the time of its formation at the end of the 1980s, partners could not agree on where to locate the firm's headquarters, primarily because many of them did not want to move from their present locations, and also because they knew they would be constantly traveling. Instead, they simply decided to incorporate in Bermuda and to meet on a periodic basis. Every six weeks Green and his 23-person, top executive team meet in some city almost anywhere in the world. "We land somewhere, meet clients in the area, meet employees, then get together as a team to make decisions—and head out again," he says.

Among the many potential difficulties faced by Accenture's top leader is trying to coordinate communication and interactions among his key subordinates when most of

them, at any given time, are not only not in one location but may not even be in any location because they are in the midst of traveling. Even with advance planning, scheduling a conference call at a particular point in time can be a problem because the participants are in multiple time zones. According to one executive, the "magic hour" for a conference call is 1 PM London time, which is 9 PM in Beijing, midnight in Australia, and 5 AM in California. However, highly sensitive matters still require in-person meetings, likely causing extended travel for one or more of the participants.

Cell phones and the Internet make it easier to manage such a sprawling global enterprise. Each day, Accenture's employees log on to the company's internal Web site to indicate where they are working that day. This way, any employee—no matter where he or she is at the moment—can eventually be reached. When employees are traveling and need to use an office, they simply find a spare desk in the closest local Accenture office. If Green is on the road, as he usually is, a phone call to his Boston office is automatically routed to the Accenture office where he is that day. When there is a need not only to hear other partners or clients but also to see them, videoconferencing provides the mechanism.

Leading any large company is difficult, and leading this kind of highly dispersed global company is especially so. Says one of Accenture's top executives: "Anyone who says managing this way is easy is lying."

Sources: Company Web site, http://newsroom.accenture.com, accessed June 25, 2010; C. Hymowitz, "Have Advice, Will Travel," *Wall Street Journal*, June 5, 2006, B1; S. Prasad, "IT Is Nothing More Than Servant to the Business," *Global Service*, March 12, 2007, http://www.globalservicesmedia.com/sections/ito/showArticle.jhtml?articleID= 197801123.

it harder or easier for leaders of particular types to be effective. From the perspective of this theory, it is more difficult for leaders to change their styles than to change the situation (or to match leaders with particular types of situations). It also clearly is a contingency theory and not a universal approach in which one type of leadership should work best in all situations.

HOUSE'S PATH–GOAL THEORY In the 1970s, House and his associates proposed what was termed a **path–goal theory of leadership**.[89] Essentially, this theory emphasized that the leader's job is to increase subordinates' satisfaction and effort by "increasing personal payoffs to subordinates for work-goal attainment and making the path to these payoffs easier to travel by clarifying it, reducing roadblocks and pitfalls, and increasing the opportunities for personal satisfaction en route."[90]

path–goal theory of leadership
a contingency theory of leadership that focuses on the leader's role in increasing subordinate satisfaction and effort by increasing personal payoffs for goal attainment and making the path to these payoffs easier

EXHIBIT 8.14

Path–Goal Theory

Source: Adapted from R. J. House, "A Path–Goal Theory of Leader Effectiveness," *Administrative Science Quarterly* 16, no. 5 (1971), pp. 321–39.

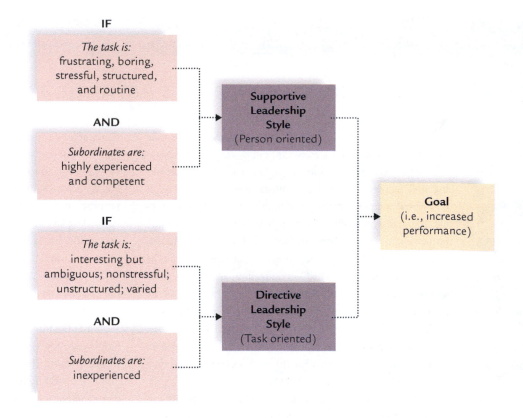

Path–goal leadership theory draws heavily from expectancy theories of motivation (discussed in the next chapter). Thus, it assumes that the leader's role is to influence subordinates' estimated probabilities for being able to convert their efforts into performance that leads to desired rewards. Also, much like several of the other leadership approaches, path–goal theory emphasizes two basic types of leader behavior: supportive leadership (people oriented) and directive leadership (task oriented).

Like other contingency-type leadership theories, the path–goal theory of leadership assumes that a particular leadership approach will work better in certain situations than in others. The theory assumes that if the tasks your subordinates are doing are frustrating, boring, or highly stressful, a supportive-leadership style will help increase their enjoyment and reduce their anxiety, thereby raising their effort and satisfaction levels. If their tasks are enjoyable and interesting, however, a supportive-leadership style won't make much difference. (See Exhibit 8.14.)

By contrast, according to this theory, a directive, task-oriented leadership style works well when your subordinates are inexperienced and their tasks are varied and unstructured. Directive behavior is assumed to reduce ambiguity and make it easier for subordinates to perform their tasks successfully. On the other hand, if your subordinates are highly experienced and their tasks are relatively structured, a directive leadership style isn't necessary, and your subordinates might even resent it.

Unlike Fiedler's contingency theory, path–goal theory assumes leaders can modify their styles to suit the situation rather than having to have the situation changed to fit the leader. In essence, path–goal theory's primary value is in helping potential leaders to think systematically about what types of behavior on their part might work best in what types of situations.

Are There Substitutes for Leadership?

In conclusion, this chapter asks the question: Is there ever a substitute for leadership?[91] The answer, at least in some circumstances, is yes. That is, a greater use of leadership behaviors is not always the only, or even the best, solution for some managerial problems. In certain work settings, other approaches can at least partially substitute for the need for leadership or can sometimes overcome poor leadership. Exhibit 8.15 shows some examples of this.

Extensive training and experience, for example, can lessen the need for a leader's direction in fast-paced and complex jobs like those held by air traffic controllers or police and emergency

Substitutes for Leadership

Ability, experience, training

Intrinsically satisfying task

Professional orientation

Advisory or staff support

Direct feedback from the task

Cohesive work group (with positive performance norms)

EXHIBIT 8.15

Examples of Possible Substitutes for Leadership

Source: Adapted from S. Kerr and J. M. Jermier, "Substitutes for Leadership: Their Meaning and Measurement," *Organizational Behavior and Human Performance* 22, no. 3 (1978): 375–403.

workers. Decisions often have to be made so rapidly in these jobs that they don't allow time for intervention by a leader. Consequently, prior employee training may be able to substitute for such influence. Furthermore, in many technical and professional jobs, high levels of formal education reduce the need for close supervision. It is safe to assume that an attorney or scientist or computer programmer working for a company will probably not need the same amount of supervision, and certainly not the same type of supervision, as an employee with few skills working in a relatively new position. Similarly, workers with intrinsically satisfying jobs, like those involving the development of an exciting new product or service, would be unlikely to need leaders to increase their motivation. These examples point to the conclusion that the amount and type of leadership required can vary considerably from situation to situation. Too much attempted leadership, or too much of a particular leadership approach, sometimes can be as dangerous for the organization— and the would-be leader—as not enough leadership.

In addition to substitutes for leadership, an aspect of the organization or work situation can serve as a **neutralizer of leadership,** that is, something that can defeat the best efforts of leaders. Examples would be inflexible organization procedures that do not give leaders sufficient freedom of choice, or an organizational compensation policy that does not allow them to appropriately reward exceptional performance. Neutralizers, like substitutes, emphasize the importance of situational contingencies and how they can impact leadership. In the case of neutralizers, however, that impact is often dysfunctional.

neutralizer of leadership
any aspect of the organization or work situation that can hinder the exercise of leadership

Managerial Challenges from the Front Line

The Rest of the Story

In her first months as a manager, Taylor Ridout Gray quickly learned that "not everybody can be friends," and decided that she had to come up with a different style of management. After giving the issue considerable thought, she concluded that she needed to use a firmer leadership approach. "I realized that we had to have clear job descriptions and expectations and then empower employees to get the job done and to take responsibility for meeting their jobs' objectives. This was a big adjustment for me, but I realized it had to be done."

So far, her revised approach to leadership has been successful, and with the spaces in the complex fully leased out, she continues to look for new sites in the north Texas area. She also has been designated one of the young leaders in her locale as part of a group honored as "40 [achievers] under 40."

Summary

- Leadership is a process of influence that can potentially occur anywhere in an organization—not just at the top. Although anyone can demonstrate leadership, those who occupy managerial positions generally have more opportunities to do so. The critical issue for both individual managers and for their organizations is how to convert leadership "potential" into actual, effective leadership.

- Leading and managing share many similarities, but they are not the same. Managing includes leading (influencing people), but it also involves various activities, such as planning and organizing, which may not directly involve influencing other people. Not all leaders are competent at managing, nor are all managers effective leaders.

- Leaders potentially have available different kinds of power. Two major types are position power and personal power. Position power is based on a person's rank in the organization and can include legitimate (formal authority), reward, and coercive power. The two primary personal powers are expertise, which is based on a person's skills and knowledge, and referent power, which occurs when people are attracted to, or identify with, someone. The use of power raises several important leadership issues such as: how much power to use, what types of power to use, how best to put power to use, and whether and to what extent power should be shared.

- A useful way to look at leadership is as a process that includes three fundamental elements: leaders, followers, and situations. The intersection of these three components has been called the "locus of leadership." Especially important for leaders are their traits and competencies, their skills, and the kinds of behaviors they exhibit. Followers are a sometimes neglected part of the leadership process. However, they often determine its effectiveness. Particularly important is the leader–follower relationship. Situational circumstances provide both opportunities and constraints that impact how effective particular leadership behaviors will be.

- Leadership is not the only way to deal effectively with managerial problems. Greater levels of education and expertise on the part of employees can often reduce the need for direct leadership. Other variables such as rigid rules and procedures can neutralize the effects of leadership.

- Even though it may be difficult for a person to become a highly acclaimed leader, almost any person can improve his or her leadership capabilities.

Key Terms

charismatic leader   218
coercive power   213
effective leadership   208
emotional intelligence   219
empowerment   216
expert power   213
Hersey and Blanchard's
    situational leadership
    model   224

influence tactic   215
leader-member exchange (LMX)
    theory   225
legitimate power (or formal
    authority)   211
neutralizers of leadership   229
organizational leadership   206
path–goal theory of
    leadership   227

personal power   211
position power   211
power   210
referent power   214
reward power   213
social intelligence   220
trait   216
transactional leadership   222
transformational leadership   222

Review Questions

1. What is leadership? Who can be expected to exhibit leadership in an organization?
2. Are leadership and management the same? Why or why not?
3. Differentiate between *position power* and *personal power.*
4. What kind of power are subordinates most likely to have? Why?
5. What is referent power, and how can it be developed? How is it related to charisma?

6. What is the role of emotional intelligence in leadership?
7. Why is it important to consider the characteristics of followers?
8. According to House's path–goal theory, what is a leader's main responsibility?
9. What is the difference between a transformational and a transactional leader? Is one necessarily better than the other? How does each bring about change?
10. What is meant by a substitute for leadership?

Assessing Your Capabilities

How Power-Oriented Am I?

Using the following scale, circle the number that best indicates the extent to which you agree or disagree with each statement.

	Strongly Disagree	Somewhat Disagree	Neutral	Somewhat Agree	Strongly Agree
1. The best way to handle people is to tell them what they want to hear.	1	2	3	4	5
2. When you ask someone to do something for you, it is best to give the real reason for wanting it rather than giving reasons that might carry more weight.	1	2	3	4	5
3. Anyone who completely trusts anyone else is asking for trouble.	1	2	3	4	5
4. It is hard to get ahead without cutting corners here and there.	1	2	3	4	5
5. It is safest to assume that all people have a vicious streak, and it will come out when they are given a chance.	1	2	3	4	5
6. One should take action only when it is morally right.	1	2	3	4	5
7. Most people are basically good and kind.	1	2	3	4	5
8. There is no excuse for lying to someone else.	1	2	3	4	5
9. Most people more easily forget the death of their father than the loss of their property.	1	2	3	4	5
10. Generally speaking, people won't work hard unless they're forced to do so.	1	2	3	4	5

Scoring

To obtain your score

1. Total your responses to questions 1, 3, 4, 5, and 9	Enter total here: _____
2. For questions 2, 6, 7, 8, and 10, reverse the score (5 becomes 1; 4 becomes 2, etc.).	Enter total here: _____
Your MACH score is the total of both partial scores	TOTAL _____

Analysis and Interpretation

This instrument was designed to compute your Machiavellianism (Mach) score. Machiavelli wrote in the sixteenth century on how to gain and manipulate power. An individual with a high-Mach score is pragmatic, maintains emotional distance, and believes that the ends can justify the means. The National Opinion Research Center, which used this instrument in a random sample of American adults, found that the national average was 25. The closer your score is to 50, the more Machiavellian you are in how you like to use power.

Source: Prentice Hall's Self-Assessment Library, eds. S. P. Robbins and T. A. Judge.

Team Exercise

The purpose of this exercise is to review the various influence tactics available to leaders and to practice using them.

Procedure

Your group will have 15 minutes to develop a role play to perform in front of the class based on the following scenario. You should pay particular attention to issues such as the tactics most likely to succeed; what to do if a chosen tactic doesn't work (what's your backup plan?); and the possibility of using more than one tactic at a time. After each presentation, the class will try to name the influence tactics used and discuss if they were effective.

The Situation

You are the head of marketing for a small but fast-growing Internet company. You love your field and are recognized as one of the industry's leading creative marketers. Your peers, top management, and clients respect you.

While reviewing the performance of your interns, you are disturbed to find that one very promising intern, Pat, has been repeatedly late to work. Also, although Pat starts out with creative ideas, this initial level of interest and creativity is not sustained, and projects are frequently late. Pat seems to be treating what you see as a career-enhancing opportunity as just another pass/fail class, not really demonstrating the effort or interest you feel the position deserves. You see a great deal of promise in this intern and feel that Pat has great potential for a very successful career in marketing. You are considering various methods to influence this intern to improve. In particular, you want to influence Pat to act more professionally, arrive at work on time, treat assignments as important work projects, and sustain the high level of creativity you know Pat is capable of.

Influence Tactics

- *Rational Persuasion:*   The agent uses logical arguments and factual evidence to show a proposal or request is feasible and relevant for attaining important task objectives.
- *Apprising:*   The agent explains how carrying out a request or supporting a proposal will benefit the target personally or help advance the target person's career.
- *Inspirational Appeals:*   The agent makes an appeal to values and ideals or seeks to arouse the target person's emotions to gain commitment for a request or proposal.
- *Consultation:*   The agent encourages the target to suggest improvements in a proposal or to help plan an activity or change for which the target person's support and assistance are desired.
- *Exchange:*   The agent offers an incentive, suggests an exchange of favors, or indicates willingness to reciprocate at a later time if the target will do what the agent requests.
- *Collaboration:*   The agent offers to provide relevant resources and assistance if the target will carry out a request or approve a proposed change.
- *Personal Appeals:*   The agent asks the target to carry out a request or support a proposal out of friendship, or asks for a personal favor before saying what it is.
- *Ingratiation:*   The agent uses praise and flattery before or during an influence attempt or expresses confidence in the target's ability to carry out a difficult request.
- *Legitimating Tactics:*   The agent seeks to establish the legitimacy of a request or to verify the authority to make it by referring to rules, formal policies, or official documents.
- *Pressure:*   The agent uses demands, threats, frequent checking, or persistent reminders to influence the target person.
- *Coalition Tactics:*   The agent seeks the aid of others to persuade the target to do something or uses the support of others as a reason for the target to agree.

Source: Adapted from G. Yukl, *Leadership in Organizations* (Upper Saddle River: Prentice Hall, 2002), 160.

Grace Reed had been working at the County Medical Society Answering Service for 18 months when she received a promotion to shift supervisor. Grace was quite excited. She had worked very hard to develop the technical skills for answering calls and the interpersonal skills for communicating with patients and their doctors. Also, she had demonstrated her desire for the promotion by volunteering for overtime and holiday work. Finally, she had been promoted.

However, now Grace faced problems she had not anticipated. How would she be able to convince her friends to take her seriously in her new role as their boss? How was she going to maintain her friendships and still maintain the discipline needed in this workplace?

The Medical Society's physicians were extremely disappointed with former county answering service companies, which handled not only physicians' calls but business and private accounts as well. Thus, the doctors had decided to start their own answering service. Their call handlers would handle only medical calls, would be better trained to recognize urgent and emergency calls, would receive better benefits, and would be paid more than the competing answering service companies paid their call handlers. The doctors believed this would allow them to attract and retain the best-possible workers.

To oversee the day-to-day operations of the service, the physicians hired a professional manager, and each shift had a supervisor whose responsibilities included scheduling workers; handling complaints from doctors, hospitals, pharmacies, and patients concerning how their calls were handled; learning how to operate new equipment, and train their call handlers to do the same; and maintaining the high level of service required by the physicians. These duties were in addition to the supervisor working her or his own eight-hour shift.

Grace was the fourth call handler hired by the organization and the first promoted from the ranks. When she was first hired, she was lucky to train with a very experienced, competent call handler. She modeled her own skills on those of her trainer and worked diligently to handle the most calls with the fewest mistakes and even fewer complaints. Whereas the other call handlers worked only 60 to 70 individual incoming lines, Grace routinely handled 100 to 120 lines, including some of those with the highest call volumes. She not only cleared her own calls but frequently assisted other call handlers in clearing their backlogged messages. When extremely difficult calls came in, such as suicide calls or nuisance calls from patients to whom even the doctors did not want to talk, often Grace was asked to handle them.

She rapidly developed excellent relationships with all of "her" doctors, their staffs, and even their families. During her first year, she was named call handler of the month five times. In her second year, she learned how to schedule workers and received other advanced operations training.

Although the work was extremely fast-paced and required concentration, there was always time to talk with other employees, joke, and have fun. Strong friendships developed among the workers, who frequently socialized after hours and on their days off. Moreover, the high levels of training and pay led to extremely low turnover rates, giving workers a sense that they were a "family" of sorts. There were always waiting lists of applicants for the positions. If a call handler wished to leave, he or she had no problem finding work at hospitals or for the phone company. Morale was generally high.

Grace's friends at the answering service threw a party for her when she received her promotion. Everyone who wasn't working attended. They were happy for her and sincerely wished her well. After all, it was proof that any one of them could be promoted from the ranks! Grace was anxious to assume her new responsibilities and even try some new procedures she had been devising.

Within a month, Grace wasn't nearly as happy with her promotion as she had thought she would be. Her friends, who were now her subordinates as well, didn't seem to pay attention to her suggestions concerning their job performance. They ignored her instructions and frequently treated them as a joke. She worked many hours planning schedules only to have the call handlers switch shifts, leave early, or arrive late, saying they were sure she wouldn't mind because she understood all their personal complications with their romantic relationships. She was their friend, after all; they knew she would cut them some slack. And her best friends seemed to be some of the worst offenders.

Grace soon realized that her new position was missing one thing—authority to go with her new responsibilities. She had no authority to sanction any of her subordinates: she couldn't dock their pay, make them work overtime, or cut back on their hours. She couldn't shorten their lunch breaks or eliminate their coffee breaks. Only the overall company manager could impose sanctions of that sort. The problem was that if she tried to insist that a call handler use a new procedure or work certain hours and the call handler balked, she had no recourse. If she complained to the manager about her situation, she would be viewed as unable to do her job. She couldn't complain to her friends because they were part of the problem.

To combat her problems, Grace tried to act with a great deal of authority. For example, she insisted employees follow the new methods she had devised. As a result, she was met with hostility, and her friends stopped talking to her. One day she had had enough and berated a group of her friends about how they gave her no respect, were uncooperative, and were not doing their jobs. After all, she never asked them to do anything she wasn't willing or able to do herself. Still, morale was plummeting and productivity was falling. Grace felt like a failure at the job she had worked so hard to get, and, even beyond that, she felt she was losing her friends.

Grace knew that something was going to have to change. She needed to try something new, to somehow regain the respect of her subordinates and find a new way to inspire them to improve their performance and efficiency and to restore morale. And she had to accomplish all of this while still maintaining her friendships.

Questions

1. Which traits, skills, and behaviors associated with successful leaders does Grace possess? Are there characteristics she could enhance to improve her leadership ability?
2. Why did Grace have problems making changes and maintaining discipline when she first was promoted to a position that required leadership?
3. Analyze Grace's leadership situation in terms of her sources of power: Are there types of power she couldn't or shouldn't use? What types of power could she draw on, and how could she use those types to greatest effect?
4. Are there substitutes for leadership present in this situation? What neutralizers must Grace overcome to be an effective leader?

Source: Personal communication with the authors.

References

1. R. M. Stogdill, "Historical Trends in Leadership Theory and Research," *Journal of Contemporary Business* 3, no. 4 (1974): 2.
2. P. Gronn, "Distributed Leadership as a Unit of Analysis," *Leadership Quarterly* 13 (2002): 423–451; M. Uhl-Bien and R. Marion, "Complexity Leadership in Bureaucratic Forms of Organizing: A Meso Model," *Leadership Quarterly* 20 (2009): 631–650. D. Ancona, and E. Backman, "Distributed Leadership," *Leadership Excellence* 27, no. 1 (2010): 11–12.
3. R. Levering and M. Moskowitz, *The 100 Best Companies to Work for in America,* rev. ed. (New York: Plume, 1993); R. Galford and A. S. Drapeau, "The Enemies of Trust," *Harvard Business Review* 81, no. 2 (2003): 88–95; A. C. Edmondson and S. E. Cha, "When Company Values Backfire," *Harvard Business Review* 80, no. 11 (2002): 18–19; T. Simons, "The High Cost of Lost Trust," *Harvard Business Review* 80, no. 9 (2002): 18–19.
4. A. Jack, "J&J Pressed over 'Phantom Recall,'" *Financial Times* June, 10, 2010, http://www.ft.com.
5. D. Katz and R. L. Kahn, *The Social Psychology of Organizations*, 2nd ed. (New York: Wiley, 1978); S. D. Dionne, F. J. Yammarino, L. E. Atwater, and L. R. James, "Neutralizing Substitutes for Leadership Theory: Leadership Effects and Common-Source Bias," *Journal of Applied Psychology* 87, no. 3 (2002): 454–464.
6. S. Finkelstein, "Seven Habits of Spectacularly Unsuccessful People," *Strategy Review* 14, no. 4 (2003): 39–51; N. Nohria, W. Joyce, and B. Roberson, "What Really Works," *Harvard Business Review* 81, no. 7 (2003): 42–52; W. G. Bennis and B. Nanus, *Leaders: Strategies for Taking Charge,* 2nd ed. (New York: Harper Business, 1997); J. P. Kotter, "What Leaders Really Do," *Harvard Business Review* 68, no. 3 (1990): 103–111; A. Zaleznik, "Managers and Leaders: Are They Different?" *Harvard Business Review* 70, no. 2 (1992): 126–135.
7. R. J. House, ed., *Culture, Leadership, and Organizations: The GLOBE Study of 62 Societies* (Thousand Oaks: Sage Publications, 2004); M. W. Dickson, D. N. Den Hartog, and J. K. Mitchelson, "Research on Leadership in a Cross-Cultural Context: Making Progress and Raising New Questions," *The Leadership Quarterly* 14 (2003): 729–768.
8. Westwood and Chan, *Headship and Leadership.*
9. S. Ronen, *Comparative and Multinational Management* (New York: Wiley, 1986), 191.
10. Westwood and Chan, *Headship and Leadership.*
11. E. Ogliastri, C. McMillen, C. Altschul, M. E. Arias, C. Bustamante, C. Davila, P. Dorfman, M. Ferreira, C. Finmen, and S. Martinez, "Cultura y Liderazgo Organizacional en America Latina: El Estudio GLOBE (Culture and Organizational Leadership in Latin America: The GLOBE Study)," *Revista Latinoamericana de Administración* (1999).
12. Dickson, Den Hartog, and Mitchelson, "Research on Leadership in a Cross-Cultural Context: Making Progress and Raising New Questions"; P. W. Dorfman and J. P. Howell, "Leadership in Western and Asian Countries: Commonalities and Differences in Effective Leadership Processes Across Cultures," *The Leadership Quarterly* 8 (1997): 233–274.
13. M. Javidan *et al.,* "In the Eye of the Beholder: Cross Cultural Lessons in Leadership from Project GLOBE," *Academy of Management Perspectives* 20 (2006): 67–90; P. Dorfman, P. J. Hanges, and F. C. Brodbeck, "Leadership and Cultural Variation: The Identification of Culturally Endorsed Leadership Profiles," eds. R. J. House, P. J. Hanges, M. Javidan, P. Dorfman, and V. Gupta, *Leadership, Culture, and Organizations: The GLOBE Study of 62 Societies* (Thousand Oaks: Sage Publications, Inc., 2004), 667–718.
14. B. Powell, R. Tomlinson, E. Nee, J. Fox *et al.,* "25 Rising Stars," *Fortune,* 2001, 140–164; B. Li, "Yifei Li Hired as Head of Publicis Groupe's Vivake in China," *Media Asia,* August 25, 2009, http://www.media.asia.
15. J. Pfeffer, *Managing with Power: Politics and Influence in Organizations* (Boston: Harvard Business School Press, 1992), 45.
16. D. A. Whetten and K. S. Cameron, *Developing Management Skills,* 4th ed. (Reading: Addison–Wesley, 1998), 229.
17. G. E. G. Catlin, *Systematic Politics* (Toronto: University of Toronto Press, 1962), 71.
18. M. Davids, "Where Style Meets Substance," *Journal of Business Strategy* 16 (1995): 48–52+.

19. Pfeffer, *Managing with Power*.

20. W. G. Bennis and B. Nanus, *The Strategies for Taking Charge* (New York: Harper and Row, 1985), 6.

21. B. M. Bass, *Leadership, Psychology, and Organizational Behavior* (New York: Harper, 1960); A. Etzioni, *A Comparative Analysis of Complex Organizations: On Power, Involvement, and Their Correlates* (New York: Free Press of Glencoe, 1961); G. A. Yukl, *Leadership in Organizations,* 3rd ed. (Upper Saddle River: Prentice Hall, 1994).

22. J. R. P. French and B. Raven, *The Bases of Social Power*, in *Studies in Social Power*, ed. D. Cartwright (Ann Arbor: Institute for Social Research, 1959), 150–167.

23. A Singh, "Organizational Power in Perspective," *Leadership and Management in Engineering* 9, no. 4 (2009): 165–176.

24. D. Mechanic, "Sources of Power of Lower Participants in Complex Organizations," *Administrative Science Quarterly* 7 (1962): 349–364.

25. B. Breen, "Trickle-up Leadership," *Fast Company 52* (2001), 70.

26. Pfeffer, *Managing with Power*, 46; N. Nicholson, "How to Motivate Your Problem People," *Harvard Business Review* 81, no. 1 (2003): 56–65; M. Mongeau, "Moving Mountains," *Harvard Business Review* 81, no. 1 (2003): 41–47

27. D. Kipnis, S. M. Schmidt, and I. Wilkinson, "Intra–organizational Influence Tactics: Explorations in Getting One's Way," *Journal of Applied Psychology* 65 (1980): 440–452; L. W. Porter, R. W. Allen, and H. L. Angle, "The Politics of Upward Influence in Organizations," in *Research in Organizational Behavior* 3, eds. L. L. Cummings and B. M. Staw (Greenwich: JAI Press, 1981), 109–139; G. Yukl and C. M. Falbe, "Influence Tactics and Objectives in Upward, Downward and Lateral Influence Attempts," *Journal of Applied Psychology* 75 (1990): 132–140; G. Yukl, R. Lepsinger, and T. Lucia, "Preliminary Report on the Development and Validation of the Influence Behavior Questionnaire," in *The Impact of Leadership*, eds. K. Clark and M. Clark (Greensboro: Center for Creative Leadership, 1992); G. Yukl and J. B. Tracey, "Consequences of Influence Tactics Used with Subordinates, Peers, and the Boss," *Journal of Applied Psychology* 77 (1992): 525–535; M. D. Mumford *et al.,* "Leading Creative People: Orchestrating Expertise and Relationships," *Leadership Quarterly* 13 (2002): 705–815.

28. Bennis and Nanus, *Leaders*; R. M. Kanter, "Frontiers for Strategic Human Resource Planning and Management," *Human Resource Management* 1, no. 2 (1983): 9–21; J. A. Conger, "Leadership: The Art of Empowering Others," *Academy of Management Executive* 3 (1989): 17–24; J. A. Conger and R. N. Kanungo, "The Empowerment Process: Integrating Theory and Practice," *Academy of Management Review* 13 (1988): 471–482; P. G. Foster-Fishman and C. B. Keys, "The Inverted Pyramid: How a Well-meaning Attempt to Initiate Employee Empowerment Ran Afoul of the Culture of a Public Bureaucracy," *Academy of Management Journal,* Best Papers Proceedings (1995): 364–368; G. M. Spreitzer, "Psychological Empowerment in the Workplace: Dimensions, Measurement, and Validation," *Academy of Management Journal* 38 (1995): 1442–1465; G. M. Spreitzer, "Social Structural Characteristics of Psychological Empowerment," *Academy of Management Journal* 39 (1996): 483–504; N. M. Tichy and M. A. Devanna, "The Transformational Leader," *Training and Development* 40, no. 7 (1986): 27–32.

29. N. Moskowitz and R. Levering, "Great Companies in Europe: Novo Nordisk," *Fortune,* 2002, 60–61; Company Web site, http://press.novonordisk-us.com, accessed May 29, 2010.

30. Bennis and Nanus, *Leaders*; R. M. Kanter, "Frontiers for Strategic Human Resource Planning and Management"; Conger and Kanungo, "The Empowerment Process"; Tichy and Devanna, "The Transformational Leader"; R. Kark, B. Shamir, and G. Chen, "The Two Faces of Transformational Leadership:

Empowerment and Dependency," *Journal of Applied Psychology* 88, no. 2 (2003): 246–255; N. Turner, J. Barling, O. Epitropaki, V. Butcher, and C. Milner, "Transformational Leadership and Moral Reasoning," *Journal of Applied Psychology* 87, no. 2 (2002): 304–311; T. Dvir, D. Eden, B. J. Avolio, and B. Shamir, "Impact of Transformational Leadership on Follower Development and Performance: A Field Experiment," *Academy of Management Journal* 45, no. 4 (2002): 735–744.

31. R. M. Stogdill, "Personal Factors Associated with Leadership: A Survey of the Literature," *Journal of Psychology* 25 (1948): 35–71.

32. R. G. Lord, C. L. De Vader, and G. M. Alliger, "A Meta-analysis of the Relation Between Personality Traits and Leadership Perceptions: An Application of Validity Generalization Procedures," *Journal of Applied Psychology* 71 (1986): 402–441; S. A. Kirkpatrick and E. A. Locke, "Leadership: Do Traits Matter?" *Academy of Management Executive* 5, no. 2 (1991): 48–60; Yukl, *Leadership in Organizations*; R. M. Kramer, "The Harder They Fall," *Harvard Business Review* 81, no. 10 (2003): 58–66.

33. Kirkpatrick and Locke, *Leadership*; Yukl, *Leadership in Organizations*; D. V. Day, D. J. Schleicher, A. L. Unckless, and N. J. Hiller, "Research Reports—Self-monitoring Personality at Work: A Meta-analytic Investigation of Construct Validity," *Journal of Applied Psychology* 87, no. 2 (2002): 390–401.

34. J. B. Miner, "Twenty Years of Research on Role-Motivation Theory of Managerial Effectiveness," *Personnel Psychology* 31 (1978): 739–760; F. E. Berman and J. B. Miner, "Motivation to Manage at the Top Executive Level: A Test of the Hierarchic Role-Motivation Theory," *Personnel Psychology* 38 (1985): 377–391.

35. Bennis and Nanus, *Leaders*; J. M. Kouzes and B. Z. Posner, *The Leadership Challenge: How to Get Extraordinary Things Done in Organizations* (San Francisco: Jossey-Bass, 1987).

36. A. Bandura, *Social Foundations of Thought and Action: A Social Cognitive Theory* (Upper Saddle River: Prentice Hall, 1986); B. M. Bass, *Handbook of Leadership: A Survey of Theory and Research* (New York: Free Press, 1990); D. C. McClelland and R. E. Boyatzis, "Leadership Motive Pattern and Long-term Success in Management," *Journal of Applied Psychology* 67 (1982): 737–743; A. Howard and D. W. Bray, *Managerial Lives in Transition: Advancing Age and Changing Times* (New York: Guilford Press, 1988).

37. Kouznes and Posner, *The Leadership Challenge*.

38. J. R. O'Neil, *The Paradox of Success: When Winning at Work Means Losing at Life. A Book of Renewal for Leaders* (New York: G. P. Putnam and Sons, 1994); M. Maccoby, "Narcissistic Leaders: The Incredible Pros, the Inevitable Cons," *Harvard Business Review* 82, no. 1 (2004): 92–100.

39. Bass, *Handbook of Leadership*; Bennis and Nanus, *Leaders*; Howard and Bray, *Managerial Lives in Transition*; C. D. McCauley and M. M. Lombardo, "Benchmarks: An Instrument for Diagnosing Managerial Strengths and Weaknesses," in *Measures of Leadership,* eds. K. E. Clark and M. B. Clark (West Orange: Leadership Library of America, 1990), 535–545; D. Goleman, R. Boyatzis, and A. McKee, *Primal Leadership: Realizing the Power of Emotional Intelligence* (Boston: Harvard Business School Press, 2002); D. L. Coutu, "Putting Leaders on the Couch: A Conversation with Manfred F. R. Kets de Vries," *Harvard Business Review* 82, no. 1 (2004): 64–71.

40. R. I. Westwood and A. Chan, "Headship and Leadership," in *Organizational Behavior: Southeast Asian Perspectives,* ed. R. I. Westwood (Hong Kong: Longman, 1992), 118–143.

41. M. Weber, *The Theory of Social and Economic Organization,* trans. A. M. Henderson and T. Parson, ed. with an introduction by T. Parsons (New York: Free Press, 1948).

42. S. Callan, "Charismatic Leadership in Contemporary Management Debates"; M. Frese, S. Beimel, and S. Schoenborn, "Action Training for Charismatic Leadership: Two Evaluations of Studies of a Commercial Training Module on Inspirational Communication of a Vision," *Personnel Psychology* 56, no. 3 (2003): 671–697; R. Khurana, "The Curse of the Superstar CEO," *Harvard Business Review* 80, no. 9 (2002): 60–66; J-C. Pastor, J. R. Meindl, and M. C. Mayo, "A Network Effects Model of Charisma Attributions," *Academy of Management Journal* 45, no. 2 (2002): 410–420; B. R. Agle, N. J. Nagarajan, J. A. Sonnenfeld, and D. Srinivasan, "Does CEO Charisma Matter? An Empirical Analysis of the Relationships Among Organizational Performance, Environmental Uncertainty, and Top Management Team Perceptions of CEO Charisma," *Academy of Management Journal* 49, no. 1 (2006):161–174; J. E. Bono and R. Ilies, "Charisma, Positive Emotions, and Mood Contagion," *Leadership Quarterly* 17, no. 4 (2006): 317–334; M. E. Brown and L. K. Trevino, "Socialized Charismatic Leadership, Values Congruence, and Deviance in Work Groups," *Journal of Applied Psychology* 91, no. 4 (2006): 954–962; A. H. B. de Hoogh, D. N. den Hartog, P. L. Koopman, H. Thierry, P. T. van den Berg, J. G. van der Weide *et al.*, "Leader Motives, Charismatic Leadership, and Subordinates' Work Attitude in the Profit and Voluntary Sector," *Leadership Quarterly* 16, no. 1 (2005): 17–38; K. S. Groves, "Linking Leader Skills, Follower Attitudes, and Contextual Variables via an Integrated Model of Charismatic Leadership," *Journal of Management* 31, no. 2 (2005): 255–277; J. J. Sosik, "The Role of Personal Values in the Charismatic Leadership of Corporate Managers: A Model and Preliminary Field Study," *Leadership Quarterly* 16, no. 2 (2005): 221–244.

43. House, *A 1976 Theory of Charismatic Leadership.*

44. M. E. Brown and L. K. Trevino, "Socialized Charismatic Leadership, Values Congruence, and Deviance in Work Groups," *Journal of Applied Psychology* 91, no. 4 (2006): 954–962.

45. C. Macrae, I. Ryder, J. Yan, J. Caswell, T. Kitchin, T. Power, M. McQuarrie, and S. Anholt, "Can Brand Leadership Recover Local Trust and Global Responsibility?" *Journal of Brand Management* 10, nos. 4–5 (2003): 268–279; R. L. Veninga, "Five Ways to Rebuild Trust," *Executive Excellence* 18, no. 10 (2001): 13–14.

46. J. E. Bono and R. Ilies, "Charisma, Positive Emotions and Mood Contagion," *Leadership Quarterly* 17, no. 4 (2006): 317–334; K. S. Groves, "Linking Leader Skills, Follower Attitudes, and Contextual Variables via an Integrated Model of Charismatic Leadership," *Journal of Management* 31, no. 2 (2005): 255–277; J. J. Sosik, "The Role of Personal Values in the Charismatic Leadership of Corporate Managers: A Model and Preliminary Field Study," *Leadership Quarterly* 16, no. 2 (2005): 221–244. M. E. Brown, and L. K. Trevino, "Leader-follower Values Congruence: Are Socialized Charismatic Leaders Better Able to Achieve It?" *Journal of Applied Psychology* 94 (2009): 478–490.

47. L. Lee, "Tricks of E*Trade: In His Drive to Create a Net Powerhouse, Christos Costakos Is Building a Culture That's Edgy, a Bit Bizarre—and Often Brilliant," *BusinessWeek,* February 7, 2000, Issue 3667, EB18–EB31.

48. Goleman, Boyatzis, and McKee, *Primal Leadership: Realizing the Power of Emotional Intelligence*; D. Goleman, "What Makes a Leader?" *Harvard Business Review* 76, no. 6 (1998): 92–103; J. D. Mayer and P. Salovey, "Emotional Intelligence and the Construction and Regulation of Feelings," *Applied and Preventive Psychology* 4 (1995): 197–208; J. D. Mayer, D. Goleman, C. Barrett, S. Gutstein *et al.*, "Leading by Feel," *Harvard Business Review* 82, no. 1 (2004): 27–37; D. Goleman, "What Makes a Leader?" *Harvard Business Review* 82, no. 1 (2004): 82–91; J. E. Dutton, P. J. Frost, M. C. Worline,

J. M. Lilius, and J. M. Kanov, "Leading in Times of Trauma," *Harvard Business Review* 80, no. 1 (2002): 54–61.

49. Goleman, "What Makes a Leader?" *Harvard Business Review* 82, no. 1 (2004) 82–91.

50. J. E. Barbuto Jr., S. M. Fritz, and D. Marx, "A Field Examination of Two Measures of Work Motivation as Predictors of Leaders' Influence Tactics," *Journal of Social Psychology* 132 (2002): 601–616; R. S. Rubin, D. Munz, and W. H. Bommer, "Leading from Within: The Effects of Emotion Recognition and Personality on Transformational Leadership Behavior," *Academy of Management Journal* 48 (2005): 845–858. P. D. Harms, and M. Crede, "Emotional Intelligence and Transformational and Transactional Leadership: A Meta-analysis," *Journal of Leadership and Organizational Studies* 17, no. 1 (2010): 5–17.

51. D. Goleman, *Emotional Intelligence* (New York: Bantam Books, 1995).

52. Goleman, Boyatzis, and McKee, *Primal Leadership: Realizing the Power of Emotional Intelligence.*

53. D. Goleman, *Social Intelligence: The New Science of Human Relationships* (New York: Bantam Books, 2006).

54. J. Misumi and M. E. Peterson, "The Performance-Maintenance (PM) Theory of Leadership: Review of a Japanese Research Program," *Administrative Science Quarterly* 30 (1985): 198–223; R. T. Lewis, "New York Times Company President and Chief Executive Officer Russell Lewis on 'The CEO's Lot Is Not a Happy One...' (with Apologies to Gilbert and Sullivan)," *Academy of Management Executive* 16, no. 4 (2002): 37–42.

55. E. A. Eagly and B. T. Johnson, "Gender and Leadership Style: A Meta-analysis," *Psychological Bulletin* 108 (1990): 235–256; J. B. Rosener, "Ways Women Lead," *Harvard Business Review* 68, no. 6 (1990): 119–125; G. N. Powell, "One More Time: Do Female and Male Managers Differ?" *Academy of Management Executive* 4, no. 3 (1990): 68–75; G. Morse, "The Emancipated Organization," *Harvard Business Review* 80, no. 9 (2002): 20–21; A. H. Eagley and L. L. Carli, "The Female Leadership Advantage: An Evaluation of the Evidence," *The Leadership Quarterly* 14 (2003): 807–834; R. P. Vecchio, "In Search of Gender Advantage," *The Leadership Quarterly* 14 (2003): 835–850; A. H. Eagly and L. L. Carli, "Finding Gender Advantage and Disadvantage: Systematic Research Integration Is the Solution," *The Leadership Quarterly* 14 (2003): 851–859.

56. "Sex and Leadership Styles: A Meta-analysis of Research Published in the 1990s," *Psychological Reports* 94, no. 1 (2004): 3–18.

57. R. R. Blake and J. S. Mouton, *The Management Grid* (Houston: Gulf Publishing, 1964); M. Wood, "The Fallacy of Misplaced Leadership," *Journal of Management Studies* 42, no. 6 (2005): 1101–1121.

58. Burns, *Leadership.*

59. B. M. Bass, "Leadership: Good, Better, Best," *Organizational Dynamics* 13, no. 3 (1985): 26–40; B. M. Bass and B. J. Avolio, "Developing Transformational Leadership: 1992 and Beyond," *Journal of European Industrial Training* 14, no. 5 (1992): 21–27.

60. W. Liu, R. Zhu, and Y. Yang, "I Warn You Because I Like You: Voice Behavior, Employee Identifications, and Transformational Leadership," *Leadership Quarterly* 21, (2010): 189–202.

61. Bass, *Leadership.* L. Hardy, C. A. Arthur, G. Jones, A. Shariff, K.l Munnoch, I. Isaacs, and A. J. Allsopp, "The Relationship Between Transformational Leadership Behaviors, Psychological, and Training Outcomes in Elite Military Recruits," *Leadership Quarterly* 21 (2010): 20–31.

62. B. M. Bass, D. I. Jung, B. J. Avolio, and Y. Berson, "Predicting Unit Performance by Assessing Transformational and Transactional Leadership," *Journal of Applied Psychology* 88, no. 2 (2003): 207–218; B. J. Avolio, "Re-examining the Components of Transformational and Transactional Leadership Using the Multifactor Leadership Questionnaire," *Journal of*

Occupational and Organizational Psychology 72 (1999): 441–463.

63. R. P. Vecchio, J. E. Justin, and C. L. Pearce, "The Utility of Transactional and Transformational Leadership for Predicting Performance and Satisfaction Within a Path–Goal Theory Framework," *Journal of Occupational & Organizational Psychology* 81 (2008): 71–82.

64. C. L. Hoyt and J. Blascovich, "Transformational and Transactional Leadership in Virtual and Physical Environments," *Small Group Research* 34, no. 6 (2003): 678–716; N. M. Tichy and M. A. Devanna, "The Transformational Leader," *Training and Development* 40, no. 7 (1986): 27–32; G. A. Yukl, *Leadership in Organizations,* 3d ed. (Upper Saddle River: Prentice Hall, 1994).

65. Bennis and Nanus, *Leaders.*

66. Yukl, *Leadership in Organizations.*

67. B. J. Avolio and W. L. Gardner, "Authentic Leadership Development: Getting to the Root of Positive Forms of Leadership," *Leadership Quarterly* 16, no. 3 (2005): 315–338. W. L. Gardner, B. J. Avolio, F. Luthans, D. R. May, and F. Walumbwa, "'Can You See the Real Me?' A Self-based Model of Authentic Leader and Follower Development," *Leadership Quarterly* 16, no. 3 (2005): 343–372; R. Ilies, F. P. Morgeson, and J. D. Nahrgang, "Authentic Leadership and Eudaemonic Well-being: Understanding Leader-Follower Outcomes," *Leadership Quarterly* 16, no. 3 (2005): 373–394.

68. P. N. Hineline, "The Several Meanings of 'Positive,'" *Journal of Organizational Behavior Management* 12, nos. 1–2 (2005): 55–66.

69. C. A. Wong, and G. G. Cummings, "The Influence of Authentic Leadership Behaviors on Trust and Work Outcomes of Health Care Staff," *Journal of Leadership Studies* 3, no. 2 (2009): 6–23.

70. "Who Nine CEOs Admire Most," *CNN.com,* April 4, 2010, http://money.cnn.com.

71. E. P. Hollander, "The Essential Interdependence of Leadership and Followership," *Current Directions in Psychological Science* 1, no. 2 (1992): 71–75; R. Stewart, *Choices for the Manager* (Upper Saddle River: Prentice Hall, 1982); cited in E. P. Hollanader, "Leadership, Followership, Self, and Others," *Leadership Quarterly* 3, no. 1 (1992): 43–54; L. R. Offermann, "When Followers Become Toxic," *Harvard Business Review* 82, no. 1 (2004): 54–60; B. van Knippenberg and D. van Knippenberg, "Leader Self-sacrifice and Leadership Effectiveness: The Moderating Influence of Leader Prototypicality," *Journal of Applied Psychology* 90, no. 1 (2005): 25–37.

72. S. Motsch, "Think Gray," *Incentive* 169, no. 4 (1995): 59–60; N. Shope Griffin, "Personalize Your Management Development," *Harvard Business Review* 81, no. 3 (2003): 113–119.

73. R. E. Kelly, "In Praise of Followers," *Harvard Business Review* 66, no. 6 (1988): 142–149.

74. R. G. Lord and K. H. Maher, "Alternative Information-processing Models and Their Implications for Theory, Research, and Practice," *Academy of Management Review* 15 (1990): 9–28.

75. B. J. Calder, "An Attribution Theory of Leadership," in *New Directions in Organizational Behavior,* eds. B. M. Staw and G. R. Salancik (Chicago: St. Clair, 1997); Lord, De Vader, and Alliger, "A Meta–analysis of the Relation Between Personality Traits and Leadership Perceptions"; A. C. Edmondson and S. E. Cha, "When Company Values Backfire," *Harvard Business Review* 80, no. 11 (2002): 18–19; B. Schyns, "The Role of Implicit Leadership Theories in the Performance Appraisals and Promotion Recommendations of Leaders," *Equal Opportunities International* 25, no. 3 (2006): 188–199.

76. Calder, "An Attribution Theory of Leadership"; J. Pfeffer, "The Ambiguity of Leadership," *Academy of Management Review* 2 (1977): 104–112.

77. P. Hersey, *Situational Selling* (Escondido: Center for Leadership Studies, 1985); P. Hersey, K. Blanchard, and D. Johnson, *Management of Organizational Behavior: Leading Human Resources,* 8th ed. (Upper Saddle River: Prentice Hall, 2001).

78. G. Thompson, and R. P. Vecchio, "Situational Leadership Theory: A Test of Three Versions," *Leadership Quarterly* 20 (2009): 837–848.

79. G. B. Graen, R. C. Liden, and W. Hoel, "Role of Leadership in the Employee Withdrawal Process," *Journal of Applied Psychology* 67 (1982): 868–872; G. B. Graen, T. A. Scandura, and M. R. Grae, "A Field Experimental Test of the Moderating Effects of Growth Need Strength on Productivity," *Journal of Applied Psychology* 3 (1986): 484–491.

80. G. B. Graen and M. Uhl-Bien, "Relationship-based Approach to Leadership: Development of Leader–Member Exchange (LMX) Theory of Leadership over 25 Years: Applying a Multi-domain Perspective," *The Leadership Quarterly, Special Issue: Leadership* 6 (1995): 219–247; M. Uhl-Bien and G. B. Graen, "Leadership Making in Self-managing Professional Work Teams: An Empirical Investigation," in *The Impact of Leadership,* eds. K. E. Clark, M. B. Clark, and D. P. Campbell (West Orange: Leadership Library of America, 1993), 379–387.

81. T. N. Bauer and S. G. Green, "Development of Leader–Member Exchange: A Longitudinal Test," *Academy of Management Journal* 39 (1996): 1538–1567; C. R. Gerstner and D. V. Day, "Meta-analytic Review of Leader–Member Exchange Theory: Correlates and Construct Issues," *Journal of Applied Psychology* 82 (1997): 827–844; Graen *et al.,* "Role of Leadership in the Employee Withdrawal Process"; Graen, Scandura, and Graen, "A Field Experimental Test of the Moderating Effects of Growth Need Strength on Productivity"; T. A. Scandura and G. B. Graen, "Moderating Effects of Initial Leader–Member Exchange Status on the Effects of a Leadership Intervention," *Journal of Applied Psychology* 69 (1984): 428–436.

82. Bauer and Green, "Development of Leader–Member Exchange"; D. A. Hofmann, S. J. Gerras, and F. P. Morgeson, "Climate as a Moderator of the Relationship Between Leader–Member Exchange and Content Specific Citizenship: Safety Climate as an Exemplar," *Journal of Applied Psychology* 88, no. 1 (2003): 170; G. Yukl, M. O'Donnell, and T. Taber, "Influence of Leader Behaviors on the Leader–Member Exchange Relationship," *Journal of Managerial Psychology* 24, no. 4 (2009): 289–299.

83. Graen and Uhl-Bien, "Relationship-based Approach to Leadership"; Uhl-Bien and Graen, "Leadership Making in Self-managing Professional Work Teams"; R. T. Sparrowe and R. C. Liden, "Process and Structure in Leader–Member Exchange," *Academy of Management Review* 22 (1997): 522–552; W. C. H. Prentice, "Understanding Leadership," *Harvard Business Review* 82, no. 1 (2004): 102–109; S. J. Wayne, L. M. Shore, W. H. Bommer, and L. E. Tetrick, "The Role of Fair Treatment and Rewards in Perceptions of Organizational Support and Leader–Member Exchange," *Journal of Applied Psychology* 87, no. 3 (2002): 590–598.

84. L. H. Nishii, and D. M. Mayer, "Do Inclusive Leaders Help to Reduce Turnover in Diverse Groups? The Moderating Role of Leader–Member Exchange in the Diversity to Turnover Relationship," *Journal of Applied Psychology* 94 (2009): 1412–1426.

85. W. Hui, *et al.,* "Leader–Member Exchange as a Mediator of the Relationship Between Transformational Leadership and Follower Performance and Organizational Citizenship Behavior," *Academy of Management Journal* 48 (2005): 420–432.

86. A. N. Turner and P. R. Lawrence, *Industrial Jobs and the Worker: An Investigation of Response to Task Attributes* (Boston: Harvard University, Division of Research, Graduate School of Business Administration, 1965); R. W. Griffin, *Task Design: An Integrative Approach* (Glenview: Scott,

Foresman, 1982); J. R. Hackman and G. R. Oldham, *Work Redesign* (Reading: Addison-Wesley, 1980).

87. L. W. Porter and G. B. McLaughlin, "Leadership and the Organizational Context: Like the Weather?" *The Leadership Quarterly* 17 (2006): 559–576.

88. F. E. Fiedler, *A Theory of Leadership Effectiveness* (New York: McGraw-Hill, 1967); M. M. Chemers and F. E. Fiedler, "The Effectiveness of Leadership Training: A Reply to Argyris," *American Psychologist* 33 (1978): 391–394.

89. M. G. Evans, "The Effects of Supervisory Behavior on the Path–Goal Relationship," *Organizational Behavior and Human Performance* 5 (1970): 277–298; R. J. House, "A Path–Goal Theory of Leader Effectiveness," *Administrative Science Quarterly* 16 (1971): 321–329; R. J. House and G. Dessler, "The Path–Goal Theory of Leadership: Some Post Hoc and A Priori Tests," in *Contingency Approaches to Leadership,* eds. J. Hunt and L. Larson (Carbondale: Southern Illinois University Press, 1974), 81–97; R. J. House and T. R. Mitchell, "Path–Goal Theory of Leadership," *Journal of Contemporary Business* 3, no. 4 (1974): 81–97.

90. House, "A Path–Goal Theory of Leader Effectiveness," 324.

91. S. Kerr and J. M. Jermier, "Substitutes for Leadership: Their Meaning and Measurement," *Organizational Behavior and Human Performance* 22 (1978): 375–403; J. P. Howell, D. E. Bowen, P. W. Dorfman, S. Kerr *et al.,* "Substitutes for Leadership: Effective Alternatives to Ineffective Leadership," *Organizational Dynamics* 19 (1990): 20–38; J. P. Howell and P. W. Dorfmann, "Substitutes for Leadership: Test of a Construct," *Academy of Management Journal* 24 (1981): 714–28; P. M. Podsakoff, S. B. MacKenzie, and W. H. Bommer, "Transformational Leader Behaviors and Substitutes for Leadership as Determinants of Employee Satisfaction, Commitment, Trust, and Organizational Citizenship Behaviors," *Journal of Management* 22 (1996): 259–298; S. B. MacKenzie, P. M. Podsakoff, and R. Fetter, "The Impact of Organizational Citizenship Behavior on Evaluations of Salesperson Performance," *Journal of Marketing* 57 (1993): 70–80; P. M. Podsakoff, B. P. Nichoff, S. B. MacKenzie, and M. L. Williams, "Do Substitutes for Leadership Really Substitute for Leadership? An Empirical Examination of Kerr and Jermier's Situational Leadership Model," *Organizational Behavior and Human Decision Processes* 54 (1993): 1–44.

9 Motivation

LEARNING OBJECTIVES

After studying this chapter, you should be able to:

Analyze the motivational forces present in a specific situation.

Identify the sources of an individual's motivation.

Differentiate between content and process theories of motivation and indicate how each can be helpful in analyzing a given motivational situation.

Explain how job enrichment can influence an employee's motivation.

Compare and contrast the various approaches to reinforcement and describe their relative advantages and disadvantages for managers.

Describe how values and attitudes toward work can influence motivation.

Courtesy of Elizabeth Hayes

Name: Elizabeth Hayes

Position: Corporate trainer/instructional designer, Fannie Mae

Alma mater: University of Texas at Austin (B.A.)

Outside work activities: Reading, movies, museums, and yoga

First job out of school: High-school teacher

Hero: Educators in general

Motto to live by: "Whether you think that you can, or that you can't, you are usually right." (Henry Ford)

What drives me: The desire to provide teachers with effective tools they can use to enhance learning

Management style: Delegator—enabling people with the tools and support they need to succeed

Ever since Elizabeth Hayes graduated from college, her career track has primarily combined the worlds of education and business. After spending her first several postgraduate years teaching high-school English, she went to work for a major college textbook publishing company as a developmental editor and associate acquisitions editor. Although the "editor" title of her jobs indicated a close association with the world of words and writing, she simultaneously had to pay close attention to the bottom line in terms of signing authors to textbook projects that would eventually contribute positively to the company's income. Mistakes in judgment about which proposed books to sign and which ones to pass on could result in wasting valuable resources. Alternatively, making the right choices could generate significant profit streams over the years through future editions of successful books.

After several years, Hayes decided to leave the publishing industry and join Texas Instruments as a product manager in the company's education division. From that job she moved to a position as a programming director of education service at America Online, Inc. (AOL). At AOL, Hayes was responsible for the editorial vision, integrity, and product direction of a no-cost Web portal that K–12 educators can use to find the right online resources and tools they need. She was also responsible for building the product and AOL's brand identity, identifying and working with strategic partners, and supervising programming staff. In this latter role, one of the biggest managerial challenges she faced was keeping her remotely located subordinates consistently motivated and challenged. As "virtual" employees, these subordinates often feel like they are left out and missing out on things happening in the office. Furthermore, with employees working at off-site locations, there is always the potential one of them will take advantage of being unobserved and avoid (for a while, at least) accountability.

Managers who can successfully motivate their employees are generally rewarded by their high performance. However, that is not so easy to accomplish. If it were, every employee would be an outstanding performer. One major obstacle is that conditions beyond a manager's or an organization's control can affect employee motivation. Furthermore, these conditions keep changing. For instance, the state of the economy constantly fluctuates, and this can influence the motivation level of many employees. Also, family and other personal circumstances can sometimes acutely affect their attitudes and level of effort.

Understanding these motivational forces has been a continuing challenge for managers ever since the beginning of the Industrial Age. However, what we want to demonstrate in this chapter is that regardless of factors not directly under one's control, it is still possible to influence the motivation of employees. Although Elizabeth Hayes faces some daunting challenges in trying to motivate her "remote" employees, she nevertheless can still exert influence. In other words, managers have many opportunities to affect the motivation of those who work with and for them—especially if they understand some of the basic principles involved in the motivational process. If you as a manager want to be able to demonstrate leadership, then you need to develop your capabilities to motivate those around you.

What Is Motivation?

When we use the term *motivation*, regardless of the setting, what does it mean? **Motivation** can be thought of as the set of forces that energize, direct, and sustain behavior. These forces can come from the person, the so-called "push" of internal forces, or they can come from the environment that surrounds the person, the so-called "pull" of external forces. It is, therefore, essential for managers to recognize the importance of both sets of factors when they are analyzing motivational causes of behavior.

motivation
a set of forces that energize, direct, and sustain behavior

However, an overemphasis on one set of forces to the exclusion of the other can lead to faulty diagnosis and to actions that do not solve motivational problems. For example, a manager might assume that her subordinate's level of sales calls is low because he is lazy, when, in fact, appropriate incentives have not been provided that tap his needs or interests. The manager would be assuming the cause to be lack of an internal, push force, whereas a more accurate diagnosis in this case would focus on inadequate pull forces. This kind of misreading of motivation, which is easy to do, could lead to the loss of a potentially valuable employee. Likewise, a supervisor might assume that due to external, or pull, forces, a clerical worker is doing an especially good job in order to please his boss, when, in fact, the employee might be a person with strong push forces who is highly motivated no matter what kind of supervision he receives. In both of these examples, a broader view of motivational factors should lead to more valid and useful assessments.

Throughout this chapter, different types of motivational forces will be examined, with particular emphasis on what psychologists and other behavioral scientists have had to say about the content and process of motivation. First, though, we begin with a framework to analyze the sources of motivational forces in the work situation. Following that, several major behavioral theories of motivation are examined. In later sections of the chapter, attention is focused on how reinforcement systems and the situational context of work can affect the strength and direction of motivation.

Sources of Motivation

As shown in Exhibit 9.1, three basic categories of variables determine motivation in the work setting:

1. The characteristics of the individual
2. The characteristics of the job or task
3. The characteristics of the work situation

EXHIBIT 9.1

Key Variables That Influence Motivation

INTERNAL (PUSH) FORCES	BOTH INTERNAL (PUSH) AND EXTERNAL (PULL) FORCES	EXTERNAL (PULL) FORCES
Characteristics of the Individual (examples)	**Characteristics of the Job/Task (examples)**	**Characteristics of the Work Situation (examples)**
Needs	• Amount of direct feedback	*Immediate Social Environment*
• For security	• Work load	• Supervisor(s)
• For self-esteem	• Variety of tasks	• Workgroup members
• For achievement	• Scope of tasks	• Subordinates
• For power	• Degree of control over tasks	*Organizational Actions*
Attitudes		• Rewards & compensation
• About self		• Availability of training
• About job		• Pressure for high levels of output
• About supervisor		
• About organization		
Goals		
• Task completion		
• Performance level		
• Career advancement		

The first category, the individual's characteristics, is the source of internal, or push, forces of motivation. This is what the employee *brings* to the work setting. Three variables contribute to an individual's push forces: The person's (1) needs, such as the need for security, self-esteem, achievement, or power; (2) attitudes—toward self, a job, a supervisor, or the organization; and (3) goals such as completing a task, accomplishing a certain level of performance, and career advancement. Martin Franklin, the CEO of Jarden Corporation, a manufacturer of a diverse array of consumer goods, represents a perhaps extreme example of the push-type forces that an individual brings to the work environment. A marathon and triathlon runner, Franklin's philosophy is: "For me, it's all about seeing how far you can go, be that in business, in helping people, or in athletics.... It would be a very sad day for me to say that I can't do more.[1]

The second category of motivational forces, which relates to both internal (push) and external (pull) forces, focuses on the characteristics of a person's job or task—what the person *does* in the work setting. These characteristics include how much direct feedback the person receives, the person's workload, the variety and scope of the tasks that make up the job, and the degree of control the person has in terms of how he or she does the job.

The third category of motivational forces also consists of external pull forces. It relates to the characteristics of the work situation—what *happens to* the individual. This category has two sets of variables: the immediate social environment composed of the person's supervisor(s), work-group members, and subordinates; and various types of organizational actions, such as, for example, the firm's reward and compensation practices, the availability of training and development, and the amount of pressure applied to achieve high levels of output.

Taken together, the three major categories of variables—individual, job, and work situation—can serve as a useful framework for analyzing the sources of motivation, whether the workplace is in Bangkok, Lima, or Chicago. The framework also forms a good basis for considering the major theories of motivation relevant to managing in organizational settings. We present these theories next.

Motivation Theories Applicable to Work Situations

Several theories of motivation are particularly relevant for work settings.[2] Each of these theories highlights one or more of the variables just discussed and displayed in Exhibit 9.1.

However, it is important to note that almost all these theories were developed by American behavioral scientists. Thus, an obvious question is: Do these theories apply only in the context of American culture and society, or can the theories be used to analyze motivation in other societies and cultures?[3] Unfortunately, the answer is not clear. Based on available evidence, the best answer is that some of the theories can be applied widely across the world whereas others cannot. However, none of the theories should be automatically rejected because they originated in a particular cultural context, nor should they be routinely accepted as always applying equally well across different cultures. Instead, managers should view them as possible ways of looking at motivational problems and issues, whatever the context.

Psychologists typically categorize motivation theories into two types: *content theories* and *process theories,* as shown in Exhibit 9.2. The two types together provide us with a deeper understanding of motivation.

Content Theories

content theories

motivation theories that focus on what needs a person is trying to satisfy and on what features of the work environment seem to satisfy those needs

A **content theory** addresses the needs a person is trying to satisfy and what features of the work environment seem to satisfy those needs. Such theories try to explain motivation by identifying both (1) internal forces, that is, particular needs, and (2) external forces, particular job and work situation characteristics that are presumed to cause behavior. Two content theories—need hierarchy and acquired needs theories—focus on identifying internal forces. A third theory, the two-factor theory, focuses on identifying external factors.

NEED HIERARCHY THEORIES The most prominent need hierarchy theory was developed a half-century ago by psychologist Abraham Maslow.[4] Maslow's theory appealed to managers because

EXHIBIT 9.2

Motivation Theories

	Content Theories	Process Theories
Focus	• Personal needs that workers attempt to satisfy • Features in the work environment that satisfy a worker's needs	• How different variables can combine to influence the amount of effort put forth by employees
Theories	• Maslow's Need Hierarchy • McClelland's Acquired Needs Theory • Herzberg's Two-factor Theory	• Equity Theory • Expectancy Theory

it was easy to remember. It contains five types of needs that are arranged in a hierarchy of strength and influence, starting with the most essential:

- *Physiological needs:*   The need for the basic essentials of life, such as water, food, and shelter.
- *Security (safety) needs:*   The need to feel safe and secure.
- *Social (belongingness) needs:*   The need to be loved and accepted by other people.
- *Esteem needs:*   The need for self-respect and respect from other people.
- *Self-actualization needs:*   The need to be personally fulfilled, to feel a sense of achievement and accomplishment and, especially, to develop one's own unique talents to their highest possible levels.

The essence of **Maslow's need hierarchy theory** is that an individual is motivated to satisfy the most basic needs first (such as physiological needs) and then, once those are satisfied, move to the next level. According to this theory, only when their most basic needs have been met will people be able to concentrate on satisfying higher-order needs. However, if these persons' basic physiological and security needs should become threatened, they would then be likely to revert to focusing on those lower-order needs. They would decrease their efforts to satisfy social, esteem, and achievement needs until or unless the threat has passed.

A good illustration of this principle was demonstrated by the effects of the recent worldwide recession. A large-scale global workforce study of over 20,000 full-time employees in 22 countries

Maslow's need hierarchy theory
a theory that states that people will first attempt to fulfill basic needs, such as physiological and safety needs, before making efforts to satisfy higher-order needs, such as social and esteem needs

SAS Institute, one of the world's leading software developers, knows it's no better than the talent of the programmers who work for it. When the company's employees leave the building for the evening, CEO Jim Goodnight knows that it's his job to motivate them to come back the next day. Toward that end, SAS offers its employees a plethora of benefits unheard of at most companies—on-site daycare, extensive healthcare, car detailing, an art museum, assistants to help employees with their day-to-day personal matters, and even live entertainment in the company's lunchroom.

Ann States\Ann States Photography

carried out by consulting firm Towers Watson at the end of 2009 showed that "The desire for security and stability trumps everything else right now, in part because employees see security as a fast-disappearing part of the deal." The survey's authors went on to say that "Mobility is at a decade-long low point—with significant numbers of employees sacrificing the prospect of career growth for a secure job right now."[5]

An even more extreme example of reverting to a focus on lower-order need fulfillment when the satisfaction of those needs is threatened occurred in the 1990s in the Los Angeles area, where young Thai nationals worked in garment workshops under conditions that approached slavery. For example, for months (and even, in some cases, years), they were not allowed to leave the building in which they lived and worked for up to 18 hours a day. Need hierarchy theory clearly would have predicted that the workers would not have been concerned with satisfying higher-order needs like belonging, esteem, and self-actualization when their most basic needs—physiological and safety—were not being met.

The key to understanding a person's motivation from a need hierarchy perspective, then, is to identify the person's most basic need that is not yet being met. For the Thai garment workers in Los Angeles, that level would be the most basic: physiological needs. Once a need has been satisfied, however, it ceases to be a motivator unless its fulfillment is threatened again. But, if it is threatened, than a more basic need becomes the focus of attention.

Many questions can be raised about need hierarchy theory. For example, do the needs occur in the same hierarchical order across all cultures and countries? Probably not. The theory was developed in an American context, and there is no convincing evidence that the hierarchy is universal, either from country to country or from one person to the next. For example, a recent study of information technology executives in India appeared to indicate that they were focused on a lower-order need—security—and the higher-order needs of esteem and self-actualization at the same time.[6]

Not only does the hierarchy of needs probably not have the same order across different cultures, it almost assuredly is not ordered the same from one individual to another. Furthermore, different individuals have quite different satisfaction thresholds for each need. For example, someone who grew up in a poor family might go to extreme lengths as an adult to satisfy her need for financial security, even though she is quite well off. Individual differences in both the order of needs and the threshold for satisfying them clearly make it harder for managers to base their actions on the theory.

A somewhat more simplified variation of need hierarchy theory was published subsequent to Maslow by behavioral scientist Clay Alderfer. Alderfer's alternative version, labeled *ERG theory* for *Existence-Relatedness-Growth*, collapsed Maslow's five levels into three and provided a more straightforward way of thinking about need hierarchies. (Exhibit 9.3 provides a graphic comparison of the two classifications of needs.) ERG theory differs from Maslow's theory in some respects. For example, it presumes that different levels of needs can be active at the same time. Thus, a lower level does not have to be completely or even mostly satisfied before higher-level needs can emerge, as shown in the study of IT managers in India, cited above. Also,

EXHIBIT 9.3

Maslow's and Alderfer's Needs Hierarchies Categories

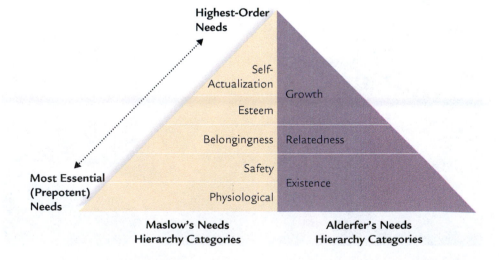

Highest-Order Needs

Most Essential (Prepotent) Needs

Self-Actualization

Esteem

Belongingness

Safety

Physiological

Growth

Relatedness

Existence

Maslow's Needs Hierarchy Categories

Alderfer's Needs Hierarchy Categories

Alderfer's version suggests that even though a lower-level need has already been satisfied, a person may revert to focusing on such a need if he gets frustrated trying to satisfy a higher-level need. ERG theory presents an interesting alternative to Maslow's earlier, more complicated version, but the key point is that both theories focus on people's attempts to satisfy particular needs and on how that can affect the amount and direction of motivation.

From the standpoint of individual managers in an organization, there is probably relatively little they can do personally to affect employees' satisfaction of basic physiological needs. Managers, however, may have some opportunities to help ensure that employees' safety needs are not threatened and that security needs are met as much as possible.

By contrast, there are probably many ways that managers and organizations can provide their employees with innovative opportunities to satisfy a variety of social, esteem, and even self-actualization needs. For example, at the Bernard Becker Medical Library at Washington University in St. Louis, managers ask employees to consider the efforts of their fellow workers who do outstanding work on behalf of the library and university, and then nominate their peers for one of several possible awards. The awards recognize not only instances of exceptional job performance, but also such contributions as suggesting new methods or ways to improve daily operations (the "bright ideas" award), or volunteering to take on unpleasant tasks that improve the working environment like cleaning up the lunchroom (the "community spirit" award). Clearly, these kinds of recognition respond to higher-order needs.[7]

ACQUIRED NEEDS THEORY Another content theory centered on needs was developed by American psychologist David McClelland.[8] His **acquired needs theory** focuses on learned, or acquired, needs that become "enduring predispositions" or tendencies of individuals, almost like personality traits, that can be activated by appropriate cues in the environment. McClelland considered three of these needs—affiliation, power, and achievement—to be especially important; hence, his theory is sometimes referred to as the *three-need theory*). However, most subsequent research has concentrated on the need for achievement.

According to McClelland's theory, a person who has a high need for achievement habitually strives for success or goal attainment in task situations (though not necessarily in other types of settings). The research data collected by McClelland and his associates indicate that individuals with high need achievement prefer to

- work on tasks of moderate difficulty
- take moderate risks
- take personal responsibility for their actions
- receive specific and concrete feedback on their performance

acquired needs theory
a motivation theory that focuses on learned needs—such as those for achievement, power, and affiliation—that become enduring tendencies

Since 1976, Habitat for Humanity has built more than 350,000 houses around the world, providing more than 1 million people with a safe, decent, and affordable place to live. Many managers encourage their employees to volunteer for Habitat for Humanity so as to give back to the community.

Isaac Brekken/Getty Images for DirecTV

In other words, high need achievers want challenges, but realistic challenges, not impossible ones. Especially important from a managerial perspective, McClelland's theory suggests that "appropriate" training, that is, showing people how to recognize and respond to relevant achievement cues, can increase the need for achievement. However, this feature of the theory is controversial; many experts doubt the extent to which permanent changes in the need for achievement can be brought about by such training.

Is a need for achievement a universal motive? Is it, for example, as prevalent in Brazil as in the United States, or in India as much as in Germany? A study that was carried out across 20 countries appeared to show that achievement, along with power, is a universal motive.[9] Although the percentage of high-achieving people varied considerably from country to country, the critical point is that there are definitely people of this type in every culture that has been studied: "It seems that the primary goal of achievers everywhere is to attain recognition for themselves."[10]

Research findings reveal fairly large changes in the level of achievement motivation in both Japan and the United States in the first several decades after World War II.[11] Achievement motivation in Japan decreased overall between the 1970s and the beginning of the 1990s, especially in younger generations. This could be due, in part, to the increase in overall prosperity in Japan during that time span. On the other hand, younger people in the United States showed higher levels of achievement motivation at the beginning of the 1990s than their counterparts did in the late 1960s and early 1970s, perhaps reflecting the decreasing levels of economic security that occurred in the United States over that time. Taken together, these findings seem to reinforce the conclusion that strong societal forces, such as changing economic conditions and changing cultural attitudes toward work, can influence achievement motivation. Incidentally, research from the mid-1990s and again in the past several years appears to indicate that achievement motivation remains somewhat lower in Japan than in the United States, although that could change again with future societal changes in the two countries.[12]

two-factor theory
a motivation theory that focuses on the presumed different effects of intrinsic job factors (motivation) and extrinsic situational factors (hygiene factors)

TWO-FACTOR THEORY In the early 1960s, American psychologist Frederick Herzberg proposed a motivation theory that came to be called the **two-factor theory**.[13] This theory focuses on the distinction between factors that can increase job satisfaction ("motivators") and those that can prevent dissatisfaction but cannot increase satisfaction ("hygiene factors"). As shown in Exhibit 9.4, motivators are intrinsic factors directly related to the *doing* of a job, such as the nature of the work itself, responsibility level, personal growth opportunities, and the sense of achievement and recognition directly received by performing the work. The other factors, hygiene factors, are extrinsic to directly performing the job. They, instead, are associated with conditions *surrounding* the job. Hygiene factors include supervision, relations with co-workers, working conditions, and

EXHIBIT 9.4

Herzberg's Two-factor Theory: Motivators and Hygiene Factors

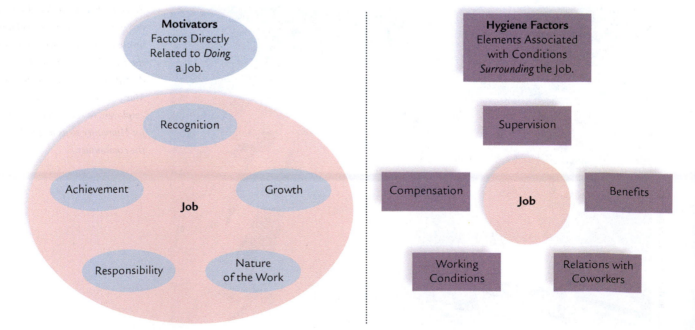

company policies and practices related to benefits and compensation.[14] As shown in Exhibit 9.5, the two-factor theory predicts that "motivator" factors actively increase satisfaction, whereas hygiene factors only decrease dissatisfaction to the point where the employee is "neither satisfied nor dissatisfied."

The theory was an immediate hit with managers when first proposed some years ago because it contains a relatively simple message: To motivate employees, focus on improving how the job is structured—what they *do*. Simply taking care of the hygiene factors can prevent dissatisfaction but will have no effect on positive motivation. Although intuitively appealing, the two-factor theory has been criticized by some scholars as overly simplistic. For one thing, the theory sometimes confuses satisfaction (positive attitudes based on the receipt of desired rewards) with motivation (the forces that energize, direct, and sustain behavior). Furthermore, subsequent research has shown that it is often impossible to distinguish clearly between variables that only decrease dissatisfaction from those that only increase motivation. Thus, for example, supervision, a hygiene factor in the theory, not only can reduce dissatisfaction, but it also potentially can contribute to increased motivation to perform at a high level. Consequently, it is likely that the supervision and leadership one receives in a job can have a whole range of effects depending on other factors in the situation and not just be a source of removal of dissatisfaction as the theory would predict. Similar dual motivation and hygiene roles can be assigned to other factors that the theory places in only one or the other category.

IMPLICATIONS FOR JOB DESIGN Despite criticisms, the two-factor theory had one very important consequence in the years after it was proposed: an increased emphasis on how jobs are designed, that is, on how different combinations of tasks are put together to form particular jobs.[15] If nothing else, the two-factor theory influenced both organizational scholars and employers to consider how the contents of jobs can affect the motivation to perform them. Managers and organizations are realizing it is possible to revise jobs to give employees a greater feeling of responsibility, accomplishment, and achievement and this in turn can affect their motivation. The general approach to designing jobs that do this is called **job enrichment.**

One of the most comprehensive approaches to designing enriched jobs with high potential for increased motivation is the "job characteristics model."[16] Developed by two organizational scientists, J. Richard Hackman and Greg Oldham, the **job characteristics model** emphasizes three components, as shown in Exhibit 9.6:

- Core job characteristics, such as skill variety and task significance
- Critical psychological states, such as experienced meaningfulness of work and experienced responsibility for outcomes of the work
- Expected outcomes, such as high internal work motivation and high work effectiveness.

Of course, not every employee wants more responsibility, autonomy, and the like—but many do. In recent years, a number of companies have paid more attention to the motivational content of their employees' jobs. It seems to be paying off. For example, in a survey of U.S. workers conducted in 1977, only 17 percent of them said the work they do "is meaningful to me." By contrast, in 2002, the percentage was 66 percent. Likewise, the percentage of workers answering "my job lets me use my skills and abilities" jumped from 28 percent to 68 percent.[17] In Europe, research carried out within the past decade has shown highly positive results for jobs that make effective use of employees'

Motivators
Intrinsic Factors
Related to the
Doing of the
Job Itself

Neither Satisfied nor Dissatisfied

**Hygiene
Factors**
Extrinsic
Factors Related
to Conditions
Surrounding
the Job

EXHIBIT 9.5

Herzberg's Two-factor Theory: Differential Effects of Hygiene Factors and Motivators

job enrichment
increasing the complexity of a job to provide a greater sense of responsibility, accomplishment, and achievement

job characteristics model
an approach that focuses on the motivational attributes of jobs by emphasizing three sets of variables: core job characteristics, critical psychological states, and outcomes

EXHIBIT 9.6 Job Characteristics Model

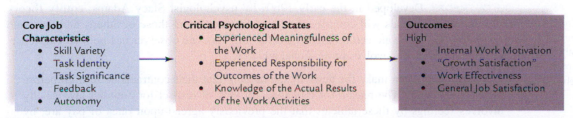

Core Job Characteristics	Critical Psychological States	Outcomes
• Skill Variety • Task Identity • Task Significance • Feedback • Autonomy	• Experienced Meaningfulness of the Work • Experienced Responsibility for Outcomes of the Work • Knowledge of the Actual Results of the Work Activities	High • Internal Work Motivation • "Growth Satisfaction" • Work Effectiveness • General Job Satisfaction

Source: Adapted from J. R. Hackman and G. R. Oldham, *Work Redesign* (Reading: Addison-Wesley, 1980).

EXHIBIT 9.7 Core Job Characteristics in Job Characteristics Model

Core Job Characteristics	Definition	Example
Skill variety	The degree to which a job requires a variety of different activities in carrying out the work, involving the use of a number of different skills and talents of the person.	The aerospace engineer must be able to create blueprints, calculate tolerances, provide leadership to the work group, and give presentations to upper management.
Task identity	The degree to which a job requires completion of a "whole" and identifiable piece of work, that is, doing a job from beginning to end with a visible outcome.	The event manager handles all the plans for the annual executive retreat, attends the retreat, and receives information on its success from the participants.
Task significance	The degree to which a job has a substantial impact on the lives of other people, whether those people are in the immediate organization or in the world at large.	The finance manager devises a new benefits plan to improve health coverage for all employees.
Autonomy	The degree to which a job provides substantial freedom, independence, and discretion to the individual in scheduling the work and in determining the procedures to be used in carrying it out.	R&D scientists are linked via the company intranet, allowing them to post their ideas, ask questions, and propose solutions at any hour of the day, whether at the office, at home, or on the road.
Feedback from job	The degree to which carrying out the work activities required by the job provides the individual with direct and clear information about the effectiveness of his or her performance.	The lathe operator knows he is cutting his pieces correctly, as very few are rejected by the workers in the next production area.

Source: Adapted from J. Richard Hackman and Greg R. Oldham, *Work Redesign* (Reading, MA: Addison-Wesley, 1980).

personal resources, such as optimism and self-esteem, and that couple those individual resources with those provided by the organization and manager, such as helpful coaching and increased autonomy where appropriate.[18] The researchers term this increased "work engagement."

The bottom-line message is that if those in managerial positions can create or adjust jobs to include more of the "core characteristics" (see Exhibit 9.7), and use more of the personal resources that subordinates bring to the work situation they may be able to increase both the motivation and satisfaction of many of those who work for them. A useful way for managers, who often have highly enriched jobs themselves, to think about enriching the jobs of their subordinates is to make those jobs more like their own!

Process Theories

process theories

motivation theories dealing with the way different variables combine to influence the amount of effort people put forth

A **process theory** of work motivation deals with the way different variables combine to influence the amount of effort people put forth. In other words, whereas content theories focus on *which* variables affect motivation, process theories focus on *how* the variables affect it. The four most prominent types of process theories are: equity theory, expectancy theory, social cognitive theory, and goal-setting theory. We discuss each next.

equity theory

a motivation theory proposing that individuals will compare their circumstances to those of others and that such comparisons may motivate certain kinds of behavior

EQUITY THEORY Developed in the early 1960s by psychologist Stacy Adams, **equity theory** proposes that individuals will compare their circumstances with those of others, and that such comparisons may motivate certain kinds of behavior.[19] As one observer has pointed out, a particularly vivid example involves professional athletes:

(Such) athletes often make the news by demanding that their contracts be torn up before their terms expire. The reason for this apparent lack of respect for contract law usually involves feelings by these athletes that the previously agreed-upon rates of pay are, by some standard, no longer "fair."[20]

EXHIBIT 9.8 Basics of Equity Theory

If	Is	Then	And I Am Motivated to
The ratio of my outcomes to my inputs	Equal to the ratio of the other's outcomes to inputs	I am satisfied	Do nothing
The ratio of my outcomes to my inputs	Less than (<) the ratio of the others' outcomes to inputs	I feel dissatisfied (inequity)	Choose between • Increasing my own outcomes • Decreasing my own inputs • Reevaluating the others' inputs • Changing the referent • Leaving the situation

Equity theory, as shown in Exhibit 9.8, assumes that people know what kind of effort and skills they put into their jobs and what kinds of outcomes (salary, promotions, etc.) they receive from their employer. The theory also assumes that individuals are likely to compare (a) the *ratios* of inputs to outcomes they receive to (b) the *ratios* of other people like their colleagues or acquaintances (within, or outside, their organization). Such comparisons determine whether the individual feels equitably treated. The most important assumption—as in the example of the professional athletes just cited—is that if the comparisons result in feelings of inequity in favor of the other persons, the individual making the observation will be motivated to take steps to reduce these feelings.

Equity theory states that people have a number of ways to reduce their feelings that others are "doing better" than they are. One way is to increase their outcomes, such as getting a salary increase or obtaining a promotion. Another response might be to decrease their inputs; for example, they might try to put less effort in the task and still receive the same level of outcomes, if possible. A third action might be to leave their jobs.

If people do not think they are being rewarded equitably, they have other ways of dealing with the situation. They might simply change the object of their comparison—that is, they might decide to compare themselves to different people, for example, neighbors instead of work colleagues. This involves no change of behavior but only a change in the way of looking at a situation. Likewise, people might reevaluate the inputs and outcomes of those with whom they are comparing themselves and rationalize that "she has more skills than I thought she did" or "his job isn't as good as I thought it was."

Unfortunately, equity theory has not been very successful in predicting *which* method people will use in a specific situation. However, the chief value of this theory is that it highlights the importance of how people's perceptions of equity, in comparison to others' circumstances, can affect their motivation. In effect, equity theory emphasizes the "social" nature of motivation.

(It should also be pointed out that comparisons can result in feelings of inequity that favor the observer. In that case, an individual could take steps, such as increasing one's own inputs, to reduce the perceived inequity. However, the common-sense assumption is that this kind of situation—where the other person's ratio of outcome to inputs is perceived as being worse than one's own—will occur relatively infrequently.)

EXPECTANCY THEORY Psychologist Victor Vroom formulated a motivation theory applicable to work settings that is based on people's expectations.[21] Although details of **expectancy theory** can get complicated, the basics are easy to understand, and Exhibit 9.9 diagrams them.

Expectancy theory focuses on the thought processes people use when they face particular choices among alternatives, particularly alternative courses of action. Simplified, the theory proposes that two kinds of beliefs affect the amount of effort people will choose to put forth. One such belief, (typically referred to as an *expectancy*), effort-to-performance, symbolized as ($E \rightarrow P$), is the probability that a certain amount of effort will lead to a certain level of

expectancy theory
motivation theory that focuses on the thought processes people use when choosing among alternative courses of action with their anticipated consequences

EXHIBIT 9.9

**Components of
Expectancy Theory**

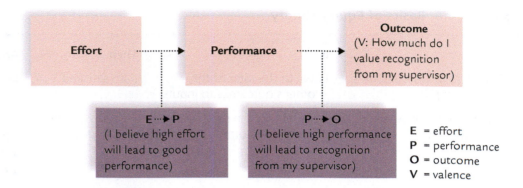

performance: "If I try to do this, will I succeed?" The other belief (often called an *instrumentality belief*), performance-to-outcome, symbolized as ($P \rightarrow O$), is the probability that a particular level of performance will lead to (will be instrumental in obtaining) particular outcomes or consequences: "If I succeed, will I get praise from the boss?" The third key variable in the theory is the valence (V), or the anticipated value a person attaches to an outcome: "How much will I like praise from the boss if I get it?" If the valence of rewards offered is high, there is potential for increased motivation; likewise, if the anticipated value of those rewards is low, or the offered rewards are seen as irrelevant, motivation is likely to be weak.

Expectancy theory states that the three key variables interact in a multiplicative, not additive, manner to determine the amount of effort people will choose to expend on a particular task:

$$\text{Effort} = (E \rightarrow P) \times (P \rightarrow O) \times V$$

Since, according to the theory, these three variables are multiplied to determine the level of effort, a low value of any one of the three would result in very low motivation. For example, even if a sales representative strongly believes that a certain level of performance (like meeting a sales quota) will lead to a very desirable reward (like a bonus), her motivation will be low if she does not also have a strong expectation that her effort will lead to that level of performance. To restate: Both expectancies *and* the anticipated value of the outcome must be high for a person to be highly motivated.

A number of implications for managerial practice flow from this theory. For each of the theory's three key variables, managers can take steps to increase employee motivation. For example, the $E \rightarrow P$ expectancy can be modified in a variety of ways: If a person believes he doesn't have the skills needed to reach a certain level of performance, these perceptions can be changed. His manager might encourage him to get additional training and further practice, and by appropriately guiding and counseling him, build his confidence (thereby influencing his $E \rightarrow P$ expectancy). Employees who believe they are capable of performing well will be more motivated to achieve their goals.[22] See the accompanying Manager's Challenge, "Sales Potential All Bottled Up," for an illustration of this principle.

Additionally, by consistently recognizing employees' accomplishments, managers can increase those employees' perceptions of the probability of obtaining a desired outcome if they have performed well (thereby influencing the $P \rightarrow O$ expectancy). How many times, however, do employees perform at a level strongly desired by the organization only to find that, from their perspective, the organization ignores or does not sufficiently recognize their accomplishment? If this happens continually, their level of motivation is certain to decrease.

On the other hand, the reverse is true: If difficult but desired levels of performance are reached and the supervisor or organization recognizes it in an explicit way, future levels of motivation can be increased. Employees are more motivated to perform well when they have a very strong belief that they will be rewarded.

Two organizational examples illustrate how $P \rightarrow O$ beliefs can be strengthened to provide positive motivational consequences: At Informa, a global business information service provider doing business in more than 30 countries, the number of available awards attached to high levels of performance has increased over recent years. As the director of Human Resources for the

A MANAGER'S CHALLENGE

GLOBALIZATION

Sales Potential All Bottled Up

Mark Johnson (a real person whose name we have changed) was in a panic. He was meeting with his company's Asia Pacific regional president in less than two weeks, and he would have to explain to him why sales were down 15 percent and profits were down 40 percent in the six months since Johnson arrived.

Johnson was the managing director of a joint venture (JV) between Pepsi and a formerly state-owned enterprise that made and bottled carbonated cola and noncarbonated fruit beverages in Vietnam. The JV was established to bottle and distribute Pepsi beverages initially in southern Vietnam and eventually throughout the entire country. To everyone's delight, the JV did well during the first couple of years of operation. During that time, the JV's managers focused on the existing customers of the Vietnamese partner. These customers were other state-owned enterprises. Johnson was sent to the JV in its third year of operation in large part to add a consumer-focused marketing and distribution strategy to the initial institutional base of customers.

Soon after his arrival, sales and profits began to decline. When Johnson asked his sales manager, marketing manager, and individual salesmen why sales and profits were declining, they simply shrugged their shoulders or blamed the rainy season. Johnson was totally frustrated. The targets for consumer sales were clear. The commissions that salesmen would receive if they hit their sales targets were very lucrative by Vietnamese standards. With unemployment at 12 percent, Johnson could not understand how the Vietnamese salesmen would not be motivated by the reward system.

In a bit of desperation, Johnson went with one of the salesmen on some sales calls. What he discovered amazed him. First, even though his Vietnamese was not good, he could tell that the salesman was not comfortable with cold calls (calling on a new customer for the first time). Second,

it was clear that Vietnam's distribution and retail industries were significantly more fragmented than in the United States. Therefore, to achieve a particular volume of sales, a salesman in Vietnam might have to make 10 times as many sales calls. Johnson also discovered that most of the roads outside the main cities of Vietnam were dirt; during the rainy season they became almost impassable for the motorcycles and bicycles that were the primary means of delivering products to retailers.

Although the salesmen acknowledged the performance expectations and lucrative rewards they would receive for meeting their targets, they were not motivated to try very hard. Why? Because they did not believe they had what it took to be successful. They knew how to deal with long-established institutional customers and take orders, but they had little experience making cold calls to small distributors and retailers.

Consequently, Johnson decided to use the JV's existing salespeople to continue to sell to institutional customers but hire a different type of person for consumer sales and marketing. For these new salespeople, one of the solutions to the motivational issue was to provide them with the information, training, and skills they needed—for example, procedures for making cold calls and how to become more efficient in consumer distribution activities. In effect, Johnson had to strengthen their effort to performance, $E \rightarrow P$, expectancies. This increased their beliefs that they could hit their sales targets with the new customers and, consequently, obtain the promised rewards.

As a result of these successful steps, sales increased substantially, and Johnson has been promoted to a larger job in the region.

Source: Personal communications to author, J. S. Black, 1998–2010.

company puts it, "As the business has developed and key performance issues have emerged, we have launched new award categories, such as 'best new initiatives in finance.' [and] 'best editorial scoop of the year.' People want to work for an organization that rewards in the broadest sense of the word."[23] Some years ago, Google launched its Founders' Awards, which can amount to millions of dollars per award in restricted stock and are given for special accomplishments. Some winning teams have had as few as a dozen or so members splitting an award. Recent winners of these awards have included the teams that developed the browser Chrome (30 million new users in its first year), Gmail, and Google Maps.[24]

The following points sum up, from an expectancy theory perspective, the key ways that managers—not just the organization as a whole—can potentially influence employees' motivation:

- Identify rewards that are valued.
- Strengthen subordinates' beliefs that their efforts will lead to valued rewards.
- Clarify subordinates' understanding of exactly where they should direct their efforts.
- Make sure the desired rewards under your control are given directly following particular levels of performance.
- Provide a level and amount of rewards that are consistent with a realistic level of expected rewards.

One final issue relating to expectancy theory should be noted: Cultural circumstances can affect its application. For instance, in certain countries in the Middle East where there is a strong emphasis on fate, attempts to change effort $\rightarrow$ performance ($E \rightarrow P$) expectancies might not succeed. Likewise, attempts to single out an individual for public praise in collectivistic cultures, such as those that exist in many Asian or Latin American countries, would not be as likely to motivate employees as it would in Germany or Australia, where individualism is a stronger cultural characteristic. (Recall from Chapter 3 our discussion of the "individualism–collectivism" dimension of culture.) A motivational approach that considers how people calculate the potential personal benefits of pursuing one course of action over another seems more relevant to most Western cultures than to cultures that place less emphasis on personal gain.

Although the psychological processes described in expectancy theory are not necessarily culturally bound, since they can occur anywhere, the frequency with which they occur probably is. For any culture, however, the key point is that expectancy theory is probably most useful in helping to understand and predict levels of motivation that involve deliberate choices in the amount of effort to be put forth, rather than forecasting routine behavior that is largely determined by habit.

SOCIAL COGNITIVE THEORY A process theory closely related to expectancy theory, and one that has received considerable recent attention among organizational scholars, is **social cognitive theory (SCT),** developed by social psychologist Albert Bandura. For our purposes, we will concentrate on one key component of SCT: **self-efficacy.** It can be defined as "an individual's... confidence about his or her abilities to mobilize motivation, cognitive resources, and courses of action needed to successfully execute a specific task within a given context."[25] In other words, self-efficacy is the extent to which a person believes he or she can accomplish a given task in a specific situation. It is roughly the equivalent of the $E \rightarrow P$ expectancy in expectancy theory. Such a belief has three dimensions: magnitude (how difficult the task to be accomplished is), strength (the certainty of its accomplishment), and generality (the extent to which similar but not identical tasks can be accomplished). Research to date appears to show conclusively that when individuals have high self-efficacy beliefs, their work-related performance is better.[26]

From a managerial perspective, you should be asking yourself this question: How can a person's self-efficacy beliefs be increased? As shown in Exhibit 9.10, SCT proposes four major determinants:

- **Enactive Mastery Experience:** Succeeding on a similar prior task *and* attributing that success to one's own capabilities rather than to luck or circumstances.
- **Vicarious Learning/Modeling:** Knowledge gained by observing or learning how others successfully perform a task and then modeling one's own behavior in a similar manner.
- **Verbal Persuasion:** Statements from others that convince a person that he or she can successfully perform the task.
- **Physiological and Psychological Arousal:** Potential energizing forces that can increase self-efficacy beliefs if the focus is directed to the task.

It should be clear from this discussion that managers have several different ways to influence positively the self-efficacy of their employees. Managers can create opportunities for employees to exhibit enactive mastery by taking on and succeeding in difficult tasks that they may have been

social cognitive theory

A process theory that, in part, describes how to increase an individual's sense of self-efficacy, thus increasing motivation

self-efficacy

an individual's confidence about his or her abilities to mobilize motivation, cognitive resources, and courses of action needed to successfully execute a specific task within a given context

EXHIBIT 9.10

Social Cognitive Theory: Methods to Increase an Individual's Feelings of Self-efficacy

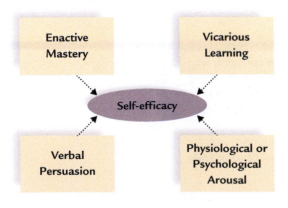

initially reluctant to try to do. They can model successful behavior for their direct reports or arrange working conditions so that they can learn from those employees most experienced and competent at the task. Managers can attempt to convince employees that they should be able to do a task successfully, but this is not always easy to do. And, they can try to increase employees' energy levels by inspiring them or directing their emotions toward specific task accomplishments. An essential point to keep in mind is that these various approaches to increasing others' self-efficacy are not mutually exclusive. Several of them can be used together.

GOAL-SETTING A somewhat different type of process theory that has attracted considerable research attention in recent years is **goal-setting theory**.[27] "Goal-setting theory assumes that human action is directed by conscious goals and intentions."[28] Therefore, as Elizabeth Hayes learned in her supervisory position at AOL, if managers can influence goals and intentions, they can directly affect performance.[29] The level at which goals are set is a potentially powerful determinant of motivation, and obtaining a person's commitment to particular goals is crucial.[30]

goal-setting theory
a theory that emphasizes the role of conscious goals and intentions in directing human actions

The findings from goal-setting research point to two basic conclusions:

- More challenging (higher or harder) goals, if accepted, result in higher levels of effort than easier goals.
- Specific goals result in higher levels of effort than general or vague goals.[31]

These two principles in action were illustrated by a manager of a retail store when she used specific goals to motivate her employees to increase their sales during the holiday season. She decided to post the sales numbers from the previous season and the sales goal for the current season where everyone could see them. In this way, she thought the sales personnel would be motivated to improve. She was gratified when the first day's sales level showed a 40 percent increase over the same day a year before, which was even higher than the percentage increase she had set as a goal.[32] Similarly, a recent study carried out in several Dutch organizations showed that when supervisors set both specific and relatively high goals for subordinates to learn new skills and knowledge, those employees were highly motivated to do so—especially when supervisors also provided appropriate learning opportunities to do so.[33]

Of course, with the particular feature of goal difficulty, several cautions are in order. The most obvious one is that goals can be set so excessively and unrealistically high that they bring on discouragement and decreased, rather than increased, motivation. However, it is not always easy to distinguish between what will be seen as a challenging difficult goal, in one instance, and an excessively difficult goal that subordinates would see as a totally inappropriate and thus de-motivating in another situation. Also, in many work situations there is often more than a single goal that needs to be accomplished. Consequently, if too many specific but difficult goals are set, organization members may face too many conflicting demands at one time and simply select one to pursue and ignore the others. Here, again, it is the total combination of number of goals together with degree of goal difficulty that will be the deciding factor in affecting both the amount and direction of motivation.[34] The accompanying table in Exhibit 9.11 poses a set of useful questions for managers to ask themselves before starting on goal-setting activities with those who report to them, and indicates why these questions are important to consider. The major conclusion regarding all of the research that has been carried out to date on goal-setting is that it offers potential advantages for motivating increased performance, but it is definitely not a simple panacea suitable for all occasions and in all types of situations.

Reinforcements and Consequences

Events that happen to people following their behavior—the consequence of their performance—can reinforce their tendencies to continue or discontinue that behavior.[35] The consequences can be positive, neutral, or negative and can vary from insignificant to overwhelming. The deliberate and appropriate application of them, however, provides a manager with a potentially powerful set of motivational tools.

Reinforcement Approaches

The two principal approaches that can be used to increase the probability of behavior desired by the manager or organization are positive and negative reinforcements, which are discussed next.

EXHIBIT 9.11 Questions to Ask Before Engaging in Goal-setting with Employees

Question	Why is this an important question?
Is the goal too specific?	The focus may be so narrow that important other features of the task environment unrelated to the specific goal are overlooked.
Is the goal too challenging?	Failure to meet the goal may harm the employee's motivation and self-efficacy, and can cause risk taking.
Who sets the goal?	Although individuals become more committed to goals they help set, sometimes they have a tendency to set easy goals for themselves.
How many goals should be set?	Individuals tend to concentrate on one goal at a time, particularly on those goals that are less difficult and can be easily measured.
Should the goal be short- or long-term?	A focus on achieving short-term goals can interfere with long-term performance.
Should I use a standard goal for all workers or tailor them to individual differences?	Because of the number of individual differences between workers, standardized goals may be ineffective; however, goals differentiated for individual abilities may appear unfair and may also harm cooperation.
Is this individual intrinsically motivated?	Goal setting can reduce motivation when an individual is intrinsically motivated.
Should this goal be focused on performance or on learning?	When employees focus closely on performance goals, they may not search for new strategies and may fail to learn.

Based on L. D. Ordonez, M. E. Schweitzer, A. D. Galinsky, and M. H. Bazerman, "Goals Gone Wild: The Systematic Side Effects of Overprescribing Goal Setting," *Academy of Management Perspectives* 23 (2009): 6–16.

positive reinforcement

a desirable consequence that, by occurring or being supplied following a behavior, increases the likelihood of that behavior being repeated in the future

POSITIVE REINFORCEMENTS A **positive reinforcement,** sometimes referred to as a reward, is a desirable consequence that increases the likelihood of a behavior being repeated in the future. In many instances, the use of positive reinforcements, such as a manager praising an employee for good performance, strengthens the likelihood of that behavior in the future, especially if the subordinate does not see such praise as routine or insincere. However, positive consequences also can inadvertently reinforce behavior that is not wanted.[36] For example, an employee might take a risky shortcut to achieve an important performance goal. If the employee's manager does not realize that the shortcut behavior occurred and congratulates the person for reaching the goal, the risky behavior is also being reinforced.[37]

Another example of a manager's unintended reinforcement of the "wrong" behavior occurred in a public relations firm. The head of the firm gave his staff the task of producing a report on their company's history to celebrate the firm's tenth anniversary. The staff members, who often procrastinated when it came to routine tasks, underestimated the time the project would require and were in danger of falling behind. The deadline could not be put off, however, so the head of the firm allowed them to drop all their other work and even hired temps to help them. After a chaotic race to the finish line, the project was done and the head of the company gave the staff a bonus to reward them for their hard work. Given these facts, it is not hard to guess what the staff members learned about the effects of their procrastination. The example demonstrates how easy it is for managers to positively reinforce undesirable behavior with the best of intentions.

One of the foremost scholarly experts on the use of rewards, Steven Kerr, suggests that for positive reinforcements (rewards) to effectively motivate people in organizational settings, the rewards should be:

- **Equitable:** The size of rewards should be roughly related to the quality and/or quantity of past job-related performance.
- **Efficient:** The rewards must have some capacity to affect future performance; for example, by making clear that a particular level of future performance will lead to a desired reward.

■ *Available (capable of being given):* Managers and organizations should not talk about or offer rewards that are not readily available, or are available in such small amounts that the recipients view them as not really rewarding at all. As Kerr states: "Organizations with minuscule salary increase pools spend hundreds of management hours rating, ranking, and grading employees, only to waste time, raise expectations, and ultimately produce such pitiful increases that everybody is disappointed and embarrassed."

■ *Not exclusive:* The possibility of obtaining rewards should not be limited to only a small percentage of employees. The more people that are "ineligible," or excluded from the possibility of obtaining the rewards, the less likely a given reward will have a wide-spread motivational effect.

■ *Visible:* The rewards should be visible not only to recipients but also to others who possibly could obtain them in the future.

■ *Reversible:* This does not refer to a reward that can be taken away once given. Rather, it refers to rewards that can be denied or not given in the future, if circumstances warrant. The classic example is a bonus. Unlike an annual pay raise, a bonus can clearly be a one-time-only reward. It also is a type of reward that can be given again in the future. That feature provides managers with a great deal of flexibility.[38]

NEGATIVE REINFORCEMENTS The *removal* of undesirable, or negative, consequences—that is, consequences a person performing an act does not want—can increase the likelihood of that behavior being repeated in the future. Removing undesirable consequences is referred to as **negative reinforcement,** just as the addition of desirable consequences is called a positive reinforcement. In both cases, they are reinforcing if they cause behavior to be maintained or increased. For example, a salesperson working in a sales territory with very difficult and demanding customers finds that, by putting in extra effort, the unpleasant experiences he has been encountering are reduced when he is transferred to a different territory. If he believes the transfer or promotion was a result of his hard work, the removal of the undesirable consequences (the difficult territory with difficult customers) has reinforced the likelihood that he will try hard to please his customers in his new territory. In this instance, both the company and the salesperson benefited from the negative reinforcement.

Negative reinforcements, however, can also work against the best interests of the organization. For example, if a supervisor finds that giving a particular subordinate an "average" rating results in avoiding unpleasant confrontations with the person that have occurred in the past—when the subordinate was given well-deserved "below-average" ratings—the supervisor's current action is negatively reinforced. Thus, the supervisor will likely continue to give the subordinate "average" ratings, while the subordinate's performance will probably continue to be sub-par.

Both of these reinforcement mechanisms—positive reinforcements and negative reinforcements—*maintain or increase* particular types of behavior and performance. Thus, they provide managers with potentially potent ways to motivate desired behavior. However, if care is not taken, their use instead can lead to the continuation of behavior that isn't wanted. In contrast to these two reinforcement mechanisms for maintaining or enhancing particular behaviors, managers can use two other methods involving consequences, discussed next, to *decrease* the probability of behaviors occurring.

PUNISHMENTS A **punishment** is an unwanted consequence that follows undesirable behavior that is intended to decrease the likelihood of that behavior being repeated. In some organizations, punishments are seen as an effective way to prevent unwanted behavior. However, many other organizations discourage punishment, often because their use is seen as either inappropriate or ineffective. Also, punishment can have the inadvertent effect of increasing behavior that isn't wanted. For example, punishing employees for absenteeism may result in more sophisticated excuses rather than better attendance. This example illustrates that it is typically quite difficult in organizations to make sure that punishments have only the intended effects managers want—and no reinforcement of undesirable behavior.

There are also many examples in organizations of punishment administered inadvertently, with possible undesirable consequences. These include giving increasing responsibility to someone who has shown that she can handle stress, or giving additional committee assignments to the person who

negative reinforcement
an undesirable consequence that, by being removed or avoided following a behavior, increases the likelihood of that behavior being repeated in the future

punishment
an undesirable consequence given following a behavior to decrease the likelihood it will be repeated

has shown that he is exceptionally dependable in meeting commitments. Unless a manager is highly alert, unintended punishments happen more often than might be expected.

extinction

the absence of positive consequences for behavior, lessening the likelihood of that behavior occurring in the future

EXTINCTION Another way to decrease undesirable behaviors is to avoid providing any positive consequences as the result of that behavior. This process is referred to as **extinction.** It is a well-demonstrated research finding, and a fact of everyday work life, that behaviors that do not lead to positive reinforcements tend not to be repeated, or at least not repeated as much. Managers can use the principle of extinction to their advantage by deliberately not reinforcing employee behavior that they consider undesirable. For example, a manager deliberately might refrain from reacting positively to a tasteless joke.

However, using extinction poses two challenges for managers. One is the inadvertent lack of attention to rewarding behavior that the manager should reinforce. A typical example of this in manufacturing organizations often occurs with respect to safety behavior. Frequently, supervisors take for granted safe work behavior and do not explicitly reinforce it. As a result, because safe behavior usually requires extra time and effort, employees gradually lose motivation to take these extra steps, and eventually an accident occurs. Another common example of the unintentional application of the principle of extinction occurs when an employee puts in extra effort on a key project but receives little or no recognition or acknowledgment from the boss. In this case, the employee is not likely to be motivated to behave similarly on the next key project—nor will other employees who observed the lack of response to the extra effort.

The second potential hazard of either the deliberate or unintended use of extinction is that it can leave the interpretation of important situations in the hands of employees rather than under the control of the manager. By contrast, explicit reinforcements and punishments provide employees with clear, or at least clearer, information regarding what their managers view as desirable or undesirable behavior and performance.

Exhibit 9.12 summarizes the effects of each of these approaches to the use of reinforcements.

Planned Programs of Positive Reinforcement

Organizations often institute programs to apply systematically the principles of reinforcement theory (often called *behavior modification* or *applied behavior analysis* programs). These programs involve four basic steps:

1. Specify desired performance precisely. (Example: "Lower and keep the accident rate below 1 percent.")
2. Measure desired behaviors. (Example: "Monitor safety actions A, B, C.")

EXHIBIT 9.12 Reinforcement Approaches and Their Effects

Reinforcement Approach	Managerial Action	Effect	Example
Positive reinforcement	Provide desirable consequence	Increase probability of behavior being repeated	Highway construction supervisor receives bonus for each day a project is completed ahead of schedule.
Negative reinforcement	Remove undesirable consequence	Increase probability of behavior being repeated	Management stops raising output quotas each time workers exceed them.
Punishment	Provide undesirable consequence	Decrease probability of behavior being repeated	Habitually tardy crew member is fined the equivalent of one hour's pay each day he is late to work.
Extinction	Removable desirable consequence	Decrease probability of behavior being repeated	Group member stops making unsolicited suggestions when team leader no longer mentions them in group meetings.

3. Provide frequent positive consequences for specified behaviors. (Example: "Give semiannual monetary rewards for performing a procedure safely 100 percent of the time.")
4. Evaluate the effectiveness of the program. (Example: "Were accidents kept below 1 percent over the previous six-month period?") Then make progress public knowledge.[39]

Programs of this type have been effective in a wide variety of work settings and in parts of the world as diverse as the Middle East, Europe, and the United States.[40] It should be emphasized, though, that formal programs aren't needed for reinforcement methods to be effective. *Any* person in a managerial position can use these methods. They will be likely to have their greatest effect on the third of the three elements that make up the definition of motivation—the persistence of behavior.

How the Situation Influences Motivation

Although the point is sometimes overlooked, understanding motivation involves more than simply analyzing individual behavior. If we are concerned about behavior in work settings, then it is crucial to recognize—as emphasized in Exhibit 9.1—the powerful influence the situational context has on motivated behavior,

Influence of the Immediate Work Group

The immediate work group affects many aspects of a person's behavior, particularly motivation. This is especially true for organizations operating in cultures and countries that have strong collectivist tendencies, such as those in Asia and Latin America.[41] In these cultures, the individual is likely to be heavily influenced by the **in-group,** that is, the group to which the person belongs, but less influenced by others who are not members of the in-group. Nonetheless, in almost any culture or organization, depending upon the circumstances, groups can strongly influence the motivation of individual members.

in-group
the group to which an individual belongs

What are those circumstances? Primarily, they involve (1) the existence of a group in which an individual is a member, the in-group, and especially (2) the strong desire of the person to be part of that group and to receive that group's approval. When this situation exists, the group's influence almost certainly will affect the level of effort or motivation a person exerts.

The direction of a group's influence on motivation will likely depend on its norms—the group's expected standards of behavior for its individual members. When those norms support the organization's goals, the group is likely to increase the motivation of its members to perform. When the norms oppose the organization's objectives, the group is likely to decrease the motivation of its members to perform. And, as originally demonstrated in a study many years ago, the more cohesive a group is, the more it can affect performance motivation in either direction—up or down.[42] (Group norms will be discussed in detail in the following chapter.)

A person's work group can affect motivational aspects of her work behavior other than just the level of performance. For example, a study of teenage workers in fast-food restaurants demonstrated that when an employee decided to leave the organization, it increased (not decreased) the desire of close friends to continue working at the restaurant. Although such a result might seem unexpected, the researchers explained the finding by hypothesizing that the friends who remained working at the restaurant had to reexamine ("justify") their reasons for staying, which resulted in a stronger determination to do so.[43] Thus, the social influence of the work-group friends in this study clearly affected the motivation of at least one type of behavior: staying with the organization.

Influence of Supervisors and Subordinates

Supervisors and subordinates, not just work-group peers, are also critical parts of the immediate social environment that can influence employee motivation—either positively or negatively. The impact of supervisors or leaders on the motivation of their employees is directly linked to their control of powerful rewards and potential punishments, as we discussed earlier. It is also strongly connected to their role in setting expectations for particular levels of employee performance, as we saw in the discussion of the effects of goal setting. In many instances, those working for the supervisor will be strongly motivated to try to meet those specifically identified objectives.[44] Additionally, managers can impact employee motivation in such realms as creativity and innovation by deliberately structuring the work environment to encourage that kind of behavior.[45]

It is also important to emphasize, however, that the motivational impact of someone in a supervisory position is not the same for all subordinates; it is often, in fact uneven. The same supervisor can be a source of increased motivation for some employees and a source of dampened motivation for others. Much depends on the one-on-one interpersonal relationships supervisors develop over time with each of their subordinates.

Subordinates can also influence the motivation of their superiors, especially through their ability to punish behavior by subtly withholding rewards. Although subordinates typically do not have the same amount of reward-punishment leverage as their superiors, they are not powerless. For example, they could withhold some specialized expertise only they have (and their supervisor does not) if they are not pleased with an action of the supervisor. A systems analyst, unhappy with the assignment she has been given, could resist pointing out some key technical details to her boss. Although such behavior is unlikely to be overt, it can affect the supervisor's motivation to act in the future in ways that produce these kinds of reactions.

Influence of the Organization's Culture

Not to be overlooked is the impact of an organization's culture on employees' motivation.[46] This influence is exercised primarily through norms—in this case, how the organization expects its employees to behave. Just as with a peer group, the more an individual wants to remain part of an organization, the more he or she will be influenced by that organization's culture. The organization can be considered simply a larger type of group, with its culture often having a less direct influence on employee motivation than the immediate work group, but an influence nonetheless. Organizations that have gone through mergers or acquisitions know only too well how the imposition of an unfamiliar corporate culture can have potentially devastating effects on the motivation of the members of the "new" entity.[47]

The Influence of Values and Attitudes Toward Work

No analysis of motivation in the work setting can be complete without considering how people's values and fundamental attitudes affect their work. These values and attitudes are especially sensitive to cultural differences within a country or across countries. Thus, to understand motivational issues in an international workforce or a diverse domestic workforce, managers need to pay attention to these differences.

Values

Chapter 3 already provided a general discussion of culture and cultural values. With that as a backdrop, we can look at the role of those values as they specifically affect motivation. Values can influence goals and intentions. They also affect what kinds of behaviors individuals will find rewarding and satisfying.[48]

Different cultures put different weights on particular values. Exhibit 9.13 shows how one set of scholars summarizes core value differences among three cultures from diverse parts of the world: American, Japanese, and Arabic.[49] The valence (desirability) of different rewards would be quite different across these three cultures. Thus, from an expectancy theory framework of motivation, for example, managers supervising employees from these three cultures would need to consider the types of rewards to offer in return for high levels of performance.

EXHIBIT 9.13 Differences in Core Values Among Three Cultures

	American	**Japanese**	**Arabic**
Core Values	Competition	Group harmony	Reputation
	Risk-taking	Belonging	Family security
	Material possessions		Religious belief
	Freedom		Social recognition

Source: Reproduced by permission. Adapted from Farid Elashmawi and Philip R. Harris, *Multicultural Management 2000* (Houston: Gulf Publishing Company, 1998), Table 3. All rights reserved.

To illustrate how cultural values can motivate particular behaviors, recall from Chapter 3 that *individualism* is the subordination of a group's goals to a person's own goals, whereas *collectivism* is the subordination of personal goals to the goals of a group.[50] An interesting line of research dealing with this dimension of culture as it affects motivation was carried out with Asian and American college students. The research project compared the preferences of the two sets of subjects for allocating rewards to members of work groups: according to "equality" (every member gets an equal share of the rewards) or according to "equity" (members are rewarded in proportion to their individual contributions). The findings showed that although both Asian and American college students generally preferred equity as the basis for rewards, students from Hong Kong and Korean backgrounds tended to put relatively more emphasis on equality than did the Americans. This is in line with the basic hypothesis that those who are raised in a culture that values collectivism will be influenced by this value when put into a work situation. They will be more likely than those raised in an individualistic culture to consider the needs of everyone in the group, even if this means deviating somewhat from the generally preferred equity reward allocation. The research also showed that while Asian student subjects had a greater tendency to use equality as a basis for allocating rewards to in-group members, they did not necessarily extend this tendency to members of out-groups. Thus, Asian students were apparently distinguishing clearly between those two types of groups.[51]

Attitudes Toward Work

Understanding how different groups or cultures view the meaning of work, that is, how much the activity of working is valued, helps us to gain additional insight into motivational differences across cultures. The famous sociologist Max Weber was one of the first persons to point out these differences. Weber contended that in the "Christian" countries of his era (the late nineteenth and early twentieth centuries), Protestant religious values emphasized hard work and the accumulation of wealth. This idea led him to coin the well-known phrase *Protestant work ethic.*[52] According to Weber, many people in the United States and in northern European countries were assumed to be guided by such an ethic, whether or not they were literally Protestants.

A body of scholarly research carried out in the last decades of the twentieth century on the meaning of work focused especially on **work centrality,** defined as "the degree of general importance that working has in the life of an individual at a point in time."[53] To measure work centrality, researchers asked working adults to rate the importance of work to them and also to compare its importance to other major life roles such as leisure, family, and religion. The findings indicated that in that time period work was relatively more important and more central to people's lives in Japan than it was in Israel, Germany, and the United States.[54]

work centrality
the degree of general importance that working has in the life of an individual at a point in time

A key issue related to work centrality is the relative balance that employees experience between the effort they devote to their jobs, on the one hand, and that which they give to their responsibilities and opportunities in non-work circumstances such as family life and recreational pursuits. Achieving an acceptable work-life balance, as this concern is termed, appears to be important to many people across different cultures, although not necessarily equally so.[55] For example, as one expert put it, "Work-family conflict is much higher in the United States than elsewhere in the developed world. One reason is that Americans work longer hours than in most other developed countries, including Japan."[56]

The work-life balance issue is salient for managers and professionals, as well as for non-managers. For instance, a study of Australian managers showed that a number of them were troubled about the increasing extent to which stress and fatigue from their jobs was intruding on their non-work lives. One manager commented: "There is a grey blur, especially with the advent of [cell] phones and home [computers], etc. I have a client who regularly calls me at 6:30 a.m. or earlier. The same person started calling my wife at 7:30 p.m. on weekdays because he couldn't instantly track me down in the office." Another noted, "Although we have excellent work/life [policies], it often depends on who the manager is at the time as to what their expectations are. Sure, we have the option to say no to additional hours, but you can pretty much assume your career won't progress as fast as those who are willing to do the hard yards."[57]

Not all features of the work environment are valued equivalently by different groups of employees.[58] One research study, for example, shed some light on this issue.[59] The study was carried out on a sample of some 4,500 "knowledge workers and managers"—arguably a segment of employees that will be one of the most important to organizations in the future—from

A MANAGER'S CHALLENGE

CHANGE

The BBs, the Xs and the Ys: Different Generational Approaches to the Work-Life Balancing Act

In decades past, someone expecting a child and wanting to reduce her workload received relatively little support from her manager or the organization. No matter what positions employees held, they were expected to put their work first. Typically, they were told to find some way to cope with the situation on their own, or leave the company. In short, in terms of work-life balance, the equation was heavily weighted toward the organization's needs, with virtually no concern on the part of the employer for family and non-work needs.

This one-sided situation has shifted considerably in recent years because of the greater prevalence of two wage-earner families, changing societal norms, and increased employee focus on the issue. For example, one survey showed employees rated work-life balance as more important than job security, financial rewards, and career advancement. In another survey, 34 percent of 200,000 workers said that "the demands of their jobs seriously interfere with their private lives." In a third survey, almost 20 percent of respondents—managerial and professional personnel—said that because of the lack of work-life balance in their current job, they planned to look for another job the following year.

It is obvious, however, that not all employees give the same degree of attention to work-life balance issues. For example, substantial differences exist across these three generations:

1. **Baby Boomers** Those born between 1946 and 1964, some of whom are already retired and others who are near retirement;
2. **Generation X (the Xs)** Those born between 1965 and approximately 1979; and
3. **Generation Y (the Ys)** Also sometimes called *Generation Next* or *Millenials,* these people were born between 1980 and 1999.

Each of these generations was shaped by a different set of events that occurred during their formative and early career years. For example, Baby Boomers were born in the post-World War II era and, as they grew older, they witnessed intense Cold War sparring between the Soviet Union and the United States, the rise of the civil rights and women's movements, and the Vietnam conflict. The economy, though, was generally prosperous during much of the period from 1946 to 1964.

The Xs experienced the sharp rise of two-income families—in which both parents work—and some experienced a less than robust economy during their early years. The Ys (basically, today's college students) have lived through the introduction of the personal computer, the cell phone, the Internet and e-mail, texting, and other social media, and the rapid expansion of the global economy.

Given these and other profound changes in organizational and external environments that have occurred over the more than six decades since World War II—just imagine college-age Baby Boomers envisioning a day when they would work with a computer *on their lap*—it is not surprising that the unique experiences of each generation have led them to different expectations and approaches regarding what they want from work and life. As a cohort group, Baby Boomers are viewed as especially driven to achieve personal and professional success and who are now at a stage in life where they focus strongly on health and related concerns. Generation X employees are seen as paying considerable attention to their work-life balance, while at the same time being more independent and willing to switch organizations than were the preceding Boomer generation. Members of Generation Y are often characterized as being especially self-confident, optimistic, and highly capable of multitasking, as well as intensely concerned with their own fulfillment, both personally and professionally.

Of course, a word of caution is in order: These generational descriptions provide only broad characterizations of behaviors and a generalized view of the more typical members of very large sets of people. Obviously, individual differences abound among members of each generation, and it is up to managers to be alert to these person-by-person differences as well as the general tendencies of each generation. Nevertheless, differences across generations appear to impact the effectiveness of specific motivational, reward, and reinforcement approaches taken by managers and organizations.

Sources: M. Macon and J. B. Artley, "Can't We All Just Get Along? A Review of the Challenges and Opportunities in a Multigenerational Workforce," *International Journal of Business Research* 9 (2009), 90–94; M. Crumpacker and J. M. Crumpacker, "Succession Planning and Generational Stereotypes: Should HR Consider age-based Values and Attitudes a Relevant Factor or a Passing Fad?" *Public Personnel Management* 36 (2007), 349–369.

Managerial Challenges from the Front Line

The Rest of the Story

Elizabeth Hayes could have chosen to have only on-site employees. However, Hayes decided not to take this route because the basic nature of the work to be done is conducive to doing it remotely. Also, AOL is well set up to facilitate remote employment, so she makes extensive use of the company's available technology. Moreover, being able to hire employees anywhere in the world gave her access to a wider pool of talent.

Nonetheless, the challenge of motivating remote employees on a steady basis is ever-present. To deal with this, Hayes set up clear performance goals and objectives for her subordinates and gave them regular, very direct feedback on how their work was going. She

did this by scheduling one-on-one meetings with each person at least once a quarter to review their performance. As a manager, Hayes also looked for opportunities to provide company-sponsored remote training classes and other growth experiences for those who reported to her. She also instituted virtual meetings to help foster a team feeling among the group. Customer use of AOL's educational Web portal increased steadily, and employee retention on Hayes's team was consistently high. After her AOL experience, Hayes made a career change and is now a corporate trainer and instructional designer for the mortgage industry firm Fannie Mae.

10 large, technology-intensive companies (including those in aerospace, software, and pharmaceutical industries) with major operations in North America, Europe, and Asia. Survey data were collected from this sample and analyzed by respondents' age, gender, and geographical region. Respondents were asked what aspects of the work situation were most important to them. The findings demonstrated that there are differences by age, gender, and region. Factors such as "career advancement" and "professional career development" were rated more important by younger versus older employees. Compared to men, women at early stages of their careers put more emphasis on job security and less on financial rewards. At later stages, women put more importance on career advancement and professional development than did men in the sample. The major difference by region involved "international opportunities" (for career advancement). Asians and Europeans viewed these opportunities as more important than did Americans.

What are the motivational and managerial implications of this kind of research? A major conclusion is that, because work does not generate the same relative degree of importance among employees, managers face different kinds of challenges in motivating employees in different cultural contexts or age groups. (See the accompanying Manager's Challenge box on different generations coping with work-life balance demands.) As a result, specific incentives—such as pay raises, time off, or opportunities for career advancement—will not have the same motivational effect on all people in all situations. The message is that managers cannot assume that everyone else will value work, and different elements of work, in the same way they themselves do. Sensitivity to these differences, therefore, can be highly useful in addressing motivational issues and problems.

Summary

- Motivation results from a set of forces that energize, direct, and sustain behavior. These forces can either be internal, or "push," forces or external, or "pull," forces. Overemphasizing one of these two sets of forces to the exclusion of the other can result in misdiagnosing the motivational situation in an organizational setting. At any point in time, either or both types of forces may be active.
- The source of internal, or push, forces is the individual. A person's needs, attitudes, and goals are major push forces. The primary sources of external, or pull, forces are the characteristics of the job, and the characteristics of the work situation. Job characteristics include

the degree of control allowed on the job, its degree of difficulty, and the feedback received from doing it. The characteristics of the work situation include a person's immediate supervisor, work-group members, and various organizational actions such as compensation and training.

■ Those who have studied motivation in organizations generally classify work-motivation theories as either content or process theories. Content theories focus on the needs that the individual brings to the situation and the features of the work setting that can potentially satisfy those needs. Process theories focus on how different variables combine to determine the amount of effort that people expend on tasks.

■ Research focused on content has helped managers understand how the design of jobs can affect the motivation of those who perform them. When a job is designed in such a way that it becomes more meaningful to the employee doing it, the result is called job enrichment.

■ The consequences employees experience following their behavior can impact the likelihood of that behavior being exhibited in the future. The applications of desirable consequences, called positive reinforcements, increase the likelihood of behavior. Similarly, the removal of undesirable consequences, called negative reinforcements, can also have this effect. Applications of undesirable consequences, called punishment, can decrease future behavior but also have other unpredictable effects. Not applying any consequences, called extinction, can decrease the likelihood of a behavior occurring in the future.

■ The values and attitudes employees bring to the work situation can strongly influence their motivation. Values vary across different categories of employees (e.g., younger versus older), and, especially, across different national cultures. Likewise, individuals' attitudes toward the importance of work in general—in other words, the "centrality of work"—can affect their reaction to various motivational attempts by their managers. The implication for anyone in a managerial role is that particular incentives that work quite well for some employees or some groups might not motivate others.

Key Terms

acquired needs theory   245
content theory   242
equity theory   248
expectancy theory   249
extinction   256
goal-setting theory   253
in-group   257

job characteristics
    model   247
job enrichment   247
Maslow's need hierarchy
    theory   243
motivation   241
negative reinforcement   255

positive reinforcement   254
process theory   248
punishment   255
self-efficacy   252
social cognitive theory   252
two-factor theory   246
work centrality   259

Review Questions

1. What are "push" and "pull" motivational forces? Give examples of each.
2. What are three major characteristics that determine motivation in organizations? What are some of the variables within each?
3. What are some of the characteristics of an individual with a high need for achievement?
4. How can managers affect motivation by changing a job's content?
5. According to equity theory, what might happen if a worker thought he or she was putting in more effort than a coworker, yet the coworker received a higher salary or larger bonus?

6. According to expectancy theory, what can a manager do to increase an employee's motivation? Does his or her culture make a difference?
7. How are content theories and process theories of motivation different?
8. What attributes do positive reinforcements need to have to motivate behavior?
9. What is the difference between a negative reinforcement and a punishment? Give an example of each.
10. What is work centrality? Why is it important for managers to understand this concept if they want to motivate their employees?

Assessing Your Capabilities

What Motivates Me?

Using the following scale, circle the number that best indicates how important each of the following items is in the job you would like to get.

	Not important	Slightly important	Moderately important	Very important	Extremely important
1. Cooperative relations with my co-workers.	1	2	3	4	5
2. Developing new skills and knowledge at work.	1	2	3	4	5
3. Good pay for my work.	1	2	3	4	5
4. Being accepted by others.	1	2	3	4	5
5. Opportunity for independent thought and action.	1	2	3	4	5
6. Frequent raises in pay.	1	2	3	4	5
7. Opportunity to develop close friendships at work.	1	2	3	4	5
8. A sense of self-esteem.	1	2	3	4	5
9. A complete fringe-benefit program.	1	2	3	4	5
10. Openness and honesty with my co-workers.	1	2	3	4	5
11. Opportunities for personal growth and development.	1	2	3	4	5
12. A sense of security from bodily harm.	1	2	3	4	5

Scoring

To calculate your score, the items in each need set are added as follows:

Items: 2, 5, 8, 11 = Growth needs   Enter your score: _____

Items: 1, 4, 7, 10 = Relatedness needs   Enter your score: _____

Items: 3, 6, 9, 12 = Existence needs   Enter your score: _____

Interpretation

If you considered all four items within a "need" category to be extremely important, you would obtain the maximum total of 20 points in each.

College students typically rate growth needs highest. However, you might currently have little income and consider existence needs to be most important. For instance, a student's scores of 20, 10, and 15 for growth, relatedness, and existence needs, respectively, would be interpreted to mean that her relatedness needs are already substantially satisfied. Her growth needs, on the other hand, are substantially unsatisfied.

Note that a low score may imply that a need is unimportant to you or that it is substantially satisfied. The implication, however, is that everyone has these needs. So a low score is usually taken to mean that this need is substantially satisfied.

Source: Prentice Hall's Self Assessment Library, eds. S. P. Robbins and T. A. Judge.

Team Exercise

1. Choose a job at least one of your group members knows a lot about. This will probably mean a job that one of you has held. Don't just pick a job at random because you really need to know all the responsibilities, drawbacks, challenges, pluses, and minuses of the job in order to do this exercise. This does not necessarily have to be the worst job you have ever held—many of those do not lend themselves well to redesign! Choose a job you feel has some potential to be redesigned.

2. Analyze the motivating potential of this job. Use the accompanying questionnaire to develop the numerical

scores to plug in to the motivating potential score (MPS) formula. Come up with an initial MPS. **Insert the initial MPS score here.** _____

3. Brainstorm ways to redesign the job so as to improve its motivating potential score. Try to think both rationally and creatively.

4. Once you have decided how you, as managers, could redesign this job so as to increase your employees' motivation to perform at a high level, compute the new MPS for the job. Use the same questionnaire items below. **Insert the revised MPS score here.** _____

5. Type a report to be handed in at the next class. The report should include

   a. The job—who held it and why you chose it.

   b. The job's initial MPS score, with your reason for scoring it the way you did.

   c. A detailed look at your job redesign strategy

   d. The job's new MPS calculation

The motivating potential score (MPS) of a given job is defined as

$$MPS = \frac{TV + TI + TS(A)(F)}{3}$$

where:

   TV = Task Variety
   TI = Task Identity
   TS = Task Significance
   A = Autonomy
   F = Feedback

Job Diagnostic Survey

How much autonomy is there in the job? That is, to what extent does the job permit a person to decide on his or her own how to go about doing the work?

1	2	3	4	5	6	7

Very little; the job gives a person almost no personal say about how and when the work is done.   _____   Moderate autonomy; many things are standardized and not under the control of the person, but he or she can make some decisions about the work.   _____   Very much; the job gives the person almost complete responsibility for deciding how and when the work is done.

To what extent does the job involve doing a "whole" and identifiable piece of work? That is, is the job a complete piece of work that has an obvious beginning and end? Or is it a small part of the overall piece of work, which is finished by other people or by automatic machines?

1	2	3	4	5	6	7

The job is only a tiny part in the overall piece of work; the results of the person's activities cannot be seen in the final product or service.   _____   The job is a moderate-sized "chunk" of the overall piece of work; the person's own contribution can be seen in the final outcome.   _____   The job involves doing the whole piece of work, from start to finish; the results of the person's activities are easily seen in the final product or service.

How much variety is there in the job? That is, to what extent does the job require a person to do many different things at work, using a variety of his or her skills and talents?

1	2	3	4	5	6	7

Very little; the job requires the person to do the same routine things over and over again.   _____   Moderate variety.   _____   Very much; the job requires the person to do many different things, using a number of different skills and talents.

In general, how significant or important is the job? That is, are the results of the person's work likely to affect significantly the lives or well-being of other people?

1	2	3	4	5	6	7

Not at all significant; the outcome of the work is not likely to affect anyone in any important way. _____ Moderately significant. _____ Highly significant; the outcome of the work can affect other people in very important ways.

To what extent does doing the job itself provide the person with information about his or her work performance? That is, does the actual work itself provide clues about how well the person is doing—aside from any feedback co-workers or supervisors may provide?

1	2	3	4	5	6	7

Very little; the job itself is set up so a person could work forever without finding out how well he or she was doing. _____ Moderately; sometimes doing the job _____ provide feedback to the person; sometimes it does not. Very much; the job is set up so that a person gets almost constant feedback as he or she works about how well he or she is doing.

Scoring

To score your questionnaire, place your responses to Questions 3, 2, 4, 1, and 5, respectively, in the blank spaces in the following equation:

$$\text{MPS} = \frac{(Q3) + (Q2) + (Q4)}{3} \times (Q1) \times (Q5)$$

If the MPS is

200–343 The MPS is high

120–199 The MPS is moderate

0–119 The MPS is low

Source: J. R. Hackman and G. R. Oldham, "Development of the Job Diagnostic Survey," *Journal of Applied Psychology* 60 (1975): 159–170.

Pamela Jones enjoyed banking. She had taken a battery of personal aptitude and interest tests that suggested she might like and do well in either banking or librarianship. Since the job market for librarians was poor around the time of her graduation, she applied for employment with a large bank, the ABC Bank of Winnipeg, and was quickly hired.

Her early experiences in banking were almost always challenging and rewarding. She was enrolled in the bank's management development program because of her education (a B.A. in languages and some postgraduate coursework in business administration), her previous job experience, and her obvious intelligence and drive.

During her first year in the training program, Jones attended classes on banking procedures and policies, and worked her way through a series of low-level positions in her branch. She was repeatedly told by her manager that her work was above average. Similarly, the training officer who worked out of the main office and coordinated the development of junior officers in the program frequently told Jones that she was among the best three of her cohort of twenty trainees.

Jones proceeded to develop a deep seated attachment to banking in general and to her bank and branch in particular. She was proud to be a banker and proud to be a member of the ABC Bank of Winnipeg. After one year in the management development program, however, Jones found she was not learning anything new about banking or the ABC Bank of Winnipeg. She was shuffled from one job to another at her own branch, cycling back over many positions several times to help meet temporary problems caused by absences, overloads, and turnover. Turnover—a rampant problem in banking—amazed Jones. She couldn't understand why so many people started careers in the service of banking only to leave after one or two years.

After her first year, the repeated promises she had received of moving into her own position at another branch started to sound hollow to Jones. The training officer claimed that there were no openings suitable for her at other branches. On two occasions when openings did occur, the manager of each of the branches in question rejected Jones, sight unseen, presumably because she hadn't been in banking long enough.

Jones was not the only unhappy person at her branch. Her immediate supervisor, George Burns, complained that because of the bank's economy drive, vacated customer service positions were left unfilled. As branch accountant, Burns was also responsible for day-to-day customer service. As a result, he was unable to perform all of the duties of his own job. The manager told Burns several times that customer service was critical, but that Burns would have to improve his performance on his own job. Eventually, Burns left the bank to

work for a trust company. This left Jones in the position of having to supervise the same tellers who had trained her only a few months earlier. Jones was surprised at all of the mistakes the tellers made, but found it difficult to do much to correct their poor work habits. All disciplinary procedures, she learned, had to be administered with the approval of Head Office.

After several calls to her training officer, Jones was finally transferred to her first "real" position in her own branch. Still eager and dedicated, Jones was soon to lose her enthusiasm.

At her new branch, Jones was made "assistant accountant." Her duties included the supervision of the seven tellers, some customer service and a great deal of paper work. The same economy drive that she had witnessed at her training branch resulted in the failure to replace customer service personnel. Jones was expected to pick up the slack at the front desk, neglecting her own work. Her tellers seldom balanced their own cash, so Jones stayed late almost every night to find their errors. To save on overtime, the managers sent the tellers home while Jones stayed late, first to correct the tellers' imbalances, then to finish her own paper work. Her manager told Jones that as an officer of the bank she was expected to stay until the work of her subordinates, and her own work, were satisfactorily completed. Jones realized that most of her counterparts in other ABC bank branches were willing to give this sort of dedication; therefore, so should she. This situation lasted six months with little sign of change in sight.

One day, Jones learned from a phone conversation with a friend at another branch that she would be transferred to Hope, British Columbia, some 100 miles east of Vancouver, to fill an opening that had arisen. Jones's husband was a professional, employed by a large corporation in Vancouver. His company did not have an office in Hope; moreover, his training was very specialized so he could probably find employment only in large cities anyway.

Accepting transfers was expected of junior officers who wanted to get ahead. Jones inquired at Head Office and learned that the rumor of her own pending transfer was true. Her training officer told her, however, that Jones could decline the transfer if she wished, but he couldn't say how soon her next promotion would come about.

Depressed, annoyed, disappointed and frustrated, Jones quit the bank.

Questions

1. Consider various need theories. What are Pamela Jones' underlying needs that motivated her? What is the basis for your answer?

2. Given the comments that Jones received from her first year trainers, what would she realistically expect after finishing her training? What did she get? Using expectancy theory, explain why the situation would not be motivating for her.

3. Burns was given extra work and told it was priority work, and he did it well. However, he was punished for not doing his other work. Analyze this situation according to reinforcement theory. What type of behavior would you expect from Burns in this situation, and why?

4. Pamela Jones was going to be transferred to another position in a branch about 100 miles from Vancouver. Do you think it is only her husband's work that makes her reluctant to take this position? What other motivational elements could be influencing her attitude toward whether to accept the new position? What could the company have done to motivate her to want to take the job?

Source: Adapted from Pinder, C.C., *Work Motivation: Theory, Issues, and Applications* (Glenview, IL: Scott, Foresman and Company, 1984), pp. 317–318.

References

1. D. Brady, "Yes, Winning Is Still the Only Thing," *BusinessWeek,* 2006, 52–55; http://www.badwater.com/results/index.html accessed April 11, 2010.

2. G. P. Latham and C. C. Pinder, "Work Motivation Theory and Research at the Dawn of the Twenty-first Century," *Annual Review of Psychology* 56 (2005): 485–516.

3. G. Hofstede, "Culture and Organizations," *International Studies of Management and Organization* 10, no. 4 (1980): 15–41; C. Sue-Chan and M. Ong, "Goal Assignment and Performance: Assessing the Mediating Roles of Goal Commitment and Self-efficacy and the Moderating Role of Power Distance," *Organizational Behavior and Human Decision Processes* 89, no. 2 (2002): 1140–1161; P. E. Spector, C. L. Cooper, J. I. Sanchez, M. O'Driscoll, and K. Sparks, "Locus of Control and Well-being at Work: How Generalizable Are Western Findings," *Academy of Management Journal* 45, no. 2 (2002): 453–466.

4. A. H. Maslow, *Motivation and Personality,* 2nd ed. (New York: Harper & Row, 1970).

5. Company Web site, "The New Employment Deal: Insights from Towers Watson's 2010 Global Workforce Study," http://www.towerswatson.com/global-workforce-study, accessed April 24, 2010.

6. N. Rajagopal, and S. Abraham, "Prominence of Higher Order Needs: An Indian IT Sector Experience," *Vilakshan: The XIMB Journal of Management.* 6, no. 2 (2009): 15–28.

7. University Web site, http://becker.wustl.edu/libdept/peer/2008PRP .html, accessed April 12, 2010.

8. D. C. McClelland, *Human Motivation* (Glenview: Scott, Foresman, 1985); D. C. McClelland and R. E. Boyatzis, "Leadership Motive Pattern and Long-term Success in Management," *Journal of Applied Psychology* 67 (1982): 734–743; D. C. McClelland and D. G. Winter, *Motivating Economic Achievement* (New York: The Free Press, 1969).

9. S. H. Schwartz and W. Blisky, "Toward a Universal Psychological Structure of Human Values," *Journal of Personality and Social Psychology* 53 (1987): 550–562; S. H. Schwartz and W. T. Bilsky, "Toward a Theory of the Universal Content and Structure of Values: Extensions and Cross-cultural Replications," *Journal of Personality and Social Psychology* 58 (1990): 878–881.

10. M. Erez and P. C. Earley, *Culture, Self-identity, and Work* (New York: Oxford University Press, 1993), 102.

11. J. W. Connor and G. A. DeVos, "Cultural Influences on Achievement Motivation and Orientation: Towards Work in Japanese and American Youth," in *Influences of Social Structure, Labor Markets, and Culture*, eds. D. Stern and D. Eichorn (Hillsdale: Lawrence Erlbaum Associates, 1989), 291–326.

12. A. Sagie, D. Elizur, and H. Yamauchi, "The Structure and Strength of Achievement Motivation: A Cross-cultural Comparison," *Journal of Organizational Behavior* 17 (1996): 431–444; K. P. Parboteeah and J. B. Cullen, "Social Institutions and Work Centrality: Explorations Beyond National Culture," *Organization Science* 14, no. 2 (2003): 137–148; K. S. Law, D. K. Tse, and N. Zhou, "Does Human Resource Management Matter in a Transitional Economy? China as an Example," *Journal of International Business Studies* 34, no. 3 (2003): 255–265; M. G. Martinson, and R. M. Davison, "Strategic Decision Making and Support Systems: Comparing American, Japanese, and Chinese Management," *Decision Support Systems* 43 (2007): 284–300.

13. F. Herzberg, *Work and the Nature of Man* (Cleveland: Worth Publishing, 1966); F. Herzberg, "One More Time: How Do You Motivate Employees?" *Harvard Business Review* 46 (1968): 54–62; F. Herzberg, B. Mausner, and B. B. Snyderman, *The Motivation to Work* (New York: Wiley, 1959).

14. J. E. LaBelle, "The Paradox of Safety Hopes and Rewards," *Professional Safety* 50, no. 12 (2005): 37–42.

15. R. W. Griffin, *Task Design: An Integrative Approach* (Glenview: Scott, Foresman, 1982); J. L. Pierce and R. B. Dunham, "Task Design: A Literature Review," *Academy of Management Review* 1 (1976): 83–97.

16. J. R. Hackman and G. R. Oldham, *Work Redesign* (Reading: Addison-Wesley, 1980).

17. J. O'Toole and E. E. Lawler III, *The New American Workplace* (New York: Palgrave MacMillan, 2005), 55–56.

18. A. B. Bakker, M. van Veldhoven, and D. Xanthopoulou, "Beyond the Demand-control model: Thriving on High Job Demands and Resources," *Journal of Personnel Psychology* 9, no. 1 (2010):3–16; A. B. Bakker, W. B. Schaufeli, M. P. Leiter, and T. W. Taris, "Work Engagement: An Emerging Concept in Occupational Health Psychology," *Work & Stress* 22, no. 3 (2008): 187–200.

19. J. S. Adams, "Towards an Understanding of Inequity," *Journal of Abnormal and Social Psychology* 67 (1963): 422–436; J. S. Adams, "Inequity in Social Exchange," in *Advances in Experimental Social Psychology*, ed. L. Berkowitz (New York: Academic Press, 1965), vol. 2, 267–299; R. T. Mowday, "Equity

Theory Predictions of Behavior in Organizations," in *Motivation and Leadership at Work,* 6th ed., eds. R. M. Steers, L. W. Porter, and G. A Bigley (New York: McGraw-Hill, 1996); J. D. Shaw, N. Gupta, and J. E. Delery, "Pay Dispersion and Workforce Performance: Moderating Effects of Incentives and Interdependence," *Strategic Management Journal* 23, no. 6 (2002): 491–512.

20. C. C. Pinder, *Work Motivation in Organizational Behavior,* 2nd ed. (New York: Psychology Press, 2008), 316.

21. V. H. Vroom, *Work and Motivation* (New York: Wiley, 1964).

22. "Integrate Corporate Culture and Employee Engagement," *Strategic HR Review* 4, no. 6 (2005): 5.

23. A. Coleman, "Local Heroes," *Employee Benefits,* February 2010, 31–32.

24. U. Bantle, "Founders Award for Google Chrome," *Linux-Magazine,* November 3, 2009, http://www.linux-magazine.com/Online/News/Founders-Award-for-Google-Chrome.

25. A. D. Stajkovic and F. Luthans, "Social Cognitive Theory and Self-efficacy: Going Beyond Traditional Motivational and Behavioral Approaches," *Organizational Dynamics* 26, no. 4 (1998): 62–74; T. A. Wright, "What Every Manager Should Know: Does Personality Help Drive Employee Motivation?" *Academy of Management Executive* 17, no. 2 (1998): 131–133.

26. A. D. Stajkovic and F. Luthans, "Social Cognitive Theory and Self-efficacy: Implications for Motivation Theory and Practice," in *Motivation and Work Behavior,* eds. L. W. Porter, G. A. Bigley, and R. M. Steers (New York: McGraw-Hill, 2003); A. Bandura and E. A. Locke, "Negative Self-efficacy and Goal Effects Revisited," *Journal of Applied Psychology* 88, no. 1 (2003): 87–99.

27. M. Erez, "Goal Setting," in *Blackwell Encyclopedic Dictionary of Organizational Behavior,* ed. N. Nicholson (Cambridge: Blackwell Business Publishing, 1995), 193–194; E. A. Locke, "The Motivation Sequence, the Motivation Hub, and the Motivation Core," *Organizational Behavior and Human Decision Processes* 50 (1991): 288–299; E. A. Locke and G. P. Latham, *A Theory of Goal Setting and Task Performance* (Upper Saddle River: Prentice Hall, 1990).

28. E. A. Locke and G. P. Latham, "Goal Setting Theory: An Introduction," in *Motivation and Leadership at Work,* 6th ed., eds. R. M. Steers, L. W. Porter, and G. A. Bigley (New York: McGraw Hill, 1996).

29. R. Ilies and T. A. Judge, "Goal Regulation Across Time: The Effects of Feedback and Affect," *Journal of Applied Psychology* 90 (2005): 453–467.

30. Erez, *Goal Setting;* A. Drach-Zachavy and M. Erez, "Challenge Versus Threat Effects on the Goal–Performance Relationship," *Organizational Behavior and Human Decision Processes* 88, no. 2 (2002): 667–682; T. W. Britt, "Black Hawk Down at Work," *Harvard Business Review* 81, no. 1 (2003): 16; N. Nicholson, "How to Motivate Your Problem People," *Harvard Business Review* 81, no. 1 (2003): 56–58.

31. Ibid.

32. L. Helliker, "Pressure at Pier 1: Beating Sales Numbers of Year Earlier Is a Storewide Obsession," *Wall Street Journal,* December 7, 1995, B1.

33. P. T. Bezuijen, K. V. D. van den Berg, and H. Thierry, "Pygmalion and Employee Learning: The Role of Leader Behaviors," *Journal of Management* 35 (2009): 1248–1267.

34. A. M. Schmidt and C. M. Dolis, "Something's Got to Give: The Effects of Dual-Goal Difficulty, Goal Progress, and Expectancies on Resource Allocation," *Journal of Applied Psychology* 94 (2009): 678–691.

35. J. L. Komaki, T. Coombs, and S. Schepman, "Motivational Implications of Reinforcement Theory," in *Motivation and Leadership at Work,* 6th ed., eds. R. M. Steers, L. W. Porter, and G. A. Bigley (New York: McGraw Hill, 1996).

36. S. Kerr, "On the Folly of Rewarding A While Hoping for B," *Academy of Management Journal* 18 (1975): 769–783.

37. LaBelle, "The Paradox of Safety Hopes and Rewards.".

38. S. Kerr, *Ultimate Rewards* (Boston: Harvard Business School Press, 1997).

39. Komaki, Coombs, and Schepman, *Motivational Implications of Reinforcement Theory.*

40. Ibid.

41. H. C. Triandis, "Collectivism vs. Individualism: A Reconceptualization of a Basic Concept in Cross-Cultural Social Psychology," in *Cross-Cultural Studies of Personality, Attitudes, and Cognition,* eds. G. K. Verma and Y. C. Bagley (London: Macmillan, 1988), 60–95; Erez and Earley, *Culture, Self-Identity, and Work.*

42. S. E. Seashore, *Group Cohesiveness in the Industrial Work Group* (Ann Arbor: Survey Research Center, Institute for Social Research, University of Michigan, 1954).

43. D. Krackhardt and L. W. Porter, "When Friends Leave: A Structural Analysis of the Relationship Between Turnover and Stayers Attitudes," *Administrative Science Quarterly* 30 (1985): 242–261.

44. P. T. Bezuijen, K. V. D. van den Berg, and H. Thierry, "Pygmalion and Employee Learning: The Role of Leader Behaviors," *Journal of Management* 35 (2009): 1248–1267.

45. C. E. Shalley, L. L. Gilson, and T. C. Blum, "Interactive Effects of Growth Need Strength, Work Context, and Job Complexity on Self-reported Creative Performance," *Academy of Management Journal* 52, (2009): 489–505.

46. C. O'Reilly, "Corporations, Culture, and Commitment: Motivation and Social Control in Organizations," *California Management Review* 31, no. 4 (1989): 12.

47. E. Schonfeld, "Have the Urge to Merge? You'd Better Think Twice," *Fortune,* 1997, 114–116.

48. Erez and Earley, *Culture, Self-identity, and Work;* Locke, *The Motivation Sequence, the Motivation Hub, and the Motivation Core.*

49. F. Elashmawi and R. R. Harris, *Multicultural Management: New Skills for Global Success* (Houston: Gulf Publishing, 1993), Table 6.2, 144; G. Morse, "Why We Misread Motives," *Harvard Business Review* 81, no. 1 (2003): 18.

50. H. C. Triandis, R. Brislin, and C. H. Hui, "Cross-cultural Training Across the Individualism–Collectivism Divide," *International Journal of Intercultural Relations* 12 (1988): 269–289.

51. K. Leung and M. H. Bond, "How Chinese and Americans Reward Task-related Contributions: A Preliminary Study," *Psychologia: An International Journal for Psychology in the Orient* 25, no. 1 (1982): 32–39; M. H. Bond, K. Leung, and K. C. Wan, "How Does Cultural Collectivism Operate? The Impact of Task and Maintenance Contributions on Reward Distribution," *Journal of Cross-Cultural Psychology* 47 (1982): 793–804; K. Leung and H. Park, "Effects of Interactional Goal on Choice of Allocation Rule: A Cross-National Study," *Organizational Behavior and Human Decision Processes* 37 (1986): 111–120; K. I. Kim, H. Park, and N. Suzuki, "Reward Allocations in the United States, Japan, and Korea: A Comparison of Individualistic and Collectivistic Cultures," *Academy of Management Journal* 33 (1990): 188–198; C. C. Chen, J. Choi, and S-C Chi, "Making Justice Sense of Local–Expatriate Compensation Disparity: Mitigation by Local Referents, Ideological Explanations, and Interpersonal Sensitivity in China–Foreign Joint Ventures," *Academy of Management Journal* 45, no. 5 (2003): 807–817.

52. M. Weber. *The Protestant Work Ethic and the Spirit of Capitalism,* trans. T. Parsons (New York: Scribner, 1958); R. Wuthnow, "Religion and Economic Life," in *The Handbook of Economic Sociology*, eds. N. J. Smelser and R. Swedbert (Princeton: Princeton University Press, 1994), 620–646.

53. G. W. England and I. Harpaz, "Some Methodological and Analytic Considerations in Cross-national Comparative Research." *Journal of International Business Studies* 14, no. 2 (1983): 49–59.

54. I. Harpaz and H. Fu, "Work Centrality in Germany, Israel, Japan, and the United States," *Journal of Cross-Cultural Research* 31 (1997): 171–200.

55. Y. P. S. Kanwar, A. K. Singh, and A. D. Kodwani, "Work-life Balance and Burnout as Predictors of Job Satisfaction in the IT-ITES Industry," *Vision: The Journal of Business Perspective* 13, no. 2 (2009): 1–12.

56. J. C. Williams, and H. Boushey, *The Three Faces of Work–Family Conflict*. (Center for Work-Life Law. UC Hastings College of the Law, 2010).

57. M. A. Parris, M. H. Vickers, and L. Wilkes, " Caught in the Middle: Organizational Impediments to Middle Managers' Work–Life Balance," *Employee Responsibilities and Rights Journal* 20 (2008): 101–117.

58. S. P. Eisner, "Managing Generation Y," *SAM Advanced Management Journal* 70, no. 4 (2005): 4–15; R. L. Lord and P. A. Farrington, "Age-related Differences in the Motivation of Knowledge Workers," *Engineering Management Journal* 18, no. 3 (2006): 20–26.

59. D. Finegold and S. Mohrman, "What Do Employees Really Want: The Perception vs. the Reality," paper presented at the World Economics Forum Annual Meeting, Davos, Switzerland, 2001.

10

Groups and Teams

LEARNING OBJECTIVES

After studying this chapter you should be able to:

Describe the similarities and differences between groups and teams.

Identify and compare different types of groups.

Name the factors that influence group formation and development.

Analyze the various structural and behavioral characteristics of groups.

Identify the advantages and disadvantages of self-managing, cross-functional, global and virtual work groups and teams.

Explain the differences in the various types of team competencies.

Distinguish between the two major types of group conflict, and discuss their causes and consequences.

Explain how managers can help their work groups develop into high-performing teams.

Courtesy of Stephen Ortiz, Prairie Band
Casino & Resort

Name: Stephen Ortiz

Position title (and company): Vice President of Marketing, Prairie Band Casino (Kansas),

Alma mater: Haskell Indian Nations University (AA); Washburn University (BBA, MBA)

Outside work activities: Bass fishing tournaments (in the Ozarks)

First job out of school: Staff Consultant, Enterprise Risk Services, Deloitte & Touche

Hero: Parents; both grandfathers; and my (late) friend Kelly D. Jones

Motto to live by: Live every day like it's your last

Management style: Instill a vision and manage to that vision; collaborative

Steve Ortiz loves to spend time outside when he is not working, especially participating in bass fishing tournaments in the Ozarks. Ortiz's fishing accomplishments have been featured in over 20 articles in outdoor magazines in the past ten years. He sees fishing as more art than sport, but he also feels that competing in bass tournaments helps sharpen his competitive edge. As he says, "Competitive fishing is much like running a business—good and bad decisions can make you a hero or a zero. The key is to learn from your decisions."

One of Ortiz's key decisions in life was to attend college. When he graduated from high school, it was not his top priority, but his father convinced him otherwise. After receiving his associate's degree, he thought about getting an undergraduate degree in environmental science. However, the experience of working on an entrepreneurial venture to bring economic development to his reservation, coupled with the advice from a faculty member at a nearby university, influenced him to change his intended major and instead obtain a BBA in accounting, and subsequently an MBA degree as well.

After graduating, Ortiz joined the accounting firm of Deloitte & Touche and worked with a number of major clients on internal auditing and business process control issues. Following four years with the firm, he was hired by Harrah's, the gaming and entertainment company, to work in the marketing department of the company's casino near Topeka, Kansas. After several promotions, Ortiz is vice president and director of marketing for the casino, which is now owned by the Prairie Band of Native Americans.

One of Ortiz's biggest challenges occurred when he first joined Harrah's as a manager, before his promotion to director of casino marketing. He was charged with growing the "VIP" customer segment of the casino's business. At the time, Ortiz had inherited a unit with subpar performance. The casino's customer service ratings (based on surveys) were some of the lowest of any Harrah's facilities. Consequently, Ortiz had to study the internal workings of the department and analyze how the group's performance could be improved. He knew from extensive data collected over the years that unless the employees who interacted with their individually assigned VIPs could become more satisfied with their jobs, these important guests would not be satisfied or willing to spend more money. Changing this situation was the challenge Ortiz faced.

In the flatter, leaner organizations of the early twenty-first century—with their increased emphasis on speed, flexibility and, especially, innovation—operating effectively in groups and teams, and managing them, is even more important than it has been in the past.[1] Organizations of all types and sizes, whether in business, government, health care, or other settings, are much more likely to use groups and teams than even a few years ago.[2] This represents a major change in the way organizations function. Consequently, it requires a change in the mind-set of both managers and their subordinates. People need to change their attitudes toward group work and emphasize teamwork instead of only individual work. This, in fact, was exactly the challenge that Steve Ortiz faced.

Of course, there will always be a place for the brilliant employee working alone who produces a remarkable innovation or creative achievement.[3] Also, not all individuals or cultures adapt equally well to a group-oriented organizational environment; nor is creating groups always the most effective way to organize work.[4] Nevertheless, operating in global markets, organizations are now depending increasingly on highly networked and interconnected relationships involving groups and teams. Managing these networked relationships requires strong collaborative skills and the ability to work successfully with, and in, groups and teams.

These skills are necessary to build social capital within an organization and with groups and organizations outside the organization as well. If they have these skills, managers are in a much better position to be able to lead and gain the acceptance and commitment of others in order to meet the important challenges faced by today's organizations.

Groups engage in a diverse set of activities, ranging, for example, from developing new products, to designing automobiles, to constructing budgets, to formulating strategic plans. Even those who are inclined to be independent entrepreneurs eventually face this reality test: If an organization is not based on high-performance groups and teams, it likely will not be able to compete effectively in the current or future competitive landscape. Therefore, it is absolutely crucial that anyone aspiring to a career in management be able to meet two fundamental challenges: how to be an effective *member* of a group or team, and how to be an effective *leader* of a group or team. This was well summed up by former eBay CEO Meg Whitman, who stated: "We hire people who aren't focused on me, me, me. One of the first questions I ask when I interview people is: 'What are the most effective teams you've been on, and how did those teams work?'"[5]

It is important to differentiate between groups and teams. Under some circumstances, the two are the same, but under other circumstances, they are not. A **group** is typically defined as a set of people, limited in number (usually from 3 to 20 or so), who have some degree of interaction and shared objectives. A **team,** on the other hand, is a type, or form, of group. It has additional characteristics beyond a "mere" group, including a higher degree of interdependent, coordinated interaction and, especially, a stronger sense of members' personal responsibility for achieving specified group outcomes.[6] Also, groups that become teams typically have created a high level of identification with the group on the part of each member. In other words, it matters to members that they are a part of the unit.

A useful way to think about the relation between groups and teams is to view it as a continuum, as illustrated in Exhibit 10.1. Individuals are put into—or put themselves into—a group. The group may or may not go on to become a team.

Put simply, all teams are groups, but not all groups are, or become, teams.[7] A major objective in most of today's organizations is to have their work groups develop and evolve quickly so that they behave more like teams.

This chapter begins by briefly identifying the various types of groups that operate in organizational settings. Then we discuss how groups are formed and developed and what some of their most important characteristics are, such as their structure, norms, and degree of cohesiveness. This is followed by an analysis of a critical issue common to many groups, namely, conflict. The chapter concludes with a consideration of the challenges involved in improving group effectiveness.

Basic Types of Groups

Most people who work in organizations are part of at least one group, and often several different groups. These groups can be of different types. One major distinction among them is simply whether they are "formal," that is, established by the organization, or "informal," established by particular individuals without direct involvement by the formal organization. The basic types of groups to which almost all organization members could belong are illustrated in Exhibit 10.2 and described here.

Formal Groups

Within and across almost any kind of organization there are typically three fundamental types of formal groups: command (supervisory), project/task forces, and committees.

COMMAND (SUPERVISORY) GROUPS A **command group** (also known as a *supervisory group*) consists of a supervisor or manager and all those who report to that person; for example, those who report to a particular production supervisor or to a sales manager in a department. These groups are usually considered to be the basic work units of an organization. Depending on the nature of the tasks assigned to each person, however, the amount of interaction among members may vary considerably from one command group to another. For example, in a clothing manufacturing plant, a group of workers may be assigned to work on a particular style of jeans. All of the

---

group
a set of people, limited in number (usually from 3 to 20), who have some degree of mutual interaction and shared objectives

team
a type of group that has additional characteristics: a high degree of interdependent, coordinated interaction and a strong sense of members' personal responsibility for achieving specified group outcomes

command group
(also known as a *supervisory group*) a group whose members consist of a supervisor or manager and all those who report to that person

---

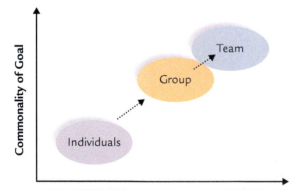

TEAMS demonstrate enhanced:
- Coordinated interaction
- Personal responsibility for group outcomes
- Individual identification with group

Commonality of Goal

Team

Group

Individuals

Degree of Interdependence and Collaboration

EXHIBIT 10.1

Individuals-to-Group-to-Team Continuum

Source: Adapted from M. E. Kossler and K. Kanaga, *Do You Really Need a Team* (Greensboro: Center for Creative Leadership, 2001).

EXHIBIT 10.2

Types of Groups

Type of Group	Features	Examples
Formal		
Command (Supervisory)	One supervisor with a number of subordinates Relatively enduring Membership changes relatively slowly	Clerical units Manufacturing assembly units Local sales managers reporting to a regional sales manager
Project/ Task Force	Temporary Specific limited purpose Group members are aware of temporary nature of group	Product design teams Management information systems teams to develop upgraded computer systems Term project groups in university classes
Committee	Either permanent or ad hoc Meet only periodically Members have different permanent jobs and/or supervisors Membership typically does not represent an employee's highest commitment	Budget committees Safety committees Promotion review committees
Informal		
Friendship	Group not originated by the organization Voluntary membership Obvious differences and boundaries between members and nonmembers	Group of employees who lunch together on Fridays Van pool group The "water cooler group"

workers construct the same garment, but because one is sewing the pocket to the leg while another is putting in zippers and yet another is topstitching the waistband, there is very little opportunity for interaction among them. Contrast this with a marketing team for a toy company, where the members meet frequently to discuss new products, schedule advertising campaigns, and decide on special promotional activities.

Command groups are usually considered relatively enduring, rather than temporary. Also, the membership in these groups changes relatively slowly. These factors together affect the nature and quality of the interpersonal associations among group members. The fact that you know that you will be interacting repeatedly with the same set of people for an indefinite length of time can have a powerful effect on your relationships with those other members.

PROJECT/TASK FORCES A **project/task force** is a group put together by an organization for a particular purpose, such as to design a new product or to work on a particular problem, and usually for a limited period of time. For example, financial services firms struggled during the dismal economic year of 2009, which led many of them to initiate layoffs and other cutbacks. To try to reduce these actions as much as possible and thereby retain the core of their talent base, Vanguard set up VATs—Vanguard Action Teams—to research specific client-oriented problems and develop solutions. These special task forces were designed to last 18 months and were composed of team members from different areas of the company who had to master

project/task force
a temporary group put together by an organization for a particular purpose

EXHIBIT 10.3

Examples of Committees Present in Many Organizations

- Governance
- Executive
- Steering
- Disaster planning
- Compensation
- Finance
- Safety
- Long-range planning
- Oversight
- Audit
- Ethics
- Public relations

different sets of skills and knowledge for this assignment. In this way, the firm was able to avoid or at least reduce layoffs in departments with excess personnel and also keep task force members motivated and challenged to develop new areas of expertise. At the end of the 18-month period, the task force members returned to the basic organizational structure, but often in units different from the ones they had worked in previously.[8]

Project teams and task forces differ from command groups in that they are deliberately intended to be temporary. They usually have a defined beginning and a specified ending date. Their members know that once they complete the project or task, the group will likely cease to exist. This feature not only changes members' perceptions and their interactions with one another, but it also changes their relationship to the appointed leader of the project or task force group.

Because of the nature and importance of the goals and objectives set for them, though, task forces and project teams (really groups that may, or may not, become true teams) constitute some of the most critical group-like activities within, and frequently across, organizations,. They often, also, involve virtual (non-face-to-face) group situations. The creation of project teams, however, is not always an ideal solution for dealing with organizational issues; they can run into various kinds of problems, such as lack of clear goals, insufficient resources to accomplish their objectives, and ineffective team leadership.[9] Nevertheless, most organizations of any size could not function for any extended period without using task forces and project teams.

committee

a group that is either permanent or temporary (ad hoc) whose members meet only occasionally and otherwise report to different permanent supervisors in an organization's structure

COMMITTEES A **committee** can be either permanent or temporary (ad hoc) in terms of its duration. Typically, the most important feature of a committee in an organization is that members meet only occasionally and otherwise report to different permanent supervisors in the organization's structure (Exhibit 10.3). Thus, interaction is episodic, and for most members this usually is not the formal organizational group to which they have the highest degree of commitment. For instance, a budget committee might meet several times during a company's fiscal year, with the members likely coming from each of the firm's major departments or divisions. The primary jobs of the budget committee members, however, are in their own organizational work units, not serving together on the budget committee. An example of a different type of committee is the Special Committee on Global Quality set up in 2010 by Toyota to investigate the causes of quality problems throughout all phases of the company's operations: design, manufacturing, marketing and service. The members of the committee are the chief quality officers for the major geographical regions (North America, Europe, China, Asia, etc.) in which the company sells its vehicles. Obviously, the intent in forming this committee is to bring concerted, as opposed to dispersed, focus on a fundamental issue: quality.[10]

formal group

a group that is designated, created, and sanctioned by the organization to carry out its basic work and to fulfill its overall mission

The preceding types of groups are all examples of a **formal group;** that is, a group designated, created, and sanctioned by an organization to carry out its basic work and to fulfill its overall mission. However, in many respects, informal groups are just as, and sometimes more, important for a manager to pay attention to, and understand, than formal groups.

Informal Groups

informal group

a group whose members interact voluntarily

An **informal group** is one whose members choose to interact voluntarily with one another, not by organizational mandate. A typical example is a friendship group. Although there is no formal "joining" process, these groups often have fairly obvious boundaries between members and non-members. At any given time, people think they know (perhaps incorrectly from the point of view of others in the group) whether they are members of a certain group or not. Just observing who eats lunch with whom, or who talks especially frequently to whom, for instance, is often a clear signal of a friendship group's boundaries. Informal groups can be fairly temporary, but more typically they last for considerable periods of time.

Most important for a manager is the fact that friendship groups and other informal groups can significantly affect the attitudes and performances of their members in relation to organizational tasks and objectives. A set of employees who were originally strangers, for example, might develop into an informal group after carpooling together over a period of time. If the conversations within this group focus on negative reactions to new organizational policies, then the group could become a source of opposition to those policies. However, informal groups often can provide considerable assistance to managers in dealing with organizational challenges. The key for the manager is whether the group can be influenced to support organizational and work group goals. To do this, managers need to be able to recognize important informal groups, gain an understanding of their norms, and identify where the leadership is within the group. If these steps are taken, then the potential exists for informal groups to become positive forces.

The Formation and Development of Groups and Teams

Groups form in organizations for many reasons and in many ways. Most often the organization deliberately puts groups together to serve stated organizational purposes. Informal groups, however, are another matter. They form more or less spontaneously on the basis of actions by their members and to serve those members' self-interests, which may or may not coincide with those of the organization.

What Influences the Formation of Groups and Teams?

The most important factors influencing the formation of groups in organizations are the goals of the organization, the opportunities for interaction and sharing mutual knowledge, and the psychological needs of potential group members.

ORGANIZATIONAL GOALS The goals and purposes of the larger organization directly affect the nature of its formal groups. The organization creates new groups, whether command, task forces, or committees, based on its judgment that needs are not being met adequately by either existing groups or the absence of any groups at all.

New groups may arise because of organizational growth, changes in the products or services the organization offers, or simply perceptions by key managers that greater efficiency and effectiveness can be gained by adding to, altering, or combining existing groups. It should also be noted, however, that occasionally companies will hire intact groups away from other companies—a practice called *lift-out*—instead of developing their own new group in order to jump start some new initiative.[11]

A key issue for organizations and managers when new groups are formed is whether they will be given adequate resources to accomplish their specific goals.[12] The leader of a team that developed the data storage system for a major product at Honeywell Defense Avionics stated, "My most important task... was to help this team feel as if they owned the project by getting them whatever information, financial or otherwise, they needed."[13]

If you are a member of a new group put together by the organization, you are likely to have a number of questions, such as

- Why was I selected, rather than someone else?
- What are the real reasons the group was put together?
- What will my new responsibilities be?
- Are the stated objectives for the group realistic and are they the actual goals that will be measured?

Such questions naturally occur to anyone who becomes part of a new group, but they don't always get asked directly or openly. Managers who form groups, therefore, must anticipate questions such as these, whether or not they are raised directly, and must be prepared to provide necessary information and explanations. If you become responsible for putting together a new organizational group, you need to recognize that, as discussed earlier, the formation of a new group does not necessarily mean that a new team has been created. You may have the hope that your new group will develop into a team with a strong sense of shared responsibility for the group's performance and output, but cohesiveness and cooperation are not something

Renowned chef Alain Ducasse owns top-rated restaurants in Monaco, New York City, and Paris. Over the course of 20 years, Ducasse has employed more than 500 people. He takes a close interest in recruiting teams for his restaurants and selects, welcomes, and trains them before encouraging them to stand on their own two feet.

that you can decree. Managers cannot simply declare new groups to be "teams" and expect that they will operate that way. Team development depends on managerial skills and follow-up actions to elicit true teamwork in more than name only.[14]

OPPORTUNITIES FOR INTERACTION AND SHARING MUTUAL KNOWLEDGE For groups to form and develop into teams, physical proximity clearly is a helpful factor. When people have the opportunity to work together closely, it can facilitate learning about similarities of interests and experiences. These similarities can provide a basis for the development of strong relationships that can assist the work of the group. However, in this age of electronic communication, groups are often highly dispersed geographically. In such circumstances, it becomes even more critical to increase the opportunities for interaction of members, even if that is only via electronic messages. In other words, in dispersed "virtual" groups, it is essential to take steps to develop mutual knowledge—to find "common ground"—among members.[15] (These and other issues related to virtual teams will be discussed in more detail later in this chapter.)

PSYCHOLOGICAL FACTORS There are many personal reasons that motivate organizational members to form closer relationships in groups, especially basic human needs for security, social support, self-esteem, and status. By belonging to groups, even virtual ones, employees are often able to fulfill needs that may not be well satisfied by the work itself. Thus, the feeling of belonging to a group at work can be highly rewarding for many individuals. It can be, in effect, a significant way for individuals to achieve a distinct social identity that is meaningful both for themselves and for others who interact with them.[16]

The Stages of Group Development

Whether groups are formed by the organization or by voluntary actions of individuals, they tend to move through distinct developmental stages as they mature.[17] One popular early statement on this issue utilizes an easy-to-remember set of terms for such stages: "forming" (getting acquainted), "storming" (expressing differences of opinion), "norming" (building consensus on basic issues), and "performing" (carrying out cooperative group actions).[18] Although this model has considerable appeal as a way to think about the phases of group development across time, it does not necessarily apply to all groups. As one set of management scholars has noted, "It seems unlikely that a single sequence can describe the development of all kinds of teams (groups)."[19]

Despite this fact, several identifiable stages do show up with some regularity in organizational contexts (Exhibit 10.4), and we will use the "forming," "storming, "norming," and "performing" labels to identify these stages.

FORMING If you are forming a new group, you will face some unique challenges. One kind of challenge is presented when potential team members are not used to a group-oriented approach to work. If they have been comfortable working alone, they are facing a significant change. Another kind of challenge in the formation stage is that the group's members will have lots of questions, whether they ask them openly or not. For example, they will want to know who is in the group and why they are there, who is leading the group, and where each person is "coming from" in terms of his or her existing attitudes and viewpoints. Nearly all new groups go through this "getting to know you" stage.

EXHIBIT 10.4
───────────

Stages of Group Development

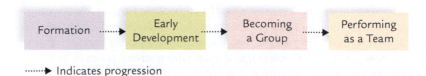

Formation ┈┈▶ Early Development ┈┈▶ Becoming a Group ┈┈▶ Performing as a Team

┈┈▶ Indicates progression

STORMING Following a group's formation and initial interactions, an early-development "storming" stage often settles in and may last for some time, depending on the nature of the group and its tasks. In this stage, members learn what is expected of them, what is acceptable behavior, and how well they relate to each other. Typically, members cautiously exchange, and sometimes jealously guard, information. If you are the group's leader, it is an important time for learning about how opinions within the group overlap or differ on key matters. Often, conflicts (hence the "storming" label for this stage) over group goals or the means to reach them may emerge in this stage. An analogy to adolescence in human development might be apt for helping to understand this stage.

NORMING In this stage, at least a minimum amount of consensus about the group's issues and norms (agreed-upon standards of behavior) begins to appear, as well as a degree of individual identity with the group and its goals. How much cohesion and group identity will actually emerge will vary widely from group to group. A critical factor will be how well the group is meeting each member's needs and how well members think the group is being led. In this stage particularly, if you are in a leadership role you can have considerable impact on the group's development of its norms (see the next section) and thus help it to become a true team.

PERFORMING In this stage, a group is able to perform like a team and take actions as a coherent entity and not just as a set of loosely affiliated individuals. Internally, this means that the group is able to influence members' attitudes and behavior on matters of importance to the group, and externally it means that others within, or outside, the organization are being affected by its actions.

Returning to the general issue of stages in the development of groups, whether a team's actions across these stages are continuously effective or not is another matter. Events internal or external to the group could still cause it to revert to an earlier stage of development, where it might need to re-form and attempt to become a "performing group" all over again. However, if a group has no specified ending point, that is, no "adjourning" phase, there is no reason why the performing stage cannot last indefinitely. To keep a group or team in this stage continually is a clear managerial and leadership challenge.

The Characteristics of Groups and Teams

All groups have certain characteristics or features that affect the degree and types of influence they have on their members and their level of collective performance. Some of these are structural, whereas others relate to the basic features of groups, such as their norms and the degree of cohesion among their members. For all these characteristics, it is important for leaders and managers to understand their likely effects. Particularly, managers need to be on the lookout for how changes, originating from both inside and outside the organization, can alter one or more of these characteristics, which in turn can have a profound impact on how well groups function and perform.

Structural Characteristics

Just as an organization has a structure (as discussed in Chapter 6), so do groups, except on a smaller scale. Four of the most essential structural features of groups are size, composition, differentiated roles, and differentiated status.

SIZE What is the optimal size for a group? This is a simple question, but the answer is complex and depends critically on the types of tasks facing the group. In the next few paragraphs we'll explore some of the advantages and disadvantages of different size groups.

The fundamental advantage of larger group size is that more resources—a more extensive pool of talent, skills and expertise—can be brought to bear on the problems or issues facing the group. Thus, a review of 30 years of research studies on creativity and innovation in groups revealed that those kinds of desired outputs are more likely to emerge from larger rather than smaller teams. The reason, according to the authors of the review is that "the production and implementation of creative ideas is an ill-defined, complex task rather than a routine task," and therefore bigger teams are, on average, more likely to include a greater variety of viewpoints and other relevant knowledge.[20] Many examples of the benefits of larger size groups come from the world of science. Increasingly over the past 50 or so years many major scientific research projects have involved increasingly larger teams. As an extreme illustration, the $6 billion Large Hadron Collider particle accelerator located near Geneva, Switzerland involves "groups" as large as 3600 individuals from over 180 institutions in 38 countries. The elected leader of one of these groups says "I cannot direct anybody to do anything they don't want to do. All decision-making is by consensus." The reason this arrangement works is because of the depth, extent, and variety of expertise that comprise the group.[21]

Even when working on much more routine group objectives, however, having too few people in a group—especially when the tasks are many—can defeat the very purpose of putting together people in the first place. Michelin America's Small Tires unit learned this lesson a few years ago when company management cut the size of sales teams in a cost-savings move, only to have to reverse course and double them just 18 months later because of increasing complaints from dealers.[22]

On the other hand, larger group size has a number of potential and often crucial disadvantages. One major one, documented by research data, is that when a group's size increases the sense of personal responsibility for its output or performance on the part of each individual member tends to decrease. This phenomenon of reduced effort per person in larger-size groups has been labeled **social loafing.**[23] Individuals in larger groups apparently are more likely than those in smaller groups to assume that other members will "carry the load." Also, in larger groups, individual members' specific contributions are less easily identified. This appears to be a major factor that encourages such "loafing."

social loafing
the phenomenon of reduced effort per person in large groups

Of course, there are approaches that can be used to counter the social-loafing tendency in larger groups. For example, it is possible to structure a group's tasks to encourage full participation by its members, as in the case of the Hadron Collider project. The key lies in being able to readily identify the contributions of each member. One experiment using college swim team members found that the athletes swam faster in individual time trials than they did during relays. When the relay race was structured so that each individual's time was announced aloud at the end of his or her lap, the individuals actually swam faster during the relay than in the individual heats. Results such as these suggest that managers may be able to encourage higher individual levels of effort on group projects by building in some form of acknowledgment of each member's contributions to the final outcome of the project.[24] Furthermore, research also seems to indicate that social loafing in groups is less likely to occur in collectivistic cultures (see Chapter 3), such as those in Asian countries, than in more individualistic cultures, such as those in the United States or Australia, because of the much stronger group orientation in collectivistic cultures.[25]

process costs
increasing costs of coordination as group size increases

Another significant disadvantage of larger groups involves the increasing **process cost**—a cost related to coordinating people—that groups suffer when their size increases. As groups become larger, the number of person-to-person relationships increases significantly, and coordination becomes more cumbersome. Also, a larger size comes with additional opportunities for interpersonal conflicts among group members.

A further managerial challenge relating to a group's relative size is that unanticipated disadvantages can appear, sometimes dramatically, when that size is increased from small to large. These effects were illustrated a few years ago by a relatively small company at that time, called Next Jump, Inc. It started out as a tiny venture organized by a group of friends. Those friends hired their friends. A "family tree" was even posted, showing the relationships among all the employees. In just three months, the company grew from 30 to 105 employees. As it grew, Charlie Kim, the company's CEO, tried to maintain the family feeling in the firm. Unfortunately, the idea of one large "team," with all members focused on the same goals, all working cohesively together, no longer worked as the company got larger. Meetings fell apart and confusion and conflict increased. People started quitting. The "family tree" was taken down. Kim, in his managerial role, was experiencing the effects that a changed size can have on a group's members and on the management of it.[26] He went on to meet this challenge of size growth and by 2010 his company was doing business with 60 percent of Fortune 500 corporations.[27] In summary, probably the best advice for managers with respect to the question of what is the best size for putting together a group is the conclusion reached in a comprehensive review of the research on groups, " use the smallest number of people who can do the task."[28] That admonition, of course, all depends on being clear about what the task actually is.

COMPOSITION Groups may be composed of individuals who are very similar or very dissimilar. If the former is the case, we describe the group as *homogeneous*. If the latter is the case, the composition would be regarded as *heterogeneous*, or diverse. Most groups these days have some degree of diversity, and many have a great deal. As Exhibit 10.5 shows, there can be different types of diversity within groups, including obvious differences such as the race/ethnicity, gender, and age of members, as well as less obvious differences such as members' values, skills, knowledge, information, and their length of time in the group and in the organization.[29] The accompanying Manager's Challenge illustrates that putting together diverse talents focused on a common goal is one possible way to create truly great teams.

Some managers deliberately take advantage of the diversity groups have to offer. For example, Jerry Hirshberg, a former president of Nissan Design who helped turn Southern California into a global center of automobile design, purposely combined employees with radically different professional and/or cultural backgrounds into teams. He believed that the natural conflict in these diverse teams results in "moments of friction and collision that lead to opportunities for breakthroughs."[30] A similar viewpoint was expressed by Hans-Paul Burkner, CEO of the Boston Consulting Group: "When we are faced with what looks like an unsolvable problem, a team with what I call 'spikes' of different talents will come up with a better solution than a team whose members have similar strengths."[31]

Demographic differences, differences in interpersonal styles, and differences in values can lend a group strength. However, the same differences can also become the source of intragroup conflict. Managers should actively emphasize the common interests of members and discourage personal conflicts between them.

The key managerial question is: Does a greater amount of diversity within groups more often help or hinder such outcomes as effective group functioning and performance? There is no simple answer to this question, especially given that there are different kinds of diversity.[32] Research findings are only suggestive and not conclusive. However, they tend to show that increased diversity potentially:

- Has somewhat negative effects on members' reactions and interactions with each other;
- Has positive effects on increasing the quality of the outputs of members' thinking together as a group—especially when innovation is a major objective—presumably because a wider range of opinions and ideas are discussed;[33] and
- Leads to decreased frequency of communication within a group but more communication with those outside the group.

In short, the challenge for a manager is to maximize the benefits that a group's diversity offers and minimize the potential disadvantages. This can be done by anticipating what some of

Types of Diversity	Potential Consequences
Observable Attributes	**Affective Consequences**
• Race	• Satisfaction
• Ethnicity	• Identification with the group
• Gender	• Conflict within the group
• Age	**Cognitive consequences**
Underlying Attributes	• Innovation
• Values	• Amount and quality of new ideas
• Skills	**Communication-Related Consequences**
• Knowledge and Information	• Decreased frequency within group
• Tenure	• Increased frequency outside of group

Source: Adapted from Frances L. Milliken and Luis L. Martins, "Searching for Common Threads: Understanding the Multiple Effects of Diversity in Organizational Groups," *Academy of Management Review* 21, no. 2 (1996), 402–423.

EXHIBIT 10.5

Examples of Diversity Within Groups and Potential Consequences

A MANAGER'S CHALLENGE

DIVERSITY

Great Teams Don't Just Happen

A manager who puts together a team in an organization always wants it to perform well, obviously, but most teams end up completing tasks and assignments in a satisfactory but not necessarily outstanding manner. The manager's challenge is how to increase the percentage of teams that perform not just competently, but exceptionally. There are no simple formulas for creating high-performing teams, but taking a look at some of the great teams that are prominent in the history of business provides a clue: Putting together the right mix of diverse talents when the team is formed is one way to increase the odds.

Several examples from past and more recent business eras serve to make the point. In the early years of the twentieth century, a revolutionary—for that time—new transportation vehicle called an "automobile" had only recently been developed. The challenge was how to manufacture such a complicated apparatus efficiently. To do this, Henry Ford, with an engineering background, put together a team that included three distinct personalities: Clarence Avery, an innovative primary designer of the assembly line process; Peter Martin, a systems thinker and head of assembly; and Charles Sorenson, an operational details expert. Together they came up with a procedure that not only could make reliably performing autos, but also—and crucially important—at a cost that was affordable for a wide range of potential customers.

An even earlier example of a great performing team of highly varied talents is the one Thomas Edison formed in the small town of Menlo Park, New Jersey, back in the 1870s. Edison enlisted the combined efforts of a small set of individuals with diverse capabilities: an American-educated mathematician, a German glassblower, an English machinist, and a Swiss clockmaker. Not only were their skills highly different, but so were their cultural backgrounds— an early global team, as it were. Out of the collaborative efforts of this group came a whole variety of products, including a dependably functioning and long-burning light bulb and an entertaining sound instrument called the phonograph powered by that newly developed source , electricity.

A much more recent example of a team that produced unparalleled accomplishments is the one that launched the Google search engine. The two founders of what has developed into a mighty firm, Sergey Brin and Larry Page, were students at Stanford in the 1990s. Starting in Page's dormitory room at the university and continuing in a garage, Brin and Page perfected the technical details that would be involved in carrying out easy-to-use searches on the Web. But, neither was a management or marketing expert. To remedy this, they brought in Eric Schmidt, an experienced technology manager, and a marketing guru, Omid Kordestani, forming a great team of different capabilities with results that became a worldwide phenomenon.

Still another relatively recent great team example comes from the world of advertising. In the late 1990s, ad agency McCann Erickson won a new contract with MasterCard, which at the time was frustrated with the ineffective results from the ad campaigns of its prior agency. The core creative team that McCann put together was small: just Joyce King Thomas, Jereon Bours, and Johnathan Cranin. They had already worked together for two years, but they brought diverse viewpoints to the challenge of completing a compelling storyline for MasterCard in its competition against its archrival Visa. They brainstormed intensively for a month, and then Cranin, while in the shower, came up with the line "some things money can't buy." Soon, Thomas was building a spot that would feature that line. Thomas and Bours further developed the idea for a setting, and settled on ordinary transactions at a baseball game and also the lead-in phrase: "Priceless." The ad campaign eventually evolved into a range of spots that have appeared in 105 countries and over 40 languages. Furthermore, since 1997, MasterCard has added users twice as quickly as Visa.

All four of these teams are legends in the history of business. Their common denominator was that they were able to integrate sets of distinctly different talents to achieve goals to which all team members, in each case, were committed. While certainly not all teams in the ordinary day-to-day world of business can or will become "great," there are lessons from these examples for managers to think about in improving any team's performance.

Sources: J. Palfini, "Four Great Teams in Business History," *BNet,* http://money.cnn.com/2006/05/31/magazines/fortune/sixteams_greatteams_fortune_061206/index.htm, accessed May 17, 2010.

those disadvantages might be and then directly addressing them. One way is for managers to give extra attention to developing strong group norms of cooperation. Also, since it is diversity in members' values and attitudes that is most likely to cause difficulties, managers need to help groups work through these initial differences and turn them into advantages rather than obstacles. The encouraging finding is that it appears that the longer a group works together, the more likely it is to find ways to do just that—to succeed in overcoming those initial differences in values and attitudes.[34] Whatever else can be said, though, one thing seems absolutely certain: The use of increasingly diverse work teams, especially—but not only—multinational groups, is becoming commonplace.[35] Therefore, for managers the opportunities for taking advantage of within-group diversity, and the necessity for coping with its potential challenges, are growing, not decreasing.

DIFFERENTIATED ROLES In groups of any size, different members perform different roles; that is, they occupy different positions with sets of expected behaviors attached to those positions. See, for example, one possible classification of different types of roles in teams, as shown in Exhibit 10.6.[36] Differences in expected behaviors attached to different positions are vividly illustrated in certain athletic teams, where players perform specialized roles when the team is on offense and different roles on defense. An example of distinctly different roles in another type of athletic team, a cycling team, is illustrated in A Manager's Challenge, "Teamwork Is Everything . . ." on page 282.

Roles in many work groups, however, are not always as clear-cut and can range from being fairly general, such as performing analytical duties, to being highly specialized with specific task assignments, such as monitoring particular pieces of equipment. More and more, however, organizations are attempting to loosen rigid job descriptions and role boundaries in groups in order to gain greater flexibility in meeting unexpected competitive and environmental challenges. The challenge for managers of teams operating in today's fast-changing circumstances is to get the members of their teams moving "outside the box"—that is, to think more creatively about how to fulfill their roles.[37]

Some roles in groups are more core, more essential, than others for team performance.[38] One such role is that of the leader. In the past, the leadership role in work groups has tended to be

	Role	Important When . . .
Task	Contractor	the task is ambiguous
	Creator	the team is new or has stagnated
	Contributor	expertise is distributed among team members or when there are high status differentials
	Completer	tasks are individually oriented
	Critic	consensus is close without adequate analysis of positive *and* negative contingencies
Social	Cooperator	the team has made a decision
	Communicator	social sensitivity is needed
	Calibrator	there are nonfunctional team processes or when team is new
Boundary Spanning	Consul	the team is dependent on external resources
	Coordinator	the team's activities must be coordinated with activities of others

EXHIBIT 10.6

Team Roles

Source: Based on T. V. Mumford, M. A. Campion, F. P. Morgeson, and C. H. Iddeking, "The Team Role Test: Development and Validation of a Team Role Knowledge Situational Judgment Test," *Journal of Applied Psychology* 93 (2008): 250-267.

A MANAGER'S CHALLENGE

GLOBALIZATION

*Team*work Is Everything in the Global Sport of Team Cycling

Nowhere is the need for intricately coordinating the efforts of a group's members more essential than in the worldwide sport of team cycling. Of course, the athletic skills and capabilities of each individual team member are a necessary and fundamental component, but unless those talents are coordinated so that real *team*work occurs, they are not sufficient to win races in this highly demanding sport.

Even such great riders as Lance Armstrong, winner of seven straight Tour de France victories, could not come close to winning that prestigious race without the elaborately choreographed efforts of his teammates. Consider the following: A typical international cycling team has 20 to 30 riders on its squad. Out of that number, the team director will select a team of nine to participate in a particular race. The nine will represent a collection of different skills, strengths, and weaknesses. The particular combination will be critical: some riders will be best at sprinting, some at mountain climbing, and some at performing as rugged work-horses. In advance of a race, the team selects a "leader," the rider who they will attempt to make sure ends up in first at the end. Usually, this person is its strongest overall rider, the one judged to have the highest probability of winning the race for the team.

The eight other riders on the team are called "domestiques," and it is their primary job to do everything they can to help the leader ultimately win the race. Although in theory any of a lead rider's domestiques could win the race, that is highly unlikely unless some unusual event occurs. What, specifically, are the tasks of domestiques? Mostly, they ride ahead of the team leader for much of each day's stage in the race. And why do they do this? To save the leader's energy for the finish line, since, on a long event, riding behind other riders—a practice called "drafting"—can save as much as 30 per cent or more of one's overall

energy expenditure. Bobby Julich, a well-known rider in international races, explained how it feels to support the leader in this way: "It's sometimes hard working for a leader because you don't receive as much personal recognition, but if the leader or your team manager comes up to you after a stage and shakes your hand or pats you on the back, that's the gratification you take from the day."

The teamwork aspect of team cycling comes into play during the different segments of a day's race where most of the time most of the riders from different teams stay tightly clustered in a large group called a "peloton." At various times, of course, a rider from a given team may attempt to break away from the peloton—known as an "attack—and it is up to a rival team's domestiques to trade off and exchange a front-riding position to try to track down the breakaway rider so that their own leader can conserve his energy while catching up. At other times, a whole team may suddenly attack and attempt to wear down a rival team as it tries to respond. It is these situations of single-rider or team attacks that call for the highly coordinated efforts and tactics of both attackers and opponents.

On long races over many stages (days), it is the cumulative effects of coordinated teamwork that add up in final victory. As the world-class Spanish rider Alberto Contador has put it, "Believe me, anybody who wants to win the Tour de France needs [the help of his teammates]. To win it on your own is really impossible."

Sources: D. Engbe, " How Do Cycling Teams Work?" *Slate News,* July 13, 2005, http://www.slate.com/id/2122645; "Tour de France: An Outstanding Case Study in Leadership and Teamwork," *Trident Leadership,* http://blog.tridentleadership.com/2010/02/an-outstanding-case-study-in-leadership-and-teamwork/, accessed May 12, 2010; and B. Julich, "How Teamwork Played a Role in First Uphill Finish of Tour," *ESPN,* http://sports.espn.go.com/oly/tdf2008/news/story?id= 3481713, accessed May 12, 2010.

specialized and concentrated in one person, the supervisor. However, the clear trend in today's highly competitive organizations is to attempt to spread leadership functions as widely as possible among group members. This occurs especially in so-called self-managing teams, but it also is becoming more common even in typical command-type groups.[39] The principle involved is that if a group's leadership functions are more broadly shared and accepted, the group will be able to respond faster and more effectively to rapidly changing pressures and circumstances.

Two particular issues that groups face with respect to roles—and that you probably have faced in your own group experiences—are role ambiguity and role conflict. **Role ambiguity** refers to a situation in which the expected behaviors for a group member are not clearly defined.

role ambiguity
a situation in which the expected behaviors for a group member are not clearly defined

This can increase the stress level for group members. **Role conflict** emerges when a member has to fulfill two or more contrasting sets of expectations, such as taking time to be friendly with customers while also meeting a certain quota of customers served. For example, a former manager at Corning, the glass company, faced this kind of role conflict. His effectiveness was evaluated on two primary criteria: (1) keeping Corning's research scientists happy, which involved adopting a relatively hands-off leadership style and letting them work when, how, and on what they wanted; and (2) keeping the company happy, which involved being a hands-on, directive leader, holding down costs and making sure research scientists were productive.[40] In such a situation, a manager has to make choices that are often very difficult.

role conflict
a situation in which a member of a group faces two or more contrasting sets of expectations

DIFFERENTIATED STATUS LEVELS Not only do members have different roles in groups, they also often have different levels of status or rank. **Status** is the standing or prestige that a person has in a group, and it can be based on a number of factors, such as perceived leadership abilities, seniority, or special skills, among others.

status
the standing or prestige that a person has in a group, which can be based on a number of factors such as perceived leadership abilities, seniority, or special skills

Research has shown that status differences can strongly influence the interactions within a group.[41] For example, higher-status members tend to receive more communications than do lower-status members, and lower-status members tend to defer to higher-status members when groups are making decisions.[42] However, a group's communication and decision making are likely to be inhibited if the status differences within the group are too extreme. In this case, information relevant to the group's members would be less likely to be widely shared and, thus, not be given sufficient attention by the group.

Behavioral Characteristics

Two chief features of groups and teams that involve behavioral-type characteristics are the norms that develop in groups and the degree to which groups are cohesive.

Norms

A **norm,** as indicated in our earlier discussion of informal groups and the stages of group development, is a standard, shared by the group, that guides the behavior of its individual members. For example, when members of a group behave similarly toward supervisors or outsiders, such as stopping nontask conversations when they enter the room, they are demonstrating the effect of group norms. It would be very difficult, if not impossible, for groups to function without norms.[43] Each person's behavior would be too unpredictable for coordinated action to take place. Norms also help to reduce ambiguity; thus, they provide members with cues and useful guidelines about how to behave.

norms
a group's shared standards that guide the behavior of its individual members

Information provided by norms is particularly important for new members of a group who need to learn what is going on in the work situation as rapidly as possible. This was illustrated in the case of a manager who left her former employer to begin work at a technology company as a supervisor of a group of project managers. Within her first few days on the new job, the manager asked her assistant to set up individual meetings with several of her project managers. To her surprise, the assistant scheduled the meetings in the subordinates' offices rather than in the manager's office. When she inquired why, the assistant replied, "That's how it's done around here." The manager realized that if she had insisted that the meetings be held in her own office, she would have violated a prevailing norm and potentially created unnecessary ill will.[44]

THE CHARACTERISTICS OF GROUP NORMS Group norms and their significance can be understood by reviewing several of their main features:

- Norms are usually established for the more important issues of concern to the group; for example, rates of minimally acceptable output or performance.
- Norms do not necessarily apply to all members of the group; some apply only to certain members (like the leader), usually based on the status or particular role of those members. For example, it may be acceptable for a senior member of a group, but not for a junior member, to arrive late for meetings.

■ Norms vary in the degree to which they are accepted by group members; some norms are accepted and endorsed by virtually all members, others by only a majority. For instance, norms regarding how to deal with work problems might be accepted by everyone, but norms regarding desirable attire might be endorsed by only certain members.

■ Norms vary in how much deviation members are permitted in following them; in other words, some norms are very loose and permit a great deal of leeway in behavior, whereas other norms, especially those regarding key group issues, are much more restrictive.[45] For example, a member of a group who talks to outsiders about the group's internal problems might receive severe censure from fellow group members. By contrast, someone who merely talks louder than normal during meetings might be tolerated (up to a degree, at least).

THE DEVELOPMENT OF GROUP NORMS Norms do not suddenly and magically appear in groups. They seldom, if ever, develop in a purely spontaneous way. Rather, they arise out of interaction among group members. An example of a typical norm development process is shown in Exhibit 10.7. Key factors that often have a major influence on the process include the following:[46]

■ *Early behaviors:* Typically, initial behaviors, especially in newly formed groups, establish standards for subsequent behavior. In committees, for example, the first few meetings help establish norms about how candid, or how indirect, the discussion of sensitive issues is likely to be. Such quickly established norms are often difficult to reshape or change later.

■ *Imported behaviors:* Members of a group often bring with them standards of behavior that were prominent in their former groups. "When in doubt, stay with the familiar" seems to be the (sometimes incorrect) watchword of many people in organizations. When a high-status member imports a norm, as in the case of those with acknowledged expertise or high power, the prominence of that norm is likely to be strong. A new CEO, for example, may believe in a norm of communication "only through channels" even though this may run counter to the organization's previous norm of "openness." However, because the new CEO's status is high, few are likely to challenge this imported norm.

■ *Critical events:* A sudden challenge to the group, such as criticism from another group, can create specific and vivid responses that form the basis for how members should be expected to respond in the future. A time of crisis makes people particularly alert to cues in their environment and tends to reinforce norms that emerge from that period. In a corporation that has announced layoffs, for example, new norms regarding the overt display of diligent work habits may emerge.

EXHIBIT 10.7

Example of the Development of Group Norms

Source: Adapted from Kenneth Bettenhausen and J. Keith Murnighan, "The Emergence of Norms in Competitive Decision Making Groups" *Administrative Science Quarterly,* Vol 30, © 1985 by permission of Administrative Science Quarterly .

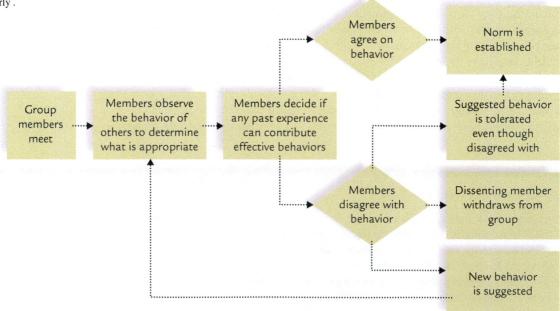

■ *Explicitly stated standards:* Not to be overlooked is the fact that leaders or high-status members of a group may simply assert that "This is how we will do it around here!" Newly appointed supervisors and athletic coaches, for example, frequently use this approach with their groups or teams.

THE EFFECTS OF GROUP NORMS The existence of strong norms tends to narrow individual differences in behavior and beliefs. This results in a certain degree of **conformity,** or close adherence to the group's norms, by individual members. In the opening profile, Steve Ortiz at Harrah's was faced with changing existing norms that seemed to be inhibiting the performance of his group. Ortiz needed the group to adopt new and different norms supportive of his unit's revised objectives.

conformity
close adherence to the group's norms by the individual members

Whether such conformity is "good" or "bad" depends on the perspective of the viewer. If the norms support a manager's goals for a group—for example, that everyone should look for opportunities to make creative suggestions to improve the group's effectiveness—then the manager would regard conformity as very helpful.[47] However, if norms conflict with the objectives a manager is trying to achieve, then greater conformity would be regarded as negative. The implication for you as a manager, therefore, is that you should be as concerned about the content or direction of group norms as about the amount of conformity to them.

From the point of view of an individual member of a group, norms can sometimes be too constraining. In that case, the individual may deviate from the group's expected attitudes and behavior. Such divergent actions or expressed views are potentially troubling to others in the group because they can threaten the group's solidarity and, perhaps, in extreme cases, even its existence. Therefore, the group sometimes imposes sanctions on the deviant in an attempt to bring about greater conformity. The classic case in certain Western work situations, particularly at the hourly worker level, is the individual who works faster or slower than the group thinks he or she should. Sometimes labeled "rate busters" or "slackers," these people are often subjected to ridicule or ostracism to persuade or force them to work at a rate more in line with the group's norms.

Cohesion

Another major behavioral property of groups is their amount of **cohesion,** "the degree to which members are motivated to remain in a group."[48] Group cohesion is usually considered to have many advantages and to be highly desirable if it can be developed.[49] When managers and organizations attempt to turn groups into teams, they are, in effect, trying to generate stronger group cohesion. However, as we will discuss later, high levels of group cohesion don't always result in positive outcomes.[50]

cohesion
the degree to which members are motivated to remain in the group

THE DEVELOPMENT OF GROUP COHESION There are no sure-fire ways for you as a manager to build strong cohesion in groups that you lead or in which you are a member. However, the available research suggests three factors that can be potentially important in developing greater group cohesion:

■ Strengthening the interpersonal attraction among group members;
■ Generating a record of high performance and past success of the group;[51] and
■ Fostering competition with other groups.[52]

The most consistently important of these factors appears to be the first, namely, whether members of the group think they have something in common with other members and tend to like being with them; that is, whether they feel like they belong to a true team. The evidence for the other two factors in bringing about cohesion is not as clear-cut. However, both past successes and current or anticipated conflicts with other groups also seem to unite members and increase their cohesion. This is especially true if a strong interpersonal attraction among members is already present. A group whose members don't especially like being with each other may disintegrate when faced with competition from external groups, rather than develop greater cohesion, which again places a premium on developing interpersonal bonds.

THE EFFECTS OF GROUP COHESION The increased cohesiveness of groups can have a number of potential advantages.[53] Chief among these is an increase in the quantity and quality of group interaction.[54] A second potential advantage of greater group cohesion is that the group has

EXHIBIT 10.8

Effects of High Levels of Group Cohesion

Positive Effects	Negative Effects
• Increased quality and quantity of group interactions	• Counterproductive norms may be emphasized
• Strengthened adherence to group norms	• Useful or creative ideas may be ignored if they deviate from established norms or values
• Increased effectiveness in achieving group goals	• Increased probability of developing groupthink
• Augmented individual satisfaction with group membership	• Potential decrease in intergroup cooperation

stronger influence on each member to conform to the group's standards or norms. Assuming—and this is a critical assumption—that those norms are positive from the manager's perspective, then this is a significant advantage. A related plus is that high group cohesion can possibly help to reduce any tendency toward social loafing on the part of individual members.[55] Still another possible advantage of higher group cohesion is that members tend to have greater satisfaction with the group.

As positive as these potential advantages might seem, high group cohesion sometimes can be a mixed blessing from a manager's point of view (see Exhibit 10.8). First, if the group has norms that do not support the organization's goals, then greater cohesion is definitely a minus. In this case, members may be more influenced in the "wrong" direction—as when, for example, a group of workers tolerates sexual harassment—than if there is little cohesion. Another possible disadvantage of strong group cohesion is that any deviance from the group's norms might not be handled well. Highly cohesive groups are more likely to reject any deviance, even if it represents creative ideas that could ultimately be useful to the group. Related to this is the danger that groupthink[56]—a tendency for a strong consensus among most group members to override any individual member's dissent—may be accentuated in highly cohesive groups. (See Chapter 12 for a further discussion of groupthink.) Dissenting viewpoints expressed by a "devil's advocate" often, however, can help a group critically examine its opinion or decisions.

Still another potential disadvantage of high group cohesion, but one that is frequently overlooked, is that the cooperation between groups may be adversely affected. For example, in developing and marketing a new product, problems may develop among a firm's production, marketing, and sales groups as they work together to develop and market a new product. If the production group is highly cohesive and has a norm of never allowing outsiders to know it has problems, it may be reluctant to notify other units that a key piece of equipment is not functioning correctly. Without this information, the marketing department might generate unrealistic expectations for the product's release date, and the sales teams then would promise higher numbers of the product to customers than would actually be available. Most organizations have many work groups; some have hundreds or more. The challenge, for higher-level managers, is to have these groups and teams work together and interact smoothly and reliably. So, it is a concern if high within-group cohesion hinders intergroup cooperation.

Emerging Types of Groups and Teams in Today's Organizations

Now that we have examined how groups form and develop and explored some of their basic characteristics, we are ready to look at some examples of particular kinds of groups and teams that are becoming increasingly prominent in today's organizations (see Exhibit 10.9). Not every organization will have each of these groups, but where they do exist they present some special managerial challenges.

Type	Potential Advantages	Potential Disadvantages
Self-managing	More team-like behavior	Not all employees want to manage themselves
Cross-functional/ New product	Increased creativity Dispersed knowledge Speed to market	Increased group conflict
Global	Increased creativity from diversity of backgrounds	Paralysis Inaction Failure
Virtual	Increased speed of communication Decreased costs	Increased misinterpretation Lack of trust Difficult to manage

EXHIBIT 10.9

Prominent Groups and Teams in Today's Organizations

Self-Managing Work Groups

A relatively recent, but increasingly important, variant of a command work group is the **self-managing work group,** also known as an *autonomous work group*—a work group that has no formally appointed supervisor. These groups are similar to command groups in that the members coordinate their work as if they all reported to the same formally appointed supervisor. However, the group manages itself on behalf of the organization's objectives, and its members usually appoint their own informal team leaders.[57] The group is made up of a number of members with diverse skills that can be applied to the group's task. It generally is responsible for decisions concerning how to accomplish the work—which members will perform which tasks and in which order. Members also frequently do jobs traditionally associated with supervision, such as conducting team meetings and solving productivity problems. A major reason why some organizations—Xerox, Procter & Gamble, and General Motors, among many others—have explored putting together self-managing units is to develop more team-like group behavior than in more traditional command groups, and eventually to gain greater efficiency and effectiveness.[58]

The idea of group self-management, however good it appears in principle, may not appeal to all employees whom it might affect. Furthermore, it cannot be assumed to fit into all types of circumstances and cultures.[59] In short, self-managed work groups are no panacea for group performance problems. Managers and organizations who want to establish such groups need to consider the potential pitfalls and resistance to this kind of arrangement, as well as the possible advantages.

Cross-Functional, New Product (or Service) Groups

Groups that draw their membership from distinctly different types of units within an organization, such as R&D and marketing, have been around for many years. However, their number and importance have increased markedly in recent years. A primary objective for such groups or teams is to bring to bear as much creativity and dispersed knowledge as possible on the task. A good example of a company's use of cross-functional teams is represented by DJO Inc., a manufacturer of orthopedics and other rehabilitation products. Given the highly competitive nature of this industry, the company needs to concentrate on new product development (NPD). To do this, it creates an NPD team for every project, consisting of members from the design engineering, manufacturing, quality, marketing, and regulatory units. Each team is given complete responsibility for the project from its start to finish and has oversight over all project tasks and elements. These cross-functional teams also are encouraged to try to solve any problems they face before having to involve higher managers to make final decisions.[60]

Other major objectives of cross-functional teams, especially in high-technology firms, are to speed the products to market while at the same time controlling or minimizing costs. This sounds good, but the reality is often that the outcomes are less favorable than expected because

self-managing work group (also known as an *autonomous work group*) a group that has no formally appointed supervisor but is similar to command groups in that the members coordinate their organizational work as if they all reported to the same formally appointed supervisor; members usually appoint their own informal team leader

of the potential for increased conflicts in groups composed of members with widely varying initial perspectives.[61] To deal with this basic issue, research results suggest that managers should try to increase the following attributes of effective cross-functional groups:[62]

- Members' feelings of ownership ("at-stakeness") of the group's decisions;
- Transparency or openness regarding members' motivations, expectations, and personal agendas;
- "Mindfulness" or, essentially, reaching high-quality decisions after examining all divergent points of view; and
- High levels of mutual cooperation ("synergy") and trust.

Global Teams

Another type of group that is becoming increasingly prominent, especially in larger organizations, is the multinational group (almost always referred to as a *multinational team*). It is usually a highly diverse group, whether or not it represents one or several functional areas, because members are often from very different cultural backgrounds. For reasons that we have already discussed, diverse teams potentially offer major advantages for organizations. However, reality is not always quite so rosy. All too frequently, the groups can end up in paralysis or even in failure.

One set of researchers divides up global teams into three general types: destroyers, equalizers, and creators.[63] Destroyers are groups that turn out to be utter disasters; they channel their members' efforts and attention into unproductive conflicts and interpersonal attacks. For example, one member of a European destroyer team described the team environment candidly: "Those Brits on our team are too serious; the Germans are so stuck-up about engineering that they don't think anyone else has a brain; and the French couldn't care less about production quotas." Equalizer teams are those that think they are doing well and have little apparent conflict, yet seem unable to produce any result other than one of mediocrity. Essentially, equalizers are underperforming teams that fail to take advantage of their cross-national diversity. Creator teams are those that directly accept and build on their differences and use them to enhance their creativity.

Virtual Teams

As mentioned earlier in this chapter, organizations are increasingly establishing virtual teams or groups composed of individuals who do not work together in close physical proximity. Members of virtual teams are often geographically dispersed, often with cross-organizational or cross-national membership.[64] As their names imply, such groups rarely, if ever, meet in person and instead conduct most or all of their business via electronic communication.

The increased speed of communication and decreased costs in meeting together are obvious advantages of these groups. Nevertheless, virtual teams have their own managerial challenges and problems.[65] First, communication, though fast and sometimes nearly instantaneous, can be incomplete and easily subject to misinterpretation by the receiver.[66] Second, trust among group members may be very difficult to develop because of the absence of the typical getting-to-know-you socialization process that occurs with nonvirtual groups that meet face-to-face.[67] Third, supervision may be more difficult than in a typical group. Also, issues that can crop up in any group, such as role ambiguity and social loafing, for example, may be intensified in virtual groups. See the A Manager's Challenge, "Stages in Virtual Teams," for an illustration of some of these issues in virtual teams that were used in FOODCO (not its real name), a large, nationwide and complex food distribution company composed of a number of different operating units.

Nevertheless, over the last decade or so organizations have, sometimes as the result of unpleasant experiences, developed some effective ways to lessen or overcome these potential problems with virtual teams. Examples would include making sure that reward incentives are explicitly attached to participating effectively in this type of group, ensuring as much as possible through technology and supervisory attention that members remain focused on the group's tasks, and creating activities – even the occasional face-to-face meeting — that promote group cohesion and commitment to its shared goals.[68]

A MANAGER'S CHALLENGE

TECHNOLOGY

Stages in Virtual Teams

Do virtual teams go through "life cycles" in the same way that many meet-in-person groups do? Do they face the same kinds of challenges at each stage of the cycle that those groups do? Those were the basic questions examined by researchers associated with the University of North Carolina (UNC).

It has been demonstrated that many teams, particularly project teams whose activities have specific beginning and ending points, go through a set of stages in their development that could be called their life cycle. Although these cycles have been studied in various groups where members are located in relative proximity to each other and can have frequent in-person, face-to-face meetings, they seldom have been investigated in virtual teams composed of members who are geographically dispersed. This was the focus of the University of North Carolina study conducted in conjunction with an executive leadership institute.

Those attending the institute held mid- and upper-level managerial positions at "FOODCO," a real company given this fictitious name to protect its anonymity. FOODCO is a large, nationwide food products distribution company with some 20 operating subsidiaries. Its clients include fast-food chains, hospitals, universities, and free-standing restaurants. With the company's participation and encouragement, the 29 managers attending the leadership program were assigned to six virtual teams of four or five persons by the instructors. Each team was given a specific project objective (for example,

to determine how to transfer the best practices from one division of the company to other divisions) and an eight-month timeline to complete their project and make concrete recommendations to top management (while continuing to do their regular jobs back at their own locations).

The researchers found that the forming-storming-norming-performing stages in a group's life cycle were relevant to the development of these virtual teams. In the forming stage, the teams exhibited extremely high levels of optimism about doing the task and being able to work with their teammates. By the storming stage, reality had set in. Problems emerged, such as a lack of team leadership, an apparent lack of commitment from some members, and difficulties related to coordinating the efforts among far-flung group members. In the third stage, only some of the teams had begun to develop consensus norms about how to proceed, do a better job of sharing relevant knowledge, and obtain commitments to time schedules. By the fourth or performing stage, definite differences had emerged across the six groups with regard to how well they were meeting their project objectives in a timely fashion and without having to make "a mad dash to the finish."

What conclusions could be drawn from the study? Many of the problems the teams faced—such as achieving agreement on responsibilities and managing a team task while also doing one's regular job—were very similar to those encountered by nonvirtual project teams, except more so! Almost all team participants agreed that the advice they would give future virtual teams was "Start [getting organized] earlier!" They found—more than they had expected to—that the "virtual" aspects of their team greatly intensified the difficulties related to finding effective ways to communicate and coordinate with one another. Also, it was clear from this study that it was extremely important for higher-level executives to intervene in a timely way to help teams. In short, "to thrive, virtual project teams must be embedded in supportive corporate cultures." Although the teams in this study were virtual, the challenges they experienced were real.

Andrey Popov/Shutterstock

Virtual teams rarely, if ever, meet in person. Instead they work toward common goals by conducting most or all of their business via electronic communication. Because they allow organizations to hire and retain the best employees around the world regardless of where they are located, virtual teams are becoming more prevalent as businesses globalize.

Sources: Based on S. A. Furst, M. Reeves, B. Rosen, and R. S. Blackburn, "Managing the Life Cycle of Virtual Teams," *Academy of Management Executive* 18, no. 2 (2004): 6–20. See also W. Combs and S. Peacocke, "Leading Virtual Teams," *T + D* 61, no. 2 (2007): 27–28; D. L. Paul, "Collaborative Activities in Virtual Settings: A Knowledge Management Perspective of Telemedicine," *Journal of Management Information Systems* 22, no. 4 (2006): 143–176; B. Rosen, S. Furst, and R. Blackburn, "Overcoming Barriers to Knowledge Sharing in Virtual Teams," *Organizational Dynamics* 36 (2007): 259–273.

Building and Managing Groups and Teams

In various places, this chapter has mentioned some of the steps that managers can take to increase the quality of group functioning and the satisfaction of group members. This section focuses on three issues particularly critical in building and managing groups and turning them into true teams: developing team competencies, dealing with team conflicts, and improving group effectiveness.

Developing Team Competencies

As emphasized throughout this chapter, working with, and in, a group is different from simply doing one's own job well. It is the interaction with other people, whether face-to-face or by electronic and other indirect means, that makes the difference. Therefore, to be able to perform effectively in a group, it is important to develop competencies in teamwork. To be a competent team member is not necessarily the same thing as being a competent individual performer. A useful way to think about what is required in a team situation is to consider three basic areas of teamwork competencies: **k**nowledge, **s**kills, and **a**ttitudes, or *KSA*s.[69] Specific examples of team competencies in these three areas are shown in Exhibit 10.10.

Knowledge (K) in the group context refers to the necessary understanding of facts, concepts, relations, and underlying relevant information necessary to perform team tasks. As shown in Exhibit 10.10, examples of the kinds of specific knowledge that are especially useful in team situations include knowledge about the team's mission and goals, the sequencing of tasks faced by the team, fellow team members' roles and responsibilities, and teammate characteristics.

Skills (S) (as noted previously) refer to highly developed behavioral and cognitive capabilities, such as emotional intelligence, that are necessary to carry out team tasks and meet team goals.[70] Among others, these skills include such competencies as adaptability and flexibility in relation to accomplishing team tasks, being able to monitor one's own performance and the performance of one's team members, being able to accept and give criticisms, and being able to assume leadership responsibilities within the group.

Attitudes (A) involve relatively stable feelings and beliefs about something. In other words, our attitudes, generally speaking, indicate how we view important parts of our environment. In group work situations, these attitudes would include those toward the concepts of teams and teamwork, the need for team cohesion, the assessment of a team's capabilities, and the level and importance of trust within a group.[71]

Dealing with Team Conflict

When people work in groups, the potential for conflict always exists within the group. Conflicts can occur for a number of reasons and can have a variety of consequences. Although the effects of group conflict, such as a marked decrease in cohesion within the group, often can be negative,

---

EXHIBIT 10.10

Examples of Specific Team Competencies in Three Areas

Knowledge	Skills	Attitudes
• Knowledge of team mission, objectives, norms	• Adaptability and flexibility	• Team orientation
• Task sequencing	• Mutual performance monitoring and feedback, self-correction	• Shared vision
• Team role interaction patterns	• Coordination and task integration	• Team cohesion
• Understanding team work skills	• Communication	• Mutual trust
• Teammate characteristics	• Decision making and problem solving	• Importance of teamwork

Sources: Adapted from J. A. Cannon-Bowers and E. Salas, "A Framework for Developing Team Performance Measures in Training," in M. T. Brannick, E. Salas, and C. Prince (eds.), *Team Performance Assessment and Measurement: Theory, Methods, and Applications* (Mahwah: Lawrence Erlbaum Associates, 1997), 47.

that is not always so. Some types of conflict, particularly task or substantive conflict (discussed next), potentially can have positive effects. For instance, a senior executive at Keane, an information technology firm based in Boston, views it this way: "We can agree our way into horrendous decisions. But when people are allowed to express their opinions, no matter how disagreeable, magic can occur. More ideas are put on the table, which can lead to more discovery, which can lead to quantum leaps in improvement and innovation...."[72]

The important point to remember is that conflict among members within groups is fairly common, and it is not always something to be avoided. In fact, the absence of any conflict at all can be a significant sign that the group is not openly generating a sufficient variety of viewpoints and potential approaches for solving problems and making good decisions.

TYPES OF GROUP CONFLICT Researchers have generally distinguished three basic types of group conflict: task, process, and relationship. **Task conflict** is conflict that focuses on differences in ideas about the nature of the issues facing a group and the group's objectives. It is also sometimes called *cognitive* (thinking) or *substantive conflict*.[73] Research indicates that sometimes, but certainly not always, some amount of task conflict can be beneficial to the group, especially for less routine and more complex tasks, and when conflict is introduced deliberately as in the use of a "devil's advocate."[74] Similarly, **process conflict**—differences of opinion about the procedures a group uses to achieve its goals—can be helpful but often may not be.

The other major type of conflict that can occur in groups, relationship conflict, is usually found to be almost always dysfunctional. **Relationship conflict** focuses on interpersonal differences and is sometimes called affective or emotional conflict.[75] It is usually a negative type of conflict for groups because it distracts focus from tasks and ideas.[76] It discourages rather than encourages members to consider multiple points of view and openly discuss ideas and solutions.

CAUSES OF GROUP CONFLICT There are many potential causes of group conflict, but they can usually be linked to the different types of conflict.

Potential causes of task and process conflicts include:

- Ambiguities regarding the task;
- Differences in goals, objectives, and perspectives (for example, stemming from differences in functional backgrounds) among group members;[77] and
- Scarcity (actual or perceived) of resources to accomplish the group's goals.

Potential causes of relationship conflicts include:

- Dissimilarities in the composition of the membership of the group, including demographic diversity (in age, ethnic/cultural background, gender, and so forth) and status/power differences;[78]
- Differences in the interpersonal styles of individual members; and
- Differences in values.[79]

Several of the potential causes of group conflict can occur together; for example, when a very diverse group that includes several people with distinctive interpersonal styles or quite different values encounters a highly ambiguous task. When there are multiple causes such as these, finding ways to deal with the conflict becomes even more difficult.

MANAGING GROUP CONFLICT If you are put in the position of leading a group, what can you do to help your group deal with conflict? Probably the most important managerial guideline for dealing with group conflict is to try to increase the ratio of substantive to relationship conflict.[80] This would mean, for example, strongly encouraging a culture of openness and cooperation that allows members to express their different opinions about task methods and objectives, and also being especially receptive to novel or creative approaches to coping with the group's task requirements.[81] In this way, maximum amounts of relevant information can be brought to bear on the issues faced by the group, and unintended groupthink tendencies can be minimized.[82] "When marketing and engineering disagree violently about something, you've got a wonderful opportunity to figure out how to make improvements by meeting both of their objectives."[83]

task conflict
conflict that focuses on differences in ideas and courses of action in addressing the issues facing a group

process conflict
differences of opinion about the procedures a group should use to achieve its goals

relationship conflict
interpersonal differences among group members

In addition to promoting and reinforcing a culture of openness, you should help to clarify and reduce task ambiguities and try to get the group to focus on larger goals beyond the individual interests of members—goals, in other words, that emphasize the common interests of all the group members. Also, there is evidence to suggest that active attempts taken to avoid relationship conflicts can be an effective way to eliminate or at least reduce their harmful effects on members' satisfaction and performance.[84] The key overall point here is that it is difficult if not impossible to avoid conflicts occurring within groups, but that conflicts of any type can be managed and potentially turned into productive group behavior.

Most of what we have been talking about so far applies to conflict *within* groups (**intragroup conflict**). In organizational settings, however, achieving coordination and reducing conflict *between* or among groups—**intergroup conflict**—is also important.[85] Strategies for managing intragroup conflict can apply equally well to intergroup conflict. Therefore, managers should look for opportunities to decrease unnecessary relational conflicts in those intergroup interaction situations and increase the focus on relevant substantive differences. Also, emphasizing larger, more organization-wide goals can help increase cooperation and, thus, performance.[86] So, for example, if sales and production can concentrate on the issue of improving customer satisfaction—to elevate it to the highest priority—then their differences on how many variations of a product to make and market can be minimized or resolved. As with intragroup conflict, the potential exists for positive effects from intergroup conflict, but again that conflict has to be faced and managed.

intragroup conflict
differences that occur within groups

intergroup conflict
differences that occur between groups

Improving the Effectiveness of Groups and Teams

Teams and groups are not static parts of organizations. They come into existence, go out of existence, and change over time. Additionally, and most important, their effectiveness and performance can be changed and improved. As a leader of a group, however, this is not necessarily easy to do. There is no magic formula to bring this about. Nevertheless, there are some useful approaches to consider that have the potential for helping to improve a group's performance in organizational settings.[87]

ASSESSING THE EFFECTIVENESS OF GROUPS What exactly do we mean by group effectiveness? What distinguishes highly effective groups from less effective ones? A survey of 61 U.S. companies revealed that about two-thirds use objective, quantifiable criteria to measure group effectiveness; these included measures of production output, quality improvements, cost reductions, and turnaround times. A number of the companies also used more subjective criteria, including member participation, cooperation, and involvement.[88]

How can we tell when a group is performing especially well? One of the foremost experts on group effectiveness, Richard Hackman, suggests there are three major indicators (Exhibit 10.11):[89]

1. Whether the group's outputs—products, services, or decisions—are valued by those that receive or use them. Are a committee's recommendations implemented? Does a product development group's creation ever get put into production? Is upper management satisfied with the performance of a customer service unit?
2. Whether the group's capacity for further cooperation among its members is maintained or increased.
3. Whether members gain satisfaction and a sense of growth and well-being from being part of the group. Outsiders are unlikely to regard a group or team as effective if the team's own members do not seem satisfied and are not experiencing feelings of accomplishment by being part of the group.

EXHIBIT 10.11

Characteristics of Highly Effective Groups

- Any product or service they develop is highly desired and valued by customers.
- Increased cooperation among members is encouraged and achieved.
- Group membership increases individual members' feelings of satisfaction, personal growth, and overall well-being.

Source: Based on J. R. Hackman (ed.), *Groups That Work (and Those That Don't): Creating Conditions for Effective Teamwork* (San Francisco: Jossey-Bass, 1990).

Most observers would probably say that the first of these criteria—acceptance of the group's outputs by others—is the most important one in organizational settings. However, if a group cannot achieve either of the other two objectives, it is highly unlikely it will be able, over time, to produce valued output. Thus, all three are important components of group effectiveness.

INGREDIENTS NECESSARY FOR GROUP EFFECTIVENESS For a group to perform effectively, it must be able to do at least three things especially well:

1. Exert enough effort to accomplish tasks at acceptable levels of quantity and quality;
2. Obtain sufficient knowledge and skills to carry out its work; and
3. Use appropriate strategies to apply effort, knowledge, and skills effectively.[90]

These three bases for achieving high levels of group effectiveness sound simple, but they pose major challenges. To ensure that these components are actually in place consistently, managers need to address several issues:

Develop Appropriate Group Structures To be effective, groups need clearly defined tasks and objectives that can motivate their members. Groups also need to be sized appropriately to their tasks, and they need a membership with a sufficient mix of skills and expertise. This means that if a leader has the option of choosing the group's members, those choices will often make a large difference in how well a group performs initially and what its capacity is to improve.

Develop Appropriate Support from the Organization[91] Groups operating within companies and organizations need support from their surrounding environment. For example, they need to be rewarded for effective collaboration.[92] They also need education and technical training for performing critical group tasks as well as relief from their other duties, and access to necessary information.[93]

Obtain Appropriate Coaching and Consultation Assistance[94] In the day-to-day world of work, most groups need outside help (whether from inside or outside the larger organization) to reduce potential conflicts, to increase their coordination in terms of dealing with problems within the group, and to develop strategies for approaching the group's tasks. Increased collaboration is an important objective, and the message here is that it is often the case that a group should not try to go it alone.[95]

Exhibit 10.12 provides a summary of the preceding points and shows how the manager's attention to the group's structure, support from the organizational context, and relevant coaching and consultation can help increase each of the three ingredients necessary for group effectiveness:

EXHIBIT 10.12 Enhancing Group Effectiveness

Necessary Processes	POINTS OF LEVERAGE		
	Group Structure	Organizational Context	Coaching and Consultation
Apply ample effort	Motivational structure of group task	Organizational reward system	Remedying coordination problems and building group commitment
Acquire sufficient knowledge and skill	Group composition	Organizational education/training system	Remedying inappropriate "weighting" of member inputs and fostering cross-training
Develop task-appropriate performance strategies	Group norms that regulate member behavior and foster scanning and planning	Organizational information system	Remedying implementation problems and fostering creativity in strategy development

Source: Adapted from J. R. Hackman (ed.), *Groups That Work (and Those That Don't): Creating Conditions for Effective Teamwork* (San Francisco: Jossey-Bass, 1990), 13.

EXHIBIT 10.13

A Checklist for Leaders of Groups

How well do you:

☐ Encourage members to learn from each other?

☐ Recognize and praise members for their contributions?

☐ Keep key people outside the group informed about its accomplishments?

☐ Promptly inform members about major developments that may affect them?

☐ Give group members authority to make at least some important decisions?

☐ Openly accept and respond to feedback from group members?

☐ Review the group's performance at the end of major tasks?

☐ Offer specific and concrete suggestions for how members can improve?

☐ Understand what motivates members to work hard?

Source: Adapted from G. L. Hallam, "Seven Common Beliefs About Teams: Are They True?" *Leadership in Action* 17, no. 3 (1997), 1–4.

high levels of effort, sufficient knowledge and skills, and appropriate strategies for applying effort and skills. The points presented and summarized in the exhibit do not provide a "cookbook" for group or team success. Rather, they are useful guidelines for managers and organizations to consider as they attempt to help groups improve their performance. Likewise, Exhibit 10.13, based on extensive research, provides a helpful checklist for those who assume leadership positions in groups and teams to measure how well they are fulfilling that role in their groups.[96] If team members concur that their leader is doing a good job in these areas, then it is likely that the group (and not just the leader) will perform well.

Managerial Challenges from the Front Line

The Rest of the Story

Steve Ortiz was confronted with the overall challenge of generating more income from the VIP customer segment of the Harrah's casino for which he works. This meant that he had to increase his employees' motivation to serve these customers better. To accomplish this, Ortiz formed a "team-based" approach. He held the entire group of employees working with the VIPs collectively accountable for the results, and he gave the team a clear-cut target on a month-by-month basis. Specifically, he developed a system whereby a VIP could be assisted by any "host" (employee), as opposed to the former system of having each host monitor only his or her "own" players. This resulted in the entire "team" receiving recognition and, most importantly, it left VIP guests with the impression that it did not matter which particular host was assigned to them—they would get great service either way.

Within two quarters following the change, the Kansas facility's customer satisfaction scores had increased above the mean scores for the company, and VIP sales ended up 18 percent over the previous year and the highest in the seven-year history of the property.

Summary

- The terms *group* and *team* are often used interchangeably. However, it is sometimes useful to make a distinction between them. A group is typically considered to consist of a small number of people, usually between 3 and 20 members who interact around some kind of shared objectives. A team can be considered a type of group that has a higher level of coordinated interaction and, especially, a higher level of individual members' identification with the group. Some groups become teams and some remain "only" groups.

- Groups operating within organizations can be classified into different basic categories. One category is "formal" groups—for example, command, project, and committee groups—assembled by the organization. The other category of groups are "informal," those formed by the voluntary actions of individuals rather than in response to an organizational directive. Informal groups often can greatly affect the success or failure of managers' actions.

- Three major factors influence the formation of groups: the organization's goals, opportunities for group members to interact and share knowledge, and people's psychological needs, such as those for security, social support, and self-esteem. Once groups are formed and their members begin to interact, they often, though not always, go through fairly predictable and sequential stages in their development. These stages have popularly been characterized as: forming, storming, norming, and performing.

- All groups, whether formal or informal, have structural and behavioral characteristics. Structural attributes include the group's size, its composition, and the different roles and levels of status of its members. A major behavioral feature of any group is its norms, or shared standards of behavior. Norms often influence the behavior of individual members in powerful ways. The level of cohesion, or the extent to which members want to remain a part of the group, is another significant behavioral characteristic.

- Several specific kinds of groups formed for particular purposes are becoming increasingly prominent in contemporary organizations, including self-managing work groups, cross-functional groups, global teams, and virtual teams. Each of these types of groups has its own advantages but also some potential problems. For example, self-managing work groups can generate a strong sense of member involvement, but not everyone may want to work in this kind of group. The other three groups are well adapted to deal with particular kinds of problems and issues, but sometimes face major problems coordinating the efforts of their members.

- Almost any type of group will perform better if its team members have good teamwork competencies. Such competencies can be classified as knowledge (for example, about one's teammates), skills (for example, communication skills), and attitudes (for example, mutual trust). Some of these competencies are "transportable" and can be used in any situation; others are sometimes specific to a particular task, particular situation, or particular combination of a task and situation.

- All groups face the possibility of conflict developing among their members. These conflicts are generally of two types: task and/or relationship. There are many possible causes of group conflicts of either type. Regardless of the specific causes, research has tended to show that an effective way to deal with group conflict is to try to reduce the amount of relationship conflict among members and to use task conflict to bring out different, even novel, approaches to task methods and goals before decisions are reached.

- The effectiveness of almost any group potentially can be increased by focusing on the following issues: the appropriateness of group processes and group structure, the nature of the organizational context, and access to external coaching and consultation where necessary.

Key Terms

cohesion   285
command group   272
committee   274
conformity   285
formal group   274
group   272
informal group   274

intergroup conflict   292
intragroup conflict   292
norm   283
process conflict   291
process cost   278
project/task force   273
relationship conflict   291

role ambiguity   282
role conflict   283
self-managing work group   287
social loafing   278
status   283
task conflict   291
team   272

Review Questions

1. What are the similarities and differences between a group and a team?
2. What are the four stages of group formation? Name the important features of each.
3. Is there an optimum group size? Why or why not?
4. What is *social loafing*? Can managers do anything to minimize or eliminate it?
5. What effects can diversity have on group members and on group functioning?
6. Provide examples of role conflict and role ambiguity that illustrate the difference between the two terms.
7. Why are norms important to groups?
8. What is meant by group cohesion? Are high levels of group cohesion always desirable?
9. What are the advantages and disadvantages of virtual teams?
10. What are KSAs, and how do they relate to team competencies?
11. Can managers eliminate group conflict? Should they try?
12. What are three major indicators that can be used to identify high-performance groups?

Assessing Your Capabilities

How Good Am I at Building and Leading a Team?

Using the following scale, circle the number that best indicates the extent to which you agree or disagree with each statement.

	Strongly Disagree	Disagree	Slightly Disagree	Slightly Agree	Agree	Strongly Agree
1. I am knowledgeable about the different stages of development that teams can go through in their life cycles.	1	2	3	4	5	6
2. When a team forms, I make certain that all team members are introduced to one another at the outset.	1	2	3	4	5	6
3. When the team first comes together, I provide directions, answer team members' questions, and clarify goals, expectations, and procedures.	1	2	3	4	5	6
4. I help team members establish a foundation of trust among one another and between themselves and me.	1	2	3	4	5	6
5. I ensure that standards of excellence—not mediocrity or mere acceptability—characterize the team's work.	1	2	3	4	5	6
6. I provide a great deal of feedback to team members regarding their performance.	1	2	3	4	5	6
7. I encourage team members to balance individual autonomy with interdependence among other team members.	1	2	3	4	5	6
8. I help team members become at least as committed to the success of the team as to their own personal success.	1	2	3	4	5	6
9. I help members learn to play roles that assist the team in accomplishing its tasks as well as building strong interpersonal relationships.	1	2	3	4	5	6
10. I articulate a clear, exciting, passionate vision of what the team can achieve.	1	2	3	4	5	6
11. I help team members become committed to the team vision.	1	2	3	4	5	6
12. I encourage a win-win philosophy in the team; that is, when one member wins, every member wins.	1	2	3	4	5	6

13. I help the team avoid "groupthink" or making the group's survival more important than accomplishing its goal.	1	2	3	4	5	6
14. I use formal process management procedures to help the group become faster, more efficient, and more productive, and to prevent errors.	1	2	3	4	5	6
15. I encourage team members to represent the team's vision, goals, and accomplishments to outsiders.	1	2	3	4	5	6
16. I diagnose and capitalize on the team's core competence.	1	2	3	4	5	6
17. I encourage the team to achieve dramatic break-through innovations as well as small continuous improvements.	1	2	3	4	5	6
18. I help the team work toward preventing mistakes, not just correcting them after the fact.	1	2	3	4	5	6

Scoring

Add your scores for each question. Your score will range between 18 and 108.

Enter your total score here: _____

Analysis and Interpretation

The authors of this instrument propose that it assesses team development behaviors in five areas: diagnosing team development (items 1, 16); managing the forming stage (2–4); managing the conforming stage (6–9, 13); managing the storming stage (10–12, 14, 15); and managing the performing stage (5, 17, 18).

Based on a norm group of 500 business students, the following can help estimate where you are relative to others:

Total score of 95 or above	=	You are in the top quartile.
72 to 94	=	You are in the second quartile.
60 to 71	=	You are in the third quartile.
Below 60	=	You are in the bottom quartile.

If you need to work on your team-building skills, see S. A. Mohrman, S. G. Cohen, and A. M. Mohrman, Jr., *Designing Team-based Organizations* (San Francisco: Jossey-Bass, 1995).

Source: Robbins, Stephen P., *Self Assessment Library 3.4 for Sales Management,* 1st, © 2009. Printed and Electronically reproduced by permission of Pearson Education, Inc., Upper Saddle River, New Jersey.

Team Exercise

Designing a Dream Team
The Situation

You have just met with the CEO of X-lent, a medium-sized clothing manufacturing company with factories in China and Mexico. X-lent sells to several large stores that carry moderately priced clothing in the United States. The CEO is concerned that her customers have expressed increasing dissatisfaction with X-lent's responsiveness to their complaints about product quality, the returned-order process, and the overall treatment by the company's employees when there is any kind of customer service problem. The CEO has asked your consulting group to make recommendations for a permanent customer service "dream team," which will develop and oversee plans and policies to address these issues.

Your team must now develop the recommendations that you will then present to the CEO and the top management of X-lent. (Remember, you are not designing or discussing your own team. You are making recommendations to the CEO as to the composition of the new X-lent team to be assigned this task.)

Assignment

Your group's assignment is to develop recommendations to present to the CEO. Your recommendations should, *at the least*, address the following issues. You are free to discuss other issues you feel may be important in the development of the new X-lent team.

Justify each of your answers. Do not just give one sentence responses. Explain *why* you believe your recommendations are appropriate and critical.

1. What type of group should this be? (Formal or informal? Command? Project? Committee?)
2. Discuss the best fit characteristics for this team (for example, size, composition, and roles).
3. How should norms be established? This may relate to the type of team you recommend.
4. How much conformity and cohesion will be needed for this team to perform effectively? What could X-lent do to help the team develop an appropriate level of cohesion?
5. What team competencies will be most critical?
6. How can the organization assist the team in developing its effectiveness?

Source: Grace B. McLaughlin, Ph.D. Reprinted with the permission of the author.

It is 3 PM on the afternoon before the written part of your team project is due to be turned in for your management class. You are about to meet with the other members of your team to put the finishing touches on your paper. Each of them had originally agreed to provide two full pages of material, on disk and with a hard copy for editing. As your group members arrive for the meeting, you find out that most don't have even one page prepared and that several of those pages are handwritten. You realize there is a lot to do if this paper is going to be in shape to turn in by tomorrow's deadline. The parts must be integrated, typed, edited, polished, and proofread. Also some of the exhibits, especially a couple of the more detailed ones, still must be completed in final form.

There are six of you on the team. The varsity athlete, who made some especially good contributions in one of the team's meetings, has tried to get several of the other past meetings postponed or cancelled in order to accommodate her practice schedule. Unfortunately, again today her coach has told her she must attend a mandatory practice session from 4 PM to 9 PM. The international student, who has good oral but poor written English, always volunteers to help and has strong ideas. For some reason, though, this student always feels resented by you. The two of you just don't seem to get along. The fraternity president was aware that planning for this weekend's upcoming major social event would provide a conflict for this meeting, and so he is anxious to get the meeting over with and leave as quickly as possible. Surprisingly, however, he has apparently spent a lot of time polishing and editing his part of the paper and has provided a hard copy and disk copy of it. Another member, a drama department major, has just gotten the lead in the school play and has absolutely no interest anymore in this class project. Frustrated by past missed deadlines, willing to settle for a so-so paper, and unwilling to miss tonight's rehearsal, the actor has submitted a handwritten rough draft that you consider to be too short and skimpy on necessary details. The sixth member has travel reservations for early this evening. A marketing major, this member just finished scribbling down some self-described creative ideas, doesn't care who writes the paper, so long as it gets done, and is willing to lend the team a laptop computer.

As the team leader, you wonder how things could possibly have gone so wrong and what you are going to do now. In the back of your mind, however, you keep reminding yourself that this group is going to have to work together again next week to develop an oral presentation to give in front of the class and the instructor. You and the other members of the group have discussed in the past the fact that the syllabus makes clear that the grade for the project will be based on a combination of both the written paper and the in-class presentation.

Questions

1. Considering what you know about each member of the group, what type(s) of conflict would you expect to exist in this group? How would the group's productivity likely be affected?
2. What stage of development does this group seem to be in?
3. Keeping in mind issues discussed in this chapter, what would you, as team leader, do now?

Source: Case developed by Grace McLaughlin and Lyman Porter. Reprinted with permission of the authors.

References

1. U. R. Hulsheger, N. Anderson, and J. F. Salgado, "Team-level Predictors of Innovation at Work: A Comprehensive Meta-analysis Spanning Three Decades of Research," *Journal of Applied Psychology* 94 (2009): 1128–1145.

2. H. J. Leavitt, "The Old Days, Hot Groups, and Managers' Lib," *Administrative Science Quarterly* 41 (1996): 288–300; L. I. Glassop, "The Organizational Benefit of Teams," *Human Relations* 55, no. 2 (2002): 225–249.

3. E. A. Locke, D. Tirnauer, Q. Roberson, B. Goldman, M. E. Latham, and E. Weldon, "The Importance of the Individual in an Age of Groupism," in *Groups at Work: Theory and Research*, ed. M. Turner (Mahwah: Erlbaum, 2001), 501–528.

4. B. I. Kirkman and D. L. Shapiro, "The Impact of Cultural Values on Employee Resistance to Teams: Toward a Model of Globalized Self-managing Work Team Effectiveness," *Academy of Management Review* 22 (1997): 730–757; D. C. Thomas and K. Au, "The Effect of Cultural Differences on Behavioral Responses to Low Job Satisfaction," *Journal of International Business Studies* 33, no. 2 (2002): 309–326; L. I. Glassop, "The Organizational Benefit of Teams," *Human Relations* 55 (2002): 225–249.

5. P. Sellers, "Get Over Yourself," *Fortune*, 2001, 76–88.

6. E. Sundstrom, K. P. de Meuse, and D. Futrell, "Work Teams: Applications and Effectiveness," *American Psychologist* 45, no. 2 (1990): 120–133.

7. M. Cotrill, "Give Your Work Teams Time and Training," *Academy of Management Executive* 11, no. 3 (1997): 87–89; R. D. Banker, J. M. Field, R. G. Schroeder, and K. K. Sinha, "Impact of Work Teams on Manufacturing Performance: A Longitudinal Field Study," *Academy of Management Journal* 39 (1996): 867–890.

8. M. Weinstein, "Investment in Success," *Training* 47, no. 2 (2010): 40–44.

9. M. Weinstein, "Coming Up Short? Join the Club," *Training* 43, no. 4 (2006): 14.

10. "Toyota Begins Radically Reshaping Operations to Meet Customer Expectations," *Wall Street Journal*, March 31, 2010, http://online.wsj.com.

11. J. McGregor, "I Can't Believe They Took the Whole Team," *BusinessWeek*, December 18, 2006, http://www.businessweek.com.

12. J. R. Hackman, "The Design of Work Teams," in *Handbook of Organizational Behavior*, ed. J. W. Lorsch (Upper Saddle River: Prentice Hall, 1987), 315–342.

13. S. Caminiti, "What Team Leaders Need to Know," *Fortune* (1995): 93–100.

14. Banker *et al.*, "Impact of the Work Teams on Manufacturing Performance."

15. C. D. Cramton, "The Mutual Knowledge Problem and Its Consequences for Dispersed Collaboration," *Organization Science* 12 (2001): 346–367; C. D. Cramton, "Finding Common Ground in Dispersed Collaboration," *Organizational Dynamics* 4 (2002): 356–371; M. K. Ahuja and J. A. Galvin, "Socialization in Virtual Groups," *Journal of Management* 29, no. 2 (2003): 161–186.

16. B. E. Ashforth and F. Mael, "Social Identity Theory and the Organization," *Academy of Management Review* 14 (1989): 20–39; Bettenhausen, "Five Years of Group Research: What We Have Learned and What Needs to Be Addressed."

17. J. S. Heinem and E. Jacobsen, "A Model of Task Group Development in Complex Organizations and a Strategy of Implementation," *Academy of Management Review* 1, no. 4 (1976): 98–111; B. W. Tuckman and M. A. Jensen, "Stages of Small-group Development Revisited," *Group and Organization Studies* 2 (1977): 419–427; Sundstrom *et al.*, "Work Teams"; Bettenhausen, "Five Years of Group Research"; A. Chang, P. Bordia, and J. Duck, "Punctuated Equilibrium and Linear Progression: Toward a New Understanding of Group Development," *Academy of Management Journal* 46, no. 1 (2003): 106–117.

18. B. W. Tuckman, "Development Sequence in Small Groups," *Psychological Bulletin* 63 (1965): 384–399; Tuckman and Jensen, "Stages of Small Group Development Revisited."

19. Sundstrom *et al.*, "Work Teams," 127.

20. Hulsheger *et al.*, "Team-level Predictors."

21. R. L. Hotz, "More Scientists Treat Experiments as a Team Sport," *Wall Street Journal*, November 23, 2009, A14.

22. B. Davis, "Michelin Unit Attempts to Satisfy Dealer Complaints," *Rubber and Plastics News* 36, no. 12 (2007): 22.

23. B. Latane, K. Williams, and S. Harkings, "Social Loafing," *Psychology Today* 13, no. 5 (1979): 104–110; P. C. Earley, "Social Loafing and Collectivism: A Comparison of the United States and the People's Republic of China," *Administrative Science Quarterly* 34 (1989): 565–581; S. M. Murphy, S. J. Wayne, R. C. Liden, and B. Erdogan, "Understanding Social Loafing: The Role of Justice Perceptions and Exchange Relationships," *Human Relations* 56, no. 1 (2003): 61–84; X-P Chen and D. G. Bachrach, "Tolerance of Free-riding: The Effects of Defection Size, Defection Pattern, and Social Orientation in a Repeated Public Goods Dilemma," *Organizational Behavior and Human Decision Processes* 90, no. 1 (2003): 139–147; H. Goren, R. Kurzban, and A. Rapoport, "Social Loafing vs. Social Enhancement: Public Goods Provisioning in Real-time with Irrevocable Commitments," *Organizational Behavior and Human Decision Processes* 90, no. 2 (2003): 277–290.

24. K. D. Williams, S. A. Nica, L. D. Baca, and B. Latane, "Social Loafing and Swimming: Effects of Identifiability on Individual and Relay Performance of Intercollegiate Swimmers," *Basic and Applied Social Psychology* 10 (1989): 73–81.

25. W. K. Gabrenya, Y. Wang, and B. Latane, "Social Loafing on an Optimizing Task: Cross-cultural Differences Among Chinese and Americans," *Journal of Cross-Cultural Psychology* 16 (1985): 223–242.

26. R. E. Silverman, "For Charlie Kim, Company of Friends Proves a Lonely Place," *Wall Street Journal*, February 1, 2001, A1 +.

27. E. Schonfeld, "Everything You Want To Know About The Most Secretive Startup in the World (Next Jump)," *Techcrunch.com*, January 14, 2010, http://techcrunch.com/2010/01/14/next-jump/.

28. Hulsheger *et al.*, "Team-level Predictors."

29. L. H. Pelled, "Demographic Diversity, Conflict, and Work Group Outcomes: An Intervening Process Theory," *Administrative Science Quarterly* 7 (1996): 615–631; L. H. Pelled, K. M. Eisenhardt, and X. R. Xin, "Exploring the Black Box: An Analysis of Work Group Diversity, Conflict, and Performance," *Administrative Science Quarterly* 44 (1999): 1–28; K. Jehn, G. B. Northcraft, and M. A. Neale, "Why Differences Make a Difference: A Field Study of Diversity, Conflict, and Performance in Workgroups," *Administrative Science Quarterly* 44 (1999): 741–763.

30. S. Caudron, "Keeping Team Conflict Alive," *Training & Development* 52, no. 9 (1998): 48–52; G. S. Van der Vegt and O. Janssen, "Joint Impact of Interdependence and Group Diversity on Innovation," *Journal of Management* 29, no. 5 (2003): 729–751.

31. S. Meier, "Building and Managing an Effective Project Team," *Defense AT&L* 37, no. 5(2008): 38–41.

32. S. G. Cohen, "What Makes Teams Work: Group Effectiveness Research from the Shop Floor to the Executive Suite," *Journal*

of Management 23 (1997): 239–290; J. T. Polzer, L. P. Milton, and W. B. Swann Jr., "Capitalizing on Diversity: Interpersonal Congruence in Small Work Groups," *Administrative Science Quarterly* 47, no. 2 (2002): 296–324; Pelled, "Demographic Diversity, Conflict, and Work Group Outcomes: An Intervening Process Theory"; Pelled *et al.*, "Exploring the Black Box: An Analysis of Work Group Diversity, Conflict, and Performance"; J. A. Chatman and F. J. Flynn, "The Influence of Demographic Heterogeneity on the Emergence and Consequences of Cooperative Norms in Work Teams," *Academy of Management Journal* 44 (2001): 956–974; D. A. Harrison, K. H. Price, and M. P. Bell, "Beyond Relational Demography: Time and the Effects of Surface- and Deep-level Diversity on Work Group Cohesion," *Academy of Management Journal* 41 (1998): 96–107; Jehn *et al.*, "Why Differences Make a Difference: A Field Study of Diversity, Conflict, and Performance in Workgroups"; J. S. Bunderson and K. M. Sutcliffe, "Comparing Alternative Conceptualizations of Functional Diversity in Management Teams: Process and Performance Effects," *Academy of Management Journal* 45, no. 5 (2002): 875–893; E. Kearney, D. Gebert, and S. C. Voelpel, "When and How Diversity Benefits Teams: The Importance of Team Members' Need for Cognition," *Academy of Management Journal*. 52, (2009): 581–598.

33. Hulsheger *et al.*,. "Team-level Predictors."

34. Harrison *et al.*, "Beyond Relational Demography: Time and the Effects of Surface- and Deep-level Diversity on Work Group Cohesion."

35. J. Gordon, M. Hequet, C. Lee, M. Picard *et al.*, "Workplace Blues," *Training* 33, no. 2 (1996): 16.

36. T. V. Mumford, C. H. Van Iddekinge, F. P. Morgeson, and M. A. Campion, "The Team Role Test: Development and Validation of a Team Role Knowledge Situational Judgment Test," *Journal of Applied Psychology* 93, no. 2 (2008): 250–267. T. V. Mumford, , M. A. Campion, and F. P. Morgenson, "Situational Judgment in Work Teams: A Team Role Typology," *in Situational Judgment Tests: Theory, Measurement, and Application*. eds. J. A. Weekley and R. E. Ployhart (Mahwah: Erlbaum, 2006), 319–342.

37. L. Thompson, "Improving the Creativity of Organizational Work Groups," *Academy of Management Executive* 17, no. 1 (2003): 96–97; G. S. Van der Vegt and O. Janssen, "Joint Impact of Interdependence and Group Diversity on Innovation," *Journal of Management* 29, no. 5 (2003): 729–751; R. Sethi, D. C. Smith, and C. W. Park, "How to Kill a Team's Creativity," *Harvard Business Review* 80, no. 8 (2002): 16–17.

38. S. E. Humphrey, M. J. Mannor, and F. P. Morgeson, "Developing a Theory of the Strategic Core of Teams: A Role Composition Model of Team Performance," *Journal of Applied Psychology* 94 (2009): 48–61

39. C. C. Manz and H. P. Sims Jr., "Leading Workers to Lead Themselves: The External Leadership of Self-managing Work Teams," *Administrative Science Quarterly* 32 (1987): 106–129.

40. C. Fishman, "Creative Tension," *Fast Company*, 2000, 359–366.

41. Shaw, *Group Dynamics*; M. C. Thomas-Hunt, T. Y. Ogden, and M. A. Neale, "Who's Really Sharing? Effects of Social and Expert Status on Knowledge Exchange Within Groups," *Management Science* 49, no. 4 (2003): 464–477; T. R. Tyler and S. L. Blader, "Autonomous vs. Comparative Status: Must We Be Better Than Others to Feel Good About Ourselves?" *Organizational Behavior and Human Decision Processes* 89, no. 1 (2002): 813–838; P. M. Valcour, "Managerial Behavior in a Multiplex Role System," *Human Relations* 55, no. 10 (2002): 1163–1188.

42. J. E. Driskell and E. Salas, "Group Decision Making Under Stress," *Journal of Applied Psychology* 76 (1991): 473–78.

43. Shaw, *Group Dynamics*.

44. E. White, "Culture Shock: Learning Customs of a New Office," *Wall Street Journal*, November 28, 2006, B6.

45. Ibid.

46. D. C. Feldman, "The Development and Enforcement of Group Norms," *Academy of Management Review* 9 (1984): 47–53.

47. Hulsheger *et al.*,"Team-level Predictors.".

48. Shaw, *Group Dynamics*; see also N. Nicholson, ed., *Encyclopedic Dictionary of Organizational Behavior* (Oxford, UK: Blackwell, 1995), 199.

49. Cohen, "What Makes Teams Work: Group Effectiveness Research from the Shop Floor to the Executive Suite."

50. D. Druckman and J. A. Swets, eds., *Enhancing Human Performance: Issues, Theories and Techniques* (National Research Council, Washington, D. C.: National Academy Press, 1988).

51. R. R. Hirschfeld, M. H. Jordan, H. S. Feild, W. F. Giles, and A. A. Armenakis, "Teams' Female Representation and Perceived Potency as Inputs to Team Outcomes in a Predominantly Male Field Setting," *Personnel Psychology* 58, no. 4 (2005): 893–924.

52. Ibid.

53. Shaw, *Group Dynamics*; Sethi, Smith, and Park, "How to Kill a Team's Creativity."

54. Ibid, 218; Sethi, Smith, and Park, "How to Kill a Team's Creativity." Hulsheger, *et al.*, "Team-level Predictors.".

55. J. McAvoy and T. Butler, "The Dilution of Effort in Self-Evaluating Development Teams: Agile Loafing." *Electronic Journal of Information Systems Evaluation* 12 (2009): 161–171.

56. D. M. Landers, M. O. Wilkinson, B. D. Hatfield, and H. Barber, "Causality and the Cohesion–Performance Relationship," *Journal of Sport Psychology* 4, no. 2 (1982): 170–183; J. A. LePine, J. R. Hollenbeck, D. R. Ilgen, J. A. Colquitt, and A. Ellis, "Gender Composition, Situational Strength, and Team Decision-making Accuracy: A Criterion Decomposition Approach," *Organizational Behavior and Human Decision Processes* 88, no. 1 (2002): 445–475.

57. M. H. Safizadeh, "The Case of Workgroups in Manufacturing Operations," *California Management Review* 33, no. 4 (1991): 61–82; A. Erez, J. A. Lepine, and H. Elms, "Effects of Rotated Leadership and Peer Evaluation on the Functioning and Effectiveness of Self-managed Teams: A Quasi-experiment," *Personnel Psychology* 55, no. 4 (2002): 929–948; L. I. Glassop, "The Organizational Benefit of Teams," *Human Relations* 55, no. 2 (2002): 225–249.

58. J. O'Toole and E. E. Lawler III, *The New American Workplace* (New York: Palgrave-McMillan, 2006).

59. Kirkman and Shapiro, "The Impact of Cultural Values on Employee Resistance to Teams," 557–569; C. W. Langfred, "The Downside of Self-management: A Longitudinal Study of the Effects of Conflict on Trust, Autonomy, and Task Interdependence in Self-managing Teams," *Academy of Management Journal* 50 (2007): 885–900.

60. R. Gildersleeve, "dj Orthopedics Adopts 'Lean' Product Developments Processes to Win," *Visions* 30, no. 3 (2006): 45.

61. K. Lovelace, D. L. Shapiro, and L. R. Weingart, "Maximizing Cross-functional New Product Teams' Innovativeness and Constraint Adherence: A Conflict Communications Perspective," *Academy of Management Journal* 44 (2001): 779–793.

62. A. R. Jassawalla and H. C. Sashittal, "Building Collaborative Cross-functional New Product Teams," *Academy of Management Executive* 13, no. 3 (1999): 50–63; J. S. Bunderson and K. M. Sutcliffe, "Comparing Alternative Conceptualizations of Functional Diversity in Management Teams: Process and Performance Effects," *Academy of Management Journal* 45, no. 5 (2002): 875–893; Sethi, Smith, and Park, "How to Kill a Team's Creativity."

63. J. J. Distefano and M. L. Maznevski, "Creating Value with Diverse Teams in Global Management," *Organizational Dynamics* 29 (2000): 45–63.

64. K. M. Chudoba, E. Wynn, M. Lu, and M. B. Watson-Manheim, "How Virtual Are We? Measuring Virtuality and Understanding Its Impact in a Global Organization," *Information Systems Journal* 15, no. 4 (2005): 279–306.

65. B. L. Kirkman, B. Rosen *et al.*, "Five Challenges to Virtual Team Success: Lessons from Sabre Inc." *Academy of Management Executive* 16 (2002): 67–79.

66. P. M. Beranek, J. Broder *et al.*, "Management of Virtual Project Teams: Guidelines for Team Leaders," *Communication of AIS* 16 (2005): 247–259.

67. S. Dani, N. Burns *et al.*, "The Implications of Organizational Culture and Trust in the Working of Virtual Teams," *Proceedings of the Institution of Mechanical Engineers* 220 (2006): 951–960; J. Goodbody, "Critical Success Factors for Global Virtual Teams," *Strategic Communication Management* 9, no. 2 (2005): 18–21.

68. J. F. Nunamaker, Jr., B. A. Reinig, and R. O. Briggs, "Principles for Effective Virtual Teamwork," *Communications of the ACM* 52, no. 4 (2009): 113–117.

69. J. A. Cannon-Bowers and E. Salas, "Teamwork Competencies: The Interaction of Team Member Knowledge, Skills, and Attitudes," in *Workforce Readiness: Competencies and Assessment*, ed. H. F. O'Neil Jr. (Mahwah: Lawrence Erlbaum Associates, 1997), 151–174; J. A. Cannon-Bowers and E. Salas, "A Framework for Developing Team Performance Measures in Training," in *Team Performance Assessment and Measurement: Theory, Methods, and Applications*, eds. M. T. Brannick, E. Salas, and C. Prince (Mahwah: Lawrence Erlbaum Associates, 1997); J. A. Cannon-Bowers, S. I. Tannenbauam, E. Salas, and C. E. Volpe, "Defining Competencies and Establishing Team Training Requirements," in *Team Effectiveness and Decision Making in Organizations*, eds. R. A. Guzzo, E. Salas, and Associates (San Francisco: Jossey-Bass Publishers, 1995); G. A. Okhuysen and K. M. Eisenhardt, "Integrating Knowledge in Groups: How Formal Interventions Enable Flexibility," *Organization Science* 13, no. 4 (2002): 370–386.

70. P. J. Jordan and A. C. Troth, "Managing Emotions During Team Problem Solving," *Human Performance* 17, no. 2 (2004): 195–218.

71. J. A. Cannon-Bowers *et al.*, "Defining Competencies and Establishing Team Training Requirements."

72. S. Caudron, "Keeping Team Conflict Alive," *Training and Development* 52, no. 9 (1998): 48–52.

73. A. C. Amason, W. A. Hochwater, K. R. Thompson, and A. W. Harrison, "Conflict: An Important Dimension in Successful Management Teams," *Organizational Dynamics* 24, no. 2 (1995): 20–35; S. Schulz-Hardt, M. Jochims, and D. Frey, "Productive Conflict in Group Decision Making: Genuine and Contrived Dissent as Strategies to Counteract Biased Information Seeking," *Organizational Behavior and Human Decision Processes* 88, no. 2 (2002): 563–586; K. A. Jehn, "A Multimethod Examination of the Benefits and Detriments of Intragroup Conflict," *Administrative Science Quarterly* 40 (1995): 256–282; Schulz-Hardt, Jochims, and Frey, "Productive Conflict in Group Decision Making: Genuine and Contrived Dissent as Strategies to Counteract Biased Information Seeking."

74. Amason *et al.*, "Conflict"; K. M. Eisenhardt, J. L. Kahwajy, and L. J. Bourgeois III, "Conflict and Strategic Choice: How Top Management Teams Disagree," *California Management Review* 39, no. 2 (1997): 42–62; K. A. Jehn and E. A. Mannix, "The Dynamic Nature of Conflict: A Longitudinal Study of Intragroup Conflict and Group Performance," *Academy of Management Journal* 44 (2001): 238–251; T. L. Simons and

R. S. Peterson, "Task Conflict and Relationship Conflict in Top Management Teams: The Pivotal Role of Intragroup Trust," *Journal of Applied Psychology* 85 (2000): 102–111; Pelled, Eisenhardt, and Xin, "Exploring the Black Box: An Analysis of Work Group Diversity, Conflict, and Performance"; Jehn, "A Multimethod Examination of the Benefits and Detriments of Intragroup Conflict"; C. K. W. DeDreu and L. R. Weingart, "Task Versus Relationship Conflict, Team Performance, and Team Member Satisfaction: A Meta-analysis," *Journal of Applied Psychology* 88 (2003): 741–749

75. Amason *et al.*, "Conflict."

76. Ibid; Jehn, "A Multimethod Examination of the Benefits and Detriments of Intragroup Conflict."

77. Pelled, Eisenhardt, and Xin, "Exploring the Black Box: An Analysis of Work Group Diversity, Conflict, and Performance."

78. Pelled, "Demographic Diversity, Conflict, and Work Group Outcomes."

79. Jehn, Gregory, and Neale, "Why Differences Make A Difference: A Field Study of Diversity," 81.

80. Amason *et al.*, "Conflict."

81. A. Somech, H. S. Desivilya, and H. Lidogoster, "Team Conflict Management and Team Effectiveness: The Effects of Task Interdependence and Team Identification," *Journal of Organizational Behavior* 30 (2009): 359–378; Eisenhardt *et al.*, "Conflict and Strategic Choice"; C. Nemeth, K. Brown, and J. Rogers, "Devil's Advocate versus Authentic Dissent: Stimulating Quantity and Quality," *European Journal of Social Psychology* 31 (2001): 707–720.

82. Jehn *et al.*, "Why Differences Make a Difference."

83. Caudron, "Keeping Team Conflict Alive."

84. Jenn and Mannix, "The Dynamic Nature of Conflict."

85. M. Hoegl, K. Wienkauf, *et al.*, "Interteam Coordination, Project Commitment and Teamwork in Multiteam R&D Projects: A Longitudinal Study," *Organization Science* 15, no. 1 (2004): 38–55.

86. D. R. Forsyth, *An Introduction to Group Dynamics* (Monterey: Brooks/Cole Publishing, 1983).

87. G. A. Neuman and J. Wright, "Team Effectiveness: Beyond Skills and Cognitive Ability," *Journal of Applied Psychology* 84 (1999): 376–389; M. A. Campion, E. M. Papper, and G. J. Medsker, "Relations Between Work Team Characteristics and Effectiveness: A Replication and Extension," *Personnel Psychology* 49 (1996): 429–452; Cohen and Bailey, "What Makes Teams Work."

88. J. Fitz-Enz, "Measuring Team Effectiveness," *HR Focus* 74, no. 8 (1997): 3.

89. J. R. Hackman, ed., *Groups That Work (and Those That Don't): Creating Conditions for Effective Teamwork* (San Francisco: Jossey-Bass, 1990).

90. Hackman, *Groups That Work.*

91. Campion *et al.*, "Relations Between Work Team Characteristics and Effectiveness"; Hyatt and Ruddy, "An Examination of the Relationship Between Work Group Characteristics and Performance."

92. R. Wageman and G. Baker, "Incentives and Cooperation: The Joint Effects of Task and Reward Interdependence on Group Performance," *Journal of Organizational Behavior* 18, no. 2 (1997): 139–158.

93. Banker *et al.*, "Impact of Work Teams on Manufacturing Performance"; Cottrill, "Give Your Teams Time and Training."

94. J. R. Hackman and R. Wageman, "A Theory of Team Coaching," *Academy of Management Review* 30 (2005): 269–287.

95. Cohen and Bailey, "What Makes Teams Work."

96. G. L. Hallam, "Seven Common Beliefs About Teams: Are They True?" *Leadership in Action* 17, no. 3 (1997): 1–4.

Communication and Negotiation

LEARNING OBJECTIVES

After studying this chapter, you should be able to:

Explain why communication is vital for effective management.

Describe the basic process of communication.

Discuss how to choose the best mode and the appropriate media richness for effective communication.

Analyze the impact of the organizational context on communication.

Identify key barriers to effective communication.

Explain various approaches to overcoming communication barriers, including intercultural barriers.

Describe the basic process of negotiation.

Bridgette Chambers

Name: Bridgette Chambers

Position title: President and CEO: The Americas' SAP Users' Group (ASUG)

Alma mater: University of Houston (BS, Education); Texas A&M (MBA)

Outside work activities: Volunteering for not-for-profit organizations; family activities; golf

First job out of school: Started my own company

Business book reading now: *Competing on Analytics* by Thomas Davenport

Hero: My grandmother; former General Electric CEO Jack Welch; Alexander the Great

Motto to live by: Get it done…do it right…and be damn proud when you are finished with it.

What drives me: Relentless desire to always grow and accomplish the next objective

Management style: Management by objectives and accountability

Pet peeve: Second place

As chief executive of an organization promoting knowledge transfer among the world's largest association of SAP customers by providing user-driven professional networking and educational opportunities, Bridgette Chambers communicates almost constantly—in person, by telephone, and by e-mail. Hers is not a desk job. She is not sitting off by herself analyzing spreadsheets. Instead, Chambers is almost daily in the center of a communication vortex. As she puts it, "Most of my day is spent communicating." If she were not a good communicator, Chambers would not last very long in her type of job.

Following college graduation, Chambers began her business career by becoming an entrepreneur, building a small company called Trans Resolve Legal Services, which she sold after seven years. With that experience and background, she moved into consulting, setting up an outside sales component for a company. She subsequently managed consulting services activities for several organizations before joining COMSYS, a $750 million publicly traded company that provides a variety of consulting and project services. Her position was in the Enterprise Business Solutions division where she managed three different service lines: business analytics, business intelligence, and enterprise resource planning. In that role, Chambers had eight direct reports and was responsible for more than 400 employees. In her current position with ASUG, she interacts almost nonstop with over 40 chapters and figures out ways to effectively utilize social media.

Chambers did not always have successful communication experiences. Earlier in her career, with a low tolerance for poor performance and task failures, she was not always aware of her impact, as a leader, on others. Consequently, she sometimes created more ill will than the situation called for and certainly more than she had intended. "I failed to understand that not everyone wakes up in the morning with the same expectations of their day and objectives. I had to begin a journey of self-awareness and seek critical feedback."

Most of us, like Bridgette Chambers early in her career, take communication for granted because we do it every day. Communicating effectively, however, is not easy.[1] Accurate and persuasive communication within and between organizations, person to person, person to group, or group to group, is frequently (and sometimes unexpectedly) difficult, as the opening example demonstrates. Receivers often do not have a complete understanding of what senders mean. But the heart of **communication** is exactly that: a process of transferring information, meaning, and understanding from sender to receiver. And carrying out that process convincingly and proficiently is an absolute essential for a manager to exercise leadership. In fact, leadership is unlikely to be successful in the absence of excellent communication skills. The first step for a manager to become an outstanding leader, therefore, is to become an outstanding communicator.

In this chapter, we start with an overview of the basic communication process, followed by an examination of the modes and media of communication. These topics provide a background for the next section on the organizational context of the communication process as it affects managers. Although the organization can facilitate managerial communication, it also can be

communication
the process of transferring information, meaning, and understanding from sender to receiver

one of the key sources of barriers to communication—interpersonal, organizational, and cultural—that are discussed in the following section. Then, the next section highlights some of the steps that managers can take to reduce or overcome these barriers.

The final parts of the chapter focus on one particular area of communication that is especially critical for managers—negotiation. In those sections, we discuss the impact of cultural influences on negotiation strategies and on the negotiation process itself. Throughout this chapter we need to keep in mind a basic perspective: Although communication is a universal human activity, successful communication is not habitual. It requires motivation, skill, and knowledge.

The Basic Model of Communication

How do people communicate? How do they send and receive messages? What factors can disrupt communication? Let's look first at the basic model of the communication process outlined in Exhibit 11.1.[2]

All communication involves four actions and five components. The four actions are encoding, sending, receiving, and decoding. The five components are sender, message, medium, noise, and receiver. The actions and components combine to transfer meaning from the sender to the receiver. The sender originates the message by **encoding** it, that is, by constructing the message. The message is the content of the communication. The sender then transmits the message through a **medium,** the method or means of transmission, not the message itself. Examples of a medium (or its plural, media) are spoken words, video, written memos, faxes, and e-mails. The receiver acquires, or receives, the message by hearing it, reading it, or having it appear on a fax or computer. The receiver then begins **decoding** the message that is, interpreting it. Sometimes distractions interfere with the message; these interferences are called **noise.** Noise contributes to misinterpretations of the original message, and it is only through feedback, or verification of the original message, that communication problems can be uncovered and corrected.

The basic model of communication is fundamental and universal. That is, it occurs whenever communication takes place regardless of the culture or organization. However, although the basic acts and components of the communication process are the same everywhere, how the acts are carried out and the *nature* of the components are deeply influenced by cultural, organizational, and even personal contexts.[3] Who can send messages to whom, what kinds and what volumes of messages are sent, by what medium are messages transmitted, what sort of interference or noise is likely to occur, and what cues are available for decoding are just some of the many examples of the types of communication issues that can vary from manager to manager, from organization to organization, and from country to country.

Modes of Communication

Communication can occur in either a verbal mode or a nonverbal mode, as shown in Exhibit 11.2. Each mode has particular characteristics and related issues that managers must understand.

Verbal Communication

Most of us think of spoken words when we think of verbal communication. The key, however, is not that the words are spoken but that the words—language—are used to convey meaning. Consequently, when we talk about verbal communication, we mean *both* oral and written communication.

ORAL COMMUNICATION The spoken word has the potential advantages of being vivid, stimulating, and commanding. In most organizational situations, it is difficult for receivers—the listeners—to

---

encoding
the act of constructing a message

medium
the method or means of transmission of a message; plural, *media*

decoding
the act of interpreting a message

noise
interference with the transmission or decoding of a message

EXHIBIT 11.1

Basic Communication Model

Sender	Noise:	Receiver
1. Encodes message	Can interfere at any point	1. Receives message
2. Chooses a medium (channel)		2. Decodes message
3. Sends the message		3. May send feedback for clarification

EXHIBIT 11.2 Modes of Communication

	VERBAL MODE (LANGUAGE USED TO CONVEY MEANING)		NONVERBAL MODE
	Oral	**Written**	
Examples	• Conversation • Speeches • Telephone calls • Videoconferences	• Letters • Memos • Reports • E-mail • Fax	• Dress • Speech intonation • Gestures • Facial expressions
Advantages	• Vivid • Stimulating • Commands attention • Difficult to ignore • Flexible • Adaptive	• Decreased misinterpretation • Precise	• Effectiveness of communication increases with congruence to oral presentation • Can emphasize meaning
Disadvantages	• Transitory • Subject to misinterpretation	• Precision loss in translation • Inflexible • Easier to ignore	• Meanings of nonverbal communication not universal

ignore either the speaker or the words spoken. Just think about the last time someone spoke to you directly. Even if you weren't interested in what the person had to say, wouldn't it have been difficult to simply ignore the person, turn, and walk away?

Also, oral communication is exceptionally flexible for both the sender and receiver. While you are speaking, you may try to make a point a certain way, but along the way you change your words in order for the listener to understand you. Because oral communication is generally interactive, it can be quite responsive and adaptive to circumstances. However, this mode of communication has the major disadvantages of being transitory (unless recorded) and subject to considerable misinterpretation. Even when individuals use the same language, the subtle nuances of the spoken word may be missed or incorrect meaning attached to them. Oral communication between those whose first languages differ, as in many management situations today, simply multiplies the chances of intended meaning going awry.

WRITTEN COMMUNICATION When messages are put in writing, as in letters, memos, e-mail, and the like, the opportunities for misunderstanding the words of the sender are reduced. The receiver may still misinterpret the intended message, but there is no uncertainty about exactly what words the sender has used. In that sense, written communication has precision. However, not everyone writes well, and so greater precision does not necessarily lead to greater understanding. This is further complicated when the words need translation from one language to another. For example, Americans often write when requesting action "at your earliest convenience," meaning that the request is somewhat urgent, but Europeans frequently interpret it to mean they can respond whenever they want. Or consider how Pepsi's slogan of "Come Alive with the Pepsi Generation" translated into Chinese: "Pepsi Brings Your Ancestors Back from the Grave."[4] Because the writer (sender) does not know immediately how well or poorly the message is getting across, written communication has the disadvantage of not being very flexible. In addition, it is often not as vivid or compelling as oral communication. Although you might find it difficult to ignore someone speaking to you, it would probably be much easier to ignore a letter you received.

Nonverbal Communication

In direct interpersonal communication, nonverbal actions and behaviors often send significant messages. A whole range of actions, or lack of them, has the potential for communicating. The way you dress, speak words, use gestures, handle utensils, exhibit facial expressions, and set the physical distance to the receiver are just some of the many forms of nonverbal communication.

A major point to emphasize regarding this type of communication is that by being more conscious of how you are communicating nonverbally you can be more in control of the types of messages you are sending. Even in an age of increasing use of electronic communication, it still is important not to lose awareness of this form of communication, and its effects, in the many work situations that still involve face-to-face interactions.[5]

As a manager, keep in mind that when verbal and nonverbal messages are contradictory, receivers often give more weight to the nonverbal signals than to the words used. For example, you might say to your employees, "I have an open-door policy. Come and talk to me whenever you need to." However, if you never seem to be able to find the time to see them or rarely look up from your work when they enter your office, they will soon come to believe the nonverbal message, "I'm busy, don't bother me" rather than the verbal message, "I encourage you to talk with me at any time."

When nonverbal messages are consistent with the spoken message, the odds of effective communication taking place are increased. For example, suppose that in addition to saying you had an open-door policy, you looked up when employees entered your office, made eye contact with them, smiled, and turned away from your computer and the report on which you were working. In combination, what sort of message do you think you would be sending?

The problem for managers in many of today's organizations where they work with employees from different cultural backgrounds and often work across international borders is that there are no universal meanings to various nonverbal actions. For example, the traditional "OK" sign in the United States is a gesture for money in Japan and is a rather rude gesture in Brazil. You might think that just toning down your nonverbal gestures would be a good way to avoid inadvertent wrong messages. Such an effort would be fine in Finland, but someone in Italy or Greece might infer from your subdued, nonverbal cues that you are uninterested in the discussion. As a manager, you should learn about the nonverbal cues and gestures of countries and cultures with which you deal the most.

Media of Communication

media richness
different media are classified as rich or lean based on their capacity to facilitate shared meaning

The means of communication, or *how* information is transmitted from sender to receiver, are typically referred to as communication media (or, in the singular, medium). In organizations, there basically are a limited number of types of media that can be used. They range from the very personal and direct, face-to-face interaction to the very impersonal and indirect, bulletin-board notice. In between are telephone conversations, electronic messages, letters, memos, and reports.

Media have different sets of characteristics, such as the following:

- Their personal–impersonal nature
- Their speed in sending and receiving
- The availability of multiple cues to assist receivers in acquiring accurate meaning from the messages
- The opportunity to receive immediate and continuing feedback from the receiver

The term used to summarize these differences is called **media richness.**"[6] Different media are classified as rich, or lean, based on their "capacity to facilitate shared meaning."[7] (See Exhibit 11.3.) Thus, interpersonal face-to-face interactions, for example, would be regarded as rich because they provide several types of information and multiple ways to obtain mutual understanding between sender and receiver. By contrast, a general e-mail message sent to a number of receivers would be regarded as leaner because it lacks some of the features listed previously. The basic principle here is that the more ambiguous and complex the issue is, the richer should be the medium of communication.[8]

Managers, consequently, should be sensitive to matching message with medium. Using face-to-face meetings to convey simple, straightforward information, such as the locations and

Hundreds of dispatchers at Burlington Northern Santa Fe Railway's Network Operations Center in Fort Worth, Texas, communicate constantly via the company's wireless network with locomotive crews across the country operating trains like this one. The dispatchers serve a function similar to that of air traffic controllers. Clear communication between the dispatchers and crews is imperative to prevent rail accidents.

James Callaghan\Alamy Images

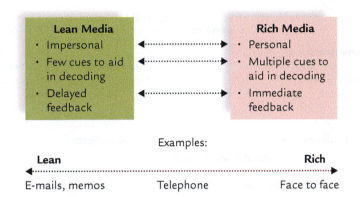

EXHIBIT 11.3

Factors Contributing to Media Richness

times of future meetings, would be an unnecessary waste of a rich medium. That is, it would involve too much time and effort of both sender and receivers to obtain shared meaning of a relatively unambiguous message. On the other hand, sending an e-mail memo, for example, rather than arranging a face-to-face meeting, would probably be a poor choice for settling a serious disagreement with one's subordinates. The medium would be too lean to enable the manager to resolve a complicated, highly ambiguous matter. As the chairman of an international law firm expressed it: "If you are going to disagree with somebody, you certainly don't want to do it by e-mail, and if possible you don't even want to do it by phone. You want to do it face-to-face."[9] A Manager's Challenge, "E-mail: Too Much of a Good Thing?" describes how one company dealt with the pros and cons of using the medium of e-mail. What is fastest may not be the best medium in all circumstances.

Often, time pressures and distance make it relatively costly for a manager to use a richer rather than a leaner medium, and there may well be circumstances such as large group meetings where using automated devices like audience response systems (i.e., electronic clickers) can counteract the potential disadvantages of a lean media environment.[10]

Another type of technology that can help provide some degree of richness in communications carried out by participants located at great distances from each other is video conferencing.[11] The key point, though, if you are a manager, is to choose a medium that best suits the degree of potential ambiguity in the message, consistent with the constraints of circumstances and the resources of you and your organization. The choice of an appropriate medium should not be left to chance.

The Organizational Context of Communication

Managers do not deal with communication in the abstract. Rather, they deal with it within an organizational context. The structure and processes of organizations powerfully shape the nature and effectiveness of communication that takes place within and between them.[12] Organizations, whether businesses, hospitals, or government agencies, have a set of defining characteristics, all of which affect communication in one way or another.[13] Thus, organizations

- Are composed of individuals and groups
- Are oriented toward goals
- Have differentiated functions
- Have intended coordination
- Have continuity through time

Organizations of any size, regardless of country, are not simply a random set of individuals who by chance come together for a brief period with no purpose. The fact that they have goal orientations, structures, and coordination greatly influences the nature and amount of communication that takes place. This influence can be analyzed in terms of directions, channels, and patterns of communication.

Directions of Communication Within Organizations

Because organizations of any degree of complexity have both differentiated functions and a number of levels of positions with differing degrees of responsibility, the potential directions of

EXHIBIT 11.4

Directions of Communication Within Organizations

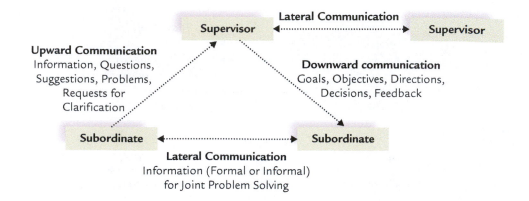

communication within organizations can be classified according to the level for which a message is intended:

downward communication
messages sent from higher organizational levels to lower levels

upward communication
messages sent from lower organizational levels to higher levels

lateral communication
messages sent across essentially equivalent levels of an organization

- **Downward communication** is sent from higher organizational levels to lower levels; for example, from the organization's top executives to its employees, or from supervisors to subordinates.
- **Upward communication** is sent from lower organizational levels to higher levels; for example, from nonmanagement employees to their supervisors, or from a manager to her boss.
- **Lateral communication** is sent across equivalent levels of an organization; for example, from one clerical assistant to another, from the manager of product A to the manager of product B, or from the marketing department to the engineering design department.

The contents of communications within organizations usually vary according to the direction of the communication activity. As shown in Exhibit 11.4, downward communication typically involves such matters as goals, objectives, directions, decisions, and feedback. Upward communication commonly focuses on information, suggestions, questions, problems, and even dissent.[14] Lateral communication is oriented toward exchanges of information—both formal and informal—that assist or affect coordination and joint problem solving.

The culture of an organization (or the culture of the country in which the organization resides) can affect the direction and nature of communication. For example, in an organization in which authority and hierarchy are stressed, upward communication might be more formal than in an organization with a more egalitarian culture. As a simple illustration, in a strongly hierarchical organization, a conversation might start with the subordinate addressing a superior several levels above as "Mr. (or Ms.) Jones." In many countries, such as Korea, the conversation might start by addressing the superior by his or her title, such as "Director Park." In organizations with less emphasis on hierarchy, the conversation might start by addressing the superior by his or her first name. Likewise, organizational or country culture can influence the frequency and flavor of upward communications. For example, in organizations with strong hierarchical values, upward communication tends to be less frequent.

Channels of Communication Within Organizations

Organizational channels, or routes of communication, consist of two fundamental types: formal and informal. Both types are essential for organizational functioning, and neither type can easily substitute for the other.

formal communication channel
a communication route authorized, planned, and regulated by the organization and directly connected to its official structure

A **formal communication channel** is a route that the organization authorizes, plans, and regulates and that is directly connected to the organization's official structure. Thus, the organization's designated structure indicates the normal paths for downward, upward, and lateral formal communication. Formal communication channels (shown in Exhibit 11.5) are like highlighted roads on a map. They specify which organizational members are responsible for communicating information to levels above and below them and back and forth to adjacent units. Also, formal channels indicate the persons or positions to whom work-related messages should be sent. Formal channels can be modified and, thus, they have some flexibility, but they can seldom be disregarded.

A MANAGER'S CHALLENGE

TECHNOLOGY

E-mail: Too Much of a Good Thing? Blessing or Curse?

The advent of e-mail in the early 1990s brought truly significant communication advantages to individuals and organizations. Almost overnight, those wishing to send written messages could do so far and wide to one person, or thousands, at virtually no cost and at almost instantaneous speed. It seemed a miracle to people who were used to communicating at a distance by postal mail or within companies by the distribution of office memoranda. Today, it's hard to imagine life without e-mail, instant messaging, or Web conferencing. Consider: When was the last 24- or 48-hour period when you did not check your e-mail?

But, as with almost anything else in life, there are downsides as well as tremendous upsides to the use of e-mail. Who among us, for example, does not complain about being bombarded with unwanted e-mail spam? Another often-heard complaint about e-mail is that it is so easy to send e-mails, and to multiple recipients at one time, that recipients feel overwhelmed by the number of messages, many of which are seen as unnecessary. One survey indicated that 75 percent of employees spend as much as half of their working day dealing with email, and another survey found that 47 percent of emails that are received at work are irrelevant to the employee's job. These are some of the obvious drawbacks of e-mail.

Are there also other important, intangible, and often hidden, costs to interacting by e-mail? Some companies are beginning to think so, particularly with regard to the issue of media richness. One of the major concerns is that the use of e-mail is a "lazy" person's way to communicate when direct phone or in-person conversations would provide much richer communication. This is especially true when there are subtleties or nuances that need to be conveyed. As one manager put it, "You can't get to know someone through e-mail."

Several years a go a company providing call-center management and other services took steps to reduce the use of casual e-mail and instead rely on relatively more person-to-person interaction. The company's CEO instituted "no e-mail Fridays" and urged his employees to reduce the use of e-mail on the other days of the week. As a result, e-mail use in the company declined by over 80 percent, and, even

Easy-to-send electronic communication has both its ups and downs. Some people feel barraged by a constant onslaught of e-mails, for example. Others can't go without checking for their messages every few minutes.

Andres Rodriguez/Fotolia

more importantly, the company's clients reacted positively and increased their communications with the firm.

"No e-mail Fridays" certainly would not work for many organizations. But one organization's need for such a policy highlights some of the unintended consequences e-mail can have. These have to be weighed against the medium's advantages. E-mail provides a great benefit—a classic case of "can't live without it"—but it is not cost-free.

Sources: D. Brady, "*!#?@ the E-mail. Can We Talk?" *BusinessWeek*, December 4, 2006, 109; "Stoned on E-Mail," *Profit,* June 2005, 115; G. Browning, "Resolve to Develop Your Email Intuition," *People Management* 11, no. 1 (2005): 102; G. Flood, "Tame the Mountain," *Information World Review 210* (2005): 18–19; S. Sweetham, "E-mail Tactics," *T&D* 60, no.1 (2006): 13; "Lack of Email Training Is Costing Employers Dearly," *Accountancy Ireland.* 40, no. 3 (2008): 102; "You've Got Mail," *Accountancy* 142, no. 1385 (2009): 43.

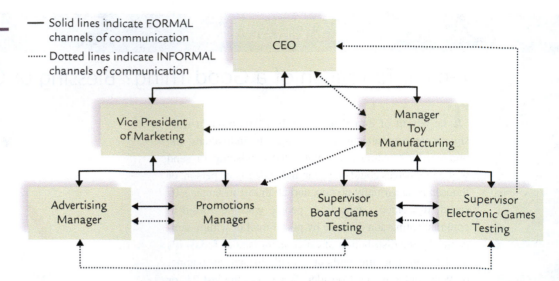

— Solid lines indicate FORMAL channels of communication

······ Dotted lines indicate INFORMAL channels of communication

informal communication channel

a communication route that is not prespecified by the organization but that develops through typical and customary activities of people at work

An **informal communication channel** is a communication route that the organization doesn't prespecify but that develops through the interpersonal activities of employees. These channels can appear, change, or disappear rapidly, depending on circumstances. However, they can also endure, especially where individuals have been working together over a period of time. If a specific pattern becomes well established, it would ordinarily be called a "network" (to be discussed later).

Several important features of informal communication channels should be noted:

- They tend to operate more laterally than vertically compared to formal channels (see Exhibit 11.6) because they are not designated by the organization and its top officials.
- Second, information flowing through informal channels is often fast-moving, principally because senders are highly motivated to pass information on. The so-called "grapevine" is a classic example.[15] In recent years, the communication capabilities of the Internet have facilitated the emergence of large-scale word-of-mouth networks. Some researchers propose that these mechanisms are poised to have a significant impact on the informal information flow in organizations.[16]
- A third feature is that informal channels carry work-related as well as nonwork information. Just because channels are informal does not mean that they carry only gossip and other messages unrelated to work. Crucial work-related information is frequently communicated this way as well. The downside is that some of the messages passed through informal channels are inaccurate or focus only on negative information. However—and this is important to emphasize—few organizations could exist for very long if they had to rely only on formal communication channels!

Formal Communication Channels	Informal Communication Channels
• Authorized, planned, and regulated by the organization	• Develop through interpersonal activities of organization members
• Reflect the organization's formal structure	• Not specified by the organization
• Define who has responsibility for information dissemination and indicate the proper recipients of work-related information	• May be short-lived or long-lasting
	• Are more often lateral than vertical
• May be modified by the organization	• Information flow can be very fast
• Minor to severe consequences for ignoring them	• Used for both work-related and nonwork information

Patterns of Organizational Communication

An identifiable pattern of communication that occurs with some regularity within and between organizations, whether using formal or informal channels, is typically called a **communication network.** Put another way, communication networks are stable systems of interconnections; networks involve consistent linkages between particular sets of senders and receivers. For example, as shown in Exhibit 11.7, a middle-level divisional marketing manager in Los Angeles might have a network that involves her boss in New York, three key managers in other departments in the company's New York headquarters, her seven subordinates located in West Coast cities, and two outside vendors of market research data. Another network for the same manager might involve two lower-level managers in other units in the firm's Los Angeles office and their former colleague and old friend who is now a sales supervisor in Chicago and who has access to inside information on how well new marketing approaches are working in that region.

An example of a larger, more organization-wide network would be the Coca-Cola Company's communication relationships between its Atlanta headquarters and its bottlers and distributors around the world. Networks can also be formed across organizations as well as within. This is what often happens, for example, when sets of managers from two companies have to work together on issues that arise in an international joint venture.[17]

The importance of communication networks to managers is that they can provide significant and regular information (both of the formal and informal type) that might otherwise take a much longer time to obtain. This is especially so if various communication links had to be set up "from scratch" each time a new issue or problem came up. Also, when managers are members of established networks, it can make it easier for them to influence the other people or groups involved in the networks. Consequently, for both of these reasons, managers need to pay particular attention to what networks they can, and want to, be a part of, and to the composition of those networks. It is no accident that the term **networking** has come to signify a process that has the potential for gaining advantages for a manager (or anyone for that matter). It helps to have one or more sets of individuals with whom one can interact easily and regularly, thereby building a sense of confidence and trust. Research has shown, in fact, that networking—building and

communication network
an identifiable pattern of communication within and between organizations, whether using formal or informal channels

networking
a process of developing regular patterns of communication with particular individuals or groups to send and receive information

EXHIBIT 11.7

Examples of Two Organizational Communication Networks

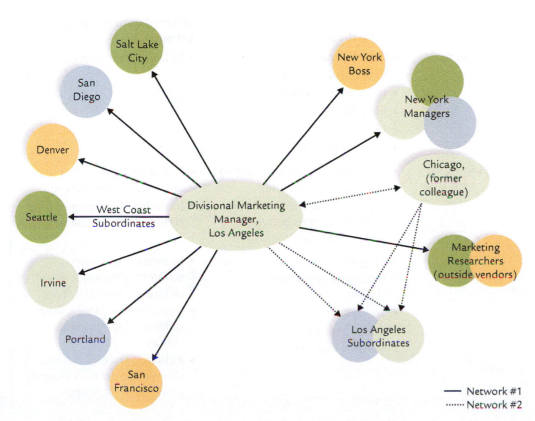

— Network #1
······· Network #2

maintaining contacts both within and outside an organizational unit—can have positive effects on salary growth and career satisfaction.[18]

In traditional Western organizations, it has always been relatively easy for men in management positions to establish various networks with other men (thus providing the basis for the phrase "old boys' network"). However, at least until very recently, it's been much harder for women and members of underrepresented ethnic groups to establish similar helpful networks. Research suggests that organizational networks involving individuals from these latter groups are different in terms of both their composition and relationships from the traditional networks composed primarily of white males.[19] It does not make such networks any less important or useful to managers from these groups, but does serve to emphasize that network patterns of communication can vary based on a number of different situational circumstances, including the age, gender, and ethnicity of the individuals involved.

Barriers to Communication

Barriers that interfere with the communication process can arise from several different sources, including interpersonal, organizational, and cultural sources, as illustrated in Exhibit 11.8. Next, we discuss each of these sources.

Interpersonal Barriers

Obstacles to interpersonal communication can occur with either the sender or the receiver. The burden is simultaneously on both the sender and the receiver to ensure that accurate communication occurs. It is, however, the sender's obligation to choose the language and words—to encode the message—with the greatest possible precision. This is the lesson that Bridgette Chambers, discussed at the beginning of the chapter, had to learn. Precision is especially important if the sender is trying to persuade the receiver to do something in a language or communication style different from what the receiver prefers. For example, if you are trying to convince your boss to authorize a new project and you use an informal style and choice of words, she may not be receptive to your request if she prefers a more formal approach. You will probably need to adjust your communication style to be effective in this case.

EXHIBIT 11.8

Barriers of Communication

Level	Origin of Barrier	Affects Communication Between:
Interpersonal	• Selective perception • Frame of reference • Individual differences • Emotion • Language • Nonverbal cues	• Individuals or groups
Organizational	• Hierarchical (barriers resulting from formal structure) • Functional (barriers resulting from differences between functional departments)	• Individuals and/or groups within an organization • Individuals and/or groups in different organizations
Cultural	• Language • High- or low-context culture • Stereotyping • Ethnocentrism • Cultural distance	• Individuals or groups in different organizations with different national cultures • Individuals or groups from different organizational cultures • Individuals or groups from diverse cultural backgrounds within an organization

The receiver, of course, often can be the source of communication breakdowns. For example, the receiver might have a **selective perception** problem.[20] That is, the receiver might unintentionally screen out some parts of the intended message because it contradicts her beliefs or desires. For example, you might stress the increased productivity that would result from a proposed project, but your boss is focusing on the estimated cost of the project. Although selective perception is a natural human tendency, it hinders accurate communication, especially when sensitive or highly important topics are being discussed. Another way to state this point is that individuals tend to adopt a **frame of reference,** or a simplified way of interpreting messages, that helps them make sense of complex communications, but these shortcuts may prevent the intended message from being received.[21]

Individual differences between senders and receivers in terms of such basic characteristics as their age, gender, ethnicity, or level of education sometimes can be the source of communication barriers. In general, it would be reasonable to assume that the fewer the differences the two parties have with regard to these kinds of attributes, the lower their communication barriers are. Research shows that even when these differences exist, they usually don't seriously impede good communication.[22] It is more a matter of a manager being very alert to the *possibility* that individual differences in sender and receiver characteristics could impose a significant obstacle to good communication, rather than assuming it will never be a barrier or, conversely, will always be a barrier.

Emotions can be another barrier.[23] How the receiver feels at the time can influence what gets heard or how it gets interpreted. You certainly have had the experience of feeling that someone was "touchy" or overly sensitive when responding to your message. As a consequence, comments that normally would be taken as mere statements get interpreted as criticisms.

Language can also be a barrier. Even for people who speak the same language, a given word or set of words can mean different things to different people.[24] For example, saying, "That's a bad haircut" to a 50-year-old means something completely different than if it were said to a 15-year-old. The 50-year-old will likely interpret the words to mean that the barber did a poor job. The 15-year-old will likely take the statement to mean he looks "cool."

Nonverbal cues can also be barriers to effective communication in two basic ways. First, people can send nonverbal signals without being aware of them, and, therefore, create unintentional consequences.[25] For example, you might make minimal eye contact with your boss while trying to convince her to approve your proposed project, and yet be unaware that you are doing so. Your boss might think the project has merit but interprets your low level of eye contact as an indication that you are hiding something. She might then reject a project that she would otherwise have authorized. Second, as we have already touched on, nonverbal cues can mean different things to different people.[26] A weak handshake might indicate politeness in Indonesia but communicate a lack of confidence in Texas.

See the "Manager's Challenge" on page 314 for an example of how multiple communication barriers, including selective perception, differing frames of reference, and unintended nonverbal cues led to the sending of mixed messages.

Organizational Barriers

Just as interpersonal barriers can limit communication, so can organizational barriers. Organizational barriers can interfere with communication between individuals or groups within the same organization, between individuals or groups from two different organizations, or between entire organizations. The basis of these barriers lies within the hierarchical structure of organizations. All organizations of any complexity have specialized functions and more than one level of authority. This specialization creates a situation that is ripe for communication difficulties. For example, one person might come from marketing and the other from R&D. The person in marketing might think nothing of exaggerating whereas the person from R&D might always understate her points. Consequently, the marketer might see the R&D employee as unimaginative and boring, whereas the R&D employee might view the marketer as superficial and careless. In addition, the two parties might come from different levels in the organization: A senior executive is likely to expect an explanation of how a proposed project broadly impacts the organization whereas a junior technical expert might be more likely to focus on the detailed schedule of the project.

A MANAGER'S CHALLENGE

COMMUNICATIONS

Communication Confusion

It was a car lover's dream. Two brothers, Jack and John Goudy, left their desk jobs to open their own auto repair shop. At first, just the two brothers did brake jobs and replaced exhaust systems. Then, as business grew, they hired a few workers and moved to a larger shop. Within a decade, Two J's Auto Repair was cranking in sales of half a million dollars per year, but then those sales reached a plateau and gradually began to decline. So John, who was in charge of sales and accounting, searched for a new way to improve business. He found it by using technology. John began integrating cutting-edge technology into the shop's office operations. But he had to convince his workers—including Jack, who spent more time in the shop than in the office—that his strategy for rebuilding Two J's would be successful.

John convened a staff meeting to communicate his new strategy to the employees. Armed with graphs and charts, he talked about profit sharing, employee involvement, and state-of-the-art technology. "From today on, we're a completely different business," he predicted. He did not know how prophetic that statement would prove to be. John's audience did not share his enthusiasm; in fact, they did not understand his message at all because they had received no previous training in the areas of finance, human resources, or the use of technology. They didn't understand the vocabulary he used or the ideas he was presenting. "It was a sea of blank faces with an occasional mutter here and there," John recalls. Thus, the flow of miscommunication at Two J's began.

John purchased a new computerized information system, which reduced the amount of paper communication generated by the office. But employees eventually discovered that the original estimates and the final invoices did not match each other, which caused them to believe that he was withholding work hours—and pay. Additionally, although John had provided his employees with an elaborate explanation of the profit-sharing plan (which they did not understand), they were skeptical of it because of mixed messages he sent: John often groaned about poor profits but would suddenly arrive at work driving a new sports car. Sensing declining morale, John started to hold daily "release meetings," designed to let employees voice their frustrations and concerns. But even these backfired. "John talked about working together like a football team," says one employee. But the meetings quickly dissolved into lectures. "John talked, we listened." Another employee observes, "It was clear John didn't care much about what we thought. He was too excited about his big ideas."

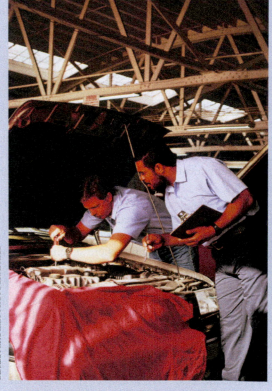

Barbara Filet/FILET PHOTOGRAPHICS

When Jack and John Goudy left their desk jobs to open their auto repair shop, it seemed like a car lover's dream. But poor communication between the two and their staff members turned their one-time dream into a nightmare. Fortunately, they realized their "failure to communicate" and were able to improve their situation.

Finally, despite John's efforts to attract new customers and provide better, faster repairs through technology, workers began to leave the shop for jobs with other companies. At first, he did not understand what had gone so wrong. He had not realized how grueling running his own business could be. He also knew that he was not a strong communicator. "Every day there were questions," he comments. "After a while, they just ground me down." When the company hit rock bottom, John started to get the message. He began to recognize the importance of communication—not only with customers, but with his own workers—and proceeded to make small changes. "Now [when I attend staff meetings], I bring a yellow pad, scribble, and listen."

Source: Based on E. Conlin, "Company Profile: Collision Course," *Inc.*, 14 no. 13 (December 1992), 132–142.

Cultural Barriers

Communication and culture are tightly intertwined. Culture cannot exist without communication, and human communication occurs only within a cultural context. Since the act of communicating is so closely connected to the surrounding environment, culture can ease or hinder it. Thus, similarity in culture between senders and receivers facilitates successful communication—the intended meaning of a message has a higher probability of getting transferred if the sender and receiver share the same culture. The greater the cultural differences between sender and receiver, the greater the difficulty in communicating you should expect. Therefore, other things being equal, it should be easier, for example, for an American manager to communicate with an Australian subordinate than with a Greek subordinate. Or, for example, consider the differences of what "yes" means in two divergent cultures, India and the United States: An Indian manager working for Infosys in Bangalore noted that: "Indians have a difficult time saying no or that you're doing it the wrong way. Indians are more hierarchical and might not say anything unless asked." Thus, some American managers have observed that when Indians say "yes" to a request or a directive, they mean they will attempt to do it, not that it will necessarily get done or that they will take responsibility for it if it does not get done.[27]

Even small and relatively subtle differences between cultures, however, can impede communication, as Jeff Skoll, a Canadian, found out. Skoll, a film company CEO and eBay's first president, recalled: "The transition from the Canadian to the U.S. workplace was really an eye-opener. I found the Canadian way to be more subdued, polite, and . . . more indirect. In the U.S. . . . it turned out that such an approach was no longer effective. Not saying what you want to say out of regard for politeness or sensitivity doesn't seem to work as well here."[28]

Organizational cultures can also differ. The industry of an organization, for example, can influence its internal culture. Therefore, it is more likely that an executive at Warner Brothers could communicate successfully with an executive at Disney than with an executive at Exxon. It is not that extreme cultural differences prevent good communication; rather, the possibilities for breakdowns in communication increase in proportion to the degree of differences in the background and customs of the two parties. See the Manager's Challenge feature on the next page, "When Different Cultures Meet, Communication Sometimes Suffers a Setback," for an illustration of the problems of both national and corporate culture differences combining to influence communication.

The extent to which a sender and receiver differ in a high-context or low-context communication style also significantly influences the effectiveness of the communication. As we discussed in Chapter 3, individuals in high-context cultures tend to pay great attention to the situational factors surrounding the communication process and as a consequence substantially alter what they say and how they say it based on the context (see Exhibit 11.9).[29] Individuals in low-context cultures tend to pay less attention to the context and so make fewer and smaller adjustments from situation to situation.[30] Although the greatest differences in high and low context occur across countries, there are also such differences across organizations. For example, Japan is a high-context culture with three distinct levels of language that speakers use depending on their status compared to that of the listener. There are five different words for "you," each one depending on relative rank and status. However, even within Japan, communication is much more high-context at Mitsubishi Heavy Industries than at Nintendo.

What is most problematic when individuals from high- and low-context cultures communicate with one another is that each often forms negative interpretations about the other's communication approach. Individuals from low-context cultures will tend to believe the wide swings in words and style indicative of people from high-context cultures is evidence of insincerity, hypocrisy, and even instability. These interpretations make trust difficult, and at the extreme, can make effective communication impossible. On the other hand, individuals from high-context cultures view the lack of change in communication style of individuals from low-context cultures as evidence of immaturity, selfishness, or lack of sophistication.

In Japan, managers are taught the old adage about effective communication—that is, to "say what you mean, and mean what you say."[31] Vague directives and instructions are seen as a sign of poor communication skills. The assumption, therefore, is that the burden of proof for effective communication is on the speaker. In contrast, in cultures such as those in Arabic countries and in Latin America, the assumption is that both the speaker and the listener share the

GLOBALIZATION

A MANAGER'S CHALLENGE

When Different Cultures Meet, Communication Sometimes Suffers a Setback

"**Y**ou'd go into a meeting and have to turn to Volume 7, Section 42, page 597." So goes the lament of an American manager from the former Chrysler Corporation about his early experiences interacting with his German counterparts during the first few months of the merger between that company and Daimler-Benz in the late 1990s. As business around the world has become more and more globalized, there are more and more interactions and mergers between companies from different countries and cultures. And as those increase, so do potential managerial communication problems for all those involved. Maintaining effective communication within large organizations is a formidable challenge by itself, but when contrasting cultures—both national and organizational cultures are involved, the difficulties multiply exponentially.

Both direct and indirect communication problems can arise . In the case of Chrysler's merger with Daimler-Benz, the date for announcing the merger was almost postponed because of a dispute over…whether the new company would use American- or European-sized business cards! Comfortable with their own long-standing traditions regarding an appropriate card size and with what this symbolically meant for ease of interactions with others from their culture, neither side would give in. The dispute eventually escalated to the very top echelons before the slightly wider European cards were finally chosen.

In the case of the DaimlerChrysler merger, the contrasting communication styles of the principal players tended to magnify an already complicated communication situation. The Americans tended to be too informal and freewheeling for the Germans' taste, whereas the Germans came across to the Americans as overly confrontational. From their view, this was exemplified by a post-merger statement of Jurgen Schrempp, the former Daimler-Benz CEO who then became the chief of the new combined DaimlerChrysler organization: "Most mergers have this deadly wish for harmony—we put the tough issues up front." Some years

before, when he was managing a Mercedes truck assembly plant in Ohio, Schrempp had said: "I know when to tell the Germans to loosen up and when to tell the Americans, 'Look, we made a decision on Monday—wouldn't it be nice if it sticks on Tuesday?' "

As might be predicted, the early stages of the merger did not go smoothly. Soon the Chrysler managers began to be annoyed by what one account reported as the Daimler managers' practice of "issuing reams of organizational flow charts." As the Chrysler manager cited earlier put it: "The Germans pride themselves on analytical research that produces a plan, while the American way is to try for the impossible and keep coming up with new ideas to make it happen." No doubt, this situation might be described differently from the German perspective. A further indication of the communication difficulties was the fact that within six months or so of the merger, the new combined corporation's communication department had to hire an outside facilitator to help members of the department to communicate with each other! For many reasons beyond communication difficulties the merger was unsuccessful. By 2007 it was sold to Cerberus Capital Management and in 2009 it was acquired out of bankruptcy by Italy's Fiat company. One could wonder whether brand-new communication difficulties will arise in this latest melding of two national and corporate cultures.

The message for managers in these types of communication challenges is not that people coming from different cultures sometimes have problems communicating with each other, but rather that those differences are only a starting point and do not represent impossible hurdles for developing strong communication links.

Sources: J. Snyder and B. Wernle, "1998–2007: Chrysler Shriveled…", *Automotive News* 83 (6347), 23; "In Tandem At Last," *Economist* 378, no. 8471 (2006): 50–52; F. Gibney, Jr. and J. R. Stuttgart, "Daimler-Benz Chrysler: Worldwide Fender Bender," *Time,* May 24, 1999, http://www.time.com.

burden for communicating effectively. In cultures in which the speaker and listener both share communication responsibilities, the chances of unpleasant encounters, direct confrontations, and disagreements tend to decrease.

Probably the greatest single cultural barrier that can affect communication across different departmental, organizational, regional, or national cultures is ethnocentrism.[32] **Ethnocentrism** is the belief in the superiority of one's own group and the related tendency to view others in

ethnocentrism
the belief in the superiority and importance of one's own group

EXHIBIT 11.9

Communication Differences in High- and Low-context Cultures

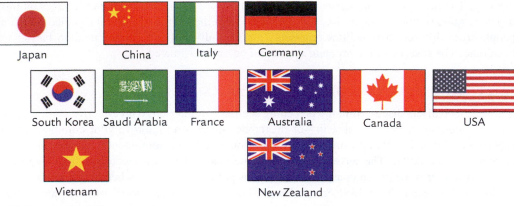

Christophe Testi/Shutterstock

High-Context Cultures
- More and greater adjustments in messages
- Rank of receiver will probably affect message and medium
- Nonverbal communication cues may be very important
- Medium may be as important as message

Low-Context Cultures
- Fewer and smaller adjustments in messages
- Rank of receiver may or may not affect message or medium
- Nonverbal communication cues not as important
- Message is more important than medium

terms of the values of one's own group. Ethnocentrism leads individuals to divide their interpersonal worlds into in-groups and out-groups. As we discussed in Chapter 10, in-groups are groups of people with whom you identify and about whom you care.[33] Members of the in-group tend to be trusted, listened to, and have information shared with them. Members of out-groups tend to be viewed with skepticism, if not suspicion, and are not given full information. This type of behavior exists in organizations as well as in interpersonal interactions.

Another cross-cultural barrier to communication closely related to ethnocentrism is **stereotyping,** the tendency to oversimplify and generalize about groups of people, especially those groups or cultures other than your own.[34] The more firmly held the stereotype by a communicator, the harder it becomes for the person to overcome preconceived expectations and focus on the specifics of the message being sent or received. A good approach for dealing with the tendency to stereotype people from other cultures was stated by an Italian management consultant: "Learn from generalizations about other cultures, but don't use generalizations to stereotype...[Stereotypes] oversimplify the complexities of human behavior and lead to poor judgment."[35]

Stereotyping, of course, can affect communication in virtually all organizational settings, whether between cultures or within the same culture. For example, suppose you are a technical service manager in a software company, and the president holds a negative stereotype of people in your position—specifically, that technical service managers are focused on details and are unable to see the big picture. With a strong stereotype of this sort, the president might not recognize that you understand and are considering the competitive implications (not just the technical ones) of a new software tool, and thus misses out on your potentially valuable input.

A third major cultural barrier to communication can be labeled **cultural distance.**[36] This concept refers to the overall difference between two cultures' basic characteristics, such as their language, level of economic development, and entrenched traditions and customs. Cultural distance was illustrated by a study that gathered 21 senior executives from major corporations in Japan, the United States, Brazil, the United Kingdom, and India for a five-week period of cultural exploration. The executives attended lectures and seminars, built rafts and climbed cliffs together, and even traveled as part of fact-finding teams to one another's countries. Nevertheless, observers reported that communication remained a problem the entire five weeks.[37] Although much of the difficulty came from obvious language differences, a more subtle difficulty came from cultural differences. Many of the Japanese managers, attempting to fit in, adopted American nicknames, but they actually hated being called by them. The Americans couldn't understand why the Japanese were so quiet, not realizing they felt it unwise to speak first at a

stereotyping
the tendency to oversimplify and generalize about groups of people

cultural distance
the overall difference between two cultures' basic characteristics such as language, level of economic development, and traditions and customs

meeting. The more senior the Japanese executive, the more he listens, and the executives on this trip were quite senior. Examples like this emphasize that the degree of cultural distance between people from different nationalities represents a potentially difficult communication barrier to overcome. The severity of the problem should not be underestimated.

Improving Your Communication Skills

The various barriers discussed in the preceding section can interfere with effective communication, but there are ways to deal with—or overcome—them, and improve your communication capabilities. First, though, how important is it for you to have a commitment to developing good communication skills? The answer: very![38] Numerous surveys of executives and corporate recruiters demonstrate the emphasis that companies put on these skills when hiring new college graduates. For example, a *Wall Street Journal*/Harris Interactive survey of recruiters found communication skills to be among the most sought-after attributes of recent graduates. As a *Wall Street Journal* article once put it: "Interpersonal communication . . . skills are what corporate recruiters crave most but find most elusive in MBA graduates." [39]

Given the obvious importance of this topic, in the remainder of this section we discuss some of the most essential approaches that are necessary for you to consider if you want to improve your communication abilities as a manager in organizations.

Improving Your Listening Skills

When it comes to improving one's communication skills, particularly verbal communication skills, most people first think of improving their speaking or writing skills. The fact, is, however, that it is also critical to do a better job of listening—an often neglected skill. It is typically overlooked as a communication skill because it is assumed to be so easy, whereas speaking and writing well are considered to be more difficult skills to master. Becoming a good listener, however, is not something to take for granted.[40]

LISTENING RATHER THAN TALKING YOURSELF The simple act of not always talking, but, instead, concentrating on listening to the other person is one way to improve your listening skills. Even those employed as recruitment interviewers sometimes lose sight of this basic principle. As David Ibarra, a human resources executive with health insurer WellPoint, has stated: "The most common mistake made by interviewers is talking rather than listening. You leave an interview not knowing who the candidate really is."[41]

BE MORE OPEN-MINDED Stereotyping, ethnocentricity, rigid frames of reference, and selective listening can all become barriers to comprehending the intended message of a sender. Consequently, one of the first things you should do to enhance your listening skills is to develop a greater awareness of your personal tendencies with regard to these barriers. Once you have a better awareness of these tendencies, you can monitor and control them during conversations. Part of the reason for direct and conscious attention to this area is that most people speak at about 120 words per minute and yet can listen at about a rate of 1,000 words per minute.[42] This creates the opportunity for our mind to wander or make judgments about what we are hearing. These tendencies then can take over and distort how we interpret what we hear.

DEVELOP EMPATHY Once you've examined your communication tendencies, the next step is developing empathy. **Empathy** is identifying with and understanding the other person's feelings, situation, and motives. To some extent, this requires thinking about the situation of other people, an activity that Bridgette Chambers had to learn to emphasize. What are their feelings relative to the topic at hand? What are their motivations? Why are they talking about what they are? These and other questions can help you enhance your understanding of the personal context of the message being sent.

empathy
the ability to put yourself in someone else's place and to understand his or her feelings, situations, and motives

LISTEN ACTIVELY The next step to improving communication is to take actions to ensure that you—the receiver—hear and understand what the sender is trying to communicate. As one writer on management has stated succinctly: "Seek first to understand, then to be understood."[43] In conversations, making eye contact is a good way to help speakers feel comfortable and convinced that you are sincerely interested in understanding what they have to say. It is important to focus on the content of the message being sent regardless of the style of its delivery. Even if people are not choosing the best words or are making grammatical errors, they may have something quite valuable to communicate. Focusing on style over substance can cause the value of the message to be missed. To make sure you understand what is being said, ask clarifying questions. Also, even when you think you have understood the message, it is a good idea to paraphrase, that is, restate what you think the message is. This can be put in the form of a question or statement. For example, you could ask, "So are you saying that…?" or you can put it more directly by saying something such as, "What I understand you to be saying is…"

OBSERVE NONVERBAL CUES As discussed earlier in this chapter, observing nonverbal cues is vital to effective communication.[44] Listening more open-mindedly and actively to the words is only part of the task. You also need to concentrate on picking up on nonverbal signals. In cross-cultural settings, this means that you need to remember that a gesture or expression can have different meanings in different cultures. There is little substitute for learning about the nonverbal cues and gestures of the culture of those with whom you will be interacting.

Improving Your Sending Skills

There are many situations in which you will be the sender of a message. You can enhance your communication ability by developing better sending skills.

SIMPLIFY YOUR LANGUAGE One of the first things a sender can do to enhance communication is to simplify the language in the message. Clearly, what is simple will vary depending on the audience. Simplifying may involve eliminating jargon that may not be familiar to all members of the audience. It may also involve choosing more succinct and active words and shorter sentences. Perhaps the best clue for spotting complicated and passive language is excessive use of prepositions. The more prepositions in a sentence, the higher the likelihood that the language could be simplified and the message could be stated more directly.

ORGANIZE YOUR WRITING Executives consistently complain about new managers' poor writing skills.[45] Their complaints lie not in spelling or grammar mistakes (though clearly these should be eliminated), but in the absence of logical thought processes. As a manager, you are likely to write more reports and memos than you may want, and the effectiveness of those written communications will have an important impact on your career. Consequently, developing good writing skills is vital to being an effective manager. Nothing substitutes for practice.

UNDERSTAND YOUR AUDIENCE Perhaps the single best thing a sender can do to enhance the effectiveness of communications is to understand the audience.[46] For example, consider the following questions, which come from the material we have covered thus far in the chapter:

- What is the direction of the communication (up, lateral, or down), and does the receiver have any expectations concerning this type of communication?
- Is the communication formal or informal, and how should it be structured to have the intended impact on the receiver?
- Does the receiver have expectations about the explicitness or implicitness of the message you want to send?
- Does the receiver have any biases for or against certain modes of communication (e.g., for or against e-mail, face-to-face conversations, and so on)?

If you do not understand the person or persons to whom you are sending a message, it is almost impossible to answer these questions. Knowing your audience is critical to improving your sending skills, particularly in cross-cultural settings. Exhibit 11.10 lists some tips to improve your cross-cultural communication.

Organization-Level Improvements in Communication

Organizations can take steps to change their policies and methods for how and when managers should communicate. Unfortunately, guidelines for this more structural approach are not as well developed as those for individual managers. A study of research and development laboratories within 14 large multinational firms, however, provides some suggestions.[47] The study produced strong evidence for the importance of a **gatekeeper,** those so-called "boundary- spanning" individuals at the

gatekeeper
an individual at the communication interface between separate organizations or between different units within an organization

EXHIBIT 11.10

Tips on Being a More Effective Cross-cultural Communicator

1. Study general principles that apply to all types of intercultural communication.
2. Learn about the fundamental characteristics of the other cultures with which you will be working.
3. For high-context cultures, learn as many details as possible in advance about the target organization(s) and their specific individual representatives.
4. For high-context cultures, use at least a few words or phrases in the listener's language.
5. For high-context cultures, be especially careful about body language and tone of voice.
6. For low-context cultures, organize written communications so that the major points are immediately and directly stated.
7. Study and respect communicators' preference for greater degrees of formality, especially compared with the typical American approach of casual informality.

communication interface between separate organizations or between units within an organization. Large companies especially need to be able to structure the activities of gatekeepers to maximize their usefulness to the communication process and to make sure that the most critical information is both sent and received. Findings from the study indicated that communication could be improved by implementing rules and procedures that increased formal communication, replacing some face-to-face communication with electronic communication, developing particular communication networks, and even creating a centralized office to manage communication activities.

Communication and Negotiation

negotiation
the process of conferring to arrive at an agreement between different parties, each with its own interests and preferences

The last sections of this chapter focus on one particular type of communication that is becoming especially crucial for a manager to master—namely, negotiation. **Negotiation** can be thought of as the process of conferring to arrive at an agreement between two parties, each with its own interests and preferences. The purpose of negotiation is to see whether the two parties can arrive at an agreement that serves their mutual interests. Since reaching an agreement inherently involves communication, negotiation and communication are inseparably linked.

Why Managers Need Good Negotiation Skills

Today's managers often find themselves in the role of negotiator. This can occur in different types of situations. One common type involves the ongoing day-to-day activities of the manager's organizational unit, where there is a need to negotiate a settlement or resolution of some kind of dispute or difference of opinion. This could be a disagreement between the manager and his own boss, between the manager and another manager from a different unit, or between the manager and one or more of his subordinates. Disagreements can also occur between subordinates or between entire departments. Typically, in these kinds of circumstances the manager would function as an individual negotiator.

The other, more specific type of negotiation situation in which managers could find themselves would be where they are part of a formally appointed negotiating team representing their unit or organization in discussions with representatives from another unit or organization. In either kind of negotiating situation, managers are taking on the role of facilitator—attempting to ensure that all parties can agree on a common course of action. Also, regardless of the particular features of the situation, the principles of effective approaches to negotiation can help settle any kind of disagreements that a manager might encounter—inside or outside an organization.

Achieving More Effective Negotiations

interest
a person's or group's concern or desire—in other words, what the person or group wants

position
a person's or group's stance regarding their interests

There are several ways managers can increase their chances of achieving successful negotiation outcomes. (See Exhibit 11.11.) One especially useful principle to keep in mind when serving as a negotiator is to focus on the two parties' *interests*, not their positions.[48] An **interest** is a person's or group's concern or desire—in other words, what the person or group wants. A **position**,

Less Effective	More Effective
◀···▶	
• Positions	• Interests
• People Involved	• Problem/Issue
• Maintaining/Increasing Competition (Win/Lose Focus)	• Decreasing/Lessening Competition (Collaborative Focus)

EXHIBIT 11.11

Improving Effectiveness of Negotiations

on the other hand, is the person's or group's stance regarding those interests. Thus, an interest, for example, would be the desire by a subordinate to receive challenging new assignments. A position, in this example, would be a statement by the subordinate that "I am the one who should receive this new sales territory because...." It is easier to get agreement on interests instead of positions because: (1) there are probably several possible outcomes that could satisfy a given interest; and (2) behind any two opposed positions are likely to be at least some interests of the two parties that are shared rather than in direct conflict with one another.[49] If these mutually compatible interests can be identified, the chances of reaching an acceptable conclusion to the negotiation are increased.

In the previous example, even though the boss is not able to give the desired new sales territory to this particular subordinate, a common interest may be identified—such as the desire of both parties to see that the subordinate's good performance in the past is rewarded with some other kind of challenging new assignment in the future—even though it can't be this particular assignment now.

As discussed in Chapter 10, a second, sound principle for negotiations is to focus on the problem or issue rather than on the people involved (see Exhibit 11.11). The key point here is that a negotiator should endeavor to concentrate on the substance of the disagreement rather than on who is doing the disagreeing or what they are like as people. This principle is well summarized in this advice to negotiators: "Be hard on the problem, soft on the people."[50]

Another helpful principle for managers who are involved in negotiation (Exhibit 11.11) is to try to lessen the competition between the two parties (an "I win, you lose" situation) by establishing an atmosphere of collaboration (a "we all win" situation). **Collaboration** is an attempt to get both parties to attack a problem and solve it together, not have one party defeat the other, as in a win-lose athletic contest. Thus, both parties should be encouraged to develop creative solutions that increase the total amount of resources available to be shared or divided by the two parties.

collaboration
part of negotiation in which parties work together to attack and solve a problem

Finally, if managers find that negotiations are extremely complex and the parties seem emotionally invested in the outcome, they can often request intervention by a neutral third party. Sometimes a disinterested manager within the organization can be asked to serve in this role. The third-party negotiator can serve the role of judge, mediator, or devil's advocate. In the role of a judge, the manager handles negotiations and decides on the best possible course of action, which the parties then agree to follow. In mediation, the manager controls the negotiation process, but someone else makes the final decision based on the arguments presented—possibly a senior executive in the organization. As discussed in Chapter 10, a devil's advocate asks questions that may oppose the positions of both parties. The attempt here is for all parties to think about positions that they may not originally have considered.

Key Factors in Cross-national Negotiations

As noted earlier, as a manager you may find yourself a member of negotiating teams. With the greater frequency of international assignments, this may particularly be the case when working in situations that require negotiations across national borders. Because of the advances in transportation and communication technologies, along with expanding capital flows worldwide, organizations are engaging in ever-larger amounts of foreign trade and international business partnerships. Together, all this activity increases the importance of your being able to negotiate successfully in cross-national circumstances as well as in your own organization or country. Three principal variables determine the outcome of negotiations in general, and especially in these kinds of cross-national situations: the people involved, the situation, and the process itself.[51]

- Listening ability
- Social intelligence
- Willingness to use team assistance
- Self-confidence
- High aspirations
- Influence at headquarters
- Language sills

Source: Based on W. H. Requejo and J. Graham, *Global Negotiation: The New Rules* (New York: Palgrave McMillan, 2008). Used with permission.

PEOPLE Individual differences play a definite role in negotiations and can affect the resulting outcomes.[52] Despite some cultural differences in preferred negotiator characteristics, some desired negotiator traits are fairly universal (see Exhibit 11.12) They include good listening skills, of course, along with such individual attributes as high social intelligence and self-confidence. In addition, though, they also include more organizationally-oriented qualities such as a willingness to use team assistance and the capability to be influential in one's home organization.

THE SITUATION SURROUNDING THE NEGOTIATIONS The second major variable affecting negotiation outcomes is the set of situational circumstances. Probably the most important are the location of the negotiations, the physical arrangements, the emphasis on speed and time, and the composition of the negotiating teams.

Location Typically, there is a strong tendency to want to negotiate on your own turf or at a neutral site, especially for critical negotiations. The so-called "home court advantage" seems to be universal: everyone feels more comfortable and confident and has greater access to information and resources when negotiating at home. For international negotiations, negotiations conducted in a manager's own offices or even in his or her home country can be a psychological advantage.

Characteristics of locations, however, can vary by culture. For example, in the United States almost all negotiations occur in a formal setting, such as an office or conference room. In contrast, in Japan and Mexico, where relationship building is crucial, major parts of the process are likely to occur in an informal or nonwork setting, such as a restaurant or on a golf course. In Korea, the final contract produced by the negotiations is likely to be signed in a formal and public setting rather than in someone's office.

Physical Arrangements The usual American approach to setting up a room for negotiations is to place the two parties on opposite sides of a table, facing each other, which emphasizes their competing interests. Other arrangements obviously are possible, though, including seating the two parties at right angles or along the same side "facing the problem" or at a round table where everyone is part of the total problem-solving effort.[53]

Emphasis on Speed and Time Americans typically avoid wasting time. They want to "get right to the point" or "get down to business." Other cultures are different. In Mexico or China, for example, the norm is to invest considerable time in relationship building and other activities not directly related to the central negotiation process. Consequently, in such cultures, speed is sacrificed, and the effectiveness and efficiency of subsequent negotiations often hinge on how well the relationships between the parties have developed.[54]

The Composition of the Negotiating Teams The composition and size of teams representing the two parties in negotiations can also influence negotiations. For example, the more people involved at the negotiation table, the more preparation that needs to be done to ensure that the team presents a united front. The composition of the team in terms of decision-making authority is also important. If individuals at the table have authority to make binding decisions, the negotiations are generally more efficient than if they do not.

Team composition can vary significantly by culture. In countries that are sensitive to status differences and ranks (for example, Singapore, India, Venezuela, and Japan), it is much more important for the members of one team to be similar in status, position, age, and authority to the team with which they are negotiating. This is less important in other countries (like New Zealand, Canada, and the United States). The size of negotiating teams also can differ markedly by culture. In the United States, where go-it-alone heroes are admired, team sizes are ordinarily much smaller than in more collectivist-oriented cultures such as those of Taiwan, China, and Japan. The problem is that the resulting mismatches in size can communicate unintended messages. The Taiwanese, for example, might interpret a single negotiator or a small team as a sign that the other party does not consider the negotiations to be important. Similarly, Americans might interpret the presence of a large team from a Taiwanese firm as an attempt to intimidate them with numbers.

THE NEGOTIATION PROCESS The third, and probably most crucial, variable determining the outcome of negotiations is the negotiating process itself. The five common stages in this process, which are basically the same across all cultures, are described next and shown in Exhibit 11.13.[55]

Stage 1: Planning and Preparation This stage involves laying the foundation through advance planning and analysis prior to any face-to-face interactions. At this stage, individuals or teams conduct background research, gather relevant information, and plan their strategy and tactics. Preliminary decisions are made about what the objectives will be and what can and cannot be conceded during the course of the negotiations.

Stage 2: Relationship Building Between Negotiating Parties This stage is commonly referred to as "nontask time," in which each side attempts to establish comfortable working relationships with the other side. As we pointed out earlier, Americans are inclined to make this stage briefer and believe such activities are relatively unimportant. On the other hand, negotiators from some other cultures such as Latin America, the Middle East, and Asia believe exactly the opposite. Research suggests three types of behaviors during this stage: developing trust, developing personal rapport, and establishing long-term association.[56]

Stage 3: Information Exchange In this stage, each party attempts to learn about the needs and demands of their counterparts. Managers from the United States often attempt to hurry through these activities with an attitude of "you tell me what you want, and I will tell you what I want."[57] In contrast, managers from Asian cultures take a much more indirect, more drawn out, and more thorough approach to acquiring and exchanging information. Arabic and Latin American managers appear to follow a similar approach, except that the latter are even more leisurely in their use of time at this stage.[58]

Stage 4: Persuasion Attempts This stage focuses on attempts to modify the position of the other party and to influence that side to accept the negotiator's desired set of exchanges (for example, an exchange of a certain price for a certain quantity or quality of goods or services). Often, behavior at this stage will differ between negotiators from low-context cultures (see Chapter 3) and those from high-context cultures.[59] American managers usually treat this as the most important stage. They are assertive and straightforward in an effort to get what they want. Sometimes this can involve the use of warnings or threats to try to force the other party to agree.[60] Managers from Arabic countries tend to show tactics similar to those of Americans at the persuasion stage, but they are less inclined to hurry. Negotiators from Asian cultures take a slow, careful approach but do not tend to be directly assertive until later in the negotiations. Managers from Latin American cultures tend to use a mixture of approaches during this stage by showing a moderate degree of assertiveness but also a willingness to use the tactic of "calculated delay" when this seems advisable.[61]

Stage 5: Concessions/Agreement At this final point, if reasonable progress has been made, compromises and concessions are made that permit each party to take away something of value. Since American managers tend to begin the negotiation process with positions fairly close to what they will finally accept, they do not have much leeway for concessions.[62] Managers from Arabic and Latin American countries seem to open negotiations from more extreme positions, which permit them to offer concessions late in the process. Managers from Asian countries often employ "normative appeals" (such as "it's your obligation") to try to get the other party to offer concessions.[63]

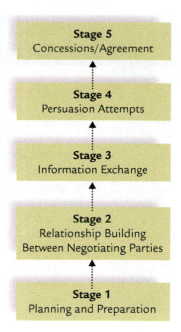

EXHIBIT 11.13

The Five Stages in the Negotiating Process

Managerial Challenges from the Front Line

The Rest of the Story

After one particularly stressful communication incident, Bridgette Chambers sought out one of her mentors in the company for advice. "She looked me in the eye and said that I did not quite do the job [of communicating successfully] that I thought I was doing," said Chambers about her mentor. "She confirmed that while I got results, I left a wake behind me that may have been, in the long run, as costly as missing my targets. The feedback she gave me was like a knife."

Using that as a learning experience, Chambers has become more alert and sensitive to the kind of responses she can create with her direct communication style. Even when she has to communicate the details of uncomfortable changes to those who will be affected, she has learned to turn the potentially difficult situations into positive and productive opportunities that contribute to successful achievement of mutual objectives. Consequently, Chambers has continued to achieve corporate results while receiving numerous accolades and awards for her leadership efforts and communication endeavors.

Summary

- Since communication involves the transfer of information, meaning, and understanding, it is an essential component of managerial effectiveness and crucial for implementing effective leadership.
- The basic communication process involves senders who encode messages and transmit them by some medium, and receivers who decode and interpret the messages. Typically, there also will be some kind of feedback (including the possibility of an apparent absence of feedback) sent by the receiver back to the sender. Throughout the process there may be some level of "noise" or distraction that interferes between senders and receivers.
- Communication can either be verbal or nonverbal, and can differ in degree of "richness"—or capacity to facilitate shared meaning—of the medium used.
- Different features of the organizational context directly impact the effectiveness of communication. These features include the direction of the communication (downward, upward, and lateral), the channels used (formal and informal), and the prevailing patterns of communication networks that exist in the organization.
- Serious barriers to effective communication include interpersonal barriers, such as emotion or differing frames of reference; organizational barriers, such as differences between the sender and receiver and their hierarchical levels or unit affiliations; and cultural barriers, such as ethnocentrism and language differences.
- Although many communication barriers are almost impossible to eliminate completely, steps can be taken to reduce their impact. Individuals can work to improve both their message sending and, especially, their listening skills. Organizations can become more aware and responsive to communication issues—such as those related to cross-cultural communications—and the need to improve their communication procedures.
- An increasingly important type of communication for managers, especially the higher they rise in their organization, is negotiation, the process of meeting with another party to arrive at an agreement. The negotiation process typically involves five key stages: planning and preparation, relationship building, information exchange, and persuasion attempts. As with any communication process, missteps can and often do occur in any or all of these stages.

Key Terms

collaboration   321
communication   303
communication network   311
cultural distance   317
decoding   304
downward communication   308
empathy   318
encoding   304

ethnocentrism   316
formal communication channel   308
frame of reference   313
gatekeeper   319
informal communication channel   310
interest   320
lateral communication   308
media richness   306

medium   304
negotiation   320
networking   311
noise   304
position   320
selective perception   313
stereotyping   317
upward communication 308

Review Questions

1. What is communication?
2. What are the basic elements of the communication model?
3. Which mode of communication is the most flexible? The least flexible? Why?
4. What is meant by "media richness"?
5. What are the typical differences in content of upward, downward, and lateral communication within organizations?
6. What is a communication network?
7. How are selective perception and frames of reference related?
8. What are the principal differences between high-context and low-context cultures relative to communication?
9. Discuss four ways to improve your listening skills.
10. What can organizations do to improve communication within them?
11. In negotiation, what is the difference between an interest and a position?
12. What are four helpful principles for effective negotiation?

Assessing Your Capabilities

How Good Are My Listening Skills?

Using the following scale, circle the number that best indicates the extent to which you agree or disagree with each statement.

	Strongly Agree	Agree	Neither Agree Nor Disagree	Disagree	Strongly Disagree
1. I frequently attempt to listen to several conversations at the same time.	1	2	3	4	5
2. I like people to give me only the facts and then let me make my own interpretation.	1	2	3	4	5
3. I sometimes pretend to pay attention to people.	1	2	3	4	5
4. I consider myself a good judge of nonverbal communications.	1	2	3	4	5
5. I usually know what another person is going to say before he or she says it.	1	2	3	4	5
6. I usually end conversations that don't interest me by diverting my attention from the speaker.	1	2	3	4	5
7. I frequently nod, frown, or provide other nonverbal cues to let the speaker know how I feel about what he or she is saying.	1	2	3	4	5
8. I usually respond immediately when someone has finished talking.	1	2	3	4	5
9. I evaluate what is being said while it is being said.	1	2	3	4	5
10. I usually formulate a response while the other person is still talking.	1	2	3	4	5
11. The speaker's "delivery" style frequently keeps me from listening to content.	1	2	3	4	5

12. I usually ask people to clarify what they have said rather than guess at the meaning.	1	2	3	4	5
13. I make a concerted effort to understand other people's points of view.	1	2	3	4	5
14. I frequently hear what I expect to hear rather than what is said.	1	2	3	4	5
15. Most people feel that I have understood their point of view when we disagree.	1	2	3	4	5

Scoring

To obtain your score

1. Total your responses to questions 1–3, 5–11, and 14.   Enter total here:_____
2. Reverse score (5 becomes 1; 4 becomes 2, etc.) questions 4, 12, 13, and 15.   Enter total here:_____
Your overall score is the total of both partial scores.   TOTAL:_____

Analysis and Interpretation

Effective communicators have developed good listening skills. This instrument is designed to provide you with some insights into your listening skills.

Scores range from 15 to 75. The higher your score the better listener you are. While any cutoffs are essentially arbitrary, if you score 60 or above, your listening skills are fairly well honed. Scores of 40 or less indicate you need to make a serious effort at improving your listening skills.

Good sources to help you improve your listening skills include:

- M. Helgessen, *Active Listening: Building Skills for Understanding* (New York: Cambridge University Press, 1994).
- M. Burley-Allen, *Listening: The Forgotten Skill* (Hoboken: Wiley, 1995).
- J. E. Sullivan, *The Good Listener* (Notre Dame: Ave Maria Press, 2000).

Source: Robbins, Stephen P., *Self Assessment Library 3.4 for Sales Management*, 1st, © 2009. Printed and Electronically reproduced by permission of Pearson Education, Inc., Upper Saddle River, New Jersey.

Team Exercise

Modeling the Might of Media Richness

This is a fun exercise that demonstrates vividly the importance of choosing the right medium for your communication needs. Your instructor will divide you into teams of teachers, learners, and observers.

Each teacher will attempt to instruct his or her learner partner in a complex task. Each team will use different levels of media richness in their instructions.

Following the demonstration exercise, the class will discuss the following questions:

1. Which method appears to have worked best?
2. Was the fastest method also the most successful?
3. What elements contributed to the success or failure of the instruction?
4. How does this exercise relate to media richness theory?
5. Give examples of unsuccessful media choices you have encountered. What was right or wrong in these situations? Were there harmful outcomes from the choice of an inappropriate medium?
6. How can you apply what you have learned to your workplace interactions?

Source: Adapted by Grace B. McLaughlin, Ph.D. (2007) from discussions with other attendees at the Organizational Behavior Teaching Conference 2002. Reprinted with the permission of the author.

Generational differences can produce challenges for managers (as has been discussed in Chapters 7 and 9). They especially can create major communication issues. The obvious question is: How best to deal with them?

Most organizations of any moderate or larger size are likely to have different generations of employees working for them: at the two ends of the spectrum are the "younger" (those in their 20s and early 30s) and "older" (those in their 60s and higher). These two extremes have been characterized, in a bit of overstatement, as "geeks" and "geezers." In between are those in the middle (those in their 40s and early 50s), and, of course there will always be some who are near a generational boundary (e.g., late 30s). As a result of their life experiences and especially their exposure to, and use of, new communication technologies in their early and teen years before becoming adults, younger employees are accustomed to communicating constantly and rapidly in short bursts utilizing multiple means. At the other end of the continuum, older employees, growing up in different conditions and before the arrival of many of the new communication technologies, are much more prone to use and respond to more formal communications, especially those in print modality. Speed, informality, and interactive are the watchwords for those in their 20s and 30s, whereas thoroughness and authenticity—a more linear style of communication—are important to those currently in their later working years.

As many observers have noted, mixing these different generations in the same organization and, especially, within the same work groups can produce unintended communication difficulties. Described below are two types of typical scenarios that can arise and present those in managerial positions with demanding challenges:

Scenario #1:

It was four PM on the third Friday of the month. Mark put down the latest company financial report, grabbed his cell phone and office key and headed out to the cookies and conversation gathering out on the back patio deck behind the cafeteria. Mark had only been with the company for six months, and he saw this kind of informal setting as a good opportunity to meet and network with other managers. He sat down with a group that was listening to the stories that Kent was telling of his early days with the company, from the early 1970s. The stories were interesting even though Kent seemed to provide just some bare factual details with very little emotional expression involved. While Mark was listening, he was also texting a couple of friends about plans for that night. Suddenly Kent just stopped, stared at him, and said, "I can see I'm boring you." Kent then got up and went over to talk to someone else. Mark immediately proceeded to send a tweet to his friends about this, and then looked for another group to join. Just then, Maria stopped him and suggested that if he really wanted to make a good impression on the group, he should probably put his cell phone away. Soon after, Mark returned to his office.

By the time he got back to his office, Mark was fairly confused about some of the comments he had received from several of the other managers. He proceeded to send off several texts to his network describing the situation and asking for feedback. Most of the feedback he received from his friends said not to worry about it. These were just older managers who didn't understand multitasking the way he and his friends did. However, he also received a phone call from Sam, a friend who worked in human resources. Though Sam is a Baby Boomer, he used electronic media frequently and well, but he also had a habit of wanting to sit down and discuss important issues face to face. Therefore, receiving a phone call rather than an e-mail from Sam wasn't that surprising to Mark. He headed over to Sam's office. The conversation was surprising. Sam talked to Mark about various methods of communicating and how different generations tend to communicate in different ways. He explained that many of the older workers view texting during meetings as extremely rude. They thought the younger workers overly needy in their insistence on constant support and feedback. The older managers valued face-to-face interactions. Sam suggested that Mark start watching how other managers communicated with each other. He said Mark would be amazed at the different communication approaches and preferences of managers from varying generations. After thanking Sam and returning to his office, Mark was left with a lot to think about. Of course, he immediately started texting several friends to tell them about this latest conversation.

Scenario #2:

After six months on the job, Whitney was generally happy as head of the marketing promotions department. Only 28, Whitney had worked hard for this chance and had introduced a number of changes to how the group interacted that were intended to make promotional planning more efficient. Most of the members of her group were in their 20s to 40s except for Brett, who was approaching retirement. Whitney seemed to have no problem communicating with most of the department, but just didn't know what to do about Brett. Brett never responded to text messages, never posted comments to the department blog that Whitney had instituted, and never shared planning documents online with the rest of the group. The former manager of the department had told Whitney that Brett was a great asset to the department, with great ideas. Whitney didn't understand why Brett wasn't living up to her expectations.

Questions

1. What kinds of barriers to communication can you find in each scenario?

2. Is anybody "at fault" in either or both scenarios? Explain your reasoning.

3. Do you think that in Scenario #2 both age and gender differences were factors, or just one and not the other, or neither (that it was just a matter of individual differences)? Explain the basis for your answer.

4. How can Mark, Kent, Whitney, and Brett improve their communication skills?

Source: G. B. McLaughlin and L. W. Porter.

References

1. S. Bing, "Business as a Second Language," *Fortune* (1998): 57–58.

2. K. Krone, F. M. Jablin, and L. L. Putnam, "Communication Theory and Organizational Communication: Multiple Perspectives," in *Handbook of Organizational Communication: An Interdisciplinary Perspective*, eds. F. M. Jablin, L. L. Putnam, K. H. Roberts, and L. W. Porter (Newbury Park: Sage Publications, 1987).

3. H. C. Triandis, *Culture and Social Behavior* (New York: McGraw-Hill, 1994); B. A. Bechky, "Sharing Meaning Across Occupational Communities: The Transformation of Understanding on a Production Floor," *Organization Science* 14, no. 3 (2003): 312; M. Becerra and A. K. Gupta, "Perceived Trustworthiness Within the Organization: The Moderating Impact of Communication Frequency on Trustor and Trustee Effects," *Organization Science* 14, no. 1 (2003): 32–44.

4. "Top 13 Worst Marketing Slogan Translations Ever," August 26, 2009, *Cosmobc.com,* http://jokes.cosmobc.com.

5. S. Hanke, "Communication Styles: What Is Your Impact on Others?" *Professional Safety* 54, no. 5 (2009): 22–25.

6. R. L. Daft and R. H. Lengel, "Information Richness: A New Approach to Managerial Behavior and Organization Design," *Research in Organizational Behavior*, eds. L. L. Cummings and B. Staw (Greenwich: JAI, 1984), 191–223; R. L. Daft and R. H. Lengel, "Organizational Information Requirements, Media Richness and Structural Design," *Management Science* 32 (1986): 554–572; K. Miller, *Organizational Communication: Approaches and Processes*, 2nd ed. (Belmont: Wadsworth, 1999).

7. L. K. Trevino, R. L. Daft, and R. H. Lengel, "Understanding Managers Media Concerns," *Organizations and Communication Technology*, eds. J. Fulk and C. Steinfeile (Newbury Park: Sage, 1990); "How to Create Communications Materials Employees Will Actually Use," *Harvard Business Review* 80, no. 1 (2002): 102.

8. S. Salmon and T. A. Joiner, "Toward an Understanding Communication Channel Preferences for the Receipt of Management Information," *Journal of American Academy of Business* 7, no. 2 (2005): 56–62.

9. J. Sharkey, "Email Saves Time, but Being There Says More," *New York Times*, January 26, 2010, B7.

10. O. B. Lowry, N. C. Romano, Jr., J. L. Jenkins, and R. W. Guthrie, "The CMC Interactivity Model: How Interactivity Enhances Communication Quality and Process Satisfaction in Lean-media Groups," *Journal of Management Information Systems* 26, no. 1(2009): 155–195.

11. "Daimler Opts for HD Conferencing," *AV Magazine,* March 2009, 8.

12. J. Yates and W. J. Orlikowski, "Genres of Organizational Communication: A Structurational Approach to Studying Communication and Media," *Academy of Management Review* 17 (1992): 299–326.

13. L. W. Porter, E. E. Lawler III, and J. R. Hackman, *Behavior in Organizations* (New York: McGraw-Hill, 1975).

14. J. K. Kassing, "In Case You Didn't Hear Me the FirstTime: An Examination of Repetitious Upward Dissent," *Management Communication Quarterly* 22 (2009): 416–436.

15. K. Davis, "The Care and Cultivation of the Corporate Grapevine," *Dun's Review* 102, no. 1 (1973): 44–47.

16. C. Dellarocas, "The Digitization of Word of Mouth: Promise and Challenges of Online Feedback Mechanisms," *Management Science* 49, no. 10 (2003): 1407–1424.

17. "BASF Launches SM/PO Venture," *Chemical Market Reporter* 262, no. 11 (2002): 23.

18. H.G. Wolff, and K. Moser, "Effects of Networking on Career Success: A Longitudinal Study," *Journal of Applied Psychology* 94, no. 1(2009): 196–206.

19. "He Said, She Said," *Communications* 46 (2003): 9, 11; H. Ibarra, "Homophily and Differential Returns: Sex Differences in Network Structure and Access in an Advertising Firm," *Administrative Science Quarterly* 37 (1992): 422–447; H. Ibarra, "Personal Networks of Women and Minorities in Management: A Conceptual Framework," *Academy of Management Review* 18 (1993): 56–87; K. A. Mollica, B. Gray, and L. K. Trevino, "Racial Homophily and Its

Persistence in Newcomers' Social Networks," *Organization Science* 14, no. 2 (2003): 123–136.

20. J. M. Beyer, P. Cattopadhyay, E. George, W. H. Glick *et al.,* "The Selective Perception of Managers Revisited," *Academy of Management Journal* 40 (2003): 716–737.

21. A. Tversky and D. Kahneman, "Rational Choice and the Framing of Decisions," *Journal of Business* 59 (1986): S251–278; "Nothing Serious? Candidates' Use of Humour in Management Training," *Human Relations* 55, no. 4 (2002): 387–406.

22. C. M. Jones, "Shifting Sands: Women, Men, and Communication," *Journal of Communication* 49 (1999): 148–155.

23. C. R. Rogers and F. J. Roethlisberger, "Barriers and Gateways to Communication," *Harvard Business Review* 69, no. 6 (1991): 105–111; L. Perlow and S. Williams, "Is Silence Killing Your Company?" *Harvard Business Review* 81, no. 5 (2003): 52–58.

24. R. Wilkinson, "Do You Speak Obscuranta?" *Supervision* 49, no. 9 (1988): 3–5; C. Argyris, "Four Steps to Chaos," *Harvard Business Review* 81, no. 10 (2003): 140.

25. J. A. Mausehund, S. A. Timm, and A. S. King, "Diversity Training: Effects of an Intervention Treatment on Nonverbal Awareness," *Business Communication Quarterly* 58, no. 1 (1995): 27–30.

26. Ibid.

27. S. Gibson, "Understanding the Indian 'Yes'," *eWeek* 23, no. 10 (2006): 32.

28. A. Mlynek, "Say Goodbye to Shy," *Canadian Business* 79, no. 18, September 11, 2006, 125–128.

29. J. H. Robinson, "Professional Communication in Korea: Playing Things by Eye," *IEEE Transactions on Professional Communication* 39, no. 3 (1996): 129–134; G. E. Kersten, S. T. Koeszegi, and R. Vetschera, "The Effects of Culture in Computer-Mediated Negotiations," *Journal of Information Technology Theory and Application* 5, no. 2 (2003): 1–28.

30. T. E. McNamara and K. Hayashi, "Culture and Management: Japan and the West Towards a Transnational Corporate Culture," *Management Japan* 27, no. 2 (1994): 3–13.

31. S. Okazaki and J. Alonso, "Right Messages for the Right Site: On-line Creative Strategies by Japanese Multinational Corporations," *Journal of Marketing Communications* 9, no. 4 (2003): 221–240; M. Rosch and K. G. Segler, "Communication with Japanese," *Management International Review* 27, no. 4 (1987): 56–67.

32. C. Gouttefarde, "Host National Culture Shock: What Management Can Do," *European Business Review* 92, no. 4 (1992): 1–3.

33. H. Triandis, "Cross-cultural Contributions to Theory in Social Psychology," in *Reading on Communication with Strangers*, eds. W. B. Gudykunst and Y. Y. Kim (New York: McGraw-Hill, 1992), 75; T. R. Tyler and S. L. Blader, "Autonomous vs. Comparative Status: Must We Be Better Than Others to Feel Good About Ourselves?" *Organizational Behavior and Human Decision Processes* 89, no. 1 (2002): 813–838; L. Huff and L. Kelley, "Levels of Organizational Trust in Individualist Versus Collectivist Societies: A Seven-Nation Study," *Organization Science* 14, no. 1 (2003): 81–90; A. C. Lewis and S. J. Sherman, "Hiring You Makes Me Look Bad: Social-Identity Based Reversal of the Ingroup Favoritism Effect," *Organizational Behavior and Human Decision Processes* 90, no. 2 (2003): 262–276.

34. J. Vaes and M. P. Paladino, "The Uniquely Human Content of Stereotypes," *Group Processes and Intergroup Relations* 13, no. 1 (2009): 23–39.

35. D. Silver, "A Broad Spectrum," *PM Network* 23, no. 1 (2009): 62–68.

36. S. Carlson, "International Transmission of Information and the Business Firm," *Annals of the American Academy of Political and Social Science* 412 (1974): 55–63; Marshall and Boush, "Dynamic Decision Making: A Cross-cultural Comparison of U.S. and Peruvian Export Managers"; Y. Luo, "Building Trust in Cross-cultural Collaborations: Toward a Contingency Perspective," *Journal of Management* 28, no. 5 (2002): 669–694.

37. J. Main, "How 21 Men Got Global in 35 Days," *Fortune* (1989): 71–79.

38. S. Datar, D. Garvin, and P. Cullen, *Rethinking the MBA: Business Education at a Crossroads*, (Cambridge, Mass.: Harvard Business School Press, 2010) 98.

39. R. Alsop, "MBA Survey: Something Old, Something New," *Wall Street Journal*, September 26, 2006, http://online.wsj.com.

40. W. E. Kraus, "The 'Cool Hand Luke' Theory of Project Communication," *AACE International Transactions* (2006): 91–94.

41. A. March, "Babbling Interviewer Disease," *Business 2.0* (2006): 54.

42. T. D. Lewis and G. H. Graham, "Six Ways to Improve Your Communication Skills," *Internal Auditor* (1988): 25.

43. S. R. Covey, *The Seven Habits of Highly Effective People* (New York: Simon & Schuster, 1989).

44. G. M. Barton, "Manage Words Effectively," *Personnel Journal* 69, no. 1 (1990): 32–40.

45. L. W. Porter and L. E. McKibbin, *Management Education and Development: Drift or Thrust into the 21st Century* (New York: McGraw-Hill, 1988).

46. S. L. Silk, "Making Your Speech Memorable," *Association Management* 46, no. 1 (1994): L59–L62.

47. A. DeMeyer, "Tech Talk: How Managers Are Stimulating Global R&D Communication," *Sloan Management Review* 32, no. 3 (1991): 49–58.

48. R. Fisher and W. Ury, *Getting to Yes* (London: Simon & Schuster, 1987); K. A. Wade-Benzoni, A. J. Hoffman, L. L. Thompson, D. A. Moore *et al.*, "Barriers to Resolution in Ideologically Based Negotiations: The Role of Values and Institutions," *Academy of Management Review* 27, no. 1 (2002): 41–57; R. B. McKersie, T. Sharpe, T. A. Kochan, A. E. Eaton, G. Strauss and M. Morgenstern, "Bargaining Theory Meets Interest-based Negotiations: A Case Study," *Industrial Relations* 47, no. 1 (2008); 66–96.

49. Ibid.

50. Ibid, 54.

51. N. J. Adler, *International Dimensions of Organizational Behavior*, 2nd ed (Boston: PWS-Kent, 1991), 185.

52. E. T. Amanatullah and M. W. Morris, "Negotiating Gender Roles: Gender Differences in Assertive Negotiating Are Mediated by Women's Fear of Backlash and Attenuated When Negotiating on Behalf of Others," *Journal of Personality and Social Psychology* 98, (2010): 256–267; D. S. DeRue, H. Moon, D. E. Conlon, and H. W. Willaby, "When Is Straightforwardness a Liability in Negotiations? The Role of Integrative Potential and Structural Power," *Journal of Applied Psychology* 94 (2009): 1032–1047; C. E. Naquin and T. R. Kurtzberg, "Team Negotiation and Perceptions of Trustworthiness: The Whole Versus the Sum of the Parts," *Group Dynamics: Theory, Research, and Practice* 13, no. 2 (2009): 133–150.

53. Fisher and Ury, *Getting to Yes*.

54. E. Giebels and P. J. Taylor, "Interaction Patterns in Crisis Negotiations: Persuasive Arguments and Cultural Differences," *Journal of Applied Psychology* 94 (2009): 5–19.

55. M. Lee, "10 Myths About Multicultural Customers," *Selling* (November 2003): 10–12; K. Kumar, S. Noneth, and C. Yauger, "Cultural Approaches to the Process of Business Negotiation: Understanding Cross-cultural Differences in Negotiating Behaviors," in *International Research in the Business Disciplines*, ed. C. L. Swanson (Greenwich: JAI Press, 1993), 79–90; B. M. Hawrysh and J. L. Zaichkowsky, "Cultural Approaches to Negotiations: Understanding the Japanese," *International Marketing Review* 7, no. 2 (1990): 28–42.

56. Kumar *et al.*, "Cultural Approaches to the Process of Business Negotiations."

57. Graham and Herberger, "Negotiators Abroad Don't Shoot from the Hip."

58. Kumar *et al.*, "Cultural Approaches to the Process of Business Negotiations."

59. E. Giebels and P. J. Taylor, "Interaction Patterns.".

60. N. Woliansky, "We Do (Do Not) Accept Your Offer," *Management Review* 78, no. 12 (1989): 54–55; Kumar *et al.*, "Cultural Approaches to the Process of Business Negotiations."

61. Graham and Herberger, "Negotiators Abroad Don't Shoot from the Hip."

62. J. L. Graham and N. J. Adler, "Cross-cultural Interaction: The International Comparison Fallacy?" *Journal of International Business Studies* 20 (1989): 515–537; C. Barnum and N. Wolniasky, "Why Americans Fail at Overseas Negotiations," *Management Review* 78, no. 10 (1989): 55–57.

63. Kumar *et al.*, "Cultural Approaches to the Process of Business Negotiations."

12

Individual and Group Decision Making*

LEARNING OBJECTIVES

After studying this chapter, you should be able to:

Explain the traditional model of decision making.

Recognize and account for the limits of rationality in the decision process.

Describe how risk and uncertainty affect decision making.

List the conditions for when it is best to make decisions individually and when it is best to make them collectively.

Name the steps to facilitate group participation in decision making.

Describe the barriers to effective decision making and ways to overcome them.

*Portions of this chapter have been adopted from *Organizational Behavior*, 5th edition, by Richard M. Steers and J. Stewart Black with permission from the authors and the publisher.

Lead Dog Productions

Name: Lurue Lord

Position: Co-owner, Lord Eye Center

Alma mater: Georgia Southern University

Outside work activities: Saltwater fishing, golf, and tennis

First job out of school: Paralegal with a Savannah, Georgia, law firm

Business book reading now: *How to Lead and Still Have a Life* and *The E Myth Revisited*

Hero: My parents because they were successful running their family business, and they taught me a strong work ethic and to act quickly.

Motto to live by: Enjoy life and enjoy your work.

What drives me: I am motivated by the challenge of success.

Management style: Total follow-through and mental toughness

Pet peeve: Dealing with low-energy people

In 1978, along with her optometrist husband, Lord established the Lord Eye Center in Statesboro, Georgia. Through the couple's hard work and dedication, the company grew to six offices in six Georgia cities (Statesboro, Savannah, Brunswick, Augusta, Rincon, and St. Mary's) from north to south across the state. Today, Lord Eye Center is the largest privately owned optometric and optical business in the state, with eleven doctors on staff.

Not unlike many small businesses, much of Lord Eye Center's early success was due to the fact that the Lords were heavily involved with its management. When they first established the business, Lord had to make most of the decisions about almost every aspect of the company's operations—from how it tried to compete to who it bought supplies from. But as the business grew and spread geographically, Lord faced an interesting challenge: Should she continue to make decisions in the same, hands-on way she always had? Or should she adopt a more employee-empowerment style of decision making?

Lord faced this choice, in part, because as Lord Eye Center grew there were simply more decisions Lord had to make. Second, as the company prospered, the Lords were able to hire and train people who could potentially take on more decision-making responsibility. "I noticed our employees' ideas and ways of doing things were often very successful and that giving them more flexibility motivated them," explains Lord. Third, making all the decisions herself took more time—time she wanted to spend enjoying some of the fruits of her labor. Fourth, as they expanded geographically, it was harder to visit all the stores frequently enough to know in detail everything that was going on and be there when specific decisions needed to be made.

Empowering your employees to make decisions is not without its risks, though. The optometric and optical business is competitive. Repeat business from existing customers is important, and "word of mouth" (positive or negative) can have a significant impact on a firm's ability to attract new customers. As a consequence, poor decisions today could affect the business far into the future.

So what should Lord do? With more and more decisions to make, employees spread across six locations from the north to the south of Georgia, and varying competitive conditions in each location, should she empower the firm's employees to make more decisions themselves, or stick with the tried-and-true approach that had driven the company to the point of success it enjoys today?

---

decision making

a process of specifying the nature of a particular problem or opportunity and selecting among available alternatives to solve a problem or capture an opportunity

In the minds of many people, decision making is *the* most important managerial activity. **Decision making** is the process of specifying the nature of a particular problem or opportunity and selecting among the available alternatives to solve the problem or capitalize on the opportunity. In this sense, decision making has two aspects: the act and the process. The act of decision making involves choosing between alternatives. The process of decision making involves several steps that can be divided into two distinct categories. The first, **formulation,** involves identifying a problem or opportunity, acquiring information, and diagnosing the factors affecting the problem or opportunity. The **solution** phase involves generating alternatives, selecting the preferred solution, and implementing the decided course of action. Following the implementation of the solution, managers monitor the situation to determine the extent to which the decision was successful.

Like Lurue Lord, as a manager you want to understand what factors affect the quality of decisions and what you can do to improve them. The models discussed next can help you better understand managerial decision making—both decisions made individually and those made in groups. Each is based on different assumptions about the nature of people at work.

Individual Decision Making

It is no easy task to outline the details of the decision-making process. Research has been mixed about how individuals and groups make decisions.[1] Even so, at least three attempts to describe the decision-making process are worth noting. These three models are (1) the rational/classic model; (2) the administrative, or bounded rationality, model; and (3) the retrospective decision-making model. As you read about these models, pay special attention to the assumptions each makes about the nature of decision makers; also note the differences in focus.

The Classical, or Rational, Model

The classical model, also known as the **rational model,** represents the earliest attempt to model decision-making processes.[2] This approach involves seven basic steps (see Exhibit 12.1).

Step 1   **Identifying Decision Situations**   In the classic model, the decision maker begins by recognizing that a decision-making situation exists; that is, that problems or opportunities exist. A **problem** exists when a manager detects a gap between the firm's existing and desired performance. This is the situation we commonly associate with decision making and why decision making and problem solving often get talked about interchangeably. For example, you might discover that your subordinates just have more work than they can get done. As a consequence, you may decide to hire an additional worker.

An **opportunity** exists when a manager sees a way for the firm to achieve a more desirable state than the one it's currently in. For example, you might see an opportunity to capture greater market share because one of your key competitors is having some production problems relative to the installation and ramp up of new equipment. In response, you might decide to increase your firm's output to fill the gap left by your competitor's lower production levels.

THE ROLE OF PERCEPTION   Managers often interpret situations differently. Some managers will see a situation as an opportunity; others will see it as a threat.[3] Your **perception**—the way you look at a situation—in large part is based on your own experiences, personality, and needs. As a result, when you first begin to examine a situation, it can be worthwhile to ask others what "their take" on it is.

The following "Manager's Challenge" illustrates how UPS tries to help its managers to make better decisions by broadening their perspective through giving them experiences that they normally would not have.

Step 2   **Developing Objectives and Criteria**   Once you have identified a problem or opportunity, the next step is to determine the criteria for selecting among the alternatives to deal with it. For example, before you can decide which job applicant to hire, you need to determine the outcome you're trying to achieve. If you need the new hire to be effective at sales, then good interpersonal skills might be a criterion. However, it is rare that a single criterion will be sufficient to guide the decision-making process, in part because one factor rarely produces all the desired results. For example, good interpersonal skills *alone* will not likely lead to great sales results; a person also needs to be motivated and understand the selling process.

When several criteria are involved, it is often necessary to "weight" the various criteria.[4] For example, you might decide that a new hire's sales depend on four things: interpersonal skills, motivation, product knowledge, and understanding of the selling process. However, the impact of these factors might not be equal. As a manager, then, you might assign a weight to each criterion: for example, motivation, 30 percent; interpersonal skills, 25 percent; understanding of the selling process, 25 percent; and product knowledge, 20 percent.

formulation
a process involving identifying a problem or opportunity, acquiring information, developing desired performance expectations, and diagnosing the causes and relationships among factors affecting the problem or opportunity

EXHIBIT 12.1

Classical Decision-Making Model

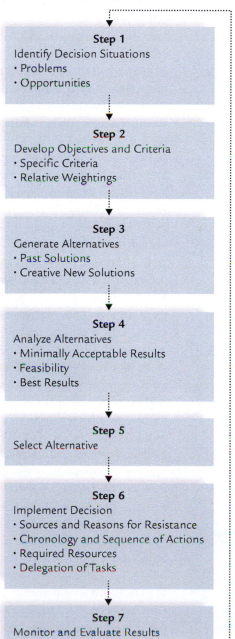

Step 1
Identify Decision Situations
• Problems
• Opportunities

Step 2
Develop Objectives and Criteria
• Specific Criteria
• Relative Weightings

Step 3
Generate Alternatives
• Past Solutions
• Creative New Solutions

Step 4
Analyze Alternatives
• Minimally Acceptable Results
• Feasibility
• Best Results

Step 5
Select Alternative

Step 6
Implement Decision
• Sources and Reasons for Resistance
• Chronology and Sequence of Actions
• Required Resources
• Delegation of Tasks

Step 7
Monitor and Evaluate Results

A MANAGER'S CHALLENGE

DIVERSITY

Gaining a New Perspective on Decisions at UPS

Managing diverse perspectives in order to make better decisions is a tough balancing act for managers at United Parcel Service (UPS). On one hand, UPS advertises that it runs the "tightest ship in the shipping business." The company has built a successful global delivery business by developing standard procedures for nearly all routine decisions, including how drivers should carry their keys when making deliveries. At the same time, UPS is increasingly a company of diverse and different employees. UPS has just over 400,000 employees and half of all UPS's new employees are not white. As one senior manager noted, "There are all kinds of personalities and all kinds of diversity. We need managers who can manage those individuals."

As a consequence, every year since 1968, approximately 50 senior managers participate in UPS's Community Internship Program (CIP): The managers leave their jobs and families for a full month to work at a CIP site in New York, Chattanooga, McAllen, Texas, and San Francisco). In these cities, UPS managers encounter a host of social and economic problems, including poverty. Whether employees spend the month cleaning up dilapidated apartments or working with migrant workers, participants say the experience drives home new lessons about diversity. For example, during a month of working in New York, Mark van Andel, a distribution manager noted, "CIP has enriched me and made me a more well-rounded manager. I have become more aware, gained a better understanding, and have become more sensitive towards issues that our people face." Patti Hobbs also did her internship in New York, working with teens who were addicted to drugs. She noted how impressed she was by the thoughtful suggestions these teens offered for keeping other teenagers off drugs. Back on the job, she broadened her use of group decision making to involve more staff members, rather than only the highest-level managers, in problem-solving discussions. "You start to think there's no one person, regardless of position, who has all the answers," she explains. "The answers come from us all."

From his experience in San Francisco, package division manager Greg Campbell said, "This has been a great experience and one that will influence me in my future in many ways. CIP enhanced our leadership skills and caused us to think and act differently." From her experience in San Francisco, human resource manager Kim Wallace noted, "I was reminded that ideas coming from a group of smart and dedicated people are better than ideas I come up with

Jim West/Alamy Images

Since 1968, UPS has invested more than $15 million to send 1,300 of its middle managers to communities that suffer from poverty and other problems. Initiated by UPS founder James Casey, the program is designed to add diversity to the company's "brown" perspective. Here UPS volunteers paint murals in a local high school.

alone. CIP gives managers an opportunity to experience firsthand the hardships that others often have to experience simply to exist. I have been much less quick to judge. I believe it will help me be a more understanding and tolerant manager throughout the rest of my career."

Allen Sawbenbauer worked on a CIP in Tennessee and commented, "The experience gave me a better understanding of how I could have a better working relationship with my employees. Since returning, I have a better understanding of some of the challenges that my team—both management and nonmanagement—may face on a day-to-day basis. As a manager, CIP gave me the tools to work out problems with my employees, rather than making things more difficult for them."

UPS has invested more than $15 million to send 1,500 of its middle managers through the program, at a cost of $10,000 per participant. Although executives cannot point to a financial return on this investment, feedback from participants indicates that they not only bring a new perspective to their work decisions, but they also come home inspired to volunteer in their own communities. "We will never really know how many lives we have touched," sums up a recent participant.

Sources: Company Web site, http://www.community.ups.com, accessed May 1, 2010; B. Leak, "UPS Delivers an Eye-Opener," *BusinessWeek,* October 10, 2005, http://www.businessweek.com.

Step 3 **Generating Alternatives** Once you've established your objectives and criteria, the next step is to generate alternatives that achieve the results you want. How exactly can you solve a particular problem or capture an opportunity? Most of us first consider alternatives we have successfully resorted to in the past. If the current situation is similar, past solutions can be effective. But if the situation isn't similar, we must generate new alternatives.

Even when a situation *is* similar, it's often worthwhile to pursue new, creative alternatives. Why? Because no two situations are exactly identical, and subtle differences may make a past solution less effective today. For example, at IBM in the past a salesperson's product knowledge and industry experience were the keys to his or her success. If you sold mainframes, you needed to know all the technical specifications and be able to convey them effectively to a technical purchasing manager in your client's organization. Over time, integrating, mainframes, servers, desktops, software, etc. became so complicated that clients wanted an integrated solution not just superior but separate components. Now instead of selling a $10 million mainframe computer, sales managers needed to sell a $100 million solution. Instead of talking to the technical purchasing manager, the sales manager had to speak to the CIO (Chief Information Officer) or the CEO. As a consequence, IBM had to use different criteria for selecting salespeople, such as the ability to talk about the business returns of purchasing the solution not the product technical specification.

Step 4 **Analyzing Alternatives** The fourth step in the process involves analyzing the alternatives generated. To begin, you need to determine which alternatives would produce minimally acceptable results. You can eliminate alternatives that are unlikely to at least achieve the minimally acceptable outcome. Next, you need to examine the feasibility of the remaining alternatives. Returning to our hiring example, you may have found three candidates for your sales position who would likely produce the minimally acceptable sales results. But one candidate's salary needs exceed your budget; therefore, that person is not feasible. Once you eliminate infeasible alternatives, the next step is to determine which of the remaining alternatives will produce the most satisfactory outcome. Typically, you apply the criteria and weights produced in Step 2 at this point. For example, of the two remaining candidates for the sales position, Jane and Martha, you might rate both people on each of the four criteria (see Exhibit 12.2).

Even though Jane scored lower than Martha on both sales and product knowledge, Jane is the better candidate. Her higher overall score is a function of scoring higher on the most important criteria (motivation and interpersonal skills).

Step 5 **Selecting Alternatives** Selecting an alternative flows naturally out of your analysis. The classical model argues that managers will choose the alternative that maximizes the desired outcome. The **subjectively expected utility (SEU) model** exemplifies this idea.[5] This model asserts that managers choose the alternative that they subjectively believe maximizes the desired outcome. The two key components of this model are the expected outcome produced by a given alternative and the probability that the alternative can be implemented. In

solution
a process involving generating alternatives, selecting the preferred solution, and implementing the decided course of action

rational model (classical model)
a seven-step model of decision making that represents the earliest attempt to model decision processes

problem
a gap between existing and desired performance

opportunity
a chance to achieve a more desirable state than the current one

perception
a way one sees a situation based on experiences, personality, and current needs

subjectively expected utility (SEU) model
a model of decision making that asserts that managers choose the alternative that they subjectively believe maximizes the desired outcome

EXHIBIT 12.2

Applying Criteria in Analyzing Alternatives

Candidate	Criteria	Rating*	×	Weight	=	Score
Martha	Motivation	8	×	.30	=	2.40
	Interpersonal	6	×	.25	=	1.50
	Sales knowledge	7	×	.25	=	1.75
	Product knowledge	6	×	.20	=	1.20
					Total Score =	6.85

Candidate	Criteria	Rating	×	Weight	=	Score
Jane	Motivation	9	×	.30	=	2.70
	Interpersonal	8	×	.25	=	2.00
	Sales knowledge	6	×	.25	=	1.50
	Product knowledge	5	×	.20	=	1.00
					Total Score =	7.20

*1=Low; 10=high

our hiring example, Jane would seem to be the candidate who will produce the greater sales because she received the higher total score on the criteria believed to lead to sales success. The SEU model suggests that before you select Jane, you should assess the probability that if you offer Jane the job, she will come work for you. If Jane is the better candidate but won't work for you, then she really isn't the better candidate; Martha is.

Step 6   **Implementing the Decision**   In the classical model of decision making, effective decision implementation has four components. First, you assess sources and reasons for potential resistance to the decision. For example, Joe, a district sales manager in your company, might resist the decision to hire Jane because Martha is his personal friend, and Joe told Martha he could help get her the sales job. Second, you determine the chronology and sequence of actions designed to overcome resistance to the decision and ensure the effective implementation of the decision. For example, you know that Joe believes that sales process and product knowledge are the most important things in hiring a new salesperson. You also know that Martha was rated higher on these criteria than Jane. Consequently, you might decide to first explain to Joe that in making your decision, you weighted motivation and interpersonal skills much higher than sales process or product knowledge and explain that company and independent studies support this weighting. Furthermore, you might assign Jane to a district sales manager other than Joe to ensure that she gets a good start with the company. You might also decide to place her in a month-long training program to better familiarize her with your products and send her to a one-week course on "The Selling Process" when it is next offered. Setting the chronology and sequence of actions leads naturally to the third step: an assessment of the resources required to implement the decision effectively. For example, you know it will cost you $5,500 for the sales training course for Jane. Moreover, you need to determine whether you could delegate implementation steps (such as scheduling Jane for "The Selling Process" course) to others and ensure these people understand and are held accountable for those steps and outcomes.

Step 7   **Monitoring and Evaluating Results**   The final step in the classical model involves monitoring and evaluating the results of your decision. To do this, you must gather information and compare it to the objectives and standards you established. This is trickier than it seems. First, you must gather the *right* information, or you will distort the evaluation, or worse, make it meaningless. For example, in the case of hiring Jane, gathering information only on the number of sick days she has taken is unlikely to help you evaluate her early job performance. You might think it is silly that anyone would gather information on sick days taken when sales are what is important, but it is not uncommon for information that is easy to collect to obscure what is important. And often, the most important information is the hardest to gather. For example, gathering information on the number of sales calls Jane makes is much easier than gathering information on the attitude she presented to customers during those sales calls. Yet the latter may be more important than the former in terms of closing the sale. If you do not gather the appropriate information, you defeat the purpose of this last step. The key point here is that it is important to monitor and evaluate results in order to detect problems with the original decision and its implementation. This will allow you to take corrective actions promptly, if need be, before it's too late.

To many, the classical model makes considerable sense. However, it is important to understand the assumptions upon which it is built:

- The problem or opportunity is clear.
- The firm's objectives are clear.
- People agree on the criteria and weights used to make the decision.
- All alternatives are known.
- All consequences can be anticipated.
- Decision makers are rational:
  - They are not biased.
  - They process all relevant information.
  - They examine the immediate and future consequences of the decision.
  - They search for the alternatives that maximize the results they desire.

The potential weaknesses of the classical model are easily exposed if you just recall your own decision about what university to attend. How clear were the problem/opportunity and your objectives? Did everyone (you, your parents, and your friends) agree on the criteria and weights

EXHIBIT 12.3 **Factors That Hamper Accurate Problem Identification and Analysis**

Factor	Description	Illustration
Information Bias	A reluctance to give or receive negative information	You are favoring Jane as the candidate and dismiss information about a performance problem she had at her last job.
Uncertainty Absorption	A tendency for information to lose its certainty as it is passed along	It is not clear how well Martha did in her previous job, but by the time the feedback gets to you, she is described as a poor performer.
Selective Perception	A tendency to ignore or avoid certain information, especially ambiguous information	Jane may have several employment alternatives and even be considering going back to school, but you ignore this and make her the offer.
Stereotyping	Deciding about an alternative on the basis of characteristics ascribed by others	Jane graduated from a private high school and went to a highly rated college on a partial scholarship so you figure she must be a great hire.
Cognitive Complexity	Limits on the amount of information people can process at one time	You initially have 200 applicants for the position but decide to eliminate anyone with less than three years' of sales experience.
Stress	Reduction of people's ability to cope with informational demands	Your company's market share is slipping because you don't have enough salespeople in the field, so you feel you just can't look at every bit of information on every candidate.

for evaluating different schools? Did you know about and consider all universities you could possibly attend? Was your evaluation of the problems and opportunities related to attending each school completely unbiased, and did you review all relevant information? Did you look at the short-term and long-term consequences of your decision? Could you fully anticipate both the short-term and long-term consequences associated with attending each school? If you answered no to some of these questions, you're not alone. Research has shown that people are not as rational as the classical model assumes.[6] We can identify a series of factors that inhibit people's ability to accurately identify and analyze problems, as shown in Exhibit 12.3.

Thus, while the rational, or classical, model shows how decisions *should* be made, it falls somewhat short of describing how decisions are *actually* made.[7]

The Bounded Rationality Model

Nobel Prize winner Herbert Simon developed an alternative decision-making model called the **bounded rationality model.**[8] It does not assume people are completely rational when they make decisions. Instead, it assumes that although people seek the best solutions, they usually settle for much less. Why? Because the decisions they face typically demand greater information and time to process than they possess. As a result, people seek a kind of "bounded" or "limited" rationality.

The concept of bounded rationality attempts to describe decision making in terms of three mechanisms. First, in the rational model, it is argued that people identify all possible solutions and then select the best alternative. Simon and other scholars have argued that this is not what people actually do. Instead, people examine possible solutions to a problem one at a time. If the first solution fails to work or they believe it is unworkable, they discard it and consider another solution. When they find an acceptable (though not necessarily the best) solution, people stop searching for new alternatives. Thus, if the first alternative is workable, the search-and-analysis effort is likely to stop.

Second, rather than using explicit criteria and weights to evaluate alternatives, the bounded rationality model argues that people use heuristics. A **heuristic** is a rule that limits the search to areas that have a high probability for yielding success. Thus, instead of looking everywhere for possible candidates for the new sales position, you might use a heuristic that says the best people for the job you have open are those already doing the job. Consequently, you might just try to hire someone away from your competitor. This could also help you make the decision more rapidly.

bounded rationality model (administrative model)
a model that assumes that people usually settle for acceptable rather than maximum options because the decisions they confront typically demand greater information-processing capabilities than they possess

heuristic
a rule that guides the search for alternatives into areas that have a high probability for yielding success

This is why we often see companies recruiting yearly from the same universities—because in the past, graduates from those schools have performed well for the companies.

The third mechanism is the concept of satisficing (not to be confused with *satisfying*). **Satisficing** involves choosing a minimally acceptable solution rather than searching exhaustively for the alternative that produces the best results. Whereas the rational model focuses on the decision maker as an optimizer, this model sees him or her as a satisficer. March and Simon explain that an alternative needs to meet two criterion to be optimal: 1) there must be a set of criteria that allow you to compare all alternatives and 2) it must be better than all the other alternatives on these common criteria. They further explain that a satisfactory alternative is one in which 1) there is a set of criteria that applies to all the acceptable alternatives and 2) the preferred alternative meets or exceeds all the criteria in this set. They stress that finding an optimal solutions is several times harder than finding a satisfactory one.

According to the bounded rationality model, the decision-making process is as follows:

1. Set the goal you want to pursue, or define the problem you want to solve.
2. Establish a minimum performance or criterion level. (When is a solution acceptable even if it is not perfect?)
3. Employ heuristics to narrow the solution to a *single* promising alternative.
4. If you cannot identify a feasible alternative, lower your aspiration level and search for a different solution (repeat steps 2 and 3).
5. After identifying a feasible alternative, evaluate it to determine its acceptability.
6. If the individual alternative is unacceptable, initiate a search for a different solution (repeat steps 3 to 5).
7. If the identified alternative is acceptable, implement the solution.
8. Following implementation, evaluate the ease with which the goal was (or was not) attained, and raise or lower the level of performance accordingly on future decisions.

This decision-making process is quite different from the rational model. We do not seek the best solution but instead look for a solution that is *acceptable*. Our search behavior is sequential—in other words, we evaluate one solution at a time. Finally, in contrast to the rational model, which prescribes how people *should* behave, the bounded rationality model is descriptive; that is, it describes how decision makers actually identify solutions to organizational problems.

The Retrospective Decision Model

A third model focuses on how decision makers attempt to rationalize their choices after they are made. It has been variously referred to as the **retrospective decision model**,[9] or *implicit favorite model.*[10]

One of the most noted contributors to this perspective was MIT professor Peer Soelberg. Soelberg observed the jobs graduating business students chose and noticed that, in many cases, that students identified "implicit favorites" (the alternative they wanted) very early on. Nonetheless, the graduates continued to explore other alternatives and also selected a second-best alternative Soelberg labeled as the "confirmation candidate." For example, a student might identify a manufacturer in Arizona as her implicit favorite and select a high-tech firm in California as her confirmation candidate. Next, the student would attempt to demonstrate after the fact that her implicit favorite was superior.

Soelberg theorized that students were engaging in **perceptual distortion**—that is, they highlighted the positive features of their implicit favorites more so than they did the positive features of their confirmation candidates. For example, a student might heavily weight the fact that housing costs are cheaper in the locale of her implicit favorite—even though the overall cost of living is no different there than in the locale of her confirmation candidate. Ironically, Soelberg noted, the implicit favorite was typically superior to the confirmation candidate only in terms of one or two dimensions. Even so, the decision makers believed they were considering all factors and, therefore, making a rational decision.

Consider how many times you've made decisions this way while shopping for clothes, cars, stereo systems, and the like. You start with an item that catches your eye and then spend a considerable amount of time convincing yourself and the people around that it's the "best" choice. If your

---

satisficing
the tendency for decision makers to accept the first alternative that meets their minimally acceptable requirements rather than push further for an alternative that produces the best results

retrospective decision model (implicit favorite model)
a decision-making model that focuses on how decision makers attempt to rationalize their choices after they are made

perceptual distortion
highlighting the positive features of the implicit favorite over the alternative

implicit favorite is the cheapest among the competition, you emphasize its price; if it is not, you emphasize its quality or styling. Ultimately, you end up buying the item you intuitively favored, feeling comfortable that you made the right choice. This type of **intuitive decision making** isn't necessarily wrong.[11] Some research shows that not only are intuitive decisions often made more quickly, their outcomes are as good or better.[12]

intuitive decision making
the primarily subconscious process of identifying a decision and selecting a preferred alternative

Types of Decisions

So which decision-making process do you think best describes your style? Are you a rational decision maker, a bounded rational decision maker, or a retrospective decision maker? Perhaps you are all three at different times depending on the type of decision.[13]

Most decisions can be divided into two basic types: programmed or nonprogrammed. A **programmed decision** is a standard response to a simple or routine problem. The nature of the problem is well defined and clearly understood by the decision maker, as are the possible solutions. For example, administrators making admission decisions often make programmed decisions. Also, at many universities admission criteria, such as grade point average and test scores, are well defined and a minimum threshold is set above which students are automatically admitted. Unions often make programmed decisions in terms of how companies treat their members—for example, using seniority to determine how the companies pay and promote union members. In all these decisions, specific criteria can be identified (grade-point averages and test scores for college admissions, and seniority levels for union promotions). High levels of certainty for both the problem formulation and the problem solution phases characterize the programmed decision-making process, and rules and procedures typically spell out exactly how people should respond.

programmed decision
a standard response to a simple or routine problem

By contrast, **nonprogrammed decisions** are made in response to problems that are either complex or novel. For example, should a university president with limited funds expand the size of the business school to meet growing student demand, or should she expand the university's science facilities to bring in more federal research contracts? No alternative is clearly correct, and past decisions are of little help; instead, you must weigh the alternatives and their consequences carefully. In most organizations, the firm's hierarchy determines who makes programmed and nonprogrammed decisions. As Exhibit 12.4 shows, top managers usually face nonprogrammed decisions, and lower level managers typically encounter mostly programmed, or routine, decisions. Middle managers fall somewhere in between.

nonprogrammed decision
a decision about a problem that is either poorly defined or novel

We need to make one final point about programmed versus nonprogrammed decisions. Programmed decisions are usually made through structured, bureaucratic techniques. For example, **standard operating procedures (SOP)** are often used for programmed decisions. SOPs specify exactly what should be done—the sequence of steps and exactly how each step should be performed. Companies have these in many cases to avoid accidents that can happen when behavior deviates from what has been established as safe and effective steps and action. For example in March 2010, Judge Gregory Ross convicted rafting company River Valley and fined the company $30,000. He also ordered the company to pay $60,000 in reparation for the death of Tor Prestmo, a trainee guide for the company. Prestmo became entrapped and died when the raft he was guiding flipped over after colliding with another River Valley raft in the grade 5 (very difficult) Fulcrum rapid. Maritime New Zealand Manager of Maritime Investigations Steve van der Splinter said, "Despite having an SOP in place to identify and mitigate known hazards on the river—such as the normal use of a safety kayak during higher water flows to help safely direct rafts through rapids—these steps were not followed on the day of the fatal accident."[14]

standard operating procedure (SOP)
established procedure for action used for programmed decisions that specifies exactly what should be done

EXHIBIT 12.4

Decision-Maker Level and Type of Decision

In part because the outcomes of nonprogrammed decisions are more uncertain, managers appear to have a tendency to let their programmed activities overshadow their nonprogrammed activities. Thus, if a manager has a series of decisions to make, he or she will tend to make those that are routine and repetitive before focusing on those that are unique and require considerable thought and have more ambiguity and uncertainty associated with their outcomes. This tendency is called **Gresham's law of planning**.[15] As a result, managers sometimes don't get to the more difficult and perhaps important decisions they must make. They either just run out of time or continue to occupy their time with programmed decisions.

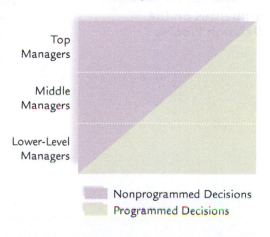

Top Managers

Middle Managers

Lower-Level Managers

Nonprogrammed Decisions
Programmed Decisions

EXHIBIT 12.5

Gresham's Law of Planning

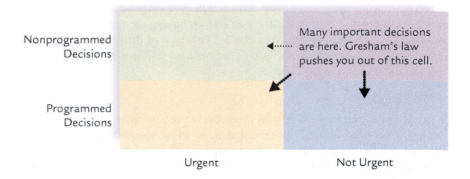

EXHIBIT 12.5

Gresham's Law of Planning

Gresham's law of planning
the tendency for managers to let programmed activities overshadow nonprogrammed activities

The implications of Gresham's law are clear. As a manager, you must make decisions in a timely fashion. Check periodically to see whether you are spending your decision-making time wisely or if you are falling prey to Gresham's law. The matrix in Exhibit 12.5 can help you with this assessment.

What Influences Effective Decision Making?

From a practical perspective, perhaps the most important question for managers is the following: "What influences *effective* decision making?" Exhibit 12.6 shows the general factors that influence a decision's quality.[16]

First are the characteristics of the decision maker. Earlier in the chapter, we discussed that we may not be as rational as we would like to believe. For example, we all have preferences and biases that we try to rationalize.[17] Moreover, we might lack familiarity with the problem or be too familiar with it and make a snap decision. There is also a limit to the amount of information we can process, which often leads us to satisfice.

Second is the nature of the problem or opportunity itself. The more ambiguous it is, the harder it is to be certain about the "right" decision.[18] Also, as we already discussed, people tend to put off making ambiguous decisions or make decisions without fully examining relevant information. The complexity of the problem can also affect the outcome. The more complex the problem is, the more challenging both the decision and its effective implementation are likely to be. The extent to which the problem is stable or volatile can also influence decision effectiveness. Clearly the more volatile the problem is, the greater the chance will be that the problem will change and the solution selected won't match the problem when it is implemented.

Third, the environment in which you make the decision will influence the decision. For example, time and resource constraints (people, money, equipment, and so forth) can influence a decision's effectiveness.[19] The more pressure you are under and the more constraints you have, the more likely it is that you will "miss" an important aspect of the decision. Finally, the importance of the decision can create its own pressures, which, in turn, can influence the effectiveness of the decision.

EXHIBIT 12.6

Influences on the Decision Process

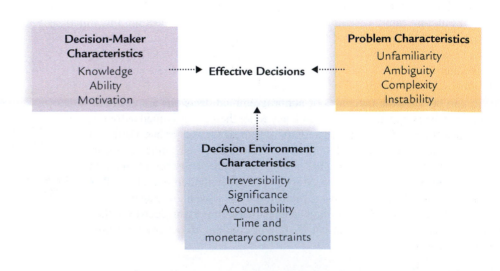

Group Decision Making

The three models described at the beginning of the chapter attempt to explain certain aspects of individual decision making. However, those models can also illuminate aspects of group decision making. Many of the basic processes remain the same. As with the classical (rational) model, both individuals and groups identify objectives. Both individuals and groups attempt to identify all possible outcomes before selecting one. Both individuals and groups satisfice and use heuristics when making decisions. Finally, both individuals and groups have implicit favorites and attempt to rationalize them.

What's different about group decision making is the social interaction, which complicates the dynamics. As shown in Exhibit 12.7, in some situations, group decision making can be an asset, but at other times it can be a liability. For example, groups are typically superior to individuals in that they bring greater cumulative knowledge to problems. But groups often arrive at decisions more slowly than individuals do.

- In *identifying alternatives,* individual efforts ensure that different and perhaps unique solutions are identified from various functional areas that the group can later consider.
- In *evaluating alternatives,* group judgment is often superior to individual judgment because it involves a wider range of viewpoints.
- In *choosing alternatives,* involving group members often leads to greater acceptance of the final outcome.
- In *implementing the choice,* individual responsibility is generally superior to group responsibility. Whether decisions are made individually or collectively, individuals perform better in carrying out the decision than groups do.

From the list in Exhibit 12.7, we cannot conclude that either individual or group decision making is superior in absolute. As a manager, you have to determine when it is best to make individual or group decisions. The discussion on the contingency model of participation, which appears later in this chapter, will help you with this. First, though, let's look at a couple of common problems related to making group decisions.

Group Decision-Making Problems: Groupthink and the Escalation of Commitment

A phenomenon called groupthink can negatively affect a group's decision making. According to research done by psychologist Irving Janis, **groupthink** occurs when agreement among members becomes so dominant that it overrides a realistic appraisal of alternative courses of action.[20] The concept emerged from Janis's studies of high-level policy decisions by government leaders. These included decisions by the U.S. government about Vietnam, the Bay of Pigs, and the Korean War. In analyzing the decision process leading up

groupthink
a mode of thinking in which pursuit of agreement among members becomes so dominant that it overrides a realistic appraisal of alternative courses of action

EXHIBIT 12.7

Assets and Liabilities of Group Decision Making

Assets +
- Groups can accumulate more knowledge and facts.
- Groups have a broader perspective and consider more alternatives.
- Individuals who participate in group decisions are more satisfied with the decision and more likely to support it.
- Group decision processes serve an important communication function, as well as a useful political function.

Liabilities –
- Groups often work more slowly than individuals.
- Group decisions involve considerable compromise that may lead to less than optimal decisions.
- Groups are often dominated by one individual or a small clique, thereby negating many of the virtues of group processes.
- Overreliance on group decision making can inhibit management's ability to act quickly and decisively when necessary.

EXHIBIT 12.8

The Groupthink Process

Source: Based on Gregory Moorhead, "Groupthink: Hypothesis in Need of Testing," *Group and Organization Studies* 7, no. 4, December 1982, pp. 429–44.

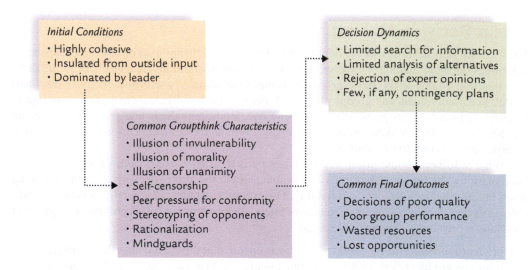

Initial Conditions
• Highly cohesive
• Insulated from outside input
• Dominated by leader

Decision Dynamics
• Limited search for information
• Limited analysis of alternatives
• Rejection of expert opinions
• Few, if any, contingency plans

Common Groupthink Characteristics
• Illusion of invulnerability
• Illusion of morality
• Illusion of unanimity
• Self-censorship
• Peer pressure for conformity
• Stereotyping of opponents
• Rationalization
• Mindguards

Common Final Outcomes
• Decisions of poor quality
• Poor group performance
• Wasted resources
• Lost opportunities

to each action, Janis found indications pointing to the development of group norms that improved morale at the expense of critical thinking. Exhibit 12.8 shows a model of how groupthink develops among groups.

SYMPTOMS OF GROUPTHINK By studying both government and business leaders, Janis identified eight primary symptoms of groupthink. The first is the *illusion of invulnerability*. Group members often reassure themselves about obvious dangers, become overly optimistic, and are willing to take extraordinary risks. For instance, in the disastrous Bay of Pigs invasion in the 1960s, the United States operated on the false assumption that it could keep its invasion of Cuba a secret. Even after news of the plan had leaked out, government leaders remained convinced of their ability to keep it a secret.

Second, victims of groupthink tend to collectively *rationalize* and discount warning signs that should lead them to reconsider earlier decisions. Motorola fell prey to groupthink when it discounted Nokia's entry into the cell phone industry in the early 1990s. Collectively, Motorola executives convinced themselves that Nokia, a Finnish company that had traditionally made rubber boots and forest-industry products, didn't stand a chance. They also doubted that Europe would adopt a unified digital standard, which would allow Nokia to sell a large number of phones. And even if Europe did adopt the new standards, the size of the market there paled in comparison to the size of the U.S. mobile phone market. Over a ten-year period, Nokia captured market share, becoming the number-one mobile phone company and the sixth most recognized brand in the world. Meanwhile, Motorola fell from its number-one global market position with a 35 percent share to the number-seven position, with only a 2.8 percent market share by early 2010.[21]

You could argue that Nokia was subject to the same dynamics of rationalizing and discounting the warning signs relative to a new competitor that had affected Motorola. While Nokia was enjoying its overtaking of Motorola as the world's number-one mobile phone company, it discounted the emergence of Samsung as a formidable competitor in part because it was not really in the mobile phone industry outside of Korea in any meaningful way until about 1999. However, from 1999 through 2009, Samsung went from being outside the top ten manufacturers of mobile phones to number two in the world with over 20 percent market share. Some of Samsung's increase in global market share came from Nokia as its global share dropped from a peak of 40 percent to about 34 percent.

Third, groups that fall prey to groupthink often have an *illusion of morality*. That is, they ignore the obvious ethical or moral consequences of their decisions. For example, tobacco companies continue to run advertisements (especially in countries in which they are not legally restricted) about free choice about smoking, completely ignoring the medical evidence on the hazards involved.

Stereotyping the enemy is another symptom of groupthink. Members often stereotype leaders of opposition groups in harsh terms and refuse to listen to their opinions or negotiate with them. Groups suffering from groupthink also tend to engage in *self-censorship*: They often minimize the seriousness of the doubts members raise and put tremendous pressure on them to agree to the group's consensus. Partly because of self-censorship, the *illusion of unanimity* forms. Members assume that individuals who remain silent agree with them. Finally, victims of groupthink often appoint themselves as *mindguards* to protect the leader and other members of the group from adverse information that could cause conflict over the correctness of a course of action. The mindguard may tell the dissident that he or she is being disruptive or nonsupportive or may simply isolate the dissident from other group members. For many years, FBI agents in Washington, D.C., who expressed views contrary to the party line found themselves transferred to less desirable locations.

CONSEQUENCES OF GROUPTHINK Groupthink can have several adverse consequences for the quality of decision making. First, groups plagued by groupthink often limit their search for possible solutions to one or two alternatives rather than all possible alternatives. Second, such groups frequently fail to reexamine their chosen action after new information or events suggest they need a change in course. Third, group members spend little time considering nonobvious advantages to alternative courses of action. Fourth, such groups often make little or no attempt to seek experts' advice either inside or outside their own organization. Fifth, members show interest in facts that support their preferred alternative and either ignore or disregard facts that fail to support it. Finally, groups often ignore possible roadblocks to their choice and, as a result, fail to develop contingency plans. This last consequence is similar to retrospective decision making—the decision is made and then data are selected that support the decision. Because peers reinforce the decision, unwillingness to reexamine and change directions is even more powerful than in individuals.

OVERCOMING GROUPTHINK Because a groupthink mentality poses such serious consequences for organizations, we must consider how to minimize its effects. Janis suggests several strategies. To begin, as a manager, you can reduce groupthink by encouraging each group member to evaluate proposals critically. Also, you can ensure that members consider a range of alternatives by not initially stating their own positions outright but instead promoting open discussion. Other strategies for preventing groupthink involve getting more suggestions for viable solutions. This can be done by assigning the same problem to two independent groups. Or before the group reaches a decision, members can seek advice from other groups in the organization. Another technique is to invite experts outside the group to challenge members' views at group meetings.

Helen Sessions/Alamy

Organizational dynamics such as groupthink can lead companies to discount competitive threats. When the Finnish company Nokia—which had traditionally manufactured forest industry products, including rubber boots—entered the U.S. mobile phone market in the 1990s, competitors like Motorola didn't take it seriously.

Groupthink can also be prevented with strategies directed at the group members themselves. For example, for each group meeting, a member can be appointed to serve as a **devil's advocate,** a person whose role is to challenge the majority position.[22] For example, after the chaos and a lethal insurgency in Iraq, blamed in no small part on poor decision making process, the U.S. Army has been quietly training its own cadre of devil's advocates. According to Greg Fontenote, the program's director, the training, "involves questioning prevailing assumptions to avoid getting sucked into that *groupthink*. This is having someone inside that says, 'Wait a minute, not so fast.'"[23] In addition to the technique of assigning a devil's advocate, after reaching preliminary consensus the group can schedule a second-chance meeting. This allows group members an opportunity to express doubts and rethink the issue.

Groups can use the steps summarized in Exhibit 12.9 to minimize the likelihood of falling into groupthink.

Escalating Commitment to a Decision

Escalating commitment occurs when decision makers adhere to a course of action after they know it's a mistake. Have you ever continued to date someone even after it was clear you

devil's advocate
a group member whose role is to challenge the majority position

escalating commitment
the tendency to exhibit greater levels of commitment to a decision as time passes and investments are made in the decision, even after significant evidence emerges indicating that the original decision was incorrect

EXHIBIT 12.9

Guidelines
for Overcoming
Groupthink

For the company
- Establish several independent groups to examine the same problem.
- Train managers in groupthink prevention techniques.

For the leader
- Assign everyone the role of critical evaluator.
- Use outside experts to challenge the group.
- Assign a devil's advocate role to one member of the group.
- Try to be impartial and refrain from stating your own views.

For group members
- Try to retain your objectivity and be a critical thinker.
- Discuss group deliberations with a trusted outsider and report back to the group.

For the deliberation process
- At times, break the group into subgroups to discuss the problem.
- Take time to study what other companies or groups have done in similar situations.
- Schedule second-chance meetings to provide an opportunity to rethink the issues before making a final decision.

were not a good match? If so, perhaps you suffered from escalation of commitment. This same phenomenon occurs when managers "throw good money after bad."[24] For example, in early 2010 several banks that had loaned billions of dollars to Greece realized that their loans were at risk because Greece had borrowed too much relative to its GDP. Even after it was clear that Greece would have great difficulty repaying their loans, the banks continued to loan the country *more* money, though they substantially raised the interest rate they charged. Or consider the case of an individual who purchased a stock at $50 a share, but the price dropped to $20. Rather than sell, the investor bought more shares at the lower price. Soon the price declined further, and the individual was again faced with the decision to buy more, hold what he already had, or sell out entirely. The investor could not bring himself to sell and go back on the original decision. No doubt you can think of other situations in which people have stuck with decisions in spite of evidence that clearly indicate the original decision was wrong. The question is, why?[25]

At least three explanations are possible. First, we can point to individual limitations in information processing. People may be limited in both their desire and ability to handle all the information for complex decisions. As a result, errors in judgment may occur. For example, the company in which our stock investor purchased shares may have significant operations in countries in which negative changes in exchange rates are occurring or in which government regulations have changed. Our investor simply may not completely comprehend these issues and how they are hurting the company's performance and subsequent stock price. A second approach is to explain decision errors as a breakdown in rationality because of group dynamics. For example, our stock investor may have received the tip from a trusted friend or he could be the friend of the company's CEO and, therefore, have a strong emotional commitment. Although both explanations may help us understand the error, the work of Professor Barry Staw suggests that these explanations do not go far enough. "A salient feature...is that a series of decisions is associated with a course of action rather than an isolated choice."[26]

Staw suggested a model of escalating commitment (Exhibit 12.10). This abbreviated model shows that four basic elements determine commitment to an action. First, people are likely to remain committed to a course of action (even when it is clearly incorrect) because of a need to justify previous decisions to others. The social psychological literature on forced compliance supports this notion. In studies of forced compliance, when individuals are made to perform an unpleasant or dissatisfying act (for example, eating grasshoppers) with no external rewards, after they comply, individuals generally bias their own attitudes to justify their previous behavior (for example, eating grasshoppers is not a bad thing because they are high in protein). This biasing of

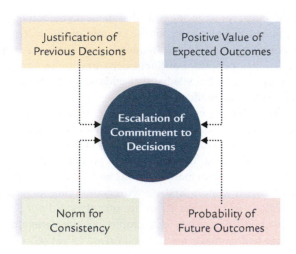

EXHIBIT 12.10

Contributing Factors to Escalation of Commitment to Decisions

attitudes is most likely to occur when individuals feel personally responsible for the negative consequences and when the consequences are difficult to undo.

In addition, a norm for consistency influences commitment to a previous decision. That is, managers who are consistent in their actions are often considered better leaders than those who "flip-flop" from one course of action to another.

Finally, two additional factors—the perceived probability and value of future outcomes—jointly influence what is called prospective rationality. **Prospective rationality** is simply a belief that future courses of action are rational and correct. When people think they can turn a situation around or that "prosperity is just around the corner," and when they highly prize the goal, they exhibit strong commitment to a continued course of action. They convince themselves that they can "pull victory out of the jaws of defeat."[27]

prospective rationality
a belief that future courses of action are rational and correct

OVERCOMING ESCALATION OF COMMITMENT Because escalation of commitment can lead to serious and negative consequences for organizations, we must consider how to minimize its effects.

1. First, as a manager, you should stress in your own mind and to others (superiors, peers, and subordinates) that investments made in the past are sunk costs—that is, you cannot recover them. All finance theory argues that managers should ignore sunk costs in making future decisions, and they should consider only future costs and future anticipated benefits.
2. Second, you must create an atmosphere in which consistency does not dominate. This requires stressing the changing aspects of the competitive, social, cultural, and commercial environment surrounding a business and focusing on the importance of matching current decisions to current and expected fixture environments rather than to past decisions.
3. Third, you can encourage each member to evaluate the prospects of future outcomes and their expected positive value critically. You can invite experts from outside the group to challenge members' future expectations.
4. As with groupthink, a member can be appointed to serve as a devil's advocate to challenge the majority position.

The Contingency Model of Participative Decision Making

Up to this point, we have noted that you cannot categorically state that individual decisions are better than group decisions or vice versa. However, most decisions aren't strictly made on an individual or group basis. The reality is that most managers face a continuum when it comes to involving others in decision making—from zero involvement (making an individual decision) to fully involving others (making a group decision). Research shows that the degree to which other people should be involved in a decision depends on the situation.[28] The key question, then, is how can you as a manager determine when to make a decision on your own and when to involve others?

Who Should Participate?

To determine some of the variables that make up good participative decisions, researchers have explored the question, "When participative decision making is effective, who should be

cross-functional team
a work group composed of employees from different departments, such as finance, marketing, operations, and human resources, to work together on problem solving

involved?" First and foremost, research suggests that those participating in the decision-making process must have sufficient knowledge about the content of the decision. Companies such as Ford, FedEx, Procter & Gamble, and Boeing frequently put together a **cross-functional team** (a work group consisting of members from different departments) to launch new products. Why? Because each member has unique knowledge that adds value to the decisions that need to be made to successfully launch these products.

However, in addition to having content knowledge, members also need to *want* to participate in group decision making. Not everyone does. However most people will want to participate if they believe (1) they have relevant content knowledge, (2) their participation will help bring about change, (3) the resulting change will produce outcomes they value or prefer, and (4) the organization values their participation, and it fits with the organization's goals and objectives. When General Motors first started encouraging more employee involvement in decision making, workers resisted the effort because they did not believe it was "for real." Historically, managers made decisions, and employees implemented them. As a consequence, GM's managers had to make a sustained effort to get workers to believe that they would take worker participation seriously.

Should the Involvement of Participants Be High or Low?

Like individual decision making, participative decision making involves related, yet separate, processes. Using the classical model of decision making, a participative group moves through the same seven steps, but the involvement of members can vary at each stage. Low involvement allows members to communicate their opinions about the problem and potential solutions but not make the final determination. High involvement allows members not only to communicate their opinions but to make final determinations. Thus, degree of involvement could range from high to low on each of the seven elements of the classical decision model. Exhibit 12.11 provides a sample in which a particular group has a high degree of involvement on the front end of classical decision making but low involvement on the back end.

So for which element of the decision-making process is high involvement more powerful? One study found that high involvement in three of the processes had strong impacts. Specifically, high involvement in generating alternatives, planning implementation, and evaluating results were significantly related to higher levels of satisfaction and work group performance.[29] The authors argued that involvement in generating alternatives was important because solutions almost always came from alternatives generated. They found that involvement in planning the implementation was important because the way a solution was implemented affected the outcome more than the solution itself. Finally, they noted that involvement in evaluating results was important because feedback is critical to beginning the decision cycle again.

One of the interesting findings from studies such as these is that members also need to understand group dynamics for participative decision making to be effective. For example, the ability of members to communicate and handle conflicts can be as important as their knowledge

EXHIBIT 12.11

Sample Configuration of Degree of Involvement and Decision Process

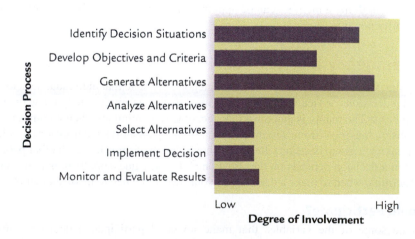

1. Do potential group members have sufficient content knowledge?
2. Do potential members have sufficient process knowledge?
3. Do members have a desire to participate?
4. Do members believe that their participation will result in changes?
5. Do members positively value the expected outcomes?
6. Do members see participation as legitimate and congruent with other aspects of the organization?
7. If the answer to any of the above questions is no, is it possible to change the conditions?

Source: Based on N. Margulies and J. Stewart Black, "Perspectives on the Implementation of Participative Approaches," *Human Resource Management* 26, no. 3 (1987), pp. 385–412.

and the desire to participate. Being able to scan one's environment to identify problems is critical. After all, it is hard to begin participative decision making without members in your group who can recognize problems and opportunities. For generating alternatives, a critical capability is creativity. It is unlikely that a group can agree on a preferred solution without some conflict. As a consequence, managing disagreement effectively is a critical process skill. In this sense, much of the information in Chapter 10 on groups and teams and their effectiveness applies to effective group decisions.

Exhibit 12.12 provides a summary of the questions managers should ask themselves to determine whether participative decision making is likely to be effective.

On the basis of a long-term research project, Victor Vroom and his colleagues Phillip Yetton and Arthur Jago also developed a theory of participation in decision making that has clear managerial implications.[30] It is possible to categorize this model as either a model of leadership or a model of decision making. The model considers how managers should behave in decision-making situations but also prescribes correct leader behavior regarding the degree of participation.

Although participative decision making is not always the best way to go, it does seem to work in many instances. Researchers have found a few key reasons for this.[31] First, participation better clarifies for employees what they can expect relative to the issue being decided. Second, participation increases the likelihood that employees will work for rewards and outcomes they value. Third, it heightens the effects of social influence on behavior. That is, peers will monitor and exert pressure on one another to conform to expected performance levels. Finally, it enlarges the amount of control employees have over their work activities. This can help not only the organization achieve its goals but its employees achieve their goals, too, which should increase their job satisfaction.[32] That said, A Manager's Challenge, "Moving from Partners to Professional Managers" might surprise you. It illustrates one instance in which the move from *more* involvement in group decision making to *less* seems to have been effective because the group just got too big and the challenges too specialized.

Decision Speed and Quality

Have you ever heard of Gavilan Computer? if you own a laptop computer, you should have, but odds are you haven't. In the early 1980s, Gavilan Computer had a virtual monopoly on the developing and soon-to-be-lucrative laptop market. But by 1984, the company had filed for bankruptcy. Despite a $31 million investment by venture capitalists, indecisiveness and long delays cost the company its early technological and market advantage.

In the early 1980s, Gavilan Computer was at the forefront of battery-operated laptop technology, having introduced the Gavilan SC laptop, shown in the photo. But by 1984, the company had filed for bankruptcy.

Photo Courtesy of The Computer History Museum

A MANAGER'S CHALLENGE

CHANGE

Moving from Partners to Professional Managers: Law Firms Change Their Decision-making Style

Traditionally in most law firms, the firm's partners have jointly participated in all decision making. But what happens when a law firm grows dramatically, both in numbers of lawyers and also in terms of its worldwide locations? In this situation, you will have dozens and dozens of partners, and as a consequence, participative decision making can lead to bottlenecks.

With 3,500 lawyers working in 67 offices across 29 countries billing over $2 billion a year, DLA Piper is such a firm. As DLA Piper grew, it realized it needed a more centralized method of decision making. Instead of bringing all the firm's partners together to vote on initiatives and then manage their implementation, the chairman of DLA Piper now relies on professional managers who specialize in particular areas of expertise, including marketing, information technology, human resources, and finance—areas the partners aren't overly familiar with. "We realized that because of our size, we had to adopt a corporate model," states joint CEO Lee I. Miller. "It streamlines our decision making. We are able to react quickly, decisively."

Sometimes, however, partners accustomed to participative decision making have a hard time delegating decisions to professional managers. "At times it's a bitter pill," says a partner at the law firm Stellato & Schwartz. "When you ascend to the position of partner, it's based upon your ability to show loyalty, longevity, and business acumen. Inherent in those qualities is a desire to lead. But sometimes that desire has to be set aside for the good of the team." For their part, the managers who make decisions on behalf of law firms must constantly and carefully evaluate how the outcome of each major decision is likely to affect the firm and its partners.

Consider the situation at Wildman, Harrold, Allen & Dixon, an Illinois law firm where John Holthaus is executive director. Holthaus has no law degree but rather is an accountant who holds an MBA degree. His experience and education provide the technical and managerial background to make the myriad day-to-day decisions that keep the law firm operating smoothly. "I view my job as that of a hospital administrator who takes care of all the details so the doctors can take care of their patients," he explains. "I'm trying to make it easier for the attorneys to focus on serving their clients." Knowing that Holthaus understands the law firm's objectives and takes care of the business details, the partners have come to rely on him rather than getting bogged down in endless group meetings to make decisions themselves.

Source: Organization Web site, http://www.dlapiper.com, accessed May 3, 2010; A. Palmer, "DLA Piper Makes Measured Progress Since Merger," *Legal Times*, June 2, 2006; J. T. Slania, "More Firms Mind Their Business: Corporate Model Helps Streamline Decision Making," *Crain's Chicago Business*, January 28, 2002, SR10.

Competitors entered the market and Gavilan failed to exploit its advantage. As one executive observed, "We missed the window."[33]

What happened to Gavilan happens frequently today—especially to companies in high-technology industries. In a series of studies of decision making in industries characterized by frequent change and turbulence—so called *high-velocity environments*—researchers Kathleen Eisenhardt and L. J. Bourgeois attempted to determine what separates successful decision makers and managers from unsuccessful ones.[34] In high-velocity industries (microelectronics, medical technology, genetic engineering, and others), high-quality, rapid decision making by executives and their companies is closely related to good corporate performance. In these industries, mistakes are costly; information is often ambiguous, obsolete, or simply incorrect; and recovering from missed opportunities is extremely difficult. What must decision makers in industries such as these do for their firms to prosper and survive?

Eisenhardt and Bourgeois found that five factors influence a manager's ability to make fast decisions in high-velocity environments (see Exhibit 12.13). Three "mediating processes" that determine the manager and group's ability to deal with the quantity and quality of information moderate the five characteristics:

1. *Accelerated cognitive processing.* The decision maker must be able to process and analyze great amounts of information quickly and efficiently. Some people and groups can

EXHIBIT 12.13 Factors of Fast Decision Making

1. *Real-time information*. Fast decision makers must have access to and be able to process real-time information—that is, information that describes what is happening right now, not yesterday.

2. *Multiple simultaneous alternatives*. Decision makers examine several possible alternative courses of action simultaneously, not sequentially (e.g., "Let's look at alternatives X, Y, and Z altogether and see how each looks."). This adds complexity and richness to the analysis and reduces the time involved in information processing.

3. *Two-tiered advice process*. Fast decision makers make use of a two-tiered advisory system, whereby all team members are allowed input but greater weight is given to the more experienced co-workers.

4. *Consensus with qualification*. Fast decision makers attempt to gain widespread consensus on the decision as it is being made, not after it is made.

5. *Decision integration*. Fast decision makers integrate tactical planning and issues of implementation within the decision process itself (e.g., "If we are going to do X, how might we do it?")

simply process information faster and better than others. The faster a manager can process information, the quicker the manager can make a decision.

2. **Smooth group processes.** To be effective, the manager must work with a group that has smooth, harmonious relations. This is not to say that everyone always agrees. Quite the contrary—members of effective groups often disagree. However, it is the way they disagree and resolve their disagreements that counts. Group members who share a common vision and who are mutually supportive and cohesive aid fast decisions.

3. **Confidence to act.** Finally, fast decision-making groups must not be afraid to act. As we noted, some people are reluctant to make decisions in the face of uncertainty and fall victim to "analysis paralysis." Unfortunately, in high-velocity environments, uncertainty is constant. Fast decision makers must be willing to make choices even in the face of uncertainty.

Remember that this research focuses on high-velocity environments, not all organizational environments. In businesses characterized by relative stability (the funeral home industry, for example), rapid decisions might prove disastrous. Because stability allows time for more complete data collection and processing, managers in stable environments have less of a need to act quickly. Thus, as a manager of a team, you need to assess the time factors that characterize your industry. This will allow you to make better decisions.

Strategies for Improving Decision Making

As a manager, how can you improve the decision-making process in your organization?[35] At the beginning of the chapter, we mentioned that decisions can be divided into two phases: problem formulation and problem solution. Strategies to improve decision making can also be divided into the same two categories.

Improving Problem Formulation

Framing a problem involves deliberately and carefully examining the problem's nature in order to better solve it. The trouble is that groups often fail to look beyond what's familiar to them and "misdefine" problems. The following steps can help groups and managers improve their problem formulation.

One of the first steps to better decision making is better decision situation assessment. Exhibit 12.14 provides a simple set of questions related to the three categories of factors

EXHIBIT 12.14 Questions Related to the Factors That Influence Decision Quality

---

Decision-Maker Characteristics

1. Do you have an implicit favorite solution?
2. Do you have a tendency to satisfice and go with the first workable solution?
3. Do you feel overwhelmed by the amount of information you have to process?
4. Do you feel a lack of knowledge about the problem?
5. Are you particularly unfamiliar or familiar with the problem?

Problem Characteristics

1. Does the problem seem quite ambiguous?
2. Is the problem substantially complex?
3. Does the problem seem stable or volatile?

Decision Environment Characteristics

1. Are you under significant time pressures to make the decision?
2. Do you face substantial resource limitations (people, money, equipment, etc.) relative to the problem and its solution?
3. Is the decision irreversible?
4. Are the problem and your decision of substantial importance?

---

structured debate

a process to improve problem formulation that includes the processes of devil's advocate, multiple advocacy, and dialectical inquiry

diagramed in Exhibit 12.6. You can ask yourself these questions in order to have a clearer picture of the situation and the potential pitfalls. In a **structured debate,** participants make use of techniques like a devil's advocate, multiple advocacy, and dialectical inquiry to better frame a problem. We discuss these techniques next.

DEVIL'S ADVOCATE As we explained earlier, a devil's advocate is a group member whose role is to disagree with the group. For example, if you asked a group of American automobile company executives why their sales are down, they might blame Japanese imports. In this case, a devil's advocate would question if the problem was not with the Japanese but with the American cars themselves and their poor product quality. This type of debate forces the group to justify its position and, as a consequence, develop a more precise and accurate picture of the problem and its underlying causes.

multiple advocacy

a process to improve decision making by assigning several group members to represent the opinions of various constituencies that might have an interest in the decision

MULTIPLE ADVOCACY **Multiple advocacy** is like the devil's advocate approach except that more than one opposing view is presented. Each group involved in making a decision is assigned the responsibility of representing the opinions of its constituents. Thus, if a university wants to enhance the campus's racial and cultural diversity, it might establish a commission including African Americans, Hispanics, Asians, women's groups, and so forth. The resulting dialogue should lead to the identification of a useful agenda for discussion.

dialectical inquiry

a process to improve decision making by assigning a group member (or members) the role of questioning the underlying assumptions associated with the formulation of the problem

DIALECTICAL INQUIRY **Dialectical inquiry** occurs when a group or individual is assigned the role of questioning the underlying assumptions of problem formulation. The group begins by identifying the prevailing view of the problem and its associated assumptions. Next, an individual is asked to develop an alternative problem that is credible but has different assumptions. By doing so, the accuracy of the original assumptions is reexamined. As a result, it forces group members to "think outside the box" and look at new ways to analyze the problem. Conducting a dialectical inquiry can be a particularly good way to overcome groupthink and escalation-of-commitment pitfalls.

Improving the Problem-Solution Process

To improve the problem-solution process, group members must be as thorough and creative as possible. Stimulating creativity expands the search for and analysis of possible alternatives. You can use the three techniques discussed next to do this.

BRAINSTORMING **Brainstorming** is a process of generating many creative solutions but not immediately evaluating their merit. It is a frequently used mechanism to provide a maximum number of ideas in a short period of time. During a brainstorming session, a group is given a problem and told to propose any ideas that come to mind to solve the problem. Once everyone's ideas are on the table, the group considers the positive and negative aspects of each proposal. Through a process of continual refinement, the best possible solution under the circumstances should emerge.

brainstorming
a process of generating many creative solutions without evaluating their merit

NOMINAL GROUP TECHNIQUE The **nominal group technique,** typically referred to as NGT, consists of four group decision-making phases.[36] First, individual members meet as a group, but they begin by silently and independently generating ideas to solve a problem. Then, a round-robin procedure follows, in which each group member presents his or her idea to the group. Initially, no discussion is allowed. The ideas are summarized and recorded (perhaps on a blackboard). After everyone has presented their ideas, the group discusses each idea. Finally, members conclude the meeting by silently and independently ranking the various ideas or solutions to the problem. The pooled outcome of the members' votes on the issue determines the final decision.

nominal group technique
a process of having group members record their proposed solutions, summarize all proposed solutions, and independently rank solutions until a clearly favored solution emerges

The NGT allows the group to meet formally, but it does not allow members as much free discussion; hence, the term *nominal* group technique. A chief advantage of the NGT is that everyone independently considers the problem without other members of the group influencing them. This technique, too, can be a particularly good way to overcome groupthink.

DELPHI TECHNIQUE The **Delphi technique** never allows decision-making participants to meet face-to-face. Instead, a problem is identified, and members are asked through a series of carefully designed questionnaires to provide potential solutions. These questionnaires are completed independently. The results of the first questionnaire are then circulated to all the group's members (who are still physically separated). After reviewing the feedback, members are again asked their opinions. This process may continue through several iterations until group members' opinions begin to show consensus.

Delphi technique
a decision-making technique that never allows decision participants to meet face-to-face but identifies a problem and offers solutions using a questionnaire

A MANAGER'S CHALLENGE

TECHNOLOGY

Streamlining Decision Making at JetBlue

JetBlue founder and CEO David Neeleman believes the airline industry underutilizes technology that could lower its costs. This is critical if you consider the fact that between 2000 and 2009, airline companies cumulatively lost $60 billion or more. During that time period, most commercial airlines cut or at least froze their IT budgets. By contrast, JetBlue nearly doubled its IT budget.

The company uses technology to make many of its daily managerial decisions. It is, in part, why JetBlue has succeeded whereas others have failed. For example, JetBlue uses workforce optimization technology called "Blue Pumpkin." Blue Pumpkin helps managers ensure the company has enough reservation agents on staff at peak call times. The first year the technology was used, the company achieved a 38 percent

Jack Hohhouse\Alamy Images

JetBlue uses technology to make many of its daily managerial decisions, which has helped JetBlue succeed whereas other airlines have failed.

(continued)

increase in service levels, a 30 percent improvement in agent productivity, and a 50 percent boost in management workload per agent.[37] The turnover among reservation agents in the airline industry overall that year was 30 percent, but JetBlue's was half that. Today, the company has about 6 percent turnover among its reservation agents, which both increases the company's effectiveness and lowers its recruiting and training costs.

JetBlue also created the first "paperless cockpit." JetBlue equips all pilots with laptops so that they, instead of a separate set of employees at the company's operations center, can access flight manuals and make pre-flight load and balance calculations. This saves JetBlue an estimated 4,800 man-hours a year.[38] It also allows the pilots to make their own decisions about load and balance adjustments when temperatures, wind strengths, and departure directions change. Each plane saves about 15 minutes prior to takeoff, translating into approximately 1,500 additional flights annually for JetBlue.

In addition, JetBlue equips both pilots and crewmembers with wireless devices that allow them to report and respond to problems such as weather delays and safety-related injuries, including those that involve passengers. The devices immediately convey the problems to JetBlue managers via BlackBerry, and employees can easily access the information via the company's intranet, JetBlue Event Management System (JEMS). In 2009, JetBlue signed a contract with Verizon to have them take over JetBlue's data center and manage its network infrastructure, including its WiFi services at JFK Airport in order to ensure that these capabilities stayed at the cutting edge of technology.

Sources: David Deans, "Managed IT Enhanced JetBlue Business Model," *Business Technology Roundtable*, October 6, 2009, http://business-technology-roundtable.blogspot.com/2009/10/managed-it-enhances-jetblue-business.html; J. Wynbrandt, *Flying High* (John Wiley & Sons, 2004); B. Peterson, *Blue Streak* (New York: Penguin Group, 2004).

The Role of Technology

Much has been made in recent years about how technology affects individual and group decision making.[39] For routine but complex decisions, such as scheduling the flow of materials and products through a factory, technology can be a godsend. Computers and software can rapidly process amounts of information that would overwhelm a human being. For example, JetBlue became a successful and profitable start-up while other airlines lost billions of dollars. Part of JetBlue's success was due to its use of new technology.[40] By putting laptops and software in the hands of its pilots, the company didn't need scores of employees to make decisions about flight paths, schedules, fuel intake, and so on.[41] A Manager's Challenge, "Streamlining Decision Making at JetBlue" looks at how JetBlue accomplished this.

A wide variety of technologies allow group members to communicate with one another and make decisions without having to meet face to face. For example, via technology, members can simultaneously review a document and make real-time changes to it. Design teams like those in the automotive industry increasingly use this type of technology, and it can significantly reduce a company's travel costs. The practice isn't without its drawbacks though. A recent study found that computer-mediated communication decreases the effectiveness of groups: Compared to face-to-face groups, these groups take longer to complete their tasks and members experience less satisfaction.[42] To be sure, organizations need to consider the pitfalls as well as the benefits associated with computer-mediated communication as a medium for group decision making.

Managerial Challenges from the Front Line

The Rest of the Story

In consultation with her husband, Lurue Lord determined that she did need to delegate some decisions as well as stop doing the lower-level tasks she had handled for many years at Lord Eye Center. Today, the company has more policies and preset procedures that help employees make routine decisions. Lord has also hired a new area manager to help her implement and manage some of the more difficult decisions and track employee and store sales. Nonetheless, Lord continues to visit the company's various offices to gather first-hand information about the competitive and operational situation each faces, and she remains involved in key decisions such as those involving pricing, technology, and new store locations.

So far, Lord Eye Center, its employees, and a more relaxed owner are adjusting well to the change. In addition to finally taking some personal time to fish, play tennis, and golf, Lord says she has more time to explore innovative ways to expand the business.

Summary

- The classical model of decision making describes how people should rationally make decisions but does not describe how people actually make decisions.
- In real life, people do not have an unlimited amount of time to gather and evaluate alternatives. Instead, they evaluate their options sequentially and stop once they find one that satisfies their minimum objectives. This is called satisficing. Satisficing is an aspect of the bounded rationality model of decision making.
- The retrospective decision model, or the implicit favorite model, of decision making explains how decision makers intuitively make choices and then rationalize their decisions after the fact. Some research shows that decisions made this way can be quite effective.
- Managers tend to let their programmed activities overshadow their nonprogrammed activities. Thus, they tend to make routine and repetitive decisions before focusing on those that are unique and require considerable thought. This tendency is called Gresham's law of planning.[43]
- Although we cannot *per se* conclude that individuals make better decisions than groups or vice versa, there are conditions under which each can lead to better decision making. It's up to managers to figure out to what extent they should involve their employees in decision making based on the situation.
- Most people will want to participate in group decision making if they believe (1) they have relevant content knowledge, (2) their participation will help bring about change, (3) the resulting change will produce outcomes they value or prefer, and (4) the organization values their participation, and it fits with the company's goals and objectives.
- Techniques such as brainstorming, NGT, and Delphi help ensure groups consider a broad range of options as well as their implications and outcomes. These techniques can help minimize group decision-making pitfalls such as groupthink and the escalation of commitment.

Key Terms

bounded rationality (administrative) model 337
brainstorming 351
cross-functional team 346
decision making 332
Delphi technique 351
devil's advocate 343
dialectical inquiry 350
escalating commitment 343
formulation 333
Gresham's law of planning 340

groupthink 341
heuristic 337
intuitive decision making 339
multiple advocacy 350
nominal group technique 351
nonprogrammed decision 339
opportunity 335
perception 335
perceptual distortion 338
problem 335
programmed decision 339

prospective rationality 345
rational (classical) model 335
retrospective decision (implicit favorite) model 338
satisficing 338
solution 335
standard operating procedure (SOP) 339
structured debate 350
subjectively expected utility (SEU) model 335

Review Questions

1. What is the basic premise of the rational (classical) model of decision making and how does it differ from the bounded rationality model?
2. How can selective perception influence decision formulation?
3. What is satisficing? How does it differ from satisfying?
4. How does the retrospective decision-making model work?
5. When are SOPs (standard operating procedures) most often used?
6. Describe Gresham's law of planning.

7. Why is analyzing the decision situation a key step in making better decisions?
8. What are the advantages and disadvantages of group decision making?
9. Describe what groupthink and the escalation of commitment are.
10. When should a manager engage in participatory decision making?
11. What techniques can managers use to improve group decision making and avoid pitfalls like groupthink and the escalation commitment?

Assessing Your Capabilities

What's Your Decision-Making Style?

Read each of the following statements. Indicate the extent to which you disagree or agree that this statement is descriptive of you. Be as candid as you can.

	Strongly Disagree	Disagree	Somewhat Disagree	Somewhat Agree	Agree	Strongly Agree
1. I double-check my information sources to be sure I have the right facts before making a decision.	1	2	3	4	5	6
2. I generally make snap decisions.	1	2	3	4	5	6
3. When making decisions, I do what seems natural at the moment.	1	2	3	4	5	6
4. I tend to put off making many decisions because thinking about them makes me uneasy.	1	2	3	4	5	6
5. I use the advice of other people in making my important decisions.	1	2	3	4	5	6
6. When making decisions, I rely on my instincts.	1	2	3	4	5	6
7. I often need the assistance of other people when making important decisions.	1	2	3	4	5	6
8. I avoid making important decisions until the pressure is on.	1	2	3	4	5	6
9. I generally make decisions that feel right to me.	1	2	3	4	5	6
10. I make quick decisions.	1	2	3	4	5	6
11. I rarely make important decisions without consulting other people.	1	2	3	4	5	6
12. I make decisions in a logical and systematic way.	1	2	3	4	5	6
13. I postpone decision making whenever possible.	1	2	3	4	5	6
14. When I make a decision, I trust my inner feelings and reactions.	1	2	3	4	5	6
15. My decision making requires careful thought.	1	2	3	4	5	6
16. I like to have someone to steer me in the right direction when I am faced with important decisions.	1	2	3	4	5	6
17. When making a decision, I consider various options in terms of specific goals.	1	2	3	4	5	6
18. I often make impulsive decisions.	1	2	3	4	5	6
19. I generally make important decisions at the last minute.	1	2	3	4	5	6
20. When I make a decision, it is more important for me to feel the decision is right than to have a rationale for it.	1	2	3	4	5	6

In scoring your responses, simply write in the number you circled beside each item. Then, add up the total numbers you wrote in within each column. What emerges is a general profile of the decision-making styles that you tend to exhibit.

Most people use more than one style but at the same time often have one or two styles they use more often, just as most people can use both hands but tend to favor using one over the other.

1. _____	6. _____	4. _____	5. _____	2. _____
12. _____	9. _____	8. _____	7. _____	3. _____
15. _____	14. _____	13. _____	11. _____	10. _____
17. _____	20. _____	19. _____	16. _____	18. _____
A Total	B Total	C Total	D Total	E Total

Column A: Logical Style

If your highest score is in Column A, this suggests that you make decisions in a logical fashion and rely on facts and information as they relate to your objectives or goals in guiding your final decision.

Column B: Intuitive Style

If your highest score is in Column B, this suggests that you trust your intuition and feelings and use them to make decisions.

Column C: Procrastinating Style

If your highest score is in Column C, this suggests that you are often uncomfortable making decisions. You tend to put them off until you are forced to make them.

Column D: Consulting Style

If your highest score is in Column D, this suggests that you value the input and perspectives of others and tend to consult with them before making important decisions.

Column E: Impulsive Style

If your highest score is in Column E, this suggests that you make decisions very quickly and do not feel the need to consult with others. Nor do you feel the need to consciously examine your own logic or feelings. Instead, you are comfortable going with what "pops" into your head.

Source: S. G. Scott and R. A. Bruce, "Decision-Making Style: The Development and Assessment of a New Measure," *Educational and Psychological Measurement* 55 (1995): 818–831. Copyright 1995 by Sage Publications, Inc. Reprinted by permission of Sage Publications, Inc.

Team Exercise

Form teams of four to six members. Read the following scenario. As a group, decide how you would answer each of the four questions at the end of the scenario.

While sitting in your office, you get a call from your company's plant supervisor. He tells you that a big customer wants you to adjust your assembly line to rush out a custom order. The plant supervisor says the decision is up to you. He needs to know what it is by tomorrow morning. The assembly line is currently in the middle of an extended standard run, producing a product for five of your mid-sized customers. Your company competes in part by offering both low-cost products and good service. The vast majority of your mid-sized customers choose to do business with you because your prices are lower. You maintain your profitability with these customers by keeping your own costs low. Your principal means of achieving this is by assembling high volumes of standardized products. Many of your large customers appreciate your low price but are willing to pay a premium for customized service and alterations to the products that come off your line.

If you stop the line to make the changes in equipment needed to run the custom order, you will incur both costs and delays to your current standard run. You are about two-thirds of the way through your standard run but need one week more to finish it. The changeover will take approximately three hours to complete, and the custom run two days to complete.

You have made this particular changeover before but not in the last six months. You know the basics of the changeover; the person most knowledgeable about the details is out sick but expects to return to work tomorrow. With the exception of two new employees, the company's nine assembly-line operators are fairly experienced and do not require close supervision. They are generally willing to be involved in decisions but are also happy just to "do their jobs."

1. Should you make this decision on your own or should you involve the group?
2. Are you inclined to stop the current run and make the changeover for the custom run? Why or why not?
3. If you insist that it's impossible to decide, what information must you have in order to make the decision?

Dov Frohman, the general manager of Intel Israel, faced a tough decision in 1991: With Operation Desert Storm looming, should he keep his plant open—especially given the fact that Iraqi Scud missiles stood ready to strike Israel in just minutes? There was also reason to believe that missiles might be equipped with chemical warheads. Moreover, Israel's civil defense authority had suggested that the country's nonessential businesses temporarily close.

Frohman said one of the top factors influencing his decision was the uncertainty of the situation: "The radical uncertainty of the situation—not knowing how many missiles would fall, where they would fall, what kind of destruction they would inflict—threatened to bring our business to a halt, even before a single missile had been launched." He also took into account the general business implications of shutting down. On one hand, he was confident senior executives at Intel's headquarters in California would understand if he decided to shut down until the crisis passed. On the other hand, he knew Intel would need to get the microprocessors his plant normally produced somewhere else in the world. From Frohman's perspective, "Managing a major unit in a global corporation is a continual fight for resources." Therefore, a production interrupt, even a temporary one, might cause the company's senior executives to think twice about making any future investments in Intel Israel.

Frohman said he was concerned not only about the survival of Intel Israel but of Israel's entire high-tech sector. Intel Israel was a key anchor of the country's still small but high-tech economy. "If we couldn't operate in an emergency situation, the trust of multinationals and venture capitalists in the stability of the Israeli business environment might crumble," he noted. Ultimately, though, Frohman's big concern was the safety of Intel Israel's employees: "People had a sealed room at home, and we had created them in all our main facilities, including the Jerusalem fab [fabrication plant]. But what about the daily commute?" He believed it was while commuting that employees would be at the greatest risk.

If Frohman decided to keep the operations running, how would he present the decision to employees? Should he order, request, strongly encourage, or simply offer them the option of showing up for work? After discussing the issues at length with his team, Frohman decided to keep the operations open. However, he would ask, not order, employees to come to work. "No one would be punished if they decided to stay home. I made it extremely clear to my direct reports that there would be no coercion: No manager was to pressure employees to come to work who did not want to."

Frohman said he communicated the decision to Intel Israel's workforce on Wednesday, January 18. The following day, with still no sign of missile attacks, most employees came to work. However, two days later, eight Iraqi Scud missiles hit Tel Aviv and Haifa around 2 AM. Fortunately, the missiles weren't laden with chemical warheads. However, at that point, Frohman had another decision to make: Should he stick with his original decision or close the plant and tell employees to stay home?

Frohman quickly met with members of his management team. The team had roughly 30 minutes to make a choice. The decision? To remain open. That morning, 75 percent of the employees scheduled to work the 7:00 AM shift at Intel's fab plant just outside Jerusalem arrived. Scud attacks continued on Saturday, but employee turnout at both the company's Jerusalem plant and its design center in Haifa remained at 80 percent.

Frohman talked to executives at Intel's headquarters about the situation. "I explained that we had decided to remain open, but we weren't forcing any employees to come to work who didn't feel comfortable doing so, and that so far turnout was quite good. They asked a lot of questions; we discussed the potential risks. But in the end, they were 7,500 miles away. Under the circumstances, they had to trust us." All totaled, the Scud attacks continued for six weeks, during which time, 39 Scuds fell in 18 separate attacks. Intel Israel operations remained open and up and running the entire time.

A few years later, Intel decided to invest in and build a second semiconductor plant in Israel. Thereafter, the Haifa design center won the assignment to develop the Centrino portable-computing microprocessor. Then in 2005, Intel announced that it would spend an additional $3.5 billion to build a new fab plant in Israel. The investment was the single largest ever made by any company in Israel. Following the investment, Intel Israel's exports soared to $1.2 billion, accounting for 14 percent of all of Israel's electronics- and information-industry exports. Today, the company is the largest foreign-owned employer in Israel.

Questions

1. Do you agree with Dov Frohman's decision in advance of the actual missile attacks to keep Intel up and running? What about after the actual missile attacks began?
2. Do you agree that Frohman should have made the decision to remain open or close or should executives at Intel's corporate headquarters have made it?
3. What criteria would you have considered if you were in Frohman's position? How would you have weighted these factors?

Sources: Adapted from D. Forman and R. Howard, *Leadership the Hard Way*, San Francisco, CA: Jossey-Bass, 2008; P. Margulies, "Dov Frohman Leads the Hard Way" *Strategy + Business*, May 26, 2009 (http://www.strategy-business.com/article/09208? gko=01786); V. Burkhardt, "Embracing Fear and Turbulence," *IdeaConnection*, May 25, 2009 (http://www.ideaconnection.com/articles/00119-Embracing-Fear-and-Turbulence.html); and D. Frohman, "Leadership Under Fire," *Harvard Business Review* (December 2006).

References

1. W. Edwards, R. Miles, and D. von Winterfeldt, eds., *Advances in Decision Analysis: From Foundations to Applications* (Cambridge: Cambridge University Press, 2007); J. F. Yates, E. S. Veinott, and A. L. Patalano, "Hard Decisions, Bad Decisions: On Decision Quality and Decision Aiding," *Emerging Perspectives on Judgment and Decision Research*, eds. S. L. Schneider and J. Shanteau (Cambridge: Cambridge University Press, 2003), 13–63; G. R. Ungson and D. N. Braunstein, *Decision Making* (Boston: Kent, 1982).

2. V. F. Reyna and S. E. Rivers, "Current Theories of Risk and Rational Decision Making," *Developmental Review* 28 (2008): 1–11; D. Miller and M. Star, *The Structure of Human Decisions* (Upper Saddle River: Prentice Hall, 1967).

3. J. Brockner and E. H. James, "Toward an Understanding of When Executives See a Crisis as an Opportunity," *Journal of Applied Behavioral Science* 44 (2008): 94–115; A. M. Isen and A. A. Labroo, "Some Ways in Which Positive Affect Facilitates Decision Making and Judgment," *Emerging Perspectives on Judgment and Decision Research*, eds. S. L. Schneider and J. Shanteau (New York: Cambridge University Press, 2003), 365–393; D. Kahneman, "A Perspective on Judgment and Choice," *American Psychologist* 58 (2003): 697–720; J. E. Dutton and S. E. Jackson, "Categorizing Strategic Issues: Links to Organizational Action," *Academy of Management Review* 12 (1987): 76–90; A. Drach-Zahavy and M. Erez, "Challenge Versus Threat Effects on the Goal–Performance Relationship," *Organizational Behavior and Human Decision Processes* 88, no. 2 (2002): 667–682.

4. J. Wallenius, J. S. Dyer, P. C. Fishburn, R. E. Steuer, S. Zionts, and K. Deb, "Multiple Criteria Decision Making, Multi-attribute Utility Theory: Recent Accomplishments and What Lies Ahead," *Management Science* 54 (2008): 1336–1349.

5. M. Machina, "Risk, Ambiguity, and the Rank–Dependence Axioms," *American Economic Review* 99 no. 1 (2009):385–92; J. Quiggin, "A Theory of Anticipated Utility," *Journal of Economic Behavior & Organization* 3 (1982): 323–343.

6. T. S. Krieshok, M. D. Black, and R. A. McKay, "Career Decision Making: Limits of Rationality and Abundance of Non-conscious Processes," *Journal of Vocational Behavior* 75 (2009): 275–290; H. A. Simon, *The New Science of Management Decisions* (Upper Saddle River: Prentice Hall, 1977); J. Parking, "Organizational Decision Making and the Project Manager," *International Journal of Project Management* 14, no. 5 (1996): 257–263.

7. M. H. Bazerman and D. A. Moore, *Judgment in Managerial Decision Making*, (New York: Wiley, 2008); D. C. Ganster, "Executive Job Demands: Suggestions from a Stress and Decision-making Perspective," *Academy of Management Review* 30 (2005): 492–502.

8. H. A. Simon, *Administrative Behavior* (New York: The Free Press, 1957).

9. R. Pieters, H. Baumgartner, and R. Bagozzi, "Biased Memory for Prior Decision Making: Evidence from a Longitudinal Field Study," *Organizational Behavior and Human Decision Processes* 99 no. 1 (2006): 34–48; F. Phillips, "The Distortion of Criteria After Decision-Making," *Organizational Behavior and Human Decision Processes* 88, no. 2 (2002): 769–784.

10. P. Soelberg, "Unprogrammed Decision Making," *Industrial Management* (1967): 19–29; D. Cray, G. H. Haines, and G. R. Mallory, "Programmed Strategic Decision Making," *British Journal of Management* 5, no. 3 (1994): 191–204.

11. E. Sadler-Smith and P. R. Sparrow, "Intuition in Organizational Decision Making," in G. P. Hodgkinson and W. H. Starbuck (eds.), *The Oxford Handbook of Organizational Decision Making* (Oxford: Oxford University Press, 2008), 287–304; G. Loveman, "Diamonds in the Data Mine," *Harvard Business Review* 81, no. 5 (2003): 109–113; E. Bonabeau, "Don't Trust Your Gut," *Harvard Business Review* 81 no. 5 (2003): 116–123.

12. E. Dane and M. G. Pratt, "Exploring Intuition and Its Role in Managerial Decision Making," *Academy of Management Review* 32 (2007): 33–54; J. Johnson *et al.,* "Vigilant and Hypervigilant Decision Making," *Journal of Applied Psychology* 82, no. 4 (1997): 614–622; Bonabeau, "Don't Trust Your Gut."

13. D. A. Rettinger and R. Hastie, "Content Effects on Decision Making," *Organizational Behavior and Human Decision Processes* 85, no. 2 (2001): 336–359.

14. "Rafting Operator Sentenced," *Maritime New Zealand,* March 23, 2010, http://www.maritimenz.govt.nz/news/media-releases-2010/20100323a.asp.

15. March and Simon, *Organizations.*

16. M. H. Bazerman and D. A. Moore, *Judgment in Managerial Decision Making* (New York: Wiley; 2008); T. R. Mitchell and J. R. Larson, *People in Organizations* (New York: McGraw-Hill, 1987).

17. R. Fryer and M. O. Jackson, "A Categorical Model of Cognition and Bias in Decision Making," *The B.E. Journal of Theoretical Economics* 8 (2008); T. A. Louie, "Hindsight Bias and Outcome-consistent Thoughts When Observing and Making Service Provider Decisions," *Organizational Behavior and Human Decision Processes* 98, no. 1 (2005): 88–95.

18. S. Venkatraman, J. A. Aloysius, and F. D. Davis, "Multiple Prospect Framing and Decision Behavior: The Mediational Roles of Perceived Riskiness and Perceived Ambiguity," *Organizational Behavior and Human Decision Processes* 101, no. 1 (2006): 59–73.

19. B. J. Weber and G. B. Chapman, "The Combined Effects of Risk and Time on Choice: Does Uncertainty Eliminate the Immediacy Effect? Does Delay Eliminate the Certainty Effect?" *Organizational Behavior and Human Decision Processes* 96, no. 2 (2005): 104–118.

20. I. Janis, *Victims of Groupthink* (Boston: Houghton Mifflin, 1972); M. E. Turner and A. R. Pratkamis, "Twenty-five Years of Groupthink Theory and Research: Lessons from the Evaluation of a Theory," *Organizational Behavior and Human Decision Processes* 73, nos. 2, 3 (1998): 105–115; J. K. Esser; "Alive and Well After 25 Years: A Review of Groupthink Research," *Organizational Behavior and Human Decision Processes* 73, nos. 2, 3 (1998): 116–141.

21. Kevin Bierfeldt, "Global Handheld Shipments up Almost 20% in Q1, Smartphone Shipments up 50%," *Brighthand.com,* May 1, 2010, http://www.brighthand.com/default.asp ?newsID=16482&news=Phone+Trends+Nokia+Apple+LG+Motorola+Q1+2010.

22. T. Greitemeyer, S. Schultz-Hardt, and D. Frey, "The Effects of Authentic and Contrived Dissent on Escalation of Commitment in Group Decision Making," *European Journal of Social Psychology* 39 (2009): 639–647; S. Schulz-Hardt, M. Jochims, and D. Frey, "Productive Conflict in Group Decision Making: Genuine and Contrived Dissent as Strategies to Counteract Biased Information Seeking," *Organizational Behavior and Human Decision Processes* 88, no. 2 (2002): 563–586.

23. A. Murline, "To Battle Groupthink, The Army Trains a Skeptics Corps," *US News & World Report* 144, no. 15 (2008): 30–32.

24. B. M. Staw, "The Escalation of Commitment to a Course of Action," *Academy of Management Review* 6 (1981): 577–587; G. Whyte, "Escalating Commitment in Individual and Group Decision Making: A Prospect Theory Approach," *Organizational Behavior and Human Decision Processes* 54, no. 3 (1993): 430–455; G. Whyte, A. M. Saks, and S. Hook, "When Success Breeds Failure," *Journal of Organizational Behavior* 18, no. 5 (1997): 415–432; D. R. Bobocel and J. P. Meyer, "Escalating

Commitment to a Failing Course of Action," *Journal of Applied Psychology* 79, no. 3 (1994): 360–363; J. Ross and M. Straw, "Organizational Escalation and Exit: Lessons from the Shoreham Nuclear Power Plant," *Academy of Management Journal* 36, no. 4 (1993): 701–732.

25. G. Whyte, "The Escalation of Commitment to a Course of Action: A Critical Test of Some Determinants," *Canadian Journal of Administrative Sciences* 5 (2009) 11–17; D. Chulkov, "Economics of Escalation: When Is Escalation of Commitment Rational for Managers and for Firms?" *International Journal of Business Research* 7, no. 5 (2007), 44–51; G. McNamara, H. Moon, and P. Bromiley, "Banking on Commitment: Intended and Unintended Consequences of an Organization's Attempt to Attenuate Escalation of Commitment," *Academy of Management Journal* 45, no. 2 (2002): 443–452.

26. Staw, "The Escalation of Commitment to a Course of Action," 578.

27. S. Schultz-Hardt, B. Thurow-Kröning, and D. Frey, "Preference-based Escalation: A New Interpretation for the Responsibility Effect in Escalating Commitment and Entrapment," *Organizational Behavior and Human Decision Processes* 108 (2009): 175–186.

28. A. Carmeli, Z. Sheaffer, and M. Y. Halevi, "Does Participatory Decision Making in Top Management Teams Enhance Decision Effectiveness and Firm Performance?" *Personnel Review* 38 (2009): 696–714; S. E. Seibert, S. R. Silver, and W. A. Randolph, "Taking Empowerment to the Next Level: A Multiple-level Model of Empowerment, Performance, and Satisfaction," *Academy of Management Journal* 47, no. 3 (2004): 332–349; R. C. Liden, S. J. Wayne, and R. T. Sparrowe, "An Examination of the Mediating Role of Psychological Empowerment on the Relations Between the Job, Interpersonal Relationships, and Work Outcomes," *Journal of Applied Psychology* 85 (2000): 407–416; N. Margulies and J. S. Black, "Perspectives on the Implementation of Participative Approaches," *Human Resource Management* 26, no. 3 (1987): 385–412.

29. J. S. Black and H. B. Gregersen, "Participative Decision Making: An Integration of Multiple Perspectives," *Human Relations* 50 (1997): 859–878.

30. J. T. Ettling and A. Jago, "Participation Under Conditions of Conflict: More on the Validity of the Vroom–Yetton Model," *Journal of Management Studies* 25 (2007): 73–83; V. Vroom and P. Yetton, *Leadership and Decision Making* (Pittsburgh: University of Pittsburgh Press, 1973); V. Vroom and A. Jago, *The New Leadership: Managing Participation in Organizations* (Upper Saddle River: Prentice Hall, 1988).

31. V. Vroom and A. Jago, "The Role of Situational Leadership," *American Psychologist*, 62 (2007) 17–24; R. Ebert and

T. Mitchell, *Organizational Decision Processes Concepts and Analysis* (New York: Crane, Russak, 1975).

32. S. S. K. Lam, X.-P. Chen, and J. Schaubroeck, "Participative Decision Making and Employee Performance in Different Cultures: The Moderating Effects of Allocentrism, Idiocentrism and Efficacy," *Academy of Management Journal* 45, no. 5 (2002): 905–914.

33. R. Hof, "Why Once Ambitious Computer Firm Quit," *Peninsula Times Tribune,* September 29, 1984, B1.

34. K. Eisenhardt and L. J. Bourgeois, "Making Fast Strategic Decisions in High Velocity Environments," *Academy of Management Journal* 32 (1989): 543–576; S. L. Brown and K. M. Eisenhardt, *Competing on the Edge: Strategy as Structured Chaos* (Boston: Harvard Business School Press, 1998); J. R. Hough and M. A. White, "Environmental Dynamism and Strategic Decision-making Rationality: An Examination at the Decision Level," *Strategic Management Journal* 24, no. 5 (2003): 481–489.

35. M. Bazerman, *Judgment in Managerial Decision Making* (Hoboken: John Wiley & Sons, 2005); W. Edwards, R. Miles, and D. von Winterfeldt, eds., *Advances in Decision Analysis: From Foundations to Applications* (Cambridge: Cambridge University Press, 2007); C. Schwenk and H. Thomas, "Formulating the Mess: The Role of Decision Aids in Problem Formulation," *Omega* 11 (1983): 239–252.

36. P. L. Roth, "Group Approaches to the Schmidt–Hunter Global Estimation Procedure," *Organizational Behavior and Human Decision Processes* 59, no. 3 (1994): 428–451; A. Van deVen and A. Delbecq, "The Effectiveness of Nominal, Delphi, and Interacting Group Decision Making Processes," *Academy of Management Journal* 17 (1974): 607–626.

37. K. Dawson, "Workforce Optimization Helps Airline Improve Service Levels by 38%," *CommWeb.com,* October 21, 2002, http://www/commweb.com.

38. Ibid.

39. J. C. Henderson, "Finding Synergy Between Decision Support Systems and Expert Systems Research," *Decision Sciences* 18 (2007), 333–349; B. B. Baltes, M. W. Dickson, M. P. Sherman, C. C. Bauer, and J. S. LaGanke, "Computer-mediated Communication and Group Decision Making: A Meta-analysis." *Organizational Behavior and Human Decision Processes* 87, no. 1 (2002): 156–179; Bonabeau, "Don't Trust Your Gut."

40. M. Wells, "Lord of the Skies" *Fortune*, October 14, 2002.

41. J. Levere, "Low-fare Airlines Aims to Build on Attitude and Hostility," *New York Times*, December 1, 2000.

42. Baltes, Dickson, Sherman, Bauer, and LaGanke, "Computer-mediated Communication and Group Decision Making: A Meta-analysis."

43. March and Simon, *Organizations.*

Part Four

Controlling

13

Operations Management

LEARNING OBJECTIVES

After studying this chapter, you should be able to:

Define *operations management* and explain its importance within service and manufacturing firms.

Describe key techniques and tools for enhancing product and service quality.

Explain common means of ensuring appropriate product quantity.

Discuss tools for managing the appropriate timing of inventory and finished product.

Describe methods for enhancing productivity and efficiency.

Explain the principle roles of effective supply chain management in the operations of organizations.

Courtesy of Michelle Jackson, BNSF
Railway Company

Name: Michelle Jackson

Position: Marketing Manager, International Intermodal
Operations, BNSF Railway Company

Alma mater: University of Oklahoma

Outside work activities: National Black MBA Association
member, volunteer for various organizations, reading,
working out at the gym, traveling, and spending time with
family and friends

First Job out of school: Advanced Financial Solutions in
Oklahoma City, Oklahoma

Business book reading now: *The Conversation*, by
Hill Harper

Heroes: My father for being successful by overcoming life's
obstacles and remaining an honest, faithful, and humble
man. And my mother for having the biggest heart that
anyone could have

Motto to live by: "Do today, what others put off to tomorrow"

What drives me: Knowing that I added value in either a
person's life or on a project

Management style: Democratic style; allow others to give
input and be a part of the decision-making process

Few people appreciate just how much of a country's
economy depends on the effective operation of railroads.
Nearly half of all freight in the United States in terms of
weight is moved by rail. The value of all the goods moved
by rail is nearly 17 percent of the value of all imports into
and exports out of the United States. Some industries are
especially dependent on rail transportation. For example,
about 70 percent of all coal and automobiles ship by rail.

Therefore, if railroad operations do not go well, it affects not
just the railroad company but the entire economy. This was
clearly felt when the economy started recovering after the
2000–2001 recession. As consumer spending increased and
imports from places in Asia, especially China, exploded, the
demand on railways in the West stretched, and in some cases
exceeded, rail capacity.

Michelle Jackson sat at the nexus of this challenge.
Jackson's customers are international ocean liners that ship
intermodal containers to and from the West Coast. In an age
where manufacturers want parts delivered at just the right
time (not too early or too late) and consumers want products
when they're hot, bottlenecks and the resulting delivery delays
cause headaches for everyone. But building new capacity cannot be done overnight. Acquiring the rights to land, satisfying
environmental impact demands, constructing new rail lines,
and the like are costly and time-intensive activities.

Jackson and other operations managers at BNSF Railway
Company faced several options to reduce bottlenecks and
thereby increase operational efficiency. They could add more
capacity by simply increasing the length of the trains and adding
more locomotives to pull the longer trains. They could increase
capacity by adding more trains, which would require purchasing
more locomotives and cars. However, adding more trains would
require hiring and training new conductors, engineers, and other
personnel. Also, if they increased capacity along the lines, they
would also have to think about managing the congestion that
would likely result at terminals and transshipment points where
cars are shifted from one train to another for their onward
journey. Through better tracking and other technologies, they
could increase the efficiency and movement of existing trains.

In the end, the actions need to not only add to the total
volume that can be moved along the lines but also the quality
of the service. This service includes both the speed of delivery
(how long it takes to get freight shipped from point A to
point B) and the reliability of delivery (how accurate the targeted delivery date is relative to actual delivery). Moving
higher volumes with worse service quality would likely *not*
lead to overall higher levels of customer satisfaction.

The Nature and Importance of Operations Management

Operations management is a specialized field of management focused on the conversion of
resources into products and services. In the past, the focus was largely on manufacturing, and
the term *production and operations management (POM)* was commonly used. With the lines
between what is strictly a manufacturing firm versus what is strictly a service firm now blurred
and with a greater portion of economic activity being devoted to services, the term *operations*

operations management
a specialized field of management
associated with the conversion or
transformation of resources into
products and services

management (OM) is a more generic one describing the activities related to producing both products and services. Because of the historic focus of operations management on manufacturing, some people incorrectly assume that the tools and techniques of operations management do not apply to service firms or service activities. However, as this chapter will illustrate, fundamentally all organizations have to deal with the same issues within operations whether they are transforming resources into physical products or intangible services. For example, billing and insurance processing account for 42 percent of all health care administration costs. On average, physicians themselves have to spend three hours a week completing health care plan paperwork at a cost of $23 billion to $31 billion each year.[1] By implementing a number of traditional operations management concepts, Jefferson Pilot Financial (now Lincoln Financial Group) reduced by 70 percent the time it took to process an insurance application and issue a policy. The company also reduced by 40 percent the number of policies that had to be reissued due to errors and reduced its total labor costs per application by 25 percent.[2]

Equally important is the strategic role of operations.[3] Just as people incorrectly think that operations management is only about making products, some also incorrectly think that operations management is just a specialized function without organizational or strategic importance. Nothing could be further from the truth. All organizations survive and thrive in large measure to the extent that they produce a service or product with the quality, in the quantity, and at a time that customers desire. For an organization to survive very long, it must do this while maintaining a positive profit margin between its costs and the revenue it receives. This is true regardless of the specific strategy the firm pursues. Whether a firm is charging a premium or discount price relative to competitors, it still needs to ensure that the costs associated with operations help the company maintain a positive profit margin and that the outcome of the operations function enhances customer satisfaction and revenues.

In this context, managers working in operations typically have four related overall objectives. First, they are concerned about and manage activities designed to ensure that the services and products produced for customers have the appropriate quality. Second, operations managers have to also use tools and techniques to ensure that the right quantities of the products and services are produced. Third, operations managers must use a number of techniques to ensure that the products and services get to the customer at the right time. Finally, operations managers must also focus on delivering the three previous objectives at the best possible cost. As we will explore in this chapter, each of the first three objectives can have direct cost implications. However, operations managers must oversee a number of other factors in order to ensure that the right quality, quantity, and timing objectives are met at the best possible cost. We will explore these factors as well.

Managing Quality

Ford Motor Company's advertising slogan, "Quality Is Job One," points out how important the concept of quality can be to an organization. However, the firm's less than stellar performance in achieving this objective against Toyota illustrates that it's not slogans but actual delivery of quality that matters to customers and influences a firm's financial performance, such as sales and market share. Toyota's quality has consistently been rated among the highest of all automobile manufacturers and this has, in part, contributed to Toyota's surpassing Ford as the number two seller of automobiles in the world. However, Toyota's troubles and recalls in 2009 and 2010 demonstrate that quality takes continuous management and cannot be put on autopilot.

quality
the reliability, durability, serviceability, and dependability of products and services; also defined as fitness for use

A popular definition of **quality** is "fitness for use," which is a measure of how well a product or service performs its intended purpose, including how reliable it is or conversely how often it breaks down and how easy it is to service or repair when it does break down. Although this might sound as though it applies most directly to products, the elements also apply to services. For example, if we consider the service element of the front desk of a hotel, all the factors mentioned previously can be directly applied. The quality of this service would be high if when people check in, the front desk clerk can consistently locate their reservation and assign a room quickly (efficiency), ensure that features of the room requested by customers match those of the room assigned (effectiveness), and do both these things in a professional and friendly manner. Increased quality has several key outcomes for the business. In the hotel example, higher service quality in terms of efficiency can influence at least two critical outcomes. First, greater *efficiency* can lead to lower costs because a given clerk could check in more customers, and, therefore, the hotel would need fewer clerks. Second, greater efficiency (that is, the speed of checking in guests) could also have a positive impact on the satisfaction of customers and their likelihood of becoming repeat customers. Higher quality in terms of *effectiveness* could also affect both current costs and future revenues. First, if the room assigned matches the room requested, this then lowers the costs associated with "fixing" mismatches. Second, the greater the match between the room requested and room assigned, the higher the customers' likely satisfaction and their probability of coming back in the future. Marriott Hotels understand this and works very hard to ensure operational effectiveness and friendliness of its front desk staff. This operational focus is reflected in its consistently receiving from customers the highest satisfaction scores including the number two rating in 2009.[4]

Exhibit 13.1 illustrates the potential outcomes of higher quality in operations. As we noted, higher quality can often enhance customer satisfaction, which in turn can lead to higher repeat business and, therefore, more revenue. If quality and satisfaction are high enough, customers may recommend the product to others—what marketers often call *positive word of mouth revenue*. The most important assessment of quality is in the eye of the customer.[5] In summary, higher quality can lower costs through higher efficiency, lower repair costs, and lower warranty costs (that is, making good on warranty guarantees relative to a product's features or performance) and can increase revenues through higher customer satisfaction through repeat business and positive word of mouth.

Given the potential benefits of higher quality, how can it be enhanced? To address this question in the following sections, the chapter first examines an overall philosophy known as **total quality management (TQM).**[6] Next, it discusses other specific tools and techniques for enhancing quality.

Total Quality Management

TQM is considered a management philosophy because it encompasses a commitment from employees at all levels to continually strive to make improvements and satisfy customers. In essence, TQM must be part of the organization's culture in order for a true commitment to quality to be realized.[7] In contrast to traditional quality control efforts where a separate team of experts inspect products or services for defects or errors after completion, TQM emphasizes "quality at the source," that is, quality inspection at all stages of production or service output. Quality at the source includes engaging in quantitative techniques, such as statistical process control, as well as nonquantitative techniques, such as employee empowerment.[8]

total quality management (TQM)

a management approach and philosophy that involves a commitment from all levels of employees to continually strive to make improvements and satisfy customers

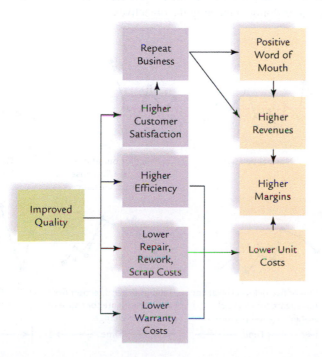

EXHIBIT 13.1

The Economic Impact of Higher Quality

statistical process control (SPC)

a quantitative tool to aid in making decisions concerning how well a process is performing

Statistical process control (SPC) provides an objective tool to make decisions concerning how well a process is performing. Although all companies ideally should have a goal of zero defects, or 100 percent customer satisfaction, in reality, slight deviations cannot be completely eliminated. Thus, organizations try to minimize their occurrence. To track and highlight results and identify unacceptable deviations, most operations managers taking an SPC approach to quality use various forms of a process control chart. Control charts are typically developed for any quality-related characteristic that may cause defective products or services. Oregon Freeze Dry (OFD) is the world's largest custom processor of freeze-dried foods.[9] It is a major supplier to the U.S. military and markets its own line of backpacking foods (Mountain House brand). If packages are overfilled during production, the company is essentially giving product away, which is not great for profits. If packages are underfilled, customers are not getting what they paid for, a situation that could damage customer satisfaction and run afoul of laws and fair trade regulations. OFD uses statistical process control to ensure that packages are consistently filled to the proper weight. The company creates a control chart by taking samples at predetermined intervals, computing the average weight measurement, and establishing the upper and lower control limits. The control limits provide an acceptable range for measurements. Any measurements outside the range are considered unacceptable and signal cause for investigation. OFD uses control charts to provide a basis for taking action to determine the causes of good or poor performance. Exhibit 13.2 provides examples of control charts and what actions should be taken based on the measurements.

continuous process improvement

incremental and breakthrough improvements in the way an organization does business; also known as business process reengineering and *kaizen*

Continuous process improvement, also known as *business process reengineering* and as *kaizen* in Japan, refers to both incremental and breakthrough improvements in the way an organization does business. The fundamental notion of process reengineering is that form influences function. In other words, the way a process is designed influences how well or poorly it functions, which in turn has an important influence on key outcomes. A common approach to process reengineering has five key elements:

1. Objective: This step focuses on determining what a process is to achieve. For example, a loan application process should result in determining whether or not a loan should be given to an individual.
2. Design: This step examines the critical sequences and seeks to maximize the objective while minimizing the number, complexity, and time required in the process.
3. Capabilities: This step determines the required capabilities for executing the design.
4. Infrastructure: This step focuses on the information and other infrastructure needed for supporting the design and capabilities to meet the objective.
5. Metrics: Finally, this step determines the key metrics that help monitor and determine how well the redesign is doing in meeting the objectives.

EXHIBIT 13.2

Quality Control Charts

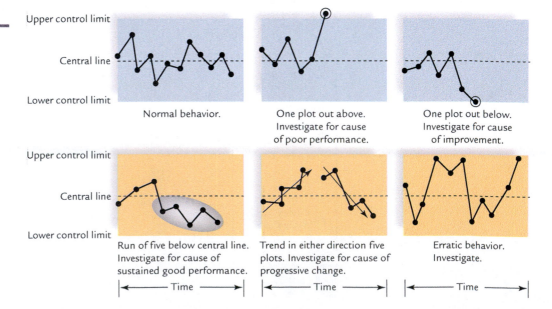

Normal behavior.

One plot out above. Investigate for cause of poor performance.

One plot out below. Investigate for cause of improvement.

Run of five below central line. Investigate for cause of sustained good performance.

Trend in either direction five plots. Investigate for cause of progressive change.

Erratic behavior. Investigate.

For example, Clorox worked on redesigning its "order to cash" process (the process of getting a customer's order through to receiving cash for the fulfillment of the order). Over a four-year period from 2002 to 2006, Clorox's late shipments fell by 70 percent, old receivables fell by 67 percent, and perfect orders (orders that hit every key target metric along the process) rose from 19 percent to 70 percent.[10] In contrast to reengineering but in the same spirit of continuous improvement, *kaizen* seeks to improve all aspects of a process. For example, at the Toyota Manufacturing plant in Georgetown, Kentucky, an employee brought in a Bass Boat seat and placed it at his station on the line. A seated position made the installation of parts under the steering wheel much easier and faster. According to the criteria for the Malcolm Baldrige National Quality Award, several types of continuous improvements are possible, including:

1. Enhancing value to customers through new and improved products and services
2. Reducing errors, defects, and waste
3. Improving responsiveness and cycle time performance
4. Improving productivity and effectiveness in the use of all resources
5. Improving the company's performance and leadership position in fulfilling its public responsibilities and serving as a role model in corporate citizenship

Six Sigma is a disciplined, data-driven approach for eliminating defects and enhancing quality with an orientation toward the impact such improvements will have on the customer.[11] Statistically Six Sigma is represented by a 99.99966 percent reliability, or not producing more than 3.4 defects per million opportunities. A defect is not a product that doesn't work or a service that fails but any result that is outside of customer specifications. As a consequence, the focus is not just on hitting a target average, but reducing the variance around that target. For example, suppose you had a customer delivery target of 6 days after an order was placed. Having the actual delivery result of 3, 6, 4, 7, 8, 2, 5, 6, 8, 10, and 11 days would result in an average of 6 days. However, this would not even achieve One Sigma (that is, 69 percent reliability). Six Sigma is focused on not just achieving the desired average but having virtually no deviation away from or variance around that target.

Within Six Sigma, quality is improved through the use of two submethodologies: DMAIC and DMADV. The DMAIC process (*d*efine, *m*easure, *a*nalyze, *i*mprove, *c*ontrol) focuses on existing processes that fall below the specification and improving them. The DMADV process (*d*efine, *m*easure, *a*nalyze, *d*esign, *v*erify) focuses on the development of new processes. According to the Six Sigma Academy, the highest level experts in Six Sigma (called "Black Belts") save companies approximately $230,000 per project and can complete four to six projects per year. General Electric estimated it saved $10 billion during the first five years of implementing its Six Sigma quality initiative.[12]

Although Six Sigma initiatives have focused largely on manufacturing environments, the principles can be applied with equal relevance and impact to service environments.[13] For example, Seyfarth Shaw LLP, is a large law firm with offices throughout the United States. The firm's Six Sigma program includes 75 attorneys and staff members (including every lawyer on the executive committee) certified as Six Sigma Green Belts, which requires completion of an intensive four-month training program and two Six Sigma projects. In less than a year, the firm increased cost predictability on more than 50 legal matters and reduced costs by 13 percent to 50 percent on those activities.[14] Albertson's, a large grocery chain, estimates that the company has saved hundreds of millions of dollars $500,000 at a time. Over several years, Albertson's tackled 556 projects, most of which yielded moderate savings individually but collectively added up to serious money. According to Jim Gentile, former senior vice president of *Six Sigma* Quality, "There are thousands of half-million-dollar ideas out there."[15]

Employee empowerment, defined in Chapter 8, is seen as being critical to the TQM philosophy. This is because however necessary the statistical monitoring and control of quality is, in the end, fixing quality problems and thereby achieving high quality requires action on the part of managers and their subordinates. The TQM philosophy is that organizations need to empower their employees so that they will take pride in and have a sense of responsibility for their individual output, as well as the output of the entire organization. By involving employees, organizations engage the expertise of those people who directly produce the product or provide the service. These individuals are the experts in their areas and should have input on how to improve the quality of the organization's product or service. In addition to employee involvement, a successful TQM philosophy requires a group of committed top managers who can effectively communicate the TQM vision and provide the strong leadership needed to implement the changes required. And, most importantly, a strong focus on the customer's needs and expectations is paramount.

The goal of exceeding customer expectations was the primary reason why Athens Insurance Center (AIC) implemented a TQM program. Part of its TQM effort helped to identify a need to cross-train its agents so that when customers called, they would be assisted immediately instead of having to wait for a particular agent. For AIC, the appeal of TQM was that it "attacks the flaws in the systems and procedures—not people." AIC reported that its TQM efforts helped instill a stronger sense of ownership and pride in their employees, which, in turn, improved customer satisfaction.

TQM efforts can also be found in nonbusiness settings such as schools. "Koalaty Kid," a program sponsored by the American Society for Quality, emphasizes TQM and continuous improvement in elementary schools worldwide. At Kingsley Elementary in Kingsport, Tennessee, writing was identified in the Kingsley School Improvement Plan as the academic subject most in need of quality improvement. School principal Dr. Sandra Ramsey reported that after implementing a plan to improve the quality of instruction provided by the school's teachers, students achieved a 58 percent improvement in their writing over a two-year period. The plan involved, among other things, recording and charting students' individual grades and recognizing students for their writing accomplishments in school announcements and during school assemblies.[16]

Quantity and Capacity Planning

Few people would debate that the right quality of a service or product is important. That said, customers also care about the right quantity. One of the principle means that operations managers use to ensure that the right quantity of product or service is produced is via **capacity planning**—determining how much a firm should be able to produce of a product or service.

Although organizations would like to be able to operate at maximum capacity at all times, no organization could possibly sustain itself at this rate. Rather than run at its **design capacity,** which is the maximum capacity that can be attained under *ideal* conditions, organizations usually run at their effective capacities instead. The **effective capacity** is the percent of design capacity actually expected, and it can be expressed as a simple formula:

$$\text{Effective Capacity} = \text{Expected Capacity}/\text{Design Capacity}$$

Organizations may need to add capacity to meet increased demand; however, it is important to consider a number of different factors including the timing, amount, and types of capacity to add. For example, if a hospital plans to increase its number of beds, it will likely have to increase its number of nurses as well. The wrong type of capacity additions might even lead to a financial disaster. For example, airlines that increase their passenger capacity by purchasing

capacity planning
the process of determining how much a firm should be able to produce of a product or service

design capacity
the maximum capacity at which a facility can run under ideal conditions

effective capacity
the percent of design capacity a facility is actually expected to maintain

Capacity planning for operations managers is tricky business—especially when it comes to corn production. Due to government subsidies, the demand for corn used to produce ethanol for cars in the United States rose sevenfold between 2001 and 2006. But it's hard to predict whether the upward trend in both demand and supply will continue.

Andy Sacks/Getty Images, Inc. / Riser

A MANAGER'S CHALLENGE

CHANGE

Corn: Fad or Fundamental Change?

The demand for corn for use in the production of ethanol for cars in the United States alone rose from 500 million bushels in 2000 to 2,500 million bushels in 2009; however, projecting future demand for corn used in making ethanol is a tricky business.

One factor that makes it difficult is that while crop-based fuel production was in the past dependent on government subsidies, it is now driven by the price of oil. As world oil prices tripled from 2003 through 2008, the price of ethanol rose to the point where its price in 2008 was more than double its cost of production. This made its conversion into fuel for cars highly profitable.

This is partly why, between October 2005 and October 2008, an astounding 85 new ethanol distilleries in the United States were constructed. This rate of construction dropped 40 percent with the recession in 2009. Nevertheless, the number of plants grew from 77 in 2005 to 197 by 2009 and capacity grew from 3.9 billion gallons in 2005 to 12.4 billion gallons by 2010.

This added demand was one of the reasons for the shortfall of 73 million tons of corn processed in 2006, and for prices rising from $2 per bushel to a peak of $7.88 in 2008. However, because they need to rotate their crops, farmers cannot simply convert all their existing acres to corn production, regardless of the price. It was estimated that farmers could increase the number of acres they devoted to growing corn by 15 percent per year. Consequently, the chances of the ethanol industry doubling or tripling corn output in any one year are not good. Whether you are an operations manager on a farm or at an ethanol company, the challenge of determining the stability of demand and, therefore, the amount of capacity needed is complicated. Oil prices peaked in 2008 at nearly $140 per barrel but then dropped back to $80 in mid-2010. Will the economy continue to recover and push oil demand and prices back up? Will consumers continue to view ethanol as a "green" alternative? Will consumers view corn as the wrong input into ethanol as compared to sugar cane or other cellulose because corn is an important food source? What will happen if instead of ethanol, consumers begin demanding hybrid cars that run on regular gasoline and rely on electric powered engines? How should the spreading shortages of irrigation water and the prospect of even more intense heat waves as the earth's temperature rises be factored into the decision to plant more corn?

For the operations managers in ethanol distilleries, how might a clash play out between U.S. motorists and the 854 million of the world's people who are chronically hungry and malnourished to the point that 24,000 of them, mostly children, die of starvation each day? On the other hand, what if the federal government continues to worry about growing U.S. dependence on imported oil and creates laws, regulations, and policies that continue to support the production and use of ethanol? The government set a goal of renewable fuels reaching 15 billion gallons by 2015. Will the government stick to that goal? Being caught short of capacity competitively can be just as damaging as being caught long on capacity.

Sources: Tom Bryan, "Rail Car Builder Offers 6351 for DDGS Transport, *Ethanol Producer Magazine,* November 2002, http://www.ethanolproducer.com; Earth Policy Institute, November 3, 2006, www.earth-policy.org/Updates/2006/Update60.htm; J. Napsha, "Corn Prices May Cause a Small Ripple in Western PA," *Pittsburg Tribune-Review,* March 31, 2007; A. Syeed and D. Pitt, "Ethanol Demand Boosts Corn Planting," *Associated Press,* March 30, 2007, http://news.yahoo.com/s/ap/20070331/ap_on_bi_ge/planting_report.

large jumbo jets may become less competitive than ones that lease the same capacity, especially if periods of increased demand are temporary. This is partly why outsourcing, or contracting with external vendors to supply products or services to cover capacity shortages, is increasingly popular because it is easier to move capacity up and down to match changing demand.

Changes in demand can create challenges for determining the needed capacity. For example, a utility company has to determine not just average demand but peak demand as well. They have to consider what would happen if one piece of equipment, one relay, one circuit failed. What level of power demand could the system handle then? Would it be enough? How much demand can be shifted around through the system and where for seasonal, daily, and hourly demands.

Sometimes determining if demand is a fad or a trend is not so easy and can make capacity planning a major challenge. Consider the accompanying "A Manager's Challenge" feature and the demand for corn. Whether you are a manager of a farm trying to determine how many acres of corn to plant or whether to purchase more land or you are an operations manager in a company considering adding ethanol-refining capacity by building new plants or expanding existing ones, clearly, determining whether the increased demand for corn is a fad or a longer lasting trend is tricky for either farmers or distillers in the ethanol industry.

materials requirement planning (MRP)

a sophisticated computer system, derived from the master production schedule and an inventory database, whose output provides schedules that identify the required raw materials, parts, and assemblies needed during each specified time period

Materials requirement planning (MRP) is a system of "getting the right materials to the right place at the right time."[17] An MRP system is a sophisticated computer system that uses information from a company's master production schedule and inventory database. The system produces schedules that identify the required raw materials, parts, and assemblies the firm needs during each specified time period. Firms that implement an MRP system can often reduce their inventory, price their products more competitively, and better respond to customers' demands. Controlling their inventory levels allows organizations to be more profitable. The reason is simple: Companies have to spend money to acquire inventory. The more inventory there is in the system and the longer it sits idle, the more money the firm has tied up in nonperforming (that is, nonearning) assets. Two of the most basic approaches to inventory management that companies can use to enhance profitability are the economic order quantity (EOQ) model and ABC analysis.

economic order quantity (EOQ)

a mathematical formula managers use to determine the most economical quantity of products to order, to minimize total inventory costs

The **economic order quantity (EOQ)** model was developed in the early 1900s and, thus, has enjoyed a rather long history in the field of operations management. The model helps managers determine the most economical quantity of products to order, to minimize total inventory costs. The actual formula is as follows:

$$EOQ = \sqrt{(2 \times AD \times OC)/(HC)}$$

where

EOQ = economic order quantity (quantity to be ordered)
 AD = annual demand
 OC = restocking or ordering cost
 HC = annual holding or carrying costs per unit

Suppose you were a retailer, and for one of your lines of suits your annual demand was 200 suits. Your ordering costs would be $50. The total unit cost of each suit was $200, and the holding, or carrying costs, related to maintaining each suit in your store until it is sold were 10 percent of the unit cost. Thus, your holding cost per suit would be $20. In this case, the economic order quantity would be 32 units (suits). So, as you can see, although the unit cost of an item is typically straightforward, true ordering costs can be harder to determine. Some research suggests that managers often underestimate the true costs of reordering, in part because they fail to consider such noncash costs as vetting vendors or processing requests for proposals (RFPs).[18] Exhibit 13.3 provides a general visual illustration of the fundamental aspects of EOQ.

Because the two major costs, ordering costs and annual carrying costs, vary inversely, there are always tradeoffs to make. For instance, a company might be able to get a discount for ordering large quantities less often, but its cost to store the items would likely be higher.

EXHIBIT 13.3

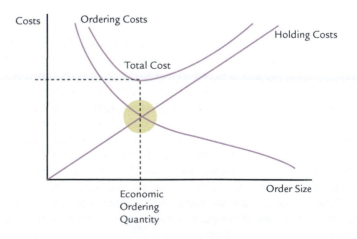

Whereas the EOQ model helps managers make decisions about when and how much of a product to order, **ABC analysis** provides information about which inventory items require the most attention. In most companies, a small percentage (15 percent to 30 percent) of their inventory accounts for the greatest percentage (70 percent to 80 percent) of their inventory dollar volume. For this reason, companies are better off putting more effort into controlling and monitoring these high-dollar-volume items compared with the lower-dollar-volume items. For example, to prevent the theft of high-priced items, many retail stores put special security tags on them. These items are likely categorized as "A" items. ABC analysis provides a way to classify inventory items into three value categories (A, B, and C):

1. "A" items typically account for the top 15 percent of the firm's dollar volume.
2. "B" items typically account for the next 35 percent of the firm's dollar volume.
3. "C" items typically account for the remaining 50 percent of the firm's dollar volume.

For a typical office supply company that sells computer equipment, office furniture, and miscellaneous supplies such as paper clips, it is likely that fax machines would be classified as an "A" item, whereas desks would be classified as "B" items, and paper clips would be classified as "C" items. Based on these categorizations, the firm would want to spend more time keeping better records of the computer equipment compared with the miscellaneous office supplies. The high dollar volume associated with "A" items occurs because either the items are low priced and have high usage rates (a high number of sales) or the items are high priced and have low usage rates (a low number of sales). In comparison, items classified as "C" result from either low demand, or sales, or low prices that result in a low dollar volume. Critical items that need a great deal of attention are likely to be categorized as "A" items regardless of the actual dollar volume of sales they generate. This would help ensure that sufficient inventory levels are kept on hand at all times. For example, hospitals would never want to run out of certain life-saving pharmaceuticals; thus, they would likely categorize these medications as "A" items to help ensure that sufficient levels are always on hand.

The Timing of Products and Services

Even if operations managers take the appropriate actions to produce the right quality and right quantity of products and services, they still have to ensure that the timing of the flow of inventory and delivery of products and services meet customers' requirements.[19] Not getting products and services to customers when they want them (often termed *stock outs*) can be as or more costly as having too much stock. Researchers have found that between 20 percent to 40 percent of customers who face a stock out leave the store and go to a competitor's store. Of those who continue shopping, 2 percent to 7 percent will leave the store without purchasing a substitute product.[20] The same researchers noted that 72 percent of all stock outs were due to poor operations management rather than unpredictable demand. The feature "A Manager's Challenge" shows how operations managers at retailer Zara have contributed to the company's overall success.

Likewise, carrying excess inventory can also be costly.[21] Under competitive pressures, surgical device maker Conmed had to decide if it was going to move more manufacturing to China or invest in automation. In the end, the company chose a third path and completely overhauled its production. Long assembly lines were changed to compact U-shaped workstations. Products were built only as orders came in and no longer languished in warehouses. Boxes with enough parts to last weeks were reduced to containing the exact number of parts needed for the next few hours. For just one product, fluid-injection devices, on-hand inventory shrank from $93,000 to just $6,000 and assembly space decreased from 33,000 square feet to just under 7,000 square feet. In addition, worker output increased 21 percent. Do the improvements yield savings superior to what could be had in China? Though vastly lower, wages there are largely offset by the costs of long lead times, inventory pileup, quality problems, and unforeseen delays. "If more U.S. companies deploy these production methods," says David A. Johnson, vice-president for global operations, "we can compete with anybody."[22]

Holding parts in dynamic industries does not just increase holding cost but like perishable fruit can go bad and have to be written off. For example, Cisco had to write off an incredible $2.5 billion in raw materials. Because the market was dynamic and rewarded Cisco for quickly meeting demand, the company stockpiled inventory to meet rush orders. But when demand declined, there was too much "perishable" stock in their system.[23]

ABC analysis
an inventory management system that categorizes items to provide information concerning which items require the most attention

TECHNOLOGY

Zara Managers Focus on Rapid Fulfillment

Zara, one of the key clothing brands within a larger company called Inditex, operates more than 1,000 stores in over 73 countries producing over 11,000 distinct items. In the fashion business, where flamboyant designs and eccentric designers grab much of the headlines, you wouldn't expect operations managers to contribute so much to a leading fashion retailer's success. However, in an industry in which customers' preferences for color, texture, cut, and other elements can change several times a year, operations timing is critical. Zara excels at this. Its operations managers have designed, redesigned, and improved the company's system. The firm can design, produce, and deliver a new piece of clothing, and put it on display in a store in just 15 days! Because customers can get the look and feel of clothes when they are in style, Zara gets full retail price on 85 percent of its products and has to mark down only 15 percent of its products. In contrast, the average in the industry is closer to a 60:40 ratio. Getting a higher price also helps contribute to a profit margin that is typically 40 percent higher than the industry average.

To keep the sense that Zara is always on the cutting edge, designers for the company create more than 40,000 new items annually, of which about 25 percent are selected for actual production. To encourage customers to buy items when they are in the store, the stock on display is kept purposely low. This way, customers think, "This shirt fits me and is in the right color and style but there are only two on the rack, so if I don't buy it now, it might not be here later." To make this possible, Zara operations managers have to ensure that they have a system that can both keep track of what is selling and resupply items quickly.

This requires the timely and constant exchange of information among the company's design, production, transportation, and retail managers. To ensure that this happens easily, Zara owns and operates all of its design, and most of its production and transportation operations. Designs are communicated directly to cutting machines at the factories for faster production. This close cooperation also allows Zara's managers to do novel things such as putting the price tags on clothes at the factory rather than at stores. Consequently, clothes can go directly from the delivery truck to the store shelves with no delay. This reduces the inventory that Zara stores have to carry, or store, by about 50 percent compared to other retailers, such as GAP or Benetton. The practice also financially benefits the company because Zara stores can be much smaller, pay less rent, and still carry as much merchandise on the floor as its competitors. Alternately, the money saved allows a Zara stores to pay a higher amount of rent but set up shop in a more expensive location—a location that attracts more affluent customers or has better customer traffic. In either case, Zara ends up with much higher sales per square foot of retail space it rents.

Although having the right designs, the right quality, and the right material are all critical in the fashion clothing business, Zara's operations managers ensure that the product gets to the customer in a timely manner. These people ensure that as shoppers' preferences change, Zara can react faster and satisfy the customer better than its competitors can.

Miguel Riopa/Agence France Presse/Getty Images

Zara is the flagship brand of the Spanish based firm, Inditex, Europe's fastest-growing apparel retailer. To be sure, Zara's clothing designs are on the cutting edge. But so are the company's operations. In a mere 15 days, the firm can design, produce, deliver, and display a new piece of clothing in its stores.

Sources: Inditex annual reports 2007 and 2008; D. Kiley, "Is Zara All That?" *BusinessWeek*, December 28, 2004; K. Ferdows, M. Lewis, and J. A. D. Machuca, "Rapid-fire Fulfillment," *Harvard Business Review,* November 2004; "Zara: A Spanish Success Story," *CNN.com,* June 15, 2001, http://edition.cnn.com/BUSINESS/programs/yourbusiness/stories 2001/ zara.

Fred Guerdin/Reporters/Redux Pictures

Just one year after a division of Baxter Healthcare Corporation implemented a JIT system and other quality initiatives, the division's defects fell by approximately one-third, and the number of days of inventory on hand fell by approximately two-thirds.

A **just-in-time (JIT) system** is an inventory management and control system that ensures the timely delivery of a product or service and related inputs. The objective is to produce the product or service only as needed with only the necessary materials, equipment, and employee time that will add value to the product or service.

The benefits of implementing JIT include:

- Reducing inventory levels to only the parts or supplies that are needed at the time and, thus, lowering the holding or carrying cost of inventory
- Improving productivity and quality by reducing labor and equipment time
- Increasing customer satisfaction by decreasing the time required to make and deliver the product or service

A number of companies that have implemented JIT have found great success. An excellent example is the Converters/Customer Sterile Business Group of Baxter Healthcare Corporation, a producer of such single-use supplies as disposable drapes and gowns for health care employees and facilities. Just one year after the division implemented a JIT system and other quality initiatives, defects fell by 32 percent and the number of days of inventory on hand fell by 66 percent. An unanticipated benefit that came from involving employees in the design and implementation of the system was a 37 percent decrease in employee turnover.

For the components to arrive just as they are needed and for the product or service to arrive as close to the time the customer needs it as possible, a high degree of integration of the components and their supply relative to the finished product or service is required. When there is a high level of repetitiveness and standardization of the production of a service or product and its related components, a JIT system tends to work well.[24] However, a JIT system is not as useful to organizations that make customized, one-of-a-kind products or services.

The **Gantt chart** is named after Henry Gantt, their inventor, who was a pioneer of the scientific management era. A Gantt chart is a nonmathematical graphical representation of a project. They are useful for determining what specific activities should be included to complete a project on time. Gantt charts are especially important because they help managers monitor progress and are most often used for projects that have a manageable number of activities (approximately 25 or fewer). This technique helps ensure that projects related to production and the production process itself delivers the designed quality and quantity to the customer at the targeted time. Projects that are much larger often require a more sophisticated technique known as PERT/CPM, which we discuss next.

The **program evaluation and review technique (PERT)** and the **critical path method (CPM)** are both useful tools for scheduling, monitoring, and controlling the timing of large, complex projects such as the expansion of a freeway system or bridge construction. Due to the complexity of such projects, a number of PERT/CPM software packages have been developed. Although Gantt charts and PERT/CPM are similar in that they both require a complete list of the

just-in-time (JIT) system
an inventory management and control system whose objective is to reduce waste throughout the production and delivery of a product or service; in manufacturing, also known as lean production or value-added manufacturing

Gantt chart
a nonmathematical graphical representation of a project; used by managers to help monitor a project's progress

PERT/CPM
program evaluation and review technique (PERT)/critical path method (CPM) is a technique for scheduling and controlling large, complex projects

specific activities involved and time estimates for each, PERT/CPM goes one step further in terms of controlling the timing. Specifically, the PERT/CPM technique requires the project manager to determine which activities must precede others and which must follow. These relationships help to determine the critical path through the network of activities. This path represents the *longest* time path for the project and the activities on the path that will delay the entire project if any one of them is delayed. For example, laying the foundation for a house would be considered a critical activity because it precedes a number of other activities, such as framing the house. Delays in laying the foundation then delay the construction of the entire house.

PERT/CPM software can also help operation managers reschedule the noncritical activities of a project, or those that can be delayed without causing the entire project to fall behind schedule. The software can even help the process get back on schedule. For example, laying the foundation for a house is a critical activity, but installing the cabinets is not. However, even though the cabinets typically come later in the building sequence, rather than having carpenters sit idle while waiting for the foundation to be poured, an operations manager might have them proceed with building the cabinets. This would both use otherwise idle workers and allow the cabinets to be installed as soon as the house is framed and wallboard installed.

Cost Reduction and Productivity

As we discussed earlier, making products of the appropriate quality, quantity, and timing can all contribute to lower costs. Nonetheless, there are additional issues that operations managers need to understand and deal with. Productivity and cost reductions are two of the most important of these issues.[25] We group them together here because one often leads to the other.

Managers are focusing on productivity and reducing costs to a greater extent, partly as a result of the greater levels of competition in the world today. The globalization of business is giving customers more choices and information about those choices. This creates less pricing power for companies. As a consequence, they have to increase their productivity and reduce their costs in order to maintain their profit margins. The simple formula for productivity is:

$$\text{Productivity} = \text{Output/Input}$$

productivity
measurement of how well an organization uses its inputs in producing its outputs

Thus, **productivity** measures how well an organization is using its resources (inputs) to produce goods and services (outputs). A useful productivity measure for a restaurant would be *the number of meals served per server*. For an automobile assembly plant, a useful productivity measure would be *the number of labor hours used to produce a car*. Productivity measures such as these can be used for two main comparative purposes. First, a firm can use the measures to compare itself with similar firms, and second, a firm can track productivity measures over time to identify trends. Most operations managers need to be concerned with both the productivity of people and the firm's assets.

Labor productivity applies to both service and manufacturing firms. If we take the case of two manufacturing firms (Toyota and GM), one of the most important measures of productivity is the labor hours required to build one complete vehicle. In 2003, GM's North American operations' labor hours per vehicle (HPV) built was 35.2. Over the next four years, GM managers worked hard to improve on that, and by the beginning of 2008, had reduced its HPV to 32.29. In 2003, Toyota's North American operations had an HPV of 30.01. Over the next four years, Toyota's managers in North America also worked to improve their productivity; however, by the beginning of 2008, their operations' HPV had remained virtually unchanged at 30.37. Improvement in productivity helped GM but its overall costs and cost increases could not be overcome with productivity improvement. With the severe decline in auto sales that came with the 2008-2009 recession, the US government ended up bailing GM out and through a capital infusion owning 70 percent of the company. In the case of services, Exhibit 13.4 provides a comparison of productivity in the postal and telecommunication industries for France, Germany, Netherlands, Canada, and the United States.[26]

work standard
the amount of time it takes a trained employee to complete a specific activity or process

Managers who are responsible for determining what a firm's productivity measures are and how improvements in them can be made often have to figure out how to measure the productivity of an employee or a group of employees. One of the common methods is via a work standard. A **work standard** is the amount of time it should take for a trained employee to complete a specific activity or process. Developing work standards involves using work measurement techniques. Two popular work measurement techniques are time and motion studies[27] and work sampling.

	Pieces of Mail Delivered per Person Employed	Number of Calls Made per Person Employed
France	37.5	17.4
Germany	21.1	19.1
Netherlands	51.5	22.3
Canada	92.4	122.6
United States	100.0	100.0

EXHIBIT 13.4

Service Productivity Differences by Country

For time and motion studies, the first step is to review each activity in detail so that unnecessary steps are eliminated. The motto "work smart, not hard" applies here. Only after each process has been carefully reviewed should standard times be developed. Stopwatches are often used to ensure accuracy. In the past, many companies used outside employees to watch and time the employees actually doing the work. More recently, teams of coworkers have begun timing their own work groups. This has been the case for the Chrysler Jeep Wrangler plant. At the plant, team members look for the safest, most efficient and effective way to complete each process at a sustainable pace while timing each other with stopwatches. This involvement has led to a greater ownership by worker for productivity and this was one of the means by which the plant increased its productivity by 38 percent in just one year and reached an HPV assembly rate of 13.57.

Work sampling is also a popular way of determining time standards, or, more commonly, the percentage of time spent on each activity during a working day or shift. This method is not as accurate as time and motion studies for setting standards for repetitive, well-defined jobs, but it works well with nonrepetitive jobs. It involves sampling the activities performed by an employee or a group of employees at random times throughout a work shift. The assumption is that the percentage of time the specific activities were observed during the observation period is the same as the percentage of time actually spent on the activity. The key to an effective work sampling study is to create an observation sheet that lists all the possible activities an employee might perform. A trained observer then marks each activity observed during predetermined random times.

To determine the percentage of time spent on a particular activity, the total number of occurrences for each activity is divided by the total number of occurrences for all activities. For example, if a nurse is observed preparing medications 10 times out of 100 observations, then the percentage of time spent on this activity would be 10 percent (10/100). Work sampling can help identify areas that need improvement. If, for example, patients complained that they rarely saw their nurses, then work sampling could help determine the percentage of time spent directly with a patient. If this time were below the goal set, then changes in processes and/or staffing levels would likely be needed. These changes, in turn, would improve the quality of patient care. As this illustrates, productivity and quality often are directly related.

Similar principles apply to asset productivity, or utilization. It is helpful to look at asset productivity separately because of the relationships that exist between asset utilization, economies of scale, and unit costs. Economies of scale occur when the per unit cost of production falls as a firm's output increases. This is commonly achieved when a company has certain fixed costs that really don't change regardless of how many units of services or products it produces. The per unit allocation of these fixed costs and, therefore, the total cost per unit go down as more units are produced. For example, a very high proportion of the costs for a hotel are fixed. Whether 10 percent or 100 percent of the rooms are occupied, the furniture, construction, heating, tax, administrative, and other costs do not change very much. Therefore, as occupancy goes up, the allocated unit cost per occupied room comes down.

The nature of the production process can directly affect a firm's economies of scale. Simplified, there are four major classifications of production processes. *Continuous flow production* is characterized by inputs that are transformed into outputs in an uninterrupted stream. This type of process is common in chemical plants, refineries, integrated steel mills, and the like. Typically, the setup costs of these operations are high as are the costs of changeovers (changes in the product being produced). *Assembly line processes* are characterized by a series of workstations at which individual steps in the assembly of a product are carried out by workers or machines as the product is moved along. Cars, computers, and cameras are all examples of products typically made through assembly line processes. *Small batch processes* are used to produce exactly that—small batches of products or services. For example, many university classes are small batch processes. A group of students (for example, 30) attends a particular class for a predetermined amount of time, and inputs are added (hopefully, knowledge). By assembling a four-year string of these small batch processes, a student emerges at the end with a degree and, hopefully, possesses the characteristics for which "customers" (employers) are looking. Finally, *job shops* are characterized by production processes that focus on the creation of small groups of products (as small as one) with features that are typically different from one job to the next. For example, most of the high-end tailors on Savile Row in London would be considered job shops. These tailors specialize in making "bespoke" suits—that is, expensive, often one-of-a-kind suits for individual customers.

As Exhibit 13.5 illustrates, typically there is a tradeoff between the flexibility, or customization, offered by each of the four basic production types and its ability to capture economies of scale and thereby reduce the unit cost as greater units are produced.

However, it is important to understand that economies of scale are not the only means of capturing lower costs through higher volumes. There are also *learning effects*. Learning effects occur when the firm gains more experience at making a product and develops greater insight about how to do the task more efficiently. This, in turn, increases productivity and lowers unit costs. For example, consider the bespoke suit tailor on Savile Row: there are essentially very few economies of scale to be captured in this business. Just because a shop makes more suits than another does not mean that its production costs will be lower. For example, most shops take 50 to 70 different measurements of one customer in order to tailor the suit to that particular customer. The time and associated cost of taking these measurements is the same for one suit as it is for 100 suits, except for the learning effects for the tailor. That is, when a tailor is new on the job, it might take him or her an hour to perform the measurements. After having done this on 100 different clients, the learning effect might enable the tailor to perform those same measurements in 30 minutes instead of an hour.

**flexible manufacturing
system (FMS)**
automation of a production line by
controlling and guiding all
machinery by computer

Many operations managers would like to capture *both* the economies of scale associated with continuous flow and assembly line production systems and the flexibility and customization benefits of small batch and job shop systems. This pursuit has led to an effort to develop a **flexible manufacturing system (FMS)**. A flexible manufacturing system has a higher degree of ability to adjust to both anticipated and unanticipated changes. This flexibility generally falls into one of two categories: station flexibility and routing flexibility. Station flexibility is either the ability to change the order of the firm's operations or the ability of a given worker or machine at a particular point in the production process to adjust quickly so as to produce different products.

Routing flexibility is the ability to use different people or multiple machines to perform the same operation on a part, as well as the overall production system's ability to absorb large-scale changes, such as changes in volume, capacity, or capabilities. Typically, computers and other automation tools centrally control the whole FMS.

EXHIBIT 13.5

**Production Types
and Trade Offs**

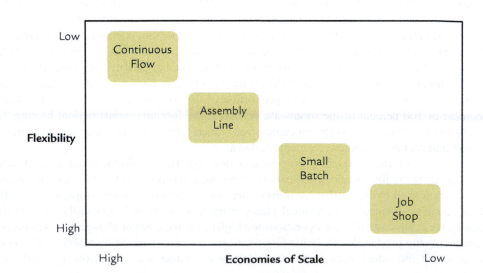

Automotive companies have been big proponents of flexible manufacturing systems, especially after seeing the productivity and revenue benefits achieved by Toyota—arguably the pioneer in this area. The cost of setting up an assembly plant for producing a car is staggering, typically exceeding $500 million and often approaching $1 billion. Moreover, the construction of such a plant often takes two to three years. Despite managers' best efforts to estimate the demand for a product produced as a result of such a massive investment, many unpredictable factors—from fuel prices to regulations—can influence actual demand. Therefore, being able to build more than one type of vehicle at a given plant and easily and quickly shift to making particular models based on changes in demand can significantly improve a company's costs and revenues.

The "A Manager's Challenge" feature describes Chrysler's attempt to implement a flexible manufacturing system and the benefits the company hopes to capture as a result. Hyundai/Kia has focused much of its FMS on robots that can change the parts they handle as different vehicle types come down the assembly line. While changing the movements of a robot are fairly easily accomplished through incorporating multiple software programs, the robot's ability to "grab" parts is highly dependent on the configuration of its "gripper" (the equivalent of human hands at the end of the arm). Having to change out the grippers with each model, especially when multiple models can be coming down the same assembly line, is costly. Hyundai solved this problem by creating grippers that can literally transform themselves by elongating the gripping ends and five other proprietary transformations that allow the same robot to grab the side panel or door panel of very different shapes and weights without any costly downtime to change tools.[28]

Computer-aided design (CAD) and **computer-aided engineering (CAE)** are computerized processes for designing new products, making modifications to existing products, and testing prototypes or models of products that can operate separately from a flexible manufacturing system or can be an important part of its design and ongoing operations. In either case, they represent important technologies for reducing costs in large part because they replace the manual and time-consuming process of drafting. The main goals of these systems are to improve the quality of the designs and to reduce the time required to produce the designs. These two objectives, in turn, reduce the costs involved in manufacturing a product because potential problems can be detected at the design stage. CAD and CAE systems also allow designs to be stored and transferred so they can be revised more easily.

computer-aided design (CAD)/computer-aided engineering (CAE) computerized systems used to design new products, make modifications to existing ones, and test prototypes

A more sophisticated form of CAD/CAE is called rapid prototyping, which uses a technique known as stereolithography to build three-dimensional models out of plastic. United Technology was able to use this technology to build a one-sixth model of its Comanche helicopter used for radar testing. The use of CAD, CAE, and stereolithography provided the information needed for designers to work quickly to perfect the helicopter's precise design specifications.

Once a product is designed via a computer, the next logical step is to allow the computer to manufacture it. **Computer-aided manufacturing (CAM)** refers to the use of computers to direct manufacturing processes. The CAM system can be programmed to guide equipment to perform various manufacturing processes, such as drilling a hole of a specified size, pouring a liquid mixture into a mold, and cutting materials at a certain speed. CAM is most beneficial when the manufacturing process is complex and when frequent design changes are made. The use of a combined CAD/CAE/CAM system can help eliminate duplication between a company's design and manufacturing groups, which not only saves time and money but also improves internal communication among employees within the organization.

computer-aided manufacturing (CAM) computerized systems used to direct manufacturing processes

Designing for manufacturing (DFM) refers to the process of designing products to both maximize their functionality for customers and to maximize their ease of production and minimize their associated costs. Designing for manufacturing often means reducing the number of parts required in a product. This often requires that a firm's various groups, such as its design or research and development groups, closely coordinate with, for example, its engineering and operations groups. For example, McDonnell Douglas Corporation has used DFM in its military and commercial divisions. Specifically, the firm captured a significant amount of savings from its F-18 fighter jet program. On one specific aspect of the program, managers reduced the number of parts by 84 percent, lowered costs by 73 percent, reduced the jet's weight by 11 percent, and increased assembly speed by 89 percent. In converting the F/A-18 C/D into F/A-18 E/F, managers reduced parts from 1,744 to 1,048. In the commercial division, by designing the MD-11 cargo liner with customer specifications and manufacturing needs in mind, managers achieved cost savings per aircraft of $86,000. In just changing and simplifying one bulkhead, managers saved $4,000 per plane. In

designing for manufacturing (DFM) designing products for ease of manufacturing so that quality is built into the design process

A MANAGER'S CHALLENGE

TECHNOLOGY

Gaining Flexibility at Chrysler

Chrysler's 2007 investment in flexible manufacturing systems has paid off in more ways than one for its 1,219 workers. That year, the automaker invested over $500 million in its Sterling Heights, Michigan, assembly plant in order to expand the company's flexible manufacturing strategy and enable the plant to produce the all-new 2008 Chrysler Sebring Convertible and the 2008 Dodge Avenger sedan alongside the Chrysler Sebring sedan.

The investment included a number of technological changes. For example, $278 million of the $500 million Chrysler invested in the FMS was used to overhaul the plant's body and paint shop and assembly areas. This included new tooling and about 620 new welding and material handling robots. Now in the body shop, only the robots' end effectors, or "hands," need to be changed in order to build a different car model. This change can now be done within the time it takes to cycle from one vehicle to the next.

"The assembly operation now has the capability to build multiple upper bodies and multiple vehicle families or architectures, which gives us the flexibility to adsd new models

© Jim West/Alamy

By investing more than $500 million in its Sterling Heights, Michigan, plant, Chrysler has been able to produce multiple vehicles faster and at a lower cost. Managers at the plant can quickly shift the production volumes of different vehicles to respond to changes in the demand for them. To further improve the plant's flexibility, employees were trained extensively and encouraged to become involved in all production and design facets.

or 'cross-load' models from other plants in order to better meet the dynamics of the market," said Fred Goedtel, the vice president of Chrysler's Small/Premium/Family Vehicle Assembly division. "In addition, the Sterling Stamping Plant can weld and assemble more than one product on the same line."

The investment allows the plant to produce a higher-quality product faster, and for a lower cost. It also allows managers to efficiently build a lower volume of certain vehicles demanded by niche market segments. Managers can also quickly shift production volumes between different models within a single plant or among multiple plants to match changes in customer demand.

In addition to technology, a new workplace organizational model was implemented to increase the flexibility of the plant's workforce. Employees were trained extensively and encouraged to become involved in all facets in the design and processing of the work stations. "We are seeing a great deal of success at the Sterling Heights facility due to the commitment of our plant employees," said Frank Ewasyshyn, Chrysler's executive vice president of manufacturing. "Their willingness to support and foster a small-team workplace model has delivered a successful launch."

The impact of the 2008-2009 recession took down not only GM but Chrysler as well. Chrysler fell into bankruptcy and the U.S. taxpayer had to bail out the company with a large capital infusion. This was followed by an investment by Fiat. However, the Sterling Heights plant was one of six left in bankruptcy and, in 2010, was scheduled to close. However, recognizing the value of the FMS investment, Fiat applied to purchase the plant, and if approved, Fiat would purchase the plant for $20 million.

Sources: Tom Krisher, "Chrysler Agrees to Buy Sterling Heights Plant for $20M," *Crain's Detroit Business,* February 19, 2010, http://www.crainsdetroit.com; Company Web site, "Two Detroit-area Chrysler Group Plants to Receive Half-billion Dollars in Upgrades," press release, www.daimlerchrysler.com/dccom/0-5-7153-1-477538-1-0-0-0-0-0-3882-7145-0-0-0-0-0-0-1.html, accessed March 30, 2007; "Flexible Manufacturing Retool Delivers New Convertible," *Just-Auto.com,* March 30, 2007, http://www.just-auto.com/article.aspx?id=90905; "Chrysler Group's Sterling Heights Assembly Plant Produces All-new 2008 Chrysler Sebring Convertible," *The Auto Channel.com,* March 30, 2007, http://db.theautochannel.com/news/2007/03/30/041715.html.

	Previous Instrument Panel	DFM Instrument Panel
Part count	74 pieces	9 pieces
Fabrication time	305 hours	20 hours
Assembly time	149 hours	8 hours
Installation time	153 hours	153 hours
Total time	697 hours	181 hours
Weight	3.00 kilograms	2.74 kilograms
Cost	74% reduction	

EXHIBIT 13.6

Instrument Panel Improvements Achieved via DFM

general the part count reduction done by McDonnell Douglas has been in the range from 36 percent to 96 percent on several of its aircraft component assemblies. Based on this, for its Longbow prototype helicopters, executives created an Integrated Product Development (IPD) team to conduct the redesign. The IPD team consisted of individuals from McDonnell Douglas' engineering, manufacturing, procurement, product support, and quality groups as well as its suppliers and others to work together to develop a product design. Initially, the team applied DFM to a limited number of items within the "crewstation." Specifically, the team focused on the pilot's instrument panel. The preexisting panel consisted of 74 parts, weighed 3 kilograms, required 305 hours to fabricate, and 149 hours to assemble. Using DFM, Exhibit 13.6 summarizes the results of the team's efforts.[29]

Managing the Supply Chain

The supply chain refers to the coordinated system of resources, information, activities, people, and organizations involved in moving a product or service from raw materials to components and into a finished product or service delivered to the end customer.[30] As a consequence, many of the activities we have already covered in this chapter related to managing the supply chain. We provide a separate discussion of this area of operations management in part because the increasing technical aspects of managing the entire supply chain and the global scope of the chain for a growing number of organizations makes an integrated discussion throughout the chapter just too complex.[31] Also, increasingly managers have to match how they manage their supply chain to the nature of the business strategy and the dynamics and complexity of the market.[32] As the complexity of managing supply chains increased, so has its potential strategic importance.[33]

Consider the complexity of the supply chain and all the coordination involved in making a Dell laptop computer. Exhibit 13.7 provides a list of the key activities, locations, and organizations involved from the time you might call in an order to the time you receive the computer at your home.[34]

Such far-flung and complicated supply chains would not be very efficient without the technological advances in information systems.[35] Operations managers can track component parts throughout the entire chain. The increasing use of *electronic data interchange* (EDI), or the integration and, in many cases, real-time exchange of supply chain information allows supply chain managers at Dell to manage such complicated relationships and processes. Sometimes the integration is so deep that customers like Dell are able to determine that they can meet an up-tick in demand for computers with certain features by instructing their suppliers to use some spare capacity in one of the supplier's plants. In other words, Dell is able to see its suppliers' currently used and spare capacity almost as easily as it can its own.

The emergence of the Internet and standard protocols is not only increasing the ease of these exchanges but lowering the costs as well.[36] Prior to the Internet, companies had to invest in and commit to expensive and restrictive proprietary software systems. Web-based systems allow these interchanges to be put into practice in short order and with little expense. One consequence of this is that small companies that previously would not have had the size or global presence to link into supply chains like Dell's can now become partners much quicker if they are able to demonstrate superior quality, reliability, and cost.

These factors create a dynamic tension between suppliers and customers.[37] On the one hand, the higher integration tends to create incentives for customers such as Dell to take a more "partnership"

EXHIBIT 13.7

Dell's Supply Chain

Activity or Component	Organization(s)	Location
Phone order	Dell	25 centers around the world, including the United States, the Philippines, and India
Assembly	Dell	Limerick, Ireland; Xiamen, China; Eldorado do Sul, Brazil; Nashville, Tenn.; Austin, Tex.; Penang, Malaysia
Notebook design	Dell (ODM) Original Design Manufacturer	United States, Taiwan
Microprocessor	Intel	Philippines, Costa Rica, Malaysia, China
Memory	Samsung	Korea
	Nanya	Taiwan
	Infineon	Germany
	Elpida	Japan
Graphics card	MSI	Taiwan
	Foxconn	China
Cooling fan	CCI	Taiwan
	Auras	Taiwan
Motherboard	Samsung	Korea
	Quanta	Taiwanese (China factory)
	Compal	Taiwan
	Wistron	Taiwan
Keyboard	Alps	Japanese (China factory)
	Sunrex	Taiwanese (China factory)
	Darfon	Taiwanese (China factory)
LCD display	Samsung	Korea
	LG Philips	Korea
	Toshiba	Japan
	Chi Mei Optoelectronics	Taiwan
	Hannstar Display	Taiwan
	AU Optronics	Taiwan
Wireless card	Agere	United States (China factory)
	Arrow	United States (Malaysia factory)
	Askey	Taiwan
	Gemtek	Taiwan
	USI	China
Modem	Asustek	Taiwanese (factory in China)
	Liteon	Taiwanese (China factory)
	Foxconn	China
Battery	Motorola	United States (Malaysia factory)
	SDI	Korea
	Simplo	Taiwan

EXHIBIT 13.7

(Continued)

Activity or Component	Organization(s)	Location
Hard drive	Segate	United States (Singapore factory)
	Hitachi	Japanese (Thailand factory)
	Fujitsu	Japanese (Thailand factory)
	Toshiba	Japanese (Philippines factory)
CD/DVD drive	Samsung	Korean (Indonesia or Philippines factories)
	NEC	Japanese (China or Malaysia factory)
	Teac	Japanese (Indonesia, China, or Malaysia factory)
Power adapter	Delta	Thailand
	Liteon	Taiwan
	Samsung	Korea
	Mobility	United States (China factory)
Power cord	Volex	United Kingdom (China, Malaysia, or India factory)
Memory stick	M-System	Israel
	Smart Modular	United States (Malaysia factory)

approach with its suppliers. In other words, the tighter Dell is integrated with its suppliers and the more it is dependent on them, the more its operations managers need to work closely with suppliers and the more they tend to need to take a longer-term perspective to the relationship and build trust between the partners.[38] On the other hand, the fact that Web-based technologies lower the entry barriers for new suppliers and lower the switching costs to new suppliers for Dell, the more Dell managers want to not get too wedded to their current suppliers and want to leave themselves open to new suppliers. In addition, there is always the threat that suppliers of core components can decide to put their own supply chain together and become a competitor to their former customer. BenQ of Taiwan did just that to Siemens in its mobile phone business and eventually bought the business in 2005.[39] Thus, there is a dynamic tension between taking a transactional and adversarial orientation on the one hand and a partnership orientation on the other.[40] Exhibit 13.8 provides a comparison of the two basic orientations along a number of different dimensions.

Today, the ever-increasing technical complexity of standard consumer goods, combined with the ever increasing size and depth of the global market has meant that the link between consumer and vendor is usually only the final link in a long and complex chain or network of exchanges. Although many companies and corporations today operate not just on a national or regional scale but also on a global scale, none are of a size that enables them to control the entire supply chain. Virtually no company controls every link in the chain, from raw material extraction to consumer.

Most of the exchanges in the supply chain are made between different companies. All of them generally seek to maximize their revenues within their areas of expertise. However, most have little knowledge or interest in the remaining players in the supply chain, except those to which they are directly linked. If not managed carefully, the supply chain becomes a chain of competitors without an overall aim. This can result in a less-attractive final product being offered to the consumer due to a combination of increased costs and decreased service levels. Consumer sales eventually decrease, and, as a result, all the links (companies) in the supply chain lose revenue.

EXHIBIT 13.8

Supplier Relationships

Source: Adapted from Richard J. Schonberger and Edward M. Knod Jr., *Operations Management*, 5th ed. (Homewood: Richard D. Irwin, 1994), 276. Reproduced with permission of The McGraw-Hill Companies.

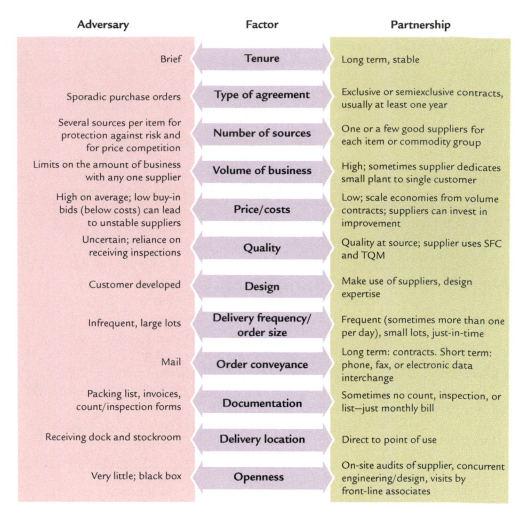

Adversary	Factor	Partnership
Brief	Tenure	Long term, stable
Sporadic purchase orders	Type of agreement	Exclusive or semiexclusive contracts, usually at least one year
Several sources per item for protection against risk and for price competition	Number of sources	One or a few good suppliers for each item or commodity group
Limits on the amount of business with any one supplier	Volume of business	High; sometimes supplier dedicates small plant to single customer
High on average; low buy-in bids (below costs) can lead to unstable suppliers	Price/costs	Low; scale economies from volume contracts; suppliers can invest in improvement
Uncertain; reliance on receiving inspections	Quality	Quality at source; supplier uses SFC and TQM
Customer developed	Design	Make use of suppliers, design expertise
Infrequent, large lots	Delivery frequency/order size	Frequent (sometimes more than one per day), small lots, just-in-time
Mail	Order conveyance	Long term: contracts. Short term: phone, fax, or electronic data interchange
Packing list, invoices, count/inspection forms	Documentation	Sometimes no count, inspection, or list—just monthly bill
Receiving dock and stockroom	Delivery location	Direct to point of use
Very little; black box	Openness	On-site audits of supplier, concurrent engineering/design, visits by front-line associates

Getting raw materials in and transformed into finished products and services for customers has long been the goal of operations managers. Increasingly, though, operations managers have begun focusing on the "reverse supply chain." The reverse supply chain relates to the activities needed to retrieve a used product from a customer and either reuse it or dispose of it. Some of these activities are being forced on to companies due to legislation and regulation. For example, since 2003, tire companies in Europe are required to arrange for the reuse or disposal of one recycled tire for every new tire they sell. As a result, reverse supply chain managers have to focus on at least five key activities: (1) acquiring the used products, (2) managing the reverse logistics to get the products to the company, (3) inspecting the product, (4) determining the disposition (destruction or reuse), and (5) distributing and selling refurbished products.[41]

Managerial Challenges from the Front Line

The Rest of the Story

Michelle Jackson relates that BNSF's operations managers undertook several actions to add capacity and increase service quality. To add capacity, they increased the length of trains and added trains. To add new trains, they needed to not only buy the equipment (locomotives and cars) but also hire and train the needed personnel.

To cope with the larger number of trains in the system, operations managers had to add rail capacity. Rather than building new lines, BNSF operations managers instead chose to increase rail capacity by "double" and in some places "triple tracking" the company's Transcon line. The Transcon line is BNSF's main track route from Southern California to Chicago. Double and triple tracking involves laying down a second or third track next to the main one to accommodate additional volume.

Although this helps increase capacity, it can create added congestion at BNSF's terminals and other transshipment points. As a result, BNSF's operations managers determined that they would also need to add more parking spaces at terminals for railcars that were being switched from one train to another as well as more cranes to lift the containers and change them from one train and track to another. Another initiative involved diverting some of the traffic to less-used ports such as those in Portland, Oregon, and Tacoma, Washington. Yet another initiative involved using fuel trucks to gas up BNSF's locomotives directly at the ports. As a result, the trains don't have to travel to nearby rail yards to fill up before leaving for their destinations.

The downturn in the economy in 2008-2009, was a double-edge sword. On one hand, with consumer spending down, manufacturers weren't producing as many goods as before, steam ship lines weren't moving as many containers, and rail lines weren't transporting as much freight. This, of course, hurt BNSF's revenues and profits. On the other hand, it diminished the capacity and congestion problems that came out of the upturn after the 2000-2001 recession. As a consequence, customers began seeing better train service and performance due to the network's fluidity. With the economy, volume started to pick up in 2010, and many of the actions previously undertaken helped improve service and train efficiencies and would yield further benefits with continued projected improvement in the economy and volume for BNSF.

Summary

- Operations management is a specialized field of management that focuses on efficiently converting resources into products and services and getting them to consumers on time. It is strategically important because it can directly affect both the costs and revenues and, therefore, the margins of a company.

- By taking steps to ensure that customers receive the quality and quantity of products or services when they want them, operations managers can improve the repeat business from customers and even the firm's revenues through positive word of mouth.

- Total quality management (TQM) is a general philosophy of enhancing quality at its source. Specific tools for enabling the desired benefits of this philosophy include statistical process control (SPC), continuous improvement (*kaizen*), and Six Sigma. SPC focuses on setting tolerances around targets, tracking performance, and eliminating unacceptable deviations. Continuous improvement techniques focus not just on hitting targets and eliminating deviations but also on increasing performance and extending targets. Six Sigma is a systematic approach ensuring that all of the firm's activities contribute to meeting customers' specifications with a 99.99966 percent reliability.

- Capacity planning, materials requirement planning (MRP), the economic order quantity (EOQ), and ABC analysis are tools and techniques that help operations managers ensure that the right quantity of products and services are available for customers. Capacity planning involves determining how much a firm should be able to produce of a product or service. MRP focuses on ensuring that the required resources to make the product or service are available. EOQ is a technique for determining the most efficient and effective quantity of an input to order. Finally, ABC is a technique for ensuring that operations managers focus their time on the inputs that have the highest impact on the company's production efforts and customer satisfaction.

- Just-in-time (JIT), Gantt charts, PERT (the program evaluation and review technique), and CPM (the critical path method) are common techniques for ensuring the timely delivery of products and projects associated with the production of products. JIT focuses on the management of inventory for the timely delivery of a product or service and related inputs. Gantt charts are used to lay out activities and their timing in order to meet deadlines. PERT and CPM are techniques that not only lay out the sequencing and timing of activities but also specify which activities are critical and could cause delays.

- Operations managers need to look for ways to capture economies of scale and learning effects as well as flexibility and the ability to customize products. Developing productivity measures involves determining work standards. Capturing both cost reductions and customization advantages likely will require managers to understand flexible manufacturing, CAD, CAE, and CAM tools, as well as DFM approaches.
- Because of the growing complexity and globalization of supply chains, managers in this area have to focus on coordinating resources, information, activities, people, and organizations involved in moving a product or service from raw materials to a finished product or service delivered to the end customer.

Key Terms

ABC analysis   369

capacity planning   366

computer-aided design (CAD)   375

computer-aided engineering (CAE)   375

computer-aided manufacturing (CAM)   375

continuous process improvement   364

critical path method (CPM)   371

design capacity   366

designing for manufacturing (DFM)   375

economic order quantity (EOQ)   368

effective capacity   366

flexible manufacturing system (FMS)   374

Gantt chart   371

just-in-time (JIT) system   371

materials requirement planning (MRP)   368

operations management   361

productivity   372

program evaluation and review technique (PERT)   371

quality   362

statistical process control (SPC)   364

total quality management (TQM)   363

work standard   372

Review Questions

1. What is operations management and why is it strategically important for all firms, regardless of their focus on or mix of products and services?

2. What are the key similarities and differences between SPC (statistical process control) and *kaizen*?

3. What are the two main Six Sigma techniques, and what is each intended to target?

4. What is EOQ and why is it a useful tool for managers in operations?

5. What are the key similarities and differences between Gantt charts and PERT/CPM techniques?

6. What is JIT, and what are its principal benefits?

7. Contrast and compare economies of scale and learning effects.

8. What is DFM, and what are its common benefits?

9. Explain the key functions of effective supply chain management and the two key tensions.

Team Exercise

Charting the End of Semester

Toward the end of each semester, students often find that there is not enough time to get things done that they need to. This is especially true during the fall semester when final exams are approaching and holiday shopping, wrapping, mailing, travel arranging, and other activities need to be done. Devise a Gantt chart listing all the possible activities and target deadlines. Use PERT and CPM concepts to arrange the activities in key sequences and to identify critical paths. If you followed the resulting plan, how different would your academic and personal results compare to what they are now?

S teve Jackson, general manager of Cranston Nissan, slowly sifted through his usual Monday-morning stack of mail. The following letter was one he would not soon forget.

Dear Mr. Jackson:

I am writing this letter so that you will be aware of a nightmare I experienced recently regarding the repair of my 300ZX in your body shop and subsequently in your service department. I will detail the events in chronological order.

August 28

I dropped the car off for repair of rust damage in the following areas:

Roof—along the top of the windshield area
Left rocker panel—under driver's door
Left quarter panel—near end of bumper
Rear body panel—under license plate

I was told it would take three or four days.

September 1

I called to inquire about the status of the car, since this was the fifth day the car was in the shop. I was told that I could pick up the car anytime after 2 P.M. My wife and I arrived at 5 P.M. The car was still not ready. In the meantime, I paid the bill for $443.17 and waited. At 6 P.M. the car was driven up dripping wet (presumably from a wash to make it look good). I got into the car and noticed the courtesy light in the driver's door would not turn off when the door was closed. I asked for help, and Jim Boyd, body shop manager, could not figure out what was wrong. His solution was to remove the bulb and have me return after the Labor Day holiday to have the mechanic look at it. I agreed and began to drive off. However, the voice warning, "Left door is open," repeatedly sounded. Without leaving the premises I returned to Mr. Boyd, advising him to retain the car until it was fixed—there was no way I could drive the car with that repeated recording. Mr. Boyd then suggested I call back the next day (Saturday) to see if the mechanic could find the problem. I must emphasize, I brought the car to the body shop on August 28 in perfect mechanical working condition—the repair work was for body rust. This point will become important as the story unfolds.

September 2

I called Jim Boyd at 10:30 A.M. and was told that the car had not been looked at yet. He promised to call back before the shop closed for the holiday, but he never did. I later learned that he did not call because "there was nothing to report." The car sat in the shop Saturday, Sunday, and Monday.

September 5

I called Jim Boyd to check on the status of the car. It was 4 P.M., and Mr. Boyd told me nothing had been done, but that it should be ready by the next day. At this point it was becoming obvious that my car did not have priority in the service department.

September 6

I called Jim Boyd again (about 4 P.M.) and was told that work had halted on the car because the service department needed authorization and they didn't know how much it would run. At the hint that I would have to pay for this mess I became very upset and demanded that the car be brought immediately to the mechanical condition it was in when it was dropped off on August 28. At this point Ted Simon, service department manager, was summoned, and he assured me that if the problem was caused by some action of the body shop, I would not be financially responsible. I had not driven the car since I dropped it off, and I could not fathom the evidence anyone could produce to prove otherwise.

September 7

Again late in the day, I called Mr. Simon, who said that Larry (in the service department) knew about the problem and switched me over to him. Larry said that they had narrowed it down to a wire that passed several spots where body work was performed. He said the work was very time-consuming and that the car should be ready sometime tomorrow.

September 8

I called Mr. Simon to check on the status of the car once more. He told me that the wiring problem was fixed, but now the speedometer didn't work. The short in the wires was caused by the body work. Larry got on the phone and said I could pick up the car, but they would send the car out to a subcontractor on Monday to repair the speedometer. He said that when the mechanic test-drove the car he noticed the speedometer pinned itself at the top end, and Larry thought that someone must have done something while searching for the other problem. I asked him if there would be charges for this, and he said there would not. My wife and I arrived to pick up the car at 5 P.M. I clarified the next steps with Larry and was again assured that the speedometer would be repaired at no charge to me.

The car was brought to me, and as I walked up to it I noticed that the rubber molding beneath the driver's door was hanging down. I asked for some help, and Mr. Simon came out to look at it. He said it must have been left that way after the search process for the bad wire. He took the car back into the shop to screw it on. When it finally came out again, he said that he would replace the molding because it was actually damaged.

When I arrived home, I discovered that the anti-theft light on the dash would not stop blinking when the doors were closed. Attempting to activate the security system did not help. The only way I could get the light to stop flashing was to remove the fuse. In other words, now my security system was damaged. Needless to say, I was very upset.

September 11
On Sunday evening I dropped off the car and left a note with my keys in the "early bird" slot. The note listed the two items that needed to be done from the agreement of last Friday—the molding and the speedometer. In addition, I mentioned the security system problem and suggested that "somebody must have forgotten to hook something back up while looking for the wire problem." On Monday I received a call from someone in the service department (I think his name was John), who said that the problem in the security system was in two places— the hatchback lock and "some wires in the driver's door." The lock would cost me $76, and the cost of the rest was unknown. The verbal estimate was for a total of $110. I asked him why he did not consider this problem a derivative of the other problems. He said that the body shop and the mechanic who worked on the wire problem said they could see no way that they could have caused this to happen.

I told the fellow on the phone to forget fixing the security system because I was not going to pay for it. At this point I just wanted the car back home, thinking I could address the problem later with someone such as yourself. I told him to have the speedometer fixed and again asked about charges for it. I was assured there would be none.

September 13
The service department called to say I could pick up the car anytime before 8 P.M. He also said that the molding had to be ordered because it was not in stock. The need for the part was known on September 8, and NOW the part must be ordered. This will cause me another trip to the shop.

When I went to the service department to pick up the car, I was presented a bill for $126. I asked what the bill was for, and I was shown an itemized list that included speedometer repair and searching for the security problem. I said my understanding was that there would be no charge. Somebody at the service desk was apprised of the problem and released the car to me with the understanding that the service manager would review the situation the next day.

My car was brought around to me by the same person who brought it to me September 8. As I got into the driver's seat, I noticed there was no rear view mirror—it was lying in the passenger's seat, broken off from its mounting. I was too shocked to even get mad. I got out of the car and asked how something like this could happen without anyone noticing. Jim Boyd said someone probably did not want to own up to it. He requisitioned a part and repaired the mirror mounting.

Mr. Jackson, I realize this is a long letter, but I have been so frustrated and upset over the past three weeks that I had to be sure that you understood the basis for that frustration. I am hoping you can look into this matter and let me know what you think.

Sincerely,

Sam Monahan
555 South Main, Turnerville

Questions

Answer the following questions from the perspective of TQM.
1. Categorize the quality problems in this case.
2. What are the probable causes of so many mishaps?
3. What specific actions should Jackson take immediately? What should some of his longer-term goals be?

Source: Lee J. Krajewski and Larry P. Ritzman, *Operations Management*, 5th ed. (Boston: Addison Wesley Longman, 1999), 241–242. © Addison Wesley Longman. Reprinted by permission of Addison Wesley Longman.

References

1. L. P. Casalino, "What Does It Cost Physician Practices to Interact with Health Insurance Plans?" *Health Affairs* 28, no. 4, May 14, 2009.
2. C. K. Swank, "The Lean Service Machine," *Harvard Business Review*, October 2003.
3. A. Hill and T. Hill, "Operations Management: Realizing Its Strategic Role." S. Dopson, M. Earl, and P. Snow, eds. *Mapping the Management Journey: Practice, Theory and Context*. (Oxford, UK : Oxford University Press, 2008), 271–288.
4. Organization Web site, http://www.theacsi.org/index.php ?option=com_content&task=view&id=194&Itemid=204; accessed June 2, 2010.
5. B. Mitra and P. N. Golder, "Quality Is in the Eye of the Beholder," *Harvard Business Review*, April 2007.
6. S. L. Ahire, R. Landeros, and D. Y. Golhar, "Total Quality Management: A Literature Review and an Agenda for Future Research," *Production and Operations Management* 4, no. 3 (2009): 277–306.

7. X. Zu, T. L. Robbins, and L. D. Fredendall, "Mapping the Critical Links Between Organizational Culture and TQM/Six Sigma Practices," *International Journal of Production Economics* 123 (2010): 86–106.

8. S. A. Black and L. J. Porter, "Identification of the Critical Factors of TQM," *Decision Sciences* 27 (2007): 1–21.

9. "Correct Packaging Weights Puts Give Away on Ice." *Packaging Digest* 46, no. 7 (2009): 40–42.

10. M. Hammer, "The Process Audit," *Harvard Business Review,* April 2007.

11. R. G. Schroeder, K. Linderman, C. Liedetke, and A. S. Choo, "Six Sigma: Definition and Underlying Theory," *Journal of Operations Management* 26 (2008): 536–554; M. J. Harry and R. Schroeder, *Six Sigma: The Breakthrough Management Strategy Revolutionizing the World's Top Corporations* (New York: Currency, 2000).

12. Six Sigma Web site, "What Is Six Sigma?" www.isixsigma .com/sixsigma/six_sigma.asp, accessed April 1, 2007.

13. A. Chakrabarty and K. C. Tan, "The Current State of Six Sigma Application in Services," *Managing Service Quality* 17 (2007): 194–208; M. L. George, *Lean Six Sigma for Services* (New York: McGraw-Hill, 2003).

14. J. Hassett, "What Every Lawyer Now Needs to Know About Project Management," *Of Counsel* 29, no.6 (2010): 5–11.

15. M. Hamstra, "Six Sigma Drove Cost Savings at Supervalu." *Supermarket News* 58, no. 4, (2010): 71.

16. Organization Web site, http://www.asq.org/edu/kkid/ highlights.html, accessed April 5, 2007.

17. S. C. Aggarwal, "MRP, JIT, OPT, FMS?" *Harvard Business Review,* September–October 1985.

18. Z. Degraeve and F. Roodhooft, "A Smarter Way to Buy," *Harvard Business Review,* June 2001.

19. J. F. Kros, M. Falasca, and S. S. Nadler, "Impact of Just-in-time Inventory Systems on OEM Suppliers," *Industrial Management and Data Systems* 106, no. 2 (2006): 224–241.

20. D. Corsten and T. Gruen, "Stock Outs Cause Walkouts," *Harvard Business Review,* May 2004.

21. R. Crandall and R. Crandall, "Managing Excess Inventories," *Academy of Management Executive* 17, no. 3 (2003): 99–113.

22. P. Engardio and J. McGregor, "Lean and Mean Gets Extreme." *BusinessWeek,* March 23, 2009, 60–62.

23. V. G. Narayanan and A. Raman, "Aligning Incentives in the Supply Chain," *Harvard Business Review* (November 2004).

24. P. H. Zipkin, "Does Manufacturing Need a JIT Revolution?" *Harvard Business Review,* January–February 1991, 4–11.

25. M. J. Benner and M. L. Tushman, "Exploitation, Exploration, and Process Management: The Productivity Dilemma Revisited," *Academy of Management Review* 28, no. 2 (2003): 238–256.

26. B. Vanark, E. Monnikhof, and C. Nannomulder, "Productivity in Services: An International Comparative Perspective," *Canadian Journal of Economics (Revue Canadienne d'Economique)* 32, no. 2 (1999).

27. P. S. Adler, "Time-and-motion Regained," *Harvard Business Review*, January–February 1993.

28. J. Buckley, "Korea's Flexible Carmakers." *Automotive Manufacturing Solutions,* May/June 2009, 18–23.

29. A. Herrea, "Design for Manufacturing and Assembly Application on the Design of the Ah64d Helicopter," paper presented at the 12th International Forum on DFMA, June 1997, Newport, RI.

30. V. A. Mabert and M. A. Venkataramanan, "Special Research Focus on Supply Chain Linkages: Challenges for Design and Management in the 21st Century," *Decision Sciences* 29 (2007): 537–552; S. Chopra and P. Meindl, *Supply Chain Management: Strategy, Planning, and Operation* (Upper Saddle River: Prentice Hall, 2001); S. Croom, P. Romano, and M. Giannakis, "Supply Chain Management: An Analytical Framework for Critical Literature Review," *European Journal of Purchasing and Supply Management* 6 (2000): 67–83.

31. M. C. Cooper, D. M. Lambert, and J. D. Pagh, "Supply Chain Management: More Than a New Name for Logistics," *The International Journal of Logistics Management* 8, no. 1 (1997): 1–14.

32. M. L. Fischer, "What Is the Right Supply Chain for Your Product?" *Harvard Business Review.* March–April 1997.

33. B. Lawson, D. Cousins, R. B. Handfield, and K. J. Petersen, "Strategic Purchasing, Supply Management Practices, and Buyer Performance Improvement: An Empirical Study of UK Manufacturing Organizations," *International Journal of Production Management* 47, no. 10 (2009): 2649–2667; M. T. Frohlich and R. Westbrook, "Arcs of Integration: An International Study of Supply Chain Strategies," *Journal of Operations Management* 19 (2001): 185–200.

34. T. Friedman, *The World Is Flat* (New York: Penguin Group, 2005).

35. S. Davaraj, L Krajewski, and J. C. Wei, "Impact of ebusiness Technologies on Operational Performance: The Role of Production Information Integration in the Supply Chain," *Journal of Operations Management* 25 (2007): 1199–1216; P. J. McGoldrick and P. M. Barton, "High-Tech Ways to Keep Cupboards Full," *Harvard Business Review,* March 2007.

36. R. A. Lancioni, M. F. Smith, and T. A. Oliva, "The Role of the Internet in Supply Chain Management," *Industrial Marketing Management* 29 (2000): 45–56.

37. R. Krishnan, X. Martin, and N. G. Noorderhaven, "When Does Trust Matter to Alliance Performance?" *Academy of Management Journal* 49 (2006): 894–917; J. T. Mentzer, S. Min, and Z. G. Zacharia, "The Nature of Interfirm Partnering in Supply Chain Management," *Journal of Retailing* 76, no. 4 (2000): 549–568; J. H. Bantham, K. G. Celuch, and C. J. Kasouf, "A Perspective of Partnerships Based on Interdependence and Dialectical Theory," *Journal of Business Research* 56 (2003): 265–277.

38. J. Yang, J. Wang, C. W.Y. Wong, and K. H. Lai, "Relational Stability and Alliance Performance in Supply Chain," *Omega* 36 (2008): 600–608; J. K. Liker and T. Y. Choi, "Build Deeper Supplier Relationships," *Harvard Business Review,* December 2004.

39. B. Arrunada and X. H. Vazques, "When Your Contract Manufacturer Becomes Your Competitor," *Harvard Business Review,* September 2006.

40. H. Ma and L. Ojala, "Benchmarking the Collaboration in the Supply Chain," *International Journal of Services and Operations Management* 2, no. 4 (2006): 367–387; M. Bengtsson and S. Kock, "'Coopetition' in Business Networks—To Compete and Cooperate Simultaneously," *Industrial Marketing Management* 29, no. 5 (2000): 411–426; T. M. Simatupang and R. Sridharan, "The Collaboration Index: A Measure for Supply Chain Collaboration," *International Journal of Physical Distribution and Logistics Management* 35, no. 1 (2005): 44–62.

41. V. D. R. Guide and L. N. Van Wassenhove, "The Reverse Supply Chain," *Harvard Business Review,* February 2002.

14

Control

LEARNING OBJECTIVES

After studying this chapter, you should be able to:

Define *control* and explain its importance in organizations.

Describe the four basic elements of the control process and the issues involved in each.

Explain the concept of scope of control.

Compare and contrast strategic, tactical, and operational controls and identify the salient issues involved in each.

Analyze the factors that determine the effectiveness of organizational controls.

Bradley Scott Carter (FASTENAL)

Name: Bradley S. Carter

Position: Strategic Accounts—Construction, East Coast Regional Sales Manager, Fastenal

Alma mater: Austin Peay State University

Outside work activities: Model aviation

First job out of school: Sales representative, Fastenal

Business book reading now: *Good to Great* by Jim Collins

Hero: Popeye

Motto to live by: "Excuses only satisfy you."

What drives me: Self-achievement, influence in positive change, developing people

Management style: "Determine your own destiny; I'll provide the tools."

Brad Carter has always been busy. Even while attending college, he worked a full-time job as an assistant manager at a local grocery store chain. After obtaining his bachelor's degree, Carter took a position as a sales representative servicing hardware stores with the retail division of a firm called Fastenal. Within a year or so, he transferred to the National Accounts division of Fastenal, again as a sales representative. A year later he was promoted to the position of regional manager in the Carolinas, where he was assigned to develop sales growth. From that position, Carter was promoted to his present job as regional manager for the East Coast in the company's Strategic Accounts group, which focuses on the construction industry. He is responsible for a team of six that produces over $12 million in sales per year.

When Fastenal first created the National Accounts division, the company used Microsoft Excel as a rudimentary way of tracking sales. Excel was used because it was both simple and low cost, and it enabled managers to monitor customer contact times and sales representatives' activity. However, as Carter's team grew in size and more customers were added, the whole operation increased in complexity and he faced a problem: It was becoming more difficult to track sales call activity in a precise way that matched each individual account with a particular sales representative. This meant that the process of combining and managing sales information was becoming increasingly cumbersome and time-consuming. Carter had a choice: Continue to hold down monitoring costs by staying with the basic Excel file format or invest in a more expensive and sophisticated customer retention software program that would involve additional—and potentially costly—training of the sales representatives, some of whom had limited computer know-how.

Managerial control problems occur in almost all types of organizations, whether they are large and complex or small and simple. Exercising effective control is a universal and exceedingly important managerial challenge, as Brad Carter found out.

Probably the most critical part of this challenge, for individual managers as well as for organizations, is where to draw the line between too much control and too little control. Most of us can think of examples from our own work or other group experiences: We have probably encountered the downside of excessive control by the actions of individuals, supervisors, or by organizations through their rules and regulations.[1] At the extreme, overcontrol conjures up images of "Big Brother," creating a situation in which you cannot make a move without first obtaining permission from someone higher up in the organizational structure.[2] More typically, too much control can result in resentment and squelched motivation.

At the other extreme, too little control can expose an organization and its managers to very costly risks. In milder forms, undercontrol contributes to sloppy operations and failure to use resources efficiently and effectively. Errors can increase, and the organization may not know where or when problems are occurring and, particularly, how to fix them. In severe cases, the potential consequences can be catastrophic for the organization, as they were for the now-infamous Enron Corporation.

Exercising **control** involves regulating activities and behaviors within an organization, or adjusting or conforming to specifications or objectives. The use of control presents not only

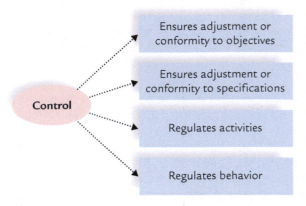

EXHIBIT 14.1

The Control Function in Management

major challenges for managers but also difficult dilemmas. The issue gets further complicated by the fact that, as we will discuss later, there are different types of control. A certain type of control may be quite effective in one situation but very ineffective or even damaging in other circumstances. The bottom line is that, no matter where they are in an organization or at what level, managers will have to deal with fundamental questions of control.

To explore the issue of control, we first look at the role that control plays in organizations and the way it relates to other managerial functions, such as strategy formulation and planning. Next, the four basic elements of the control process—establishing standards, measuring performance, comparing performance against standards, and evaluating results (and, if necessary, taking action)—are reviewed. Following this is a discussion of the different levels of control (strategic, tactical, and operational) and the various forms of control. The chapter concludes with an examination of factors that can influence the effectiveness of controls, such as their focus, amount, and the cost of implementing them. How these factors lead to crucial managerial choices is also explored.

The Control Function of Management

control
regulation of activities and behaviors within organizations; adjustment or conformity to specifications or objectives

On the face of it, the word *control* sounds negative. It can mean restraints, constraints, or checks. This clearly connotes restricted freedom of action—an idea that many people, especially in some cultures, may find troublesome. Certainly, within the context of organizations, **control** involves regulation of activities and behaviors (see Exhibit 14.1). To control, in an organizational setting, means to adjust or bring about conformity to specifications or objectives that have been set. In this sense, then, the control responsibilities of managers are bound to restrict someone's freedom. A manager cannot control without restricting. However, whether this is good or bad depends on the consequences of the control and whose perspectives are being considered.

Some amount of control in organizations is unavoidable. The very essence of organizations is that individuals give up total independence so that common goals and objectives may be accomplished. As one organizational scholar put it, "The coordination and order created out of the diverse interests and potentially diffuse behaviors of members is largely a function of control."[3] Thus, control is a fundamental characteristic of organized activity. Managers should always keep in mind, however, that control is a means for achieving a goal—and is not the goal itself (as the "A Manager's Challenge" feature, "Steak Right," illustrates).

The managerial function of control comes at the end of a chain of the other major functions of planning, organizing, and leading. (That is why a chapter on control is almost always found toward the end of most management textbooks.) If those prior functions are carried out well, generating positive responses to controls will be much easier. Conversely, if major problems exist in planning, organizing, and leading, almost no amount of attention to control is likely to work very well. In this sense, effective control is a managerial function that depends heavily on the other functions that precede it. When these preceding functions work well, control tends to work well. When they don't, control can become a major headache for a manager.

EXHIBIT 14.2

Control's Feedback Loop

Control can also be thought of as a "causal" variable because the results of control efforts can inform and improve the planning process of the organization. Control is thus part of a feedback loop into planning and organizing (see Exhibit 14.2) that can help managers adapt to changing circumstances and conditions. When either the internal or external organizational environment changes, good control systems let managers know if the current ways of operating are still meeting the organization's objectives. For example, some years ago, certain sales agents within a major life insurance company tried to increase their revenues and bonuses based on larger sales through "churning." The churning involved persuading customers who had long-standing policies with built-up cash value to take out new, bigger policies on the promise that these new policies would not cost them more. Customers were not told that the cash value of their

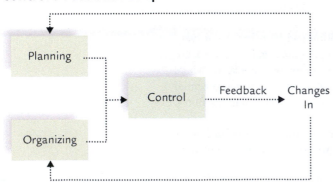

old policies were being used to pay the higher costs of the new policy. So, although customers were not laying out any more cash in monthly premiums than they did before, the new policies were, indeed, costing them. An external audit at one point warned senior managers about the problem. Unfortunately for the insurance company, however, while this control provided an early warning signal, managers did not do enough to follow up and investigate, and the company was hit by a raft of lawsuits.[4]

A MANAGER'S CHALLENGE

CHANGE

Steak Right

For fine restaurants, cooking is an art, not a science. The reputation of the food at these restaurants is usually a function of the chef's creativity. So the ideas of standardization and tight control are generally alien to upscale restaurants.

This is not the case with Morton's Restaurant Group, a company that started in 1978 in Chicago and now owns and operates more than 70 upscale steak houses in the United States and several other countries. Morton's operates many aspects of the restaurants with McDonald's-type precision, and the company firmly believes that tight controls have been the key to its financial success. It has always faced a challenging external environment due to ups and downs in the economy

and tough competition from other high-end steak restaurants, such as Ruth's Chris Steak House and Smith & Wollensky. Morton's has always been under pressure to make changes that would reduce costs. Nonetheless, it has retained loyal customers and attracted new fans by refusing to compromise its strict controls on food preparation and presentation.

Morton's controls start with the "bible." This phone-book-thick illustrated binder prescribes, ingredient by ingredient, the preparation of the 500 items coming from the kitchen. The binder exactly specifies everything from the sauces to a medium-rare Porterhouse steak. The presentation of the food is also not open to individual interpretation. Color photographs line the wall of every Morton's kitchen. Evaluating the presentation of a dish then becomes a relatively easy matter. Either the dish to be served looks like the photograph, or it doesn't.

The push for control is so stringent that each restaurant has a food and beverage controller who spends 12 hours a day tracking the movement of every item. Even the potatoes must meet rigorous standards. "I weigh every potato," says Andrew Moger, a food and beverage controller in the Manhattan Morton's. "They have to be at least a pound apiece."

The adherence to portion regulation and presentation is coupled with an effective cost control and inventory tracking system. Morton's is said to be able to track a single lost steak, which is no small matter with such valuable inventory.

The result is a consistent atmosphere and a dependable menu that brings customers back again and again. "I like knowing what to expect," says one regular customer who brings clients to Morton's for business entertaining. "You never worry about the food or service. When business is involved, you can't trust things to chance."

Morton's consistency through tough times paid off when a mad-cow disease scare hit the industry early in 2004. The company's sales didn't suffer, and its revenues actually climbed. The consistency produced by its highly

The Morton's Steak House chain adheres to strict portion regulation and entrée presentation coupled with an effective cost control and inventory tracking system. The company is said to be able to track a single lost steak.

Rachel Weill/Getty Images, Inc - Dex Images

(continued)

developed control system has also made Morton's a desirable tenant in the buildings in which it rents space.

"Landlords want to use us as an anchor," explained its chairman emeritus. "We're in demand because developers can get other tenants if we're there. Of course, they want their new Morton's to be like the old ones in every way." And—regardless of changes in the external business environment or increased competitive pressures—the steak house intends to be just that. Even changes in the company's top management haven't changed the stringent control policies at Morton's.

Sources: Company Web site, Morton's annual report, http://phx .corporate-ir.net/External.File?item=UGFyZW50SUQ9Mzg4 NjR8Q2hpbGRJRD0tMXxUeXBlPTM=&t=1, accessed June 25, 2010; company Web site, "Morton's Restaurant Group, Inc., Investment Conference," press release, March 6, 2007, http://www .mortons.com; company Web site, "Morton's Restaurant Group's Spectacular Italian Restaurant, Trivi, Opens in Las Vegas," press release, February 5, 2007; C. Hymowitz, "Managers Are Starting to Loosen Budgets as Optimism Grows," *Wall Street Journal,* January 6, 2004, B1; R. Smith, "Castle Harlan Completes Acquisition of Morton's," *Feedstuffs,* August 12, 2002, 6; G. Collins, "A Big Mac Strategy at Porterhouse Prices," *New York Times,* August 13, 1996, C1, C4.

The Basic Control Process

The basic elements of the control process in an organizational setting are simple and straightforward (see Exhibit 14.3):

1. Establish standards
2. Measure performance
3. Compare performance against standards
4. Evaluate results (of the comparison) and, if necessary, take action

Each of these basic components involves important managerial attention and decisions.

Establish Standards

Specifying what management expects is absolutely critical at each step of the control process. This starts at the top of the organization and, ideally, should eventually involve every level of employee. First and foremost, those at the highest levels should be able to articulate a vision and formulate broad strategic goals for the organization. For instance, the motto of Dart Transit Company, a long-haul company that for 75 years has operated with a network of independent truckers, is "to exceed the expectations of our customers." In recent years it has done that, and has received several awards for safety and operational excellence, and a "Best Fleet to Drive For" award from a truck carriers association.[5] From this example of a strategic mission statement, it is easy to see how a particular **standard,** or performance target, might be developed. Without a strategic vision and goals for the overall organization, managers in various parts of the organization will find it difficult to develop meaningful and agreed-upon performance yardsticks.

The establishment of standards—wherever they exist throughout the organization—requires as much specificity as possible. The reason for this is that measuring performance against standards cannot readily be accomplished if the standards are vague. A standard of "efficiently responds to customer complaints," for example, does not provide usable guidelines for determining whether the standard has been met. A standard of "responds, on average, to three customer complaints per hour" would permit an objective measurement of performance.

However, for some aspects of performance, especially in higher-level and more complex jobs, such as those in research laboratories, it is often not possible nor even desirable to set up easily quantified standards (such as number of discoveries per year). In these kinds of positions, the most important elements of performance may be the most difficult to measure, such as the probable long-term impact of a given discovery. Moreover, as in the example in the preceding paragraph, the quality of response to customer complaints may be more important than the rate of response. However, quality is often more difficult to measure. As shown in Exhibit 14.4, the more abstract the standard, the greater the possibility of confusion in measuring performance, and the greater the problem of gaining the acceptance of those measurements by members whose performance is being assessed.

Other issues also can arise in the establishment of standards (see Exhibit 14.5). One issue revolves around who should set the standards. In general, research has shown that in setting

standard
a performance target

EXHIBIT 14.3

The Basic Elements in the Control Process

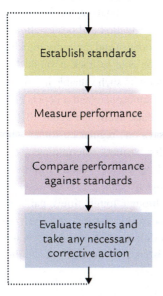

If anyone knows how to put on the "ritz," it's Ritz-Carlton employees in the company's 70 hotels located in 24 countries. Each Ritz employee gets over 100 hours of customer service training annually. A daily "SQI" (Service Quality Indicator) in every hotel is displayed on TV screens for hotel personnel to see. The SQI monitors production and service processes up to the minute so problems are apparent and can be immediately remedied.

standards participation by those who will be affected is beneficial in two respects.[6] First, because they have had some opportunity to influence the standards being set, those affected are more likely to be committed to meeting them. Second, involving those who have to meet the standards often results in a useful exchange of information and expertise that, in turn, results in more appropriate standards.

Another issue is the degree of difficulty of the standards themselves. As we saw in the chapter on motivation, the research on goal setting points to the conclusion that difficult but achievable goals seem to result in the highest levels of performance.[7] Similar views have been expressed regarding goals in the budgetary process. Thus, "the ideal budget is one that is challenging but attainable."[8] Achievable budget standards are regarded as desirable because they reduce the motivation to manipulate data or to focus only on short-term actions at the expense of long-term objectives. Such budgets also have the potential for increasing morale and generating a "winning atmosphere."[9] This assumes, as noted, that the budgetary targets are not only attainable but also reasonably difficult. Here, again, where to draw the line between goals that are too challenging and those that are not challenging enough is itself another type of managerial challenge.

An interesting side note on the topic of budgets is that some companies have rejected the use of budgets, and the wrangling over what the data indicate. In the absence of budgets, they use alternative financial and nonfinancial goals and measures. Companies that have rejected budgets require employees to measure themselves against the performance of competitors and against internal peer groups. Because employees do not know whether they have succeeded until they can look back on the results of a given period, they must make sure that they beat the competition. A key feature of many companies that have rejected budgets is the use of rolling forecasts, which are created every few months and typically cover five to eight quarters.[10]

Measure Performance

The second step in the basic control process is the measurement of performance—the actions of people and equipment that the organization wants to monitor (see Exhibit 14.6). If specific and concrete standards have been set, measurement is facilitated and there is more likely to be agreement on how performance is to be measured.

When readily quantifiable criteria do not exist, however, it becomes especially important to obtain as much consensus as possible about the way in which performance is to be assessed. To use an analogy, when true-false or multiple-choice tests are used in a class, the score a student receives is seldom contested (even though the quality

EXHIBIT 14.4

The Effect of Specificity of Standards on Performance Measurement

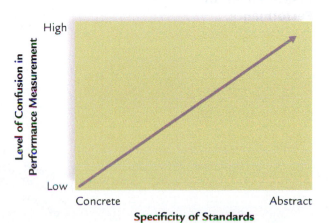

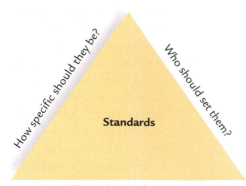

EXHIBIT 14.5

Issues in Establishing Standards

of the questions often is). On the other hand, the score given to the answers on tests composed of essay questions is frequently the cause of disputes between students and their teachers. The more an instructor and the class members can agree in advance about the qualities of good answers and on how the essay questions will be graded, the more likely that the measurement process will be accepted. This occurs even though that process is clearly subjective. Similarly, in work situations, gaining an up-front commitment to the performance measurement methods—what are often called key performance indicators (KPIs)[11]—is critical and will reduce later complaints about what those measurements showed and what they mean to individuals and to the organization.

Most jobs involve multiple activities. Thus, it is important for the measurements taken to be comprehensive. If only some aspects of performance are measured, the results can be misleading; they can skew the data that are used for the next two steps in the control process, especially taking action to change the performance. Companies such as Kellogg, Medtronic, Johnson & Johnson, and General Electric use a comprehensive control technology called "stage-gate" throughout the life of a project. Each project is divided into several stages with "gates" between them. Collectively, the gates act as comprehensive quality control checks that have to be passed before the gate will open, allowing the project to move on to the next stage. This allows management, at each gate, to review the progress of the project and decide whether it merits continued funding.[12] A potential danger, though, is that promising new products might be killed too soon by over-eager, stage-gate keepers.

Finally, even though measurement should be comprehensive, not everything that possibly could be measured should be measured. Measurement has a cost, and the usefulness of the information obtained may not justify the costs. The issue here is one of criticality, that is, what is measured should be highly relevant to the goals of the organization. Activities that are necessary but that do not provide relevant indicators of progress toward goals do not justify the expense to measure them. What is easy to measure may not be what is most important to control (as we also noted in Chapter 7).

Compare Performance Against Standards

Comparing performance results against previously set standards is the third step in the control process. Just as performance measurement is strongly influenced by the standards, so are comparisons affected by the kinds of measurements available. If key measurements have not already been built into the system, it is usually not possible to go back and reconstruct them for purposes of comparison. Sometimes managers realize too late that appropriate comparisons cannot be made.

When several dimensions of performance have been measured, this step in the process can involve multiple comparisons. If those comparisons all point in the same direction, interpretation

EXHIBIT 14.6

Issues in the Measurement of Performance

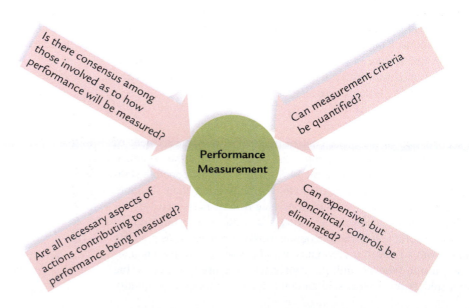

is relatively straightforward. However, the picture of performance that emerges from a set of comparisons may be inconsistent or contradictory. That is, some comparisons may show good adherence to standards and targets, and others may reveal problems. So managers need to know how to interpret the patterns of comparisons and to draw appropriate conclusions. A single negative comparison may outweigh a number of positive comparisons, or vice versa.

For example, after a major restructuring, a large grocery store chain found that its sales per store had nearly tripled and sales per employee had risen by 70 percent. Overall, profits were up, but customer satisfaction scores were down. What were managers to make of this? In this particular case, sales and overall profits were up because the organization had sold off or closed its least profitable stores (many of which had been operating at a loss). All of this might paint a very positive picture. However, the fact that customer satisfaction was down was potentially a bad sign. Grocery stores make money through volume. Therefore, if dissatisfied customers were to start spending less at this chain's stores and more at competitors' stores, positive results could deteriorate rapidly. Consequently, for any grocery or other type of retail store chain, placing too much emphasis on per-store sales compared with customer satisfaction could be a control mistake.

In this step, managers need to compare expected performance with actual performance. These comparisons often involve both subjective estimates as well as objective ones. However, even if the comparison involves only objective, quantitative numbers, judgment is still needed. For example, suppose the grocery chain's average customer satisfaction numbers were down from 5.5 to 5.2. Anyone can compute that customer satisfaction had declined by 0.3. However, the key question is, "Is this drop significant?" The answer to this question requires managerial judgment.

Evaluate Results and Take Action

The fourth step, evaluate results and take action, is arguably the most difficult managerial task in the entire control process. The results that emerge from the performance comparisons may or may not require action. Managers need to consider whether any single comparison or a pattern of comparisons requires action to be taken. If actual performance deviates from expected performance, how much of a difference is required before something is done about that difference? That question has no single answer. It requires evaluation of the importance and magnitude of the deviation.

An analogy illustrates what is involved in this type of judgment. In industrialized countries, the directors of the national banking system—in the case of the United States, the Board of Governors of the Federal Reserve System—periodically receive the most current data about the national economy, including the unemployment rate, the consumer price index, the index of consumer confidence, the rate of new starts in home building, and the like. These data are compared against predetermined benchmarks, and then a decision must be made about whether to take action (for example, to increase interest rates). The problem for the board, as for any manager in an organization, is to determine which data are most important and how much of a change is significant. However, the issue is even more complicated. Managers must determine whether a slight change in the same direction for all of the indicators is more or less important than a major change in just one indicator. As any macroeconomist would testify regarding the national economy, this type of judgment is not easy.

The other basic judgment that must be made in this fourth step is what action to take if the pattern and size of deviations from expected performance are determined to be significant. Managers need knowledge about the causes of the deviation as well as about the potential actions that are possible.

The evaluation and action step of control requires managers to have strong diagnostic skills as well as a certain level of expertise. Sometimes, the causes of a problem may be easily recognized, but the decisions about which actions to take to correct them may be extremely difficult. Conversely, the most effective actions may be well-known, if only the causes could be clearly identified.

If a manager discovers major negative differences between performance and standards, some type of action is clearly needed because failure to act can lead to more severe problems in the future. However, if the deviations are major but positive, the necessity for action is usually much less (see Exhibit 14.7). Such positive differences, though, may provide valuable insights about unexpected opportunities that should be pursued. For example, a major maker of baby

EXHIBIT 14.7

**Outcomes of
Performance
Measurement**

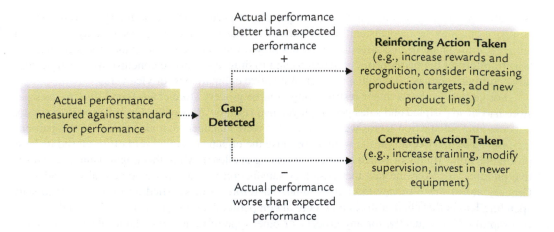

food discovered stronger-than-expected sales of its new line of toddler foods in Florida. Further investigation revealed that the increased sales were not due to a higher-than-expected number of toddlers; rather, they were due to older customers with teeth problems who bought the product because it was easier to chew. This led to a whole new line of packaged foods targeted at this particular consumer segment.

To help maintain positive performance, employees who are doing better than expected can be given increased recognition and rewards to reinforce their excellent performance. Likewise, sales that exceed their forecast may mean that production should be increased or the product line should be extended. Costs that are below target may suggest an efficient practice that could be duplicated for other employees to follow to reduce the costs even further. In short, it is as important to evaluate surprises on the upside as it is on the downside.

One other issue is involved in determining what action managers should take in the case of significant deviations from standards (either in the positive or negative direction). This is the judgment about whether the standards are correct and the performance is the problem, or whether the performance is appropriate but the standards are too difficult or too easy. That is why a broken-line feedback arrow is shown from "Evaluate Results" to "Establish Standards" in Exhibit 14.3, indicating that the standards may need to be adjusted.

Over time, standards are sometimes modified as experience is gained and the feasibility of existing standards is better understood. If a great deal of effort and care has been used in setting the standards and participation in setting them was broad, then the issue is probably likely to be one of performance. If, though, the standards have been set hastily or without appropriate input from the relevant parties, performance may not be the problem. This kind of issue points out once again the tight interconnection of the four basic steps of the control process.

Scope of Control in the Organization

Even though the four steps of the control process are similar wherever they occur in organizations, the scope of what is being controlled can vary widely. This, in turn, affects how the steps are actually put into use. A bank provides a simple illustration. The bank manager may need to assess whether she has an adequate level of deposits relative to outstanding loans. The scope is quite broad because the outcome of this assessment could affect the entire organization. If the ratio is too low, the bank may need to reduce its level of lending or try to get more deposits. On the other hand, the manager may also need to evaluate the ratio of human bank tellers to automatic teller machines at each branch. In this case, the scope is much narrower because the issue only involves a small part of the bank's total set of activities. In the former instance we would label the scope as "strategic," and in the latter instance it would be regarded as an "operational" control issue. These represent two of the three major categories of control scope. The third, and intermediate level between strategic and operational, is a category typically called "tactical." (Refer to Chapter 5 for a discussion of these three categories.)

In the remainder of this section, we look at the issues involved in each of these three types of control classified by the breadth of their scope. However, it is useful to remember that no

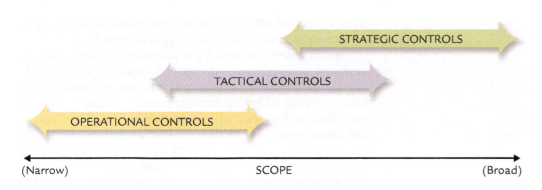

EXHIBIT 14.8

Types and Scope of Control

hard-and-fast boundaries separate the three types (see Exhibit 14.8). The differences between strategic and tactical control issues often are blurred, and likewise, it is not always clear whether a control issue should be considered tactical or operational. Nevertheless, the three categories help remind managers where they should focus their attention.

Strategic Control

As discussed in Chapter 4, strategy refers to the direction for the organization as a whole. It is linked to the mission of the organization and to the basic plans for achieving that mission. Thus, **strategic control** is focused on how the organization as a whole fits its external environment and meets its long-range objectives and goals.[13] Strategic control systems, where they exist, are designed to determine how well those types of objectives and goals are being met.

A particular challenge in formulating strategic controls is the fact that strategic goals are broad and, especially, long term. This means that such goals typically are more abstract than goals for particular units. Consequently, setting strategic standards and measuring strategic performance can be especially challenging.[14] For this reason, research has shown that only a relatively small number of firms in both Europe and the United States have yet set what could be termed strategic control systems.[15] The numbers will undoubtedly increase in the future, but important obstacles interfere with establishing such systems.

A significant factor that affects whether strategic control systems can be set up, and whether they will be effective, is the unpredictability of the external environments in which many organizations operate and from which they obtain resources. This also makes it difficult to develop standards and measures that are relevant for more than short periods of time. It is particularly problematic for firms to try to develop useful criteria for assessing the long-term performance of individual managers.[16]

The environmental conditions of large companies affect how much leeway each division or unit is given to determine its own competitive strategies for dealing with its particular markets.[17] The issue is essentially one of how much strategic control systems should be centralized versus decentralized, and how much variation should be allowed by unit. Such a decision involves not only matters of strategy but also of organization structure (Chapter 6).

Sometimes, because of changes in the external environment, companies find they have to reverse course on their overall strategic approach to controls. Thus, McDonald's had to restructure its U.S. operations to reinstate controls it had abandoned in the mid-1990s. Why? Because it was suffering a decreased earnings trend. To deal with this, the company began controlling not only its ingredients but also shaping the experience customers have in its restaurants. It has gone back to more inspections of every store and the use of mystery shoppers, both in the United States and abroad. It is also making more use of extensive customer surveys.[18]

Research indicates, however, that "the efficiencies of managing through centralized control may be greater . . . when the operating environments of divisions in multidivisional organizations are relatively stable and predictable" (see Exhibit 14.9).[19] When there is more uncertainty in the environment, centralized control becomes less efficient. In other words, in relatively turbulent environments, it is difficult for centralized strategic control systems to keep up with events. Consequently, more responsibility for control must be delegated to major units. When the environment is changing rapidly, as it is for many companies these days, too much reliance on organization-wide strategic goals and standards of performance that are set too far in advance can interfere with the needed speed and flexibility of the various operating

strategic control
assessment and regulation of how the organization as a whole fits its external environment and meets its long-range objectives and goals

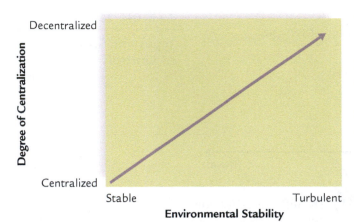

EXHIBIT 14.9

Degree of Centralization of Control in Relation to Environmental Stability

units to respond effectively to the environment, especially in complex organizations with many types of units.[20]

Both the degree to which it is possible to measure precisely how well performance conforms with strategic goals and the degree of turbulence or uncertainty in the environment can affect the value of having strategic control systems.[21] They are most likely to be useful when measurement is easy and operating environments are relatively calm, as in the case of the cement industry, for example. Although this industry basically follows the ups and downs of the construction industry, the factors that significantly affect these movements are relatively well known. For instance, changes in interest rates have a significant impact on building booms and busts. As rates go down and money is cheaper to borrow, construction increases. As rates go up and money becomes more expensive to borrow, construction decreases. Thus, for a concrete firm, strategic controls such as being number one in sales in a region can be relatively useful.

Conversely, strategic controls are probably least useful when exact measurement is difficult and the environment is fluctuating rapidly. As recently as five years ago, putting up a Web site for a company involved contracting with a vendor that specialized in the unique and various languages used on the Internet. Companies providing such services have seen their world change dramatically. New languages and tools have emerged so that almost anyone with a little skill and knowledge can create a professional-looking Web site. In such a turbulent environment, strategic goals do not last long. Therefore, strategic controls are of more limited value in these types of organizations.

Strategic control is especially challenging in international organizations. Even with advances in communication and transportation technology, Sydney is still a long way from Paris, so to speak. Consequently, maintaining strategic control across a worldwide organization that crosses cultural, economic, social, political, and religious borders as well as 13 different time zones is significantly more difficult than it is for a purely domestic organization.

Tactical Control

tactical control

assessment and regulation of the day-to-day functions of the organization and its major units in the implementation of its strategy

Tactical control focuses on implementing strategy. Thus, this level of control forms the heart—and, one might say, the soul—of an organization's total set of controls. Tactical control involves the fundamental control arrangements of the organization, those with which its members have to live day to day. Four of the most important types of tactical control systems are financial controls, budgets, the supervisory structure, and human resource policies and procedures.

Financial and budgetary control contains elements of both strategic and tactical control systems. To the extent they focus on the entire organization, they tend to be more toward the strategic end of the continuum (see Exhibit 14.10), and the more they focus on specific units within an overall organization, they tend to be toward the tactical end. We have chosen to discuss them in this section since they most often focus on organizational units, but keep in mind that they, especially financial controls, can also be used as well for some strategic control considerations.

FINANCIAL CONTROLS Financial controls include several important quantitative ratios involving key financial statistics.[22] Although these statistics are always generated at the organization-wide level as well as at the organizational-unit level, they are especially useful at the unit level as a form of tactical control.

The data used for the most important financial controls involve a basic cost-benefit analysis. For example, ratios relevant to the profitability of a given unit are constructed from revenue data (benefit) in relation to given amounts of investment (cost). The ratio is called *return on investment (ROI)*, or alternatively, *return on equity (ROE)*, and compares the amount of net profit before taxes (the numerator of the ratio) to the total amount of assets invested (the denominator). Thus, a unit that earns a profit of $500,000 in a given year from invested assets of $10 million would have an ROI of 0.05 for that year. If another unit generated that same amount of profit on invested assets of only $5 million, its ROI would be 0.10. This unit's financial performance would be superior because it generated an equal benefit for less cost.

Other financial ratios that are commonly used to assess unit performance include, in addition to profitability ratios, those related to liquidity (current assets in relation to current liabilities),

Tactical Controls	Strategic Controls
Time Frame	
Limited	Long, unspecific
Objective	
Controls relate to specific, functional areas	Controls relate to organization as a whole
Types of Comparisons	
Comparisons made within organization	Comparisons made to other organizations
Focus	
Implementation of strategy	Determination of overall organizational strategy

EXHIBIT 14.10

Characteristics of Strategic and Tactical Controls

which provides an indication of how well the unit can meet its short-term cash requirements; leverage (a firm's total debt to its total assets), which provides an indication of a company's ability to meet its long-term financial obligations; and efficiency or activity (for example, the amount of sales in a given period relative to the cost of inventory used to generate those sales), measuring how efficiently assets are used.

Exhibit 14.11 shows examples of these four types of ratios for two organizations in the retail industry for the year 2009. As seen in the exhibit, The Limited had a lower ROI than The GAP that year, somewhat more liquidity, a less favorable leverage ratio, and a slightly less efficient use of inventory. If these had been two units within the same larger organization, one would say that for this year The Gap unit was generally doing better overall insofar as its financial performance was concerned.

The important point regarding financial ratios is not the detailed steps that need to be taken to calculate them. Rather, it is that when the ratios are calculated, they can be used to compare one organization, or one unit, to another. It is the comparative nature of the ratios that provides the information managers need to take action during the control process. The numbers used to calculate a ratio, such as inventory turnover, for example, will show whether the ratio is relatively unfavorable, and if so, an examination of the two components used in the ratio will also

EXHIBIT 14.11

Examples of Company Financial Ratios

RATIO	FORMULA		The GAP, Inc. 2009 (in $ millions)		The Limited, Inc. 2009 (in $ millions)	
Profit						
Return on Investment	Net Profit Before Taxes / Total Assets		1102 / 7895	0.14	859 / 7173	0.12
Liquidity						
Current Ratio	Current Assets / Current Liabilities		4664 / 2131	2.19	3250 / 1322	2.50
Leverage						
Debt to Asset	Total Liabilities / Total Assets		3004 / 7985	0.38	4990 / 7173	0.70
Activity						
Inventory Turnover	Sales / Inventory		14197 / 1477	9.61	8632 / 1037	8.32

indicate whether the problem seems to be in the amount of sales (too low), or in the amount of inventory (too high), or both. In other words, financial ratios are a very useful diagnostic control tool for managers.

Another financial measure is sometimes used for control purposes in business organizations. That measure is called the **break-even point (BEP).** Essentially, the BEP is where the selling price of a unit of a product (or service) minus its variable costs exceeds the fixed costs for that unit. The lower the fixed costs, the fewer the units of goods or services that need to be sold for a break-even point to be reached. Likewise, the lower the variable costs, the higher the profit per unit and, therefore, the fewer the units that need to be sold to reach that point. Break-even analysis, then, provides a way for managers to gauge whether new products or services have a potential to turn a profit. Managers can, therefore, exercise control *before* new ventures are undertaken. Even more important, for ongoing operations, a break-even point analysis focuses managers' attention on reducing or controlling the two categories of costs—fixed and variable—to take the pressure off the need to sell larger volumes.

The airline industry provides an example of where a break-even point analysis can illustrate comparisons between two organizations or business units. Many of the larger airlines have set up separate subsidiary airlines. For example, American Airlines set up American Eagle to handle its short-haul commuter routes. These commuter airlines can operate on relatively small volumes of passenger traffic because their costs—like lower wage bases for their pilots—produce lower break-even points. Similarly, certain independent airlines—if they are especially efficient—can charge very low fares on many of their routes and still make a profit. Southwest Airlines is another example. Southwest avoided the cost of passengers' meals by serving only snacks long before other airlines did. It also maintained its highly flexible point-to-point route system instead of adopting the hub-and-spoke system of most major airlines.[23]

Although a BEP analysis can provide extremely useful information for managers for control purposes, such an analysis also has limitations. Looking strictly at the numbers of a BEP analysis may discourage certain decisions that could ultimately result in very profitable activities that do not initially appear to be profitable. Also, it is not always easy to allocate costs between fixed and variable categories, and it is sometimes difficult to project costs accurately, especially variable costs. Like other financial controls, a break-even point analysis can be an aid to exercising effective control, but it is not by itself a guarantee of wise decisions. What it does, however, is highlight the potential advantages to be gained by controlling specific types of costs.

BUDGETARY CONTROLS Budgets are used in almost every organization (as we discussed in Chapter 5), and, like financial controls, can sometimes be considered elements of a strategic system. A **budgetary control,** however, is more usefully viewed as a significant form of tactical control because it focuses on how well strategies are being implemented. In contrast to purely strategic control, budgetary controls:

- Typically cover a relatively limited time frame (usually a 3- or 12-month period).
- Focus exclusively on one type of objective (financial).
- Usually cannot be used to compare a total organization's progress relative to its competitors.[24]

Anyone occupying a managerial position is controlled by budgets and uses budgets to control others. A budget is a commitment to a forecast to make an agreed-upon outcome happen.[25] Thus, it is more than a forecast, which is simply a prediction. A budget is designed to influence behavior so that forecasts or plans for expenditures and (where relevant) revenues can be achieved. It "controls" by assigning responsibility for meeting financial targets and for evaluating how well those targets have been met. It would be difficult indeed to maintain an organization if none of its members were held accountable for limits on expenditures.

When using budgets as a form of control, managers face several important issues, as shown in Exhibit 14.12. One is the question of whether to use a fixed budget for a specific period, usually 12 months, and stick with those numbers, or to revise it midway during the period based on changes in operating conditions. Some companies have dealt with this problem by adopting a rolling planning and budgetary process. This kind of budgetary process with relatively frequent revisions has the advantage of being more current and, therefore, more accurate; on the other hand, however, it also can take more managerial time and effort.

break-even point (BEP)
amount of a product that must be sold to cover a firm's fixed and variable costs

budgetary control
a type of tactical control based on responsibility for meeting financial targets and evaluating how well those targets have been met

EXHIBIT 14.12

Issues in Budgetary Control

Issue	Questions
Rolling budgets and revision	Should the budget period be for 12 months followed by another 12-month budget a year later, or should a calendar quarter be added each time a new calendar quarter begins?
	Should the budget remain fixed for the budget period or should it be revised periodically during the period?
Fixed or flexible budgets	Should performance be evaluated against the original budget or against a budget that incorporates the actual activity level of the business?
Bonuses based on budgets	Should incentive compensation, if any, be based on actual versus budgeted performance, or on actual performance against some other standard?
Evaluation criteria	Should the budget used to evaluate performance include only those items over which the evaluated manager has control, or should it include all unit costs and revenues appropriate to the managerial unit?
Tightness of the budget	What degree of "stretch" should there be in the budget?

Source: Adapted from N. C. Churchill, "Budget Choices: Planning vs. Control," *Harvard Business Review* 62, no. 4 (1984), pp.150–64 (p. 151).

Another budget issue is whether compensation bonuses should be based on the achievement of budgetary targets. This sounds good, but it has the great disadvantage of encouraging budget game playing. Why? Because the person being evaluated has an incentive to provide high cost and low revenue estimates when the budget is first developed. By creating "budgetary slack" with relatively easy targets, the person has a higher probability of hitting the targets and earning a bonus. Thus, managers who supervise the preparation of budgets need to be alert to how a bonus system of this type can distort estimates and thus undermine control. Managers also need to make sure that they don't inadvertently create a short-term focus on the part of subordinates attempting to meet budgetary targets at the expense of more important, longer-term organizational goals.[26]

A third budgetary control issue involves the question of whether those responsible for meeting specified targets should be evaluated only on expenditures and revenues over which they have direct control, or whether they should be evaluated on a final "net" figure based on all costs and revenues for a given unit. The former results in a more direct link between managerial behavior and budgetary responsibility, but the latter is the ultimate "bottom line," especially for publicly held corporations. For example, as a manager of a sales unit, you might have strong control over the revenues that your unit generates and the money spent on travel expenses. When these travel expenses are subtracted from sales, your unit might look very good. However, if your unit also uses marketing and promotional materials to get these sales, those costs may need to be factored into the overall assessment. Otherwise, you may overspend on marketing and promotion.

The final, and perhaps most important, managerial control issue regarding budgets is how tight or loose to make them. Should a budget require those charged with meeting it to make an extra "stretch"? As we have said before, research indicates that the best performance results from goals that are challenging but achievable. Since budgets represent goals, this conclusion seems highly relevant to the issue of budgetary control.

SUPERVISORY STRUCTURE CONTROLS The basic **supervisory structure** of an organization is probably the most widespread tactical control system that a typical employee encounters. The amount and form of such control, as well as how employees react to it, varies considerably from organization to organization but almost always exists in some form.[27] In organizations of any size, there is always someone or some group to which an employee or manager reports. (Recall the discussion of span of control in Chapter 6.) Even in the least bureaucratic types of work organizations, such as research laboratories and nonprofit enterprises, some sort of reporting

supervisory structure
a type of tactical control based on reporting levels in an organization

structure almost always regulates the activities of each member. However, such supervisory control structures, like other controls, can fail.

This was demonstrated several years ago at the Ohio division of the American Cancer Society. Until 2000, the organization had enjoyed a great deal of success but that year the society's board of directors announced that its chief administrative officer had embezzled $7.5 million over a period of approximately three years. This had occurred even though a new CEO had checked all security arrangements when he started a few years before. The administrative officer had used a variety of schemes to steal the funds, such as billing for imaginary services, charging personal home repairs and expenditures to the organization, and transferring money to secret accounts in Europe. The board and top managers were shocked to find out that, in this instance, their controls had failed. The administrative officer had never undergone a background check (which would have revealed previous problems); he was the only person authorized to sign checks in large amounts and, especially, had no direct supervision of his day-to-day activities.[28]

HUMAN RESOURCE CONTROLS **Human resource policies and procedures** are a fourth major type of tactical control that affects everyone working in an organization. These are discussed in detail in Chapter 7, but what is important to stress about them here is that they provide a number of different opportunities for control (see Exhibit 14.13):

■ Selection procedures can specify the range of abilities and knowledge that will be brought into the organization.[29]
■ Training can improve people's skills and performance levels so that they meet standards.
■ Appraisal and evaluation methods can reinforce desired behavior and discourage undesirable levels of performance.
■ Compensation can be used to motivate employees and increase their efforts in particular directions.

An example of using human resource procedures to reinforce desired behavior occurred a few years ago when DTE Energy's Detroit Edison subsidiary, operator of a nuclear generating facility, employed a consulting firm to help it assess the effectiveness of its senior team (of 15 members) in charge of the plant. The assessment found that there were major problems in such team activities as timely sharing of information across departments and giving assistance to other departments. As a result of the assessment process, several key changes were made, - including weekly team "alignment" meetings and the creation of specific action plans with follow-up monitoring. Re-assessment data obtained two years after these human resource type of changes were implemented showed significant improvements in sharing of information and cross-functional teamwork, and, especially important, the plant had demonstrated improved operational performance and a better safety record.[30]

Because the effects of human resource policies and procedures are so extensive, they are a very powerful means of control. When used with skill and deftness, they are a significant aid to the achievement of organizational objectives, as the Standard Life of Scotland example illustrates. When used ineptly, and with heavy-handedness, however, they can hinder organizational progress.

CONTRASTING APPROACHES TO USING TACTICAL CONTROLS The ways in which tactical control systems are implemented say a great deal about an organization—what it is like to work there and how effective the control is. These control systems characterize an organization and are a critical part of its identity. For these reasons, it is important to specify and discuss the two fundamental approaches to tactical control: (1) imposed, or bureaucratic, control and (2) elicited, or commitment or clan, control (see Exhibit 14.14).[31] Most organizations use a combination of these two approaches but also tend to emphasize one over the other.

Bureaucratic control stresses adherence to rules and regulations and a formal, impersonal administration of control systems. For instance, many companies provide thick operating manuals for their managers. Such manuals specify everything from which types

---

human resource policies and procedures
a type of tactical control based on the organization's overall approach to utilizing its human resources

bureaucratic control
an approach to tactical control that stresses adherence to rules and regulations and is imposed by others

EXHIBIT 14.13

Opportunities for Control in the Human Resource Function

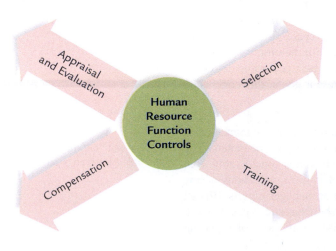

Type of Control	Social Requirements[a]	Control Approach	Informational Requirements
Bureaucracy	• Norm of reciprocity • Legitimate authority	• Adherence to rules and regulations • Formal and impersonal • Emphasis on detecting deviance • Imposed on the individual	• Rules
Clan	• Norm of reciprocity • Legitimate authority • Shared values, beliefs	• Stresses group consensus on goals and their measurement • Mutual assistance in meeting performance standards • Uses deviations as guidelines in diagnosing problems • Control comes from the individuals or groups	• Traditions

[a]Social requirements are the basic agreements between people that, at a minimum, are necessary for a form of control to be employed.

Source: Adapted from William G. Ouchi, "A Conceptual Framework for the Design of Organizational Control Mechanisms," *Management Science* 25, no. 9 (1980), pp. 833–47 (p. 838).

EXHIBIT 14.14

Control in Bureaucracy and Clan Structures

of capital budget requests need which type of approval to equipment maintenance schedules. This approach highlights rational planning and orderliness. It heavily emphasizes detecting deviance from standards. The *failure* to follow standard operating procedures in this type of bureaucratic control can create serious problems in cases where safety of operations is paramount. Regardless of whether this type of control is effective or not, however, its foremost feature—in a control sense—is that control is *imposed on* the person, group, or activity. From an employee's perspective, "others" do the controlling.

Commitment, or clan, control stresses obtaining consensus on what goals should be pursued and then developing a shared sense of responsibility and self-control for achieving those goals.[32] It is called a "clan" approach to control because of the emphasis on generating shared and deeply held values, as in a set of close relatives, and on mutual assistance in meeting performance standards. Unlike the bureaucratic approach, the clan approach tends to treat deviations from standards more as a basis for diagnosis than for taking corrective action. Its foremost feature, in a control sense, is that control is viewed as being *elicited from,* rather than imposed on, the person, group, or activity. From an employee's perspective, the employee or his or her group, rather than others, does the controlling.

You might wonder why every organization doesn't use a commitment approach. It sounds as if it would function better for both the organization and those who work in it. However, things are not that simple. Creating a genuine clanlike atmosphere among employees, especially in large organizations, is extremely difficult. It takes time and also considerable managerial effort. It may not succeed, or, more likely, succeed only partially. If a true clanlike, high-commitment culture is not created, an organization cannot rely on self-control by individuals or groups to exercise sufficient control. However distasteful it may sound, some amount of bureaucratic managerial control seems necessary for most complex organizations.

Even from the perspective of the organization member or employee, self-imposed clan control may not be as satisfying as it would seem at first glance. A detailed study of a small manufacturing company illustrates the point.[33] This company converted its traditional hierarchical structure, which emphasized a high degree of supervisory control, to a structure that was built around self-managing work teams. In the first phase of the transition, the teams spent a good deal of time developing consensus on what constituted, both collectively and individually, good work for the teams and good patterns of behavior that would translate those standards into action. In the second phase, the teams developed strong norms regarding expected behavior. Experienced team members expected new workers to buy into the teams' values and act according to their norms.

Under the old system, supervisors tolerated some slackness among the workers. But in the team system, the members exercised their newfound authority with much less patience. The clan approach to control tended to formalize the teams' norms and create ironclad, self-imposed rules.

commitment (clan) control
an approach to tactical control that emphasizes consensus and shared responsibility for meeting goals

EXHIBIT 14.15

Operational Controls

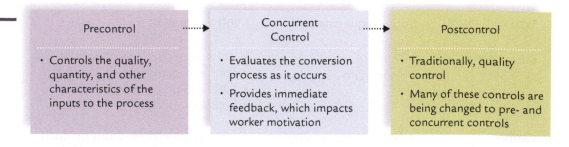

The researcher studying this company stated, "The teams had now created, in effect, a nearly perfect form of control... an essentially total system of control almost impossible to resist.... The team members had become their own masters and their own slaves." For these teams, clan control had become an "iron cage," as the researcher put it.

The previous example serves to emphasize the point that no single approach to managerial control will work well in all situations. It also shows that whatever approach is chosen will have its own unique problems as well as advantages.

Operational Control

operational control

assessment and regulation of the specific activities and methods an organization uses to produce goods and services

precontrol

a type of operational control that focuses on the quality, quantity, and characteristics of the inputs into the production process

concurrent control

a type of operational control that evaluates the conversion of inputs to outputs while it is happening

postcontrol

a type of operational control that checks quality after production of goods or services outputs

As its name implies, **operational control** regulates the activities or methods an organization uses to produce the goods and services it supplies to customers and clients. It is control applied to the transformation of inputs into outputs, such as the actions that produce a car, administer therapy to an ill patient, cook and serve a restaurant meal, send a satellite into the sky, or write computer software. In short, operational control "is where the rubber meets the road."

The overall management of operations involves a number of critical and often technical issues. Here, we focus specifically on an overview of the control process relating to operations. Operational control can be analyzed by relating it to the three basic elements involved in any type of service or goods production: inputs, transformation, and outputs (Exhibit 14.15).[34] These three elements can be related to the location of control in the production process: before transformation occurs, or **precontrol;** during transformation, or **concurrent control;** and after transformation takes place, or **postcontrol.**

PRECONTROL OF OPERATIONS This form of operational control focuses on the quality, quantity, and characteristics of the inputs into the production process—for example, the purity of steel, the grade of beef, the number of passengers, the age of patients, the test scores of entering students, the aptitudes of job applicants.[35] Such precontrol is illustrated by the actions of a company called South West Trading, which manufactures yarns made from bamboo, corn, and soybeans. It controls its raw materials at the point of origin and utilizes the services of United Parcel Service (UPS) to combine orders from various factories into one container for shipment.[36] Another example of pre-control in an entirely different realm is the increased inspections that several companies that own large construction cranes are instituting before their giant cranes are allowed to be put into action. These pre-operation inspections are becoming more rigorous, and they also are becoming more effective because of digitization procedures. As one executive explained: "We have to be diligent in... erecting equipment that we truly know—not that we believe—but that we truly know is safe.[37]

The more stringent the control over the quality of inputs, the less need for control at the later two stages. The higher the quality of army recruits, for example, the easier it is to train them to be competent soldiers. However, there is a cost involved in exacting precontrol standards. Higher-quality inputs typically cost more, and the effort to ensure that the quality is high also increases costs. Nevertheless, those costs in many cases may be well justified. In other words, customers may be willing to pay more for better products and services.

CONCURRENT CONTROL OF OPERATIONS Concurrent control involves real-time assessment of the quality of the transformation process, that is, evaluation of the conversion of inputs to outputs while it is happening. For example, Koch Pipeline Company uses concurrent information provided by its central computers that model 125,000 data points from its pipeline networks. This system allows the monitoring safety managers to spot leaks within seconds and to prevent catastrophic incidents before they can occur. The result of this concurrent control is that pipeline accident incidents fell by

94 percent between 1995 and 2005.[38] Another example of concurrent control is the use of GPS technology by Union Pacific (UP) railroad to track the fuel efficiency of each train engineer. The importance of this to the organization is shown by the fact that UP rewards the most fuel efficient engineers with a portion of the savings they achieve.[39] Still another good illustration of concurrent control in action in different types of organizational settings is presented in the "A Manager's Challenge" feature on the use of RFID technology.

Other typical examples of concurrent control are the monitoring of a customer service representative's performance while handling a telephone inquiry or the inspection of fruit while a batch of it is proceeding along a conveyer belt. This type of control is designed to provide immediate feedback so that operations can be changed rapidly to decrease errors or increase quality. To have effective concurrent control procedures, however, managers must give considerable attention in advance to how such systems are designed and implemented. Also, managers need to be aware that this kind of control can have strong impacts on the motivation of those carrying out the operations since the feedback is so immediate and often very direct.

POSTCONTROL OF OPERATIONS Postcontrol was the traditional form of control in manufacturing—checking quality *after* a product (TV sets, shoes, furniture, and so forth) was produced. Under that arrangement, companies had quality control inspectors or a quality department that checked the rate of defective products and then decided what to do if those rates were too high. In recent years, however, quality control at many companies has been greatly diminished in favor of pre- and concurrent controls instead. The adage has been: "*Build* quality into the product, rather than inspect quality into the product."[40] Also, the more contemporary approach to operational control has been to shift control responsibilities to operations personnel and away from separate evaluators at the end of the process.

Control-Effectiveness Factors

Regardless of good intentions, control systems in organizations can break down completely or at least not work very well. There can be many reasons for this, but alert managers can take the initiative to lessen the possibility of this occurring. The effectiveness of control is very much under their control. Again, there are no automatic prescriptions or rules of thumb for managing the control process well. Instead, managers can use certain potential sources of influence to increase the probability of success. In this section, we look at some of the key factors that make controls effective (see Exhibit 14.16).

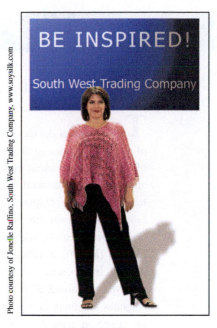

South West Trading, which manufactures yarns made from bamboo, corn, and soybeans, focuses on operational precontrol—that is, the strict control of inputs into the production process. The firm controls its raw materials beginning with their point of origin and utilizes the services of United Parcel Service (UPS) to combine orders from various factories into one container for shipment.

Photo courtesy of Jonelle Raffino, South West Trading Company, www.soysilk.com

EXHIBIT 14.16

Key Factors in Determining the Effectiveness of Controls

Key Factor	Concerns
Focus of control	• What will be controlled?
	• Where should controls be located in the organizational structure?
	• Who is responsible for which controls?
Amount of control	• Is there a balance between over- and undercontrol?
Quality of information collected by the controls	• Is the information useful?
	• Is the information accurate?
	• Is the information timely?
	• Is the information objective?
Flexibility of controls	• Are the controls able to respond to varying conditions?
Favorable cost–benefit ratio	• Is the information being gathered worth the cost of gathering it?
Source of control	• Is control imposed by others?
	• Is control decided by those who are affected?

A MANAGER'S CHALLENGE

TECHNOLOGY

RFID: The Ultimate Tracker?

Technological devices over the years have always been of major assistance to the control systems of organizations of all types—business companies, government agencies, and health care institutions, to name a few. Recent years have seen the development of a technological method that holds great promise for reducing costs of control and, especially, for increasing accuracy. It is radio-frequency identification (RFID), an automatic identification method using tags or transponders to send data that can be remotely retrieved and stored. RFID tags with silicon chips containing antennas are small enough to be inserted into—or attached to—a person, animal, or product for identification purposes using the emitted radio waves. Larger transponders are used currently in everyday activities, such as the automatic identification of cars on toll roads.

Initially, there were no agreed-upon standards for "passive" RFID tags (that is, tags with no internal power source), and this fact was a major hurdle that had to be overcome before RFID could be more widely used, particularly by global companies. Until countries could agree on those standards, the technology would enjoy only minimal efficiencies and costs would be prohibitively high. However, this problem was mostly resolved when a number of countries—including China, a significant exporter—agreed to an RFID standard in 2006.

[Photographer]/Agence France Presse/Getty Images

Radio-Frequency Identification tags like the one shown here are allowing Wal-Mart and other firms to track the movement of their inventory with greater precision.

As with any technology, especially relatively new ones, there are always pluses and minuses. On the positive side: RFID opens up many new approaches for managers and organizations—in industries as diverse as cleaning, auto manufacturing, aircraft, coal mining, and retail stores—to enhance their control actions. For example, two major retail chains, Wal-Mart and Marks & Spencer, have been especially active in adopting this technology. Wal-Mart has applied it to the issue of how to avoid the perennial "out-of-stock" problem that plagues all stores of any size. Shortly after trying out RFID technology, the firm was able to reduce the incidences of the problem by 13 percent in its inventory of mid-price items. A few years later, that percentage reduction was 62 percent and is still improving. Wal-Mart has also used RFID tags to track high-cost items in its stores to prevent them from being shoplifted. Likewise, Marks & Spencer uses the technology to help manage inventory turnover by precisely tracking its merchandise. As a Marks & Spencer executive explained: "Most people think that the benefits of RFID are around cost reduction and speed, but the main benefit is control. Sending the right product in the right quantity to the right depot at the right time is far more important."

In the health care industry, RFID is being increasingly used. Specifically, the tagging procedure has been used to control the supply chain flow of pharmaceuticals from their point of origin through their dispensation to patients. As in retail stores, the technology has been used in hospitals to keep track of, and reduce the theft of, high-cost drugs and other items. Additionally, RFID has been used to keep track of patients and the location of personnel within the hospital.

On the downside, three major concerns have slowed down wide-scale adoption of RFID technology. The first of these, as we mentioned, was the lack of agreed-upon standards. To some extent, this problem has been solved. A second deterrent has been the high costs related to purchasing the tags and their sophisticated readers. Experience has shown, however, that if the initial investment can be made, the subsequent return-on-investment results of RFID have more than justified the costs. Finally, and perhaps the most difficult problem to solve, has been the public's concerns with privacy: It is one thing to track the movement of goods, and quite another thing to track the movement and activities of individual people. This "Big Brother is watching you" issue is likely to be a continuing topic of discussion in the coming years.

Sources: "RFID Users Will Increase Their Budgets in 2010," *Material Handling Management* 65, no. 1 (2010): 8; B. Trebilcock, "RFID: 6 Key Trends," *Modern Materials Handling* 61, no. 13 (2006): 43–46; W. McKnight, "RFID for the Information Management Professional, Part 2," *DM Review* 11, no. 13 (2006): 41; W. Hadfield, "RFID Tags Overtake Barcodes in M&S Food Business Supply Chain," *Computer Weekly*, March 28, 2006, 5; D. Power, "RFID Aids Inventory Control at Wal-Mart," *Women's Wear Daily* 191, no. 113 (2006): 27; R. A. Perrin and M. B. McAndrew, "RFID: The New Strategy in Healthcare IT," *Healthcare Purchasing News* 30, no. 10 (2006): 13–19; J. Silva, "RFID Tracking Gets 'Thumbs Down' from Government Panel," *Wireless News*, November 27, 2006, 3–4; "EC's Reding: RFID Policy Must Address Privacy Fears," *Telecommunications Reports*, November 1, 2006, 22.; B. Chatterjee (June, 2010), "RFID in Pharma Today," *Pharmaceutical Processing, 18–19*.

The Focus of Control

The decision about where to focus control in an organization involves critical choices based on which actions and outcomes should receive the greatest attention. In other words, the focus of control refers not only to *what* is to be controlled but also to *where* control should be located in the organizational structure. This means paying careful attention to which people or positions in the structure have responsibility for different types and areas of control and how broad or narrow is their scope of responsibility. Control responsibility that is too broad can lead to omissions, and responsibility that is too concentrated can result in bottlenecks and decision delays. On one hand, if too many people are responsible for quality control of a complex set of equipment, each may assume that one of the others has taken care of a particular problem, and, as a consequence, some aspect of control gets left undone. On the other hand, if only one person is charged with inspecting all the pieces of equipment, he or she may get overloaded, with the result that some critical detail gets inadvertently overlooked. Either way, effective control could be compromised.

The guiding principle for focusing control is that it should be closely linked to the strategic goals and, particularly, the planning process of the organization. For example, Nordstrom's strategic focus is customer service. As a consequence, while the company would probably not be wise to ignore inventory controls, the focus would need to be on how to maintain a high level of customer satisfaction.

To be most effective, planning should be part of the control process, and control should be part of the planning process. Priorities should be set regarding what should be intensely monitored and controlled and what should be given less attention. As software firms have found out, for example, little is to be gained from requiring star programmers to come to work on a precise schedule, given that the real objective is to produce innovative software. It is worth considerable control effort in that kind of organization, however, to make sure that the software that is written is as absolutely error-free as possible.

One approach to determining the focus of control that has become popular in recent years is the **balanced scorecard**.[41] Advocates of this approach argue that historically there has been an "over-focus" on financial ratios and budgetary controls and a corresponding neglect of other important areas of measurement of a company's performance.[42] To remedy this, the developers of the balanced scorecard approach proposed an integrated and "balanced" set of measures for four critical areas ("perspectives" as they called them):[43]

balanced scorecard
an integrated and "balanced" set of measures for four critical areas or perspectives: financial, customers, internal business, and innovation and learning

1. The (traditional) financial perspective: How do shareholders perceive the company?
2. The customer perspective: How do customers perceive the company?
3. The internal business perspective: Does the company excel in its internal business operations and procedures?
4. The innovation and learning perspective: How well is the company doing at innovating, improving, and creating value?

Balanced-scorecard proponents argue that financial perspective approaches primarily pay attention to the past and that the other three categories are much more future oriented. In effect, a presumed significant advantage of the balanced scorecard is that it requires managers to link measures of organizational success more closely to strategic objectives.[44] It also encourages managers to assess whether success in one area may be coming at the expense of poor performance in another area(s). It is intended, therefore, to bring greater focus and concentration on a total set of the most important areas of evaluation and control.

Many companies—perhaps as many as 50 to 60 percent of large U.S. firms—appear to have adopted some form of the balanced-scorecard approach.[45] Executives at a wide range of organizations such as ExxonMobil, Cigna Insurance, Port Authority of Valencia, Spain, and Kiwibank of New Zealand, for example, believe the balanced-scorecard approach has helped to improve overall corporate performance. Nonetheless, some questions have been raised about the approach. One is whether or not there are only four major areas to measure and whether these areas are the "correct" ones. A missing area, for example, is how employees perceive the organization: Is it doing a good job of attracting and retaining talent? Also, should a company concentrate on only one or two of the areas or some other sort of mix?[46] Still another issue—which is common to any system or overall approach to control measurement—is how difficult it is to design and implement the types of measures called for in this comprehensive approach.[47] Regardless, it is clear that the balanced scorecard has introduced a significant and innovative approach to control—one that focuses on more than just financial numbers.

The Amount of Control to Apply

As we discussed at the beginning of this chapter, one of the greatest control challenges for any organization or manager is to determine the amount of control to apply—a choice that can mean the difference between the life and death of an organization. The "A Manager's Challenge" feature illustrates such a situation: A company that almost went out of existence not only because of deliberate flouting of controls by the top executive, but also because there had been too little control virtually throughout the organization for an extended period of time.

Effective control involves finding a balance between overcontrol and undercontrol. Often, less-experienced managers tend to apply more control than is necessary in their eagerness to demonstrate that they are "in charge." This, in turn, can produce unintended resentment and resistance. Thus, new managers need to be aware of this tendency and moderate it. Issues of over- or under-control, however, can occur with even the most experienced managers or companies. Toyota found this out in recent years in their overzealous controls of costs. Although the company disputes that cost reductions in parts and manufacturing were the cause, by early 2010 it faced 109 class actions and 32 individual-filed cases in North America involving safety-related failures of equipment.[48]

Ordinarily, when managers have more experience, they would be expected to have a better basis for gauging the minimum levels of control that will get the job done without incurring unjustified risks. Even seasoned managers, however, often find it difficult to judge correctly the degree of control required, and problems of under- or over-control can crop up where least expected. No predetermined "right" amounts of control apply to all work situations. The best guideline for a manager to follow is to view the amount of control as something that, within limits, can be adjusted. Additionally, the undesirable consequences of excessive control and the dangers of too little control need to be made part of careful assessments of performance requirements and not inadvertently or casually overlooked. As we have already mentioned, involving those who will be directly influenced by the control measures in setting the amount of control increases the chances that an appropriate level of control is set from the outset. Furthermore, if adjustments need to be made, this initial involvement will likely reduce the resistance to needed changes.

The Quality of Information

Effective control requires using knowledge that is based on accurate data, a situation that Brad Carter faced in deciding whether to invest in new customer retention software; that is, it requires good information. Four characteristics that determine the quality of information are usefulness, accuracy, timeliness, and objectivity.

A MANAGER'S CHALLENGE

ETHICS

Collapse of Control—or Worse?

Sometimes, the breakdown of controls in an organization can be deliberate on someone's part, and sometimes it can be inadvertent. In the case of the software company CA (formerly, Computer Associates) in the last few years, it seems to have been both. The "deliberate" aspect was confirmed by the guilty plea of former CEO Sanjay Kumar in April 2006, and his subsequent sentencing in November of that year to 12 years in federal prison.

What were the charges against Kumar that constituted deliberate flouting of the organization's control systems? Among them were falsely reporting revenues to the U.S. Securities and Exchange Commission (SEC) over at least a three-year period. These revenues, from licensing agreements, were reported in a given quarter, despite the fact that some of the deals were not formally closed until at least the following quarter, a practice referred to colloquially as a "35-day month." This was done in order to make the company's revenue picture look more impressive than it actually was, which of course helped its stock price. Additionally, Kumar had conspired with other company officials to back-date contracts and other documents. All of this was further compounded by the fact that he then "obstructed justice" by lying about these activities to the SEC and the FBI.

Clearly, unethical behavior was involved in Kumar's actions. However, the company also had major control problems that were unrelated to the fraudulent activities described previously. A truly great irony at CA was the fact that although it was a company that specialized in providing extremely complex software systems in areas such as database management and storage to over 95 percent of the *Fortune* 500 companies, it had never installed sophisticated business software in its own company! A classic example of "do as I say (sell to you), but not as I do!"

The lack of adequate control systems in its own operations resulted in at least two accounting restatements, a late filing of an SEC 10-K form, and a botched sales commission program. The latter had been developed by the CEO who succeeded Kumar. The program was designed to alter the reward basis for commissions in order to create better and longer-term relationships with customers. However, the revised commission plan turned out to be very complex and overwhelmed the company's archaic computer systems. So much so that as one report put it, "[15 people in the finance department] were assigned the unenviable task of individually calculating each commission for the company's 4,000 salespeople." Or, as one former CA executive said: "A lot of the [company's] systems were internally developed and had not been updated...so it was very much a spaghetti code of an application. And no one could believe any of the data."

A new CEO, John Swainson, was recruited from IBM in 2004 and took a number of steps to improve CA's operations and controls, as well as its ethical climate. However, as he indicated in late 2005, "It took a long time for the company to get screwed up, and it will take a long time to get it 'unscrewed' up." Since then, though, definite progress has been made in that direction, and the revitalized company (which has about 13,000 employees and which recently changed its brand name to CA Technologies) has done relatively well in a demanding competitive environment. Nevertheless, making up for prior ethical lapses (by others) and inadequate control systems has never been an easy managerial task.

Sources: S. E. Ante, "Software Maker CA Changes Name," *Wall Street Journal,* May 14, 2010, http://online.wsj.com; "CA Makes Headway," *BusinessWeek Online*, February 5, 2007; N. Varchaver, S. Kaufman, and D. Burke, "Long Island Confidential," *Fortune*, November 27, 2006, 172–186; "Ex CA CEO Gets Prison," *Network World*, November 6, 2006, www.networkworld.com; W. Atkinson, "CA's Procurement Overhaul Focuses on Global Expertise," April 6, 2006, www.purchasing.com, 17–20; A. N. Stuart, "Sins of Commission," *CFO* 22, no. 9 (2006): 20; R. J. Newman, "Debugging CA," *U. S. News & World Report*, 2006, EE12.

USEFULNESS Not all data collected for control purposes are equally useful in managerial operations and decisions. Sometimes data that were once useful continue to be collected, even though the original purposes for obtaining that information have disappeared. Consider a situation in a division of a major manufacturing company. Because of major changes in the operating environment at one of its units, the company decided to find out which accounting reports, if any, were actually helpful to managers. Did the information contained in the reports actually help managers do their jobs better? The answer was a resounding "no." Investigation indicated the accounting department thought it was gathering data that two separate groups could use: corporate managers and plant managers. Yet, it turned out that the information being disseminated was of assistance only to the first group. As a result, the accounting department worked with operations managers in the plants to develop control reports that would help them do their particular jobs more effectively.

ACCURACY Data or numbers that are inaccurate or misleading not only fail to provide a good basis for control steps but also breed cynicism among those whose performance is being measured. Since control actions, especially those designed to change behavior that does not meet agreed-upon standards, can have such powerful effects, it is vital that substantial effort be put into obtaining data that are absolutely valid. Otherwise, no information is better than inaccurate information.

TIMELINESS Even accurate data, if they arrive too late, are not useful. This is true for any organizational actions but especially so for purposes of control. In the fast-paced world of global business, data that are out of date are of virtually no use. For effective control, information must arrive on time to those who can take action and make any required changes. In everyday life, for example, information that arrives to truck drivers 10 minutes after the wrong route has been taken is not very useful. Effective control systems require speed.

OBJECTIVITY Objectivity, especially as it relates to control, is something of a two-edged sword. Almost everyone would agree that objective facts are better than subjective, and possibly biased, opinions. However, for some kinds of performances, objective data may not be possible to obtain or even may be misleading. In a diving competition, the exact height that a diver jumps off a springboard may be much less important than the subjective opinion of an experienced judge about the form of the dive. Similarly, in organizations, some of the most easily measured activities, and, therefore, the most easily controlled, may be relatively insignificant for the achievement of major, strategic goals. All other factors being equal, objective information would be preferred, but in many situations, those other factors may not be equal, and thoughtful judgments rather than unimportant "facts" may provide the best basis for action decisions.

For example, in a customer service call center, it is relatively easy to gather objective data on the length of time a customer service agent spends on the phone with each caller. However, comparing the number of callers served by each agent may not tell you the most important thing—how well each customer was served. If the number of calls answered becomes the key performance measure, customer service agents may begin to provide poor service in order to get customers off the phone quickly and move on to the next customer, thereby maximizing the number of calls they take in a day. In this case, it is clear that the objective data (the number of calls taken) may not be the most important data (that is, how well the customer is served). To measure customer service effectively may require having a supervisor randomly listen in on service calls or going to the cost and effort of trying to measure customer satisfaction by polling customers who have called in to the service center.

Flexibility

For control to be effective, its procedures must respond to changing conditions. Organizations and managers get accustomed to control procedures that are already in place. It is a human tendency to stay the course when things appear to be going well. But that tendency can defeat effective control. Well-designed control systems should be able to account for changing circumstances and adjust accordingly. Rigidity of control systems usually is not a feature to be prized. Flexibility often is.[49]

Favorable Cost-Benefit Ratio

The designs of some control systems look good on paper, but they prove to be impractical or costly to use. To be effective, the benefits of controls must outweigh both the direct financial costs and the indirect costs of inconvenience and awkwardness in implementation. Elaborate, complicated control systems immediately raise the issue of whether they will be worth the expense involved. Sometimes, the simplest systems are nearly as effective. Consider again the customer service call center example. Obtaining satisfaction ratings directly from customers may cost significantly more and not provide much better information than feedback that well-trained supervisors can provide.

Managerial Challenges from the Front Line

The Rest of the Story

Brad Carter decided that it was worth it to invest in the new customer retention software. The software was installed across the board on all the sales representatives' computers, and an additional investment was also made to train each of the representatives to use it. Along with the installation of this new tracking aid, the sales representatives were given explicit targets of how many customer contacts they should make each week. Furthermore, they were told that the actual number of contacts that were made would be compared against the target number on a monthly basis.

With the new software, the number of actual customer contacts could be precisely tracked both by Carter as a manager and by each salesperson. As a result of this enhanced method of accountability, sales soon increased by 60 percent, more than repaying the investments made in the new system.

Some situations, however, require that intricate and complex controls be implemented because not doing so could be disastrous. (See the Closing Case for a discussion of the 2010 "Disaster in the Gulf of Mexico" in this regard.) Nuclear power plants, military weapons units, and federal air traffic control agencies need to invest heavily in control systems that ensure an exceedingly high degree of reliability. Consequently, they have to make costly investments—in, for example, continual training, back-up staffing, and very expensive equipment—to control operations and reduce the possibility of a catastrophic accident to absolute minimum levels.[50] In such cases, high control costs are obviously justified.

Sources

The source of control often affects the willingness of organization members to work cooperatively with the system. As we discussed earlier, in recent years many organizations have changed from bureaucratic control to control that relies more on members' monitoring their own or their team's performance. Thus, the source of control is shifted, and the change may increase positive reactions because employees have more trust in a process over which they have some influence.

Similarly, controls that provide information from equipment or instruments often seem less resented and more fair than controls involving what can be viewed as the sometimes arbitrary actions of supervisors. For any type of control, the source has a great deal to do with the acceptability of the system. Acceptability, in turn, affects how well control systems work in practice and not just in theory.

Summary

- The word *control* often has negative connotations. However, control has an essential role in the overall process of management. It involves the regulation of activities and behavior to determine the degree of conformity to an organization's objectives. In other words, without controls there is very little coordination that can take place within an organization. Control is a necessary function that follows, but complements, the other major functions of management: planning, organizing, and leading.
- There are four basic elements of any control process in organizations: establishing standards, measuring performance, comparing performance against standards, and evaluating the results of the comparisons and taking any necessary follow-up action. Each of these elements of the control function has its own problems and issues, such as: how stringent the standards should be, what aspects of performance should be measured, whether comparisons against standards should be judged on an overall basis or a standard-by-standard basis, and whether any deviations from standards are major enough to cause a change in policies or procedures.

■ A significant dimension of control in organizations is the breadth of scope of controls. Generally, the degree of scope falls under three major categories: strategic, or very broad controls addressed to long-range goals; tactical, or controls that are intermediate in breadth and that focus on the implementation of strategy; and operational, or very concrete controls that assess and regulate specific activities or methods against very well-defined immediate objectives.

■ Strategic controls are very broad and, thus, it is often difficult to measure their effectiveness. They can also be affected by unexpected changes in the organization's external environment, This can cause problems when it comes to setting standards that are applicable across extended periods of time. Generally, the greater the degree of environmental uncertainty, the more decentralized an organization's control system will be.

■ Tactical controls are intermediate in scope. They are typically the fundamental part of the overall set of controls that apply to specific units of the organization in connection with the implementation of strategy. Some of the major types of tactical controls are financial controls, budgetary controls, supervisory structure controls, and human resource controls. Two general orientations to how tactical controls are applied in practice are: a rules-and-regulation, or bureaucratic-oriented, approach; and a commitment, or clan, type of self-control approach.

■ Operational controls relate to the transformation of organizational inputs into outputs. Operational controls can be applied at three different stages of a process: before the transformation takes place (precontrol), during the actual transformation (concurrent controls), or after the transformation is completed (postcontrol). In recent years, organizations have attempted to place more emphasis on pre- and concurrent control instead of relying only on postcontrol.

■ A number of factors, such as the focus of control, the quality of information, and the flexibility of controls, can determine the effectiveness of control systems. A particularly difficult issue for organizations that can impact control effectiveness is to decide on the amount of control. An error in either direction—either too little or too much control—can lead to potentially severe consequences.

Key Terms

balanced scorecard 405	concurrent control 402	precontrol 402
break-even point (BEP) 398	control 388	standard 390
budgetary control 398	human resource policies and	strategic control 395
bureaucratic control 400	procedures 400	supervisory
commitment (clan)	operational control 402	structure 399
control 401	postcontrol 402	tactical control 396

Review Questions

1. What is meant by *control* in organizations?
2. How is the control function linked to other managerial functions?
3. Who is responsible for setting standards?
4. What key issues must managers consider when establishing standards?
5. When measuring performance, can nonquantifiable data be helpful? How?
6. What is the limiting factor in comparing performance against standards?
7. Compare strategic, tactical, and operational control. Why are the boundaries between each not always clear?
8. Describe four managerial control issues involving budgets.
9. What is the fundamental difference between bureaucratic control and commitment (clan) control?
10. What is the relationship between pre-, concurrent, and postcontrols of operations? Which type is best?
11. What are the advantages and the problems involved in using a balanced-scorecard approach?
12. What factors determine the usefulness of information to the control process?

Assessing Your Capabilities

How Willing Am I to Delegate?

Using the following scale, circle the number that best indicates the extent to which you agree or disagree with each statement. If you have not worked in a supervisory role, consider a supervisor you have had. Evaluate that individual on these questions. Then, consider how you reacted to the type of control used by your supervisor. You can also apply this to student groups or teams where you have been in charge.

	Strongly Agree	Agree	Neither Agree nor Disagree	Disagree	Strongly Disagree
1. I'd delegate more, but the jobs I delegate never seem to get done the way I want them to be done.	1	2	3	4	5
2. I don't feel I have the time to delegate properly.	1	2	3	4	5
3. I carefully check on subordinates' work without letting them know I'm doing it, so I can correct their mistakes if necessary before they cause too many problems.	1	2	3	4	5
4. I delegate the whole job—giving the opportunity for the subordinate to complete it without any of my involvement. Then I review the result.	1	2	3	4	5
5. When I have given clear instructions and the task isn't done right, I get upset.	1	2	3	4	5
6. I feel my staff lacks the commitment that I have. So any task I delegate won't get done as well as I'd do it.	1	2	3	4	5
7. I'd delegate more, but I feel I can do the task better than the person I might delegate it to.	1	2	3	4	5
8. I'd delegate more, but if the individual I delegate the task to does an incompetent job, I'll be seriously criticized.	1	2	3	4	5
9. If I were to delegate a task, my job wouldn't be nearly as much fun.	1	2	3	4	5
10. When I delegate a task, I often find that the outcome is such that I end up doing the task over again myself.	1	2	3	4	5
11. I have not really found that delegation saves any time.	1	2	3	4	5
12. I delegate a task clearly and concisely, explaining exactly how it should be accomplished.	1	2	3	4	5
13. I can't delegate as much as I'd like to because my subordinates lack the necessary experience.	1	2	3	4	5
14. I feel that when I delegate, I lose control.	1	2	3	4	5
15. I would delegate more, but I'm pretty much a perfectionist.	1	2	3	4	5
16. I work longer hours than I should.	1	2	3	4	5
17. I can give subordinates the routine tasks, but I feel I must keep nonroutine tasks to myself.	1	2	3	4	5
18. My own boss expects me to keep very close to all details of my job.	1	2	3	4	5

Scoring

To obtain your score:
Add your responses to all 18 items.
Enter score here: _____

Analysis and Interpretation

Managers get things done through other people. To do so, they need to be able to delegate, but many managers find difficulty in doing this. This instrument taps most of the excuses new managers give for failing to delegate. It also addresses some of the errors used when delegation is done improperly. In conjunction with this chapter, this instrument gives you insight into whether you tend to overcontrol situations.

Your score can be interpreted as follows:

72–90 points =	Effective delegation
54–71 points =	You still have room to improve
36–53 points =	Delegation skills need substantial improvement
18–35 points =	Ineffective delegation

Source: Adapted from *Prentice Hall's Self Assessment Library*, ed. S. P. Robbins and T. A. Judge.

Team Exercise

Controlling Your Team

Your group has just been formed as a permanent new-products development team at X-Lent Corporation. X-Lent is the industry leader in new-product development but is lagging behind others in the industry in controlling for the costs of new-product development. The members of your team have a great deal of experience and are all highly committed to doing the best possible job both in developing new products and in controlling the costs involved.

Your group is meeting today to determine what elements of the process should be controlled and how to control them. You realized that there are many possible elements to control. These might include the obvious such as materials and technology costs, but also could include team process costs (individual contributions, absenteeism, turnover, etc.), and maybe even other items.

Your group should try to determine all the possible areas where maintaining control will help to reduce overall costs. Then, remembering that you need to maintain a favorable cost–benefit ratio, you should determine which controls should be put in place. Then make a report of your findings. You will need to justify all the controls you have included and why you felt others should be omitted.

Source: Copyright © Grace B. McLaughlin. Reprinted with permission.

Closing Case

Disaster in the Gulf of Mexico:
A Case of "An Ounce of
Prevention..."?

At 9:50 PM on April 20, 2010, massive explosions occurred on the giant oil drilling rig Deepwater Horizon located in the Gulf of Mexico and operating on behalf of the global oil company BP PLC. Eleven of the 126 people working on the rig were killed, and the fire resulting from the explosions sank the rig within the next two days. This catastrophic event raises many different kinds of issues (such as effects on marine life and other elements of the coastal environment), but certainly a major issue that pertains to the topic of management is that of controls. Were the right kinds of controls in place before the incident? Were they sufficient in amount and scope? Were they effective once the explosions had taken place? These are just some of the many control-type questions that could be asked.

In evaluating what happened, or didn't happen, in the months, weeks, and days leading up to the series of developments on the Deepwater Horizon that culminated in the explosions, it is useful to consider some background context. The Gulf incident and events and decisions preceding it occurred in an organizational environment where BP, in the last several years, had been putting increased emphasis on controlling costs. For instance, in an address to top managers in 2008, a senior executive of BP emphasized the importance of establishing a "much stronger performance culture" in the company and the need to strictly monitor and, if possible, reduce expenses for greater efficiency. Thus, from a financial perspective, in the case of the Deepwater Horizon situation two years later, BP managers clearly had an incentive to make as rapid progress as possible on completing the well and moving the rig to another drilling location. Nevertheless, as of April 20, BP was already 43 days late in finishing the job and was paying the rig owner, Transocean, some $500,000 per day for each additional day of its lease.

To review the timeline of events and decisions leading up to the pipeline blowout:

- June 2009: BP engineers note concerns in internal company correspondence regarding the type of casings being used for the well because they failed to meet the company's own safety and design specifications. Nevertheless, those casings were used.
- March 2010 [all dates hereafter are in the year 2010]: Sudden and unexpected bursts of gas, called "kicks," occur on the drilling rig. Several workers express to their wives their worries about the increasing number of these kicks.
- March: Also around this time, the "blowout preventer" that was supposed to seal the well in an emergency is found to be leaking fluids on three different occasions. The U.S. government's drilling oversight regulatory agency, the Minerals Management Service (MMS), permits a requested delay in the testing of the blowout preventer. When testing starts again, the MMS allows BP to use a lower pressure (6,500 pounds per square inch) than the 10,000 psi pressure that was used in the tests that were carried out before the delay.
- April 1: An employee of Halliburton, the firm subcontracted to provide pipeline cementing services, notes in his job log that the way BP is using the cement "is against our best practices."
- April 16-18: BP engineers decide to use only six "centralizers" to stabilize the well before cementing it, instead of the 21 recommended by Halliburton, because "it will take 10 hours to install them," according to an email from a BP official. Halliburton again warns BP about the cementing practices being used and states that a "severe" gas flow could occur if the pipeline casings were not better centered.
- April 20, 5 PM: Tests of the adequacy of the hardening of the cement plug that is being poured are either unsatisfactory or inconclusive.
- April 20, 8 PM: After additional cementing tests are run, BP decides to end tests, remove the mud in the pipe, and replace it with lighter seawater.
- April 20, 9:49 PM: Mud suddenly flows out of the top of the rig's derrick, and an initial small explosion occurs.
- April 20, 9:50 PM: The large explosion erupts.

Prior to the explosions, there appeared to have been confusion about who was in charge. An official panel convened a few weeks after the incident pursued this question intensively, given that four organizations—BP, Transocean, Halliburton, and MMS—were involved in activities on the rig. In answer to the question, the rig's captain responded: "It's pretty well understood amongst the crew who's in charge." A panel member (from the Coast Guard) insisted: "How do you know that?" The rig captain replied: "I guess I don't know... but it's pretty well... everyone knows." This vital question had in fact been tested in the immediate aftermath of the April 20 explosions. Once the events had occurred with sudden, unexpected, and tremendous force that evening, the captain of the rig quickly got together with eight others (managers and crew members) to try to decide what to do. However, confusion reigned. According to press reports, one of the participants, from Transocean, wrote in a log afterward that he had heard the captain scream at a worker "because she had pressed the distress button without authorization." The Transocean employee also reported that he had asked someone if he had contacted the shore for help, but that person said he did not have the authority to do so.

Questions

1. Was the Deepwater Horizon accident a clear and unequivocal case that illustrates the proverb "An ounce of prevention is worth a pound of cure"? Why or why not?

2. What is the most important control issue in this case?

3. Keeping in mind costs, what is the single most effective control step BP could have taken in advance to prevent or reduce the possibility of a blowout?

4. Aside from problems relating to control, name three other important sets of management issues that were involved in this incident. Justify your choices and provide a ranking of those issues.

Sources: G. Chazan, B. Faucon, and B. Casselman, "Safety and Cost Drives Clashed as CEO Hayward Remade BP," *Wall Street Journal*, June 30, 2010, A1+; N. King, "BP Focused on Costs: Congress," *Wall Street Journal*, June 15, 2010, A1+; C. Kirkham, "Deepwater Horizon Oil Well Was Increasingly Out of Control Before Explosion, Widows Testify," *The Times Picayune*, June 7, 2010. I. Urbina, "At Issue in Gulf: Who Was in Charge?", *New York Times*, June 6, 2010, 1+; R. Gold and N. King, "Red Flags Were Ignored Aboard Doomed Rig," *Wall Street Journal*, May 13, 2010, A6.

References

1. G. Mars, "From the Enclave to Hierarchy – and on to Tyranny: the Micro-political Organization of a Consultant's Group," *Culture and Organization* 4 (2008): 365–378.

2. G. Orwell, *1984: A Novel* (New York: New American Library, 1950); D. E. W. Marginson, "Management Control Systems and Their Effects on Strategy Formation at Middle-management Levels: Evidence from a U.K. Organization," *Strategic Management Journal* 23, no. 11 (2002): 1019–1031; M. Goold and A. Campbell, "Do You Have a Well-designed Organization?" *Harvard Business Review* 80, no. 3 (2002): 117–124; W. Nasrallah, R. Levitt, and P. Glynn, "Interaction Value Analysis: When Structured Communication Benefits Organizations," *Organization Science* 14, no. 5 (2003): 541–557.

3. A. S. Tannenbaum, ed., *Control in Organizations* (New York: McGraw-Hill, 1968); Marginson, "Management Control Systems and Their Effects on Strategy Formation"; Campbell, "Do You Have a Well-Designed Organization?"; Nasrallah, Levitt, and Glynn, "Interaction Value Analysis."

4. L. Seism, "Prudential Auditor Gave Early Warning Signals About Sales Abuses," *Wall Street Journal*, August 7, 1997, A1, A4.

5. Company Web site, http://www.dartadvantage.com/new.htm, accessed June 25, 2010.

6. B. Govrindarajan, "Impact of Participation in the Budgetary Process on Managerial Attitudes and Performance: Universalistic and Contingency Perspectives," *Decision Sciences* 7 (1986): 496–516.

7. E. A. Lock, "The Ubiquity of the Technique of Goal Setting in Theories of and Approaches to Employee Motivation," *Academy of Management Review* 3 (1978): 594–601; A. Drach-Zachavy and M. Erez, "Challenge Versus Threat Effects on the Goal–Performance Relationship," *Organizational Behavior and Human Decision Processes* 88, no. 2 (2002): 667–682.

8. R. N. Anthony and J. S. Reece, *Accounting Principles,* 7th ed. (Chicago: Richard D. Irwin, 1995).

9. Ibid.

10. J. Hope and R. Fraser, "Who Needs Budgets?" *Harvard Business Review* 81, no. 2 (2003): 108–115.

11. "Measuring the Immeasurable," *Strategic HR Review* 4, no. 5 (2005): 7.

12. F. D. Buggie, "Set the 'Fuzzy Front End' in Concrete," *Research Technology Management* 45, no. 4 (2002): 11–14; R. G. Cooper, "Managing Technology Development Projects," *Research*

Technology Management 49, no. 6 (2006): 23–31; J. E. Ettlie and J. M. Elsenbach, "Modified Stage–Gate Regimes in New Product Development," *Journal of Product Innovation Management* 24, no. 1 (2007): 20–33.

13. Y. Li, L. Li *et al.,* "Linking Management Control System with Product Development and Process Decisions to Cope with Environment Complexity," *International Journal of Production Research* 43, no. 12 (2005): 2577–2591.

14. R. I. Delgado and J. R. Langabeer, II, "Strategic Performance Evaluation in Cancer Centers," *Journal of Healthcare Management*. 54, no. 6 (2009): 369–382.

15. Marginson, "Management Control Systems and Their Effects on Strategy Formation"; M. Goold and J. J. Quinn, "The Paradox of Strategic Controls," *Strategic Management Journal* 11 (1990): 43–57.

16. J. Hogan and B. Holland, "Using Theory to Evaluate Personality and Job-performance Relations: A Socioanalytic Perspective," *Journal of Applied Psychology* 88, no. 1 (2003): 100; P. Lorange and D. C. Murphy, "Strategy and Human Resources: Concepts and Practice," *Human Resource Management* 22, nos. 1–2 (1983): 111–135.

17. J. A. Alexander, "Adaptive Change in Corporate Control Practices," *Academy of Management Journal* 34 (1991): 162–193; V. Govindarajan and J. Fisher, "Strategy, Control Systems, and Resource Sharing: Effects on Business-unit Performance," *Academy of Management Journal* 33 (1990): 259–285.

18. A. Zuber, "McD Restructures to Beef Up Performance," *Nation's Restaurant News* 35, no. 44 (2001): 1, 6; K. Benner, "Consumer Confidential: Get Paid to Shop," CNNMoney.com, November 29, 2005, http://money. cnn.com/2005/11/29/pf/ secret_shop/index.htm.

19. Alexander, "Adaptive Change in Corporate Control Practices," 181.

20. G. Hamel and L. Valikangas, "The Quest for Resilience," *Harvard Business Review* 81, no. 9 (2003): 52–63; Goold and Quinn, "The Paradox of Strategic Controls."

21. Ibid, figure 2, 55.

22. Li *et al.*, "Linking Management Control System with Product Development and Process Decisions to Cope with Environment Complexity."

23. L. Strauss, "Come Fly with Me," *Barron's* 82, no. 33 (2002): T8.

24. Goold and Quinn, "The Paradox of Strategic Controls."

25. N. C. Churchill, "Budget Choice: Planning vs. Control," *Harvard Business Review* 62, no. 4 (1984): 150–164.

26. W. A. Van der Stede, "The Relationship Between Two Consequences of Budgetary Controls: Budgetary Slack Creation and Managerial Short-term Orientation," *Accounting, Organizations and Society* 25 (2000): 609–622.

27. C. Bendersky, C. Morill, *et al.,* "Fair Control: Complementarities Between Types of Managerial Controls and Employees' Fairness Evaluations," *Academy of Management Proceedings* (2006): F1–F6.

28. M. Gallagher and V. S. Radcliffe, "Internal Controls in Nonprofit Organizations: The Case of the American Cancer Society, Ohio Division," *Nonprofit Management and Leadership* 12, no. 3 (2002): 313–325.

29. P. Kibort, "Raising the Bar of Safety for Your Medical Staff," *Physician Executive* 22, no. 1 (2007): 48–51.

30. M. J. Rogers and C. M. Walker, "Evaluation of Leadership Teamwork Interventions at DTE Energy – Fermi 2 Nuclear Power Station," *Electric Light & Power* 88, no. 3 Special Section, (2010): 6–8.

31. J. R. Barker, "Tightening the Iron Cage: Concertive Control in Self-managing Teams," *Administrative Science Quarterly* 38 (1993): 408–437; Goold and Quinn, "The Paradox of Strategic Controls"; W. G. Ouichi, "A Conceptual Framework for the Design of Organizational Control Mechanisms," *Management Science* 25 (1979): 833–848; W. G. Ouichi, "Markets, Bureaucracies, and Clans," *Administrative Science Quarterly* 25 (1980): 129–141; R. E. Walton, "From Control to Commitment in the Workplace," *Harvard Business Review* 63, no. 2 (1985): 76–84.

32. T. R. Tyler and S. L. Blader, "Can Businesses Effectively Regulate Employee Conduct? The Antecedents of Rule Following in Work Settings," *Academy of Management Journal* 4 (2005): 1143–1158.

33. Barker, "Tightening the Iron Cage."

34. W. H. Newman, *Constructive Control: Design and Use of Control Systems* (Upper Saddle River: Prentice Hall, 1975).

35. N. Panagopoulos and S. Dimitriadis "Transformational Leadership as a Mediator of the Relationship Between Behavior-based Control and Salespeople's Key Outcomes," *European Journal of Marketing* 43 (2008): 1008–1031.

36. J. Sloane, "Small Companies That Play Big," *Fortune Small Business,* 2006: 26–38.

37. T. Van Hampton, "Crane Owners Step up Inspections to Meet Tighter Quality Controls," *Engineering News Record* 264, no. 3 (2010): 28–35.

38. "Koch Pipeline Reaches Safety Milestone," *Pipeline and Gas Journal* 223, no. 12 (2006): 2–4.

39. Gunther, M., "Union Pacific: Building America," *Fortune* 162 (1): 120–124.

40. R. N. Anthony, J. Dearden, and V. Govindarajan, *Management Control Systems*, 8th ed. (Burr Ridge: Richard D. Irwin, 1995).

41. R. I. Delgado and J. R. Langabeer, II, "Strategic Performance Evaluation in Cancer Centers."

42. R. S. Kaplan and D. P. Norton, "The Balanced Scorecard— Measures That Drive Performance," *Harvard Business Review* 70, no. 1 (1992): 71–80; A. Neely and M. Bourne, "Why Measurement Initiatives Fail," *Quality Focus* 4, no. 4 (2000): 3–6.

43. Kaplan and Norton, "The Balanced Scorecard."

44. R. S. Kaplan, D. P. Norton and B. Rugelsjoen, "Managing Alliances with the Balanced Scorecard," *Harvard Business Review* 88, no. 1/2 (2010): 114–120; W. B. Tayler, "The Balanced Scorecard as a Strategy-evaluation Tool: The Effects of Implementation Involvement and a Causal-chain Focus," *The Accounting Review* 85 (2010): 1095–1117; J. A. Aparisi-Caudell, A. Giner-Fillol and E. M. Perez-Garcia, "Evidence on Implementing a Balanced Scorecard System at the Port Authority of Valencia," *Global Business Research* 3, no. 2 (2009): 93–116.

45. Neely and Bourne, "Why Measurement Initiatives Fail"; E. M. Olson and S. F. Slater, "The Balanced Scorecard, Competitive Strategy, and Performance," *Business Horizons* 45, no. 3 (2002): 11–16; "Zen and the Art of the Balanced Scorecard," June 23, 2010, http://www. cio.com/white-paper/595891/.

46. Olson and Slater, "The Balanced Scorecard, Competitive Strategy, and Performance."

47. Neely and Bourne, "Why Measurement Initiatives Fail."

48. A. Ohnsman, J. Green, K. Inoue, D. Welch, M. C. Fisk, D. Levin, I. Rowley, M. Kitamura and Y. Hagiwara, "The Humbling of Toyota," *BusinessWeek.* (4171), March, 22, 2010, 32–36.

49. G. A. Bigley and K. H. Roberts, "The Incident Command System: High-reliability Organizing for Complex and Volatile Task Environments," *Academy of Management Journal* 44 (2001): 1281–1299.

50. K. H. Roberts, "Managing High Reliability Organizations," *California Management Review* 32, no. 4 (1990): 101–113.

15

Organizational Change and Development

LEARNING OBJECTIVES

After studying this chapter, you should be able to:

Identify the internal and external forces for change in an organization.

Discuss the focus of change, including strategy, structure, systems, technology, culture, and staff.

Analyze the process managers should use in evaluating the need for change.

Describe the process of organizational change.

Explain common sources of resistance during the process of change.

Discuss key approaches to overcoming such resistance.

Outline the choices managers must make in managing change.

Describe the most important elements involved in evaluating change outcomes.

Describe three approaches to comprehensive organizational change and compare their similarities and differences.

Courtesy of Chris Haenen

Name: Chris Haenen

Position: Director, PricewaterhouseCoopers Advisory Services

Alma mater: Leiden University, the Netherlands

Outside work activities: Family, sports (shooting and fitness), wining and dining

First job out of school: Junior consultant at Deloitte

Business book reading now: *It Starts With One* by Stewart Black

Hero: My grandfather, who was always able to do the right thing, in harsh times and against the odds

Motto to live by: Enjoy the journey, not the destination

What drives me: New experiences, new people, learn something new every day

Management style: No guts no glory, manage by objectives, empower people as much as possible

Pet peeve: Other people's disorder

Chris Haenen was one of three directors (including the managing director) in the Netherland office of PricewaterhouseCoopers (PwC), a global accounting firm. Since 2005, the office's results varied from great to poor, but overall the team had managed to reach budgets. Locally, however, the 18-member office had been particularly successful, winning several large accounts at the expense of its main competitor, a Dutch boutique firm. In the summer of 2008, the team won another big account, a large Dutch multinational corporation. This created significant competitive pressure for the boutique firm. The PwC office proposed a joint venture with the boutique firm, which refused, and countered with an offer to acquire the PwC Netherlands office. The boutique named a price that PwC's managing director—the company's senior executive—found attractive.

On September 18, 2008, Haenen received a phone call from the managing director, informing him that he had sold the office to the boutique firm; the sale would be effective October 1. The following day, the managing director visited the Netherlands office to explain his decision—an explanation that Haenen felt added little clarity. That afternoon, the boutique firm CEO visited the PwC office to provide further explanation and to discuss integration plans. The reaction in the acquired office varied from anger and crying to disbelief—but no enthusiasm.

Haenen had some key decisions to make in dealing with this unexpected and very large change. First, should he personally stay in his job with the office and become an employee to the new owner? And, independent of what he personally chose to do, should he encourage his team to stay independent of what he personally decided to do with the new owner? If Haenen decided not to stay with the new owner, should he help his team find new jobs if they also decided not to stay?

As the real case of Chris Haenen illustrates, organizations never stay the same because the world around them never stays the same. From ancient times, all organizations and individuals have had to foster the capacity to change.[1]

Making changes and managing that process have been essential to the vitality of all organizations throughout history but today they are arguably more important than ever. However, managing the change process is no easy task. While the need to change is often obvious, making successful changes presents formidable managerial challenges. For example:

- How much change is enough?
- How fast should change take place?
- How should the need for continual changes be balanced against the need for a minimum level of stability and continuity?
- Who should be the major players in change processes, and what should their roles be?
- Who, exactly, is likely to benefit and who could be harmed by particular changes?

How these and similar questions are answered will determine the fate of attempted changes in any organization.

Throughout this book, we have emphasized understanding change as a major theme because it is so critical to managerial success. This final chapter focuses specifically on bringing about change in organizational settings. As a result, the chapter addresses specific means and methods used in changing the overall organization as well as units within it. The chapter presumes a basic knowledge of the other topics covered in this book. This knowledge will be helpful in analyzing the significant issues involved in organizational development and transformation.

Organizational contexts, because of their complexity, provide managers with many opportunities as well as challenges for making changes. Sometimes the changes that need to be made are unplanned and unpleasant. For example, even with more than $50 billion pumped into General Motors by the U.S. government, the economic downturn forced GM to lay off nearly 70,000 hourly workers (or entice them to retire) from 2006 through August 2009.[2] Other changes, like that undertaken by Chris Haenen, involve more planning and are designed to change fundamental aspects of the organization so that sudden, drastic changes, like layoffs, will not be necessary.

The first parts of this chapter examine general issues and principles relating to organizational development and transformation. We first review why organizations change—focusing on the forces that can cause changes. Particular attention is given to analyzing internal and external forces of change as well as recognizing and diagnosing those forces. The specific areas of change a company might undertake—its technology, shared values and culture, strategy, structure, systems, and staff—are considered next. These sections, in turn, provide a background for an examination of managerial choices regarding the preparation, implementation, and evaluation of the change process.

We conclude the chapter with an analysis of three major, typically organization-wide, approaches to planned change frequently used in contemporary organizations. These include the organizational development (OD) approach, process redesign (also known as reengineering), and the development of the learning organization. We will look at how these approaches are used, and at their relative strengths and weaknesses.

What Causes Organizations to Change?

The causes of organizational change originate from both external and internal forces, and a manager must be alert to all of them (see Exhibit 15.1). Sometimes those causes arise almost totally from factors outside the organization, such as economic or business conditions, technological developments, demographic shifts, and the like. At other times, the forces of change arise inside the organization. These forces include changes initiated by managers and employees. Often, the causes of change are a combination of both external and internal forces.

Forces Outside the Organization

A major driver of organizational change is the external environment in which the organization exists. A whole host of forces outside the organization can bring about changes inside it. Here, we discuss several of the most important.

ECONOMIC CONDITIONS Obvious forces for change affecting business organizations are developments in the economic environment. If the economy weakens, many companies reduce their workforce or at least limit hiring; prune low-profit product lines; and make other cost-cutting decisions. In 2009, economic conditions hurt sales enough that Dell moved a major production facility from Ireland to less costly Poland, leaving 1,900 Irish workers unemployed.[3]

Conversely, if the economy is vibrant and expanding, many firms consider adding new services or products, creating new units or divisions, increasing their geographic areas of operations, and undertaking similar growth changes. For example, foreign companies more than doubled their investments in China as the country's economy boomed from 2000 through 2009.[4]

Analogous to these business-world examples, many nonbusiness organizations, especially governmental agencies, contract or expand in relation to economic conditions because external forces directly impact their budgets. For example, the downturn in the economy in 2008-2009 hit the state of Michigan particularly hard, in part because of the high concentration of businesses related to the auto industry. The city of Flint felt the pain as city revenues (via taxes and other sources) declined, forcing Flint mayor Dayne Walling to announce a layoff of 23 percent of the

EXHIBIT 15.1

Forces for Change

city's firefighters.[5] While this change was viewed as necessary, Flint residents had to hope that the incidence of fire didn't rise with fewer firemen to fight them.

COMPETITORS' ACTIONS Regardless of the state of the economy, most businesses and many other organizations are likely to be extremely sensitive to moves made by their direct competitors, especially those in response to changes in the market or customers' preferences. The actions of other significant players in the immediate environment often can trigger changes inside a given organization, even when that organization would prefer not to make any changes. For example, once Apple decided to move into the mobile phone space, Google started pushing its alternative software and strategy. Strangely, Eric Schmidt, CEO of Google, formerly sat on Apple's board of directors and the two companies used to cooperate. With the release of the Apple 4G phone in 2010, Google pushed its Android software and EVO 4G made by HTC of Taiwan. Whereas Apple's software was proprietary and would work only on Apple's iPhones, Google decided not to make hardware, to distribute its software widely, and to let partners modify its code however they like.[6]

TECHNOLOGICAL DEVELOPMENTS Changes in technology developed outside an organization frequently require it to respond, whether it wants to or not. Technological advances offer both opportunities and threats to organizations. If managers are slow to respond to technological changes, the consequences can be dire. The "A Manager's Challenge" feature illustrates how a company that dominated its industry for nearly 250 years nearly disappeared because it did not respond appropriately to technological change. The company is Encyclopædia Britannica. As you read this example, ask yourself why the firm's managers were so slow to respond. What might they have done differently and how would it have affected the outcome? Keeping in mind that hindsight is 20/20, what arguments would you have made for change before the fateful events left the company with too few options?

TECHNOLOGY

Two Centuries of Dominance End for Encyclopædia Britannica

First published about 1770, Encyclopædia Britannica arguably invented the category in which it competes. For 200 years Encyclopædia Britannica was considered the most authoritative encyclopedia in the market, and in the 1970s, a full set of the books sold for as much as $2,000. In the mid-1980s, however, a little-known company called Microsoft (only 10 years old at the time) approached Britannica to discuss a potential collaboration but was turned down flat. Why would a company like Britannica, with such a stellar brand and a reputation more than 210 years old at the time, team up with an unknown with no reputation or publishing experience?

Rebuffed, Microsoft used content from *Funk & Wagnall's Standard Encyclopedia* to create *Encarta*. Executives at Britannica could only smile as the desperation of one of its more lowly esteemed competitors drove it into the arms of such a strange and immature bedfellow as Microsoft. This view was only reinforced as Britannica's sales grew, hitting $650 million in 1990.

However, just three years later in 1993, Microsoft began bundling *Encarta* with its Office suite of products. Although *Encarta*'s content was not nearly as good as Britannica's, it was essentially free. Britannica's sales dropped like a rock. Determined to survive, Britannica executives decided to publish a CD-ROM version of the product, but all the information could not fit on one disk. It came on three disks, making it inconvenient for customers because depending on what information you wanted, you had to make sure you put in the correct disk. What's more, Britannica executives priced their CD offering at $995. The hope was that such a high price for three CDs would encourage customers to continue to buy the company's nicely bound volumes.

The plan did not work, and in 1994, executives decided to launch an online version of its famed encyclopedia. However, they priced a user's subscription at $2,000. Again, the hope was that such a high-priced online subscription would encourage customers to continue to buy traditional book sets. But sales at Britannica plummeted yet further. In 1996, only 20,000 hard copy versions were sold compared with 117,000 in 1990.

At this point, in just 2 percent of Britannica's total lifespan, its revenues had shrunk by more than 80 percent. However, in the end, Britannica's fate was sealed not by Microsoft but by another organization, called Wikipedia. The ironic point of this tale is that virtually all the information we have conveyed about Encyclopædia Britannica can be found at www.wikipedia.org—a free, online encyclopedia that relies on literally tens of thousands of writers, who voluntarily contribute to the site for free.

Neither Britannica, as it struggled just to stay alive, nor Microsoft, as it continued to bundle *Encarta* with its Office suite of products, envisioned this online form of encyclopedia. When Wikipedia was launched in 2001, who would have predicted that by 2010, Wikipedia would have over 3 million articles in English consisting of over 1 billion words or that it would have nearly 200 different language editions? To put this in perspective, Wikipedia's English articles are five times larger than the largest Encyclopædia Britannica set. Who could have foreseen this blinding pace of change? The pace has been so rapid that Microsoft decided to terminate Encarta and exit the encyclopedia space. Britannica was determined to survive in the industry it launched, and in 2009, announced it would accept edits and additions to the online Britannica Web site from the public. However, this content will sit in a separate section of its Web site so that people can easily distinguish content produced and edited by its professional staff versus that generated and edited by

Myrleen Ferguson/PhotoEdit Inc.

Beginning in the 1990s, Microsoft's Encarta software, followed by Wikipedia, the web-based encyclopedia, practically rendered obsolete Encyclopædia Britannica—a firm that had dominated its industry since the 1700s.

the public. The company determined that the published edition of the encyclopedia would undergo the rigorous process of verification that has been the hallmark of the published edition for 240 years. Will these changes be sufficient for Britannica to survive and keep up with the changing times? Only time will tell, but given the rate at which content is added to Wikipedia, you could not keep up with it even if you read all the *new and edited* material seven days a week, 24 hours a day.

Sources: Adopted from J. S. Black and H. B. Gregersen, *Leading Strategic Change* (Upper Saddle River: Financial Times Prentice Hall, 2007); "Wikipedia," http://en.wikipedia.org/wiki/Wikipedia; accessed June 22, 2010; "Encyclopædia Britannica," http://en.wikipedia.org/wiki/Encyclopedia_britannica, accessed June 20, 2010.

LEGAL AND POLITICAL DEVELOPMENTS When governments make new laws or courts issue new interpretations of those laws, managers need to respond, even when the solutions or types of changes that should be made are not obvious. In the United States, the passage of Title IX of the 1964 Civil Rights Law required universities to provide equal resources and opportunities to male and female students (in relation to their proportions in the student body). Directors of intercollegiate athletics at U.S. universities eventually realized that this would have major implications for their area of activities. Because of tight budgets, however, these particular managers, the athletic directors, found it difficult to add enough women's sports to equalize the proportion of men to women athletes. Nevertheless, some managers handled this situation much better than others and made the changes more quickly and with less conflict within their organizations. Clearly, however, the external force of law in this instance caused changes that would likely not have come about for any other reason. Also, in this example, the political climate added a force to the legal enactment that hastened the need to make these changes.

SOCIETAL AND DEMOGRAPHIC SHIFTS Other types of external forces for change can take longer to develop and be more subtle and difficult to detect, such as changing societal attitudes toward various products, services, and practices. Many employers around the United States, as well as many restaurants and bars, for example, recently have had to change their practices regarding indoor smoking. In response to both tighter legal restrictions and changing levels of public tolerance to smoking in confined areas, these organizations have had to pay attention to an area of employee-customer behavior they had long ignored. In fact, Oregon's new law that went into effect in 2009 requires all of the following to be smoke-free: bars and taverns, including bar areas of restaurants, bowling centers, bingo halls, and private and fraternal organizations; employee break rooms; restaurants; private offices and commercial office buildings; retail and wholesale establishments; manufacturing plants and mills; truck stops; child and adult day-care; assisted living facilities; movies theaters and indoor entertainment venues; hotels and motels (exception: up to 25 percent of guest rooms may be designated as smoking rooms by the owner or entity in charge); and work vehicles that are not operated exclusively by one employee. The law also prohibits smoking within ten feet of entrances, exits, windows that open, and ventilation intakes of workplaces or public places.[7]

Shifting demographic patterns, such as the aging of populations in the United States and Japan in recent years, are another type of slow-moving external force. For example, the U.S. Bureau of the Census projects that between 2010 and 2020, the number of people in the United States over age 60 will jump by over 30 percent, whereas almost all other age groups will stay roughly the same in numbers.[8] Such alterations in the age makeup of society will, for example, challenge retailing and other consumer-oriented firms to change their product mixes and take new approaches to sales and marketing. These kinds of demographic shifts do not take place overnight, but they can exert a powerful force nevertheless.

Forces Inside the Organization

As with external factors, many potential forces inside the organization can cause changes to take place. Two of the most important are (1) managerial decisions and (2) employee preferences and pressures.

The percentage of people over the age of 60 is increasing rapidly in the United States and other developed countries. A potential shortage of workers and changing demand for products are just two of the side effects managers are likely to struggle with because of this demographic shift.

Simone van den Berg\Shutterstock

MANAGERIAL DECISIONS Managers at any level of an organization operate under certain constraints that limit what they can change. However, in many instances they have considerable authority to make changes in their particular parts of the enterprise. Even in flatter organizational structures, the higher up managers are in an organization, the more leeway they typically have to institute changes. Managers are often reluctant, though, to use their power for this purpose. Some experts argue that managers tend to *underutilize* their power to make changes.[9] The risk is that an attempted change will be unsuccessful, and the manager will end up with less power than before. This is why in the next section we discuss one of the most critical leadership issues facing you as a manager: accurately evaluating the need for change.

EMPLOYEE PREFERENCES AND SUGGESTIONS Managers are not the only source of change inside organizations. Lower-level employees often are an excellent source of innovative suggestions for change.[10] For example, Virginia Credit Union instituted an old-fashioned employee suggestion box with a 2010 twist in that employees submit "Continuous Improvement Requests" via e-mail or from the employee portal. The process improvements or new technologies are viewed weekly by senior leaders, who then responds to the submitter as to the feasibility of the request. In all, 38 of 185 requests from 86 employees have been implemented since the program began in November 2008. "The requests come from all employees, from tellers to senior executives, with five or six people who seem to participate most frequently," said Thompson, VP-strategy and governance. Up to three employees annually are awarded $500 each for requests that generate significant measurable savings, and certificates are presented to everyone who participates. In one year, the changes saved the company $250,000.[11]

In extreme instances, employees can exert overt pressure for changes. For example, workers at the Port of Los Angeles opposed the introduction of new cargo handling technologies. Their "work slow down" efforts basically stopped traffic into the Port of Los Angeles for several weeks and caused losses approaching $2 billion, which demanded management's attention.[12]

Managers need to distinguish between employee pressures that address legitimate needs for change and pressures that attempt to obstruct or intimidate. Making such judgments wisely and responding appropriately are essential managerial skills, as discussed in the next section. Regardless of the extent to which managers have that skill, however, employees can be a stimulus for change that frequently cannot, and should not, be ignored.

Determining Where Organizational Changes Should Occur

When managers decide that change is needed, or when they realize that they have no choice but to make changes, one of the first issues they face is: What to change? While not exhaustive, a reasonably comprehensive set of areas to consider include, technology, shared values and culture, strategy, structure, system, and staff. Any change will almost certainly involve at least one of these areas of focus, and the larger the change the more likely several areas will be involved. (See Exhibit 15.2.) The "A Manager's Challenge" feature regarding Sony on the next page is a good example of change involving multiple areas of focus. Particularly complex and comprehensive changes—"transformational changes"—will involve all six (see Exhibit 15.3).

Strategy

Changes in many of these external forces mean that managers must alter their organizations' strategy.[13] For example, if your competitors introduce a popular new product to the market, you may have no choice but to change your organization's strategy in response.[14] Top managers more than lower-level managers are typically charged with determining an organization's strategy. Lower-level managers are more involved in implementing that strategy.[15]

Announcing a change in strategy is vastly different from actually bringing about such a change, though. For example, a few years ago, Honda sought to convert itself from "a local company in Japan, with a global viewpoint, into a global company with a local viewpoint." In other words, Honda's new strategy was to be as flexible as a small local company while developing and using all the strengths of a large, global company. To support the strategy, the organization developed a global product supply network, a new flexible manufacturing system, and a global standard layout. This was no easy task. Today, however, Honda is noted for its flexible manufacturing capabilities. Its major North American production facilities can assemble nearly any vehicle it sells, depending on what consumers on that continent are demanding. As a consequence, in 2009 when Toyota lost $4.9 billion and Nissan Motor lost $2.6 billion, Honda made a profit of $1.5 billion.[16]

Structure

Changing the structural makeup of organizations is sometimes one of the most valuable tools managers have to create other desired changes. Many structural changes like reorganizing the firm on a product rather than a geographic basis or consolidating a company's major divisions can affect how different units interact and how information flows in the organization. Nokia, which has offices on multiple continents, had formerly been organized on a geographic basis, but reorganized by product in 2004. It made another major restructuring in 2008. In 2008, Nokia

EXHIBIT 15.2

Focus of Organizational Changes

EXHIBIT 15.3

Some Specific Examples of Focus of Change

Focus	Examples
Strategy	• Change from niche market to general market focus
	• Change focus from individual customer to large corporate customer
Structure	• Change from a geographic to a customer structure
	• Implement an international division
Systems	• Replace batch with continuous flow manufacturing
	• Change from last in-first out to first in-first out inventory valuation
Technology	• Update computer systems
	• Use holography in product design
Shared Values and Culture	• Implement diversity awareness program
	• Institute participatory decision making throughout organization
Staff	• Encourage cooperation through cross-training program
	• Increase number and availability of training workshops for lower-level employees

recombined all its handset activities into one unit, called Devices. Before, they were divided into three units (Mobile Phones or basic handsets, Multimedia, and Enterprise). Executives established two other business units: Software & Services and Markets. Markets will include all sales, marketing, logistics, and manufacturing operations. Financially, Nokia announced that it will report just two operations: Devices and Software & Services.[17]

Other structural changes can be made at the intermediate level. They can include combining or dividing departments or changing locations and reporting relationships within or among business

A MANAGER'S CHALLENGE

CHANGE

Saving Sony

Sony is famous the world over for its Walkman music player, PlayStation game console, TVs, and other electronic products. Unfortunately, success rarely lasts forever: From 2000 to 2003, Sony's hot-under-the-collar shareholders watched the value of their shares drop from $150 to $25. It was enough to force some major changes at the company.

In 2005, Howard Stringer became the first non-Japanese head of the company in its history and one of the few to ever lead any major Japanese company. Stringer was born in Wales in 1942 but moved to the United States in 1965. He joined Sony in 1997 as the head of Sony America, turning around the performance in that unit by establishing higher levels of integration and cooperation across its electronics, game, and entertainment units.

However, after taking over as CEO of the global enterprise, Stringer determined that Sony's problems were both broad and deep. It was facing mounting financial losses and increasing pressure from relatively new products, such as Samsung's LCD and plasma televisions and Apple's category-killer iPod. To compete, Stringer decided Sony had to streamline its businesses into five groups focusing on electronics, TVs cameras and camcorders, digital imaging, DVD recorders, and portable audio. As part of that restructuring over the next five years, Sony closed 8 of its 57 manufacturing sites and laid off 16,000 employees. It goal was to reduce its annual operating cost by $3 billion.

Stringer was determined to make the change a success. A key part of the initiative involved giving Sony's Electronics division central decision-making authority over key areas. Previously each unit had its own planning, human resources, finance, and sales functions and operated with considerable autonomy. Stringer believed the new structure would streamline and speed up decision making across Sony's product lines. It would also permit uniform software development across the lines so Sony's products would operate seamlessly

with one another. This would, of course, also eliminate design and product redundancies and optimize the firm's R&D spending. In 2009, Sony announced that it aimed to make 90 percent of its electronic product categories network-enabled and wireless-capable by March 2011.

Stringer also hoped the change in structure would help change Sony's corporate culture. Sony had a tradition of engineering the best products. This approach had worked wonders for years. However, the development of Apple's iPod highlighted the fact that consumers were not just interested in technical superiority but the easy use of products. And some of Sony's products had become too complicated for customers to operate.

The change plan also affected specific technologies. For example, Sony executives declared that television was of the utmost importance to the company. The firm would scrap the production of cathode ray tube (CRT) television sets and focus on LCD and rear-projection TVs and technology. Furthermore, Sony would focus on self-luminous flat-panel organic light-emitting diode (OLED) displays, on high-definition technology Blu-ray, and on mobile technologies.

The cost of all this restructuring? An estimated $1.8 billion. Is it working? More than five years into the transformational change, there are signs of progress. For example, even though sales decreased from $77 billion in 2008 to $72 billion in 2009, losses also decreased from $989 million to $410 million. Sony forecast 2010 sales of $76 billion and a profit of $500 million—a nearly $1 billion turnaround in profits. However, skeptics remain, which the Stringer acknowledged, "We have made promises before, but we failed to execute them." He was confident this time would be different.

Sources: Company Web site, consolidated financial statements, 2009, 2008, 2007, 2006, and press release, 2005, www.sony.net/SonyInfo/News/Press/200509/05-050E/index.html, accessed July 22, 2010.

units. Still other structural changes can be made at very micro-levels, such as forming new project groups or altering the composition of particular jobs or positions. For example, several years ago, the Mayo Clinic formed a group of 13 examining physicians and 17 staff members as part of the clinic's new Executive Health Program. Today, the group oversees the annual physical examinations of over 4,500 U.S. corporate executives.[18]

As with changes in strategy, changes in structure are not especially difficult to pull off initially, but making them generate the desired effects can be particularly challenging for managers. Research shows that almost no other event in an organization can create as much political maneuvering as potential, or rumored, reorganization changes.[19] The ambiguity of the effects of such changes, coupled with their potential importance for the jobs of those who may be directly affected, causes high levels of anxiety and frequent politicking by employees.

Systems

Another major object of change can involve the firm's system of formal processes or procedures. These changes involve the sequence and manner in which work activities are carried out. For example, Intel has changed its procedure for opening new plants. Its new procedure is to exactly duplicate each and every one—even, for example, down to the color of the gloves workers wear, including one of its newest plants in Dalian, China.[20]

Changes in a firm's processes and procedures often come about because of earlier changes in the organization's strategy or structure. The purchase of new equipment, for instance, would be a primary change, and the adoption of new procedures because of this equipment would be the secondary change.

Technology

For many organizations—from the corner dry cleaner to the largest multinational—the most obvious and most frequent object of change is technology. This has always been the case in manufacturing and capital-intensive companies, where replacing and upgrading equipment and technology have been the keys to organizational survival and an ability to keep ahead of the competition. In recent years, however, virtually all types of firms, government agencies, and nonbusiness organizations have been paying increasing attention to improving and expanding their information technology.[21] Sometimes that change may not go as smoothly or as fast as predicted. For example, in June 2003, Wal-Mart's then CIO Linda Dillman announced the start of the retailer's RFID tag (Radio Frequence ID) compliance program, saying Wal-Mart would ask its top 100 suppliers to begin tagging pallets and cases starting in January 2005. In April 2006, Linda Dillman left as CIO to take an executive role in Human Resources and Rollin Ford, previously head of supply chain and logistics, became CIO. Ford subsequently took a much lower profile approach to RFID. By October 2007, Wal-Mart announced a major change in its RFID strategy, largely abandoning the initial pallet/case focus on shipments going to Wal-Mart stores in favor of focusing on shipments going to Sam's Club. By January 2008 Wal-Mart announced its first real compliance "penalties" of $2-$3 for failure to tag products, specifically for shipments to its Sam's Club chain. By 2009 it had reduced the penalties to 12 cents and issued no formal press releases on the subject over the next two years.[22]

Usually a change in technology will have ripple effects on other parts of the organization that can be a real challenge for managers. New equipment, for example, can result in entirely different patterns of work relationships among employees, and that, in turn, can create considerable confusion. If these effects are significant or persistent, they can take a toll on the improvements the firm is trying to make. Therefore, focusing solely on technology as a source of change isn't always the answer.

Shared Values and Culture

The shared values and culture of the organization are another major focus for change. Changing an organization's culture can be as potent as making major changes in the firm's strategy or technology. Despite its potential, however, changing an organization's embedded traditions and accepted ways of doing things can be extremely difficult. For example, when China Development Industrial Bank bought Grand Cathay Brokerage of Taiwan, over 100 of Grand Cathay's key employees left within the first year as a result of the new culture that had been imposed. As one departing employee put it, "Grand Cathay had a very democratic culture. When policies were made, we were always invited to give feedback. Our opinions mattered. But the new management has a very autocratic style."[23]

Putting the firm's new values into a mission statement is easy enough. However, making them part of the basic fabric of the organization is exceedingly difficult and can take a long time. More likely than not, it is easier and less costly for managers to attempt to change other factors, such as the firm's strategy or structure. Nevertheless, a firm's culture does represent a significant, if difficult, target for making fundamental changes.

Staff

Finally, people—both individuals and groups—can be the focus of major changes. Essentially, changes that focus on people involve one or more of the following four elements:

- Who the people are.
- What their attitudes and expectations are.
- How they interact interpersonally.
- How they are trained or developed.

In the first instance, change can be brought about by adding, subtracting, or interchanging people. Bringing in a new supervisor or transferring a difficult employee from one unit to another is an example of change focusing on the selection and placement of people.

The second element, people's attitudes and expectations, can sometimes be modified without excessive effort or cost by the manager. For example, providing people with new information or a new way to look at problems, issues, or events can potentially create significant changes in their behavior. There are no guarantees that this will occur, however.[24]

Attempting to change how staff members relate to one another—such as by being more cooperative and supportive of their co-workers—represents a third, people-oriented change focus.

The fourth and often most lasting people-change approach involves directly enhancing their knowledge, skills, and abilities—typically through education, training, and personal development activities. This can improve the performance of individuals, groups, and even larger units, regardless of any other changes a manager might initiate.

As with other types of changes, efforts to change people can be costly and time consuming. Managers need to weigh these costs against the potential benefits, such as having a more capable, creative, and innovative workforce, better morale, and, perhaps, lower turnover.

Evaluating the Need for Change

Is change always necessary? To answer that question, you should undertake two critical steps. One is to recognize the possible need for change and to correctly assess the strength of that need. The other is to accurately diagnose the problems and issues that the change or changes should address. Misjudgments at either step can lead to severe problems, if not outright disaster.[25] Jumping in to make changes before taking *both* these steps is a recipe for almost certain failure.

Recognizing and Assessing the Need for Change

As we have stressed earlier, making changes is definitely not a cost-free activity (see Exhibit 15.4). This puts a premium on not making changes if the costs will outweigh the potential benefits. It also means that it is crucial to make an accurate assessment of the strength of the forces behind the need for change.

PROACTIVE RECOGNITION Effective managers, no matter where they are in the organization's structure, are those who can recognize the need for change at the earliest possible time. To do this, they must have systems and methods in place to monitor the environment in which they and their units operate. They need to be able to detect trends before they become obvious warning signs.[26]

Collecting this information can be done in a number of ways. Sophisticated information systems can be used. So can gathering the information via more mundane activities such as spotting trends or anomalies in sales reports and actively seeking out the opinions of one's clients, customers,

EXHIBIT 15.4

Relative Cost of Change

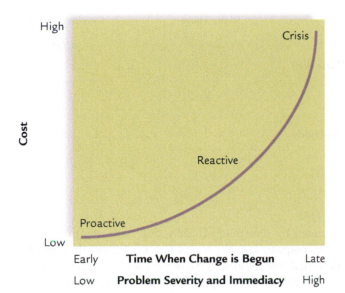

and employees. Starbucks, the coffee house giant, tries to spot trends by proactively studying various ways to retain its current customers and attract the next generation of young coffee drinkers. The company even hypnotized a group of volunteers in their twenties, to try to find out what they *really* think about Starbucks. As a result of these assessments, the company established Starbucks Express. Starbucks Express allows customers to e-mail their orders to the stores they patronize. The stores then have their coffee waiting for them in personalized cups when they arrive.[27]

REACTIVE RECOGNITION Not *all* needs for change can be identified in advance, regardless of how much proactive recognition is attempted. Invariably, some developments in the internal or external environment will take place so quickly, or reach critical mass so unexpectedly, that managers must react to them in real time rather than plan for them in advance.[28] For example, Starbucks really never saw itself competing with McDonald's and therefore did not anticipate that a move by McDonald's would require a reactive countermove by Starbuck. However, when McDonald's decided it would offer a premium coffee and *Consumer Reports* rated it better than Starbucks at half the price, Starbucks had to react. The need for a reaction got amplified when McDonald's decided to add free WiFi to its locations in an effort to get people to sit longer as they surfed the Web or answered email, drink their coffee, and hopefully buy a few unintended items off the McDonald's menu. Because McDonald's has about 11,000 locations across the United States—about as many as Starbucks—Starbucks felt it had no choice but to offer free WiFi at all of its locations as well.[29]

Diagnosing Problems

The recognition that change needs to take place is only a starting point. Much like a physician, noting that a patient has a fever without diagnosing that an infection is causing the fever can lead to the wrong treatment. Initiating changes that do not improve the underlying problems is sometimes worse than making no changes at all. Thus, managers need to avoid premature conclusions about causes. Instead, they should obtain information from a variety of sources, if possible; compare the information to uncover consistent patterns or trends; and, most important, attempt to determine what are the most likely causes. The end result of a comprehensive analysis of this type should be an accurate, valid diagnosis of what, and who, needs to change.

The Change Process

One of the most enduring, simple, and yet comprehensive frameworks of the change process was proposed by psychologist Kurt Lewin over 50 years ago.[30] He argued that change (personal, team, or organizational change) went through three distinctive phases: unfreezing, movement, and refreezing.

EXHIBIT 15.5

Change Failure Framework

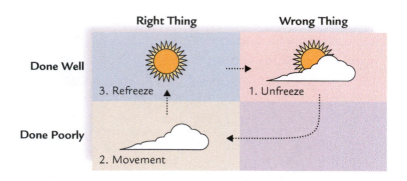

Phase 1—Unfreezing

Most change is preceded by something. Usually, that "something" is success. In other words, individuals, teams, or companies usually have a history of doing the right thing and doing it well before a change is needed (see Exhibit 15.5). In general, the longer a previous "right thing" has proven itself successful, the more likely people are to want to hang on to it.[31] Change is typically stimulated when something is anticipated to change or actually changes in the environment (external or internal). Simplistically, the change in the context causes the previous right thing for the past to become the wrong thing for the future.

For example, suppose you had the pattern of making decisions on your own without seeking input from subordinates. This pattern worked for you for many years, in part because the decisions you faced as a manager were fairly routine. You had all the knowledge you needed to make the decisions without seeking the input of others. Your individual decision-making approach was right, and you were good at it.

Then something happens. The nature of your company's customers changes. They require much more sophisticated products. These new products involve technologies that are new to you. You now need to involve others more in decision making because you don't have all the information or answers yourself. The environment has shifted and what used to be the right thing—individual decision making—is now the wrong thing. However, you are still very good at it.

A similar pattern can happen at the organizational level. For example, for more than a decade NEC, a large Japanese electronics firm, was one of the leading makers of computer displays. NEC's displays were based on the cathode ray tube (CRT) technology of TVs. At the time, Lucky Goldstar (LG), a Korean electronics firm using LCD technology, was not a major player in computer displays.

But NEC's long history of success made it difficult for its executives to see the advantages of LCD technology or the threat posed by LG. By the time they did see a need for change, they were left with virtually no options but to drop out of the computer display market and let LG rise to become one of the largest suppliers in the world.

Several factors can cause people to not see or resist seeing the initial need for change and create problems for the unfreezing state of change, including:

- **Inertia.** Simply being comfortable with their present ways of doing things. Without significant incentive to change or high-perceived risks for not changing, people simply find it easier to do things the way they always have rather than to operate or behave differently.
- **Mistrust.** Mistrust of those communicating the need for change by those affected by the proposed change can be a significant barrier to unfreezing.
- **Lack of Information.** Lack of adequate information about both the need for the change and what its effects are likely to be can be a third powerful force of resistance.

Fundamentally, the unfreezing process involves recognizing that what was right for the past is wrong for the future and why. However, even if you recognize the need for change, Lewin argued that unless we undo or unfreeze these old patterns, it is difficult to change to something new. To better appreciate Lewin's notion, you might think about an ice sculpture. Suppose you wanted to change an ice sculpture of a bird into a sculpture of a fish. You could try to chip away at the old bird and fashion the new fish, but it's a difficult process. Instead, what would happen if you unfroze or melted the bird sculpture? You could then use the water to create a new bock of ice from which you could carve a fish. Trying to simply carve a fish out of the original bird sculpture is perhaps possible but not very efficient or effective.

This was part of the problem for managers at NEC. Since the technology for producing flat-panel screens is completely different than that used in CRTs, you have to let go of the old technology in order to get your mind around the new technology. In NEC's case, both senior executives as well as managers in the R&D area resisted letting go of the old. Some of the strongest champions of the new technology were younger scientists, but in a very hierarchical organization such as NEC, they were unable to get older managers to unfreeze their notions about what customers wanted in a computer screen—which was for it to provide good resolution but take up less space.

Phase 2—Movement

Unfortunately, even if people accept that the old right thing is now the wrong thing, they may still resist moving or changing. Specific sources of resistance to the movement stage of the change process include the following:

- *Lack of Clarity.* If the new right thing or the target of change is not clear to people, they are likely to resist movement toward it. Why? Because to them it is like shooting in the dark.
- *Lack of Capabilities.* As we discussed in the chapter on motivation (Chapter 9), if people believe they lack the capabilities needed to implement the change, they may resist movement (even if they see the need for change).
- *Lack of Sufficient Incentives.* If those affected by the change believe that the anticipated negative consequences of the change outweigh the positive consequences, resistance to movement is almost guaranteed.

As Exhibit 15.5 illustrates, change typically requires people to go from doing the wrong thing well to doing the right thing poorly. For example, if you have made decisions on an individual basis for many years, even if you recognize the need to make decisions in a more participative manner by involving others, you are not likely to be great at participative decision making at first. Research has demonstrated that one of the biggest determinants of resistance during the movement stage of the change process is the level of uncertainty associated with the change.[32] The greater the uncertainty of what will happen, generally the greater the resistance to move or change. Moreover, in general, there is a relationship between the magnitude of the change and the level of uncertainty.[33] If the magnitude of the change increases, so too will the level of uncertainty. Both, in turn, will likely lead to higher levels of resistance by employees.[34] As a consequence, you will have to do more planning and preparation in order to make the change a success. In the end, unless people are confident that they can go from doing the new right thing poorly to doing it well, they will fail to move.[35]

Phase 3—Refreezing

But suppose you are successful getting people to see the need to unfreeze and you are also able to get them moving toward the desired change, what are the odds that the change will last? To appreciate why Lewin stressed this third stage of change, you only need to think about the percentage of people who start a new diet or exercise program and subsequently stick with it past the first few weeks. Less than one in four people sustain this type of personal change. If it is hard to sustain change in ourselves, we can appreciate the managerial challenge, which is to sustain change in others.

PULL OF PAST COMPETENCIES Lewin contended that the "pull" of old, successful patterns was strong and that simply making the move from the old to the new was not enough to ensure lasting success.[36] This was in part because, whatever the "old" pattern, it existed in the first place because it was positively rewarded. In other words, most people have the communication patterns, a leadership style, a decision-making approach or companies have a specific strategy, structure, or culture because they worked in the past. In this sense, you can think of past patterns as having a kind of gravity that will pull us back to them unless a greater force is in place to keep us moving forward.

This is why Lewin stressed the refreezing stage of the change process. However, when most people hear the term *refreezing*, they usually get images of things frozen solid and unmovable. By *refreezing*, Lewin did not intend to imply that the new state should be static with no movement. He did not mean for the term to imply that once change is made that there should be no monitoring or adjusting. Instead, the term was designed to reflect the notion that after a change is made, forces need to be put in place to keep people and behaviors from giving in to the gravitational pull of the past and reverting back to old patterns.

As a consequence, refreezing involves monitoring the change to see if it is producing the anticipated and desired results. To the extent the change is succeeding, the refreezing phase should involve reinforcing the change so that it becomes more established.[37] This is important because as Lewin recognized, and research has confirmed, without reinforcement people will return to past habits and patterns.[38]

NONIMMEDIATE RESULTS   This is especially true if the results from the change are slow in coming, which is the case with change initiatives of moderate or greater magnitude. This is in part why people have difficulty changing their diet or exercise habits. They want the envisioned changes in their fitness or appearance, but when those results are slow in coming, people often return to the old habits. The inconvenient truth is that most significant change does not produce instant, positive consequences. As a consequence, managers that only pay attention to the first two phases of change tend to find that the overall change initiative fails to deliver the desired results because of problems in the third phase.

Overcoming Resistance to Change

With the overall framework of unfreeze, move, and refreeze, practicing managers want to know how they can overcome common challenges and successfully lead and manage change in themselves and others. That's precisely what this section addresses.

Overcoming Resistance to Unfreeze

As we stated, if people cannot see the need for change, the entire change process doesn't even get going. Most needed changes for an individual, team, or organization are stimulated by some anticipated or existing change outside that person, team, or organization. For example a needed change in an individual's behavior might stem from a change in the organization's strategy. A change in the organization's strategy might stem from an anticipated change in technology. As a consequence, one of the keys to unfreezing is helping people see what has changed in the larger context that requires a change from them. Getting this contrast clear between how things were before and why the past approach was successful and how things are different going forward and why what worked in the past may not in the future is a critical first step in managing change. Consider the case faced by Tom Alexander of Hewlett-Packard, illustrated in the feature, "A Manager's Challenge." What do you think of the way Alexander tried to illustrate the contrast between how HP made printers in the past and what consumers needed in the future? What do you think of the outcome? Would you have taken the same approach?

This process of illustrating the contrast can involve communicating to people the reason for the change or getting those affected by the change to analyze the stimulus for the change. Because involvement and participation generally take more time, managers often have to take time pressures into account in order to determine what level of involvement is appropriate. As we discussed in Chapter 12, "Individual and Group Decision Making," if there is time and participants have the needed information and capabilities, involving them can often increase their level of buy in and reduce their resistance to the change.

Overcoming Resistance to Move

Even though unfreezing is a necessary step in the change process, it is not sufficient by itself. More to the point, even if managers are successful in getting others to see the need for change, they still may encounter resistance in the moving stage of the change process. As we discussed, one of the prime sources of resistance to move is lack of clarity about what people are moving toward. Thus, one of the first means of overcoming the failure to move is to educate people as to what the desired change is. For example, if you want to change from an individual decision-making style, you need

A MANAGER'S CHALLENGE

CHANGE

Changing the Crown Jewels at HP

Hewlett-Packard (HP) is a well-known technology company. One of its most important businesses is printers. Printers account for about two-thirds of its profits. As recently as 2004, HP's printer division accounted for almost *all* of the firm's market value because its two other major divisions (services and computers) were generally losing money. In short, printers were the crown jewels of HP.

Beginning in the late 1990s, however, HP managers saw their strong position begin to slip away, especially the position of its low-end products. Specifically, Lexmark, a key competitor, introduced good quality printers that sold for a retail price of under $100. Soon Lexmark saw its share of the market double to 14 percent.

In response to this change in the environment, the head of HP's printer division, Vyomesh Joshi, determined that HP had to change. Joshi determined that HP needed to build a new line of printers, including a printer that HP could manufacture for $49 or $30 cheaper than its least expensive printer at the time. This would then allow the printer to retail for under $100. He also challenged his group to go from "concept to shelf" (from the idea to putting the printer on retailer's shelves) in three years rather than the normal four.

Most HP managers said they thought building a printer for $49 instead of $79 was impossible. Tom Alexander, a key project manager, knew he needed to "explode their complacency." In a team meeting, he created a high contrast that helped people see the need for change and unfreeze the past.

After listening to people say how impossible it was to build a significantly less expensive printer, Alexander grabbed an HP printer, put it on the floor, and stood on it—all 200 pounds of him. In that instant, the people in the room broke through the failure to see barrier and got the message: HP printers were overengineered. Printers did not

Hewlett-Packard Development Company, L.P.

In the 1990s, Lexmark chewed away at the profits of Hewlett Packard, the dominant player in the printer business. HP's managers initially had a hard time convincing employees that the firm needed to design smaller, less-expensive copiers like the one shown here.

need to be engineered and constructed sturdily enough to be stepping stools. The extra engineering, material, and manufacturing costs were significant, making it impossible to bring down the cost and be competitive with Lexmark.

In the end, HP managers delivered a line of 14 inkjet printers and seven "all-in-one" printers based on just two cost-efficient platforms. The new line was produced on time and at the desired cost. It also included a printer that cost HP $49 to make and retailed for under $100. Following their introduction, HP sold $5.6 billion of the new printers (a 12 percent year-over-year increase) at a profit margin of 16.5 percent (a 14 percent increase in profitability). HP took 70 percent of the market share, and much of it came from Lexmark.[39]

to not only recognize the need to change, but you have to see and understand the new, participative approach. You may have to educate yourself as to how effectively to involve others in gathering and processing information. Until the new destination is clear, you are likely to stay where you are.

However, simply making the alternative or new destination clear may not be sufficient to get the desired movement or change. For example, suppose you are the manager of a group of customer service representatives. You have helped your team see the changes in customers' expectations and, therefore, the need to switch from focusing on how many customers you can service in a given time period to how delighted you can make customers with the service you provide. You clearly describe the new destination of customer service. You explain that the objective is to be sure you understand the customer's questions and then answer the questions without having to pass the customer on to someone else. But even if people now see the need to change and can clearly envision the new destination, they may fail to move.

In addition to helping your people see the new destination, you have to make sure they have the needed capabilities (information, tools, resources, and skills) to change. This typically requires an assessment of what is required and what exists. Based on this gap analysis, as the manager of the customer service representatives, you would need to help your subordinates bridge the gap through training, tools, or other resources.[40]

Finally, call representatives need to perceive that the anticipated benefits of the change will outweigh any negative outcomes. Simply communicating how the change will directly affect them in a positive way can often increase support and reduce resistance during the movement stage. For example, you might highlight how the installation of new equipment will make their work easier, or how the additional training will add to their repertoire of skills and general future employability. At other times, providing incentives might involve conferring benefits directly to those affected. This could include, for example, either nonmonetary incentives, such as praise, or the use of some form of monetary incentives, such as increased compensation for increased customer satisfaction.

Overcoming the Failure to Finish

Suppose you have been able to get your team to see the need for change and have gotten them moving toward the change. How can you ensure that movement continues and avoid the failure-to-finish problem? How can you, in Lewin's terms, refreeze the change and ensure that it lasts?

As we discussed earlier, the pull of past patterns and the lack of early, natural positive consequences often assures that change doesn't last. Refreezing is not an instant process because instant expertise in a new behavior is almost never possible. For example, improvement in customer service versus call processing comes gradually. Early attempts by your customer service representatives to answer customers' questions and not transfer them to another department are likely to produce less-than-stellar results at first. Early on, when call representatives' proficiency at the new approach is low, customers might even ask to be transferred: "Well, if you can't answer my question, then connect me with someone who can." Initial low proficiency at customer service will produce negative consequences that, in general, tend to drive out the desired behavior. Consequently, one of the key things managers need to do to refreeze change is compensate for the early negative consequences that naturally follow from low proficiency.

This compensatory action to provide positive reinforcement of desired efforts even when results are below the target is the subject of a number of authors and studies. This is often referred to as "celebrating early wins." Whether this or another term is used, the idea is the same: When people engage in change, they need early and consistent reinforcement to overcome the gravitational pull of past patterns and build momentum in moving toward establishing new patterns.[41] Managers are likely to need to celebrate and reinforce early correct efforts and not just desired outcomes. As we previously described, proficiency at new activities does not come instantly and so neither do the positive consequences naturally associated with high proficiency. Therefore, early on managers need to reinforce the desired behaviors so that they get repeated and eventually lead to higher proficiency, which, in turn, will lead to a higher frequency of desired results.

However, even if managers use reinforcement to sustain early efforts and help push the change into the early portion of the refreezing stage, it may not be sufficient to move completely through it. This is, in part, because typically progress and improvement are made in small enough increments that without feedback, people can underestimate their progress. If they underestimate sufficiently, they can feel like they are making no progress and give up on the change. Thus, in addition to reinforcing early and desired efforts, managers also need to provide feedback on progress—both to individuals as well as groups. Many of the principles of feedback and performance management that we discussed earlier in the chapter on human resources apply to this aspect of managing change.

Managing Change

So far in this chapter, we have focused on the background and context of change in organizations: That is, the forces and targets of change, the process of change, and, especially, managers' roles in understanding, assessing, and evaluating the need for change. Now, we turn to the

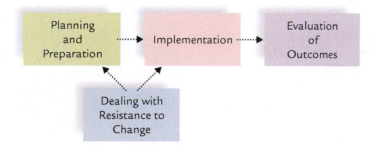

EXHIBIT 15.6

The Change Process

processes of managing change, including planning and preparing for it, implementing it, and evaluating its outcomes (see Exhibit 15.6).

Planning and Preparing for Change

Once a manager (or a group of managers) is convinced that change is necessary and that an accurate diagnosis has been made of the causes requiring change, preparation for the changes can begin. Exhibit 15.7 shows the issues related to this planning.

FORCE FIELD ANALYSIS One very useful way of looking at the change challenge is what is called a **force field analysis,** as Lewin proposed some years ago. This analysis, as depicted in Exhibit 15.8, uses the concept of equilibrium, a condition that occurs when the "driving forces" of change are roughly balanced by the "restraining forces" of change. Such a condition results in a relatively steady state that is disrupted only when the driving forces for innovation become stronger than the restraining forces for inertia (the two forces are sometimes called the "in" forces).[42] If we apply this analysis to typical organizational changes, we see that managers basically face two choices: add more force for change, such as putting more pressure on subordinates to conform to new procedures; or reduce the resistance forces, such as convincing informal leaders that they will benefit from the change. The basic problem with increasing the driving forces is that this often results in increasing the opposing forces. Therefore, Lewin's analysis suggests that weakening restraints may be the more effective way to bring about change.

With this general framework in mind, managers still have a variety of key decisions and judgments to make relative to planning and implementing a change. Sadly, there are no magic formulas to map out exactly what choices should be made under which conditions. However, deliberately thinking about the choices rather than just falling victim to one's own biases, tendencies, fears, preferences, and the like increases the chances that you will make a better judgment and decision.

TIMING Managers are often tempted to initiate something quickly, especially if the need for change seems exceptionally strong. Whether rapid implementation is a good idea or not represents

force field analysis
uses the concept of equilibrium, a condition that occurs when the forces for change, the "driving forces," are balanced by forces opposing change, the "restraining forces," and results in a relatively steady state.

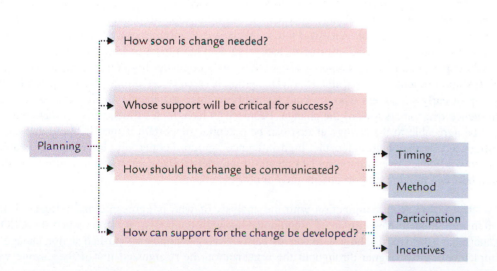

EXHIBIT 15.7

Planning Choices for Change

EXHIBIT 15.8

Force Field Analysis

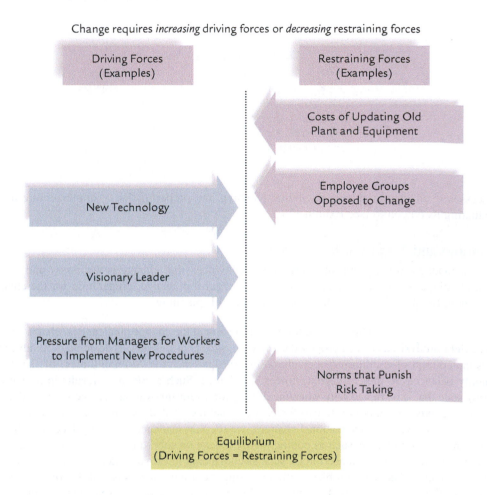

Change requires *increasing* driving forces or *decreasing* restraining forces

a difficult judgment call. Acting too quickly can lead to changes that are not well planned and that often fail because they lack sufficient support. On the other hand, waiting too long to make necessary changes can also be a recipe for failure. For example, in 2009 General Motors CEO Rick Wagoner was forced out because GM's board, which by then included representatives from their largest shareholder, the U.S. government, did not feel he was willing to make the magnitude of changes that were needed. Wagner was succeeded by Chief Operating Officer Frederick "Fritz" Henderson. Less than a year later, Henderson resigned, under pressure from the board, for not being more aggressive; GM chairman Edward Whitacre took over as CEO.[43]

BUILDING SUPPORT Whereas the previous section focused on overcoming resistance in general, this aspect of managing change focuses on building support. Developing this foundation requires especially careful analysis. First, it involves determining who are more likely to be in favor of the change. Second, it involves analyzing who has power or influence over others. The ideal people to build early support with are those who come out high on both criteria of agreeability and influence (see Exhibit 15.9). This group is often referred to as a **leading coalition,** a group of early supporters who are both favorably inclined toward the change and can exercise influence over others toward the change. People who have high influence over others but may not be agreeable to the change at first can be potential supporters if they listen to and can be influenced by the "high agreeable, high influence" group. People who have high agreeability but low influence over others can be potential supporters if there are many of them; their sheer numbers can provide support and momentum for the change.

leading coalition
a group of supporters who are favorably inclined toward change and can influence others toward change

COMMUNICATION In conjunction with the analysis of who is agreeable and influential, it is often important to have a plan of communicating with them. For example, when the CEO of Caterpillar (the world's largest maker of earth-moving equipment) pushed major change by implementing Six Sigma throughout the organization, he recognized that if the change were

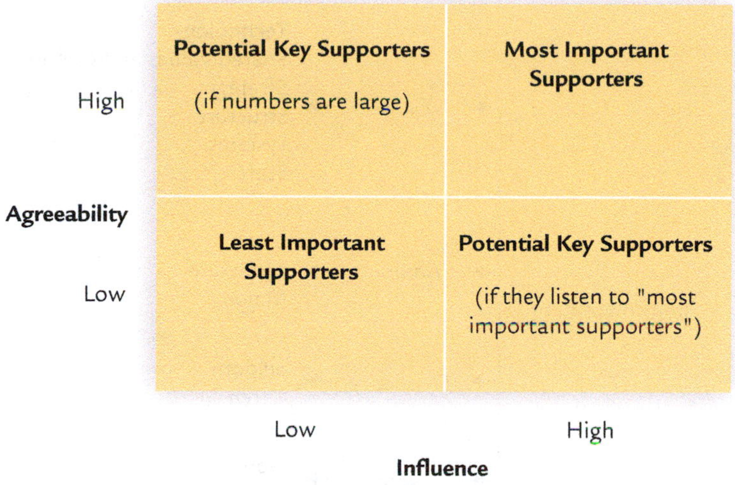

EXHIBIT 15.9

Matrix of Agreeability and Influence

	Low Influence	**High** Influence
High Agreeability	**Potential Key Supporters** (if numbers are large)	**Most Important Supporters**
Low Agreeability	**Least Important Supporters**	**Potential Key Supporters** (if they listen to "most important supporters")

Agreeability

Influence

to be sustained, he would have to communicate with and involve Caterpillar's dealer network. (The company sells its machines not directly but through a dealer network of nearly 200 organizations worldwide, which together employ 131,000 employees.) In the process of making this significant change over more than five years, Caterpillar established not only 2,000 Six Sigma Black Belts internally but communicated the need for Black Belts among its dealers and eventually helped nearly 1,000 of its dealers qualify as Black Belts.[44]

PARTICIPATION During the planning stage, obtaining the participation of those who are agreeable and influential can help strengthen their support. Plans can often be improved and commitment gained through such participation.[45] The use of participation is not cost-free. As mentioned in the previous section, it takes time and effort, and participation can backfire if participants' suggestions diverge widely from managers' goals. Furthermore, if those asked to participate sense that their input is not really wanted and that a manager is only "going through the motions," this can quickly lead to a feeling of being "manipulated." In such cases, participation typically erodes rather than supports change.

INCENTIVES Giving leading coalition members incentives to make the change also can help build support for it. For example, offering a set of lead call representatives a bonus based on customer satisfaction scores rather than the number of calls they answer may be a way to motivate them to engage in new behavior. Here, managers should take care because providing incentives may make the beneficiaries feel as if they are being "bought off." Thus, the use of incentives for change, especially monetary incentives, can potentially boomerang by increasing the skepticism and cynicism of managers' motives for the changes.

Implementation Choices

Where planning for change leaves off and implementation of change begins is often difficult to specify because the process is—or should be—more or less continuous. Regardless of where that boundary is, however, implementing change involves several critical choices for managers (see Exhibit 15.10). Three of the most important are discussed here.

CHOICE OF FOCUS Earlier, this chapter identified six targets on which change can be focused: strategy, structure, systems, technology, shared values, and staff. To initiate the change process, one or more of these targets needs to be selected. The choice depends in large part on the objectives to be accomplished which, in turn, are linked to the problems identified in the assessment of the need to change. If the major problem is outdated equipment, then, obviously, changing the technology will be the focus of choice. However, if the problem is one of sluggish growth in sales compared with competitors, then the choice of focus is not so self-evident. It could be that the organization is not sufficiently market oriented, which could indicate a need for change in strategy and culture of the organization.

EXHIBIT 15.10

Implementation Choices

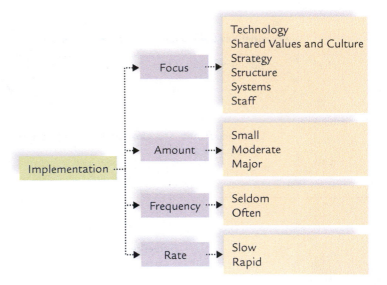

CHOICE OF AMOUNT   Even after managers have decided what approach to take and have started to implement those choices, they must also confront another, but related, set of issues: How much change should take place? That is, how comprehensive should the change be, and what parts of the unit or the whole organization should be affected? These questions have no easy answers.

When change is too little, the benefits are not likely to outweigh the costs involved. Even modest changes can take a great amount of effort and cause disruptions that are almost as great as if the change were much more sizable. Thus, managers must decide whether implementing minimal changes is worth the cost or simply wait until the problems are large enough to justify the substantial investments required. The argument in favor of making minimal changes, however, is that even though the immediate cost–benefit ratio may not be favorable, changes postponed until later will be much more expensive; therefore, the longer-term benefits can easily prove the worth of making small changes early. The old adage of "pay me now, or pay me later" comes to mind here.

Changes can be too massive or too small. Although managers are sometimes tempted to make big changes, they often overlook the potential costs. For example, large-scale changes can be confusing and difficult to coordinate because they affect multiple parts of the organization in different ways. Very large changes are sometimes what are called for, especially when major changes are occurring in the unit's or organization's environment. Changes such as these can also help "galvanize the troops" by inspiring their best efforts. However, as already discussed, any change can cause resistance, and significant changes can cause immense resistance. For example, Dirk Jager was CEO at Procter & Gamble for only 18 months, in part, because he pushed for what were likely needed changes but harder and faster than the organization could tolerate. P&G's share price plummeted. Instead of pushing employees to excel, Jager's torrent of slogans and initiatives almost brought P&G to its knees.[46] Thus, too great a change, in effect, can create more chaos and more problems than existed initially. When this happens, no change at all would have been better than the change that failed.

The lesson for managers is that they must take great care in deciding how much change they should implement.[47] Potential problems exist in making changes so small that they either don't justify the costs or they produce minimal effects. Similarly, there can be other kinds of dangers in making changes that are too large. In particular instances, however, one of these extremes may be the best alternative. The general guideline, therefore, is that the amount of change should fit the severity of the problems, and this should be determined by a sound analysis of the strength of the need for change.

CHOICE OF FREQUENCY   Another aspect of change that needs to be considered is the frequency of changes. Because today's competitive pressures are shifting more frequently, changes must be implemented much more often than in the past. In some sense, change is a more or less constant condition. However, this can become mentally and physically exhausting for the organization's members. Imagine, for example, that you are a member of a sales department in a large, geographically dispersed company. Suppose your company decides that its sales data should be centralized, so a new information system linking all of the sales regions is installed. Next, the company reorganizes the sales department by geographic region rather than by type of product as well as institutes a team sales structure. Each of these changes, by itself, might improve customer satisfaction and employee performance. However, if they all occur within a short space of time, you might not have time to completely adjust to any one of them. Therefore, the frequency of changes must be considered along with their size.

CHOICE OF RATE Just as the amount and frequency of change are important, so is the rate of change. If the pace of change is too slow, conditions that created the need for it in the first place might again shift significantly. Also, change that is too slow can frustrate many people who want to see at least some early and tangible results in return for their efforts. For instance, suppose a company spends several months putting together new work teams and training employees in decision-making techniques, group processes, conflict resolution, and computerized tracking techniques. Then, however, suppose it delayed installing the new equipment and software. Employees would likely be frustrated by not being able to put their new knowledge and skills to immediate use.

Change that is too rapid can also cause major problems. Whether the change is primarily technological, structural, procedural, or some other focus, people need to adapt to the rate. Rates that are excessively fast can exceed the typical person's ability to cope and increase resentment and resistance. It has even been suggested that in situations of rapid change, the work experience may be so stressful and so damaging to a person's self-identity as to trigger violent behavior.[48]

Managers sometimes make rapid changes deliberately and appropriately. One obvious case is when the forces for change are so overwhelming that swift change is essential. Furthermore, managers sometimes institute a fast rate of change precisely to determine who can keep up and who cannot. In such circumstances, a rapid rate may be a viable change tactic—if the manager has carefully considered what is to be accomplished and what the potential negative consequences or costs might be. In many other cases, however, managers have not adequately assessed the possible costs and benefits and may have simply implemented an abrupt change because of their eagerness to see results quickly.

As with choices about the amount of change, managers often face clear options about the rate of change they can choose. However, there is one major difference. When dealing with the rate of change, managers can make midcourse corrections more easily than they can when it comes to the amount of change. (It is very difficult, for example, to suddenly convert a large change into a small change.) If the initial pace has started slowly, managers can increase it if this appears desirable. Likewise, a change that has started out rapidly can be slowed, allowing for adaptation to catch up with events. Thus, just as the rate of speed of a car can be increased or decreased depending on road conditions, so can the rate of change in organizational settings. Just as in a car, if the rate is changed too often or too drastically, it can be very uncomfortable for those required to adapt. This, in turn, can reduce confidence in the person responsible for the changes.

Evaluating Change Outcomes

Once change has been carried out, whether throughout the entire organization or within one unit, managers need to evaluate the outcomes. If the effects of changes are not appraised in some manner, managers have no way of knowing whether additional changes are needed and also whether the particular approaches implemented should be used again in similar circumstances. To carry out the evaluation process, three things must be done: data must be collected, the results of the data must be compared against the change's goals, and ultimately the results must be communicated to those affected by it. (See Exhibit 15.11)

DATA COLLECTION The data that can be collected to evaluate the outcomes of change essentially come in two forms: objective (or quantitative) data and subjective (or attitude) data. Both types can be useful to a manager who has implemented change, and often it will be necessary to tap several sources of each type. For example, after introducing new information technology, a manager could evaluate its effectiveness by measuring changes in output per employee, the speed of response to customers, and the attitudes of employees and clients who deal with them.

EXHIBIT 15.11

Evaluating Change Outcomes

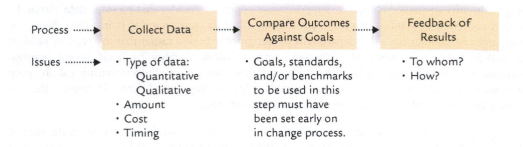

It is important to keep in mind that the collection of different sets of data, such as these, to measure change outcomes may well require significant costs. Therefore, not every type of data that could be collected *should* be collected. As with other organizational actions, the benefits should be weighed against the costs. The point, though, is that significant sources of data should not be overlooked, and the more types of data that can be collected, the more likely the analysis of the effects will be informative. Also, in most cases, data should be collected at periodic intervals to measure the lasting power of the change. A recent survey showed that two-thirds of companies are using some form of scorecard software to measure everything from financial progress to customer satisfaction. These scorecards can be customized to reflect only the measures the company wishes to track. Then, by targeting the distribution of this kind of data, a company can ensure, for example, that managers from marketing, finance, and research and development are all discussing the same measures in meetings.[49]

COMPARING THE OUTCOMES AGAINST THE CHANGE'S GOALS Collecting data is only a first step in evaluating outcomes. The next step is comparing the outcomes against the goals and various benchmarks, or standards, set in advance of the change. Without those standards, interpreting the data will be almost meaningless. To know that sales increased by 3 percent isn't enough unless the result can be compared with some explicit goal, such as a 5 percent increase. In other words, absolute results are not as informative as relative results. Goals and benchmarks that have been specified in advance of change efforts provide the basis for making meaningful relative comparisons.

COMMUNICATING THE RESULTS OF THE CHANGE The final step in evaluating change outcomes is communicating the findings to those who are involved with or affected by the change. As we discussed earlier in the chapter, this is one of the keys to ensure that the change lasts (the refreeze stage in Lewin's model). Managers seldom, if ever, neglect to provide this information to their superiors. Their subordinates are another story. This may be short-sighted. Not providing feedback can frustrate employees. They may even question a manager's motives for not supplying it, thereby creating an element of distrust and hampering successful changes in the future.

The "A Manager's Challenge" feature on the transformation of PricewaterhouseCoopers LLP (PwC) provides insight into how senior executives made choices around these key dimensions when implementing change.

Specific Approaches to Planned Change

Earlier, this chapter presented general issues and principles relating to organizational change and renewal. This final section looks at three specific, usually organization-wide, approaches to planned change. The first is *organizational development*, an approach with a strong behavioral and people orientation. The second is the more engineering-based approach called *process redesign* (or *reengineering*). The final part of this section describes what is almost more a particular framework or perspective than a change approach as such, namely, *organizational learning*.

The Organizational Development (OD) Approach to Change

The essence of an **organizational development (OD)** approach to change is its emphasis on planned, strategic, long-range efforts focusing on people and their interrelationships in organizations.[50] Although "organizational development" may seem like a general term that could be applied to almost any aspect of the topic of organizational change, as we noted at the beginning of this chapter, it refers

organizational development (OD)

approach to organizational change that has a strong behavioral and people orientation, emphasizing planned, strategic, long-range efforts focusing on people and their interrelationships in organizations

A MANAGER'S CHALLENGE

CHANGE

Changing the DNA at PwC

PricewaterhouseCoopers LLP (PwC) is one of the world's largest accounting firms, with more than 163,000 employees in 151 countries. In fiscal 2009, these workers generated approximately $26.2 billion in revenue. The right quality and quantity of human capital matters in any firm but is critical in a professional services firm like PwC. However, when your turnover rate is 50 percent higher than that of your competitors, turnover is costing you $40 million annually, and satisfaction is so low that staff at *Fortune*'s "100 Best Companies to Work For" list advised PwC executives not to apply again until they had significantly transformed the culture, you know you're in trouble.

Senior associate Kimberly Liu explained, "We had a hard time keeping up with the work because the high turnover created a revolving door on my teams. Some of our stars couldn't see futures for themselves at the firm and didn't feel free to talk about it." PwC leaders took this as a personal challenge, vowing to achieve a quick turnaround. As operations leader and CFO Mike Burwell said, "Turnover was not just a matter of cost, but also quality. There's a deep connection between the experience our people have and the experience they provide to our clients. For us, attracting and retaining top talent is a strategic imperative."

Many partners and staff were skeptical, so the first task for senior executives was to listen to staff regularly through biannual surveys. Executives then openly shared survey results in town hall meetings to foster a two-way dialogue.

To ensure that managers felt accountability for the needed changes, human resource leaders developed scorecards featuring retention, employee satisfaction, and other survey results and reported the results of their teams to each manager.

While turnover was a critical symptom, executives knew that they had to get to the root causes. They conducted a study and found:

- Only 20 percent of new hires joined PwC intending to build a long-term career there.
- Current compensation was competitive, but perceived opportunities to engage in challenging work and continually develop knowledge and skills were not.
- Among PwC staff members who intended to leave, key predictors were work/life balance, pay, and job satisfaction.

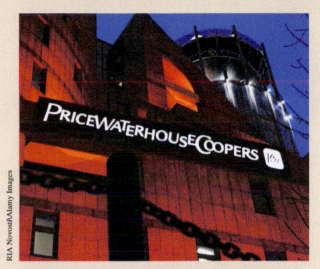

RIA Novosti/Alamy Images

PricewaterhouseCoopers LLP (PwC) is one of the largest accounting firms with more than 163,000 employees in 151 countries. However, they had a turnover rate that was 50 percent higher than their competitors. After changing their focus to smaller, more cohesive market-oriented and industry-based teams, employee satisfaction improved to the point that PwC ranked among Fortune's "100 Best Companies to Work For."

- Future compensation growth relative to other potential jobs was more important than current compensation in predicting retention.
- Employees who stayed at PwC to gain management experience experienced greater long-term financial and career gains than those who left earlier, regardless of whether they became partners. The challenge: retaining and developing employees as they become increasingly valuable in the marketplace.

Based on these deeper insights, U.S. sourcing leader Robert Daugherty said, "We had to strengthen our fundamental approach to retaining our people—by really understanding their goals and aspirations and providing the coaching, connectivity and experiences that would both develop and challenge them and improve the quality of our client service."

Yet in a firm run by partners—that is, individuals with an ownership stake in the organization—a new way of operating requires both changing the way partners understand their accountability and their capabilities. Each office had to generate concrete action plans. For example, one

(continued)

PwC office in California found that many employees considered leaving because they were receiving little feedback, and therefore, created a plan that included regular one-on-ones between partners and managers and managers and associates.

As the Tax and Advisory practices shifted their focus from large practices with pools of staff to smaller, more-cohesive market- and industry-based teams, employees began to feel a deeper understanding of clients and the ability to exercised greater influence.

By 2010, key outcomes included:

- Employee satisfaction that improved to the point that PwC ranked among *Fortune*'s 2010 list of "100 Best Companies to Work For" at #71 overall and #25 among large companies.
- Turnover that declined by 70 percent and now is well below that of its competitors.

Sources: M. J. Fenlon and S. A. Mohrman, "Where Counting Counts," *HRmagazine* 55, no. 1 (2010): 30–35; organization Web site, press release, January 21, 2010, http://www.pwc.com.

to a specific approach to bringing change to organizations. It grew out of behavioral science research aimed at improving the communication and quality of interactions among individuals in groups. Researchers put together groups of individuals in sessions away from the workplace in what they call a *basic skill training group* or, as it came to be called, a **T-group**.[51] The T-group orientation over time broadened into a focus on interpersonal relationships throughout the larger organization, and hence the attention to *organizational*, not just group, development.

VALUES AND ASSUMPTIONS   The early formulation of what eventually evolved into the OD approach placed particular importance on certain values and assumptions, and they have remained at the heart of this approach to change to this day.[52] One set of these values related to the people in organizations: First and foremost is the assumption that "people are the cornerstone of success in any organizational endeavor."[53] A second value or assumption is that most people want opportunities for personal growth and enhancement of their capabilities. Another basic belief that underlies this approach is that people's emotions are as important as their thoughts. Therefore, the open expression of these emotions can be critical in facilitating real change.

The fundamental assumption about organizations in the OD approach is that they are systems composed of interdependent parts. Thus, a change in one part can affect other parts.[54] Another assumption is that the way organizations are designed and structured will influence the interpersonal relationships among the people within them. In other words, the behavior of people in organizational settings is at least partly caused by the conditions they encounter there—and these conditions can be changed.

BASIC APPROACH TO THE PROCESS OF CHANGE   The basic OD approach to organizational change fundamentally follows the three stages of change outlined earlier in the chapter: Unfreezing, movement (changing), and refreezing.[55] Thus, in an OD approach to change, the initial challenge is to critically examine existing behavioral patterns by getting people not to take them for granted but to question them and look at their effects.

In the traditional OD approach, both the first and second steps—unfreezing and movement—call for the use of change agents. A **change agent** is an individual specifically responsible for managing change efforts.[56] They can be internal change agents, that is, working inside the organization—often from the human resource area—or they can be external change agents from outside the organization. In either case, the OD change agent is someone who is not a member of the particular groups or units directly involved. Frequently, this person is a consultant, someone with expertise in helping groups see the need for and make changes.

The changes themselves are achieved by the use of one or more interventions. An **intervention** is a set of structured activities or action steps designed to improve an organization.[57] Some of these interventions, such as fact finding, begin in the unfreezing stage, and others, such as team building and coaching or counseling, take place in the changing stage. Exhibit 15.12 shows several of the more common types of interventions.

T-group
a group of individuals participating in organizational development sessions away from the workplace; also called a basic skills training group

change agent
an individual responsible for implementing change efforts; can be either internal or external to the organization

intervention
a set of structured activities or action steps designed to improve an organization

EXHIBIT 15.12 **Types of OD Interventions**

Intervention	Objective	Examples
Diagnostic Activities	To determine the current state of the organization or the parameters of a problem	Interviews Questionnaires Surveys Meetings
Individual Enhancement Activities	To improve understanding of and relationships with others in the organization	Sensitivity training (T-groups) Behavior modeling Life and career planning
Team Building	To improve team operation, abilities, cohesiveness	Diagnostic meetings Role analysis Responsibility charting
Intergroup Activities	To improve cooperation between groups	Intergroup team building
Technostructural or Structural Activities	To find solutions to problems through the application of technological and structural changes	Job enrichment Management by objective New technology introduction
Process Consultation	To disseminate information concerning the future diagnosis and management of human processes in organizations including communication, leadership, problem solving and decision making, and intra-and intergroup relationships	Agenda setting Feedback and observation Coaching and counseling Structural change suggestions

Source: Adapted from Wendell L. French and Cecil H. Bell Jr., *Organization Development: Behavioral Science Interventions for Organizational Improvement*, 5th ed. (Upper Saddle River: Prentice Hall, 1995),165.

The priority in the second change stage is on exploring new forms of behavior and relationships. Particularly important at this point is an emphasis on behavioral processes, such as leader–group relations, decision making, intergroup cooperation, and the like. This **behavioral process orientation** is a key distinguishing feature of the OD approach to organizational change.

Merely engaging in new and different ways of behaving, relating, and interacting is not enough for changes to have lasting effects. This is the reason for the third stage, refreezing. As we discussed earlier in this chapter, the intent of this third stage is to make sure that the changes "stick" and that behavior and relationships don't easily return to their former—less effective—states. However, since the time of the original formulation of the three-stage change process many years ago, the goal of refreezing has been broadened into the objective of **organizational renewal.** The idea behind organizational renewal recognizes that in a fast-changing, competitive world, new habits and patterns rapidly become outdated. Therefore, the emphasis has shifted from simply locking changes into place and instead to developing a *capacity* for renewal, that is, the flexibility to change more or less continually.

In recent years, the OD approach to change, which formerly was almost a rigid set of procedures, has evolved into a more general approach—one that emphasizes line managers as potential change agents. Also, many OD intervention methods, such as team-building, have now become day-to-day activities for firms. Other comprehensive approaches to change have attracted increasing attention in the last decade or so. Two of these are process redesign and organizational learning, discussed next.

Process Redesign (Reengineering)

Process redesign, or **reengineering,** involves redesigning a firm's processes to achieve dramatic improvements.[58] Technology, especially information technology, usually plays a central role

behavioral process orientation
key distinguishing feature of the OD approach to organizational change that focuses on new forms of behavior and new relationships

organizational renewal
a concept of organizational change that proposes a goal of flexibility and capability for continual change

process redesign (reengineering)
involves a fundamental redesign of business processes to achieve dramatic improvements

EXHIBIT 15.13

Issues in Process Redesign

Objectives	Coverage	Potential Drawbacks
• Reduce costs • Shorten cycle times • Improve quality	• Breadth • Depth	• Requires high level of persistence and involvement of top management • Effort may be greater than results • High chaos factor • High levels of resistance

in such reengineering efforts. However, the human and managerial issues related to process redesign are also extremely crucial. (See Exhibit 15.13).

Reengineering first appeared in the late 1980s, and seemed to peak in popularity in the mid-1990s.[59] The approach is based on two key principles: Many companies have business processes that are inefficient and structures that involve more people than necessary. The goal is to reduce costs, shorten cycle times, and improve quality.[60] IBM was one of the first companies to take a reengineering approach. In the 1990s, the company shortened its credit approval process from two weeks to just two hours with no increase in staff.

The most successful process redesign efforts appear to have both breadth and depth.[61] Breadth of reengineering involves redesigning a set of processes rather than a single process. Depth of reengineering involves changing a host of core elements, such as the roles and responsibilities, structure, incentives, and shared values, within an organization.

But breadth and depth are not enough for a reengineering effort to succeed. Key executives in the organization must also make a major commitment to it. For example, they must supply the necessary resources to implement the activities and demonstrate that they are personally involved in the effort. Like any comprehensive change approach, reengineering requires enormous energy, planning, a coordinated effort, persistence, and attention to detail. Otherwise, it is likely to fail.

Even under the best circumstances, however, reengineering does not always produce effective changes. This has led to some disillusionment with the approach.[62] For one, the amount of effort it requires has not always been commensurate with the results obtained. One European commercial bank, for example, saw its reengineering effort yield only a 5 percent cost reduction rather than an anticipated 23 percent reduction.[63] A second reason that some managers have become disenchanted with the approach is that it can cause continual disorder, or, as some managers call it, "mass chaos."[64]

As the history of companies' attempts to implement process redesign illustrates, it is an approach or organizational renewal that is not exactly embraced by many of those who have to take part in it. Michael Hammer, one of the coauthors of the book *Reengineering the Corporation*, which was most influential in popularizing this approach, has stated that the people aspects of reengineering were not always given enough attention. "I was insufficiently appreciative of the human dimension. I've learned that's critical."[65] Nevertheless, despite its problems, at least some CEOs and other corporate leaders appear to remain positive about the potential of this comprehensive approach to change.[66]

Organizational Learning

organizational learning
exhibited by an organization that is skilled at creating, acquiring, and transferring knowledge, and at modifying its behavior to reflect new knowledge and insights

Although the concept has been around for some time, it was not until relatively recently that **organizational learning** has become a major approach to organizational change and renewal.[67] A firm that is good at organizational learning is said to be "skilled at creating, acquiring, and transferring knowledge, and at modifying its behavior to reflect new knowledge and insights."[68] Such an organization would be called a *learning organization*.

Several factors have been shown to facilitate learning by organizations:

- Employees with well-developed core competencies.
- An organizational culture that supports continuous improvement.
- The capability (such as managerial expertise) to implement necessary changes.[69]

Managers and organizations cannot simply decide, or declare, that learning should take place. The elements listed previously need to be in place as a starting point if organizational learning is going to lead to any real benefits. Then, a number of activities need to take place to implement fully an ongoing learning process in organizations. Five of the more important ones are explained here.[70]

A SYSTEMATIC, ORGANIZED, AND CONSISTENT APPROACH TO PROBLEM SOLVING Rather than relying on assumptions or guesswork to solve problems and make decisions, learning organizations systematically and continually collect data related to them.

EXPERIMENTATION TO OBTAIN NEW KNOWLEDGE Learning organizations experiment with new methods and procedures to expand their knowledge and gain fresh insights. They engage in a steady series of small experiments to keep acquiring new knowledge consistently and to help employees become accustomed to change. Corning, Allegheny Ludlum, and Nucor Steel are examples of companies that constantly try new methods and processes to improve their productivity.

DRAWING ON PAST EXPERIENCES Enterprises with strong learning cultures pay particular attention to past failures as well as successes. For example, because of problems with the development of its 737 and 747 planes, Boeing initiated a three-year project to compare the development of these planes to the earlier, more reliable 707 and 727 planes. This project resulted in a booklet of "lessons learned," which was then used in the development and manufacture of 757s and 767s.

LEARNING FROM THE BEST PRACTICES AND IDEAS OF OTHERS Learning organizations and their managers consistently scan their environments for information and knowledge from a variety of external sources, including their competitors, customers, and even other industries. One increasingly common form of this is benchmarking, where the best practices of competitors are identified, analyzed, and compared against one's own practices.[71] Exhibit 15.14 shows some of the business processes that are commonly being benchmarked by companies today. Xerox, Corning, the U.S. Army, and the U.S. Social Security Administration are among the major U.S. organizations that make frequent use of benchmarking.

Other ways of generating this kind of learning include putting together focus groups. A **focus group** typically consists of customers who spend time in small groups for intense discussions of the positive and negative features of products or services.

focus group
a small group involved in intense discussions of the positive and negative features of products or services

TRANSFERRING AND SHARING KNOWLEDGE Learning organizations also ensure that the knowledge they gain is disseminated throughout their organizations. This can include such activities as distributing reports, developing demonstration projects, initiating training and education programs, and rotating or transferring those with the knowledge.

As an approach to change, an organizational learning perspective has much to offer. It emphasizes paying constant attention to potentially needed changes, and it embodies the goal of renewal—of pushing organizations to continually reinvent themselves through the purposeful and persistent acquisition of new knowledge. One of the best ways to keep abreast of changing environments is for managers to focus intently on instilling a learning culture within their work groups.

Business Process
Employee development training
Billing
Information systems technology
Customer service
Process improvement management
Facility management
Human resources
Project management

EXHIBIT 15.14

Commonly Benchmarked Business Practices

Managerial Challenges from the Front Line

The Rest of the Story

After considering that PwC and the boutique firm acquiring his office were radically different in terms of their vision, strategy, client experience, quality standards, culture, and more, Chris Haenen decided not to join the boutique firm. Haenen made it clear to his people that they should decide what was best for them and not be influenced by his decision. To his surprise, the other director decided to stay with the new owner in part because he was offered a specific position with the new "parent."

Because the consulting world is a small one, another global firm, a PwC rival, approached Haenen and he started talks with them. Because the takeover was effective October 1, Haenen (and any others who had

not yet committed to stay) were required to move out of their Amsterdam office and return laptops and phones by the end of September 30. This was rather disquieting to several staff, many of whom had worked for the firm for more than 10 years.

Meanwhile, the global firm that had approached Haenen also entered into negotiations with six other people from the PwC Netherlands office. By the end of October, he and five others joined the rival global firm.

One lesson Haenen learned from the whole affair: in today's unpredictable environment, professionals must be prepared to make changes, not just with their team but sometimes in terms of their own career path.

Summary

- The forces for change are primarily external or internal. Key external forces include economic conditions, competitors, technology, legal and political contexts, and societal and demographic trends.
- Change can be focused on or directed to one or more of the following key targets: strategy, structure, systems, technology, culture, and staff.
- In analyzing and evaluating the need for change, managers may take a proactive, reactive, or crisis approach. In any case, it is critical to diagnose the real problem so that the changes actually improve the situation the organization faces.
- The three major stages in the process of change include unfreezing, moving, and refreezing.
- Resistance to change in each stage is common. In the unfreezing stage, inertia, mistrust, and lack of information are often common causes of resistance. During the movement stage, lack of clarity regarding the change, lack of capabilities, and lack of sufficient incentives are core sources of resistance. During the refreezing stage, the pull of past competencies and the nonimmediate nature of results both can contribute to resistance and ultimately the failure of change.
- Four key actions can help managers overcome the resistance to change: First, it is usually critical to help people understand the rationale for the change. Second, it is vital that people clearly understand the change and know what they will do differently. Third, if people are to make the desired changes, they need the capabilities to implement the change, including knowledge, information, skills, and other resources. Finally, managers must ensure that they reinforce early correct efforts and not just desired results.
- Managing change involves a number of key choices that managers need to make. In the planning stage, managers need to decide on the timing of the change, build a leading coalition, determine how to communicate the plan, the levels of participation, and types of incentives. Before implementing the change, managers must determine the focus, amount, frequency, and rate of change.
- Making changes is time consuming and costly. Therefore, ensuring that the benefits outweigh the costs is critical. This process typically involves gathering data, comparing it to goals, and then providing feedback to involved parties on the progress.

- Organizational development (OD) is a large-scale change that focuses on interventions designed to change people's behaviors. These interventions are led by a designated change agent or group of agents.
- Process redesign, or reengineering, is a general change approach that focuses on improving an organization's work processes (and thereby productivity) by changing what people do and how they do it. Changes in how work is done often involve changes in or additions of technology.
- Organizational learning is more of a general framework for continual organizational change. Companies that are good at it have a systematic approach to problem solving, experiment, learn from the past as well as others, and share that knowledge broadly within their organizations.

Key Terms

behavioral process orientation   441
change agent   440
focus group   443
force field analysis   433

intervention   440
leading coalition   434
organizational development
   (OD)   438

organizational learning   442
organizational renewal   441
process redesign (reengineering)   441
T-group   440

Review Questions

1. List the forces from outside an organization that act to bring about change within it.
2. What are an organization's internal forces for change?
3. What components within an organization can be changed? (Hint: The chapter discusses six of them.)
4. What is the key to changing an organization's culture?
5. Is it more difficult to change an organization's strategy or its culture? Why?
6. What is meant by proactive and reactive change?
7. Name the three major stages in the change process.
8. What are the key sources of resistance in each major stage of the change process?
9. Describe some of the considerations managers face when planning change.
10. What are the key considerations and choices in implementing change?
11. What two criteria are key in determining targeted supporters for change?
12. Why is it important to be careful in choosing the amount and rate of change? What are the benefits and drawbacks

involved in large-and small-scale change? In rapid or slow change?
13. List the drawbacks to using incentives to gain cooperation during a change.
14. What are some of the ways managers can overcome employees' resistance to change?
15. Define the term *force field analysis*.
16. In evaluating the outcome of a planned change, what types of data are used?
17. Name and describe the three steps in evaluating the outcome of a planned change.
18. What is the emphasis of the OD approach to change?
19. Name and describe the key steps in the OD approach to change.
20. What is a change agent? Where do change agents come from?
21. What is the difference between the breadth and the depth of reengineering?
22. Describe a learning organization.
23. How can you tell when you are encountering a learning organization?

Assessing Your Capabilities

Select a change initiative to assess. It is best to select a change initiative that you are currently facing or will soon face. However, you can also choose a past change that you were part of. Once you have the change initiative in mind, simply follow the step-by-step assessment instructions.

    For each of the following statements, indicate the extent to which you agree or disagree by circling the appropriate number

to the right. In responding to each item, use as a reference group those people who will be most directly and significantly impacted by the change initiative you have in mind. The reference group might be as small as a team or as large as all the employees in an organization. Whatever is the case, simply use that group as your reference as you respond to the following statements.

	Strongly Disagree	Disagree	Somewhat Disagree	Somewhat Agree	Agree	Strongly Agree
See the Need						
1. The contrast between where we are and where we need to be is clear.	1	2	3	4	5	6
2. The reason for the needed change is clear to those most affected by it.	1	2	3	4	5	6
3. How things will be after the change is clear—people can envision the destination.	1	2	3	4	5	6
Make the Move						
4. A powerful and capable team to lead the change is in place.	1	2	3	4	5	6
5. Those who need to change understand the path forward.	1	2	3	4	5	6
6. Those who need to change have the tools, resources, and capabilities to make the required changes.	1	2	3	4	5	6
Reinforce the Finish						
7. Capable champions are in place who will reinforce early efforts and successes.	1	2	3	4	5	6
8. Systems are in place to chart and communicate progress to individuals and groups.	1	2	3	4	5	6
9. Key systems (e.g., rewards, performance appraisal, training, etc.) have been aligned to support (not work against) the required changes.	1	2	3	4	5	6

Now, record your totals for each section by simply adding your scores:

Add all three scores together:

See	(Q1 + Q2 + Q3) = _____
Move	(Q4 + Q5 + Q6) = _____
Finish	(Q7 + Q8 + Q9) = _____

TOTAL   = _____

Use the following table for a rough interpretation of your scores:

	3–8 points Bad News	8–12 points Not Good News	13–15 points Good News	16–18 points Great News
See	Change initiatives with these scores tend to fail on the launch pad. If they do get off the pad, they tend to come crashing back to earth.	Change initiatives with these scores tend to get started but then fizzle and fade.	Scores in this range often indicate enough fuel to get off the launch pad, but the change may lose momentum while breaking through the first barrier.	Scores in this range often indicate enough fuel to get off the launch pad and make it successfully through the first barrier.
Move	Change initiatives with these scores (if they make it through the first barrier) slam to a stop at the second.	Change initiatives with these scores (if they make it through the first barrier), sputter and usually die before making it through the second barrier.	Scores in this range often signal enough momentum to push the envelope of the second barrier but tend to break through only for small to moderate change initiatives.	Scores in this range usually lead to success in breaking through the second barrier.

Finish	Scores in this range occur even when scores for See and Move are high. Unfortunately, with scores in this range, the change initiative still is likely to be among the 70% that ultimately fail.	Scores in this range suggest that while the change might achieve initial success, it will fall far short of its goal and has a high chance of ultimate failure.	If the scores for See and Move were high, there's hope; but if they were only good, this is likely to be the end—with the destination in sight but just out of reach.	While nothing is guaranteed, scores in this range in combination with strong See and Move scores put you in the elite group whose change initiative likely succeeds.
TOTAL	**9–24 points Bad News**	**25–37 points Not Good News**	**38–47 points Good News**	**48–54 points Great News**
	The odds of your change initiative succeeding are as good as a motorcycle breaking through a thick concrete wall.	You may feel like you've got the odds of success on your side, but you don't. You have a 70% chance of failure.	You're close enough that if there's time, you can strengthen some aspects of the change initiative and still succeed.	With total scores in this range, the odds are on your side. You have a better than 70% chance of success.

Team Exercise

Leading Change at GenCom

Divide into groups of three to five members each. Each group should take one of two perspectives. One group should take the perspective of the review committee while the other group should take the perspective of the general employees. Each group should read the following short scenario and then prepare for a dialog. Use the questions at the end to help guide your preparations. (Note: The objective is to bring out the dynamic of change and key issues, not for either side to fabricate data, past experiences, etc. in order to win their point.)

Two years ago GenCom gave its production review committee responsibility for developing and implementing procedures to improve manufacturing productivity. Jerry, the manager of GenCom's engineering department, co-chairs the committee with Gene, GenCom's production manager. They and the three other committee members jointly decide on any major productivity changes.

A monthly meeting of the production review committee had already begun when Gene hurried in. "Have you seen these production figures?" he asked. "They are incredible—just look at the increase in productivity in this department!"

Jerry was surprised at Gene's enthusiasm and said, "Wait a minute. Just what are you talking about that has you so excited?"

Gene realized the other members of the committee hadn't yet seen the new report and quickly handed copies of it around. He then took a deep breath and started explaining. "Several months ago, I told Kim, the manager of extract processing, that I was somewhat disappointed by the latest productivity figures and wished someone could figure out a way to improve them. I didn't think about that statement until just this morning when Kim walked into my office and handed me this report. It seems she has had her team working on the problem for the last four months. They collected information on productivity levels at other similar companies and carefully studied the procedures of the most successful. They worked with several of the ideas in their group, testing the ideas separately and in combination and with new additions until they found a method that seemed to work. Wow! I'll say it seems to work. Just look at those figures. I think we ought to immediately implement their idea in all the production units. Just think of the profit improvements that would result from across-the-board performance improvements matching these."

Jerry and the other members of the committee were pleased with the report and decided to accept Gene's recommendation for a company-wide application of the new procedures developed by Kim's team. They had all been anxious to find a new initiative that would really work since their last two change attempts had been unsuccessful. Both previous initiatives had been scrapped rather quickly. The first one had not worked because the plant didn't have the right type of equipment and infrastructure to support it. The second had failed because of high levels of resistance from employees. However, after discussion, the committee members were convinced that this new approach would definitely work, and they decided to implement it throughout all relevant units. After all, it had worked out exceedingly well in Kim's department.

However, before the review committee could formulate its plan, the firm's employees heard both about the result in Kim's department and rumors that the committee was considering another "flavor of the month" change based on what happened for a short period of time in Kim's department.

1. As a member of the review committee, analyze the forces for and against this change (force field analysis). Based on this, what early actions might you take?

2. What would be the basic elements and choices in your change plan?

3. As an employee, why might you resist this change? What might make you less resistant to the change?

Leading Signal Processing (LSP)—a disguised name but a real company—produces diagnostic instruments primarily for the health care industry. Over most of its history, its leading-edge products, based on state-of-the-art analog signal technology, were used by scientific and hospital researchers in diagnostic tests and cellular and blood chemical analysis.

After years of success, the company's CEO noticed digital signal processing emerging as a potential new technological platform, though initially it seemed unable to rival LSP's analog technology at the moment. He also recognized a shift in customers and end users. In the past, MDs and PhDs had performed diagnostics and analyses in research labs and hospitals; now technicians in clinics were increasingly performing these tests. Many of LSP's largest customers were likely to be slow to make this transition, but midsize and small customers were more likely to quickly change over and save money. In addition, the market was moving away from separate tests and analyses toward integrated systems and analyses.

Although LSP's CEO recognized that these environmental shifts would require the company to change, many of the firm's scientists—analog technology experts—resisted, seeing digital technology as a threat to their jobs. The more the CEO talked about environmental shifts, the harder these scientists worked on customized analog products for customers, especially big customers. This was, in part, because it took years to become an accomplished analog scientist, and analog and digital science were like Greek and Chinese—knowing Greek did you very little good in mastering Chinese and vice versa. Moving from the top of the analog learning curve to the bottom of the digital learning curve was very unappealing, especially to the more senior and influential scientists in the company.

The CEO also realized that the trend toward integrated systems would require LSP's workforce to collaborate using both cross-product and cross-functional teams composed of employees from research, development, marketing, and manufacturing. Such teamwork was rare within LSP. Each department did its own thing, and the R&D department was clearly the most important. From their perspective, the company had succeeded in the past because their products were so leading edge that they essentially sold themselves; marketing and sales were simply "order takers."

As a few competitors brought new digital products to market, LSP's research scientists scoffed at their initially lower reliability and inferior performance. Although the manager of the R&D group was more favorably inclined

to the changes, he was only 6 to 12 months away from retirement. And his most senior signal processing scientist, Dr. Lee, was completely opposed to the changes. This was critical because Dr. Lee was, without question, the most brilliant of all the scientists and his innovations in analog signal processing were used in virtually all of LSP's current products. Most of the more junior scientists had been exposed to digital signal processing in their studies, but many of them had joined LSP in part because of Dr. Lee's fame and reputation.

The head of marketing thought that small- and medium-sized clinics, labs, and other enterprises constituted a large and growing set of potential customers LSP was not currently tapped into. He was fully in favor of digital technology and felt it "represented the only way the company was really going to grow."

The head of manufacturing was more neutral on digital technology and the potential changes it implied. Production was working fairly well at the moment. And although LSP's manufacturing costs were slightly higher than other firms' manufacturing costs, the leading edge nature of its products allowed it to enjoy pricing premiums that offset the higher costs.

The CEO wondered what he should do and how he should approach this challenge. If he waited too long to make a move, LSP might lose its reputation as a technology leader. He might also see his traditional customer base decline relative to the total size and nature of the market and its segments. On the other hand, he was up against some very powerful resistors. Dr. Lee had visibility to and credibility with the CEO's boss—the board of directors. In the past, Dr. Lee had made several presentations to the board on technical matters, and his recommendations had generally proven correct. Would the board listen to the CEO or Dr. Lee?

Questions

1. What is your analysis relative to a potential leading coalition?
2. At the three different stages of change, what are the likely sources of resistance?
3. Why is Dr. Lee so opposed to the potential change? Can anything be done to reduce his resistance?
4. What would your general recommendations be relative to building a leading coalition, communication plan, levels of participation, and types of incentives?
5. What would be your general recommendations relative to the focus, amount, frequency, and rate of change?

References

1. P. F. Drucker, "The New Society of Organizations," *Harvard Business Review* 70, no. 5 (1992): 95–104; C. K. Wagner, "Managing Change in Business: Views from the Ancient Past," *Business Horizons* 38 (1995): 812; G. Hamel and L. Valikangas, "The Quest for Resilience," *Harvard Business Review* 81, no. 9 (2003): 52–63; H. Tsoukas and R. Chia, "On Organizational Becoming: Rethinking Organizational Change," *Organization Science* 13, no. 5 (2002): 567–582.

2. N. Bunkley, "After 6,000 Take Buyouts, GM to Lay off Thousands," *New York Times*, August 3, 2009, B4.

3. http://www.npr.org/templates/story/story.php?storyId=99276446; accessed February 2, 2009.

4. U.S.-China Business Council, "Foreign Investment in China," http://www.uschina.org/statistics/fdi_cumulative.html, accessed June 15, 2010.

5. http://www.emsresponder.com/online/article.jsp?siteSection=1&id=12152; accessed February 20, 2010.

6. D. Lyons, and N. Summers, "Phone Fight!," *Newsweek*, June 12, 2010, http://www.newsweek.com/2010/06/12/phone-fight.html.

7. State Web site, http://www.oregon.gov/DHS/ph/smokefree/thelaw.shtml accessed June 10, 2010; CDC, "State Smoking Restrictions for Private-sector Worksites, Restaurants, and Bars—United States, 1998 and 2004," www.cdc.gov/mmwr/preview/mmwrhtml/mm5426a1.htm, accessed January 17, 2007; "Workplace Smoking Ban Would Help Kick Habit," *Occupational Health* 54, no. 9 (2002): 7.

8. U.S. Census Bureau, "Population Projections Program, Population Division," Washington, D.C: 20233 (301) 763–2428.

9. J. Pfeffer, "Understanding Power in Organizations," *California Management Review* 34, no. 2 (1992): 29–50.

10. M. Moon, "Bottom-up Instigated Organization Change Through Constructionist Conversation," *Journal of Knowledge Management Practice* 9, no. 4 (2008):

11. K. Jones, "How CU Saved $250K with Process Improvement," *Credit Union Journal* 14 no. 3 (2010): 1, 10.

12. E. Iritani and M. Dickerson, "Tallying Port Dispute's Costs," *Los Angeles Times*, November 25, 2002, B1.

13. A. D. Chandler, *Strategy and Structure: Chapters in the History of the Industrial Enterprise* (Cambridge: MIT Press, 1962); T. L. Amburgey and T. Dacin, "As the Left Foot Follows the Right? The Dynamics of Strategic and Structural Change," *Academy of Management Journal* 37 (1994): 1427–1452; M. T. Hannan, L. Polos, and G. R. Carroll, "Cascading Organizational Change," *Organization Science* 14, no. 5 (2003): 463–482.

14. M. A. Hitt, R. D. Ireland, and R. E. Hoskisson, *Strategic Management: Competitiveness and Globalization* (Cincinnati: South-Western Publishing Co, 2005).

15. D. A. Nadler and M. L. Tushman, "Beyond the Charismatic Leader: Leadership and Organizational Change," *California Management Review* 32, no. 2 (1990): 77–97; Hannan, Polos, and Carroll, "Cascading Organizational Change."

16. I. Rowley, "What Put Honda in the Passing Lane," *BusinessWeek*, October 19, 2009, 57–58; Company Web site, "Summary of 2006 Mid-year CEO Speech," press release, http://world.honda.com/news/2006/c060517MidYearCEOSpeech, accessed December 12, 2006; M. Wall, "Manufacturing Flexibility," *Automotive Industries* 183, no. 10 (2003): 44–46.

17. Nokia Annual Report, 2008.

18. D. Tuller, "Get a Check Up," *Menatrisk.com*, June 13, 2010, www.menatrisk.org/health/checkup.html; organization Web site, "Executive Program," http://www.mayoclinichealthmanagementresources.com/products/executiveprogram.cfm, accessed July 22, 2010; L. A. Armour, "Me and the Mayo," *Fortune*, 2006, 86–89.

19. D. L. Madison, R. W. Allen, L. W. Porter, P. A. Renwick *et al.*, "Organizational Politics: An Exploration of Managers' Perceptions," *Human Relations* 33, no. 2 (1980): 79–100; M. C. Kernan and P. J. Hanges, "Survivor Reactions to Reorganization: Antecedents and Consequences of Procedural, Interpersonal, and Informational Justice," *Journal of Applied Psychology* 87, no. 5 (2002): 916–928.

20. "Intel Dalian Chip Plant To Be Put into Operation in October 2010," http://www.ciipp.com/en/index/view-117074.html, accessed June 22, 2010; D. Clark, "Inside Intel, It's All Copying," *Wall Street Journal*, October 28, 2002, B1.

21. R. Barkerville, *Business Agility and Information Technology Diffusion* (New York: Springer, 2005); N. Venkatraman, "IT-Enabled Business Transformation: From Automation to Business Scope Redefinition," *Sloan Management Review* 35, no. 2 (1994): 73–87.

22. "The Up and Down of Wal-Mart RFID Implementation," http://ecosensa.com/rfidblog/2009/03/24/wal-mart-rfid-implementation, accessed June 12, 2010.

23. J. Evans, "Grand Cathay's Assets Take a Walk," *Asiamoney* 13, no. 9 (2002): 49.

24. S. Ghoshal and C. A. Bartlett, "Rebuilding Behavioral Context: A Blueprint for Corporate Renewal," *Sloan Management Review* 37, no. 2 (1996): 23–36.

25. T. G. Cummings and C. G. Worley, *Organizational Development and Change* (Florence, KY: Cengage Learning, 2008); W. Weitzel and E. Johnson, "Decline in Organizations: A Literature Integration and Extension," *Administrative Science Quarterly* 34 (1989): 91–109.

26. B. Dumaine, "Times Are Good? Create a Crisis," *Fortune* 1993: 123–130.

27. B. Nussbaum, "Learning to Be Like Apple, Nike, Starbucks, Nokia, P&G and Other Creative Companies," *BusinessWeek*, April 7, 2006; I. Isidro, "10 Lessons Small Businesses Can Learn from Starbucks," *PowerHomeBiz.com*, www.powerhomebiz.com/vol144/starbucks.htm, accessed October 5, 2004; S. Holmes, "Planet Starbucks," *BusinessWeek*, September 9, 2002, 100–110.

28. M. L. Tushman, W. H. Newman, and E. Romanelli, "Convergence and Upheaval: Managing the Unsteady Pace of Organizational Evolution," *California Management Review* 29, no. 1 (1986): 29–44.

29. T. Bradley, "McDonald's Free Wifi a No-Brainer Win-Win," *PCWorld Online*, December 17, 2009, http://www.pcworld.com/businesscenter/article/184939/mcdonalds_free_wifi_a_nobrainer_winwin.html.

30. K. Lewin, "Frontiers in Group Dynamics," *Human Relations* 1 (1947): 5–41.

31. A. C. Amason and A. C. Mooney, "The Icarus Paradox Revisited: How Strong Performance Sows the Seeds of Dysfunction in Future Strategic Decision Making," *Strategic Organization* 6, no. 4, (2008): 407–434; F. Gavetti and D. Levinthal, "Looking Forward and Looking Backward: Cognitive and Experiential Search," *Administrative Science Quarterly* 45 (2000): 113–137.

32. D. M. Macri, "A Grounded Theory for Resistance to Change in Small Organizations," *Journal of Organizational Change Management* 15 (2002): 292–309.

33. F. Yuan and R. W. Woodman, "Formation of Expectations Regarding Change Outcomes: Integrating Information and Social Effects," in R. Woodman, W. Pasmore, and A. B. Shani (eds.) *Research in Organizational Change and Development*, vol. 16 (Bingley, UK: Emerald Group Publishing Limited, 2007), 81–104; T. L. Saaty and L. G. Vargas, "Uncertainty and Rank Order in the Analytic Hierarchy Process," *European Journal of Operational Research* 32, no. 1 (1987): 108–118.

34. L. Jones, B. Watson, E. Hobman, P. Bordia, C. Gallois, and V. J. Callan, "Employee Perceptions of Organizational Change: Impact of Hierarchical Level," *Leadership & Organization Development Journal* 29, no. 4 (2008): 294–316.

35. S. A. Furst and D. M. Cable, "Employee Resistance to Organizational Change: Managerial Influence Tactics and Leader–Member Exchange," *Journal of Applied Psychology* 93, no.2 (1993): 453–462; L. L. Paglis and S. G. Green, "Leadership Self-Efficacy and Managers' Motivation for Leading Change," *Journal of Organizational Behavior* 23 (2002): 215–235.

36. Lewin, "Frontiers in Group Dynamics"; M. L. McDonald and J. D. Westphal, "Getting by with the Advice of Friends: CEOs' Advice Networks and Firms' Strategic Responses to Poor Performance," *Administrative Science Quarterly* 48, no. 1 (2003): 1–32.

37. Lewin, "Frontiers in Group Dynamics."

38. S. A. Sackman, P. M. Eggenhofer-Rehart, and M. Friesl, "Sustainable Change," *The Journal of Applied Behavioral Science* 45, no. 4 (2009): 521–549; R. Cacioppe, "Using Team–Individual Reward and Recognition Strategies to Drive Organizational Success," *Leadership and Organization Development Journal* 20 (1999): 322–331.

39. J. S Black and H. B. Gregersen, *It Starts with One: Changing Individuals Changes Organizations* (Philadelphia: Wharton School Publishing, 2008); B. Dobbin, "Kodak Enters Inkjet-Printer Market," *Star-Telegram.com*, February 6, 2007; N. Watson, "What's Wrong with This Printer?" *Fortune*, 2003, 120C–120.

40. D. Blankenship, "Preparing Employees for Change," *Baylor Business Review* 13, no. 2 (1995): 14+; M. Cortsjens and J. Merrihue, "Optimal Marketing," *Harvard Business Review* 81, no. 10 (2003): 114–122.

41. J. Oldham, "Achieving Large Scale Change in Health Care," *Journal of American Medical Association*, 301 no. 9 (2009):965–966; J. Covington and M. L. Chase, "Eight Steps to Sustainable Change," *Industrial Management* 44, no. 6 (2002): 8–11.

42. K. Lewin, *Field Theory in Social Science; Selected Theoretical Papers* (New York: Harper, 1951).

43. N. King and J. D. Stoll, "Government Forces Out Wagner," *Wall Street Journal*, March 30, 2009, http://online.wsj.com/article/SB123836090755767077.html; J. D. Stoll and K. Linebaugh, "GM's Chairman Seizes the Wheel," *Wall Street Journal*, December 1, 2009, http://online.wsj.com/article/SB10001424052748704107104574569613149594076.html.

44. J. Gillett, R. Fink, and N. Bevington, "How Caterpillar Uses Six Sigma to Execute Strategy," *Strategic Finance*, April (2010), 25–28.

45. N. L. Jimmieson, M. Peach, and K. M. White, "Utilizing the Theory of Planned Behavior to Inform Change Management: An Investigation of Employee Intentions to Support Organizational Change," *Journal of Applied Behavioral Science* 44 (2008): 237–262.

46. J. Reingold, "CEO Swap," *Fortune*, 2009,. http://money.cnn.com/2009/11/19/news/companies/procter_gamble_lafley.fortune/index.htm

47. C. R. Leana, "Stability and Change as Simultaneous Experiences in Organizational Life," *Academy of Management Review* 25 (2000): 753–762; Q. N. Huy, "Emotional Balancing of Organizational Continuity and Radical Change: The Contribution of Middle Managers," *Administrative Science Quarterly* 47, no. 1 (2002): 31–69.

48. V. Baxter and A. Margavio, "Assaultive Violence in the U.S. Post Office," *Work and Occupations* 23 (1996): 277–296.

49. B. K. Spiker and E. Lesser, "We Have Met the Enemy," *Journal of Business Strategy* 16, no. 2 (1995): 17–21.

50. S. Mohrman, "Having Relevance and Impact: The Benefits of Integrating the Perspectives of Design Science and Organizational Development," *The Journal of Applied Behavioral Science* 43, no. 1 (2007): 12–22; J. Kurtzman, "Is Your Company Off Course: Now You Can Find Out Why," *Fortune* (1997): 58–60.

51. W. L. French, C. H. Bell Jr., and R. A. Zawicki, *Organizational Development and Transformation: Managing Effective Change*, 4th ed. (Burr Ridge: Richard D. Irwin, 1994).

52. Ibid.

53. R. Beckhard, *Organization Development: Strategies and Models* (Reading: Addison-Wesley, 1969); R. D. Smither, J. M. Houston, and S. D. McIntire, *Organization Development: Strategies for Changing Environments* (New York: HarperCollins, 1996); B. Pitman, "Leading for Value," *Harvard Business Review* 81, no. 4 (2003): 41–46.

54. Smither *et al., Organization Development: Strategies for Changing Environments.*

55. Ibid.

56. K. Lewin, "Frontiers in Group Dynamics," *Human Relations* 1 (1947): 5–41; A. Clardy, "Learning to Change: A Guide for Organization Change Agents," *Personnel Psychology* 56, no. 3 (2003): 785–788.

57. Smither *et al., Organization Development: Strategies for Changing Environments;* N. J. Foss, "Selective Intervention and Internal Hybrids: Interpreting and Learning from the Rise and Decline of the Oticon Spaghetti Organization," *Organization Science* 14, no. 3 (2003): 331+.

58. W. L. French and C. H. Bell Jr., *Organization Development: Behavioral Science Interventions for Organizational Improvement*, 5th ed (Upper Saddle River: Prentice Hall, 1995), 156; M. J. Benner and M. L. Tushman, "Exploitation, Exploration, and Process Management: The Productivity Dilemma Revisited," *Academy of Management Review* 28, no. 2 (2003): 238–256; M. J. Benner and M. Tushman, "Process Management and Technological Innovation: A Longitudinal Study of the Photography and Paint Industries," *Administrative Science Quarterly* 47, no. 4 (2002): 676–706.

59. D. A. Garvin, "Leveraging Processes for Strategic Advantage," *Harvard Business Review* 73, no. 5 (1995): 76–79; M. Hammer and J. Champy, "Reengineering the Corporation," *Small Business Reports* 18, no. 11 (1993): 65–69. M. Hammer and J. Champy, *Reengineering the Corporation*, (1993), New York: HarperCollins.

60. D. Rigby, "Management Tools and Techniques: A Survey," *California Management Review* 43, no. 2 (2001): 139–161.

61. Ibid.

62. G. Hall, J. Rosenthal, and J. Wade, "How to Make Reengineering Really Work," *Harvard Business Review* 71, no. 6 (1993): 119–131.

63. J. B. White, "Next Big Thing: Reengineering Gurus Take Steps to Remodel Their Stalling Vehicles," *Wall Street Journal*, November 26, 1996, A1, A10; Rigby, "Management Tools and Techniques: A Survey"; D. Elmuti and Y. Kathawala, "Business Reengineering: Revolutionary Management Tool, or Fading Fad?" *Business Forum* 25, nos. 1–2 (2000): 29–36.

64. Hall and Rosenthal, "How to Make Reengineering Really Work"; M. J. Benner and M. L. Tushman, "Exploitation, Exploration, and Process Management: The Productivity Dilemma Revisited," *Academy of Management Review* 28, no. 2 (2003): 238–256.

65. Elmuti and Kathawala, "Business Reengineering: Revolutionary Management Tool, or Fading Fad?"; M. C. Kernan and P. J. Hanges, "Survivor Reactions to Reorganization: Antecedents and Consequences of Procedural, Interpersonal, and Informational Justice," *Journal of Applied Psychology* 87, no. 5 (2002): 916–928; D. A. Buchanan, "Demands,

Instabilities, Manipulations, Careers: The Lived Experience of Driving Change," *Human Relations* 56, no. 6 (2003): 663–684.

66. White, "Next Big Thing: Reengineering Gurus Take Steps to Remodel Their Stalling Vehicles"; M. J. Benner and M. Tushman, "Process Management and Technological Innovation: A Longitudinal Study of the Photography and Paint Industries," *Administrative Science Quarterly* 47, no. 4 (2002): 676–706; Q. N. Huy, "Emotional Balancing of Organizational Continuity and Radical Change: The Contribution of Middle Managers," *Administrative Science Quarterly* 47, no. 1 (2002): 631–691; A. E. Akgun, G. S. Lynn, and J. C. Byrne, "Organizational Learning: A Socio-Cognitive Framework," *Human Relations* 56, no. 7 (2003): 839–868.

67. D. M. Rousseau, "Organizational Behavior in the New Organizational Era," *Annual Review of Psychology* 48 (1997): 515–546; C. Argyris and D. A. Schoen, *Organizational Learning II: Theory, Method, and Practice* (Reading, MA: Addison-Wesley, 1996); D. A. Garvin, "Building a Learning Organization," *Harvard Business Review* 71, no. 4 (1993): 78–91; E. C. Nevis, A. J. DiBella, and J. A. Gould, "Understanding Organizations as Learning Systems," *Sloan*

Management Review 36, no. 2 (1995): 73–85; F. A. Schein, "How Can Organizations Learn Faster? The Challenge of Entering the Green Room," *Sloan Management Review* 34, no. 2 (1993): 85–92; P. M. Senge, "The Leader's New Work: Building Learning Organizations," *Sloan Management Review* 32, no. 1 (1990): 7–23; P. M. Senge, *The Fifth Discipline* (New York: Doubleday, 1990); S. F. Slater, "Learning to Change," *Business Horizons* 38, no. 6 (1995): 13–20.

68. A. D. Ellinger, A. E. Ellinger, Y. Bayin, and S. W. Howton, "The Relationship Between the Learning Organization Concept and Firms' Financial Performance: An Empirical Assessment," *Human Resource Development Quarterly* 13, no. 1 (2002): 5–21.

69. Garvin, "Building a Learning Organization," 80.

70. Nevis *et al.,* "Understanding Organizations as Learning Systems."

71. G. Francis and J. Holloway, "What Have We Learned? Themes from the Literature on Best-practice Benchmarking," *International Journal of Management Reviews* 9, no. 3 (2007): 171–189; J. Levinson, "Benchmarking Compliance Performance," *Environmental Quality Management* 6, no. 4 (1997): 49–60.

Appendix

The History of Managerial Thought and Practice

Taken from J. Stewart Black and Lyman W. Porter, *Management: Meeting New Challenges*
(Upper Saddle River: Prentice Hall, 1999).

General Motors: How Pioneering Managers Struggled to Organize a New Industry

When the American auto industry came into being just after the beginning of the twentieth century, new car manufacturers soon faced emerging problems, among them how to organize the work and lines of communication. For each of these companies to survive the tumultuous changes of the new century, including rapid growth, changes in technology, and market shifts, executives had to find a rational way to manage the workforce as well as the structure of the organization. One such top manager was Alfred P. Sloan, Jr., who served as CEO of General Motors from 1923 to 1946.

General Motors was founded in 1908. It is important to keep in mind that management theories, as they related to the new industrial era, were in their infancy then. By the early 1920s, when Sloan took over at General Motors, many manufacturers had adopted an approach called "scientific management" (discussed later in this appendix), which was designed to organize factory floor tasks. But usable and systematic approaches to management that dealt with the total organization had yet to evolve to any extent. Thus, Sloan and his colleagues struggled to find a solution.

Sloan recalled that, at General Motors, "It was . . . management by crony, with the divisions operating on a horse-trading basis." In the first few years immediately following the end of World War I, divisions were competing against each other for available funds, which were often allocated based on top managers' preferences rather than unbiased evaluation. "The important thing was that no one knew how much was being contributed—plus or minus—by each division to the common good of the corporation. And since, therefore, no one knew, or could prove, where the efficiencies and inefficiencies lay, there was no objective basis for the allocation of new investment," observed Sloan.

Sloan recognized that the organization had to change. "I became convinced that the corporation could not continue to grow and survive unless it was better organized, and it was apparent that no one was giving that subject the attention it needed." With Sloan's support, late in 1920, General Motors' new president Pierre du Pont and its new executive committee began to implement "a highly rational and objective mode of operation." Using the findings from an "organizational study" conducted by Sloan, they developed a new policy, which Sloan ultimately called a "trend toward a happy medium to industrial organization." General Motors' new policy was designed so that the organization could evolve in a strong yet flexible manner. The policy included decisions about the amount of responsibility that individual divisions would retain—and "thus initiated for the modern General Motors," Sloan wrote in 1964, "the trend toward a happy medium in industrial organization between the extremes of pure centralization and pure decentralization." Finding that "happy medium" is still a managerial problem that faces many organizations, including General Motors, even today, some 90 years later!

Source: Alfred P. Sloan, Jr., *My Years with General Motors* (New York: Doubleday & Company, Inc., 1964), 27, 42, 48, 52, 65; General Motors Web site, "General Motors History," http://www.gm.com, accessed November 3, 1998.

As this opening story about the trials and tribulations of General Motors at the beginning of the 1920s demonstrates, industrial and other leaders throughout the twentieth century struggled with how to approach the challenge of managing their organizations. In this task, they were assisted by various writers and scholars who contributed ideas and theories about this complex topic. Some of those more important thinkers and their ideas are covered in this appendix.

It is important to keep in mind a basic proposition: To understand the present, you must know something about the past. A review of the history of management thought, especially during the twentieth century, can help us to gain a better understanding of different approaches to management—how those approaches have changed over the years and why they are the way they are now. Although, as we will see, there have been ideas about management since antiquity, so-called "modern" management is only roughly 100 years old.

We begin with a brief look at the earlier origins of organized and systematic thinking about management, especially those that arose from the Industrial Revolution in England and later in the United States. Then we trace the development of the scientific management approach, classical management theory, and neoclassical theory. Later in the appendix, three more contemporary approaches are discussed: behavioral, decision-making, and integrative approaches. To give you some perspective, Exhibit A.1 provides a timeline of the developments in management thought that places them in the historical context of other events that were occurring at the same approximate period of time. The exhibit emphasizes the point that conditions and

EXHIBIT A.1 History of Events and Managerial Thought and Practice Through the End of the Twentieth Century

Date	General Events	Industrial Events	Management Thought/Practice
700–0 B.C.	First written laws of Athens Mayan civilization Greek civilization Rise of Rome	Canal between Nile and Red Sea Sundials, water clocks Mediterranean trade Great Wall of China (215 B.C.)	Sun Tzu, *The Art of War* (4th century B.C.)
A.D. 1–1450	London founded (A.D. 43) Fall of the Roman Empire (455—Vandals sack Rome) Dark Ages in Europe Mohammed (570–632) Oxford University founded(1167) Black Death decimates European population (1347–1349)	Applicants for public office in China required to take examinations (606) Postal and news services in the Caliph's empire (945) Trade between Asia and Western Europe via Venice (983) Coal mining begins in Newcastle, England (1233) Guild system Standardization of measurements in England Bankruptcy of Florentine banking houses (1345)	
1450–1700	Renaissance in Europe Spanish Inquisition (1478–1834) Columbus lands in the Americas (1492) Age of Exploration Slave trade begins in Europe and Americas Plague in Europe (1563) New York City founded (1626) Harvard College founded (1636) Great Fire of London (1666) Newton's theories (1687)	Printing press (1455) Regular postal service in Europe (Vienna to Brussels to Madrid) (1500) Beginning of textile industry in England (1641) Hudson Bay Company founded (1670) Mitsui family trading and banking house in Japan founded (1673)	Machiavelli, *The Prince* (1513)
1700–1800	Yale University founded (1701) American Revolution (1776) French Revolution (1789)	Bernoulli's work on hydrodynamics (1738) Benjamin Franklin invents the lightning conductor (1752) First iron mill in England (1754) Industrial Revolution begins London Stock Exchange founded (1773) Steam engine (1775) New York Stock Exchange founded (1790) Whitney invents the cotton gin (1793) First telegraph, Paris-Lille (1794)	Smith, *An Inquiry into the Nature and Causes of the Wealth of Nations* (1776) Malthus, *Essay on the Principle of Evolution*(1798)

EXHIBIT A.1 (Continued)

Date	General Events	Industrial Events	Management Thought/Practice
1800–1900	Century of Steam Luddite riots in England (1811) Trade union movement Darwin, *On the Origin of the Species by Natural Selection* (1859) American Civil War (1861–1865) Transcontinental railroad (1869) First U.S. business school: Wharton at the University of Pennsylvania (1881) Nobel Prizes established (1896)	First battery (1800) Robert Owen institutes social reforms at the Lanarck Mills (1800) Steam locomotive (1814) First typewriter patented (1830) Faraday works with electromagnetism (1831) British Factory Act provides system for factory inspection (1833) Morse demonstrates electric telegraph (1837) Standard Oil Company founded by John D. Rockefeller (1870) Telephone invented (1876) Phonograph invented (1877) Introduction of electric lights (1880) AT&T formed (1885) Eastman produces box camera (1888)	Babbage, *On the Economy of Machinery and Manufacturers* (1832) Cournot, *Researches into the Mathematical Principles of the Theory of Wealth* (1838) Engels, *The Condition of the Working Class in England* (1845) Marx and Engels, *The Communist Manifesto* (1848) Towne, *Engineer as Economist* (1886)
1900–1920	Century of electricity First MBA program established at the Tuck School, Dartmouth College (1900) Wright brothers' flight (1903) Einstein's special theory of relativity (1905) World War I (1914–1918) Russian revolution (1917)	U.S. Steel organized (1901) Ford Motor Company founded (1903) General Motors formed (1908) Weekends become popular (1910) Woolworth Co. founded (1912) Ford introduces assembly line (1913) Airmail service established from New York to Washington, D.C. (1918)	Taylor, *The Principles of Scientific Management* (1911) Fayol, *Administration Industrielle et Générale* (1916) The Gilbreths, *Applied Motion Study* (1917)
1920s	Lindbergh flies across Atlantic (1927) Stock market crash (1929)	Sloan reorganizes General Motors into multidivisional structure Beginning of chain stores	Mary Parker Follett, *Creative Experience* (1924) Hawthorne studies (1924–1932)
1930s	Great Depression Social Security Act (1935)	First supermarkets Sit-down strikes Industrial unionism as a challenge to managerial control	Mooney and Reiley, *Onward Industry* (1931) Mayo, *The Human Problems of Industrial Civilization* (1933) Barnard, *The Functions of the Executive* (1938) Roethlisberger and Dickson, *Management & the Worker* (1939)

(continued)

EXHIBIT A.1 (Continued)

Date	General Events	Industrial Events	Management Thought/Practice
1940s	World War II (1939–1945) Atomic age begins (1945) First session of the United Nations (1946) Partition of Palestine, creation of state of Israel (1947)	Commercialization of television ENIAC—Birth of general purpose computing (1946) Xerography process invented (1946) First supersonic flight (1947) Transistor invented at Bell Labs (1947) Creation of the World Bank and IMF	Weber, *Theory of Social and Economic Organization* (trans. 1947) Simon, *Administrative Behavior: A Study of Decision-Making Processes in Administrative Organization* (1947) Lewin, *Resolving Social Conflicts* (1948)
1950s	Korean War Colonial independence movements Suburbanization U.S. interstate highway system USSR launches *Sputnik* (1957) European Common Market (1958)	Color television introduced in United States (1951) Electric power produced from atomic energy (1951) Transatlantic cable telephone service (1956) AFL merges with CIO (1955)	Maslow, *Motivation and Personality* (1954) Drucker, *The Practice of Management* (1954) Argyris, *Personality and Organization* (1957) March and Simon, *Organizations* (1958) Herzberg *et al.*, *The Motivation to Work* (1959)
1960s	Civil rights movement Women's movement Vietnam War Campus protests Assassinations of John Kennedy, Robert Kennedy, Martin Luther King, Jr. Berlin Wall constructed (1961) Cuban missile crisis (1962) Rachel Carson, *Silent Spring* (1962) Nobel prize for discovery of structure of DNA to Watson, Crick, and Wilkins (1962) Six Day War in Middle East (1967) First moon landing (July 20, 1969)	Conglomerates emerge as organizational form "Military-Industrial Complex" Jet travel Franchising Environmental Protection Agency Equal opportunity legislation	McGregor, *The Human Side of Enterprise* (1960) Likert, *New Patterns of Management* (1961) Chandler, *Strategy and Structure* (1962) Cyert and March, *A Behavioral Theory of the Firm* (1963) Sun Tzu, *The Art of War* (trans. 1963) Lawrence and Lorsch, *Organizations and the Environment* (1967)
1970s	U.S. withdraws from Vietnam Western trade opened with China Oil embargo Airline deregulation	Dow Jones Index at 631 (1970) Birth of Apple Computer Handheld calculators Fiber optics	Major growth in number of MBA graduates Quality circles Mintzberg, *The Nature of Managerial Work* (1973)
1980s	Deregulation Berlin Wall falls (1989)	Breakup of AT&T Major growth in personal computing Wal-Mart	M. Porter, *Competitive Strategy* (1980) Ouchi, *Theory Z: How American Business Can Meet the Japanese Challenge* (1981)

EXHIBIT A.1 (Continued)

Date	General Events	Industrial Events	Management Thought/Practice
			Peters and Waterman, *In Search of Excellence* (1982)
			M. Porter, *Competitive Advantage* (1985)
			Just-in-time inventory systems
1990s	Soviet Union dissolves	Internet	Corporate downsizing
	NAFTA	Electronic commerce	Rightsizing
	European Union near reality	Microsoft Corporation dominance in software	Empowerment
			Reengineering
			Corporate governance issues
			Total quality management (TQM)
			Outsourcing
			Learning organizations
			Increasing emphasis on teams

Source: J. Stewart Black and Lyman W. Porter, *Management: Meeting New Challenges,* 1st edition, copyright 2000. Reprinted and electronically reproduced with permission of Pearson Education, Inc., Upper Saddle River, NJ.

events in society and industry existing in a given time period strongly influence the type of management theories and approaches being proposed.

The appendix concludes with a look at the status of management thought as the twenty-first century unfolds. As you read the appendix, keep in mind two key questions to enhance your understanding: (1) What preceded the development of a particular way of thinking about management? (2) What was the world—in particular, the world of work—like at the time the theory or approach emerged?

The Origins of Managerial Thought

The topic of how to manage organizations did not receive systematic and wide-scale attention until virtually the start of the twentieth century. However, writers have been commenting on, and even analyzing, managerial issues throughout the past 3,000 years. As we will see in the next few pages, a scattering of writers and recorded examples from a small number of organizations in different places in the civilized world did leave their mark on management thought and practice before the beginning of the twentieth century.

Pre-Industrial Revolution Influences

As the feature "Even Ancient Civilizations Faced Managerial Challenges" shows, as far back as roughly 1000 B.C., perceptive officials in China were writing about how to manage and control organized human activity. Five hundred or so years later, in approximately the fourth century B.C., an illustrious Chinese military leader of the time, Sun Tzu, wrote about his views of principles of leadership (for example, the need for the leader to promote unity within an organization), ideas that many consider are still relevant to today's organizations.[1]

Other civilizations, such as those of ancient Egypt and, later, Rome, were able to organize large numbers of people to carry out coordinated activities that required a form of what today we would call "management." The Egyptians built pyramids as far back as 2700 B.C., and the Romans in the early centuries A.D., and even before, were able to develop highly organized and well-led armies that exercised control over wide areas of territory. Thus, although relatively little was written systematically at the time about how these feats of organization and leadership were carried out, the results demonstrated that management was being successfully practiced in terms of achieving goals and objectives.

In the late Middle Ages (fifteenth and sixteenth centuries), city-states in Europe such as Venice and Florence were managing certain activities with procedures that today we would consider "modern." For example, Venice had a large shipyard at that time that, in effect, adopted such managerial control procedures as the standardization of parts, inventory control, and analysis of costs of materials.[2] Also in this era, Machiavelli (in 1513) published his famous treatise—*The Prince*—on opportunistic and, some would say, crafty techniques for leaders of state to rule their subjects.

Although these and other developments relevant to management thought and practice took place before the eighteenth century, it was not until the middle of that century that the issue of how to manage organizations started to become a more prominent concern. Until that time, most organizations (with a few exceptions such as those noted, the Catholic Church, and military organizations), were still relatively small and simple in structure. For this reason, it had been unnecessary to give serious thought to the way jobs were carried out, work divided among people, and their efforts coordinated. All this was about to change around 1750 when the Industrial Revolution began in England. (This period of societal transformation was not called by that name at the time but was given that label by historians many decades later.) It would take some years, however, before that "revolution" would spread to other places, including the Western Hemisphere and Asia.

The Industrial Revolution in England

The fundamental changes that took place in human work performance in the latter half of the 1700s received that impetus from one key source: advances in technology, especially those related to

Even Ancient Civilizations Faced Managerial Challenges

Although this appendix primarily focuses on the history of management thought and practice dating from the eighteenth century, we can turn even further back in time to gain an understanding of how organizations function. Four thousand years ago, Chinese rulers faced the same challenge that today's managers face: how to organize people (including different levels of officials) in order to complete tasks and achieve goals. Until 250 B.C., China was made up of many states of differing sizes, populations, and natural resources. In fact, China resembled a modern, large, multidivisional corporation. Then, between 250 B.C. and 206 B.C., China became a centralized empire with tight control from the top, a structure that is not totally unfamiliar in some of today's large companies.

What methods did Chinese rulers develop over centuries to meet the challenge of governing such a large country, and how do they relate to today's methods? *The Officials of Chou*, developed either by King Ching of Chou or the Duke of Chou sometime around 1100 B.C., outlines in great detail many of the features that management experts now think of as tenets of a true bureaucracy, including clear, specific job descriptions for officials at every level; explicitly stated rights, powers, and obligations of senior officials; division of labor based on specialization (and, ultimately, technical competence in those areas); clear hierarchy of authority; clearly defined work procedures; and promotion or advancement based on merit (technical competence). King Ching also outlined several important "rules of good management," including personal qualities such as carefulness and economy, the quest for self-improvement, the necessity of making bold decisions as well as conforming to rules, and the importance of promoting subordinates.

All of these characteristics probably sound quite familiar, as if they might be found in an employee's or manager's handbook for a large, contemporary corporation.

Leadership style also played an important part in the governing of ancient China. In addition to the rules of good management, high-level officials were encouraged to be benevolent in their methods of governing because this behavior would, in the end, engender support from the people. E Yin, who was prime minister around 1750 B.C., wrote, "Do not slight the concerns of the people: Think of their difficulties.... Be careful to think about the end at the beginning. When you hear words against which your mind sets itself, you must inquire whether these words are not right. When you hear words that agree with your own thinking, you must ask whether these words are not wrong." Being able to communicate effectively with subordinates and citizens and win their support was crucial to the survival of a leader's power—and perhaps his life. China's social system was clan based, and many of the clans had their own armies. Apparently, a number of rulers were overthrown simply because their behavior and style of governing were unacceptable to the clans.

With their global reach and capacity for instantaneous communication, today's corporations may not appear to resemble ancient China's agrarian civilization. But it is clear that even four thousand years ago, rulers searched for efficient, effective ways to manage people. In some respects, they came up with answers that sound very familiar today.

Source: V. P. Rindova and W. H. Starbuck, "Ancient Chinese Theories of Civilization," *Journal of Management Inquiry* 6, no. 2 (June 1997), 144–159; copyright 1997 Sage Publications, Inc.

mechanized power. Up to that time, work was accomplished almost solely through human or animal effort, sometimes supplemented by wind or water power. Consequently, work was organized around the family and was located typically within each family's dwelling. The nature of this system—subsequently labeled the "domestic system" by historians—made it difficult to perform more complex work, to produce more complex products, and especially to turn out goods in high volumes.[3]

The beginning of the end of the domestic production system was signaled by the introduction of power-driven machinery, especially the steam engine. Although the now-famous inventor James Watt produced the first functional steam engine in 1765, it was another 20 years before it was put into general use.[4] From then on the steam engine, and what it could do, rapidly altered the ways many types of goods were produced. Its development was perhaps the single most important step in the rise of the factory system. The steam engine made it possible to increase vastly the volume of production; however, increased production also required more materials and hence more capital. To put those resources to more efficient use, in turn, required more people working together in one location. This meant, in effect, bringing people to the work rather than bringing work to the people. Hence, the factory seemed to answer the emerging question of how to take the greatest advantage of the potential of steam power for increased productivity.

Once factories were established at the end of the 1700s in England, it became clear that although they solved one problem, they created another: how best to coordinate workers' efforts for maximum efficiency. One approach was to divide up the work so that each person performed a limited number of tasks; in other words, specialized tasks. This idea, which came to be called **division of labor,** was especially championed by one of the founders of modern economics, Adam Smith. In 1776, about the time the Revolutionary War was beginning in America, Smith published his seminal work, *The Wealth of Nations*. That book (consisting of several volumes) contained a very clear description of the advantages of the division of labor:

> *This great increase of the quantity of work which, in consequence of the division of labour, the same number of people are capable of performing, is owing to three different circumstances: first, to the increase of dexterity in every particular workman; secondly, to the saving of the time which is commonly lost in passing from one species of work to another; and lastly, to the invention of a great number of machines which facilitate and abridge labour, and enable one man to do the work of many.[5]*

Interestingly, some people today forget that Smith also had great insight in anticipating the potential *dis*advantages of the implementation of the division of labor idea, especially as it related to the workers who would be involved:

> *The man whose whole life is spent in performing a few simple operations...naturally loses, therefore, the habit of [mental] exertion, and generally becomes stupid and ignorant as it is possible for a human creature to become...His dexterity at his own particular trade seems...to be acquired at the expense of his intellectual, social, and martial virtues.[6]*

In addition to the issues of how to divide up the work efficiently, the other problem relating to factories was how to coordinate the efforts of all of the workers—in other words, how to manage them. There were a number of aspects to the management problem. The owners of early factories and their immediate family were also the managers. As factories grew in size, however, it became impossible for family members to supervise all the workers. This meant that other people had to be hired for supervision. But who was to do this?

At the beginning of the Industrial Revolution, there were no trained supervisors or managers, because this task had never existed before. The early nonfamily supervisors were usually "illiterate workers promoted from the ranks because they evidenced a greater degree of technical skills or had the ability to keep discipline."[7] As management historian Daniel Wren has summed up the situation: "The transformation of England from an agrarian to an industrial society meant that there was no managerial class or, in modern terms, no professional managers. First, there was no common body of knowledge about how to manage.... Second, there was no common code of management behavior, no universal set of expectations about how a manager should act."[8]

The need for attention to the process that would come to be known as "management" became more acute as England entered the nineteenth century and the Industrial Revolution became more

division of labor
the division of work so that each person performs a limited number of tasks (specialized tasks); first used early in the Industrial Revolution

widespread and affected more people. Several prominent individuals, typically entrepreneurs or factory owners themselves, in the early 1800s in England and Scotland did consider how best to organize the activities of factories and direct the work of the people employed in them. Some of these earliest management thinkers, such as Robert Owen and Charles Babbage, even published their ideas in books. Consequently, they can be thought of as the first "management writers" of modern times, but their impact was relatively limited. Book reading in that era was not widespread, and the typical factory manager was busy coping with his own day-to-day problems, not worrying about other people's thoughts on how to run factories more efficiently. Also, much of this early writing focused on techniques applicable to specific firms rather than on general principles or theories about management. Formal writing about principles of management was still more than half a century away.[9]

The Industrial Revolution in America

While the Industrial Revolution started in England, it was in the New World in America that it flourished. One contributing factor to its success was the abundance of raw materials and natural resources, such as water, timber, and minerals. Another factor was the general absence of old traditions to slow the adoption of new methods. Also, American manufacturers gained an advantage from the early trial and error of their English counterparts, some of whom migrated to the United States and brought their most successful methods with them.

Three types of industrial enterprises in the first half of the nineteenth century accounted for most of the improvements in managing enterprises in the United States: textile manufacturing, arms manufacturing, and railroads.[10] As one historian has noted, "The American Industrial Revolution began in textiles."[11] Textile manufacturing was the principal industrial activity that benefited most from a large number of people working together in one location. Manufacturers of arms and weapons, on the other hand, were the key developers of interchangeable parts. In doing so, they advanced the practice of using division of labor and high degrees of employee specialization and significantly increased the ability of a manufacturer to turn out products requiring precision work.

In the railroads, however, the first systematic thinking emerged about how to *manage* a company more effectively. The critical challenge to railroads, from a management standpoint, was quite different from that faced by manufacturers. Railroads had to organize, coordinate, and supervise multiple operations in widely dispersed geographical locations. Although armies and the Catholic Church had been coping with such problems for many years, those organizations had unique sources of discipline and control unavailable to private-sector industrial organizations. In the decades just before and after the Civil War, several far-sighted individuals connected with railroads began to propose specific methods to deal with organizational problems. One such person was David McCallum, general superintendent of the Erie Railroad in the 1850s. McCallum instituted a number of procedures and policies that we now take for granted, but for the time they were quite innovative. He developed organizational charts, regular reports from lower and middle managers, formal job descriptions, and promotions based on merit.[12] The issue of how best to run railroads efficiently and safely set the stage for more formal, systematic approaches to managerial activities. We turn next to a review of the insights and ideas of those who contributed such systematic approaches, the pioneers of modern management theory.

Pioneers: The Scientific Management Approach

The rapid growth in the number and size of factories following the end of the American Civil War in 1865 resulted in increased attention to the issue of how to improve industrial efficiency. By the 1880s, professional engineers were beginning to address this problem directly. A paper delivered in 1886 in Chicago at a meeting of the American Society of Mechanical Engineers is regarded as the beginning of "modern" management in the United States.[13] This paper, titled "The Engineer as Economist," was presented by engineer Henry R. Towne, who was the co-founder of the Yale Lock Company. The significance of Towne's paper is that it represented one of the first formal calls for serious attention to the business aspects of engineering activities. Specifically, Towne urged engineers to consider that "the matter of shop management is of equal importance with that of engineering as affecting the successful conduct of most, if not all, of our great industrial establishments, and...the *management of works* [Towne's italics] has become a matter of such great and far-reaching importance as perhaps to justify its classification...as one of the modern arts."[14]

Frederick W. Taylor (1856–1915)

Towne's call was not immediately heeded by most of his engineering colleagues. However, at roughly the same time period (that is, the 1880s), an engineer working at the Midvale Steel Company in Philadelphia was thinking along somewhat the same lines. His name was Frederick Winslow Taylor, and he was to become one of the most famous people in the Western world in the early years of the twentieth century.

To put Taylor's ideas into perspective, it is necessary to take a brief look at what the United States was like around the turn of the century. At that time, the typical education level of an industrial worker was less than the sixth grade, and there were only about 15,000 college graduates per year in a population of over 58 million. (Compare education levels over 100 years later in the early years of the new century, when the respective numbers are 1.3 million degrees conferred and a population of about 290 million. The ratio of college graduates per year to the total population has thus changed from .03 percent to .4 percent.) It is crucial to keep such facts in mind when considering what Taylor proposed and why he advocated the ideas and procedures he did.

Taylor began his life's work as a common laborer and as an apprentice tool and die maker. Thus, hard-earned, on-the-job experience in blue-collar jobs provided his initial ideas and motivation about how to improve the efficiency of industrial plants. Taylor developed a strong belief that only through rigorous scientific experimentation could better methods be developed. He was particularly keen on time study and analysis of workers' individual tasks—a truly innovative concept for its day. As noted management author Peter Drucker has written, "Taylor was the first man in history who actually studied work seriously."[15] In some respects, the emphasis on gathering factual data about tasks and jobs might be regarded as Taylor's greatest contribution to the advancement of the practice of management.

TAYLOR'S PRINCIPLES OF SCIENTIFIC MANAGEMENT Even though most of Taylor's fact-finding studies concentrated on the hourly employee and the first level of supervision, his total approach as it evolved and expanded over the years came to be called **scientific management.**

> **scientific management**
> approach developed by Frederick Winslow Taylor focusing on basic principles for improving performance, such as studying jobs by using objective measurements in order to determine the one best way, selecting the best persons for the job, training them in the most efficient methods, and providing sufficient monetary incentive to those performing the work

Frederick Winslow Taylor, 1856–1915

Frederick Winslow Taylor was born in 1856 in Germantown, Pennsylvania. His father was a prosperous lawyer, and Taylor grew up in an affluent family. Taylor's family was of Puritan descent, arriving in the United States in 1629 at Plymouth, Massachusetts. This ancestry instilled in Taylor many Puritan values, including the need to search for the truth, to avoid waste of any type, and to judge by observation of the facts. These values in part drove Taylor's search for the "one best way" even in his youth. For example, while just a boy, Taylor searched for the one best way to play croquet and the best way to make a cross-country walk covering the greatest distance with the least fatigue.

Although he enrolled in Harvard Law School to follow his father's footsteps, he had to withdraw because of poor health and poor eyesight. After leaving Harvard, Taylor started as an apprentice at Enterprise Hydraulic Works of Philadelphia and finished his apprenticeship in 1878 at the age of 22.

During this time he developed an appreciation for workers' points of view and saw problems with worker "soldiering" (that is, loafing), poor quality of management, and poor relations between workers and management.

In 1878, Taylor moved to Midvale Steel (Pennsylvania) and worked as a common laborer. Within six years he moved from laborer to clerk, to machinist, to gang boss of machinists, to foreman of the machine shop, to master mechanic, to chief engineer. While working full-time at Midvale, Taylor also enrolled in a home study course from Stevens Institute of Technology in New Jersey, attending classes only to take examinations. Two and a half years after enrolling, Taylor graduated in 1883 with a degree in mechanical engineering.

Source: F. B. Copley, *Frederick W. Taylor: Father of Scientific Management*, 2 vols. (New York: Harper & Row, 1923).

EXHIBIT A.2 **Basic Elements of Scientific Management**

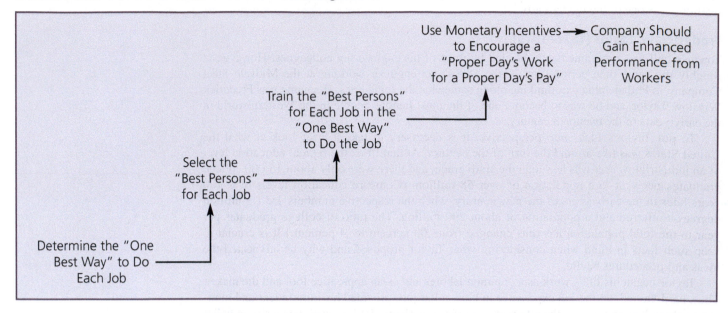

The essence of Taylor's scientific management approach focused on a few key principles that gradually evolved over years of extensive study of task and supervisory practices and how they could be combined for improved performance. The basic elements of scientific management (shown in Exhibit A.2) were the following:

- *Determine the one best way to do each job through precise, objective measurement:* Taylor's entire approach was fundamentally based on meticulously studying and measuring the efforts involved in performing each task and movement that constituted a job, and then determining from the data the single best way to carry out the total set of procedures.

- *Select the "best persons" for the job:* For many of the blue-collar jobs Taylor investigated, such as loading pig iron, the best person meant the strongest person with the strongest desire to do a good job. For other jobs not involving sheer strength, this meant the person with the most aptitude for a particular set of tasks.

- *Train the "best person" in the most efficient methods of performing the task(s)—the one best way:* Taylor stressed that it was management's—not the worker's—responsibility to study the task and determine scientifically the optimal way to perform it. This might mean retraining workers who had already been performing the task.

- *Provide sufficient monetary incentive to the workers to perform the task correctly and meet a defined hourly or daily target rate of output (a "proper day's work"):* Taylor believed that it was only fair for workers to share directly in the rewards of higher levels of output that would result when correct methods were used and when the prescribed rate of performance was achieved. These rewards were to be in the form of sharply higher take-home wages for individuals who met or exceeded the standards, compared with the wages of workers who produced at slower rates and did not meet assigned targets.

TAYLOR'S IMPACT By the time Taylor's major work, *The Principles of Scientific Management*, was published in 1911, he already had attained considerable notoriety, both within the business world as well as in the wider society. Companies were beginning to explore ways to implement versions of Taylor's approach in order to increase the performance level of their operations. At the same time, however, some of the labor unions of the day were becoming more concerned and vocal about the possible exploitation of workers if Taylor's methods were used widely. Even the U.S. Congress took note of Taylor, when hearings were held in 1911 and 1912 by the House Labor Committee. The committee examined Taylor's views on how scientific management was affecting the ordinary worker, among other matters.

EXHIBIT A.3 Contributions and Criticisms of Scientific Management

CONTRIBUTIONS	• Emphasized the Gathering of Factual Data Concerning Jobs and Tasks • Persuaded Managers to Abandon Haphazard Approaches to Planning and Organizing Work • Stressed the Role of Management in Organizing Work, Training Workers, and Instituting Incentives	
	FROM ORGANIZED LABOR	**FROM BEHAVIORAL SCIENTISTS**
CRITICISMS	• Too Much Pressure to Perform Placed on the Workers • Unfair Division of Rewards Between Management and Labor	• Presents an Oversimplified Approach to Worker Motivation • Pays Insufficient Attention to Social Factors in the Workplace that Affect Worker Behavior • Too Authoritarian in Approach • Demands Excessive Specialization of Jobs and Tasks

The major criticism of Taylor and his overall approach (see Exhibit A.3) was that his methods not only placed undue pressure on workers but also disproportionately rewarded management compared with employees. Taylor himself maintained that companies and their workers should have a joint and mutual interest in improving output through scientific management principles and that increased levels of efficiency and production would benefit both parties.[16] He also argued that he was not anti-union, but that unions would become unnecessary if management fairly shared productivity gains with workers. What constitutes an equitable sharing of gains (including protection against layoffs caused by increased rates of production) has never been resolved, and, thus, organized labor has always remained extremely wary of many features of scientific management.

In later years, some behavioral scientists criticized Taylor and the scientific management approach on several grounds (as shown in Exhibit A.3), including the following: (1) scientific management was an oversimplified approach to motivation that emphasized the importance of wage incentives; (2) it paid insufficient attention to other, especially social, factors that affect employee behavior in work settings; (3) it was an authoritarian, management-dominated approach; (4) it placed too much emphasis on specialization of tasks and jobs; and (5) Taylor failed to give credit to those who helped develop the ideas and procedures commonly identified with "scientific management."[17] Some of these criticisms have been challenged by other management scholars, and, thus, the validity of the criticisms is still disputed.

Nevertheless, several facts ought to be kept in mind about Taylor and the impact of his contributions:

1. *The influence of his times:* Just as we all are products of our own times, so was Taylor. He was strongly influenced by many factors at the turn of the century (for example, the average education level of the workforce) that have changed considerably in the intervening 90-plus years. Were today's conditions present then, he undoubtedly would have modified some of his views.

2. *Order out of chaos:* Taylor spent a great amount of effort, as we have noted earlier, on systematically studying jobs and work. As a result of his research and demonstrations, he helped persuade managers to abandon a haphazard approach to planning and organizing work and instead to base it on facts, especially at the hourly worker's level and the first level of supervision.

3. *Managerial responsibilities:* Taylor continually stressed that it was management's responsibility to organize the work, train the workers, and institute an effective incentive system. In his own words, he wanted to bring about "a complete mental revolution," not only on the part of the workers but also, and particularly, "on the part of those on the management's side—the foreman, the superintendent, the owner of the business, the board of directors— a complete mental revolution as to their duties toward their fellow workers in the management, toward their workmen, and toward all of their daily problems."[18] This, perhaps, was Taylor's most enduring legacy to the development of management thought.

Other Leaders of Scientific Management

Although Frederick Taylor was the acknowledged founder and central figure in the scientific management movement, several others played important roles in advancing and extending the general approach to fact-based and orderly processes for managing industrial organizations. Three of those, whom we briefly mention here, were Henry L. Gantt and Frank and Lillian Gilbreth.

H. L. GANTT (1861–1919) Gantt was a young engineering colleague of Taylor's at the Midvale Steel Company at the end of the 1880s, but by the early 1900s he was well launched in his own career as one of the first bona fide management consultants. He was heavily influenced in his early career by Taylor's views, but he subsequently became known chiefly for developing graphic methods to aid in organizing and coordinating multiple tasks in complex production jobs. While serving as a volunteer consultant to the U.S. government during World War I, he perfected a type of bar chart that showed the order in which tasks had to be initiated and the time allotted for each. Versions of this graphic display, now called Gantt charts, have been widely used and were the direct forerunner of modern-day Program Evaluation and Review Techniques (PERT) methods. The importance of Gantt's graphic approach was that it reinforced the need for systematic planning in order to sequence tasks efficiently and for more direct control over the time allotted to them, which, in turn, directly lowered costs and increased performance.

FRANK AND LILLIAN GILBRETH (1868–1924 AND 1878–1972) This husband-and-wife team were strong advocates of Taylor's general approach, but they were able to add their own unique contributions. Frank Gilbreth was a contractor who became intensely interested in studying how various construction tasks could be performed more efficiently and with reduced fatigue for the worker. Using the recently invented motion picture camera, he developed techniques to analyze each motion that went into performing a task, such as bricklaying. Eventually, Gilbreth was able to categorize any motion into one of 17 basic types (which he called "Therbligs," a reversal—with *t* and *h* transposed—of the spelling of *Gilbreth*). In theory, this categorization of motions made it possible to develop the most effective combination for performing any physical task. Lillian Gilbreth was one of the first doctoral-level industrial psychologists in the United States. In her early career, she worked closely with her husband on his analytical studies of motions. She concentrated on the "mental" tasks facing management and on how psychological principles could further the application of a scientific management approach that would benefit both worker and manager. Lillian Gilbreth (who died in 1972 at the age of 93) achieved many "firsts": she was the first woman member of both the Society of Industrial Engineers and the Society of Mechanical Engineers, and in later years her peers called her "the first lady of management."[19] Not the least of the two Gilbreths' many joint accomplishments was their success in raising 12 children, the story of which was immortalized in a book, *Cheaper by the Dozen*, and a movie (1950) of the same name. The Gilbreths, thus, applied scientific management principles in the home as well as in their extensive investigations of industrial jobs. It was in the latter area, however, where their individual and combined efforts had worldwide impact.

Pioneers: Classical Management Theory

While Taylor and various associates were spreading the gospel of scientific management in the United States and Europe in the first two decades of the twentieth century, others also were beginning to think seriously and insightfully about how to manage organizations. Four of those who had the greatest impact on subsequent management thought and practice will be discussed here. Two of them essentially worked and wrote individually, and the other two jointly authored a book. One was French, one was German, and the other two were Americans (see Exhibit A.4). Their ideas, together with some of the emerging concepts identified with the scientific management approach, have come to be called *classical management theory*.

classical management theory

ideas concerning the management of organizations arising from pioneers such as Taylor, Fayol, Weber, and Mooney and Reiley, together with emerging concepts identified with the scientific management approach

Classical management theory focuses on the study of the principles and functions of management and the authority structures of organizations. In some cases, the term *administrative theory* could be used interchangeably with *management theory*. The term *classical management theory* was never attached to this broad set of ideas during the era in which they appeared (from roughly 1900 to the early 1930s). It has only been more recently

EXHIBIT A.4 Contributors to Classical Management Theory

	HENRI FAYOL (FRENCH)	MAX WEBER (GERMAN)	J. D. MOONEY AND A. C. REILEY (AMERICAN)
WROTE	*General and Industrial Management*	*The Theory of Social and Economic Organization*	*Onward Industry!*
STATED/DEFINED	• Five Functions of Management • 14 Principles of Management	• Three Basic Types of Authority Relationships • Bureaucracy	• Four Basic Principles of Management
(COMMENT)	Focused on middle and upper management activities in multi-unit organizations	Writings aimed more for scholars than practicing managers, but ultimately influenced society as a whole	Fayol and Weber had not yet been published in America, so the similarity of Mooney and Reiley's descriptions of management was used to argue the universality of management principles

applied. The ideas and thoughts are considered classical because they had some relatively enduring qualities and served as a springboard for others' thinking and action. As we will see later in this appendix, they even served as a model against which newer and quite different theories and approaches were contrasted.

Henri Fayol (1841–1925)

Henri Fayol, a French mining engineer, rose rapidly in his company to become president at age 37. Under his leadership, his company became a large, integrated mining, iron, and steel organization, taking raw materials and transforming them into finished product. Fayol's relatively early and extended exposure to the top management position of a sizable firm gave him an opportunity to reflect on what was required to manage the total enterprise. Using his experience to good advantage, Fayol put some of his ideas on management into written form, culminating with the publication of his most famous work in 1916, a monograph entitled *Administration Industrielle et Générale* ("General and Industrial Management").

Fayol's publication had lasting impact for two reasons. First, his attempt to define management as consisting of five key elements was a major advance.[20] His approach was analytical and focused attention on management as a legitimate, specialized set of activities, and it identified what those activities were: planning (in French, "prévoyance"), organizing, command, coordination, and control. These "elements," as Fayol termed them, have subsequently been called (in English) **functions of management,** and in slightly modified form, they have prevailed to the present day. The alert reader will recognize that Fayol's list of elements is quite similar to the major sections of this text and nearly all other contemporary management texts. The most common current version of the list collapses the functions to four (allocating coordination activities across the other four functions) and changing the term *command* to *influencing* or *leading.* In short, even with the passage of about 90 years since the publication of *Administration Industrielle et Générale,* few improvements have been made on Fayol's "classic" list of management functions.

The other reason Fayol's work received a great deal of attention in later years was that it also presented a list of 14 management "principles," or, more accurately, guidelines that he found effective and thought could be used to improve the performance of a wide variety of organizations. Some of the more important of these (paraphrased) were division of labor (specialization of work); unity of command (each person in the organization should receive orders from only one other person); unity of direction (all persons in a part of the organization must govern their actions by the same, single plan); and "scalar chain" (there must be a clear line of authority from the bottom to the top of the organization). Exhibit A.5 provides a complete list of Fayol's principles. These principles have been challenged in recent years, but they appeared at a time when business and industrial activity was quite different from that of today and the context (government, society, technology, etc.) in which such activity took place was profoundly different.

functions of management basic elements of management as originally identified by Henri Fayol, consisting of planning, organizing, command, coordination, and control

EXHIBIT A.5 Fayol's 14 Principles of Management

1. Division of Work	Divide work into specialized tasks and functions, each assigned to specific individuals.
2. Authority	Authority must be accompanied by responsibility.
3. Discipline	Sanctions are necessary to minimize or prevent the recurrence of behavior that violates agreed-upon expectations.
4. Unity of Command	"For any action whatsoever, an employee should receive orders from one superior only."
5. Unity of Direction	There should be "one head and one plan for a group of activities having the same objective."
6. Subordination	"The interest of one employee or group of employees should not prevail over that of the [organization]."
7. Remuneration	". . . should be fair and, as far as is possible, afford satisfaction both to personnel and firm (employee and employer)."
8. Centralization	The amount of centralization or decentralization necessary to a firm is a function both of the size of the firm and the ability of the manager(s). Organizational effectiveness is increased by determining the optimal level of centralization.
9. Scalar Chain	"The scalar chain is the chain of supervisors ranging from the ultimate authority to the lowest ranks. The line of authority is the route followed—via every link in the chain—by all communications which start from or go to the ultimate authority."
10. Order	There must be order in both material and personnel. For material: "things [must] be in their place suitably arranged . . . so as to facilitate all activities." For personnel: "Perfect order requires . . . that the place be suitable for the employee and the employee for the place . . . the right man in the right place."
11. Equity	To encourage employee loyalty and performance, employers must treat employees fairly, combining kindness and justice, but not excluding forcefulness or sternness.
12. Stability of Tenure of Personnel	It requires time for an employee to develop the skills necessary to perform his or her work well. Therefore, successful companies are those with low turnover (high stability of tenure) of personnel. "Instability of tenure is at one and the same time cause and effect of bad [management]."
13. Initiative	"At all levels of the organizational ladder zeal and energy on the part of employees are augmented by initiative [the thinking out and implementation of plans]. The initiative of all, added to that of the manager, and supplementing it if need be, represents a great source of strength for businesses."
14. Esprit de Corps	"Union is strength. Harmony, union among the personnel of a concern is great strength in that concern. Effort, then, should be made to establish it."

Source: Adapted from H. Fayol, *General and Industrial Management* (London: Pitman, 1949), chap. 4. (Translation by C. Storrs from 1916 French edition, *Administration Industrielle et Générale.*)

The importance of Fayol's contributions was not fully recognized in the English-speaking world until later translations appeared (e.g., in 1949), but the originality of his ideas and the clarity and systematized way in which they were presented endure. Also, it should be noted that Fayol's focus, in contrast to much of Taylor's work, was directed toward the middle and upper levels of managerial activities of multi-unit enterprises rather than toward shop floor supervision and the management of individual factories. In that sense, Fayol's ideas were consistent with Taylor's, but they covered new ground—ground that would be especially relevant to the types of firms and corporations prominent in the last half of the twentieth century.

Max Weber (1864–1920)

Although Max Weber lived at approximately the same time as Taylor and Fayol, he neither influenced them nor was influenced by them. Weber was a German academic and scholar who never managed an organization, or even part of one, but who was one of history's most perceptive organizational observers. As one of the early forerunners of modern sociology, Weber was an organization theorist and not a management theorist *per se*. He is mentioned here, however, because by the mid-twentieth century he had become extremely influential in how leading thinkers viewed the management process in organizations—industrial or otherwise.

Although originally published in 1922 after his death, Weber's most significant work dealing with organizations, *The Theory of Social and Economic Organization*, was not translated into English until 1947. He was a product of the German culture and society of his era, and this background no doubt had a strong bearing on the kinds of intellectual issues he chose to analyze. With respect to organizations, those issues centered on the concept of authority, especially the questions of "Why do individuals obey commands?" and "Why do people do as they are told?"[21] He theorized that three basic types of authority relationships or structures could be used to classify organizations:

1. *Traditional authority:*   authority exercised on the basis of custom or past practice. According to Weber, its weakness as a source of authority in organizations was that it emphasizes precedent for its own sake rather than making the best possible decisions.
2. *Charismatic authority:*   based on "devotion to the specific and exceptional sanctity, heroism, or exemplary character of an individual person."[22] The weakness of charismatic authority, as stressed by Weber, is that it does not provide a basis for succession of authority relationships when the charismatic leader leaves the scene, and hence this threatens the continuity of the organization.
3. *Rational-legal authority:*   authority exercised to achieve specifically designated goals and based on the legal right of the person in a particular office (*buro* in German) to issue commands. In Weber's analysis, this type of authority is best suited for larger, complex organizations because it emphasizes obedience to orders issued by someone—*whoever that person is*—fulfilling an official position and acting on the basis of powers conferred on that position (and not to a particular person). This basis for authority overcomes, in Weber's view, the disadvantages of the other two forms of authority.

Weber went on to describe the type of organization that would result if the use of rational–legal authority were maximized: namely, a "bureaucracy." In describing bureaucracies, Weber was not necessarily advocating that every organization should become one, only that if this type of authority were put into place throughout an organization, it would have certain features; for example:

- An explicit set of rules to govern official actions
- Clearly defined duties for each office (that is, position)
- Competence and technical qualifications as the basis for selection of officeholders
- Comprehensive training for people occupying particular positions

In assessing the impact of Weber and his writings on the history of management thought, several points should be made. To begin with, it should be reiterated that Weber has affected society's views about the management of organizations by influencing scholars rather than by directly addressing managers. Nevertheless, although Weber wrote independently of others who concentrated specifically on ways to improve the performance of managerial activities, his analysis of the advantages of bureaucratic organization was consistent with the prescriptions for managers provided by Taylor and Fayol. It is also necessary to keep in mind that Weber's concept of a bureaucracy was that of a form of organization based on a specified type of authority and not the caricature of a sluggish, rule-strangled organization that the term has come to mean in recent years. If Weber were alive today, he would probably think of that type of organization as a sort of bureaucracy run amok and not at all what he envisioned.

J. D. Mooney (1884–1957) and A. C. Reiley (1869–1947)

The final set of classical management theorists to be discussed here are two American executives, James D. Mooney and Allan C. Reiley. Both were upper-level managers within the General Motors Corporation, with a particular interest in the historical evolution of organizational principles. In the depths of the Great Depression (in 1931), they published a book that had the bold title of *Onward Industry!* This book, which gained considerable visibility for its authors, attempted to demonstrate how all great organizations of the past and present tended to follow several fundamental principles, principles we now refer to as the center of the classical approach to management:

1. The *coordinative principle:* the need to obtain a high degree of coordination of actions toward a common purpose.
2. The *scalar principle:* the need to designate the precise delegation of authority from the top to the bottom of the organization.
3. The *functional principle*: the need to achieve a tight grouping of specialized functions or duties.
4. The *staff principle:* the need to provide managers in the direct chain of command (the line) with ideas and information from specialized experts (the staff), and the related need to distinguish clearly between the two types of positions.

Although Mooney and Reiley apparently had never read the works of either Henri Fayol or Max Weber (since their works had not yet been translated into English), their managerial and organizational principles were remarkably similar to those that these two theorists had developed in other countries and cultures some two decades earlier. Some management writers later took this to be evidence for the universality of management principles.

The Impact of Classical Management Theory

As we said at the beginning of this section, the term *classical management theory* is a label applied in recent years to the collection of ideas put forth by such people as Fayol, Weber, Mooney and Reiley, and others in the first 35 years of the twentieth century. Those ideas do not constitute "theory" in the strict, scientific sense of that word. Rather, they are a loosely held set of concepts and principles that have provided a coherent and, above all, rational way to think about how organizations should be structured and managed. Because this cluster of ideas—along with those of Taylor and the scientific management approach—amounted to such an advance in thinking, they were indeed influential. They provided guidance for those who wanted to develop and operate effective and efficient organizations. Furthermore—and this should not be overlooked—many of these notions have persisted to this day in one form or another. Anyone who has ever worked in a company, a government office, or in almost any organization cannot help but notice how often and how widespread is the attempted application of many of the so-called principles of classical management theory even 90 years after they were first proposed.

Despite the progress in management thinking that classical management theorists represent, there were (and are) major problems with their basic approach. To obtain a sense of some of those problems, we need only to consider the underlying assumptions, which are listed in Exhibit A.6. First and foremost, as summarized in Exhibit A.7, the underlying assumptions implied an extremely limited view of the role of people in organizations. Second, and also quite important, the classical management approach was essentially a static view of how organizations should be managed and did not deal sufficiently with the effects of changing conditions. Classical theory implicitly assumed that all organizations should be managed in "the one best way." As with its close cousin, scientific management (often classified as a classical theory), it was clearly a product of its times, even though this fact was not apparent to those who proposed its principles nor especially to those who to this day still believe that what worked in 1925 will still work just as well in 2025!

Neoclassical Administrative Theory

By the beginning of the 1920s, the world of work was changing. The size and complexity of organizations were increasing, as shown in the General Motors example presented earlier, and the skills, abilities, and expectations of employees were also becoming more complex. These changes made it obvious that the traditional approach to managing was not adequate nor always appropriate. Revisions in the ways of thinking about how to manage organized work activity began in the 1920s and continued to the 1940s. As might be expected, the new thinking drew from the accepted wisdom of basic management principles, even though it went beyond those principles in interesting new directions. Because these ideas had at least some links to past thinking, this approach is

1. "Efficiency of an undertaking is measured solely in terms of productivity."
2. "Human beings can be assumed to act rationally."
3. "[Employees] are unable to work out the relationships of their positions without detailed guidance from their supervisors."
4. "Unless clear limits to jobs are defined and enforced, [employees] will tend to be confused . . ."
5. "Human beings prefer the security of a definite task and do not value the freedom of determining their own approaches to problems . . ."
6. "It is possible to predict and establish clear-cut patterns of future activities and the relationships among activities."
7. "Management involves primarily the formal and official activities of individuals."
8. "The activities of [employees] should be viewed on an objective and impersonal basis . . ."
9. "Workers are motivated by economic needs . . ."
10. "People do not like to work, and therefore, close-supervision and accountability should be emphasized."
11. "Coordination will not be achieved unless it is planned and directed from above."
12. "Authority has its source at the top of a hierarchy and is delegated downward."
13. "Simple tasks are easier to master and thus lead toward higher productivity by concentrating on a narrow scope of activity."
14. "Managerial functions . . . have universal characteristics and can be performed in a given manner regardless of the environment and qualities of the personnel involved."

Source: J. L. Massie, "Management Theory," in *Handbook of Organizations*, ed. J. G. March (Chicago: Rand McNally, 1965). Reprinted with permission of J. G. March.

now often called neoclassical management theory. **Neoclassical management theory** continued to emphasize the study and analysis of managerial functions and organizational structures but expanded to include situational and social considerations such as communication and cooperation. Two individuals closely associated with this label were Mary Parker Follett and Chester Barnard (Exhibit A.8).

neoclassical management theory

thinking about organized work activity and how to manage that drew from classical theory in its emphasis on study and analysis of the workplace but expanded to include situational and social considerations (i.e., communication and cooperation)

Mary Parker Follett (1868–1933)

Lillian Gilbreth was not the only prominent woman who contributed to management thought in the early part of the twentieth century. Mary Parker Follett was a writer, lecturer, and independent consultant who was interested in political philosophy early in life but later turned her attention to the management of organizations. She was especially influential in the 1920s.

EXHIBIT A.7 Contributions and Criticisms of Classical Management Theory

CONTRIBUTIONS	• Provided a coherent and Rational Way to Think about the Structure and Management of Organizations • Provided Directions for Managers Attempting to Increase Effectiveness and Efficiency in Their Organizations • Many of the Principles Have Persisted in One Form or Another to the Present
CRITICISMS	• Assumed an Extremely Narrow View of the Role of People in Organizations • Assumed There is "One Best Way" to Manage Businesses • Assumed (implicitly) a Static Role for the Business Environment

EXHIBIT A.8 Contributors to Neoclassical Management Theory

	MARY PARKER FOLLETT	CHESTER BARNARD
WROTE	*Creative Experience*	*The Functions of the Executive*
AGREED WITH CLASSICAL THEORISTS ON	• Importance of Detailed Analysis of Work Settings • Coordination of Work Activities	• Importance of Detailed Analysis of Work Settings
EMPHASIZED	• Cooperation Between Managers and Subordinates • Integration of Interests of Organization and Employees • The Use of the Type of Authority Appropriate to the Situation	• A View of Organizations as Cooperative Social Systems • The Need for Managers to Obtain Voluntary Cooperation from Their Workers • The "Zone of Indifference" • The Need for Efficient Organizational Communication
(COMMENT)	Forerunner of many modern ideas of management, particularly the contingency approach	Views on authority were innovative and anticipated later behavioralist thinking

law of the situation

Mary Parker Follett's emphasis on the need to generate a spirit of cooperation between managers and their subordinates with a focus on the authority (based on a person's knowledge and experience) that seems appropriate to the circumstances

In many respects, Follett's thinking was consistent with Taylor's and the scientific management movement in that she placed great importance on detailed study and analysis of the work setting and on the necessity for careful coordination of activities. However, she also emphasized the need to generate a spirit of cooperation between managers and their subordinates and to integrate the interests of the organization and its employees. In this regard, her ideas differed from the typical views of many contemporary advocates of scientific management. Also, in contrast to Weber's analysis, Follett focused not on the formal powers conferred on an office but rather on the dictates of the **law of the situation,** that is, the authority—based on a person's knowledge and experience—that seems appropriate to the circumstances. This type of thinking anticipated by some 40 years a prominent modern approach to management, the contingency approach, which is discussed later in this appendix. In summary, although Mary Parker Follett and her ideas are often classified as being associated with classical management theory, she was someone who was a clear forerunner of much of modern management thought that has dominated the last half of the twentieth century. Thus, we have placed her here in the neoclassical category of management thinkers.

Mary Parker Follett, 1868–1933

Mary Parker Follett was born in Boston and although she was a contemporary of Taylor, Follett was much more a philosopher than manager. She was educated at what is today called Radcliffe College. Her early interest in John Fichte (1762–1814), a German philosopher who espoused a nationalism in which freedom of the individual had to be subordinated to the group, led her to write the book *The New State*. In this book, Follett argued that an individual could find his or her true self only through group orientation.

She began to be more of a business philosopher after publishing her book, *Creative Experience,* in 1924. This book was widely read by businessmen of the day. In 1924 and 1925, Follett gave a series of lectures in New York that were sponsored by the Bureau of Personnel Administration. The lectures were well received and led Follett to focus most of her later writings and lectures on principles of business organization and administration.

Source: H. C. Metcalf and L. Urwick, *Dynamic Administration: The Collected Papers of Mary Parker Follett* (New York: Harper & Row, 1940).

Chester Barnard (1886–1961)

A long-time executive at AT&T and ultimately president of then New Jersey Bell Telephone company, Chester Barnard spent a considerable amount of time and thought in formulating his unique and detailed ideas regarding the nature of organizations and the role of their managers and leaders. This effort resulted in a highly regarded book published in 1938, *The Functions of the Executive*, which has influenced the field of management ever since.

As did most classical management theorists, Barnard provided a systematic but nonempirical (nondata) analysis of the tasks of management. In this sense, the starting point for his analysis could be considered somewhat similar to that of classical theorists. However, Barnard differed sharply from the standard classical approach by viewing organizations as cooperative social systems. As it was for Mary Parker Follett, cooperation was at the center of Barnard's thinking about the nature of organizations. He believed that all organizations, no matter what type, required (1) willingness to cooperate, (2) common purpose, and (3) communication. In particular, he stressed the need for managers in organizations to obtain the voluntary cooperation of those they lead. Additionally, his strong focus on the need for communication as an essential ingredient in any organization was also a ground-breaking notion for its day.

It was in his discussion of the concept of authority, however, where Barnard probably achieved his greatest influence on others. He argued that the source of a manager's authority depends on subordinates' acceptance of the manager's orders. This was a truly radical idea for its time, because until then traditional management theory had always insisted that the source of authority was solely determined by the position of the manager and that the higher the position, the greater the authority possessed by the person occupying it. Barnard elaborated on his perspective by defining what he called the "zone of indifference" (which others later labeled the "zone of acceptance"). This zone consisted of orders that would be accepted by the subordinate without question. Barnard did believe (in line with classical theory) that this zone was wider the higher the position of the order giver, but he also contended that a manager's leadership skills and abilities were critical to broaden the scope of orders that a subordinate would accept without dispute or resistance. His thinking, thus, foreshadowed later behavioral approaches to the process of management.

Behavioral Approaches

Early management theorists, especially Frederick Taylor and the proponents of a scientific management approach, did not entirely ignore the human component of organizations. Rather, they viewed the human dimension of organizations in very specific and limited ways. Scientific management and classical management approaches placed great emphasis on initial selection of workers for jobs and in effect, on individual capabilities, such as differences in physical agility or strength. They also believed that worker motivation stemmed almost solely from the financial incentives offered by hourly and piecework wages linked directly to the amount of output. What was not given much, if any, attention in these approaches were the following:

- Capacities of employees for further development after they are hired for particular jobs
- Other sources of employee motivation in addition to financial rewards
- The impact of relationships among employees and with their supervisors

While it is easy to say with the benefit of hindsight that even the earliest management theorists ought to have paid more attention to these factors, remember that the average person's level of education was much lower then than now and that the social and cultural conditions that existed in those times resulted in different employee and management expectations compared with those of today. Put another way, traditional ways of operating were much different then, and those traditions exerted a powerful influence on management theories of that era.

Neoclassical theorists like Mary Parker Follett and Chester Barnard, with their strong focus on the need for cooperation in organizations, did begin to bring the human element more to the forefront in discussions of how enterprises should be managed. Nevertheless, it took the dramatic findings of a years-long set of research studies, the Hawthorne studies, to focus a spotlight on how the human factor impacted work performance at the shop floor level. These findings led to a whole new approach called the human relations approach.

Chester Barnard, 1886–1961

Chester Barnard was born to a farming family in Malden, Massachusetts. Through his talent and hard work, he earned a scholarship to Harvard University, where he studied economics. As a student, Barnard supplemented his income by tuning pianos and managing a small dance band. He completed his studies in three years but was not granted a degree because even though he had passed a certain course with distinction, he had been too busy to take the laboratory section.

Barnard left Harvard in 1909 and joined the Statistics Department of American Telephone and Telegraph. He worked hard and applied both his formal education from Harvard and knowledge from his own studies. Despite being a Harvard "drop-out," Barnard was a scholar who read Vilfredo Pareto in French and Kurt Lewis and Max Weber in German. In 1927 he was named president of New Jersey Bell.

Barnard also spent considerable time and energy working in voluntary organizations. He helped David Lilienthal establish the policies of the U.S. Atomic Energy Commission. He worked with the United States Service Organization and served as its president for three years. He also served as the president of the Rockefeller Foundation for four years.

After ten years as president of New Jersey Bell, Barnard gave a series of lectures at the Lowell Institute in Boston. An expansion of the lectures was published in Barnard's famous book, *Functions of the Executive*, published by Harvard University Press in 1938.

Source: W. B. Wolf, *How to Understand Management: An Introduction to Chester J. Barnard* (Los Angeles: Lucas Bro. Publishers, 1968).

The Human Relations Approach

human relations approach
approach springing from the findings of the Hawthorne studies that focused on the importance of relationships among people in the workplace.

Hawthorne studies
a series of research studies at the Hawthorne plant of the Western Electric Company that focused a spotlight on the importance of the human factor in productivity

The **human relations approach** to management did not suddenly emerge full-blown. Instead, it evolved as findings from the **Hawthorne studies** began to achieve prominence toward the end of the 1930s, with the publication of Roethlisberger and Dickson's *Management and the Worker* in 1939. The research began as a series of investigations in the mid-1920s at the Hawthorne plant of the Western Electric Company (a manufacturing subsidiary of the American Telephone and Telegraph Company [AT&T] at the time) outside Chicago. They were directed initially by researchers from the Massachusetts Institute of Technology.[23] However, as time went by, the research program became more associated with two well-known Harvard professors, the Australian social scientist Elton Mayo and management professor Fritz Roethlisberger.

Befitting the times, the first studies at the Hawthorne plant were designed to determine the effects of changes in the physical working environment, namely lighting, on productivity. However, when researchers analyzed their early findings, it became apparent that what seemed to be causing the largest effects on worker performance was not the amount of light in the workplace, but rather the relations among the workers and between them and their supervisors. (Analyses of the data carried out some years later suggested that changes in the wage incentive system at the time also may have played a role in determining changes in worker output in some of the test conditions.[24])

These initial results led to other studies during the late 1920s and early 1930s at the Hawthorne plant designed to gather more detailed data on the nature of these relationships among workers and supervisors and on how they affected employee output. The additional studies included observations under researcher-controlled conditions about how a group of workers could act together to exert considerable influence on the performance of individual members of the group. The researchers also carried out extensive interviewing of employees regarding their attitudes toward their work. The overall findings from the series of studies that spanned some eight years were then summarized in the 1939 Roethlisberger and Dickson book. Among other prominent outcomes of the Hawthorne studies, incidentally, was the demonstration of the apparent effect on worker behavior of having that behavior observed and given special attention. That phenomenon became known as the *Hawthorne effect*.

Although the Hawthorne studies have received criticism for inadequacies in research design and in the way in which some of the data were analyzed, the highly publicized findings did strongly impact many managers.[25] In effect, as management historians have put it, "the Hawthorne studies…introduced a new way of thinking about the people factor."[26] It became evident that if those who ran factories or companies were interested in improving productivity, more attention—than had been the case in most organizations up to that time—would have to be paid to the way in which the people relationships were handled, thus, leading to the origin of the term *human relations approach*. Simply instructing employees on how to operate machines or equipment and providing them with a wage incentive for doing so was not sufficient.

Those advocating more attention to human relations concentrated particularly on the role of the first-line supervisor and his (since in those days it usually was a "he") interactions with subordinates. The advice was to treat subordinates not as impersonal cogs in a machine but as individual human beings with feelings and emotions and needs other than just financial. This approach also stressed that it was the task of upper management to provide the necessary support and backing for the first-level supervisors, or foremen, in the time and effort they devoted to improving relations. The logic involved was that if workers felt better about their relationships with their supervisor and their working conditions, they would have a greater desire to produce more—or, at least, have less of a desire to try to restrict output.

The Human Resources Approach

The human relations movement flourished in the 1940s and 1950s, as many organizations attempted to implement a more human and humane approach to their treatment of employees. Again, it must be emphasized that the assumption—sometimes explicit but often implicit—was that improved worker satisfaction would result in better performance. By the 1960s, as a result of continuing research carried out in a variety of work circumstances, the human relations approach was shown to be incomplete at best and highly misleading at worst. In effect, the findings from these studies demonstrated that there was seldom a direct connection between satisfaction and performance and that, furthermore, from a psychological perspective, it should not be presumed that more satisfied workers necessarily will be more productive workers. Such results, coupled with additional analyses, led to new behavioral formulations relevant to the management process. One of these, called the human resources approach, provides a distinct contrast to the human relations approach and puts particular emphasis on starting from a different set of managerial assumptions concerning people. Exhibit A.9 shows the basic differences between these two approaches.

In essence, the core of the **human resources approach** to management thinking—led by such scholars as Douglas McGregor, Rensis Likert, and Chris Argyris—stresses a fundamental belief that most people possess and want to use more talent and capabilities in their work than may be readily apparent from their past or present job assignments. If so, it becomes management's primary role to develop these untapped human resources through increased opportunities for self-direction and self-control. The logic is that if human resources are better used, performance will be enhanced. Increased satisfaction, if it occurs, becomes the by-product rather than

human resources approach approach involving a basic belief that people possess and want to make greater use of their talents and capabilities and that if allowed to do so, performance and satisfaction will increase

EXHIBIT A.9 Differences Between Human Relations and Human Resources Approaches to Management

HUMAN RELATIONS APPROACH PROPOSED:

HUMAN RESOURCES APPROACH PROPOSED:

the cause of this improved performance. Direct evidence for the effectiveness of the human resources approach is not easy to obtain, but this general orientation toward the human component of organization underlies the basic behavioral approach to management in a large number of organizations as the new century begins.

Decision-Making Approaches

The behavioral approaches just described emphasize the motivation of individuals to excel at their jobs. Although it is hard to deny the importance of such perspectives, other processes taking place in organizations also have considerable consequences for their overall effectiveness. One of the most crucial is decision making. Good decisions can mobilize many people, and bad decisions can undercut and even jeopardize the continued existence of the organization. Despite the importance of decision making for the fate of organizations, it was not until after World War II that this process received concerted attention from management theorists. When this did happen, two lines of inquiry developed, one more behavioral and one more mathematical. We will look at both briefly here but only in terms of their historical significance.

Behavioral Decision-Making Approach

The emphasis on decision making as a critical element in the management process is generally credited to Herbert Simon, a Nobel laureate in economics, who originally received his doctoral training in political science. Early in his academic career, Simon turned his attention to the concept of "economic man," the notion that individuals are totally rational and that in their decisions they can evaluate all alternative courses of action and their consequences and then select that one that has the best chance of maximizing goal attainment (for example, profit). Simon was particularly interested in how this concept worked in real organizational settings. His analyses led him to develop an alternative model, "administrative man." In contrast to economic man, administrative man—managers in real-life organizations—does not have information on all possible alternative courses of action and also does not have complete information on the probabilities of various consequences arising from particular actions. Simon did not dispute the idea that managers attempt to make rational decisions, but he proposed that such thinking is constrained by human limitations and results in what he called **bounded rationality.** Because of their "bounded," or constrained, rationality, according to Simon, managers do not search indefinitely for the best alternative (that is, goal maximization) but rather make a decision that "satisfices." **Satisficing** is a decision process that results in an acceptable course of action, although not necessarily the best course. Satisficing is necessary, in actual situations, according to Simon, because managers almost always must operate under conditions of uncertainty rather than certainty.

Although Simon's ideas probably have had more direct effect on academics who study management than on managers themselves, they nevertheless have been extremely influential, as attested to by his receiving a Nobel Prize in economics. Simon's 1940s writing on decision making led to additional important work on this topic in the 1950s and 1960s by himself and James March and Richart Cyert, his colleagues at Carnegie Mellon University. March and Cyert authored an important book in the early 1960s, *A Behavioral Theory of the Firm,* which provided an all-encompassing view of organizations from a decision-making perspective.

Quantitative Decision-Making Approaches

Quantitative, or mathematical, approaches to managerial problems, especially problems requiring specific decisions, did not emerge until after World War II. Using techniques developed during wartime, a new field of study was developed called **management science, or operations research.** Each of these terms caused some confusion, the former because of its similarity to the term *scientific management* and the latter because it did not convey precise meaning. Nevertheless, the field (which we will refer to as *management science*) grew rapidly in popularity for its ability to provide precise solutions to decision problems involving many variables and complicated connections among those variables. In effect, management science techniques such as linear programming (a mathematical procedure for determining the optimal combination of resources under specific constraining conditions) and various mathematical modeling procedures provided valuable tools to managers to assist in planning and forecasting activities. Along with **simulation** techniques, where various potential combinations of variables can be

bounded rationality
Herbert Simon's concept that managers attempt to make rational decisions, but their thinking is constrained by human limitations

satisficing
a type of decision that results in an acceptable course of action rather than necessarily the best alternative, or goal maximization

management science (operations research)
quantitative or mathematical approaches to managerial problems, especially those requiring specific decisions

simulation
a set of techniques in which various potential combinations of variables can be mathematically manipulated in advance of actual decisions to determine the possible effects of changes in one or more variables

mathematically manipulated in advance of actual decisions to determine the possible effects of changes in one or more variables, such mathematical modeling approaches have greatly improved the quality of managerial analyses of complicated decisions. However, such techniques do not in themselves provide comprehensive theories of management and hence have not had the same impact as some of the other major conceptual approaches to management covered earlier in this appendix. Nevertheless, their introduction did bring a much stronger analytical approach to some management tasks.

Integrative Approaches

The final set of approaches to management that we consider in this appendix are more recent and can loosely be labeled **integrative approaches,** that is, approaches that attempts to combine a number of different variables or elements into a more wholistic approach to the broad process of management. Since such approaches are relatively recent, it is questionable whether they should be included in a chapter on the *history* of management thought. But we include them to provide background on current management thinking and to show how historical approaches have been modified to the present. Also, they are presented in one form or another throughout this book, and, therefore, are introduced briefly here. The two most encompassing integrative approaches that most widely affect contemporary management thinking are systems theory and contingency approaches.

integrative approaches
recent approaches to management that include systems theory and contingency approaches and emphasize a consideration of a wide range of factors

Systems Theory

What has been called General Systems Theory (GST) was developed as early as the 1920s and was especially used in biology ("living systems") and engineering ("mechanical systems"), among other scientific areas of endeavor.[27] This approach was not applied to organizations until the 1960s, but since then it has been a prominent form of organizational analysis with considerable implications for understanding the process of management. A **system** refers to an interconnected set of elements that have orderly interactions that form a unitary whole. Thus, **systems theory** in the organizational context refers to the process involved in how "inputs" get transformed by the organization into "outputs," as illustrated in Exhibit A.10. Organizational inputs are generally considered to be of three major types: financial, material, and human resources. These inputs are combined and modified by technological and managerial actions into the two major types of organizational outputs, goods and services. Thus, from this perspective, management can be viewed as a type of transformation process, with the manager's role being one of converting a collection of resources into useful output. Understanding how all of these elements relate to each other and effectively integrating units and processes provide two major challenges for managers.

Systems theory also distinguishes between a **closed system** and an **open system,** as shown in Exhibit A.11. In the former, the system elements do not interact with the outside environment, and in the latter they do. Therefore, organizations can be considered open systems if they constantly interact with their environment, importing resources from it into the organization, and

system
an interconnected set of elements that have orderly interactions that form a unitary whole

systems theory
the processes involved in how "inputs" get transformed by the organization into "outputs"

closed system
a system in which there is no interaction of the elements with the outside environment

open system
a system in which there is interaction of the elements with the outside environment

EXHIBIT A.10 Systems Theory Applied to Organizations: An Example

INPUTS	TRANSFORMATION PROCESSES	OUTPUTS
FINANCIAL, MATERIAL, AND HUMAN RESOURCES Ideas of Artists, Writers, and Directors	**ACTIONS OF EMPLOYEES, MANAGERS, AND TECHNOLOGY** Through Use of Latest Computer Technology, Combined with Employee Motivation and Managerial Leadership	**GOODS AND SERVICES** New Animated Motion Picture

EXHIBIT A.11

Open System

exporting goods and services back out into the outside world. Since traditional management theory often seemed to treat organizations as if they were more or less closed systems, it tended to overlook many of the important impacts that relations with the outside environment could have on functions inside the company or plant. Viewing organizations as open systems, on the other hand, provides an appropriate, and necessary, perspective for any manager operating in the rapidly changing world of the twenty-first century.

Contingency Approaches

A cornerstone of scientific management and classical management theories was that there was *one best way* of doing a job, including the various functions of management. Performing tasks in any other way—according to those theories—would result in reduced effectiveness. Furthermore, these approaches specified what should characterize this one best way as it related to managerial jobs and roles: namely, unity of command, clear hierarchy of authority, precise specification of job duties, and so forth. The central theme of the "one best way" persisted for decades after Taylor and others first proposed it.

What was challenged over the years, particularly in the 1940s and 1950s, was the nature of what the one best way should be. That is, in some organizations a version of a human relations approach replaced the traditional way of operating. Thus, for such firms and agencies there was an effort to substitute a more responsive and employee-centered approach that stressed increasing employee satisfaction and morale and providing more flexible rules and regulations. It was almost as if some organizations had made 180-degree turns in their attempts to do things differently. Sometimes this change met with success, but often companies and other organizations found that they had simply exchanged one type of problem (employee dissatisfaction) for another type (casual or sloppy performance).

By the end of the 1960s, interesting research findings suggested that perhaps what was being overlooked was how well different management approaches (for example, the highly structured traditional approach versus the flexible, employee-centered approach) worked in different circumstances.[28] In effect, the findings tended to indicate that the highly structured approach (sometimes called the **mechanistic approach**) was better suited to stable external environments, highly repetitive tasks, and employees with limited technical or professional expertise. On the other hand, the flexible approach (often labeled the **organic approach**) seemed better suited for rapidly changing and complex environments, nonrepetitive tasks, and employees with considerable training and competence. Collectively, the research findings led many management scholars to the view that the most effective type of management would be a **contingency approach** that took into account the circumstances that existed, especially the nature of the organization's environment, its technology, the tasks to be performed within the organization, and the types of individual members—with their particular capabilities— the organization could attract and retain.

In its narrower sense, then, the term *contingency approach* refers to a choice between more traditional forms of organizational structure and methods of management and more flexible and less specified structure and methods. This choice, as it relates to the process of management, is well summed up in the often-quoted statement of Tommy Lasorda, former manager of the Los Angeles Dodgers: "Management is like holding a dove: squeeze it too hard and it dies; hold it too loose and it flies away."

In its broader sense, the contingency approach simply means that there are no general principles of management that can be applicable to *all* situations. What is best will depend on a whole host of variables, many of them beyond the manager's direct control, but most of which should be considered in deciding how to proceed. Interestingly, in management theory, we have gone from one extreme—"one best way"—to another extreme—"it all depends." Although this latter stance does not appear on the surface to provide much obvious guidance, it is clearly more suited to the current era of exceedingly rapid and often discontinuous change. It also puts the burden squarely where it belongs: on managers themselves to develop their diagnostic and analytical skills to provide effective approaches for changing circumstances.

mechanistic approach
highly structured traditional management approach, which may be better suited to stable external environments, highly repetitive tasks, and employees with limited technical or professional expertise

organic approach
a flexible, employee-centered management approach that seems better suited for rapidly changing and complex environments, nonrepetitive tasks, and employees with considerable training and competence

contingency approach
a management theory that emphasizes matching a structured or flexible management style to the organization's environment, its technology, the tasks to be performed, and the types of employees

Looking Back and Looking Forward

The history of management thought and practice up to this point in time can be compared to a flowing river. In the centuries before 1900, there was only a relatively tiny stream of ideas about how to manage organizations of any size and complexity. Like small brooks forming the source of a river, the ideas of ancient writers made their individual contributions to the development of management thought, but it was not until other events occurred, in this case the Industrial Revolution, that a major river was formed.

The needs of expanding industrial societies provided the setting and the impetus for concentrated attention on the subject of management. Even within this fertile context, however, it took the exceptional efforts and dedication of a relatively small number of people, such as Taylor, Follett, the Gilbreths, and Barnard, to increase the flow of ideas. They not only increased the size of the river, but they also changed its course, while always being strongly affected by events and circumstances of the times in which they lived. They brought greater rationality to a former haphazard process and, over time, a broader and more complex view of what the process of management was all about. It took the Hawthorne studies and the publication of their findings in the late 1930s, however, to bring additional clarity to the river of management ideas by emphasizing the centrality of the people component of organizations and the importance of the human relations that existed within them.

In the years following World War II, the management river broadened considerably with the input of such major tributaries as the behavioral, decision-making, systems, and contingency theory approaches to management. Each of these sets of ideas added to those that preceded them and often opened up whole new ways of thinking about managerial issues. Now, at the start of a new century, the river of management history has, in effect, arrived at a sort of delta, with a very large spread of ideas and practices. With all of the influences of significant forces for change in the external environment—such as leapfrog advances in information technology, an increasingly diverse workforce, expanding globalization of business, and the growing use of "voice" (that is, speaking up) by employees and society at large—it is extremely difficult to chart the future of management.

It is useful to take an overview of where management thought is currently. One conclusion that can be stated unequivocally: There is no single, grand theory or all-encompassing approach that dominates the thinking about management. Rather, as we have seen in the preceding sections, there are a variety of perspectives that have been developed in recent years that have shaped how both academic scholars and practicing managers view the challenge of managing organizations effectively. Many of these more recently developed frameworks discussed in the past few pages have been based on rigorous research and related analysis; that is, they have been based on attempts to develop a science of management (not to be confused with "scientific management" or "management science"). Such research and analysis are continuing at a brisk pace and could lead to new insights and major innovations within the next decade or so.

To reiterate, the reality today is that the competitive world of organizations, especially business organizations, is so complex and so fast-changing that no single, overall theory or approach to management can be expected to provide *the* way of thinking about this topic. Managers, and those who expect to be managers in the future, need to draw their ideas from many different sources and be able to take into account—but critically evaluate—multiple approaches to managing. That would seem to be the clear message and challenge in the years ahead.

Key Terms

bounded rationality   474
classical management theory   464
closed system   475
contingency approach   476
division of labor   459
functions of management   465
Hawthorne studies   472
human relations approach   472

human resources approach   473
integrative approaches   475
law of the situation   470
management science (operations research)   474
mechanistic approach   476
neoclassical management theory   469

open system   475
organic approach   476
satisficing   474
scientific management   461
simulation   474
system   475
systems theory   475

References

1. C. A. Rarick, "Ancient Chinese Advice for Modern Business Strategists," *SAM Advanced Management Journal* 61 (1996): 38–43; H. W. Vroman, "Sun Tzu and the Art of Business," *Academy of Management Executive* 11 (1997): 129–130; C. H. Wee, "Fighting Talk," *People Management* 3, no. 21 (1997): 40–44; Y. Y. Wong, T. E. Haher, and G. Lee, "The Strategy of an Ancient Warrior: An Inspiration for International Managers," *Multinational Business Review* 6 (1998): 83–93.

2. C. S. George, *The History of Management Thought* (Upper Saddle River: Prentice Hall, 1972).

3. Ibid.

4. D. Wren, *The History of Management Thought*, 5th ed. (New York: Wiley, 2005): 41.

5. Ibid., 34. From Adam Smith, *An Inquiry Into the Nature and Causes of the Wealth of Nations*, Great Books of the Western World, vol. 39 (Chicago: Encyclopædia Britannica, 1952; originally published in 1776).

6. Wren, *The History of Management Thought*, 36. From Smith, *An Inquiry Into the Nature and Causes of the Wealth of Nations*.

7. Wren, *The History of Management Thought*, 50.

8. Ibid., 50–51.

9. George, *The History of Management Thought*.

10. Wren, *The History of Management Thought* (see especially Chapter 5).

11. Ibid., 77.

12. George, *The History of Management Thought*, p. 83; Wren, *The History of Management Thought*, 77.

13. D. A. Wren, ed. and J. A. Pearce II, assoc. ed., *Papers Dedicated to the Development of Modern Management: Celebrating 100 Years of Modern Management: 50th Anniversary of the Academy of Management* ([S.I.]: Academy of Management, 1986).

14. From *Transactions* 7 (1886), pp. 428–432, published by the American Society of Mechanical Engineers. Reprinted in Wren, *Papers Dedicated to the Development of Modern Management*, 3–4.

15. P. F. Drucker, "The Coming Rediscovery of Scientific Management," *Conference Board Record* 13, no. 6 (1976): 26.

16. Edwin A. Locke, "The Ideas of Frederick W. Taylor: An Evaluation," *Academy of Management Review* 7, no. 1 (1982): 15.

17. Charles D. Wrege and Amede Perroni, "Taylor's Pig Tale— A Historical Analysis of Frederick W. Taylor's Pig-Iron Experiment," *Academy of Management Journal* 17, no. 1 (1974): 6–27; Locke, "The Ideas of Frederick W. Taylor," 18–19.

18. U.S. House of Representatives, Labor Committee, "Hearings on House Resolution 8662, A Bill to Prevent the Use of Stop Watch or Other Time-Measuring Devices on Government Work and the Payment of Premiums or Bonuses to Government Employees," (Washington: Government Printing Office, 1994), 1387. Quoted in Wren, *The History of Management Thought*, 127.

19. Ronald G. Greenwood, Regina A. Greenwood, and Jay A. Severance, "Lillian M. Gilbreth, First Lady of Management," in Jeffrey C. Susbauer, ed., *Academy of Management Proceedings*, San Francicso, 1978, 2. Cited in Wren, *The History of Management Thought*, 143.

20. D. S. Pugh, D. J. Hickson, and C. R. Hinings, *Writers on Organizations* (Beverly Hills: Sage, 1985), 64.

21. Ibid., 15.

22. A. M. Henderson and T. Parsons, eds. and trans. *Max Weber: The Theory of Social and Economic Organization* (New York: Free Press, 1947), 328.

23. R. G. Greenwood and C. D. Wregge, "The Hawthorne Studies," in Wren, *Papers Dedicated to the Development of Modern Management*.

24. Ibid.

25. A. Carey, "The Hawthorne Studies: A Radical Criticism," *American Sociological Review* 32 (1967): 403–416.

26. Greenwood and Wregge, "The Hawthorne Studies."

27. Ludwig von Bertalanffy, "General Systems Theory: A New Approach to the Unity of Science," *Human Biology* 23 (1951): 302–361.

28. Tom Burns and G. M. Stalker, *The Management of Innovation* (London: Tavistock Publishers, 1961); Joan Woodward, *Industrial Organization: Theory and Practice* (London: Oxford University Press, 1965); and Paul R. Lawrence and Jay W. Lorsch, *Organization and Environment: Managing Differentiation and Integration* (Homewood: Richard D. Irwin, 1967).

Glossary

360-degree feedback appraisal system in which information about an individual's performance is gathered from supervisors, coworkers, subordinates, and sometimes suppliers and customers

ABC analysis an inventory management system that categorizes items to provide information concerning which items require the most control

above-average return profit that is above the average for a comparable set of firms

acquired needs theory motivation theory that focuses on learned needs—such as those for achievement, power, and affiliation—that become enduring tendencies

affirmative action program a hiring and training program intended to correct past inequalities for certain categories of people based on gender, race and ethnicity, age, or religion

approved budget a budget that specifies what the manager is actually authorized to spend money on and how much

at-risk compensation pay that varies depending on specified conditions, including the profitability of the company; hitting particular budget, revenue, or cost savings targets for a unit; or meeting specified individual performance targets

balanced scorecard an integrated and "balanced" set of measures for four critical areas or perspectives: financial, customers, internal business, and innovation and learning

behavioral process orientation key distinguishing feature of the OD approach to organizational change that focuses on new forms of behavior and new relationships

behaviorally anchored rating scales (BARS) a performance appraisal system in which the rater places detailed employee characteristics on a rating scale

benchmarking investigating the best results obtained by your competitors and noncompetitors and the practices that led to those results

bona fide occupational qualification (BFOQ) a qualification that has a direct and material impact on job performance and outcomes

bounded rationality Herbert Simon's concept that managers attempt to make rational decisions, but their thinking is constrained by human limitations

bounded rationality model (administrative model) a model that assumes that people usually settle for acceptable rather than maximum options because the decisions they confront typically demand greater information-processing capabilities than they possess

brainstorming a process of generating many creative solutions without evaluating their merit

break-even point (BEP) amount of a product that must be sold to cover a firm's fixed and variable costs

broadband system a pay structure in which the range of pay is large and covers a wide variety of jobs

budget a tool used to quantify and allocate resources to specific activities

budgetary control a type of tactical control based on responsibility for meeting financial targets and evaluating how well those targets have been met

bureaucratic control an approach to tactical control that stresses adherence to rules and regulations and is imposed by others

cafeteria-style plan a benefit plan in which employees receive a set number of "benefit dollars" that they can use to purchase benefits that fit their particular needs

capacity planning the process of determining how much a firm should be able to produce or service

capital expenditure budget a tool that specifies the amount of money to spend on specific items that have long-term use and require significant amounts of money

career path a set and sequence of positions and experiences

centralized organization an organization in which decision-making authority resides with only a few individuals, usually at the top of the organization

change agent an individual who is responsible for implementing change efforts; can be either internal or external to the organization

charismatic leader one who has influence over others based on individual inspirational qualities rather than formal power

classical management theory ideas concerning the management of organizations arising from pioneers such as Taylor, Fayol, Weber, and Mooney and Reiley, together with emerging concepts identified with the scientific management approach

closed system a system in which there is no interaction of the elements with the outside environment

code of ethical conduct a formal statement that outlines types of behavior that are and are not acceptable

coercive power a type of position power based on a person's authority to administer punishments, either by withholding something that is desired or by giving out something that is not desired

cognitive differentiation the extent to which people in different units within an organization think about different things or about similar things differently

cohesion the degree to which members are motivated to remain in the group

collaboration part of negotiation in which parties work together to attack and solve a problem

collectivism the extent to which identity is a function of the group(s) to which an individual belongs (e.g., families, firm members, community members, etc.) and the extent to which group members are expected to look after each other

command group (also known as a *supervisory group*) a group whose members consist of a supervisor or manager and all those who report to that person

commitment (clan) control an approach to tactical control that emphasizes consensus and shared responsibility for meeting goals

committee a group that is either permanent or temporary (ad hoc), whose members meet only occasionally and otherwise report to different permanent supervisors in an organization's structure

communication the process of transferring information, meaning, and understanding from sender to receiver

communication network an identifiable pattern of communication within and between organizations, whether using formal or informal channels

compensatory justice if distributive and procedural justice fail, those hurt by the inequitable distribution of rewards are compensated

competitive advantage the ability of a firm to win consistently over the long term in a competitive situation

computer-aided design (CAD)/computer-aided engineering (CAE) computerized systems used to design new products, make modifications to existing ones, and test prototypes

computer-aided manufacturing (CAM) computerized systems used to direct manufacturing processes

concentration of effect the extent to which consequences are focused on a few individuals or dispersed across many

concurrent control a type of operational control that evaluates the conversion of inputs to outputs while it is happening

conformity close adherence to the group's norms by the individual members

content theory a motivation theory that focuses on what needs a person is trying to satisfy and on what features of the work environment seem to satisfy those needs

contingency approach a management theory that emphasizes matching a structured or flexible management style to the organization's environment, its technology, the tasks to be performed, and the types of employees

contingency plan a plan that identifies key factors that could affect the desired results and specifies what actions will be taken if key events change

continuous process improvement incremental and breakthrough improvements in the way an organization does business; also known as business process reengineering and *kaizen*

control regulation of activities and behaviors within organizations; adjustment or conformity to specifications or objectives

controlling regulating the work of those for whom a manager is responsible

core competence an interrelated set of activities that can deliver competitive advantage in the short term and into the future

cost leadership strategy a strategy in which a firm is the lowest-cost producer of a product or provider of a service while charging only slightly less than industry average prices

critical incident a specific incident in which the employee's behavior and performance were above or below expectations

cross-border acquisition the acquisition of a local firm made by a foreign firm to enter a new international market

cross-functional job rotation an arrangement in which an employee has an opportunity to work in different functional areas and gain additional expertise

cross-functional team a work group composed of employees from different departments, such as finance, marketing, operations, and human resources, to work together in problem solving

cultural context the degree to which a situation influences behavior or perception of the appropriateness of behaviors

cultural distance the overall difference between two cultures' basic characteristics such as language, level of economic development, and traditions and customs

culture a learned set of assumptions, values, and beliefs that members of a group have accepted and that affect human behavior

customer segment a group of customers who have similar preferences or place similar value on product features

decentralized organization an organization in which decision-making authority is pushed down to the lowest-possible level

decision making a process of specifying the nature of a particular problem or opportunity and selecting among available alternatives to solve a problem or capture an opportunity

decoding the act of interpreting a message

Delphi technique a decision-making technique that never allows decision participants to meet face-to-face but identifies a problem and offers solutions using a questionnaire

design capacity the maximum capacity at which a facility can run under ideal conditions

designing for manufacturing (DFM) designing products for ease of manufacturing so that quality is built into the design process

devil's advocate a group member whose role is to challenge the majority position

dialectical inquiry a process to improve decision making by assigning a group member (or members) the role of questioning the underlying assumptions associated with the formulation of the problem

differentiation the extent to which tasks are divided into sub-tasks and performed by individuals with specialized skills

differentiation strategy a set of actions under which a firm works to gain competitive advantage by making a product or service different from those of its competitors

directing the process of attempting to influence other people to attain an organization's objectives

distributive justice the equitable distribution of rewards and punishment, based on performance

division of labor the division of work so that each person performs a limited number of tasks (specialized tasks); first used early in the Industrial Revolution

downward communication messages sent from higher organizational levels to lower levels

dual-career couple a couple in which both partners work full-time in professional, managerial, or administrative jobs

economic order quantity (EOQ) a mathematical formula managers use to determine the most economical quantity of products to order, to minimize total inventory costs

effective capacity the percent of design capacity a facility is actually expected to maintain

effective leadership influence that assists a group or organization to meet its goals and objectives and perform successfully

efficiency perspective the concept that a manager's responsibility is to maximize profits for the owners of the business

emotional intelligence an awareness of others' feelings and a sensitivity to one's own emotions and the ability to control them

empathy the ability to put yourself in someone else's place and to understand his or her feelings, situations, and motives

empowerment the sharing of power with others, especially by those with high amounts of position power

encoding the act of constructing a message

entry barrier an obstacle that makes it difficult for firms to enter a particular type of business (industry)

environmental complexity the breadth and depth of differences and similarities in an organization's external environment

equity theory a motivation theory proposing that individuals will compare their circumstances to those of others and that such comparisons may motivate certain kinds of behavior

escalating commitment the tendency to exhibit greater levels of commitment to a decision as time passes and investments are made in the decision, even after significant evidence emerges indicating that the original decision was incorrect

ethical dilemma having to make a choice between two competing but arguably valid options

ethical lapse a decision that is contrary to an individual's stated beliefs and policies of the company

ethnocentrism the belief in the superiority and importance of one's own group

expectancy theory a motivation theory that focuses on the thought processes people use when choosing among alternative courses of action with their anticipated consequences

expense budget a budget that includes all primary activities on which a unit or organization plans to spend money and the amount allocated for the upcoming year

expert power a type of personal power based on specialized knowledge not readily available to many people

exporting manufacturing products in a firm's home country and shipping them to a foreign market

externality an indirect or unintended consequence imposed on society that may not be understood or anticipated

extinction the absence of positive consequences for behavior, lessening the likelihood of that behavior in the future

flat organization structure an organizational structure that has relatively few layers in its hierarchy

flexible manufacturing system (FMS) automation of a production line by controlling and guiding all machinery by computer

focus group a small group involved in intense discussions of the positive and negative features of products or services

focus strategy a set of actions that targets a particular market segment; may be a focused cost leadership strategy or a focused differentiation strategy

focused differentiation strategy a strategy to gain a competitive advantage by making a product or service different from those of your competitors

force field analysis uses the concept of equilibrium, a condition that occurs when the forces for change, the "driving forces," are balanced by forces opposing change, the "restraining forces," and results in a relatively steady state

Foreign Corrupt Practices Act (FCPA) a law prohibiting employees of U.S. firms from corrupting the actions of foreign officials, politicians, or candidates for office

formal communication channel a communication route authorized, planned, and regulated by the organization and directly connected to its official structure

formal group a group that is designated, created, and sanctioned by the organization to carry out its basic work and fulfill its overall mission

formalization the official and defined structures and systems related to decision making, communication, and control in an organization

formulation a process that involves identifying a problem or opportunity, acquiring information, developing desired performance expectations, and diagnosing the causes and relationships among factors affecting the problem or opportunity

frame of reference an existing set of attitudes that provides a quick way to interpret complex messages

functions of management basic elements of management as originally identified by Henri Fayol, consisting of planning, organizing, command, coordination, and control

Gantt chart a nonmathematical graphical representation of a project; used by managers to help monitor a project's progress

gatekeeper an individual at the communication interface between separate organizations or between different units within an organization

gender focus the extent to which people in a country value masculine or feminine traits

general environment the sum total of the sociocultural, technological, economic, political-legal, and global forces that can influence the effectiveness of an organization's strategy

glass ceiling an invisible barrier that prevents women from promotion to the highest executive ranks

global approach integrating the firm's activities on a coordinated, worldwide basis

global mind-set a set of cognitive attributes that allows an individual (e.g., manager) to influence individuals, groups, and organizations from diverse sociocultural and institutional environments

globalization the flow of goods and services, capital (money), and knowledge across country borders

globally focused organization an organization that invests the primary authority for major strategic decisions in the home office

goal-setting theory a belief proposing that human action is directed by conscious goals and intentions

Gresham's law of planning the tendency for managers to let programmed activities overshadow nonprogrammed activities

group a set of people, limited in number (usually from 3 to 20), who have some degree of mutual interaction and shared objectives

groupthink a mode of thinking in which pursuit of agreement among members becomes so dominant that it overrides a realistic appraisal of alternative courses of action

Hawthorne studies a series of research studies at the Hawthorne plant of the Western Electric Company that focused a spotlight on the importance of the human factor in productivity

Hersey and Blanchard's situational leadership model a model proposing that different types of appropriate leadership are contingent on some other variable, in this case, followers' readiness to learn new tasks

heuristic a rule that guides the search for alternatives into areas that have a high probability for yielding success

high-context culture a culture in which people pay close attention to the situation and its various elements

human relations approach approach springing from the findings of the Hawthorne studies that focused on the importance of relationships among people in the workplace

human resource policies and procedures a type of tactical control based on the organization's overall approach to utilizing its human resources

human resources approach approach involving a basic belief that people possess and want to make greater use of their talents and capabilities and that if allowed to do so, performance and satisfaction will increase

incentive plans a system that ties some compensation to performance

incremental budgeting approach a budgeting approach whereby managers use the approved budget of the previous year and then present arguments for why the upcoming year's budget should be more or less

individualism the extent to which people's identities are self-oriented and people are expected to take care of themselves and their immediate families

industry and competitor forces the five environmental forces (also known as Porter's Five Forces) that can significantly influence the performance of organizations in an industry

influence tactic a specific behavior used to affect the behavior and attitudes of other people

informal communication channel a communication route that is not pre-specified by the organization but that develops through typical and customary activities of people at work

informal group a group whose members interact voluntarily

informal organization the unofficial but influential means of communication, decision making, and control that are part of the habitual way things get done in an organization

in-group the group to which an individual belongs

institutional environment the country's rules, policies, and enforcement processes that influence individuals' and organizations' behaviors that operate within the country boundaries

institutional force a rule, policy, or enforcement process that influences individuals' and organizations' behaviors within a country's borders

integrated differentiation cost leadership strategy a set of actions designed to differentiate the firm's product in the marketplace while simultaneously maintaining a low-cost position relative to its competitors

integration the extent to which various parts of an organization cooperate and interact with each other

integrative approaches recent approaches to management that include systems theory and contingency approaches and emphasize a consideration of a wide range of factors

interdependence the degree to which one unit or one person depends on another to accomplish a task

interest in negotiation, a person's or group's concern or desire—in other words, what the person or group wants

intergroup conflict differences that occur between groups

intervention a set of structured activities or action steps designed to improve an organization

intragroup conflict differences that occur within groups

intuitive decision making the primarily subconscious process of identifying a decision and selecting a preferred alternative

job analysis determination of the scope and depth of jobs and the requisite skills, abilities, and knowledge that people need to perform their jobs successfully

job characteristics model an approach that focuses on the motivational attributes of jobs by emphasizing three sets of variables: core job characteristics, critical psychological states, and outcomes

job design the structuring or restructuring of key job components

job enrichment increasing the complexity of a job to provide a greater sense of responsibility, accomplishment, and achievement

job posting an internal recruiting method in which a job, its pay, level, description, and qualifications are posted or announced to all current employees

job sharing situation in which two people share the same job by each working part-time

justice approach focuses on how equitably the costs and benefits of actions are distributed

just-in-time (JIT) system an inventory management and control system whose objective is to reduce waste throughout the production and delivery of a product or service; in manufacturing, also known as lean production or value-added manufacturing

lateral communication messages sent across essentially equivalent levels of an organization

law of the situation Mary Parker Follett's emphasis on the need to generate a spirit of cooperation between managers and their subordinates with a focus on the authority (based on a person's knowledge and experience) that seems appropriate to the circumstances

leading coalition a group of supporters who are favorably inclined toward change and can influence others toward change

leader-member exchange (LMX) theory a belief proposing that leaders develop different levels of relationships with different subordinates, and that the quality of these individual relationships affects the subordinate's behavior

legitimate power (also known as *formal authority*) a type of position power granted to a person by the organization

liaison an individual or unit designated to act as a "bridge" or connection between two or more areas of a company

licensing the process of a company arranging for a local firm in the new market to manufacture and distribute its product

line of authority specifying who reports to whom

local approach differentiating the firm's activities country by country

low-context culture a culture in which contextual variables have much less impact on the determination of appropriate behaviors

magnitude of the consequences the anticipated level of impact of the outcome of a given action

management the process of assembling and using sets of resources in a goal-directed manner to accomplish tasks in an organizational setting

management science (operations research) quantitative or mathematical approaches to managerial problems, especially those requiring specific decisions

managerial ethics the study of morality and standards of business conduct

Maslow's need hierarchy theory a set of beliefs proposing that people will first attempt to fulfill basic needs, such as physiological and safety needs, before making efforts to satisfy higher-order needs, such as social and esteem needs

materials requirement planning (MRP) a sophisticated computer system, derived from the master production schedule and an inventory database, whose output provides schedules that identify the required raw materials, parts, and assemblies needed during each specified time period

mechanistic approach highly structured traditional management approach, which may be better suited to stable external environments, highly repetitive tasks, and employees with limited technical or professional expertise

media richness a communication medium's capacity to facilitate shared meaning

medium the method or means of transmitting a message; plural is *media*

mission statement a statement that articulates the fundamental purpose of the organization; often contains several components

moral intensity the degree to which people see an issue as an ethical one

moral rights approach focuses on examination of the moral standing of actions independent of their consequences

motivation a set of forces that energize, direct, and sustain behavior

multiple advocacy a process to improve decision making by assigning several group members to represent the opinions of various constituencies that might have an interest in the decision

multipoint competition strategy a set of actions that involves competing with firms across markets by using strengths in one market to overcome weaknesses in another market

negative reinforcement an undesirable consequence that, by being removed or avoided following a behavior, increases the likelihood of that behavior being repeated in the future

negotiation the process of conferring to arrive at an agreement between different parties, each with its own interests and preferences

neoclassical management theory thinking about organized work activity and how to manage that drew from classical theory in its emphasis on study and analysis of the workplace but expanded to include situational and social considerations (i.e., communication and cooperation)

network structure the formal or informal relationships among units or organizations (for example, along the firm's value chain)

networking a process of developing regular patterns of communication with particular individuals or groups to send and receive information

neutralizer of leadership any aspect of an organization or work situation that can hinder the exercise of leadership

noise interference with the transmission or decoding of a message

nominal group technique a process of having group members record their proposed solutions, summarize all proposed solutions, and independently rank solutions until a clearly favored solution emerges

nonprogrammed decision a decision about a problem that is either poorly defined or novel

norm a standard, shared by a group, that guides the behavior of its individual members

objective an end state or target that a company's managers aim to achieve

open system a system in which there is interaction of the elements with the outside environment

operational control assessment and regulation of the specific activities and methods an organization uses to produce goods and services

operational plan a plan that translates tactical plans into specific goals and actions for small units of the organization and focuses on the near term

operations management a specialized field of management associated with the conversion or transformation of resources into products and services

opportunity a chance to achieve a more desirable state than the current one

organic approach a flexible, employee-centered management approach that seems better suited for rapidly changing and complex environments, nonrepetitive tasks, and employees with considerable training and competence

organizational chart a graphic illustration of the relationships among a firm's units and the lines of authority among supervisors and subordinates

organizational design the process of assessing an organization's strategy and environmental demands and then determining the appropriate organizational structures

organizational development (OD) approach to organizational change that has a strong behavioral and people orientation, emphasizing planned, strategic, long-range efforts focusing on people and their interrelationships in organizations

organizational leadership an interpersonal process that involves attempts to influence other people in attaining organizational goals

organizational learning exhibited by an organization that is skilled at creating, acquiring, and transferring knowledge, and at modifying its behavior to reflect new knowledge and insights

organizational renewal a concept of organizational change that proposes a goal of flexibility and capability for continual change

organizational structure the sum of the ways an organization divides its labor into distinct tasks and then coordinates them

organization an interconnected set of individuals and groups who attempt to accomplish common goals through differentiated functions and their coordination

organizing systematically integrating resources to accomplish tasks

outsourcing the practice of contracting out a significant activity within the organization to an independent party

path-goal theory of leadership a contingency theory of leadership that focuses on the leader's role in increasing subordinate satisfaction and effort by increasing personal payoffs for goal attainment and making the path to these payoffs easier

pay structure a range of pay for a particular position or classification of positions

perception a way one sees a situation based on experiences, personality, and current needs

perceptual distortion the act of highlighting the positive features of an implicit favorite over an alternative

personal power power based on a person's individual characteristics

PERT/CPM program evaluation and review technique (PERT)/ critical path method (CPM) is a technique for scheduling and controlling large, complex projects

physical force an element of a country's infrastructure, such as its roads, telecommunications, air links, or deepwater harbors, that can affect existing and potential business operations

planning a decision-making process that focuses on the future of an organization and how it will achieve its goals

plan the means by which managers hope to hit a desired target

pooled interdependence the collective contribution of several largely independent groups to a common output

position in negotiation, a person's or group's stance regarding their interests

position power power based on a person's position and rank in an organization

positive reinforcement a desirable consequence that, by occurring or being supplied following a behavior, increases the likelihood of that behavior being repeated in the future

postcontrol a type of operational control that checks quality after production of goods or services outputs

power the capacity or ability to influence

power distance the extent to which people accept power and authority differences among people

precontrol a type of operational control that focuses on the quality, quantity, and characteristics of the inputs into the production process

primary activity an activity that is directly involved in the creation of a product or service, getting it into the hands of the customer, and keeping it there

probability of effect the moral intensity of an issue rises and falls depending on how likely people think the consequences are

problem a gap between existing and desired performance

procedural justice ensuring that those affected by managerial decisions consent to the decision-making process and that the process is administered impartially

process conflict a difference of opinion about the procedures a group should use to achieve its goals

process cost the increasing cost of coordination as group size increases

process redesign (reengineering) involves a fundamental redesign of business processes to achieve dramatic improvements

process theory a motivation theory dealing with the way different variables combine to influence the amount of effort people put forth

productivity measurement of how well an organization uses its inputs in producing its outputs

profit center a unit or product line whose related expenses are deducted from the revenue it generates

programmed decision a standard response to a simple or routine problem

project/task force a temporary group put together by an organization for a particular purpose

proposed budget a budget that outlines how much money an organization needs; submitted to a superior or budget review committee

prospective rationality a belief that future courses of action are rational and correct

proximity the physical, psychological, and emotional closeness the decision maker feels to those affected by the decision

punishment an undesirable consequence given following a behavior to decrease the likelihood that behavior will be repeated

quality the reliability, durability, serviceability, and dependability of products and services; also defined as fitness for use

rational model (classical model) a seven-step model of decision making that represents the earliest attempt to model decision processes

reciprocal interdependence the dependence of two or more groups on one another for inputs

reengineering fundamental rethinking and radical redesign of business processes to achieve dramatic improvements in critical, contemporary measures of performance, such as cost, quality, service, or speed

referent power a type of personal power gained when people are attracted to, or identify with, that person

region–country focus a situation in which primary authority for determining competitive strategy rests with the management of the international subsidiary based in a region of the world or a specific country

relationship conflict interpersonal differences among group members

retrospective decision model (implicit favorite model) a decision-making model that focuses on how decision makers attempt to rationalize their choices after they are made

reward power a type of position power based on a person's authority to distribute rewards

role ambiguity a situation in which the expected behaviors for a group member are not clearly defined

role conflict a situation in which a member of a group faces two or more contrasting sets of expectations

satisficing a decision process that results in an acceptable course of action among several alternatives rather than pushing to achieve the altogether best solution

scientific management an approach developed by Frederick Winslow Taylor focusing on basic principles for improving performance, such as studying jobs by usng objective measurements in order to determine the one best way, selecting the best persons for the job, training them in the most efficient methods, and providing sufficient monetary incentive to those performing the work

selective perception the process of screening out some parts of an intended message because they contradict our beliefs or desires

self-efficacy an individual's confidence about his or her abilities to mobilize motivation, cognitive resources, and courses of action needed to successfully execute a specific task within a given context

self-managing-work group (also known as an *autonomous work group*) a group that has no formally appointed supervisor but whose members coordinate their organizational work as if they all reported to the same formally appointed supervisor; members usually appoint their own informal team leader

sequential interdependence a relationship in which one group's outputs become the inputs of another group

simulation a set of techniques in which various potential combinations of variables can be mathematically manipulated in advance of actual decisions to determine the possible effects of changes in one or more variables

social cognitive theory a process theory that, in part, describes how to increase an individual's sense of self-efficacy, thus increasing motivation

social consensus the extent to which members of a society agree that an act is either good or bad

social intelligence the ability to "read" other people and their intentions and adjust one's own behavior in response

social loafing the phenomenon of reduced effort expended per person in a large group

sociocultural force a force consisting primarily of the demographics and the cultural characteristics of the societies in which an organization operates

solution a process involving generating alternatives, selecting the preferred solution, and implementing the decided course of action

span of control the number of employees reporting to a given supervisor

stakeholder an individual or group who haa an interest in and is affected by the actions of an organization

standard operating procedure (SOP) established procedure for action used for programmed decisions that specifies exactly what should be done

standard a performance target

statistical process control (SPC) a quantitative tool to aid in making decisions concerning how well a process is performing

status the standing or prestige that a person has in a group, which can be based on a number of factors such as perceived leadership abilities, seniority, or special skills

stereotyping the tendency to oversimplify and generalize about groups of people

strategic alliance a cooperative arrangement between two firms in which they agree to share resources to accomplish a mutually desirable goal

strategic control assessment and regulation of how the organization as a whole fits its external environment and meets its long-range objectives and goals

strategic corporate social responsibility perspective a three-criteria model that can help managers focus on social areas where there is the highest possibility of creating shared value for the business and society

strategic objective an objective that turns the strategic intent and mission of a firm into concrete and measurable goals

strategic plan a plan that focuses on the broad future of the organization and incorporates both external environmental demands and internal resources into managers' actions

strategic scope the size, depth, or breadth of a firm's strategy or focus

strategic vision a view of the firm over the long term that describes what it should achieve in the future

structured debate a process to improve problem formulation that includes the processes of devil's advocate, multiple advocacy, and dialectical inquiry

structured interview one in which interviewers ask a standard set of questions of all candidates about qualifications and capabilities related to job performance

subjectively expected utility (SEU) model a model of decision making that asserts that managers choose the alternative that they subjectively believe maximizes the desired outcome

substitution the ability to fulfill a customer's need by alternative means

superior value characteristic of a product or service whose value to customers is greater than that of a competitor's product or service

supervisory structure a type of tactical control based on reporting levels in an organization

support activitiies activities that facilitates the creation of a product or service and its transfer to the customer

swift trust the rapid development of trust in teams with positive and reciprocal communications about the team's task activities

SWOT analysis an analysis of the firm's strengths, weaknesses, opportunities, and threats (SWOT) to its continued operation

system an interconnected set of elements that have orderly interactions that form a unitary whole

systems theory the processes involved in how "inputs" are transformed by the organization into "outputs"

tactical control assessment and regulation of the day-today functions of the organization and its major units in the implementation of its strategy

tactical plan a plan that translates a strategic plan into specific goals for specific parts of the organization

tall organization structure a structure that has multiple layers of hierarchy or significant vertical differentiation

task conflict a difference of opinion about ideas and courses of action for addressing the issues facing a group

task differentiation differentiation by what employees do

team a type of group that has additional characteristics: a high degree of interdependent, coordinated interaction and a strong sense of members' personal responsibility for achieving specified group outcomes

temporal immediacy a function of the interval between the time the action occurs and the onset of its consequences

T-group a group of individuals participating in organizational development sessions away from the workplace; also called a basic skills training group

total quality management (TQM) a management approach and philosophy that involves a commitment from all levels of employees to continually strive to make improvements and satisfy customers

trait a relatively enduring characteristic of a person

transactional leadership leadership that focuses on motivating followers' self-interests by exchanging rewards for their compliance; emphasizes having subordinates implement procedures correctly and make needed, but relatively routine, changes

transformational leadership leadership that motivates followers to ignore self-interests and work for the larger good of the organization to achieve significant accomplishments; emphasizes articulating a vision that will convince subordinates to make major changes

transnational organization an organization that strives to be simultaneously centralized and decentralized

two-factor theory a motivation theory that focuses on the presumed different effects of intrinsic job factors (motivation) and extrinsic situational factors (hygiene factors)

uncertainty the extent to which organizations cannot accurately forecast future input, throughput, and output factors

uncertainty avoidance the extent to which a culture needs clarity or tolerates ambiguity

unity of command the notion that an employee should have one and only one boss

universal approach choosing a course of action that you believe can apply to all people under all situations

upward communication messages sent from lower organizational levels to higher levels

utilitarian approach focuses on the consequences of an action

valid selection technique a screening process that differentiates those who would be successful in a job from those who would not

value chain the set of key activities that directly produce or support the production of a firm's products and service offered to customers

values fundamentally important behaviors, activities, and outcomes

virtual team a team that relies on electronically mediated communication

whistle-blower an employee who discloses illegal or unethical conduct on the part of others in the organization

wholly owned subsidiary a direct investment that establishes a business in a foreign market in which the local firm owns and controls 100 percent of the business

work centrality the degree of general importance that working has in the life of an individual at a point in time

work standard the amount of time it takes a trained employee to complete a specific activity or process

zero-based budgeting approach a budgeting approach that assumes that all funding allocations must be justified from zero each year

Name Index

Subject Index